SIXTH EDITION

THE
WELL-CRAFTED
ARGUMENT
A Guide and Reader

FRED D. WHITE
Santa Clara University

SIMONE J. BILLINGS
Santa Clara University

CENGAGE
Learning·

Australia • Brazil • Mexico • Singapore • United Kingdom • United States

CENGAGE
Learning®

**The Well-Crafted Argument:
A Guide and Reader,
Sixth Edition**
Fred D. White
Simone J. Billings

Product Director:
Monika Eckman

Product Manager: Kate Derrick

Content Developers:
Kathy Sands-Boehmer,
Chad Kirchner

Marketing Director: Stacey
Purviance

IP Analyst: Ann Hoffman

IP Project Manager:
Nick Barrows

Manufacturing Planner:
Betsy Donaghey

Art and Design Direction,
Production Management,
and Composition:
Cenveo® Publisher Services

Cover Image:
© JoeyPhoto/Shutterstock.com

For product information and technology assistance, contact us at
Cengage Learning Customer & Sales Support, 1-800-354-9706

For permission to use material from this text or product,
submit all requests online at **www.cengage.com/permissions**.
Further permissions questions can be emailed to
permissionrequest@cengage.com.

Library of Congress Control Number: 2015947509

Student Edition:
ISBN: 978-1-305-63412-1

Loose-leaf Edition:
ISBN: 978-1-305-66271-1

Cengage Learning
20 Channel Center Street
Boston, MA 02210
USA

Cengage Learning is a leading provider of customized learning solutions with employees residing in nearly 40 different countries and sales in more than 125 countries around the world. Find your local representative at **www.cengage.com**.

Cengage Learning products are represented in Canada by Nelson Education, Ltd.

To learn more about Cengage Learning Solutions, visit **www.cengage.com**.

Purchase any of our products at your local college store or at our preferred online store **www.cengagebrain.com**.

Printed at CLDPC, USA, 08-22

BRIEF CONTENTS

CONTENTS

4   Using the Rogerian Model in Your Arguments   134

5   Reasoning: Methods and Fallacies   173

7 Researching Your Argument   243

8 Documenting Your Sources: MLA and APA Styles   275

PART II Reading Clusters   319

1 Masterpieces of Argument: What Do They Teach Us About the Art of Persuasion?   320

2 Athletics and Academics: How Do They Benefit Each Other?   348

5 Media Matters: What Are the Key Issues? 481

6   Biomedical Research: What Role Should Ethics Play?   513

PREFACE

The ability to plan and write a well-crafted argument has always been highly prized, but never more so than in these times of rapid scientific and technological development and social change. Mastery of argumentative writing brings tremendous advantages in academia, in the workplace, and in life generally. It can also provide the satisfaction that comes with thoughtful self-expression and effective, responsible communication. For these reasons, we wrote *The Well-Crafted Argument: A Guide and Reader*. A textbook was clearly needed that could equip students with the comprehensive set of skills necessary for writing argumentative essays in a wide variety of contemporary social contexts. *The Well-Crafted Argument* is based on a process pedagogy that encourages individual voice and vision. At the same time, it introduces models of good writing that provide grounding for inexperienced writers.

Features

Over the years we have used a number of argumentation textbooks in our courses. Time after time, we found that these books left out too much—or put in too much—that was not essential in helping students to master argumentative writing. This textbook is distinctive because it contains the following:

- **A thorough discussion of critical reading strategies.** Critical reading skills help students to understand and evaluate arguments, perform successful peer critiquing, and draft and revise their own arguments.

- **An introduction to the three principal methods of argument.** Detailed explanations of Classical, Toulmin, and Rogerian methods of constructing arguments are presented. The Toulmin method, and its relationship to Classical argument, has been explained more clearly. Similarities and differences among the three methods are discussed in detail.

- **Extensive use of student essays to represent the full range of argumentative writing.** In both Part I, The Rhetoric of Argument, and Part II, Reading Clusters, student argumentative essays are among the selections that illustrate different topics and strategies and form the basis for discussions, exercises, and writing projects. No other textbook on argument contains so many student-written argumentative essays covering so many different topics and strategies. Students are thus reminded that their voices are important in the world of argumentative discourse.

- **A focus on the writing process as it applies to argumentative writing.** Chapter 1, The Nature and Process of Argument, and other chapters within Part I, The Rhetoric of Argument, consider the writing process—gathering ideas, drafting, and revising—in the context of structuring and writing effective arguments.

- **Comprehensive instruction in conducting research for purposes of argument.** Chapter 7, Research Your Argument, helps students to locate and use print, database, and Internet resources; to use effective search strategies; and to avoid plagiarism. This chapter also introduces students to interviewing, conducting surveys, and designing questionnaires as ways of obtaining information. Chapter 8, Documenting Your Sources, presents Modern Language Association (MLA) and American Psychological Association (APA) citation styles with examples.

Divided into two parts, a rhetoric and a reader, *The Well-Crafted Argument* provides instructors and students with a wealth of materials and tools for effective argumentative writing, thinking, and reading.

Part I: The Rhetoric of Argument

- **Practical Coverage.** Eight thorough and readable skill-building chapters cover (1) planning, drafting, and revising strategies for argumentative essay writing; (2) critical reading strategies using (3) Classical/Toulmin, and (4) Rogerian models to develop an argument; (5) reasoning effectively and recognizing pitfalls in reasoning; (6) argument in the major academic disciplines, including literary and fine arts, natural sciences, technology, health and nutrition; (7) researching arguments and locating and integrating outside information using print, electronic, and interpersonal resources; and (8) documenting sources (both print and electronic) following MLA and APA formats.

- **Reasoning skills covered in context.** This book combines methods of effective reasoning with instruction in identification and avoidance of *errors* of reasoning. Most argument texts present only an out-of-context discussion of the latter.

- **Thorough and pedagogically sound apparatus.** Exercises appear throughout each chapter to help students reinforce for themselves what they have just learned in a particular section. Each chapter concludes with a summary, a checklist of protocols relevant to each chapter, and a set of writing projects.

Part II: Reading Clusters

- **Timely topics.** Part II presents a plethora of readings, organized thematically into six clusters. Popular debate topics include athletics vs. academics, media censorship, freedom of speech, and multicultural learning. Other topics include biomedical ethics and immigration reform. Each cluster includes a wide range of contrasting (not just opposing) views on issues that students will find intriguing and challenging, as well as refreshing.

- **Readings drawn from a wide range of sources.** Following the first chapter of classic readings, each cluster includes essays from both mainstream periodicals and academic journals, and features at least one student essay on that cluster's topic.

- **Famous essays well represented.** The first cluster contains masterpieces of argument, including Plato's "Allegory of the Cave," Jonathan Swift's "A Modest Proposal," and Frederick Douglass's "I Hear the Mournful Wail of Millions." We include this cluster so students can become acquainted with historically important arguments and consider ways of incorporating masterful argumentative techniques into their own arguments.

- **Readings from many disciplines.** Readings come from political science, international relations, biotechnology, athletics, education, literature, law, communication, and cultural studies. A separate chapter (6) is devoted to writing across the disciplines. Students thus are made dramatically aware of the fact that argumentative writing is vital to all fields.

- **Effective and interesting apparatus.** Each cluster begins with a brief introduction to the cluster topic and ends with Connections Among the Clusters questions, Writing Projects, and Suggestions for Further Reading. Each reading selection has a contextualizing headnote and is followed by Reflections and Inquiries questions and Reading to Write assignments.

New to the Sixth Edition

We have reinforced the strengths of the first five editions by updating, enhancing, and adding new features that will help students better understand the nature of argumentative writing and more readily gain mastery in constructing their own arguments. These features include the following:

- Expanded commentary on formulating an arguable thesis

- Expanded commentary on the common problems associated with composing an argument and ways to avoid them

- Expanded commentary on researching a topic using the Internet and on the role of ethics in research

- Expanded coverage of visual argument throughout the text, with special attention to the use of visual aids as a heuristic device and the uses of visuals in the context of Toulmin and Rogerian modes of argument

- Part II retains popular thematic clusters from the previous editions, from athletics and academics to international relationships to multicultural learning to media matters to national security issues to biotechnical research. Also for this new edition, we have updated several selections, including student selections.

Online Resources

MindTap® English for White/Billings's *The Well-Crafted Argument* 6th edition engages your students to become better thinkers, communicators, and writers by blending your course materials with content that supports every aspect of the writing process.

- Interactive activities on grammar and mechanics promote application in student writing

- Easy-to-use paper management system helps prevent plagiarism and allows for electronic submission, grading, and peer review

- A vast database of scholarly sources with video tutorials and examples supports every step of the research process

- Professional tutoring guides students from rough drafts to polished writing

- Visual analytics track student progress and engagement

- Seamless integration into your campus learning management system keeps all your course materials in one place

MindTap lets you compose your course, your way.

Acknowledgments

We wish to thank Santa Clara University and our current and former department chairs John Hawley and Phyllis Brown for their ongoing support of this project. We are also grateful to our colleagues Don Riccomini and Aparajita Nanda for their feedback. To our spouses, Terry M. Weyna and William R. Billings, we express our deepest gratitude for their inspiration, patience, understanding, and caring. We extend a special thanks to Devorah Harris, who expressed enthusiasm for the book from the very beginning.

Throughout the development of this text, many of our colleagues have been extremely helpful with their suggestions and generous with their time. We gratefully acknowledge the assistance of the following reviewers for the first, second, third, fourth, and fifth, and sixth editions:

Susan Achziger, *Community College of Aurora*; Edmund August, *McKendree College*; Julie Baker, *Northeastern University*; Joseph E. Becker, *University of Maine at Fort Kent*; Geraldie Cannon Becker, *University of Maine, Fort*

Kent; Lynnette Beers-McCormick, *Santiago Canyon College;* Marck L. Beggs, *Henderson State University;* L. Bensel-Meyers, *University of Denver;* Ellen Bernabei, *Grossmont College;* Drew Bixby, *University of Colorado, Denver;* Nancy Blattner, *Southeast Missouri State University;* Arnold Bradford, *Northern Virginia Community College;* Peter Burton Ross, *University of the District of Columbia;* Paul Cockeram, *Harrisburg Area Community College;* Sydney Darby, *Chemeketa Community College;* Barbara Davis, *Yavapai College;* Susan Davis, *Arizona State University;* Kimberly Del Bright, *Pennsylvania State University;* Christy Desmet, *University of Georgia;* Rodney F. Dick, *Mount Union College;* Josh Dickinson, *Jefferson Community College;* Adrienne Eastwood, *San Jose State University;* Bonnie L. Ehmann, *Gateway Community College;* Susan Garrett, *Goucher College;* Tom Ghering, *Ivy Tech Community College of Indiana;* Emily Golson, *University of Northern Colorado;* Lorien J. Goodman, *Pepperdine University;* Nate Gordon, *Kishwaukee College;* Rachael Groner, *Temple University;* Keith Gumery, *Temple University;* Robert W. Hamblin, *Southeast Missouri State University;* Susan Hanson, *Southwest Texas State University;* Katherine Harris, *San Jose State University;* William A. Harrison, III, *Northern Virginia Community College;* Barbara Heifferon, *Louisiana State University;* Carl Herzig, *St. Ambrose University;* Eileen Hinders, *University of Memphis;* Karen Holleran, *Kaplan College;* Tom Howerton, *Johnston Community College;* Michael Hustedde, *St. Ambrose University;* J. Allston James, *Monterey Peninsula College;* Alex M. Joncas, *Estrella Mountain Community College;* Karen J. Jones, *St. Charles Community College;* Erin Karper, *Purdue University;* Eleanor Latham, *Central Oregon Community College;* Cathy Leaker, *Empire State College;* Michael Levan, *University of Tennessee, Knoxville;* Debbie Mael, *Newbury College;* Rita Malenczyk, *Eastern Connecticut State University;* Linda Marquis, *Daniel Webster College;* Linda McHenry, *University of Oklahoma;* JoAnna Stephens Mink, *Minnesota State University;* Amy Minett, *Madison Area Technical College;* Amy Minervini, *Western Arizona College;* Bryan Moore, *Arkansas State University;* Heather Moulton, *Central Arizona College;* Troy Nordman, *Butler Community College;* Marcia Ribble, *University of Cincinnati;* Barbara Richter, *Nova University;* Libby Roeger, *Shawnee College;* Vicki Santiesteban, *Broward Community College;* Nina Scaringello, *Suffolk County Community College;* Ana Schnellmann, *Lindenwood University;* Wayne Stein, *University of Central Oklahoma;* Daniel Sullivan, *Davenport University;* Daphne Swabey, *University of Michigan;* Paul Van Heuklom, *Lincoln Land Community College;* Cynthia Van Sickle, *McHenry County College;* Jim Wallace, *University of Akron;* Kathleen Walsh, *Central Oregon Community College;* Taryn R. Williams, *Johnston Community College;* Will Zhang, *Des Moines Area Community College;* and Jason Whitesitt, *Yarapai College.*

We also wish to thank our students at Santa Clara University and at other academic institutions. Their help has been essential to the creation of this text, and we have learned a great deal from them. We owe a special debt of gratitude to the talented student writers who have given us permission to include their work: Gaby Caceres, Melissa Conlin, Kate Cooper, Joseph Cotter, Bryan Crook, Joseph Forte, Chris Garber, Daniela Gibson, Jarrett Green, Scott Klausner, Yung Le, Matthew Netterer, Regina Patzelt, Lauren Silk, Kiley Strong, and Sara Vakulskas.

Finally, we thank the remarkable staff of Cengage Learning: Monica Eckman, Kate Derrick, and Kathy Sands-Boehmer. We have made a special effort to present this challenging and complex material in an engaging, stimulating fashion, and we welcome all feedback on how this book can continue to be improved in the future. We invite you to email us with any questions or suggestions you might have.

Fred D. White (fwhite@scu.edu)
Simone J. Billings (sbillings@scu.edu)
Santa Clara University

PART I

The Rhetoric of Argument

1 | The Nature and Process of Argument

Give me the liberty to know, to utter, and to argue
freely according to conscience, above all liberties.

—John Milton

The freedom to think for ourselves and the freedom to present and defend our views rank among the most precious rights that we as individuals possess, as the great poet and essayist John Milton knew. The more we know about argument— what it involves, how a strong argument is constructed, and what a weak argument lacks—the more likely we are to benefit from this liberty.

Why Argue?

All of us find occasions to argue every day. Sometimes we argue just to make conversation. We argue casually with friends about which restaurant serves the best food, which movies are the most entertaining, or which automobile performs the best or most reliably for the money. Sometimes we engage in arguments presented in the media, taking positions on topics debated in newspapers and magazines, or on television, radio, and the Internet. And sometimes we argue in a more analytical manner on issues we have thought a lot about, such as which political party is most sympathetic to education reform, whether the Internet is a reliable research tool, or how we might solve a particular problem. When more is at stake, as in this last type of argument, the chances are greater that we will fail to be persuaded by what we hear or read or become frustrated by our own failure to persuade. We often fail to persuade because we lack evidence to back up our claims, because the evidence we do have is inadequate, or because we did not clearly or thoroughly show why challenging views are inadequate.

In other words, while casual arguments often consist of little more than exchanges of opinions or unsupported generalizations, more formal arguments are expected to include evidence in support of generalizations if they are to succeed in making strong points, solving real problems, or changing minds.

What Is an Argument?

People sometimes say that *everything* is an argument. That is quite true in the sense that whatever is communicated represents an individual point of view, one compelling enough to be accepted by the audience. Thus, if you're writing on a seemingly neutral topic, such as a day in the life of an emergency room nurse, you are implicitly arguing that your portrayal of the nurse is accurate and that nurses play a vital role in emergency rooms.

But *argument* as we use the term in this textbook is more explicitly an effort to change readers' minds about an issue—a topic of concern or urgency that is not easily agreed upon due to its complexity or controversy. Thus, we would generally call a day-in-the-life article mainly explanatory or reportorial writing. However, if your aim is to show that people often have the wrong idea about the role or importance of hospital nurses, you would be raising an issue in need of resolving. You would then be engaged in argumentative writing.

Arguments, in other words, arise when people disagree on what is true or false, accurate or inaccurate, sufficient or insufficient, about the subject being discussed. Keep in mind that an argument is indeed a *discussion* (implying civil discourse, not some tumultuous quarrel). A point often overlooked about argument is that it is necessary if one is to fully understand a particular issue. Note that the word *argue* comes from the Latin *arguere*, "to make clear."

An argument must possess four basic ingredients to be successful. First, it must contain as much *relevant information* about the issue as possible. Second, it must present *convincing evidence* that enables the audience to accept the writer's or speaker's claim as authentic. Third, it must fairly represent *challenging views* and then explain why those views are wrong or limited. And fourth, it must lay out a *pattern of reasoning*; that is, it must logically progress from thesis to support of thesis to conclusion. Before we examine these four elements, though, let us consider a formal definition of argument.

A Formal Definition of Argument

An argument is a form of discourse in which the writer or speaker tries to persuade an audience to accept, reject, or think a certain way about a problem that cannot be solved by scientific or mathematical reasoning alone. The assertion that the circumference of a circle is a product of its diameter times pi is not arguable because the assertion cannot be disputed; it is a universally accepted mathematical fact. At the other extreme, asserting an unsubstantiated opinion is not stating an argument; it is only announcing a stance on a particular issue. For example, someone in a casual conversation who asserts that public flogging of robbers would be a more effective deterrent than jailing them is voicing an opinion, not presenting an argument. If you respond by saying, "Yeah, probably," or, "No way—that would contribute to a culture of violence," you are also stating an opinion. If you respond instead by requesting evidence, such as statistics that show a correlation between public punishment and crime rate, you are helping to shape the conversation into a true argument. It is useful to keep in mind that *arguere*, in addition to meaning "to make clear," also means "to prove."

A good argument is not casual. It takes considerable time and effort to prepare. It not only presents evidence to back up its claim but also acknowledges the existence of other claims about the issue before committing to the claim that corresponds most closely to the arguer's convictions. A good argument also guides the audience through a logical, step-by-step line of reasoning from thesis to conclusion. In short, a good argument uses an argumentative structure.

Amplifying the Definition

Let us now amplify our definition of argument: An argument is a form of discourse in which the writer or speaker presents a pattern of reasoning, reinforced by detailed evidence and refutation of challenging claims, that tries to persuade the audience to accept the claim. Let us take a close look at each of the elements in this definition.

". . . a pattern of reasoning . . ."   This element requires that a good argument disclose its train of thought in a logical progression that leads the reader or listener from thesis to support of thesis to conclusion. It also implies that any unfamiliar terms or concepts are carefully defined or explained and that enough background information is provided to enable readers or listeners to understand the larger *context* (interacting background elements) contributing to the argument. For example, to make the claim that gas-guzzling sports utility vehicles (SUVs) are selling better than fuel-efficient subcompacts does not qualify as an argument because no context for the claim is given. Readers or listeners would ask, "So what?" But if the assertion is placed in the context of an urgent problem—for example, that the enormous popularity of SUVs is rapidly increasing gasoline consumption nationally, which in turn is leading to greater dependence on foreign oil—then a valid argument is established.

". . . reinforced by detailed evidence . . ."   In a formal argument, any assertion must be backed up with specific, compelling evidence that is accurate, timely, relevant, and sufficient. Such evidence can be data derived from surveys, experiments, observations, and firsthand field investigations (statistical evidence) or from expert opinion (authoritative evidence).

". . . that tries to persuade the audience to accept the claim."   This last element of the definition brings to mind the ultimate aim of any argument: to convince the audience that the arguer's point of view is a sensible one, worthy of serious consideration if not outright acceptance. To accomplish this aim, arguers often reinforce their evidence with what are known as *appeals*—appeals to

authority and traditional values, to feelings, and to reason. In an ideal world, evidence (the hard facts) alone would be enough to persuade audiences to accept the truth of a claim, but, in reality, more persuasive force often is needed, and appeals are drawn in.

What Is an Arguable Thesis?

As we noted in our formal definition of *argument*, statements of fact are not arguable because they are beyond dispute. One cannot challenge the fact that Homer's *Iliad* is about the Trojan War; however, one can challenge the assertion (or claim) that the Trojan War actually occurred. Merely to assert that you don't believe the Trojan War occurred would be expressing your *opinion*, but it is not an arguable thesis. Consider what is necessary for this opinion to qualify for both criteria.

For an opinion to become a thesis, it must be presented as *a problem capable of being investigated*—for example, "Judging from the latest archaeological evidence, I wish to argue that the fabled Trojan War did not occur." Moreover, the thesis must be counter-arguable. In other words, it should at least be conceivable that the evidence used to support the thesis could be interpreted differently or that new evidence could negate the old or at least lead to a very different interpretation of the old. We now have a thesis because (1) we have characterized the subject matter as a problem (that is, experts have been trying to determine for a long time whether the Trojan War occurred) (2) that is capable of being investigated at least through archaeological evidence (and perhaps through other forms of evidence as well—accounts by contemporary historians, for example) and (3) that has a thesis that is refutable.

The next step is to ensure that the argument to be presented is substantive. Merely referring to "archaeological evidence" will not do because it is too generalized; it's like the advertising phrase, "Doctors everywhere recommend . . ." or "A million satisfied customers prove . . ." To make the thesis substantive, reference to evidence needs to be more specific: "Archaeological evidence from the latest excavations in Turkey suggest that the fabled Trojan War did not occur."

"Wait," you say. "Doesn't evidence from excavations qualify as 'fact' and therefore become beyond dispute?" No. Facts are self-evident: The square root of 144 will always equal 12, no matter who does the calculating. Archaeological findings are subject to interpretation. One archeologist will study newly discovered artifacts and construct one historical scenario; another archaeologist will study the same artifacts yet construct a completely different scenario. That's because the evidence uncovered (a potsherd, a sculpture fragment, or the like) does not shed enough light on the historical event being investigated.

Using Evidence in Argument

Argumentative writing uses two kinds of evidence, indisputable (or factual) and disputable. The first kind refers to matters of public record that anyone can verify. No one is going to dispute the fact that the earth revolves around the sun every 365.25 days, say, or that the state of California was admitted to the Union on September 9, 1850. How such facts are applied is another matter, but the facts themselves are beyond dispute.

But what about disputable evidence? Imagine that a friend's room is filled with art books and reproductions of paintings. If someone asks about this friend's interests, you would reply, "Art!" without hesitation and cite as evidence the books and paintings. But that evidence is disputable: The books and paintings could belong to a roommate, could be a mere inheritance, or could represent a former interest recently abandoned.

Just the fact that evidence is disputable, however, does not mean it is unreliable. Such evidence often represents the closest one can get to the truth. Will banning handguns prevent tragedies like the Columbine school shootings? One researcher might discover statistical evidence of a correlation between banning guns and reduced crime; yet another researcher could find evidence of a contrary correlation. Different parts of the country or the world, different years, different times of year, different age groups—all represent constantly changing variables that can affect such a correlation. The more aware you are of the possible ways in which evidence may be disputed, the less likely you are to reach facile or premature conclusions.

EXERCISE 1.1

1. Consulting an unabridged dictionary, prepare a critical summary of the terms *argument*, *debate*, *dispute*, and *quarrel*. In what ways do the definitions differ? Where do they overlap, and how do you account for the overlap?

2. Supplement these definitions with examples, drawing from your own experiences.

3. Which of the following assertions could be developed into a formal argument, and which could not? Explain your reasons.

   a. A clear link has been established between secondhand cigarette smoke and lung cancer.

   b. The surgeon general has determined that smoking is a health hazard.

   c. Studying a foreign language gives children a greater command of their native language.

   d. The more video games children play, the less likely their abstract reasoning skills are to develop properly.

4. List the topics of recent disputes you have had with friends or family. Under each topic, note the claims asserted by each side, followed by any support that had been attempted for each. Next, go back over these topics and list additional support you would give to one or more of these claims if you had been asked to elaborate on them in a more formal manner.

5. Discuss the kinds of evidence writers would want to use to resolve the following controversial assumptions. What problems with definitions might arise in some of these claims?

    a. Adults are safer drivers than teenagers.

    b. The many species of birds that still inhabit the Everglades suggest that this ecosystem is not as endangered as environmentalists say it is.

    c. The greater number of violent shows you watch, the more likely you are to commit acts of violence.

    d. Male smokers are three times more likely to become impotent than male nonsmokers.

    e. Obscene books should be banned from public school libraries.

Refuting Challenging Views

Perhaps the most commonly overlooked or ignored element of a successful argument is the refutation or rebuttal—the acknowledgment and fair representation of those claims that oppose or in some way challenge the claim you are arguing. Remember that the very reason for engaging in argument is to try and resolve a disagreement, to show that one claim is more deserving of acceptance than other claims. To succeed in this goal, you need to do more than present compelling evidence; you must also show why your challengers' views (together with the evidence they present) are either incorrect or flawed.

Incorrect evidence is easy to refute, assuming you can pinpoint the error. All you need to do is produce the correct evidence. Flawed evidence, however, is more difficult to refute. Evidence is flawed when it relies on data that may well have been reliable at one time but have since become unreliable. ("Getting a suntan is healthy" might have been supportable by reliable evidence fifty years ago; today, the evidence suggests that getting a suntan is unhealthy due to potentially cancer-causing ultraviolet radiation.) Or the data may still be correct or relevant but the challenger did not *interpret* them properly. For example, it is statistically true, according to the 2015 edition of *The World Almanac and Book of Facts*, that in 2013 the United States had one and a half times as many personal computer users than China (340.6 million compared to 269.5 million).

But one can interpret that fact in different ways. If your challenger argues that fewer people use personal computers in China because fewer people can afford personal computers there than in the United States, you might refute that conclusion by arguing that availability, not affordability, is the cause (or at least the principal cause). Of course, you would need to demonstrate that claim with additional specific data. Thus, a challenging view may be flawed (a) because a certain fact or set of facts was overlooked or (b) because inappropriate criteria were being applied. For another example, to judge a movie by box office success alone may be an inappropriate criterion for determining the quality of that movie.

To frame an effective refutation for your argument, follow these steps:

1. Ask yourself, "What are the possible objections to my claim?" See if you can anticipate refutations to your claim even if you cannot readily locate them.

2. Search for actual arguments that challenge your own. Be sure to summarize these arguments fairly; that is, do not omit parts of the claim that you think you would not be able to counterargue. *Note:* It is entirely possible that a challenging view will strike you as so convincing that you may want to revise or even abandon your original claim.

3. Look for common ground—places where the challenging claim intersects with your own. *Note:* The Rogerian method of argument (see Chapter 6) requires you to give special emphasis to common ground.

4. Explain why the challenging claim is incorrect or flawed.

EXERCISE 1.2

Suggest one or two ways in which each of the following claims might be refuted:

a. E-book readers are growing rapidly in popularity; clearly, print books are becoming obsolete.

b. Doing away with music programs in the public schools to increase teachers' salaries, reduce class size, and upgrade equipment is not a great sacrifice; it's better to have private music lessons at home anyway.

c. The fewer taxes corporate executives have to pay, the better able they will be to hire workers.

d. Children should learn to do basic math in their heads or on paper the old-fashioned way before being permitted to use calculators; otherwise, their mental agility will suffer.

FIGURE 1.1

The Aristotelian
or Communication
Triangle

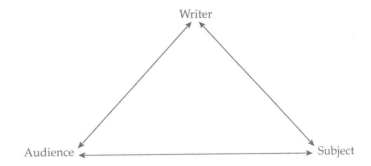

Communicating with a Purpose

Before we turn to writing effective arguments, consider the elements in an act of communication. Any communication act consists of the *writer* or *speaker*, an *audience*, and the *subject* being communicated. This is known as the *Aristotelian* or *Communication Triangle* (Figure 1.1).

The Aristotelian Triangle reminds us that the act of writing, virtually by definition, involves writing about something to someone—that writing never occurs in a vacuum.

Any act of communication involves a writer or speaker conveying a particular viewpoint to a particular audience in a particular way. We have all had the experience of describing something one way to one person and quite another way to someone else. For example, we might discuss a romantic relationship one way with a friend, quite another way with a parent, and yet another way with a minister, rabbi, or psychologist. The writer or speaker, subject, and audience all shape the communication.

A fourth major element that shapes communication is *purpose*. There are three basic kinds of communication, each with a different purpose:

1. *Referential* or *expository*: communication that primarily aims to inform and explain;

2. *Expressive*: communication that primarily aims to stimulate the imagination, create mood or "atmosphere," and evoke feelings; and

3. *Argumentative*: communication that primarily aims to help skeptical readers or listeners make up their mind about a debatable issue.

These three modes of communication are not mutually exclusive. For instance, writers of arguments must take time to inform readers about the facts underlying a problem. They also must try to make such explanations interesting—perhaps by dramatically re-creating a moment of discovery or by describing the beauty of an observed phenomenon. But argumentative writing does have a distinct purpose, which is to present, support, or challenge a debatable

FIGURE 1.2

Rhetorical Rhombus

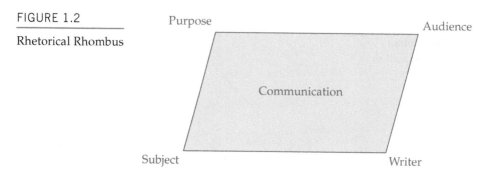

proposition (such as a conflict in ethical behavior or policymaking). Such views cannot be proven with experiments or made compelling through descriptive writing alone.

To incorporate this element of purpose, we can transform Aristotle's triangle into a square or, to be a bit more alliterative (to help remember it better), into a *rhetorical rhombus* (Figure 1.2). Simple as this diagram may seem, it calls to mind a subtle interconnection among the elements; that is, any one element is indispensable to the other three. Thus, the writer's way of seeing the world is made significant by the fact that he or she has a particular purpose for writing; a subject is enriched by the way in which it is made relevant to a particular audience; and so on.

Let us examine each element of the rhetorical rhombus separately, in depth, as it pertains to writing effective arguments. Once you establish that your primary purpose is not expository (to inform) or expressive (to evoke feelings) but rather argumentative (to persuade your audience to agree with your claim), you will want to consider purpose in that context.

Purpose in an Argumentative Context

The purpose of your argument is the reason *why* you want your audience to agree with your claim and take whatever action is necessary to carry it out. Often, the purpose for wanting to communicate anything is complex. For example, if your claim is that wolf hunting must be stopped (say, by passing laws that prohibit wolf hunting), your purpose might consist of the following:

- The facts make it clear to you that wolves are rapidly becoming an endangered species.
- You are convinced that such species endangerment poses a serious threat to the environment.
- You love wolves, and it distresses you to see these beautiful, intelligent animals slaughtered by those who cannot appreciate them.

Purpose, then, is the motivational force that imbues the mere potential for communication with the desire to communicate. In a required writing course, however, purpose becomes even more complicated. Unlike working writers, whose purpose for writing a given piece is intrinsically related to the subject, student writers are often motivated by extrinsic matters, such as getting a good grade on the assignment or in the course. Although there is nothing wrong with this kind of motivation, it does not quite constitute a bona fide purpose for writing about a given topic.

It is preferable, however, to adopt a professional sense of purpose toward your subject matter. The best way to accomplish this involved, engaged stance is to role-play. *Become* the writer you would like to be. Instead of thinking of yourself as a student in a composition course, think of yourself as an expert in the field about which you are writing—one who genuinely cares about the topics at hand enough to want your audience to understand them and appreciate them the way you do.

Audience in an Argumentative Context

The people at whom you aim your argument can significantly influence the way you present that argument. For example, two arguments supporting the prohibition of wolf hunting, one aimed at legislators and the other aimed at hunters, would differ greatly from each other. If you were addressing an audience of legislators, you would want to focus on the need for laws that would better protect the environment. If you were addressing an audience of hunters, you would want to explain why it is in the hunters' best interest to stop hunting wolves. You could argue that damage to the habitat would ultimately cause the wolves to die out.

Audience also affects the writing and reading of arguments, in that some arguments may be classified as academic (or scholarly) and others as nonacademic (or popular). Academic arguments are written for fellow scholars affiliated with higher education, although some scholars are "independent"— that is, they are not employed by a college or university yet pursue similar research projects. The purpose of such writing is knowledge sharing or idea sharing; academic arguers say, in effect, "Here is what fellow researchers have determined thus far about the issue at hand; now, here are my views on the matter." A research paper is the student version of the professional scholarly article, in which the scholar carefully and explicitly articulates a claim and provides support for that claim.

Types of Academic Arguments   As a college student, you are probably experiencing several different audiences for arguments. In a literature course, you are asked to write papers in which you argue for what you consider to be an important theme in a poem, work of fiction, or play. This type of argumentation is known as *literary criticism*. The evidence you would gather for such an argument would consist of specific passages from the literary work in question (and possibly other works by the same author as well), relevant information about the author's life and times, and commentary from other scholars.

In a science course, you learn to write *scientific papers* in which you analyze, say, the properties of newly observed phenomena or *laboratory reports* in which you accurately describe and interpret the results of physics, chemistry, or psychology experiments. "The Need to Regulate 'Designer Babies'" (Cluster 6, Biomedical Research, pages 529–531), the Editors of *Scientific American* explain genetic diagnosis in a way that lay readers can understand.

Another type of academic argument is the *ethnographic study*, common to sociology and anthropology. The ethnographer closely observes the behavior of individuals of a particular community or group and derives inferences from what has been observed.

One of the most common types of academic writing is the *position paper*, in which you take a stance on a debatable issue, making sure that you represent each challenging view as fairly as possible before demonstrating the limitations of those views and proceeding to support your own view. "Two Languages Are Better Than One," by Wayne Thomas and Virginia Collier (pages 452–457), is one of several position papers that appear in this textbook.

Your history courses present you with the opportunity to conduct a *historical inquiry* into a particular period or event. New archaeological discoveries or lost documents brought to light can profoundly change the way a historical event or even an entire period is interpreted.

Students as well as professionals in the fields of engineering, business administration (management, finance, marketing), and law all must produce documents that have an argumentative component: A *proposal* describes a work in progress, often to receive approval for its completion; a *feasibility study* demonstrates the need for a new program or facility; and a *progress report* chronicles, as the name implies, the progress that has been made on a given project. Of course, many of these forms of academic writing exist outside the academy. Magazines publish literary criticism, specialized companies submit proposals to large manufacturers or agencies, and so on.

Nonacademic Arguments   On the other hand, nonacademic arguments focus more on reporting the "gist" of new developments or controversies. Academic arguments examine issues in depth and use specialized language to ensure precision, whereas nonacademic arguments tend to gloss over the technicalities and use nonspecialized language, which is less accurate but more accessible to the general public. The chief distinguishing features between academic and nonacademic arguments are outlined in Table 1.1.

The more aware you are of your target audience's needs and existing biases, the greater the likelihood that you will address their particular concerns about the topic and, in turn, persuade them to accept your *thesis*. To heighten your audience awareness, ask yourself these questions:

1. What do my readers most likely already know about the issue? Most likely do not know?

2. How might the issue affect my readers personally?

TABLE 1.1   Distinction Between Academic and Nonacademic Arguments

Academic Arguments	Nonacademic Arguments
Specialized (i.e., discipline-specific), precise language	Nonspecialized, less precise but more accessible language
Formal or semiformal tone	Less formal, more personal tone
All primary and secondary sources explicitly cited and documented, using standard formats (MLA, APA, etc.)	Sources are acknowledged informally, without footnoting
Contributions by other scholars in the field are discussed formally and in detail	Contributions by other writers in the field are discussed briefly
Scholarly audience	General audience

3. What would happen to my argument if my conclusions or recommendations are accepted? If they are not accepted?

4. Why might readers not accept my conclusions or recommendations?

Note that this last question leads you to think about counterarguments and the way you might respond to them. See "Refutation" in Chapter 3.

Writer in an Argumentative Context

How, you may wonder, is the writer a variable in the communication, aside from the obvious fact that the writer is the one who presents the argument (the "Communication" that lies at the center of the rhetorical rhombus and is its very reason for being)? Actually, the writer can assume one of many roles, depending on the target audience. Say, for example, you are trying to convince a friend to lend you $500 to use as a down payment for a summer trip to Europe. Your role here is that of trustworthy friend. If instead you are trying to convince your bank to lend you that same $500, your role becomes that of client or applicant. You are likely to use different language and different support in making your argument to the bank's loan officer than to your friend. Similarly, writers often are obliged to play different roles, depending on the particular needs of different audiences.

Subject in an Argumentative Context

The subject refers to what the argument (the text) is about. Although the subject remains identifiably constant, a writer might shift the *focus* of a subject to accommodate a particular audience or situation. For example, to convince your friend to lend you $500 for the down payment on that European trip (your argument's subject), you might focus on how the friend could come with you to make for an even more rewarding trip. To convince the bank, you might shift the focus to emphasize future job security and the likelihood of your paying back the loan.

As you study the Classical, Toulmin, and Rogerian models of argument in the chapters that follow, think about how the rhetorical rhombus applies to each and about how different models place different emphasis on **p**urpose, **a**udience, **w**riter, or subject (PAWS).

The Process of Composing an Argument

Unlike cooking, which follows a rather fixed sequence of steps, writing arguments (or essays of any kind) is mainly a dynamic, recursive process rather than a linear one. That is, you can start anywhere and return to any stage at any time. You can *brainstorm* for additional ideas, rework the organizational scheme, wad up and rewrite part of the existing draft, or walk over to the library or log on to the Internet to conduct additional research—and you can do any of these activities whenever you feel the need. Some writers simply do not feel comfortable composing in a linear fashion; some like to compose their endings first, or "flesh out" particular points of an argument as they leap to mind, and then organize them into a coherent sequence later on. Some writers need to map out their ideas in clusters, write outlines, or simply let loose their spontaneous flow of associations via freewriting.

Freewriting to Generate Ideas Rapidly

As you may recall from your earlier composition studies, freewriting is a good way to generate material for an argument. Start writing without any advance planning. Let your thoughts run loose on the page; do not concern yourself with organization, sentence structure, word choice, or relevancy to the topic of your argument. You might surprise yourself with how much you already know!

There are two kinds of freewriting, unfocused and focused. In *unfocused freewriting,* let your pen move across the page, recording whatever comes to mind. Try not to pause. In the following example, a student, Janis, engages in some unfocused freewriting to stir up ideas about a subject for her argument. She is thinking spontaneously with a pencil, you might say, making no effort to develop a thesis:

```
Let's see, I'm supposed to write an argument that would
persuade first-year college students what would be the best
major in preparation for a particular career. Well, I'm
undeclared myself, but want to study law after I graduate,
so maybe I could do a comparative analysis of three or four
majors that would seem to offer the best preparation for
law school (hey, this could help me make up my own mind).
Poli sci seems like an obvious possibility, since lawyers
```

```
need to have a basic knowledge of the way governments work,
the nature of public policy, how laws are passed.... Also,
English, because lawyers need strong communication skills and
need to acquire the kind of deep insight into the human heart
that great works of literature offer.... Then I might talk
to law students as well as professors in the four different
majors—and maybe even practicing attorneys to find out what
they majored in as undergraduates, and why. Hey, my aunt is a
lawyer! I could talk to her.
```

Janis knows that she likely will discard most, if not all, of her freewriting; her goal was not to whip out a rough draft or even test out a topic but to help her mind tease out ideas and associations that otherwise might have remained buried. The goal of freewriting is greater than overcoming not knowing what to say; it includes becoming more receptive to what is possible.

In *focused freewriting*, you write spontaneously as well but attempt something resembling an actual draft of the essay. Your goal is to generate as much as you know about the topic. It is an excellent way of discovering gaps in knowledge.

Here is an example of focused freewriting:

```
Maybe I'll limit the scope of my essay to how liberal arts
courses such as history, English, or political science can
serve as excellent preparation for a legal career. First
I'd want to show how courses in these majors train students
in basic skills such as thinking critically, communicating
clearly, researching (Internet, library, interviewing),
acquiring a solid understanding of key periods in world
history; what else? Maybe how federal, state, local govs.
operate; finally, how these skills serve as a foundation for
the study of law.
```

Using the Journalist's 5Ws/H

The heuristic device 5Ws/H has long been favored by journalists because it serves as a quick reminder for answering the key questions—Who, What, Where, When, Why, and How—when reporting a news story, but it also serves writers of argument. After all, reporting the facts underlying a debatable issue will make your views more convincing. Thus, if you argue that critical thinking skills should be taught to children as early as first grade, you might use the 5Ws/H heuristic as follows:

WHO: Who are the teachers already teaching critical thinking to children?

WHAT: What kinds of activities or materials do these teachers use to teach critical thinking?

WHERE: (1) Where in the country (or abroad) is this instruction taking place? (2) In which grades is this instruction being used with greatest effectiveness?

WHEN: (1) When during the school year should critical thinking skills be taught? (2) When should this instruction be presented in the lesson plan for the day? For the semester?

WHY: (1) Why should anyone teach critical thinking to preadolescent children? (2) Why would preadolescent children need critical thinking skills?

HOW: (1) How are instructors teaching critical thinking—their methods? (2) How *should* instructors teach critical thinking?

Immersing Yourself in the Subject

Imagine spending twenty minutes or so freewriting and getting down on paper everything that comes to mind; you produce several scraggly pages in long-hand or neater ones on a computer. You read them over, highlighting with a marker or with your computer's highlighting tool what seems most relevant and useful. Then, you ask yourself these questions: What seems to be the dominant or recurrent trend? What more do I need to know about my topic to write persuasively about it? What kinds of evidence do I need to back up my thesis, however tentative it may be at this stage? In taking these steps, you are preparing to immerse yourself in your subject.

Having relevant information available is important to all writers. Once you know what more you need, you can start looking for information. An enormous quantity of information can be accessed quickly on the Internet, so it is a good place to begin your research. A strong search engine such as Google, Dogpile, or Yahoo! can bring material from any subject onto your screen in seconds. On the other hand, a large percentage of Internet sources are superficial, dated, or not very relevant to your needs. Balance your Internet research by examining a variety of reliable print sources, such as books, articles, encyclopedias (general as well as subject specific), handbooks, and specialized dictionaries. For more information about using sources, see Chapter 9, Researching Your Argument.

Your goal in reading and researching should be to learn all you possibly can about your topic. Familiarize yourself with the differing views experts have about it. Talk to experts. As a college student, you are surrounded by them; get in the habit of contacting professors who can give you timely and in-depth information about your topic or suggest material to read. Read and explore as many sources as possible. In other words, immerse yourself in the subject matter of your argument. This involvement will show in your writing and will give the finished paper added depth and vigor.

Using Listing and Clustering

Like freewriting, listing and clustering tap into writers' natural inclination to take a mental inventory of what they already know about a topic as well as to discover what they do not know about it. To list, jot down as quickly as you can ideas (or idea fragments) or names of people, places, events, or objects. One student prepared the following list as a prelude to writing about the increasing problem of childhood obesity:

> Fast-food chains aggressively target their products to preteen kids.
>
> TV commercials give wrong impressions.
>
> Parents too busy to cook.
>
> Hamburgers often loaded with mayonnaise.
>
> Burgers, fries, milk shakes, ice cream loaded with fat.
>
> Parents not paying close enough attention to their kids' diets.

You can use lists to make notes to yourself or to ask questions the moment they occur to you:

> Check how many calories are in a typical fast-food burger.
>
> How much fat content in a bag of fries?
>
> What do nutritionists and pediatricians say about the increasing obesity problem?
>
> Find out how often kids eat fast food, on the average.
>
> How can kids learn more about this problem in school?

Clustering helps writers take an inventory of what they know, but it also helps them discover relationships among the ideas they list by seeing how the cluster bubbles connect. This discovery helps writers organize their ideas more efficiently when they begin outlining or drafting their arguments.

   To cluster an idea for an argumentative essay, take a sheet of paper and write down words or phrases; at the same time, keep similar words and phrases close together and draw large circles around them to form "clusters." Next, draw lines between bubbles that seem to go together. Figure 1.3 shows how one student clustered her thoughts for an argumentative essay on why teenagers should spend more time reading books.

FIGURE 1.3   Student Cluster Diagram

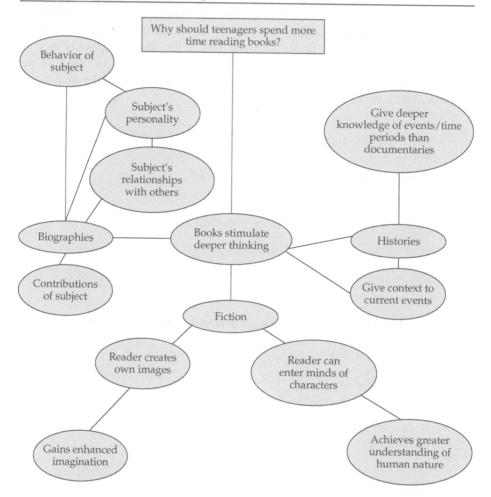

EXERCISE 1.3

1. Your science instructor asks you to evaluate the benefits and dangers of vitamin C. Using the Internet, locate information that both supports and challenges claims about the benefits and dangers of this vitamin. Keep a record of the websites that you visit.

2. List things you might say in a paper arguing for or against the benefits or dangers of vitamin C.

3. Having gathered potentially useful information about vitamin C and listed things you might want to include in your argument, do a focused freewrite. Do not pause or organize your thoughts or choice

of words and phrases. Write rapidly until you have filled at least two handwritten pages.

4. Maggie Jackson, author of *Distracted* (Prometheus Books, 2008), the book from which the following paragraph is taken, argues that the new technologies are causing social fragmentation and eroding attention spans. After reading the passage, make two lists: one consisting of possible defenses of her premise, the other consisting of possible challenges. Later, you may wish to read the book to determine how convincingly the author makes her case.

> We can tap into 50 million Web sites, 1.8 million books in print, 75 million blogs, and other snowstorms of information, but we increasingly seek knowledge in Google searches and Yahoo! headlines that we gulp on the run while juggling other tasks. We can contact millions of people across the globe, yet we increasingly connect with even our most intimate friends and family via instant messaging, virtual visits, and fleeting meetings that are rescheduled a half dozen times, then punctuated when they do occur by pings and beeps and multitasking. Amid the glittering promise of our new technologies and the wondrous potential of our scientific gains, we are nurturing a culture of social diffusion, intellectual fragmentation, sensory detachment. In this new world, something is amiss. And that something is attention.

Workable Topics for an Argumentative Essay

What kinds of topics make strong argumentative essays? In a nutshell, the topics are on substantive issues that are timely or perennially relevant (see Cluster 1, Masterpieces of Argument) and that stir up a healthy, heated debate. Good topics also give readers insight into the issue being discussed or invite readers to test their long-held values and beliefs. No matter what point of view you wish to defend or challenge, if the issue matters deeply to many people, it is likely to be a successful topic. Avoid topics that cannot be logically defended, such as those involving culinary or aesthetic taste ("Oranges taste better than apples"; "Jackson Pollack's abstract paintings are more aesthetically pleasing than Mark Rothko's"), or those that are too speculative to be either defendable or refutable ("Everything in the universe has been predetermined").

Sometimes your instructor will assign you a topic just to see what you can do with it; other times, you will be responsible for coming up with your own topics. Follow these suggestions when working up a topic for your assignments:

1. *Keep the scope manageable.* That is, aim for depth rather than breadth. If you're planning a four-page (1,000-word) paper, a topic such as the effects of video games on the attention spans of preadolescent children

would be too ambitious—more appropriate for a master's thesis. A more manageable topic would be the effects of one particular type of video game on the attention spans of sixth graders or a paper that considers a possible correlation between time spent video gaming and development of reading skills among sixth graders.

2. *Make sure you can come up with a defendable thesis for your topic, backed with solid evidence.* If your topic is residence hall safety and you want to argue that better security is needed, be sure you can obtain data on security breaches (obtainable from your school's public safety or campus police office) to support your thesis.

3. *Anticipate ways your thesis may be refutable.* Is it possible to come up with a counterargument to your thesis? In the case of residence hall security, is it possible to argue that the security breaches could have occurred no matter how well the security measures were enforced? Or that the breach in security was merely due to the rare oversight of one public safety officer? Try to anticipate as many counterarguments to your thesis as possible and be prepared to refute them.

EXERCISE 1.4

Determine whether the following topics are appropriate for a four-page argumentative essay or even appropriate for argument. If not, suggest how the thesis can be modified to make it appropriate or suggest what a writer may want to argue instead.

1. Some campus buildings pose a serious fire hazard.
2. All first-year students should be required to take a course in environmental science.
3. One day, we will be able to cure cancer just by swallowing a pill.
4. Kindergarten is a waste of time.
5. Adopt-a-pet programs can help senior citizens improve their quality of life.
6. Football is more enjoyable than baseball.
7. Protesters such as the Women in Black on Sundays who are urging world peace should be applauded and continue their silent protests because clearly their efforts are having the desired effect.

Taking a Fresh Approach to Your Topic

Even though you may be asked to write on a specific topic, you should always aim for a fresh approach to that topic. What do we mean by "fresh"?—a way of thinking about the topic that likely has been given little or no previous attention. For example, say you have been asked to argue whether reading fiction helps develop critical thinking skills. Instead of merely taking a "yes-it-does" or "no-it-doesn't" stance, you might argue that it all depends on the complexity of the fictional work—and proceed to give examples of complex fictional works versus simplistic fictional works. Another approach would be to examine the whole notion of "complexity" in the context of fiction: does it (or should it) apply to the psychological aspects of the characters? The twists and turns of the plot? The historical context?

Using Appeals in Argument

To argue successfully, a person does not rely solely on facts; facts need to be explained, be placed into a particular context (that is, related to the problem being argued), or have their importance validated. Successful writers of argument often demonstrate the importance of these facts to persuade their audience that the facts are important. For such a demonstration, these arguers turn to strategies of *persuasion* known as appeals.

The ancient Greek philosopher Aristotle in his *Rhetoric* identifies three kinds of appeals:

1. *Ethical:* the appeal to tradition, authority, and ethical and moral behavior, which Aristotle terms *ethos;*

2. *Emotional:* the appeal to feelings and basic human needs, such as security, love, belonging, and health and well-being, which Aristotle terms *pathos;* and

3. *Rational:* the appeal to reason and logic, which Aristotle terms *logos.*

As Figure 1.4 shows, these three appeals correspond to Aristotle's three modes of communication, Writer, Audience, and Subject (look again at Figure 1.1). In other words, Ethos (character, values, trusted authority) is the attribute of a responsible Writer. Similarly, Pathos (emotion, compassion) suggests appealing to the needs and desires of the public—that is, of the Audience. Finally, Logos (reason) corresponds to the factual, rational truth content of the Subject.

FIGURE 1.4

Aristotelian Appeals
in Correspondence
with the Elements
of Communication

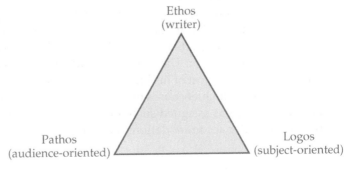

How do appeals reinforce evidence? Say that a writer wishes to argue that if acid rain fallout continues to increase, agriculture in a certain region will be threatened. To argue this claim convincingly, a writer first needs to bring in indisputable facts—those derived from scientific experiments. These facts would suggest a correlation between increased acidity and rainfall and decreased crop yield. Note that the correlation may be disputable, but it still constitutes valid evidence.

Use of appeals can enhance the persuasive force of the thesis. The writer above, for example, might use one or more of the following appeals:

- An ethical appeal that introduces the testimony of an expert, such as a farmer whose crops have been affected or an industrial chemist who has a professional understanding of the way in which acidity in rainfall reacts with soil nutrients.

- An emotional appeal that discusses the basic human need for uncontaminated food or justifies the fear of cancer many people will have if the situation is not corrected.

- A rational appeal that emphasizes the logical and inevitable consequences of what happens to soil and crops when acid rainfall goes untreated.

Appeals such as these go a long way toward reinforcing the evidence and strengthening the writer's argument.

Combining appeals in a given argument can be especially effective. In the following excerpt from *The Souls of Black Folk* (1903), the educator and pioneer sociologist W. E. B. Du Bois (1868–1963)—the first African American to earn a PhD from Harvard University—calls attention to the living conditions of black people in the post–Civil War South, specifically in Dougherty County, Georgia. Note how Du Bois appeals to both reason and emotion to convince readers of the injustice of such living conditions:

> Above all, the cabins are crowded. We have come to associate crowding with homes in cities almost exclusively. This is primarily because we have so little accurate knowledge of country life. Here in Dougherty County one may find families of eight and ten occupying one or two rooms, and for every ten rooms of house accommodation for the Negroes there are twenty-five persons. The worst tenement abominations of New York do not have above twenty-two persons for every ten rooms. Of course, one small, close room in a city, without a yard, is in many respects worse than the larger single country room. In other respects it is better; it has glass windows, a decent chimney, and a trustworthy floor. The single great advantage of the Negro peasant is that he may spend most of his life outside his hovel, in the open fields.
>
> There are four chief causes of these wretched homes: First, long custom born of slavery has assigned such homes to Negroes; white laborers would be offered better accommodations, and might, for that and similar reasons,

give better work. Secondly, the Negroes, used to such accommodations, do not as a rule demand better; they do not know what better houses mean. Thirdly, the landlords as a class have not yet come to realize that it is a good business investment to raise the standard of living among labor by slow and judicious methods; that a Negro laborer who demands three rooms and fifty cents a day would give more efficient work and leave a larger profit than a discouraged toiler herding his family in one room and working for thirty cents. Lastly, among such conditions of life there are few incentives to make the laborer become a better farmer. If he is ambitious, he moves to town or tries other labor; as a tenant-farmer his outlook is almost hopeless, and following it as a makeshift, he takes the house that is given him without protest.

First, Du Bois appeals to reason by providing "accurate" information about country life to reverse the assumption that crowding occurs only in city life; he also appeals to reason by examining the "four chief causes" of such housing. But appealing to reason is not enough: It is important to address the heart as well as the mind. Hence, Du Bois appeals to emotion by referring to the urban tenements as "abominations," adding that they are less extreme than the country housing situation, and by calling the prospects for tenant-farmers "almost hopeless."

In the following passage, from "Civil Disobedience" (originally delivered as a lecture to his fellow townspeople in 1848), we see Henry David Thoreau using all three appeals—ethical, emotional, and rational—in his effort to convince his audience, although the ethical appeal dominates:

Under a government which imprisons any unjustly, the true place for a just man is also a prison. The proper place to-day, the only place which Massachusetts has provided for her freer and less desponding spirits, is in her prisons, to be put out and locked out of the State by her own act, as they have already put themselves out by their principles. It is there that the fugitive slave, and the Mexican prisoner on parole, and the Indian come to plead the wrongs of his race, should find them; on that separate, but more free and honorable ground, where the State places those who are not *with* her but *against* her,—the only house in a slave-state in which a free man can abide with honor. If any think that their influence would be lost there, and their voices no longer afflict the ear of the State, that they would not be as an enemy within its walls, they do not know by how much truth is stronger than error, nor how much more eloquently and effectively he can combat injustice who has experienced a little in his own person. Cast your whole vote, not a strip of paper merely, but your whole influence. A minority is powerless while it conforms to the majority; it is not even a minority then; but it is irresistible when it clogs by its whole weight. If the alternative is to keep all just men in prison, or give up war and slavery, the State will not hesitate which to choose. If a thousand men were not to pay their tax-bills this year, that would not be a violent and bloody measure, as it would be to pay them, and enable the State to commit violence and shed innocent blood. This is, in fact, the definition of a peaceable revolution, if any such is possible. If the tax-gatherer, or any other public officer, asks me, as one has done, "But what shall I do?" my answer is, "If you really wish to do any thing, resign your office." When the subject has refused allegiance, and the officer has resigned his office, then the revolution is accomplished. But even suppose blood should flow. Is there not a sort of blood shed when the conscience is wounded? Through this wound a man's real manhood and immortality flow out, and he bleeds to an everlasting death. I see this blood flowing now.

I have contemplated the imprisonment of the offender, rather than the seizure of his goods,—though both will serve the same purpose,—because they who assert the purest right, and consequently are most dangerous to a corrupt State, commonly have not spent much time in accumulating property. To such the State renders comparatively small service, and a slight tax is wont to appear exorbitant, particularly if they are obliged to earn it by special labor with their hands. If there were one who lived wholly without the use of money, the State itself would hesitate to demand it of him. But the rich man— not to make any invidious comparison—is always sold to the institution which makes him rich. Absolutely speaking, the more money, the less virtue; for money comes between a man and his objects, and obtains them for him; and it was certainly no great virtue to obtain it. It puts to rest many questions which he would otherwise be taxed to answer; while the only new question which it puts is the hard but superfluous one, how to spend it. Thus his moral ground is taken from under his feet. The opportunities of living are diminished in proportion as what are called the "means" are increased. The best thing a man can do for his culture when he is rich is to endeavour to carry out those schemes which he entertained when he was poor. Christ answered the Herodians according to their condition. "Show me the tribute-money," said he;—and one took a penny out of his pocket;—If you use money which has the image of Caesar on it, and which he has made current and valuable, that is, *if you are men of the State*, and gladly enjoy the advantages of Caesar's government, then pay him back some of his own when he demands it; "Render therefore to Caesar that which is Caesar's, and to God those things which are God's,"—leaving them no wiser than before as to which was which; for they did not wish to know.

When I converse with the freest of my neighbors, I perceive that, whatever they may say about the magnitude and seriousness of the question, and their regard for the public tranquility, the long and the short of the matter is, that they cannot spare the protection of the existing government, and they dread the consequences of disobedience to it to their property and families.

For my own part, I should not like to think that I ever rely on the protection of the State. But, if I deny the authority of the State when it presents its tax-bill, it will soon take and waste all my property, and so harass me and my children without end. This is hard. This makes it impossible for a man to live honestly and at the same time comfortably in outward respects. It will not be worth the while to accumulate property; that would be sure to go again. You must hire or squat somewhere, and raise but a small crop, and eat that soon. You must live within yourself, and depend upon yourself, always tucked up and ready for a start, and not have many affairs. A man may grow rich in Turkey even, if he will be in all respects a good subject of the Turkish government. Confucius said,—"If a State is governed by the principles of reason, poverty and misery are subjects of shame; if a State is not governed by the principles of reason, riches and honors are the subjects of shame." No: until I want the protection of Massachusetts to be extended to me in some distant southern port, where my liberty is endangered, or until I am bent solely on building up an estate at home by peaceful enterprise, I can afford to refuse allegiance to Massachusetts, and her right to my property and life. It costs me less in every sense to incur the penalty of disobedience to the State, than it would to obey. I should feel as if I were worth less in that case.

Thoreau's appeal to ethics is revealed in his allusions to the injustice of the State, to what constitutes proper and honorable behavior when the State has exercised unethical judgment. He also appeals to ethics by invoking Christ's example regarding Roman tribute money.

We can detect Thoreau's subtle appeal to emotion in at least two ways: by presenting seemingly nonviolent acts such as taxation as acts of violence that can "shed innocent blood" as easily as cannons and by presenting the State as harassing its citizens rather than protecting them whenever those citizens dare to challenge the State's authority.

Finally, Thoreau appeals to reason by tracing the logical consequences of a tax-bill: "it will . . . waste all my property and so harass me and my children, which in turn makes it no longer worth the while to accumulate property."

EXERCISE 1.5

1. What types of appeals would be most appropriate for persuading readers of the following assumptions?

    a. Reading stories to children greatly enhances their mental skills as well as their emotional stability.

    b. All work and no play makes Jill a dull girl.

    c. More severe penalties should be imposed on those who abuse animals.

   d. Safety should be anyone's top priority when purchasing a
       family car.

   e. This painting is definitely a Picasso because an art historian from
       Yale authenticated it as such.

2. Determine the appeals at work in each of the following passages. What
    words or images show the appeals at work?

   a. My mistress was . . . a kind and tender-hearted woman, and in the
       simplicity of her soul she commenced, when I first went to live
       with her, to treat me as she supposed one human being ought to
       treat another. In entering upon the duties of a slaveholder, she did
       not seem to perceive that I [was] mere chattel, and that for her to
       treat me as a human being was not only wrong, but dangerously
       so. Slavery proved as injurious to her as it did to me. When I went
       there, she was a pious, warm, and tender-hearted woman. There
       was no sorrow or suffering for which she had not a tear. She had
       bread for the hungry, clothes for the naked, and comfort for every
       mourner that came within her reach. Slavery soon proved its abil-
       ity to divest her of these heavenly qualities. Under its influence,
       the tender heart became stone, and the lamblike disposition gave
       way to one of tiger-like fierceness. The first step in her downward
       course was in her ceasing to instruct me. . . . Nothing seemed to
       make her more angry than to see me with a newspaper. —Frederick
       Douglass, *The Narrative of the Life of Frederick Douglass, an American
       Slave* (1845), Chap. 7.

   b. Most films and television shows are produced by men for men.
       Their main purposes are to show white males triumphant, to
       teach gender roles, and to cater to men's delight in male preda-
       tion and victimization, especially young, pretty, near-naked
       women with highly developed breasts and buttocks (parts that
       are usually the locus of attack). Like the men of the proto-Nazi
       German Freikorps that waged between the wars, shooting
       women between the legs because they carried grenades there (!),
       American men's most satisfying target is women's sexuality, the
       area of men's greatest fear. Pornography is a systemic abuse of
       women because the establishment colludes in this male sadism
       toward women, which fits its purposes. Case in point: the Indian
       government, which does censor films for political content, *for-
       bids scenes of lovemaking or kissing but allows rape;* indeed, a rape
       scene has been "all but requisite" in Indian films for some years,
       writes Anita Pratap. —Marilyn French, *The War Against Women*
       (New York: Ballantine, 1992) 175.

c. There is no single way to read well, though there is a prime reason why we should read. Information is endlessly available to us; where shall wisdom be found? If you are fortunate, you encounter a particular teacher who can help, yet finally you are alone, going on without further *mediation*. Reading well is one of the great pleasures that solitude can afford you, because it is, at least in my experience, the most healing of pleasures. It returns you to otherness, whether in yourself or in friends, or in those who may become friends. Imaginative literature is otherness, and as such alleviates loneliness. We read not only because we cannot know enough people, but because friendship is so vulnerable, so likely to diminish or disappear, overcome by space, time, imperfect sympathies, and all the sorrows of familial and passional life. —Harold Bloom, *How to Read and Why* (New York: Scribner, 2000) 19.

3. Read the magazine ads on pages 28–35 and consider the images they use. Then answer these questions:

    a. What are the basic arguments of the magazine ads?

    b. What appeals can you identify in them?

    c. Is there more than one appeal in a given ad?

Organizing the Argument

All writing must be organized or structured. Whether you are relating an experience (*narration*), or explaining an idea or process (*exposition* or *explanation*), or defending a thesis (*argumentation*), you must structure your writing to communicate best with an audience.

Organizing your writing means that you do the following:

1. Introduce the topic (the situation in a narrative; the subject matter to be explained in an exposition or explanation; the problem in an argument).

2. Present the particulars of the situation (the sequencing of incidents in a narrative; elements of a phenomenon in an exposition or explanation; the nature of the problem, followed by the body of evidence, in an argument).

3. Conclude (the outcome in a narrative; the "whole picture" in an explanation; the interpretation, assessment, and recommendations, if appropriate, in an argument).

IT'S AS CLOSE TO
THE GROVE
AS YOU CAN GET

Florida's Natural® Premium Brand Orange Juice is made only from our fresh oranges, *not* from concentrate. In fact, we own the land, the trees, and the company. So you can be sure our personal best goes into every carton.

www.floridasnatural.com

Looks fast standing still.
That's called truth in packaging.

YOU JUST CAN'T DOWNLOAD THIS.

All the

world's a stage.

Performances daily.

250 cities.

40 countries.

One airline.

 We know why you fly° **AmericanAirlines°**

AA.com

South China Sea / Pacific Ocean / PHILIPPINES

Palawan Hornbill *(Anthracoceros marchei)*
Size: Head and body length, 55 - 65 cm (21.7 - 25.6 inches) **Weight:** 601 - 713 g (1.3 - 1.6 lbs)
Habitat: Primary and secondary evergreen forest; also found in mangrove swamps and cultivated areas
Surviving number: Estimated at 2,500 - 10,000

Photographed by Kurt W. Baumgartner

WILDLIFE AS CANON SEES IT

The forest has a friend. The Palawan hornbill fulfills that role beautifully thanks to its dining habits. It gathers fruits in a gular pouch, then processes and spits out seeds where they are able to thrive, away from the competing parent tree. Living in pairs or small groups, the hornbill nests in large trees and ranges from undergrowth to canopy. But trees are in shorter and shorter supply these days — three islands in the hornbill's range are now largely deforested. With the forest disappearing, poaching persisting and eggs and young being captured for pets or food, the hornbill needs some friends of its own if it is to have a future.

As we see it, we can help make the world a better place. Raising awareness of endangered species is just one of the ways we at Canon are taking action—for the good of the planet we call home. Visit **canon.com/environment** to learn more.

Canon

GOD, I'M STARVING!

GOD, SO AM I.

☐ Yes, I would like to make a donation to Catholic Charities of Chicago. My donation is $ _____ ☐ Please send me more information on wills and estate planning. Name: _____ Address: _____ City: _____ State: _____ Zip Code: _____ Send to: Rev. Edwin M. Conway, Administrator, Catholic Charities, 126 N. Desplaines St., Chicago, Illinois 60606	"Starving." So easy to say when you sit down to satisfy your appetite. But it's an empty, hopeless reality for many. Please. Send a check now; leave a bequest in your will later . . . your willpower can work miracles. At Catholic Charities, 98.8¢ of each dollar goes to help the needy through 189 services at 96 locations. We helped over a half a million people last year. People of all faiths. The homeless, addicted, abused . . . and hungry. Victims of unfortunate circumstances who need our help. Next time you feel "starved," consider those who really are, and help. Write Rev. Edwin M. Conway, Administrator, 126 N. Desplaines, Chicago, IL 60606, or call 236-5172. PHOTO: BILL EMRICH

The CATHOLIC CHARITIES OF THE ARCHDIOCESE OF CHICAGO

© Catholic Charities, Chicago

How you meet these three organizational requirements in an argument depends on the type of model you adopt: the Classical (or Aristotelian/Ciceronian), the Toulmin, or the Rogerian. The chapters that follow examine each model in depth, but for now you merely need to be aware of each one's distinguishing organizational features.

In the *Classical model*, the organizational scheme is predetermined. One begins with an introduction that establishes the problem and states the thesis; next, one analyzes the evidence and refutes opposing views in light of the evidence collected; finally, one draws conclusions and provides recommendations.

In a variation of the Classical model known as the *Toulmin model* (named for the philosopher Steven Toulmin), truth is not absolute but value dependent. Accordingly, the logic content of the argument is scrutinized for its underlying values. Evidence does not operate in a vacuum but must be tested according to the values (called *warrants*) of the arguer. These values always come into play during the argument, meaning that no one argues for timeless, eternal truths.

In the *Rogerian model* (named for the psychologist Carl Rogers), one shifts emphasis to the social act of negotiating difference through argument. Truth is not only value based, it must be negotiated cooperatively if argument is to have any constructive social function.

Drafting the Argument

There are several ways to compose a draft. One way of drafting (and, alas, too common) is to put off the task until the day or night before it is due and then to dash off a single draft and proofread it hastily. In general, this is the least productive way of writing. The best writers tend to revise *most* often, not least often.

Another way of drafting is to use an outline as a template. By elaborating on each section of the outline, the drafter takes an important step toward substantive *development* of the essay. The subsequent rethinking of the argument and the additional research that results become more apparent using this method.

A third way is to produce a *discovery draft*, which is like freewriting in its spontaneity and in its goal of getting down on paper as much as possible about the topic. However, discovery drafters do have a rudimentary sense of structure and purpose in mind. They believe that, to some extent at least, the things they want to say will fall into place through the very act of writing, and if not, they can rearrange, revise, and edit once they have a rough draft in hand.

Whichever drafting method you choose, allow yourself enough time to reread the draft two or three times and to make marginal notations about possible changes. Mark up a printout of your draft with reminders of what else to include, questions that might help you identify and gather additional evidence, and ideas for changes that will strengthen your argument.

Common Problems in Composing an Argument and Ways to Resolve Them

Most writing projects seem more like obstacle courses than walks through the park. The obstacles also can be difficult to anticipate because they usually arise from the particular demands of the subject at hand. That said, here are five common problems that arise during drafting, along with suggestions for resolving them:

1. *The basis for the argument—the problem—has not been clearly or fully articulated.* Let the initial response to a problem be your starting point for laying the foundation, not the foundation itself. Angry that your local library has cut its hours? Use that as the catalyst for framing the problem of public library closures in your area, describing the underlying causes, and explaining why the problem deserves urgent attention.

2. *The thesis is not sufficiently forceful or urgent.* If you're arguing that your school needs to improve its health care services, be sure that you are able to pinpoint specific improvements and why the reasons are needed.

3. *The evidence to support your claim is faulty or missing.* For your claim to be convincing, you must present compelling evidence to support it. How can you determine what constitutes compelling evidence? Check to see that the evidence is relevant, current, sufficient (in other words, not just an isolated, atypical case), and accurate.

4. *The appeal(s) to emotion, logic, and/or authority (laws, customs, and the like) ought to be used to greater advantage.* Appeals provide the dimension of persuasion to an argument. To convince readers of your views, go beyond detached logic to stir their hearts, their minds, their souls.

5. *Opportunities to represent and refute challenging views have been overlooked, ignored, or slighted.* Develop the habit of "testing" your thesis by imagining how it could be refuted; by doing so, you will be better prepared to locate counterarguments. Keep in mind, too, that some counterarguments may be so compelling that you will want to at least modify your original thesis.

Composing Openings

Openings can be difficult to write because they usually lay out the terrain for the whole argument. Nobody likes to spend a lot of time writing an introduction, only to realize later that it has to be scrapped because the claim or approach has shifted during drafting. But no rule says that you must write your opening first. You can postpone writing the full opening until you have written part of the body of the paper or until you have a firm sense of your paper's shape.

Openings serve two purposes, to introduce the topic and the background information needed to understand or appreciate the topic's seriousness and to state the thesis.

Consider the following types of openings. Keep in mind that one type can overlap the other (for example, startling openings can be partly anecdotal):

- **Occasional opening.** An occasional opening refers to a current event or local incident and uses it as the occasion for writing the essay. "In light of the current crisis in Addis Ababa . . ."

- **Startling opening.** A startling opening grabs the attention of readers with unexpected information. "While you are reading this sentence, fifty people will die of cigarette-related illnesses in this country."

- **Anecdotal opening.** An anecdotal opening uses a brief story to engage the reader's attention quickly. An argument against the continuous use of all the technology available on one's tablets or smartphones might begin with an anecdote about the hours an individual can play Angry Birds without realizing that he or she has spent two hours trying to achieve three stars on every level.

- **Analytical opening.** An analytical opening launches immediately into a critical discussion of the issue. An argument on the effects of alcohol on the body might open with an explanation of how alcohol damages certain bodily functions.

What makes one opening more appropriate than another? When choosing, consider the four interconnected elements of communication discussed earlier in the rhetorical rhombus. You may find that your subject lends itself more to an analytical opening. Or perhaps the writer's personal experience with the issue leads to an anecdotal opening. Or your purpose to shock readers into accepting the urgency of the matter suggests a startling opening. Maybe the kind of audience you are targeting (impatient to learn the facts? uncertain about the relevance of the topic?) justifies the use of an occasional opening.

Therefore, weigh the purpose of your argument, the kinds of readers you are targeting, and the nature of the subject matter when considering your opening.

EXERCISE 1.6

Discuss the rhetorical techniques used in each of the following openings:

1. The opening to an argument that one learns good writing mainly from reading well, by a Harvard psychologist and linguist.

    "Education is an admirable thing," wrote Oscar Wilde, "but it is well to remember from time to time that nothing that is worth knowing can be taught." In dark moments . . . I sometimes feared that Wilde might be right. When I polled some accomplished writers about which style manuals they had consulted during their apprenticeships, the most common answer I got was "none." Writing, they said, just came naturally to them.

    I'd be the last to doubt that good writers are blessed with an innate dose of fluency with syntax and memory for words. But no one is born with skills in English composition per se. Those skills may not have come from stylebooks, but they must have come from somewhere. That somewhere is the writing of other writers. Good writers are avid readers. —Steven Pinker, *The Sense of Style*. New York: Viking, 2014: 12.

2. The opening to an argument about the potential significance of discovering life elsewhere in the universe, by a professor of natural history.

    The recent discovery of abundant water on Mars, albeit in the form of permafrost, has raised hopes for finding traces of life there. The Red Planet has long been a favorite location for those speculating about extraterrestrial life, especially since the 1890s, when H. G. Wells wrote *The War of the Worlds* and the American astronomer Percival

Lowell claimed that he could see artificial canals etched into the planet's parched surface. Today, of course, scientists expect to find no more than simple bacteria dwelling deep underground, if even that. Still, the discovery of just a single bacterium somewhere beyond Earth would force us to revise our understanding of who we are and where we fit into the cosmic scheme of things, throwing us into a deep spiritual identity crisis that would be every bit as dramatic as the one Copernicus brought about in the early 1500s, when he asserted that Earth was not at the center of the universe. —Paul Davies, "E.T. and God," *Atlantic Monthly* Sept. 2003:112.

3. The opening to an argument about the merits of urban public schools, by a newspaper columnist:

   I was terrified. It felt as if I were shoving my precious 4-year-old into a leaky canoe and pushing him off into croc-infested waters. My friends acted as if they thought I was crazy. I was enrolling my little boy in a mob scene, sending him off to a place as dangerous as it was crowded. Didn't I see the newspaper that showed students crammed into shower-stall study halls or watch the television report where box-cutter-wielding delinquents were barely contained by exhausted security guards? Hadn't I read Jonathan Kozol? My tow-headed treasure was poised at the edge of the blackboard jungle, a place where the stairwells were as dangerous as the banks of the Amazon. It was 10 years ago, and I was sending my son off to kindergarten in the infamous New York City public school system. —Susan Cheever, "Thriving in City's Schools—Until 9th Grade?" *Newsday* 12 Nov. 2003:32.

4. The opening to an argument about how best to curtail obesity among young people, by two medical researchers:

   Obesity in children has tripled in the past 20 years. A staggering 50 percent of adolescents in some minority populations are overweight. There is an epidemic of type 2 (formerly "adult onset") diabetes in children. Heart attacks may become a disease of young adults. In response to this public health crisis, federal and state officials are seeking ways to protect children from the ravages of poor diet and physical inactivity. National legislation on the prevention and treatment of obesity is being considered. California and Texas are working to remove snack foods from schools. There are proposals for the regulation of food advertising to children. —Kelly D. Brownell and David S. Ludwig, "Fighting Obesity and the Food Lobby," *Washington Post* 9 June 2002.

Composing the Body of the Argument

If you think of your argument's opening as the promise you make to your readers about what you are going to do, then the body of the argument is the fulfillment of that promise. Here you deliver the goods that comprise the subject node of the rhetorical rhombus: the detailed support—facts, examples, illustrations—as well as the emotional, logical, and ethical appeals that collectively demonstrate to your readers that the claim you set forth in your introduction is valid.

Let's consider the development strategy of a famous argument, "Allegory of the Cave." In this famous allegory from *The Republic*, Plato aims to convince his audience of the difference between appearance (or illusion) and reality. (You may wish to read the allegory on pages 322–328 before continuing.) After introducing his statement of purpose to his pupil Glaucon—"Let me show in a figure how far our nature is enlightened or unenlightened"—Plato first describes the setting of the cave (or underground den) and the condition of the prisoners: They are chained so that they see only the shadows that are cast on the walls, and they can hear voices but are unable to determine who is speaking because they cannot turn their heads toward the actual source. Plato is now ready to elaborate on his thesis, which is in two parts: (1) Even though, when released, the prisoners would be temporarily blinded by the actual light (from the fire in the cave and then, even more so, after being dragged against their will outside the cave, from the light of the sun), their eyes would eventually grow accustomed to the true reality of things; that is, "the journey upwards [represents] the ascent of the soul into the intellectual world." (2) It is not enough to take the journey upwards; once accomplished, one should return to the cave to acquire a clearer judgment of the quality of life down there and to persuade the prisoners that a better life exists above.

How should you proceed in writing out the body of your argument? First, check that the sequence you developed in your outline includes everything you want to say about the issue. Jot down additional notes in the margins if necessary. If you have completed a freewrite or rough draft, now is the time to retrieve those pages and decide what to keep. You may already have more of the draft of your argument completed than you realize!

Many writers find it productive to move back and forth from draft to outline. The outline gives a bird's-eye view of the whole scheme; the draft concentrates on the minutiae of point-by-point discussion and exemplification.

Composing Conclusions

A good conclusion enables readers to grasp the full impact of the argument. If the introduction states the claim and the body argues for the validity of the claim by citing evidence for it, the conclusion encapsulates all those points of evidence, leaving readers with a renewed sense of the argument's validity.

To write an effective conclusion, then, aim for conciseness: Capture in just one or two paragraphs the gist of your argument. Conclusions of short papers need not be long and could be just three to four sentences.

What might you do in a conclusion? Here are three possibilities:

1. Reflect on the paper.
   - Return to the image or analogy or anecdote you discussed in the introduction and provide a frame for the piece.
   - Restate the thesis to underscore the argument of your essay.
   - Summarize your main points if the argument is complex or the paper is longer than six pages.

2. Broaden the scope beyond your paper.
   - Forecast the future if your main points should prove to be true.
   - Point out the implications of the ideas presented.
   - Exhort your readers to action.

3. Reinforce your readers' emotional involvement in the matter at hand. Keep in mind that "emotional involvement" can refer to feelings of security, hope, happiness, self-confidence, optimism, or overall well-being.
   - Introduce or reintroduce in a different way appropriate rational, ethical, or emotional appeals.
   - Aim for conciseness. Less is more when it comes to striking an emotional chord with readers.

EXERCISE 1.7

Discuss the strengths or weaknesses in the body and conclusion of the following essay, in which the author argues that video games are doing a better job than schools of teaching kids to think:

High Score Education | James Paul Gee

The United States spends almost $50 billion each year on education, so why aren't kids learning? Forty percent of students lack basic reading skills, and their academic performance is dismal compared with that of their foreign counterparts. In response to this crisis, schools are skilling-and-drilling their way "back to basics," moving toward mechanical instruction methods that rely on line-by-line scripting for teachers and endless multiple-choice testing. Consequently, kids aren't learning how

Source: James Paul Gee, "High Score Education: Games, Not School, Are Teaching Kids to Think," *Wired* 05 2003, pp. 91–92. Reprinted by permission of the author.

to think anymore—they're learning how to memorize. This might be an ideal recipe for the future Babbitts of the world, but it won't produce the kind of agile, analytical minds that will lead the high tech global age. Fortunately, we've got *Grand Theft Auto: Vice City* and *Deus Ex* for that.

After school, kids are devouring new information, concepts, and skills every day, and, like it or not, they're doing it controller in hand, plastered to the TV. The fact is, when kids play videogames they can experience a much more powerful form of learning than when they're in the classroom. Learning isn't about memorizing isolated facts. It's about connecting and manipulating them. Doubt it? Just ask anyone who's beaten *Legend of Zelda* or solved *Morrowind*.

The phenomenon of the videogame as an agent of mental training is largely unstudied; more often, games are denigrated for being violent or they're just plain ignored. They shouldn't be. Young gamers today aren't training to be gun-toting carjackers. They're learning how to learn. In *Pikmin*, children manage an army of plantlike aliens and strategize to solve problems. In *Metal Gear Solid 2*, players move stealthily through virtual environments and carry out intricate missions. Even in the notorious *Vice City*, players craft a persona, build a history, and shape a virtual world. In strategy games like *WarCraft III* and *Age of Mythology*, they learn to micromanage an array of elements while simultaneously balancing short- and long-term goals.

That sounds like something for their résumés.

The secret of a videogame as a teaching machine isn't its immersive 3-D graphics, but its underlying architecture. Each level dances around the outer limits of the player's abilities, seeking at every point to be hard enough to be just doable. In cognitive science, this is referred to as the regime of competence principle, which results in a feeling of simultaneous pleasure and frustration—a sensation as familiar to gamers as sore thumbs. Cognitive scientist Andy diSessa has argued that the best instruction hovers at the boundary of a student's competence. Most schools, however, seek to avoid invoking feelings of both pleasure and frustration, blind to the fact that these emotions can be extremely useful when it comes to teaching kids.

Also, good videogames incorporate the principle of expertise. They tend to encourage players to achieve total mastery of one level, only to challenge and undo that mastery in the next, forcing kids to adapt and evolve. This carefully choreographed dialectic has been identified by learning theorists as the best way to achieve expertise in any field. This doesn't happen much in our routine-driven schools, where "good" students are often just good at "doing school."

How did videogames become such successful models of effective learning? Game coders aren't trained as cognitive scientists. It's a simple case of free-market economics: If a title doesn't teach players how to play it well, it won't sell well. Game companies don't rake in $6.9 billion a year by dumbing down the material—aficionados condemn short and easy games like *Half Life: Blue Shift* and *Devil May Cry 2*. Designers respond by making harder and more complex games that require mastery of sophisticated worlds and as many as 50 to 100 hours to complete. Schools, meanwhile, respond with more tests, more drills, and more rigidity. They're in the cognitive-science dark ages.

We don't often think about videogames as relevant to education reform, but maybe we should. Game designers don't often think of themselves as learning theorists. Maybe they should. Kids often say it doesn't feel like learning when they're gaming—they're much too focused on playing. If kids were to say that about a science lesson, our country's education problems would be solved.

Revising the Argument: A Form of Reevaluation

You have written a draft of your argument, using one of the above methods. Now it is time to revise. "I love the flowers of afterthought," the novelist Bernard Malamud once said. The wonderful thing about writing is that you do not need to get it right the first time. In fact, you can try as many times as you wish, which is not the case with speaking. Malamud, you will notice, is commenting on the opportunity that revision provides to writers: the opportunity to say it better—more clearly, effectively, or convincingly. And for most writers, the very best "flowers" of thought occur only *after* they have written something down.

In revising argumentative essays, attend closely to the ways you have presented the problem, stated your claims, reported the evidence and testimony, represented the challenging views, drawn inferences, and reached reasonable conclusions. What follows is a closer look at each of these steps:

- **Presenting the problem.** Unless you capture the exact nature and full complexity of the problem you are examining, your entire argument is built on a shaky foundation. To determine whether the problem is represented well, question whether the introduction suits the audience and subject (recall the PAWS rhombus) and whether you establish sufficient ethos and pathos for readers to care to read on and to trust you, the writer.

- **Stating the claim.** Just as the problem must be stated clearly, so must the assertions that presumably solve the problem. Ask yourself whether your claim is realistic, practical, and sensible in light of the nature of the problem and the circumstances underlying it.

- **Reporting the evidence.** Facts and statistics—the raw data that comprise evidence—do not carry much meaning outside of a context of discussion. In presenting evidence in support of a thesis, the writer aims to communicate the significance of those facts and figures, not simply to drop them on the page. The writer also aims to present facts and figures in a way that readers can easily absorb, ideally in a visual configuration of some kind, such as an attractively designed chart or graph. When revising your discussion of evidence, ask yourself whether you interpret the data accurately, relate one cluster of data to another clearly enough (through visual representation of the data), and establish your ethos as a careful researcher and thinker on the issue.

- **Refuting challenging views.** When revising refutations, make sure that your writing represents the claims and evidence of the other side as fairly as possible. If you argue from a Rogerian perspective, think of establishing common ground with the audience in terms of shared values (warrants) or of cooperating to reach shared goals. Resist the temptation to omit parts of a challenging perspective because you are not sure how to refute it. Also, double-check the reliability of your refutation: Does it reveal the limitations or falsity of the challenging view?

- **Drawing inferences and conclusions.** How do you interpret your findings? How clearly do your underlying warrants emerge? Should you give more attention to them? How willing will your readers be to cooperate with you, based on your interpretation of the findings? What else can you say to ensure their cooperation—assuming that you would find such cooperation desirable?

Pulitzer Prize–winning journalist and teacher of writing Donald Murray, in *The Craft of Revision*, 5th ed. (2013), identifies three cardinal virtues of revision:

1. Revision allows one to identify problems to be solved.

2. Revision enables writers to explore the topic more deeply to arrive at new insights into the topic.

3. Revision enhances the brain's capacity for recall and patterning.

Reading to Revise

Reading well, especially in the context of writing, provides you with a wider perspective of your subject and of the many divergent views that give it depth and richness. As a well-read writer, you are in the position of integrating the ideas of different authors into your own views on the subject. Reading and reflecting critically on what you have read also help you to revise more successfully because they force you to get into the habit of reading your own writing as if it were someone else's. The advantage to beginning your project well in advance of the due date is that you will have the time to do such a critical reading of your drafts.

Using Your Reading Skills in Peer-Critiquing Workshops

You may be given the opportunity to respond critically to other students' drafts. Always read the draft as carefully as you would any published argument. Consider the following criteria as you read the first draft of a peer:

- **Purpose-related issues.** Is the purpose of the draft apparent? Stated clearly enough? Is the thesis (claim) well-stated? Directly related to the purpose?

- **Content-related issues.** Is the scope of the topic sufficiently limited? Does the writer provide enough background information? Provide enough evidence in support of the claim? Provide enough examples and illustrations to support the evidence? Represent challenging views fully and fairly before pointing out their flaws? Are the writer's interpretive and concluding remarks thorough? Does the writer offer clear recommendations, if appropriate?

- **Issues relating to style and format.** Is the writing concise? Easy to read? Are the sentences coherent, well-constructed, varied? Is the level of usage consistent and appropriate for the intended audience? Is the word choice accurate? Are unfamiliar terms defined? Does the writer use subheadings and visual aids where appropriate? Follow proper documentation format? For a discussion of the way incorporating visuals can enhance your argument, see "Reading Visuals Critically in the Digital Age," in Chapter 2, pages 73–74.

Types of Revision Tasks

Revising an argument involves a lot more than just "fixing things up"; it also involves *reseeing* the entire draft from a fresh perspective, checking to make sure that each assertion is fully discussed and that the discussion follows a logical sequence. Here are some different types of revision strategies.

Holistic Revision   F. Scott Fitzgerald liked to speak of "revising from spirit"— that is, revising from scratch after realizing that the first draft is on the wrong track or just does not seem to "click" in your mind. This kind of holistic revision—of revision as reseeing—makes it more likely that new energy and insights will be infused into the argument. For this kind of revision to work best, you often need to set aside (though not necessarily scrap) the original draft and start afresh.

Content Revision   When revising for content, you examine your ideas in greater depth than you did during the earlier draft. Typically, you gather more information or return to the original information to process it more efficiently. You may discover that you have underdeveloped an idea, so you would need to provide specific detail to support your claim. Usually, such revisions can be pasted into the original draft.

Organizational Revision   Writers often revise to strengthen the structure of their argument. When you revise for organization, pay close attention to the logical progression of your ideas. An argument can be made more effective, for example, by saving the most compelling point for last. As for moving coherently and smoothly from one point to the next, make sure you include transitional markers such as "on the other hand," "nevertheless," "in spite of," "according to," "however," and so on. Strive for the best possible order of ideas, not just the order in which the ideas occurred to you. When an argument unfolds logically, you create what is casually referred to as *flow*. The smoother the flow, the more likely your readers are to follow along and comprehend your argument.

Stylistic Revision   When revising to improve your style, pay attention to the way you sound on paper—to the manner in which you convey your ideas. Stylistic problems include inconsistency in tone of voice (too informal here, excessively formal there), lack of sentence and paragraph variety and emphasis, and use of jargon.

One of the pleasures of writing is projecting something of your individual personality and your own manner of emphasizing ideas, of relating one point to another, and of making colorful or dramatic comparisons. As Sidney Cox writes, "What you mean is never what anyone else means, exactly. And the only thing that makes you more than a drop in the common bucket, a particle in the universal hourglass, is the interplay of your specialness with your commonness" (*Indirections*, 1981:19).

One way to become more adept at constructing sentences and paragraphs is to play around with them. Take any paragraph, your own or someone else's from a magazine article, and rewrite it in different ways, discovering what is possible. You can sense a personality behind Cox's tone of voice, can you not? Look at his syntax, his peculiar word choice. But the point is, if *you* were the one asserting Cox's point, you would have done so in your own manner. For example, you might have expressed the point like this:

> People communicate ideas differently because each person sees the world differently. Each person uses language differently. At the same time, all of us who belong to the same culture share a common language. It is a writer's special blending of his or her individual voice with a commonplace voice that makes for a memorable writing style.

In this "revised" passage, the voice has become less conversational and more impersonal. The syntax and word choice seem more formal, which create the impression that the author is speaking to a large audience rather than to a single person.

Proofreading   One of our students once referred to proofreading as *prof-reading*—making sure the essay is ready for the prof's critical eye. Some students mistakenly equate proofreading with copyediting or even with revision in general, but proofreading refers to a very careful line-by-line scrutiny of the semifinal draft to make sure that no errors of any kind are present. The term *proofreading* comes from the profession of printing; a proof is an initial printing of a document that is used for correcting any mistakes. Most desk dictionaries list common standardized proofreaders' marks, or symbols and abbreviations that professional compositors use to indicate changes. You already know some of them: the caret (^) to indicate insertion of a word or letter; the abbreviation *lc*, which means change to lowercase (a diagonal line drawn through a capital letter means the same thing). Proofreading is not reading in the usual sense. If you try to proofread by reading normally, you will miss things. An ideal way to proofread is slowly and orally.

Chapter Summary

An argument is a form of discourse in which a writer or speaker tries to persuade an audience to accept, reject, or think a certain way about a problem that cannot be solved by scientific or mathematical reasoning alone. To argue well, a writer uses the three appeals of ethos, pathos, and logos—personal values and ethics, feelings, and logical reasoning—to supplement the facts themselves. The rhetorical rhombus reminds us that every communication act involves targeting a particular audience, whose particular needs and expectations regarding the subject must be met by the writer, and that every act of communication must have a clear, often urgent purpose for establishing communication in the first place.

Good argumentative writing is carefully structured. The three models of argumentative structure—Classical, Toulmin, and Rogerian—represent three different views about the nature and purpose of argument. *Classical argument* follows a predetermined structure consisting of an introduction and statement of the problem, presentation of evidence, refutation of opposing views, and a conclusion derived from the evidence presented. *Toulmin argument*, a modern form of Classical argument, growing out of the practicalities of political and legal debate, emphasizes the context-dependency of argument and the arguer's underlying values associated with the data the arguer brings forth to support a claim. *Rogerian argument*, growing out of modern humanistic psychology, emphasizes the need for human cooperation when viewpoints differ; hence, a basic assumption underlying the Rogerian argument is that a common ground can be found between the arguing parties, no matter how irreconcilable their differences may seem to be.

Composing arguments is a dynamic process that involves generating ideas, organizing the argument, drafting, revising, editing, and proofreading. These phases of composing overlap and are recursive. Understanding the composing process also means being aware of using different strategies for different parts of the argument, such as openings and conclusions. One final and vitally important phase in the composing process is acquiring feedback from peers. Feedback on first drafts is usually immensely valuable in helping writers think more deeply about the purpose, audience, and subject of their arguments.

Checklist

1. Do I clearly understand the four elements of the rhetorical rhombus that comprise the communication act? How each element interacts with the others?
2. Do I understand how the three appeals of ethos, pathos, and logos function in argumentative writing?
3. Do I understand the nature of evidence? Of refutation?
4. Am I familiar with the strategies that comprise the composing process?
5. Have I prepared an outline to prompt me in my drafting?
6. Am I familiar with the different kinds of revision?
7. Have I learned to proofread my drafts carefully?
8. Do I know the definitions of Classical, Toulmin, and Rogerian arguments?

Writing Projects

1. Conduct an informal survey of students' study habits by talking to your fellow students. How many of them "cram" for exams or write their papers immediately before the assignment is due? What specific strategies do students use when they study? (For example, do they make marginal glosses in their books? Write notes on index cards? Make flash cards? Get together with other students in regular study groups?) Can you correlate methods or habits of study to levels of academic success? Write an essay in which you argue for or against such a correlation, using the responses you have gathered.
2. Write an essay on the role that argumentative writing can play in helping people who disagree about a given issue to arrive at better understanding—or at least at a greater willingness to cooperate. What likely obstacles must initially be overcome?
3. Keep a "writing process log" the next time you write an argument. Describe in detail everything you do when prewriting, composing each draft, revising, and proofreading. Next, evaluate the log. Which facets of the composing process were most useful? Which were least useful?
4. Compose four possible openings, each a different type (occasional, anecdotal, startling, analytical), for your next argument writing assignment. Which opening seems most appropriate for your essay, and why?

5. Prepare an outline (Classical, Toulmin, or Rogerian) for an essay taking a position on one of the following topics:

    a. All places of business should (should not) block the Facebook site to keep employees on task.

    b. This college should (should not) sponsor formal skateboarding competitions.

    c. More courses or programs in ethnic and gender studies need (do not need) to be offered at this college.

2 Methods of Critical Reading

> **A reader must learn to read.**
>
> —Alberto Manguel

Reading and writing are intimately related modes of thinking—so intertwined that you really cannot do one without doing the other. Just as writers determine how to approach their subjects by considering their purpose and their readers, so too do readers determine how to approach *their* purpose for reading by considering how to approach the subject, often working along similar lines to those intended by the author.

Reading as the Construction of Meaning

Some researchers refer to the symbiotic relationship between reading and writing as the *construction of meaning*. That is, readers must process meaning from those symbols on the page that, by themselves, possess no intrinsic meaning.

As readers, we also construct meaning beyond what we see on the page before us. For example, when we read through a draft of an argument to revise and edit it, we monitor our sense of direction, the development of the ideas, the coherence (that is, the logical progression of ideas), the clarity, and the larger concerns of persuasiveness and originality.

All of these activities are context dependent. As the example in Table 2.1 reveals, reading strategies that work well, say, in drafting an essay that objectively analyzes the strengths and weakness of a high school exit test may not work when drafting a more subjective essay on why the school should retain or abandon such tests. In the first essay, you need to read for such elements as logical progression of ideas, thorough support of assertions, and fair representation of challenging or alternative views. In the second essay, aware that you are presenting an individual preference, you need to keep an eye out for sufficiently clear (if not always logical) reasons behind your preferences.

Thus, whenever we read, we do a great deal more than simply absorb words like a sponge. In reading others' work, we sometimes think to ourselves,

TABLE 2.1   Sample Perspectives from Which We Read

Topic	Perspective 1 (neutral outsider)	Perspective 2 (offensive)	Perspective 3 (defensive)
Value of exit tests	To weigh pros vs. cons to pass a fair judgment	I've always been held back by these biased tests!	Tests have always enabled me to show how much I know!

"If I had written this essay, I'd have made this introduction much shorter and put in more examples in the third paragraph—I barely understood it, after all!" Such thinking is comparable to what we do as we revise our own work, so clearly we are reading another's text from the writer's perspective.

We might also "revise" another's writing when someone asks us about a book or article we've read: "What is Leslie Jamison's *The Empathy Exams* about?" In summarizing that contemporary work of creative nonfiction, we would use our own words to shorten a 225-page work to one or two paragraphs. In fact, while you are reading such a text, you are summarizing it to yourself—during the actual reading or during breaks between readings. Thus, to understand a text means, in a sense, to rewrite the author's ideas so that we blend them with our own ideas. Such rewriting is built into the very nature of reading. We cannot truly comprehend a text without doing so.

Active Versus Passive Reading

In the sense that "to read" means processing written language to understand it, all reading is "active." But some forms of reading represent a greater challenge to the comprehension process than others. A letter from a loved one may be processed relatively swiftly and efficiently, almost as a photograph would, whereas a demanding legal or technical document of the same length may need to be processed in a much more methodical manner.

When we read primarily for pleasure—whether a novel, a work of nonfiction, or a friend's email—we are concerned primarily about content: What is going to happen to the characters in the novel? What is the author's premise in the work of nonfiction? What fun activities did the friend experience in London over the summer?

But when we read for a purpose other than (or in addition to) pleasure, we need to think more consciously of our reading process so that we can make necessary modifications. Such reading is task oriented: to find out certain information, to summarize the work, to analyze the structure of the work, to assess the merits of the argument, to determine how the information coincides with our position on the issue.

You can adopt certain strategies to become a more active reader. It may seem strange to think of a "strategy" of reading. The only strategy that leaps to mind is moving our eyes across the page from left to right and top to bottom (for readers of most Western languages). But from a psychological and linguistic perspective, we are pulling off complex feats of cognition. At the simplest level, we are doing any or all of the following, more or less simultaneously:

- *Linking* one part of a sentence with another; for example, linking a subordinate clause to a main clause or nouns and verbs to their respective adjectival or adverbial modifiers, or linking the data in a visual aid such as a graph or diagram to the discussion of those data in the body of the argument. Visuals themselves possess components that need to be linked together when they are read. Imagine a pie chart that breaks down someone's college-related expenses for a given month. The reader links each slice of the chart with the others, reflecting on proportions. If 40 percent of the pie is given over to the cost of meals, for example, the reader may agree or disagree with your claim that food costs on this campus are disproportionate relative to food costs on other college campuses.
- *Tracking* the constantly shifting parameters of meaning from word to word, phrase to phrase, sentence to sentence, paragraph to paragraph
- *Relating* any given sentence or paragraph to a premise or theme, whether implied or explicitly stated

Those are just some of the *basic* strategies. As students of writing, you read not just for understanding but for insight into the way in which an author organizes and develops an argument. This type of active reader needs to do the following:

1. Determine the *framework* of the author's argument. What are the claim, data, and warrant?

2. Evaluate the *data* (evidence) presented. Are they accurate? Sufficient? Appropriate? Relevant?

3. Evaluate the author's *organizational strategy*. Why does the author bring in X before Y and after W? Is the sequence beyond dispute, or is there no clear rhetorical purpose behind the sequence? Should the author have arranged things differently?

4. Speculate on the *significance* of what is being argued. What are the short- and long-term consequences of the author's views? If the author argues that student athletes are treated unfairly in the classroom, for example, and uses compelling evidence to back up that claim, then the significance of the argument is that it could persuade classroom teachers to be more flexible, say, in permitting student athletes to miss class to participate in out-of-town athletic competitions.

5. Analyze the *logic* of the argument. Has the writer inadvertently committed any of the logical fallacies covered later on in Chapter 7? Each of these cognitive acts works together to comprise active reading. Passive reading, by contrast, means reading without reflecting or "talking back" to the text—that is, without forming questions that can and should be asked of an author who is trying to communicate with us.

EXERCISE 2.1

1. Assess your reading process. What kinds of material do you read actively? Passively? What about the material encourages one mode of reading rather than another?
2. Select a short piece such as a magazine feature or editorial on a social or political issue and discuss it in terms of the four concerns of an active reader (framework, data, organizational strategy, and significance).
3. Read a short piece for coherence alone. Explain how the author "glues" sentences and paragraphs together to make them interrelate clearly and meaningfully.

Reading with a Purpose

As a student, you are preparing yourself to read with a critical eye and to retain a healthy skepticism when encountering strong views on controversial issues—that is, to demand that any claim on such an issue requires compelling evidence to be convincing. To read with a purpose means to demand from an argument evidence that is relevant, timely, accurate, and clearly presented. It also means to be able to spot errors in reasoning—overgeneralizations, faulty analogies, false dichotomies, red herrings, and so on—errors that are discussed in Chapter 5.

Reading as a Writer of Arguments

Chapter 1 describes the role supporting data and expert opinion play in building your argument. As you read to find sources of support for your argument, use the following strategies: previewing, in-depth reading, and postreading.

Previewing

Imagine Bob, a first-year student, trying to study for a political science quiz the next day. He's having trouble reading the textbook chapter being tested. It seems to have more pages than he has time or inclination to absorb. So he finds his classmate Julie in the library and tells her he's having trouble motivating himself to do all that reading. Julie, who's already read the chapter, encourages him by saying, "Oh, Bob, the chapter essentially covers only four points about the economic conditions on the Greek islands comprising Santorini." Relieved that the chapter highlights only four main points, Bob returns to his room motivated to read but also with a sense of how to read the chapter productively. Julie has given him a *preview* of what to expect. Previewing is typically a two-stage process: (1) prereading and (2) skimming.

Anything worth reading typically requires several readings, so you approach this previewing stage knowing that you will read the assignment more thoroughly later on.

To read as critical thinkers and writers, you must read to ensure that you

- understand the content and progression of the story or argument,
- can determine the rhetorical strategy (for example, the validity and significance of the claim, the data, and the warrant), and
- are able to incorporate the author's views into your own.

Prereading   You preread the text to determine its central purpose and approach. You may do this at the beginning of the term when, standing in line to purchase your textbook, you peruse the table of contents and the introductions to each of the chapters. You also preread when you read the topic sentences of the paragraphs in the introduction. (The topic sentence usually is the first, second, or last sentence.)

To preread an article or chapter from a work of nonfiction, you can rely on the structure that writers in the Western tradition have used for centuries and handed down to the modern college composition course:

- Introduction
- Thesis statement
- Topic sentences
- Transitional paragraphs
- Conclusion

Remember that the purpose of prereading is not to understand the whole piece but to identify the key points of the piece so that, when you do read it in its entirety, you already have a clear sense of its framework.

After reading the introduction in full, read the topic sentences of the body paragraphs. These tend to be in one of three spots: first, last, or second. Topic sentences most frequently appear as the first sentences of the paragraphs, just where you have been taught to put them. But they also may occur as the last sentence in the paragraph when the writer has organized the content of the paragraph by presenting his or her evidence before the claim. And the topic sentence sometimes is the second sentence of the paragraph (the third most frequent position) when the first sentence is transitional, linking the paragraph before to the one that follows. In these cases, you will read both the transitional sentences and the topic sentences. You may need to read a bit of the article or essay to gain a sense of the writer's style—that is, where he or she tends to position the topic sentence.

Here is an example of a paragraph in which the topic sentence appears at the very end, a technique that this particular author, Carl Sagan, uses quite commonly in his writing. This selection is from Sagan's *The Demon-Haunted World: Science as a Candle in the Dark* (1995):

> What do we actually see when we look up at the Moon with the naked eye? We make out a configuration of irregular bright and dark markings—not a close representation of any familiar object. But, almost irresistibly, our eyes connect the markings, emphasizing some, ignoring others. We seek a pattern, and we find one. In world myth and folklore, many images are seen: a woman weaving, stands of laurel trees, an elephant jumping off a cliff, a girl with a basket on her back, a rabbit,...a woman pounding tapa cloth, a four-eyed jaguar. People of one culture have trouble understanding how such bizarre things could be seen by the people of another.

The pattern Sagan uses in this paragraph is this: He opens with a question, gives a string of examples to illustrate the basis of the question, and then answers the question, that is, posits the topic sentence. Such rhetorical patterning provides a coherence that enables readers to follow the strands of a complex discussion.

The final step in prereading is paying close attention to concluding paragraph or paragraphs of the argument. Writers often summarize their main points here. They may also point out implications of the ideas or perhaps let readers know what steps they should take. To return to the chapter from *The Demon-Haunted World* that focuses on the difficulty of observing nature objectively, we arrive at Sagan's conclusion:

> By and large, scientists' minds are open when exploring new worlds. If we [scientists] knew beforehand what we'd find, it would be unnecessary to go [there]. In future missions to Mars or to the other fascinating worlds in our neck of the cosmic woods, surprises—even some of mythic proportions—are possible, maybe even likely. But we humans have a talent for deceiving ourselves. Skepticism must be a component of the explorer's toolkit, or we will lose our way. There are wonders enough out there without our inventing any.

Sagan not only stresses his central idea about the need to maintain objectivity in the search for truth but also assures us that the search for truth will reward us with discoveries every bit as wondrous as anything we could concoct.

By following a pattern of prereading, you may not yet fully understand the text, but at this stage you are just trying to provide yourself with an overview.

You are also giving yourself a sense of how much energy you will need to invest before reading the piece fully.

Skim-Reading   At this stage, read the article in full, including the parts you have preread. But read swiftly, keeping alert for the key words in each sentence. To skim well, take advantage of your peripheral vision: You do not have to look directly at a word to see it; your eyes notice it just by looking in its general vicinity. Also, you already have an idea of the general parts of the article, and you are fleshing out those generalizations via the specifics that the writer provides. This enables you to grasp more readily the writer's logical progression of ideas and use of evidence.

By the time you reach the conclusion, you should feel more comfortable with whatever the author is summarizing or exhorting readers to do.

If the piece you are reading is printed in columns, you probably will make your eyes stop once every line, approximately following a pattern indicated by the x's in the passage that follows:

As you read these two columns, you'll notice that there are x's above the typed lines, one to the left on the first line and then one to the right on the second line. The x's continue to alternate down the columns. Fixing your eyes on those x's, you can see the words written below them—not just the words directly below the x's but the words before and after those as well. If you were looking just for a particular date, such as June 20, 2000, then you would be looking just for that particular configuration of numbers. Looking somewhat above the lines rather than directly at the words on the lines helps you not to read the words but more to focus on the particular pattern of words or numbers that you are looking for. (The date of June 20, 2000, was chosen because that's the wedding date of two British friends, Dave and Jenny.) You see how you could systematically skim for just the two occasions of a date-like configuration. Essentially, that's skimming.

When skimming a page with visuals, return to the visual after skimming the text. First look for connections between the text and the visual; then look for points of comparison and contrasts within the visual itself—for example, in a multiple-bar graph that shows changes in use of coal versus oil for heating in three different decades in the United States (represented by three different-colored bars), you want to notice the degree of difference between coal and oil and whether such a difference is significant in arguing, say, that the United States has been doing a good job in becoming less oil-dependent from one decade to the next.

In-Depth Reading

The previewing strategies detail methods that you can follow if you wish to locate specific, brief information or to quickly scope out the gist of a piece. As a writer of arguments, you read for other reasons as well:

- *Summarizing* to demonstrate an ability and willingness to present another's ideas in a fair, unbiased way (see "Writing a Summary," pages 58–59)
- *Analyzing* the structure of the piece to understand precisely the logic the writer uses, to determine whether the writer omits some important causal or temporal element, or whether the writer fairly and accurately represents all major viewpoints regarding the issue
- *Assessing* the strengths and weaknesses of the argument and determining the extent to which the writer's position influences your own
- *Annotating* in the margins to maintain an ongoing critical-response dialogue with the author as you are reading (see "Reading with a Pencil," pages 63–64)

Postreading

You follow the full reading with a postreading. Essentially, you read the same parts of the piece that you read for the preread. The purpose of a postread is to reinforce the framework of the whole in your mind and to distinguish between details and main points of a piece. In a postread, you cement in your mind the structure and logic of the piece by going back over it and reviewing its contents. During the postread, follow these steps:

1. Ask yourself, "What is the most important thing I learned from this piece, and where is it most clearly expressed?" At this stage, not any earlier, you begin to mark the text. Highlight this passage with a marker and make a marginal note briefly summarizing the passage in your own words. Summarizing helps you reinforce what you have read.

2. Now ask, "What evidence does the author use that supports the claim most convincingly?" Highlight and annotate this passage as well.

3. Finally, ask, "What concluding insight does the author leave me with?" Again, highlight and then annotate this segment of text in your own words.

Once you get into the habit of previewing, in-depth reading, and postreading articles and essays, you will find it an efficient and satisfying process.

EXERCISE 2.2

1. Choose an article from your campus newspaper. First, preview the article and jot down what you remember immediately afterward. Next, read the article in depth and jot down new things you had not obtained during the preread. Finally, postread the article and answer the questions posed in the three steps on the previous page.

2. Preview an article in one of your favorite magazines or from the Clusters in Part 2. Write down all the information you obtain from this preview reading. Next, read the article as you normally would and write down any information you had not obtained from the prereading. Write a brief assessment of the value of prereading based on this experience.

Writing a Summary

One of the most effective ways of reinforcing your comprehension of a piece is to write a formal *summary* of it shortly after you read it. As you already know, a summary is a concise but accurate rephrasing, primarily in your own words, of the premise of a work. Writing summaries of works you read is a valuable exercise for three reasons:

1. To summarize is to demonstrate (to yourself and to others) the degree to which you understand the piece as the author means it to be understood—realizing, of course, that there is no way of knowing whether one's understanding of an argument corresponds *exactly* to what the author has in mind. Unfortunately, readers sometimes praise or criticize a work based on a misreading or a misunderstanding of what the author is trying to convey. Writing a concise summary of the thesis statement and the principal support statements can help you avoid that problem.

2. Writing summaries of arguments that challenge your own is a good way to pay closer attention to both the strengths and the shortcomings of the challengers' lines of reasoning.

3. Summaries of related articles and books serve as an important resource for a research paper. You may be reading many different sources on a given topic. Summarizing each one immediately after you have read the work helps you to internalize the material better and keep various sources straight in your mind. Sometimes, you will use these summaries when preparing an annotated bibliography. (See Chapter 8 for how to format an annotated bibliography.)

Typically, a summary is about one-fourth the length of the original, but a special type of summary is referred to as an *abstract*. Abstracts of books are generally a single page long and those of articles, a single paragraph. Volumes of abstracts, such as *Resources in Education* (which summarizes thousands of articles on education collected in a vast *database* known as ERIC) and *Chemical Abstracts* (which maintains a similar service for articles on chemistry), are located in your school library and often online.

Writing a summary returns you to the skeletal outline of your essay, where you are better able to isolate the key points. The procedure of summarizing is relatively simple in principle, but in practice it can be tricky. Some pieces are more difficult to summarize than others, depending on whether the key ideas are presented explicitly or implicitly. Here are the steps you should take:

1. Determine the thesis of the essay, rephrase it in your own words, and make that the opening sentence of your summary.

2. Locate the supporting statements. Sometimes these are the topic sentences of each paragraph, but some writers are inventive with paragraph structure. Rephrase the supporting statements in your own words.

3. Write a concluding sentence, paraphrasing the author's own conclusion if possible.

Read the following short argument at least twice. During the second reading, underline key passages and make marginal notations as needed. Next, write a summary of the article. After completing your summary, compare it with the summary that follows the article.

Death to the Classics!
Is it time to update the reading list? | Melissa Slager

To be, or not to be.
That is the question—not only asked by Hamlet, but increasingly asked about the de facto reading list that has enshrined him in high school English classes for decades.

Teach only these time-tested classics—your Shakespeare, Dickens and Hawthorne? Or take up arms against tradition and bring in some new blood—your Cisneros, Tan and Hosseini? And what exactly makes up "the canon," anyway?

These are questions that draw plenty of slings and arrows. And that may be because there is no right answer, says David Kipen, director of literature for national reading initiatives with the National Endowment for the Arts.

Source: "Death to the Classics! Is it time to update the reading list?" by Melissa Slager from Encarta.msn.com. Used by permission.

"A canon is a useful thing until you start treating it like one," Kipen says, "and then it becomes slightly dangerous."

Ye Olde Canon

There appears to be nothing dangerous, however, about William Shakespeare. The English bard has dominated high school reading lists, unquestioned, for decades, and there's still no sign of the curtain falling.

"Shakespeare isn't going anywhere," says Carol Jago, a past president of the National Council of Teachers of English.

In many schools, neither are other old standbys—*To Kill a Mockingbird*, *The Great Gatsby* and *Of Mice and Men*, to name a few. For teachers such as Diane Bahrenburg, a Vermont Teacher of the Year at Colchester High School, the syllabus of must-teach titles also includes Homer's *Odyssey* and Dante Alighieri's *Inferno*. To most people's minds, these are what make up "the canon." They are the classics, and there are good reasons for teaching them.

"They're the foundation of so much of the rest of literature—it's our base," Bahrenburg says.

The New Canon

But that base has been slowly shifting alongside cultural and educational fads. While the 1980s saw a movement to preserve cultural heritage by teaching foundational Western classics, the 1990s ushered in an era of multiculturalism to depict the women and minorities frequently left out.

In many ways, the reading list is merely expanding to include the faces that have appeared on the literary map since the Calvin Coolidge administration. Among these so-called modern classics, for example, are *Their Eyes Were Watching God* by Zora Neale Hurston, a black woman, and *Bless Me, Ultima* by Chicano author Rudolfo Anaya.

Today, with video games and TV crowding out reading habits, there's a move to put just about any book in kids' hands—so long as they're reading it.

As a result, many 19th-century texts, such as Dickens' *Great Expectations*, are disappearing completely from classrooms, deemed "too long, too hard" for attention-deficit teenagers of the 21st century. "Teachers are giving up," Jago says.

A Quasi Canon

Researcher Sandra Stotsky of the University of Arkansas says this trend to get teens to read, no matter what's between the covers, reveals a different kind of canon altogether—one where Harry Potter supplants Macbeth.

"The (traditional) canon is being taught in some schools, in some places, in some grades. But it's like the tail of an emaciated dog," she says.

She points to a 2007 study of 162,000 high school students who took online quizzes on books they'd read during the school year through a program called Accelerated Reader.

To Kill a Mockingbird was the most-read book, reflecting its continuing popularity among teachers. But also cracking the top 20 were all seven books in J. K. Rowling's *Harry Potter* series, as well as Stephenie Meyer's vampire-romance hit, *Twilight*.

Likely, these best-sellers are self-selected books that students read to earn extra class credit and are probably not assigned by teachers. But it's no less horrifying, Stotsky says.

"This has turned out to be a disaster," she says. "Most of what these kids are reading is at an arrested intellectual level. That's not what you want."

The Coming Canon

And yet, at times, what the kids choose is exactly the direction you should head, some teachers say.

At Billings Senior High School, teachers are required to teach a core curriculum that includes all the usual suspects, from *The Old Man and the Sea* to *Macbeth*. Beyond that, teachers are allowed to add works of their choosing.

For Steve Gardiner, a Montana Teacher of the Year, that means letting students pick their own books during "sustained silent reading." He sees kids pull everything from Stephenie Meyer to John Steinbeck out of their backpacks. He also sees a lot of nonfiction—something fiction-heavy English departments often overlook.

"We're very good about teaching poetry and fiction, and not so good about teaching nonfiction. And a lot of kids want nonfiction—that's how their minds work," Gardiner says.

There also are lessons in the protagonists students choose to follow, characters that tend to be brooding teenagers rather than brooding adults, says Kylene Beers, president of the National Council of Teachers of English.

"Because the characters are still in childhood, there's this inclination to still be interested [in and] worried about [them], and [to] develop an empathetic bond," Beers says. "That's what really moves a kid through a book. It's sometimes hard to develop that bond with Daisy in *The Great Gatsby*."

Beers and colleague Robert Probst conducted a survey in 2008 of about 1,200 teachers, asking them what they assign their students. She was disappointed to find that only about one-quarter of teachers assigned books from the young adult market with regularity, books such as Walter Dean Myers' *Fallen Angels*, a 1988 novel published by Scholastic about the Vietnam War.

"To me, that's the bravest teacher," Beers says.

Seeking a Story, a Fight

But what follows this expansion? Should graphic novels also be added to the canon? Cell-phone serials? English professor Mark Bauerlein of Emory University says the background college freshmen bring to class is already helter-skelter.

"You can't refer to a core set of texts anymore and expect that all students have read it," he says.

Bauerlein, author of *The Dumbest Generation*, blames the unclear goals of the politically correct and a dumbed-down digital culture. But he adds that the solution doesn't necessarily mean a classics-only catholicon.

"The important thing is this: Students need to leave a classroom with a deep sense of a tradition—whatever that tradition is. They need to walk out of class with a story," he says.

And, from there, refrain from setting it in concrete.

This thing we call a canon is really this "endlessly elastic, flexible, argument-worthy thing," says Kipen of the National Endowment for the Arts.

Kipen directs the NEA's Big Read, which seeks to tie readers together from across the country like one gigantic book club. None of the three books in his "personal pantheon"—Alan Paton's *Cry, the Beloved Country*, Charles Dickens' *Bleak House*, and Thomas Pynchon's *Gravity's Rainbow*—have yet made that list.

"Is this a canon—these three books? Are my three books better than your three books? I don't know," Kipen says. "All I know is I want to fight about it with you."

One Possible Summary

Despite the endurance of canonical works of literature like Homer's *Iliad* and *Odyssey*, Shakespeare's plays, and modern works like Harper Lee's *To Kill a Mockingbird*, the traditional canon has been slowly eroding since the 1980s in an effort to get today's students to become more committed readers. Some teachers feel that it's more important *that* students read than *what* they read. But for Emory University professor Mark Bauerlein, the most important thing is that students acquire a sense of tradition.

EXERCISE 2.3

1. Do an in-depth reading of the article you preread for the second item in Exercise 2.2. How does the prereading help you to absorb the discussion as you encountered it in the in-depth reading?

2. Write a summary of Martin Luther King Jr.'s essay, "Letter from Birmingham Jail," found in Chapter 4.

3. After everyone in class has written a summary of the King essay, compare the summaries in small groups. How do they differ? How are they alike? How do you know? What accounts for the similarities among the summaries? What accounts for the dissimilarities? Are the differences and similarities significant? In what way?

4. Consider the differences and similarities found in question 3 above to see whether they account for greater accuracy of some summaries.

5. Explain the relationship between summary writing and reading comprehension.

Reading with a Pencil

To help you pay special attention to key ideas during a postreading, write marginal comments, underline text, or use visual icons such as asterisks, checkmarks, or arrows. Such annotations, or *marginalia*, enhance your involvement with the reading material and reinforce understanding. (*Note:* Of course, if you are reading library books or books belonging to someone else, do not put a mark of any kind in them. Instead, jot your notes down in a journal.) If you are not in the habit of writing in the margins or in journals, it is a valuable habit to cultivate. Here are some types of marginalia to try:

- *Glosses:* One-sentence summaries of what each paragraph is about.

- *Comparisons:* Notes to yourself reinforcing correspondences you notice. Say you want to compare a passage with something you have read earlier in the piece or in a different piece. The abbreviation *cf.* (Latin for "compare") is most often used; it means compare and/or contrast this passage with such-and-such a passage on such-and-such a page.

- *Questions or reactions:* Spur-of-the-moment concerns you have about an assertion, the validity of the data or other kinds of evidence, or something the author overlooks or overstates.

- *Icons:* These are your own personal symbols—asterisks, wavy lines, check marks, bullets, smiley faces, and so on—that instantly convey to you on rereading whether the passage marked is problematic or especially noteworthy.

Let us take a look at one possible way of annotating a piece. Study the example that follows.

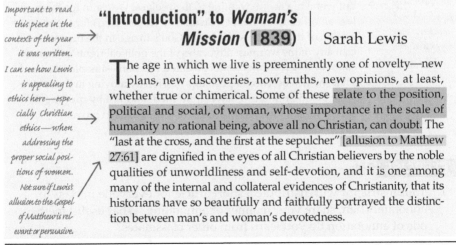

Important to read this piece in the context of the year it was written.

I can see how Lewis is appealing to ethics here—especially Christian ethics—when addressing the proper social positions of women. Not sure if Lewis's allusion to the Gospel of Matthew is relevant or persuasive.

"Introduction" to *Woman's Mission* (1839) | Sarah Lewis

The age in which we live is preeminently one of novelty—new plans, new discoveries, now truths, new opinions, at least, whether true or chimerical. Some of these relate to the position, political and social, of woman, whose importance in the scale of humanity no rational being, above all no Christian, can doubt. The "last at the cross, and the first at the sepulcher" [allusion to Matthew 27:61] are dignified in the eyes of all Christian believers by the noble qualities of unworldliness and self-devotion, and it is one among many of the internal and collateral evidences of Christianity, that its historians have so beautifully and faithfully portrayed the distinction between man's and woman's devotedness.

This book was first published anonymously in London; despite its having been influential for its time, nothing is known about the author.

What support for women's rights from previous ages is she referring to here, I wonder? →

Lewis is aware of male anxiety over allowing women greater participation in public discourse. →

Women back then sometimes refrained from taking advantage of opportunities to break free of their stereotyped roles. →

That the sex, characterized by such noble moral development, is destined to exercise no unimportant influence on the political and social condition of mankind, we must all believe, indeed, the united testimony of ages leaves this an undoubted fact. There is a popular cry raised of injustice and oppression on the part of the other sex. Yet men, in all ages, have shown a sufficient willingness to allow woman a share of influence, sometimes a very undue share. There is no hyperbole in the phrase—"Vainqueurs des vainqueurs de la terre" [Conquerors of the conquerors of the earth], and this influence is so powerful, and so generally felt, that it becomes a question whether it is used as it ought to be—for good.

But, it is said, it is degrading to work by influence instead of by power—indirectly instead of directly—as subordinates, not as principals. Here is the question at issue. Would mankind be benefited by the exchange of influence for power in the case of woman? Would the greatest possible good be procured by bringing her out of her present sphere into the arena of public life, by introducing to our homes and to our hearths the violent dissensions, the hard and rancorous feelings, engendered by political strife? It is really difficult to approach the subject in the form to which it has by some writers been reduced, with any degree of gravity, and it is somewhat to the credit of the other sex, that it has not more frequently been treated with the keen and indelicate satire which it deserves, and might provoke. Yet we are not one iota behind these fiery champions of womanhood, in exalted notions of its dignity and mission. We are as anxious as they can be that women should be roused to a sense of their own importance, but we affirm, that it is not so much social institutions that are wanting to women, but women who are wanting to themselves. We claim for them no less an office than that of instruments (under God) for the regeneration of the world—restorers of God's image in the human soul. Can any of the warmest advocates of the political rights of woman claim or assert for her a more exalted mission—a nobler destiny! That she will best accomplish this mission by moving in the sphere which God and nature have appointed, and not by quitting that sphere for another, it is the object of these pages to prove.

EXERCISE 2.4

1. Your instructor will distribute a short article for everyone in class to annotate. Then, share your manner of annotating. What useful methods of annotation do you learn from other classmates?

2. Clip a relatively short newspaper story, paste or photocopy it on a sheet of paper, leaving very wide margins, and then annotate the article fully.

Reading with an E-Reader

For the past several years, e-readers such as Amazon's Kindle and Barnes & Noble's Nook have been revolutionizing the way people read. It is now possible to download, for a nominal fee (sometimes for no fee at all), most books in print. A single e-reader can hold hundreds of books, making it exceptionally convenient because the readers are lightweight and easy to carry around.

But what about annotating? Well, most e-readers have an annotating device. It may not be as easy to do as penciling in notes in the margins of a print book, but it can be done. Unlike annotating online documents, which can be done only if you download the file and type in your annotations or simply print out the document, you can add your notes directly to the text of the e-book you are reading.

Reading Visuals in an Argumentative Essay

You might be thinking, "Who needs to be shown how to read a visual? All you need to do is look at it!" Well, that might be true for the consumer—in fact, advertisers *hope* that consumers will simply look at their images so that the hidden persuasive appeals can work their alchemy. As writers of argument, however, you need to read visuals critically, just as you would read any book or article critically. But how does one read an image critically? Graphs and charts are virtually self-explanatory; their captions in effect tell you how to read them, so let's set this type of visual aside for the moment and focus instead on photographs and drawings.

As simple and unified as a photograph or drawing might be, it generates several different kinds of relationships: external, internal (that is, the interplay of particular visual elements within the whole image), and rhetorical (that is, what the different elements in the visual communicate or seem to communicate to the audience).

External Relationships

- The relationship of the visual to the text surrounding it and/or to the text referring to it
- The relationship of the visual to other visuals in the article, if any

Internal Relationships

- The interplay of figure and ground
- The terms *figure* and *ground* refer to the object of focus (the figure), which dominates the photograph or drawing, and what is in the background. In a visual, everything in an image establishes a relationship of some sort with everything else, simply by its presence.
- The expression of mood and attitude

David Plowden

Study David Plowden's photograph, "The Hand of Man on America." It conveys a *mood and attitude,* the visual equivalent of point of view. Note, for example, how the telephone poles are misaligned and uneven, as if placed carelessly on the land. Note, too, how the wires seem to reinforce this misalignment. Together the poles and the wires project a dark or solemn mood and convey an attitude of disdain toward the telecommunication industry: It is not "aligned" with the harmonious shape of the Statue of Liberty.

Before deciding on including a particular visual for your article, ask yourself these two questions:

1. Do the figure and ground elements interconnect in ways that enhance the purpose of the image? Look again at Plowden's photograph. Notice how the foreground objects interact with the background object, the Statue of Liberty. One of the many ironies of this image is that the Statue of Liberty not only dominates the image, even though it's in the background (the telephoto lens used to take the photograph makes it appear larger than it would otherwise), but it also embodies the implicit conflict between the precious liberties it symbolizes and the ways in which those liberties are sometimes abused by environmentally damaging technology and industry.

2. Do all the objects in the foreground or background serve a unifying purpose? Are there extraneous elements in the ground that could prove to be distracting? Test the criterion of unity on Plowden's photograph. Can anything be deleted from the image without diminishing its impact? The cranes in the background? No; they, along with the telephone poles and the piles of refuse, contribute to the ironic contrast between the dark images of abuse and the bright image of liberty.

Visuals need not be specifically connected to an argument to be useful to that argument. Consider the role played by the visuals in the following piece about the relevance of traditional Jesuit liberal arts courses to modern-day students. What implicit point is being made by the photograph of the students playing tug-of-war? How do the portraits of the saints relate to the photograph? To the premise of the article?

Philosophers, Theologians, Postmodern Students
Why They Need Each Other | Joseph J. Feeney, S.J.

In November 2001, *Newsweek* interviewed a Princeton undergrad about his education, and with palpable regret he said "he had been taught how to deconstruct and dissect, but never to construct and decide." Reading his comment, I acutely felt his sense of loss, and wondered whether a similar loss affects undergrads at Jesuit universities. This issue of *Conversations* prompts me to ask how much our professors of philosophy, theology, and religious studies help students to "construct," to "decide," and even to *affirm*—specifically, to affirm *meaning* and *faith*. I write, then, to propose a dialogue with philosophers and theologians about our students.

A number of my own students, I find, are "postmodern"—skeptical about truth, emotionally wary, prone to parody. Since 1993 I've taught "Modernism and Postmodernism" at Saint Joseph's University (we study literature, music, art, and architecture, but not formal theory), and for their final essay I ask if they are modernist, postmodern, traditional, or some mix of these. Such a personal essay first baffles, then entrances them, as they discover aspects of themselves they never noticed. Probing their own lives, they tell me about themselves (I am always touched and honored by their trust in me), and a fair number call themselves postmodern in whole or in part. Thus allowed to know them, I find it my role as, well, professor of postmodernism, to raise this issue with my colleagues in philosophy and theology, I offer, then, a three-part invitation to dialogue: (I) What is postmodernism? (II) What do my recent students (Fall, 2006) say about themselves? (III) What kind of dialogue do I propose?

Source: "Philosophers, Theologians, Postmodern Students" by Joseph J. Feeney, S.J. from *Conversations on Jesuit Higher Education*, No. 32 (Fall 2007): 22–24. Reprinted by permission.

I

The word "postmodern" resists easy definition. Some dictionaries just omit the word, others focus on philosophy or architecture. The New Oxford American Dictionary (2001) is more encompassing, defining postmodernism as

> *A late 20th-century style and concept in the arts, architecture, and criticism that...*
> *has at its heart a general distrust of grand theories and ideologies as well as a problem-*
> *atic relationship with any notion of "art." Typical features include a deliberate mixing*
> *of different artistic styles and media [and] the self-conscious use of earlier styles and*
> *media [and] the self-conscious use of earlier styles and conventions...*

In my own teaching, I begin postmodernism with a 1967 essay from *The Atlantic Monthly* where the novelist John Barth asserts that traditional art forms are tired, used-up, worn out, and can be used only "with ironic intent" as a wry comment on, or parody of, the past. As postmodernism develops, such suspicion of the past affects attitudes and convictions, and both art *and* life seem worn out, random, incoherent, meaningless. With little depth or stability, postmodern works glitter with surface verve: bright colors, bizarre collages, playful contradictions, references to their own artifice. For example, John Fowles' novel *The French Lieutenant's Woman* (1969) parodies Victorian prose, mixes past/present and fiction/reality, and has three endings. In Jeff Koons' sculpture "Three Ball 50/50 Tank" (1985) three basketballs just float on water in a glass tank. Boundaries are pushed, freedom reigns. No longer able to be surprised or shocked, postmodernists grow cool and detached, their dulled emotions relieved by laughter and parody. I must say, though, that I find postmodern works fun to read, see, hear, and teach. But such freedom has its cost: like that Princeton student, people "deconstruct and dissect" but find it hard to "construct and decide."

In the recent *Postmodernism: A Very Short Introduction* (2002), Christopher Butler of Oxford University reviews both theory and practice, finding the "party" of postmodernists "not particularly united in doctrine" yet "certain of its uncertainty." "A deep irrationalism [lies] at the heart of postmodernism," he writes, and "a kind of despair about the Enlightenment-derived public functions of reason." Yet, he concludes, "I believe that the period of its greatest influence is now over."

II

But postmodernism is not over for our students—the fragile, lovely people who sit before us in our classrooms. Many live with the emotions dulled, trust and meaning limited, religious faith lost. Let me quote (with permission, for which I thank them) two of my postmodern students from last fall. One writes,

> *Life is completely random. Life is chaos. By acknowledging this simple truth I can ele-*
> *vate myself above the bullshit and find some meaning in life, and by that I mean I can*
> *make life mean to me virtually whatever I want....I can choose to interpret my life and*
> *the world around me in whatever way I see fit. That is a great power.*

(6) to each individual student. To help our students, I suggest, we professors need a dialogue on academic and religious cura personalis.

About what might we talk? About how best to offer our students—postmodernists and all the others—a worldview that questions *and* affirms. Literature offers them a rich humanism; philosophy, meaning and synthesis; theology, a belief that is intellectual, centrist-Catholic, ecumenical. Outside the classroom, campus ministry, service-learning, and semester-beak trips offer their own invitations. To end, I return to my title: Why do philosophers, theologians, and postmodern students need each other? So philosophers can offer meaning, so theologians can offer belief, so students can discover—and affirm—both meaning and belief. We don't want our students to be like that disappointed Princeton undergrad in *Newsweek*.

© Sky Light Pictures/Shutterstock

To give another example of the way visuals can reinforce a point of view, consider the following ad for IAmBiotech.org, part of a public information project produced by the Biotechnology Industry Organization (BIO). What do the visual elements contribute to the assertions that appear in the advertising copy?

The first image, that of a parent (or medical professional?) holding a child presumably suffering from some form of cancer (suggested by her lack of hair) reinforces the idea that biotechnology research is people centered, compassionate, implicitly refuting the idea that such research is excessively clinical, and indifferent to the human element. The second image, that of specimen tubes being organized by a researcher, comes closer to the commonplace image of "scientific research"—which in its own way is generally regarded as a source of progress and hope. Note how the designer of the ad cleverly links the two images together, as if to say, "Scientific research is never separate from human caring and compassion." Thus, even before readers take in the information presented in the ad copy, they are predisposed to the implied thesis that biotech research works on behalf of people and is not merely research for its own sake.

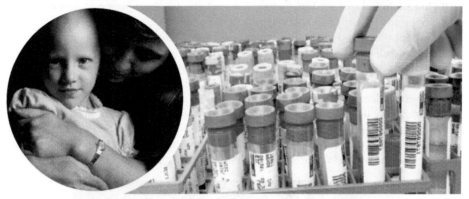

Cancer · Alzheimer's · HIV/AIDS · Parkinson's

Where is the world finding answers?

Biotechnology

More than 325 million people worldwide have been helped by the **more than 200 drugs and vaccines** developed through biotechnology. **Future breakthroughs** may lead to **treatments** and even **cures** for some of the world's most debilitating and rare diseases.

Biotechnology also helps drive our nation's innovation economy, creating high-wage, high-value jobs with a high multiplier effect. The more than **1.3 million Americans employed in the biosciences** help **create an additional 6.2 million jobs**, for business services, contractors and other vendors.

And we're just getting started.

If you are looking for answers to some of our biggest challenges visit www.IAmBiotech.org/learnmore

We're working on answers. For all of us.

Let's work together.

www.IAmBiotech.org/learnmore

BIOTECHNOLOGY
INDUSTRY ORGANIZATION

© Biotechnology Industry Organization

EXERCISE 2.5

Write an analysis of the compositional technique of one of your favorite photographs or paintings. Pay attention to the interplay of foreground objects with background objects and the way each object in the image contributes to a central idea.

EXERCISE 2.6

Consider the advertisements in Chapter 1. In each case, decide whether the appeal is basically visual or basically verbal—that is, whether the photographs or the words are most important to the impact of the ad. Why do you think as you do?

Reading Visuals Critically in the Digital Age

Images have always played an important role in mass communication, but in today's technologically sophisticated world, images appear everywhere—on our smartphones and tablets, on computer and television screens, as well as in print periodicals, advertising flyers, and billboards. Public monuments and statues are images to be read critically as well. Buildings and houses are also images that convey a point of view. The image on the dust jacket or front cover of a novel, textbook, biography, or manifesto not only advertises the content of the book but also reflects the author's (and the publisher's) attitude toward the subject matter. Everywhere we look, we confront images that persuade us to buy things, attempt to shape our tastes and lifestyles, and help us to absorb information from articles and reports. Moreover, we ourselves regularly transmit images (mostly photographs) that not only convey information about our personal and public lives and interests but also convey our values. If we share images of animals with friends and family, for example, we are implicitly letting them know we love animals, that it is important to love animals, that animals should be nurtured and protected, and so on.

Strategies for Critically Reading Internet Materials

You may be wondering, why should reading Internet documents be any different from reading print documents? Aside from possible neurological differences between reading off a screen versus reading a printed page (it's possible that the brain processes information differently when reading off a screen), there are rhetorical considerations to keep in mind when you read material on the Internet—not just documents per se, but websites, blogs, social networking posts, and so on.

You may have discovered that some Internet materials are quite lengthy and that it would be counterproductive to print out the entire document just for a few paragraphs or relevant information that you may need to support an assertion. In such a case, simply use the copy-and-paste function of your word processor to download the passage(s) into your notes.

Although plenty of print sources may be of questionable reputation, there are far more questionable Internet sources—that's because it is much easier to post things online than it is to publish in print journals. Authors of print articles and books must go through varying kinds of editorial screening and peer review, but anyone can post his or her material directly to the web. Note, however, that not everything on any given web site, even a web journal, is necessarily peer reviewed. As a result, you need to examine the documents you access with skepticism as well as scrutiny. More specifically, consider the following:

- *Credentials of the author.* Is the author a recognized professional in his or her field? You can quickly determine this by "Googling" the author and learning about his or her qualifications. *Note:* Sometimes the authors who contribute to a website are anonymous and impossible to locate. For example, the articles comprising the vast online encyclopedia, Wikipedia, are all written anonymously.

- *Authenticity of the research.* Are the author's methods and findings well documented? Have they been acknowledged by valid authorities or published in recognized journals? Again, you can determine these criteria by locating the sources themselves.

- *Effectiveness of the argument.* Has the author backed assertions with sufficient, timely, and relevant evidence? Have challenging views been fairly represented and examined for their shortcomings?

- *The Internet domain.* The domain of a website can be a first clue as to the nature of the document. The .edu domain indicates an academic website; .gov indicates a government agency; .org tells you that the website is from a nonprofit organization; and .com tells you the website is that of a company or corporation.

EXERCISE 2.7

1. What is the point of view being conveyed by the cover designs of your college textbooks, including the cover of this argument textbook?

2. Evaluate the credentials of the authors associated with the following blog on torn ACL (knee ligament) recovery: http://aclrecuperation .blogspot.com/

3. Bring one of your own photographs to class and analyze it in terms of its internal elements (mood, attitude, figure, and ground relationships).

Becoming a Highly Motivated Reader

People read for many reasons: to be entertained; to be informed of global, local, and job-related events; to enhance their general knowledge of fields such as history, science and technology, commerce, politics, social developments, and the arts; and to improve their personal lives and health.

You, however, have an additional reason to read: to become a better writer. To realize this goal, you must become not only an alert, active reader but a highly motivated one as well.

To acquire a sense of the rich possibilities of argumentative writing, begin to read (if you don't already) any or all of the following material:

- Newspaper editorials and op-ed pieces (familiarize yourself not only with the editorial section of your local newspaper but with those of the *New York Times* and the *Washington Post* as well)

- Essays that appear in magazines and journals noted for high-quality commentary on important issues, such as *Newsweek, Time, Harper's Magazine*, the *Atlantic Monthly*, and the *New York Review of Books*

- Books that take a strong stand on current, intensely debated issues, such as John Mueller's *Overblown: How Politicians and the Terrorism Industry Inflate National Security Threats, and Why We Believe Them* (Free Press, 2006) or Victoria de Grazia's analysis of the influence of the United States on Europe after World War II, in *Irresistible Empire: American's Advance Through Twentieth-Century Europe* (Belknap Press/Harvard University Press, 2006)

You likely are already a motivated reader, or you could not have made it into college. Your goal now is to capitalize on your already strong reading skills by reading even more widely and avidly. Here are a few suggestions to consider:

1. Begin by thinking of each reading experience—each opportunity to scrutinize an argument—as a chance to recruit more brain cells. It is said that we use only 10 percent of our brain capacity, so there's no danger in running out of cells!

2. Think of each reading experience as yet another opportunity to study a talented writer's craft, an important step toward helping you develop your own craft.

3. Select books for reading that you have intended to read but "never got around to." Do not be overly ambitious; you do not want to disappoint yourself. It is not necessary to give yourself page quotas (for example, a hundred pages a night); that has a way of backfiring when you have an already busy schedule. The key is to read *regularly*, every day, at the same time, just as you might with exercising, so that reading becomes a habit.

And be patient with yourself: It sometimes takes a while for a habit to take hold. After about three or four weeks of "forcing" yourself to read, say, one hour of non-course-required reading every morning, the ritual will become so ingrained that it will feel as natural (and as enjoyable) as eating.

4. Finally, take the time to keep a reading journal. This does not have to be elaborate. After each reading session, take about fifteen minutes to jot down your reflections on or reactions to the reading you have just finished. In addition to reinforcing your comprehension of the material and your insights into it, the journal will serve as a logbook of your reading experiences.

Once again, it is impossible to overemphasize the importance of reading to learning, to the life of the mind, and to what it means to be educated in this complex, information-driven, competitive world. Reading is truly your ticket to the treasures of knowledge and understanding.

EXERCISE 2.8

1. Write a reading autobiography in which you describe your childhood and early adolescent reading experiences and tastes. Note how your tastes in and habits of reading have changed over the years.

2. Keep a record of your reading activities over the next four weeks. Record the time you spend reading each day. List everything you read, but only after you finish reading it (individual chapters can count as separate pieces). Divide the material into "required" and "nonrequired" reading. Do an "active reader" critique of each work (refer to the list on page 52). At the end of the fourth week, evaluate your reading. Did your motivation to read improve? When? Did your reading become more efficient? Be as honest with yourself as you can.

3. If you consider yourself a slow or inefficient reader, make a special effort to improve. If it takes you longer than an hour to read fifty pages of a book, you are probably subvocalizing (sounding out one word at a time in your head, as if you were reading aloud). Practice reading *clusters* of words and be sure your pacing is swift and smooth, not jerky. Check to see whether your campus offers classes in speed reading or efficient reading.

4. Keep a reading improvement log. Each day for the next four weeks, record the number of pages you read in a given time (say, half an hour). Do not sacrifice your comprehension as you work on improving your efficiency. The more efficient your reading process, the more your comprehension should improve.

Reading Responsibly

To read arguments responsibly is to engage in a three-step procedure:

1. Read to learn the author's position on the issue.

2. Reread to understand fully that position.

3. Reread to compare and contrast the author's views with the views of others.

Every time we read or listen to someone's views about an issue, we may feel prematurely inclined to agree or disagree. Remaining neutral is sometimes difficult, especially if the writer or speaker presents his or her ideas with passion, eloquence, and wit. As a responsible reader, you do not need to maintain neutrality permanently, only to delay judgment. Before judging an issue, regard any argument as but one perspective and assume that many perspectives must be considered before a fair judgment can be made.

Reading well is like listening well. Good readers give writers the benefit of the doubt, at least momentarily, and respect the author's point of view, believing it worthy of serious attention (unless the author demonstrates negligence, such as distorting another author's views). But disagreement should never be confused with contentiousness, even if the author comes across as adversarial. You will comprehend and subsequently respond more successfully if you read the argument attentively, if you assume that the writer has considered the argument's assertions with great care, and if you are willing to give the writer the benefit of any doubts, at least for the time being. Once you have read the argument and reflected on it, go over it again, making sure you have understood everything. Then, before you do a third reading, place the writer's point of view in the context of others' views. The third reading is the critical one in which you ask questions of every assertion, questions that reflect the larger conversation produced by other essays.

EXERCISE 2.9

Use active reading strategies to read the following editorial on the need to combat global warming. *Preread* the editorial to get a sense of its premise and key points. *Skim* it straight through without critical questioning, allowing the author to present his or her case without interruption, so to speak. Then *read* the essay in depth, paying close attention to the way in which the writer develops the argument. Finally, *postread* it to reinforce full comprehension, making notes in the margins as recommended above.

1. Write a one-paragraph summary of the article to ensure that you accurately understand the author's premise and line of reasoning. What is

the most important insight you gain from this editorial? What do you most agree with? Least agree with?

2. How does the editorial compare with other commentary on global warming, such as Al Gore's book and film, *An Inconvenient Truth* (2006)? Do a subject or key word search using your library's online catalog or your Internet search engine or consult one of the periodical indexes in your library's reference room, such as the *Environmental Index* or the *Reader's Guide to Periodical Literature*. Keep in mind the simple but easily overlooked fact that a single argument is but one voice in a multitudinous conversation. As John Stuart Mill wisely states, "He who knows only his own side of a case knows little." Before you can fully understand the complexities of an issue, let alone take a stance on it, you must become thoroughly familiar with the ongoing conversation, not just with one or two isolated voices.

3. If you had the opportunity to address this topic in an essay of your own, what would be your thesis? How would you defend it? Is there anything missing from the editorialist's argument that should be included? Why do you suppose he omitted it? Out of ignorance? His wish to hide a persuasive contrary view? His assumption that it is irrelevant? Do you find anything in the writer's treatment of the topic that seems especially illuminating or, on the contrary, misleading or confusing?

4. Discuss how well the EPAs 2014 summary of climate change reinforces the claim that climate change is real and urgent.

5. Rewrite the opening paragraph of the editorial. What expectations does your paragraph set up for your readers? How do they differ, if at all, from the expectation the editorialist sets up with his original opening?

6. Consider the author's style, identifying as many stylistic elements as you can. Examples include use of metaphor, manner of incorporating or alluding to outside sources, manner of emphasizing a point, devices used to connect one idea with another, orchestration of sentence patterns, choices of words and phrases, manner of integrating outside sources, overall readability, and concision. What about his style most delights you? Annoys you? What would you do differently and why?

7. Describe the author's concluding paragraphs. Suggest an alternative conclusion for the editorial.

8. Locate up-to-date information about the Kyoto Protocol. How justifiable is the editorialist's faith in this treaty? How would you rewrite the editorial, if at all, in light of your findings?

High Noon

Global warming is here. It is moving as fast as scientists had feared. If it is not checked, children born today may live to see massive shifting and destruction of the ecosystems we know now. They may witness the proliferation of violent storms, floods, and droughts that cause terrible losses of human life.

The good news is that we are not helpless. We can still curb the greenhouse trend. Our next, best chance will come November 13–24 in the Netherlands, when the nations of the world negotiate again over the terms of the global warming treaty called the Kyoto Protocol. If we lose this chance, we may lose momentum for the entire protocol, and with it five or more years of precious time. But if we win a strong treaty in the Netherlands, it will start real movement on the long road to change.

Evidence and Damage

Like trackers on the trail of a grizzly, scientists read the presence of global warming in certain large-scale, planet-wide events. Over the last century, the surface of the planet heated up by about one degree Fahrenheit. More rain and snow began falling worldwide, an increase of 1 percent over all the continents. The oceans rose 6–8 inches. If these numbers applied to local weather, they would be trivial. As planetary averages, they are momentous. The past decade was the warmest in at least a thousand years. A graph of average global temperatures since the year 1000 shows a precipitous rise that starts at about the time of the Industrial Revolution and shoots upward to our own time.

The results may be profound and unpredictable. In altering the climate of the planet, we are playing with a vastly complicated system we barely understand. As Columbia University scientist Wallace Broecker has said, climate is an angry beast, and we are poking it with sticks.

We may already be feeling its anger. Of course, weather happens in spurts, _5_ with or without global warming. It is impossible to know whether this storm or that drought was an ordinary event, say the effect of a little extra moisture carried over the West Coast by El Nino, or whether it was a flick of the tail of the global warming beast.

What is certain is that the kinds of catastrophes global warming will cause are already happening all over the world. Hundreds of people died in exceptionally high monsoon floods in India and Bangladesh this fall. Three dozen died last month in mud slides in the Alps; the floodwaters rushing out of the mountains were said to have raised one lake to its highest point in 160 years. A heat wave last year across much of this country claimed 271 lives. Penguins in the Antarctic are finding it harder and harder to find food for their chicks, as the shrimplike krill they eat grow scarcer in warmer waters. Disease-bearing mosquitoes have moved to altitudes and longitudes they usually never reach: malaria has come to the Kenyan highlands; the West Nile virus thrives in New York City.

If global warming continues unchecked, the next hundred years will be a century of dislocations. Ecosystems cannot simply pick up and move north. Many will break apart as temperatures shift too far and too fast for all their plants and animals to follow. Others, such as alpine tundra, will die out in many places because they have nowhere to go.

According to some climate models, by the year 2100 the southern tip of Florida may be under water and much of the Everglades may be drowned. Vermont may be too warm for sugar maples; wide swaths of the forests of the Southeast may become savannah; droughts may be frequent on the Great Plains. Meanwhile, according to the UN's Intergovernmental Panel on Climate Change, heat-related human deaths will double in many large cities around the world and tropical diseases will spread. Deaths from malaria alone may rise by more than a million a year.

Problem and Solution

There is no scientific question about the cause of global warming. Carbon dioxide and other "greenhouse gases" in the atmosphere trap heat. For millennia, the planet's temperature has moved in lockstep with the concentration of carbon dioxide in the atmosphere. Humans have now increased that concentration by 30 percent since the preindustrial era, principally by burning oil, coal, and other fossil fuels. Today we have the highest atmospheric carbon concentration since the evolution of Homo sapiens.

10   The United States is the world's biggest greenhouse gas polluter. We have only 5 percent of the world's population, but we produce more than 20 percent of its greenhouse gases. In the face of climate chaos, we continue to increase our pollution. Power plants are the fastest-growing source of U.S. carbon dioxide emissions, primarily because we are increasing the output from old, inefficient coal plants, many of which don't meet current standards. Cars are another major and growing source.

To stop piling up carbon dioxide, we need to shift to cutting-edge technologies for energy efficiency and for renewable energy from the sun, wind, and geothermal sources. Prosperity doesn't require fossil fuels. According to the American Council for an Energy-Efficient Economy, U.S. carbon intensity (carbon emissions per unit of gross domestic product) has been cut almost in half since 1970. Even during 1997–1999—at the height of an economic boom and with the subsidies and policies that reinforce fossil fuel use still deeply entrenched—the United States achieved a steep decline in carbon intensity, partly through the use of advanced efficiency technologies.

Just tightening up national fuel economy standards would eliminate 450 million tons of carbon dioxide per year by 2010.

As the biggest polluter, the United States should take the lead in dealing with global warming. Instead, for most of the past decade, we have obstructed progress. One reason is obvious: the enormously powerful and wealthy fossil fuel lobby, whose campaign contributions subvert the relationship between Congress and the public.

As a result, the Kyoto Protocol is far weaker than it should be. Though many other industrialized countries had pushed for deep cuts in greenhouse gas pollution, U.S. intransigence kept the final agreement conservative. The protocol requires the industrialized nations to reduce their greenhouse gas emissions only 5 percent below 1990 levels by 2012. But for the moment, the protocol is our best hope for nationwide and global progress.

What happens in the Netherlands will be critical in making the Kyoto   *15* Protocol work, because the rules on exactly how countries can meet their targets have yet to be written. Three issues stand out:

- The protocol allows a country to meet part of its target by buying greenhouse gas "credits" from nations that emit less than their quota. The negotiators at the Netherlands must make sure that any credits traded represent real pollution cuts, not just paper-pushing.

- The protocol needs strong rules on enforcement. Countries that fail to act and countries with slipshod accounting cannot be permitted to undermine the effort.

- Growing trees absorb carbon, and the protocol allows a nation to meet some of its target by planting trees. The negotiators must make sure that the rules do not permit countries either to raze ancient forests and replant (which releases more carbon than it takes up) or to start counting all the plantings they would have undertaken anyway as new, climate-friendly tactics.

The United States must push to eliminate all of these carbon loopholes. If we get a good treaty, it could be the impetus we need to start modernizing our power plants, vehicles, factories, and buildings. Study after study has shown that these steps will create thousands of new jobs and reduce consumers' energy bills. And, for the sake of future generations, it is our responsibility to change our ways.

We have an enormous job to do. It's time to roll up our sleeves and get to work.

To support a strong U.S. position in the Netherlands, contact Undersecretary Frank Loy, State Department Building, 2201 C Street, N.W., Washington, D.C. 20520; phone 202-647-6240; fax 202-647-0753. For more information as the negotiations proceed, see the global warming homepage.

Active Reading as Shared Reading

Most of the reading you do is in solitude. However, a significant chunk of learning takes place in social contexts such as classrooms or college learning assistance centers, book discussion groups, or student-coordinated study groups. Whenever possible, arrange to have an in-depth discussion of an assigned essay with another classmate or friend, ideally with two or three other classmates or friends. Here is how to make your reading discussion group most productive:

1. After the group reads the piece once, have each person go through it again, following the annotating suggestions given in "Reading with a Pencil," pages 63–64.

2. Discuss each writer's strategies identified by the group.

3. Discuss the strengths and weaknesses of the argument, keeping tabs on any common ground that is mentioned (see the discussion of Rogerian argument in Chapter 6).

4. Also keep tabs on any outside sources mentioned by group members. If at all possible, everyone in the group should consult these sources before trying to reach a consensus (see following point).

5. Attempt to reach consensus, despite differences of opinion. What unified position statement can your group produce that fairly represents the view (by now quite likely modified) of each individual member?

EXERCISE 2.10

1. Reflect on your private reading experience in relation to your public one. What does each reading context contribute toward your understanding and enjoyment of the text? Draw from actual reading experiences that included both a private and a public phase.

2. Does reading with others increase or decrease your comprehension of the text? What do you think accounts for this difference?

Using the Modes of Argument as a Schema for Analysis

To analyze the logic and merits of an argument, first determine which of the predominant general patterns of argument introduced in Chapter 1 and discussed in detail in Chapters 4 through 6—Classical, Toulmin, Rogerian—the argument fits into:

• If the piece follows the Classical (Aristotelian) model, you might ask: Is the intended audience uninformed or well informed on the issue?

• If the piece follows the Toulmin model, you might ask: Are the warrants on solid or shaky ground? Do they need to be made more explicit?

• If the piece follows the Rogerian model, you might ask: Is the tone sufficiently conciliatory to reduce the possibility of reader hostility?

The Importance of Open-Mindedness When Reading

One of the most important attributes that an education affords, along with self-discipline and attentiveness, is open-mindedness—the willingness to suspend judgment until one considers as many differing viewpoints as possible.

Learning to be truly open-minded takes effort. Everyone has deeply rooted beliefs, some of which even border on superstition. When these beliefs are challenged for whatever reasons, no matter how logical the reasons offered are, we resist—sometimes against our own better judgment. Beliefs often operate outside the realm of intellectual control and are entwined with our values and emotions. If, for example, someone in your family earns his or her livelihood in the Pacific Northwest logging industry, you may find it difficult to sympathize with environmentalists who advocate putting an end to logging in that region, even though a part of you wishes to preserve any species threatened with extinction due to continued deforestation.

Being predisposed toward a certain viewpoint is to be expected. Rare is the individual who goes through life with a neutral attitude toward all controversial issues. But one can be predisposed toward a certain view or value system and still be open-minded. For example, you might be highly skeptical of the existence of extraterrestrial creatures yet be willing to suspend that skepticism to give a writer a fair chance at trying to change your mind. Your willingness to be open-minded may increase, of course, if the author is a scientist or if the body of evidence presented has been shared with the entire scientific community for independent evaluations.

Sometimes we feel defensive when a long-held conviction is suddenly challenged. We may wish to guard the sanctity of that conviction so jealously that we may delude ourselves into thinking that we're being open-minded when we're not. When Galileo made his astronomical discoveries of the lunar craters and the moons of Jupiter known in 1610, he was promptly accused of heresy. We may think, from our enlightened perspective in the twenty-first century, that the church was narrow-minded and intolerant, neglecting to realize that at the dawn of the seventeenth century, modern science had not yet come into being. Most people's conception of "the heavens" was literally that: The night sky was a window to Heaven. And celestial (that is, heavenly) objects like planets, stars, and the moon all occupied divine niches in that Heaven; they were called the *crystal spheres*. Galileo's modest telescopic observations revolutionized our conception of the universe, but it did not happen overnight, particularly because Galileo recanted his "heresy"—or, rather, was persuaded to recant by the threat of execution. We know that Galileo never wavered in his convictions because, even while under house arrest, he continued to write about his discoveries.

The moral of Galileo's story, and the stories of many other daring thinkers throughout history, is that open-mindedness is precious, despite its difficulties.

Take a few steps to ensure that you will not judge an argument prematurely or unfairly:

1. Identify and perhaps write down in your notebook the specific nature of the resistance you experience toward the author's point of view. Is it that you're a Republican reading a Democrat's evaluation of a Republican presidential administration? A strict vegetarian or vegan and animal-rights activist reading an article about the importance of preserving the cattle industry? An evolutionist reading an article by a creationist questioning the validity of the hominid fossil record? Consciously identifying your predisposition helps you approach neutrality and open-mindedness.

2. Allow yourself to accept the author's premise at least temporarily. What are the consequences of doing so? Are there any reasonable facets to the argument? Can you establish some kind of common ground with the author? Does the author perhaps expose weaknesses in the viewpoint that you would advocate?

EXERCISE 2.11

Read the following excerpt from *How to Read a Book*, which illustrates the importance of reading with an open mind, and respond to the questions that follow:

> You must be able to say, with reasonable certainty, "I understand," before you can say any one of the following things: "I agree," or "I disagree," or "I suspend judgment." These three remarks exhaust all the critical positions you can take. We hope you have not made the error of supposing that to criticize is always to disagree. That is a popular misconception. To agree is just as much an exercise of critical judgment on your part as to disagree. You can be just as wrong in agreeing as in disagreeing. To agree without understanding is inane. To disagree without understanding is impudent.
>
> Though it may not be so obvious at first, suspending judgment is also an act of criticism. It is taking the position that something has not been shown. You are saying that you are not convinced or persuaded one way or the other.
>
> The rule seems to be such obvious common sense that you may wonder why we have bothered to state it so explicitly. There are two reasons. In the first place, many people make the error...of identifying

Source: Mortimer J. Adler and Charles Van Doren, from *How to Read a Book*. New York: Simon & Schuster, 1940; revised and updated edition, 1972: 142–143.

criticism with disagreement. (Even "constructive" criticism is disagreement.) In the second place, though this rule seems obviously sound, our experience has been that few people observe it in practice. Like the golden rule, it elicits more lip service than intelligent obedience.

1. Why is it sometimes a challenge fully to understand a discourse before a person thinks critically about it?

2. Do you agree that suspending judgment is an act of criticism, as Adler and Van Doren claim? Explain.

3. Give examples that show how "constructive" criticism can be a form of a disagreement.

Chapter Summary

Reading and writing are interconnected modes of thinking. We critically read our own writing (for sense of direction, development of ideas, coherence, clarity, persuasive force, and so on) as well as the writing of others. We construct meaning (a kind of internal writing) when we read in depth—that is, we read actively rather than passively whenever we read critically. Today, effective reading must include the ability to analyze and evaluate digital documents, such as those accessed on the Internet. To read effectively also means to read in stages: previewing (prereading and skim-reading) to grasp the central purpose of the piece; in-depth reading to understand the content, progression, and rhetorical strategies at work in the piece; and postreading to reinforce the framework of the whole argument. To read effectively also means to respond spontaneously with a pencil, writing marginal glosses, comparisons, and questions in the margins. Finally, reading effectively means to read with an open mind, in a highly motivated manner, as if you are interacting with the author on paper, attempting to reconcile your views with the author's.

Checklist

1. Have I read the assigned essays, as well as the drafts of my fellow students, in three stages: first previewing, then reading in depth, and then postreading?

2. When reading in depth, do I determine the framework of the argument? Evaluate the data presented? Evaluate the author's organizational strategy? Speculate on the significance of what is being argued?

3. Do I understand what it means to read responsibly? Open-mindedly?

4. Have I considered including visuals that would enhance the reading experience and reinforce the key ideas of my argument?

5. Have I analyzed and evaluated Internet materials in the different ways they need to be examined?

Writing Projects

1. Write a critical response to one of the following quotations about reading.
   a. "To write down one's impressions of *Hamlet* as one reads it year after year would be virtually to record one's own autobiography, for as we know more of life, Shakespeare comments on what we know." (Virginia Woolf)
   b. "We read often with as much talent as we write." (Ralph Waldo Emerson)
   c. "The greatest part of a writer's time is spent in reading." (Samuel Johnson, as quoted by James Boswell)
   d. "To read well...is a noble exercise....It requires a training such as the athletes underwent, the steady intention almost of the whole life to this object." (Henry David Thoreau)
   e. "A reasoning passion." (How the French novelist Colette described her experience of reading Victor Hugo's *Les Miserables*.)

2. Write an essay in which you propose ways of improving one's reading strategies. You may want to discuss these strategies in relation to particular types of reading materials.

3. How well do young people in elementary grades read today compared to their counterparts twenty years ago? Fifty years ago? Prepare an investigative study, using at least two visual aids (charts, graphs, tables) to illustrate your findings.

3 Using the Classical Model in Your Arguments

> We need the capacity effectively to urge contradictory
> positions...not so that we may adopt either of the two
> (it is quite wrong to persuade men to evil), but that we
> should be aware how the case stands and be able, if our
> adversary deploys his arguments unjustly, to refute them.
>
> —Aristotle

Rhetoric, or the art of using language persuasively, has a long history. The work of ancient rhetoricians such as Plato, Aristotle, Quintilian, and Cicero has influenced Western education and literature for nearly two thousand years, shaping public discourse and public life. Though rooted in the past, rhetoric plays an integral role in today's judicial, political, religious, and educational institutions.

Argument in the Ancient World

In the ancient world, rhetoric was taught as oratory (public speaking) and was basic preparation for students entering law, politics, and teaching. Students learned how to communicate a point of view clearly and convincingly. There were three categories of argumentative oratory in the ancient world, corresponding to three different functions. Two of these functions were professional or quasi-professional, such as presenting lectures and debates emulating professional situations; one function was political (*deliberative*), such as deliberating over military and civic policies; the other was legal (*forensic*), such as courtroom prosecution or defense motions. The third category of oratory—celebratory (*epideictic*)—generally falls outside the scope of argument. This kind of oratory was used in eulogies, commendations, dedications, and so on. Early rhetoricians, itinerant teachers known as *Sophists*, emphasized the pragmatic skills to be developed in winning an argument. Later, the Platonic school gained ascendancy, valuing philosophical reasoning over mere "training." Plato's student, Aristotle, achieved a sort of middle ground between the idealistic truth seeking of his mentor and the mercenary pragmatism of the Sophists by viewing rhetoric as the art of finding the best available means of persuasion in a given case—that is, by applying the rigors of philosophical reasoning to actual problems.

Another important element of ancient rhetoric was its system of topic development. For ancient orators, topics were preestablished "modes of thought" regionalized in the mind (the word *topic* comes from the Greek *topos*, meaning "place") to aid the memory when speaking. The first topic, logically enough, is definition, followed by comparison, temporal/causal connection, circumstance (for example, what is capable or incapable of happening), and testimony (use of authority, laws, or concrete examples to establish authenticity).

In addition to the ancients' everyday uses of argument in law, politics, religion, athletics, and the military, oratorical competitions were held. Individuals or teams would argue an issue, and an impartial judge would determine the winner based on each argument's strengths (much like what happens in debate tournaments today). Debating, we might say, is the "sport" side of argument—a show of argumentative skill for its own sake and valuable for the development of such skill.

The Classical Model of Argument

The Classical model for structuring an argument is both simple and versatile. First, here is a look at it in outline form:

   I. Introduction
       A. Lead-in
       B. Overview of the situation
       C. Background
  II. Position statement (thesis)
 III. Appeals (ethos, pathos, logos) and evidence
       A. Appeals: to ethics, character, authority (ethos); to emotions (pathos); to reason (logos). Usually, one type of appeal is used, although it is possible for an argument to employ all three appeals in more-or-less equal measure.
       B. Evidence: citing of statistics, results, findings, examples, laws, relevant passages from authoritative texts
  IV. Refutation (often presented simultaneously with the evidence). There are two parts to a refutation: a fair and accurate summary of the challenging view, followed by a discussion of the erroneousness or the limitations of those views.
   V. Conclusion (peroration)
       A. Highlights of key points presented (if appropriate)
       B. Recommendations (if appropriate)
       C. Illuminating restatement of thesis

Aristotle (384–322 BCE) wrote *Rhetoric*. It was the first systematic study of argument and reasoning for practical purposes—political, judicial, and ceremonial.

Argument structure was given its fullest examination by the Roman rhetorician Quintilian, who not only described the five parts of a discourse—the introduction, the statement of facts relating to the issue, the evidence, the refutation of challenging views, and the conclusion—but stressed the importance of exercising judgment in using them. Rhetorical arrangement, after all, is an art, not a rote computer program. Hence, not all introductions are alike in scope or tone; in fact, the orator may sometimes dispense with an introduction altogether— as when someone wants to hear only "the bottom line." Similarly, the orator may want to refute opposing views before presenting the evidence. The orator may also decide whether the evidence should be strictly factual—that is, appeal exclusively to reason—or should include ethical and emotional appeals as well. Writers of argument may choose to use the Classical model when they, too, write to audiences that are invested in a topic (such as the judges in the ancient debates) because, perhaps, they do not know why they should care about the topic or they lack much information about the issue.

Organizing Your Argument Using the Classical Model

The Classical argument introduces the problem and states the thesis; it next presents background information in the form of a narrative. It then presents the evidence in support of the thesis, including refutation of opposing views. Finally, it reaches a conclusion.

Consider the case of Paul Ferrell, who has set out to structure an op-ed piece (see Exercise 3.1) with the premise that population growth is a more serious problem than climate change. First he presents the problem—the rapid rate of population growth; the ongoing lack of concern over the impact of our rapidly growing population on earth's resources; that Big Oil is poised to defeat efforts to stop fossil-fuel consumption; etc.; then he presents his thesis that we must tackle the real culprit, overpopulation, and cites expert opinion (*Scientific American*; Jeremy Grantham, etc.). Quite likely, Farrell used a set of guiding questions similar to the following to help structure his argument:

1. What is my reason for writing this piece?

2. What is the most effective way to open the piece, securing the reader's attention?

3. What wrong assumptions need to be identified and refuted?

4. How can my stance on the issue be presented most persuasively?

5. How will my readers react to my assertions? Negatively? Indifferently? Skeptically? Enthusiastically? How can I deal with these reactions in advance? For example, if my readers would be against controlling overpopulation, what might I say to change their minds?

EXERCISE 3.1

Read Paul Farrell's article on the effects of population growth on our planet and then answer the questions that follow.

Opinion: Climate Change Isn't the Problem. A Population Bomb Is Killing Us | Paul B. Farrell

The dinosaurs went extinct without knowing what hit them. But human beings know what's coming and refuse to act.

Overview; lead-in → The human race is in a suicidal rush to self-destruction. We can't blame some grand conspiracy of climate-science deniers, Big Oil, Koch Bros, U.S. Chamber of Commerce, GOP governors and Congress.

Thesis → We are the problem. You. Me. Too many of us. Population is out of control worldwide. Seven billion today. Ten billion by 2050, in one generation. Too many babies. Too many old folks. An out-of-control civilization committing mass suicide. We are responsible for destroying the planet.

iStockphoto.com/ugurhan

Examples to →
support thesis

We keep buying gas guzzlers, keep investing retirement money in Big Oil, forever in denial of the widening gap between perpetual economic growth and runaway population living on a planet of rapidly diminishing resources. We're in denial, suicidal, blind. Forget global warming…until we face this deadly population bomb.

Refutation of
challenging →
views

We're solving the wrong problems. Yes, even the United   5
Nations and the 2,500 elite scientists in the Intergovernmental Panel on Climate Change (IPCC). They've updated us with 2,000-page technical reports, every five or six years since 1988. They estimate global population out to 2150 with 12 billion people on the planet. Then, politicians, economists, businesses, and families just ignore the disastrous impact of too many people.

As problem solvers, the U.N.'s climate scientists aren't much different than Exxon Mobil's CEO Rex Tillerson. He admits climate change is real, just an "engineering problem and there will be an engineering solution." Same with the IPCC. But Tillerson doesn't trust those "climate models to predict the magnitude of the impact." At least Tillerson has faith that humans will "adapt to a sea-level rise." After all, humans "have spent our entire existence adapting. We'll adapt."

The U.N. says we're 97% certain climate change is human-caused. So what? Even if the U.N. has 20,000 scientists who are 100% certain that climate change will wipe human civilization off the planet like dinosaurs...still you can bet your Big Oil retirement stock that Tillerson and every other science denier will keep fighting for free-market capitalism, subsidies, and deregulation, keep investing $37 billion annually in exploration. And with their war chest of $150 billion annual profits, they can still pay off all the politicians and investors they need to make sure Big Oil keeps beating all the U.N.'s climate scientists.

Even 2,500 scientists are in denial about the killer problem

What's wrong? Everybody on Earth is in denial about our biggest problem—runaway population. Too many new babies, a net of 75 million a year. Admit it, we're all closet deniers—leaders, billionaires, investors, the 99%, everybody. Even Bill McKibben's 350.org global team. Everybody knows overpopulation is Planet Earth's only real problem.

Demographic growth is the one key dependent variable in the IPCC's scientific equation. But we refuse to take action. So, yes, even IPCC scientists are science deniers too. They know population growth is the killer issue, yet we avoid it.

10   Thousands of scientists have brilliant technical solutions for their narrow specialties, so many solutions to reduce the impact of global warming. But they keep avoiding the root cause. They keep focusing on Band-Aid solutions to climate-change science equations. Warning, population growth is the cause of the Earth's problem, not the result.

Time to stop, shift, focus on the real problem. Stop focusing on the wrong variables. Your scientific method makes this clear... we are making too many babies, building an aging civilization. Out of control. Deal with it: Population is out of control. That's the world's No. 1 problem. Yet we're trapped in mass denial. Nobody's dealing with the world's biggest problem. Listen:

Appeal to reason (logos) using statistics →

- *Scientific American* says global population growth is "the most overlooked and essential strategy for achieving long-term balance with the environment." By 2050 world population will explode from today's 7 billion to 10 billion, with 1.4 billion each in India and China. With China's economy nearly three times America's. Billionaire philanthropists met secretly in Manhattan five years ago: Bill Gates, Warren Buffett, George Soros, Michael Bloomberg, Ted Turner, Oprah Winfrey and others. Each took 15 minutes to present their favorite cause. Asked what was the "umbrella cause?" They all agreed: Overpopulation, said the billionaires. But they're still silent today.

Appeal to authority (ethos) →

- Our collective conscience is trapped in a massive conspiracy. In "The Last Taboo," Mother Jones columnist Julia Whitty hit the nail on the head: "What unites the Vatican, lefties, conservatives and scientists in a conspiracy of silence? Population." But this hot-button issue ignites powerful reactions. Yet politicians won't touch it. Nor will U.N.'s world leaders. Even when it's killing us. Cowards talking a good game.

- Jeremy Grantham's investment firm GMO manages about $110 billion in assets. He also funds an Institute of Climate Change at London's Imperial College. He warns, population growth is a huge "threat to the long-term viability of our species, when we reach a population level of 10 billion." Why? It's "impossible to feed 10 billion people." We don't need more farmers, we need fewer small mouths to feed.

But how? Bill Gates says we must cap global population at 8.3 *15* billion, even as his vaccine and contraceptive plans extend life expectancy. But Columbia University's Earth Institute Director Jeff Sachs says even 5 billion is too many. Stop adding more babies? Virtually impossible. So how do we not add a billion? Or subtract two billion from today's seven billion total? Voluntary? Remember how China's one-child plan failed.

World's biggest problem—out-of-control population—has no solution?

Appeal to emotion (pathos) → Worst-case scenario: There is no solution. Overpopulation is going to drive the world off a cliff. And seems nobody really cares. Nobody's working on the real solution. No one has the courage. Not U.N. leaders, scientists or billionaires. No one. It's taboo. All part of a conspiracy of silence. A denial that's killing us.

Any real solutions? Just wait for wars, pandemics, starvation to erase billions? Wait in denial? But will wars, disease, poverty solve Earth's biggest problem, the problem no one wants to talk about? Meanwhile, Big Oil's marketing studies keep telling CEOs like Tillerson the truth about the inconsistent behavior of irrational humans living in denial. To Big Oil, population growth is good, more customers, essential for economic growth.

Yes, we just keep telling ourselves we're recyclers, green, love hybrids, eat organic.

Even as we just keep adding to the billion autos on the planet, keep buying Big Oil stocks for retirement, keep stocking up on carbon polluting products. Why? Our subconscious secretly endorses Big Oil's strategy. As Tillerson once told Charlie Rose in Business Week: "My philosophy is to make money. If I can drill and make money, then that's what I want to do," making "quality investments for our shareholders." It's a subtle conspiracy.

Conclusion; author re-invokes opening metaphor →

Is it already too late? Will we ever stop our insane suicidal obsession?

Don't bet on it. Watching how America's dysfunctional government solves problems lately is not encouraging.

Appeal to emotion (pathos) →

Millennia ago dinosaurs disappeared. Didn't know what hit them in the last great species extinction. They vanished forever. Forever. The planet never brought them back. Today humans know what's ahead. We can make the big, tough decisions...if only we wake up in time...if only we have the will to act... before it really is too late.

1. How convincingly does Farrell support his thesis? What additional evidence, if any, should he have included? What, if anything, should he have excluded?

2. Comment on the usefulness of the statistical evidence Farrell provides.

3. How relevant is Farrell's allusion to dinosaur extinction?

4. Evaluate the effectiveness of Farrell's refutation of challenging views?

5. Comment on the overall structure of Farrell's blog post. How might he have reorganized the piece, if at all?

Elements of a Classical Argument in Action

Now let us examine each element in detail and see how it operates in a particular argument. Keep in mind that outlines serve to remind writers of the basic strategy for developing a sound argument; they should not be followed slavishly as if they were some unalterable blueprint for constructing a house.

Introduction   A good introduction accomplishes three things:

1. It presents the topic of inquiry or the problem requiring attention, and perhaps briefly states the thesis.

2. It establishes a clear context for the problem.

3. It engages the reader's attention and desire to get "the whole picture."

Consider the following introduction to an argument against the use of school vouchers, a system whereby the state promises to pay parents a percentage of tuition for attending a quality school of the parents' choice:

Most Americans believe that improving our system of education should be a top priority for government at the local, state, and Federal levels. Legislators, school boards, education professionals, parent groups and community organizations are attempting to implement innovative ideas to rescue children from failing school systems, particularly in inner-city neighborhoods. Many such groups champion voucher programs. The standard program proposed in dozens of states across the country would distribute monetary vouchers (typically valued between $2,500 [and] 5,000) to parents of school-age children, usually in troubled inner-city school districts. Parents could then use the vouchers towards the cost of tuition at private schools— including those dedicated to religious indoctrination.

Superficially, school vouchers might seem a relatively benign way to increase the options poor parents have for educating their children. In fact, vouchers pose a serious threat to values that are vital to the health of American democracy. These programs subvert the constitutional principle of separation of church and state and threaten to undermine our system of public education.

How well do these two paragraphs meet the criteria for a strong introduction to an argument? First, the author (an anonymous writer for the Anti-Defamation League) introduces the problem: the need to improve our educational system and the fact that vouchers are considered to be a promising solution of that problem. The second paragraph presents the thesis: Vouchers are a bad idea. Finally, the author engages the reader's attention by using strong, dramatic language to convey a sense of urgency to the matter: Vouchers "pose a serious threat to values that are vital to the health of American democracy" and "subvert the constitutional principle of separation of church and state." Such language not only piques interest but also heightens anticipation: How is this writer going to convince me that such an assertion makes sense?

Appeals and Evidence   At the heart of any Classical argument is the evidence, reinforced by the persuasive appeals (see pages 21–25) that will ideally demonstrate, beyond doubt, the validity and reasonableness of the thesis. To be persuasive—that is, to change the minds of readers who otherwise would reject your thesis—facts and appeals must be conveyed in a way that allows readers to see the path by which they lead directly to the thesis.

Let us consider the way in which the three appeals are applied to the argument on school vouchers.

1. *Ethos* (the appeal to ethics, character, valid authority). When the school vouchers author argues that a voucher program would undermine the ideals on which this country was founded, he or she is evoking the appeal of ethos: It would be unethical, or a sign of bad character, to undermine what are considered the fundamental ideals of American democracy and liberty. It should be taken for granted, the author implies, that the authority of the U.S. Constitution must always be upheld.

2. *Pathos* (the appeal to emotion, compassion, sympathy). By alluding to "a serious threat" that vouchers pose to American values, the author is evoking the appeal of pathos—specifically, the fear of what might happen if states violated the U.S. Constitution.

3. *Logos* (the appeal to logic, to sound, reason-based decision making). Note how the author sets up a logical connection between separation of church and state and the American system of public education: If the former is violated, the integrity of the latter is threatened. This is an example of the appeal to logic and reason: There is a logical connection to be made between *A* and *B*.

Appeals go a long way toward persuading readers, but strong evidence is also needed. Two kinds of evidence are appropriate to Classical argumentative writing—direct and indirect. *Direct evidence* consists of data from surveys, scientific experiments, and cases-in-point—phenomena that clearly point to a causal agency ("where there's smoke, there's fire"). Facts represent evidence that anyone can check firsthand at any time. *Indirect evidence* consists of formal analytical and mathematical reasoning. Here, the author takes the reader through a step-by-step analysis of causes that lead to inevitable effects.

Reinforcing Aristotelian Appeals with Visuals

Good argumentative writing makes its claims convincing by appealing to readers' emotions, values, and reason (as Aristotelian appeals demand), as well as by providing "hard" evidence through data—and even hard data should be "warranted" on a platform of values as the Toulmin method of argument (discussed later in the chapter) demands. Images, especially photographs, are an especially powerful tool for transmitting appeals because, unlike verbal appeals, images tend to trigger an instantaneous emotional response. Some images are so effective they stay with us indefinitely. We have all seen such images: charity ads depicting hungry or homeless wide-eyed children; animal protection ads depicting abandoned dogs and cats; home security ads depicting burglars breaking into a bedroom window.

Using Visuals to Reinforce Ethical Appeals

Many of the public service ads published by humanist and religious organizations to help raise public consciousness demonstrate how visuals can appeal to one's sense of ethics. The UNICEF ad, for example, dramatically illustrates the unethical practice of child-labor exploitation in sweatshops.

Using Visuals to Reinforce Emotional Appeals

Sometimes, raising reader consciousness needs to be reinforced with an emotional jolt appealing to our deepest psychological needs: safety, love, youth,

For many women and children, there is no more dangerous place to be than home. Call **1.877.868.4JOE** or go to **www.joetorre.org** to help make home safe again.

Before you start your career,
give it a little firepower.

Responsibility.
Motivation.
Teamwork.
In a national survey, more than 850 employers said these are the
qualities they desire most in employees.
But where can you develop these qualities?
One of the best places is the Army.
Whether you're driving a tank or leading a fire team, you'll learn
what it takes to do the job—any job—and do it well.
So when you start looking for a job, you'll
already have what employers really want.
The things that can give your career
some firepower.
The things that can give you an edge
on life.
If you're looking for an edge, call
1-800-USA-ARMY.

ARMY.
BE ALL YOU CAN BE.

© U.S. Army

tradition (for example, family, custom), longevity, strength or power, or compassion. Here are some examples:

- **Security, freedom from fear.** Say you wanted to incorporate visuals for an
  essay on the seriousness of domestic violence. You might consider using the
  photograph on page 97 of a run-down city block with the words "It's safer
  here" [superimposed on the street] "than here" [superimposed beneath an
  upstairs window].

- **Strength, Power.** If you plan to write an essay on the ways in which the armed
  forces help develop leadership skills, you may want to consider matching
  expectations (as reflected in the U.S. Army ad) against actualities.

- **Appeal to youth.** For an essay arguing that keeping in shape will keep you youthful, you might incorporate an image similar to the photograph of two runners.

- **Appeal to compassion.** World events that affect large numbers of people may generate strong feelings of compassion. These emotions can be stirred up for years to come by using evocative imagery. The memorial of American flags photograph marked the first anniversary of 9/11. The layout of the flags, appropriate for a cemetery, presents a powerful and

moving visual reminder of those who lost their lives on that day in 2001.

Using Visuals to Reinforce Logical Appeals

In argumentative writing, it is frequently necessary to provide hard data such as statistics or findings from surveys or experiments to support a claim.

Using charts, graphs, and tables to capture in images what you analyze in the body of your argument aids in comprehension and in turn makes your claim more convincing. If you happen to be writing about population growth, for example, and wanted not only to support your claim that the world population has grown exponentially in recent history but also to convey the fact as dramatically as possible, you might choose to use this graph:

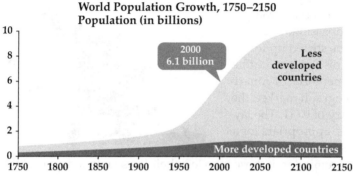

World Population Growth, 1750–2150
Population (in billions)

Source: Population Reference Bureau. Reprinted with permission.

Note how the data is laid out in a way that emphasizes the relationship between the variables on each axis—in this case, the quantity variable on the horizontal (*x*) axis and the temporal variable on the vertical (*y*) axis. What would take readers 30 seconds or more to read in a paragraph-long explanation can be perceived—and understood with greater clarity—in just two or three seconds via the graph. By the way, there's no reason why you need to restrict yourself to just a line graph. You can, for example, combine drawings and graphs into what are known as pictographs, as shown in the example on page 101.

Combining the Appeals

Most arguments combine all three appeals, *although one appeal generally will predominate*. Here is a case in point: Imagine that your instructor has assigned the class to investigate the issue of the arts funding in public school education. As state educational budgets are cut back, school boards tend to target arts programs—music, dance, theater, applied arts-and-crafts classes in painting or illustration, and so on—for elimination. Your task is to write an argument defending or challenging a decision to eliminate an arts program. What kinds of appeals might you use to persuade readers to accept your point of view? What kind of visual will you select or design that would reinforce those appeals?

To get the research ball rolling, your instructor shows you the ad on page 102 by an organization called Americans for the Arts.

First, take a few moments to contemplate the ad, noticing how the visual elements interact with the text in order to enhance the persuasive force of the

U.S. Higher Education Trends: Bachelor's Degrees Conferred

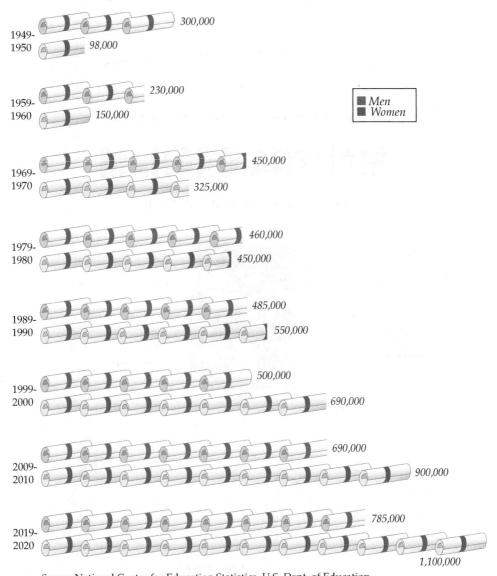

Source: National Center for Education Statistics, U.S. Dept. of Education.

message. For example, you notice how the image of the box of graham crackers is labeled, absurdly, "Martha Grahams"; directly on the other side of the first column of text is a larger image of Martha Graham herself in a classic dance pose—one of her skills being that of using dance to tell a story. The caption wittily recontextualizes the original aim of that photograph: "Ms. Graham told

THERE'S NOT ENOUGH ART IN OUR SCHOOLS.

NO WONDER PEOPLE THINK

MARTHA GRAHAM

IS A SNACK CRACKER.

Hardly a fitting legacy for the woman who, despite getting a late start at the positively elderly age of 17, became the mother of American interpretive dance.

A misconception. Not to mention an overlooked marketing opportunity.

With verve and nearly single-handedly, Martha Graham brought her dance style into the 20th century. She did nothing less than create an entirely new genre of dance, while shattering the expectations of audiences and critics alike with her percussive, angular movement style. She was one of the first dancers to collaborate with contemporary composers instead of using the 18th- and 19th-century compositions her predecessors favored. Her dances have been called "motion pictures for the sophisticated"; her theories on movement and kinesthetics are still vital today; and there is scarcely a dancer alive who doesn't

Ms. Graham told stories using movement. Here, she tells us how sad it is that kids aren't getting enough art.

owe a huge debt to her sharp creative mind and fierce perfectionism.

And to think she could have made it her entire life without experiencing the arts. Just like so many kids today.

Each day, more and more of the arts are being completely drained from our children's schools. Yet studies show parents believe dance and music and art and drama make their kids better students and better people. So what can you do to reverse this trend?

Speak up now. Demand your child's fair share of the arts. To find out how to help, or for more information about the benefits of arts education, please visit us at AmericansForTheArts.org. Otherwise, even a legacy as rich as Martha Graham's can crumble to nothing.

READIN'
ART
'RITING
'RITHMETIC

Let art borrow some brain. It'll return it in better condition.

ART. ASK FOR MORE.

 For more information about the importance of arts education, contact www.AmericansForTheArts.org

©Barbara Morgan, from "Martha Graham: Sixteen Dances in Photographs" by Barbara Morgan.

ID
DORIS DUKE
CHARITABLE FOUNDATION

AMERICANS for the ARTS

© Americans for the Arts

stories using movement. Here, she tells us how sad it is that kids aren't getting enough art." The third image, positioned within the second column of text and below the Martha Graham photo, is the schematic of the human brain. Perhaps you will incorporate the ad into your argument.

The next step, you decide, is to access the Americans for the Arts website, www.AmericansForTheArts.org.

Here you discover a wealth of links to information resources, field services, events, and ways to become involved with their cause. Here you will find the support data you need to make your claim convincing. You will also find testimonials from parents and teachers describing the impact of an arts education on children's success in and out of school.

Visuals can be effective in argumentative writing because they seem to demonstrate something irrefutable about the nature of what is being represented. As Susan Sontag says in her book-length essay *On Photography* (Delta, 1977), "Photographed images do not seem to be statements about the world so much as pieces of it" (4). That is why they so effectively convey evidence, despite the fact that photographs can be faked or misrepresented.

No matter what type of evidence is used, it must be tested for its relevance, accuracy, thoroughness, and timeliness.

- **Relevance.** The evidence must relate directly to the claims being made. If an argument claims that high school teachers tend subtly to discourage young women from pursuing careers in science or engineering but then cites instances of that problem only from colleges or private schools, critics would argue that the evidence is not relevant to the claim.

- **Accuracy.** Inaccurate evidence is worse than useless: It can deceive—and even harm. Facts and figures must always be double-checked. Quotations from experts or passages from texts must be quoted or paraphrased accurately. Accuracy also requires a degree of precision relevant to what is being argued. It may be acceptable to say "water was brought to a boil" in reference to a recipe, but when describing a chemical experiment involving a water temperature to a precise fraction of a degree, such a statement would be problematic.

- **Thoroughness.** The evidence must cover every facet or implication of the claim. If a writer claims that teenagers in the United States have fewer traffic accidents today than they did ten years ago but then cites accident statistics from only three states, readers rightly would argue that the evidence could be made more thorough by including statistics from all 50 states.

- **Timeliness.** The evidence must be appropriately recent. If a writer argues that teenagers are safer drivers "today" but presents statistics from 1995, then one rightly could argue that the evidence needs to be updated.

Managing Your Data

It takes time and patience to locate relevant evidence—statistics, testimonials, experimental findings, and the like—from reliable sources to make your argument credible. But gathering these data is only the first step; you also need to manage them properly. Managing data includes the following: (1) Evaluating the data to ensure that they are relevant, reliable, accurate, and up-to-date; (2) deciding which data you will use (typically, you will gather more data than needed, so you must determine which data are most useful); (3) deciding where the data should appear in your paper; and (4) deciding how to introduce the data—that is, how to integrate the data into the body of your paper.

Refutation

Closely associated with evidence is refutation, or referring to opposing views and then rebutting them. Refuting viewpoints that challenge our own is seldom easy; quite often, it is the most difficult stage in writing an effective argument. To refute effectively, we must assume that the challengers are equally convinced of their views. We may be tempted to trivialize or misrepresent an adversarial point by leaving out certain information or giving a faulty interpretation. Disagreements tend to be rooted in deeply personal values and beliefs, so we instinctively try to protect these beliefs. They have worked for us, have stabilized our sense of the world, have helped us cope. Any challenges are avoided. Yet, unless we have the courage to permit these beliefs to be challenged, perhaps modified, maybe even abandoned, learning and personal growth cannot take place.

Knowledge consists not of disembodied facts but of negotiated ideas. What we know we have assimilated from innumerable points of view. The health of our own ideas depends on a steady influx of fresh viewpoints, just as a body of water must be continuously replenished to avoid becoming stagnant. Such receptivity to new ideas requires courage, of course. It is never easy to say of those who argue against us, "Maybe there is some validity to these challenging views; maybe I should adopt some of them."

If after a careful and critical analysis of opponents' arguments we still hold to our overall stance and, in fact, have found flaws in theirs, we are ready to refute them. The aim of refutation is to demonstrate the limitations or errors of challenging views. It is not necessary to establish a distinct boundary between evidence and refutation because evidence may be brought in as part of the refutation process. Notice that in the body of the article on school vouchers (reprinted on pages 106–109), the author refutes the provoucher argument by first stating the opposition's rationale and then showing why that rationale is in error:

> Proponents of vouchers argue that these programs would allow poor students to attend good schools previously only available to the middle class. The facts tell a different story. A $2,500 voucher supplement may make the difference

for some families....But voucher programs offer nothing of value to families who cannot come up with the rest of the money to cover tuition costs.

The refutation is clearly articulated, but is it convincing? Skeptics probably would demand that the antivouchers author supply more in the way of evidence to substantiate the claim that vouchers undermine the integrity of American public schools.

How thorough is the evidence in support of the Anti-Defamation League's thesis that vouchers are harmful? The author brings in important facts that appear to demonstrate the unconstitutionality of vouchers, such as the Supreme Court's quoting of the Establishment Clause or its striking down "education programs that allow parents of parochial school students to recover a portion of their educational expenses from the state." However, much of the argument relies on speculation. There is no way of knowing for sure that the Supreme Court would judge vouchers to be unconstitutional, nor is there any way of knowing for sure that voucher programs "would force citizens— Christians, Jews, Muslims and atheists—to pay for the religious indoctrination of schoolchildren."

Effective argument depends on not only the kinds of evidence used but the degree to which that evidence resolves the stated problem. For further discussion of refutation and its importance in argument, see Chapter 1.

Conclusion

The minimal task of a conclusion is to provide a final wisdom about the thesis just argued. Some conclusions summarize the key points of the argument, a strategy that can be much appreciated in a long and complicated argument but may be unnecessary otherwise. Quite often, such summary statements are followed by recommendations for what actions to take. Other conclusions are more speculative: Instead of recommending what should be done, they focus on what *might* be done. And still other conclusions are more open ended, offering not summative statements but questions for the readers to consider.

The Anti-Defamation League writer on school vouchers does not present as full-fledged a conclusion as he or she does an introduction. Is the conclusion sufficient?

> School voucher programs undermine two great American traditions: universal public education and the separation of church and state. Instead of embracing vouchers, communities across the country should dedicate themselves to finding solutions that will be available to every American schoolchild and that take into account the important legacy of the First Amendment.

The author succinctly restates the problem and leaves the reader with the provocative suggestion found in the concluding sentence. But what sort of solution will solve that complex problem? The author brings the readers no closer to a real solution.

Read the complete text of "School Vouchers: The Wrong Choice for Public Education." Then answer the questions that follow.

School Vouchers
The Wrong Choice for
Public Education | Anti-Defamation League

Introduction

Most Americans believe that improving our system of education should be a top priority for government at the local, state and federal levels. Legislators, school boards, education professionals, parent groups and community organizations are attempting to implement innovative ideas to rescue children from failing school systems, particularly in inner-city neighborhoods. Many such groups champion state or local school voucher or "neo-voucher" programs.

The standard school vouchers program proposed in dozens of states, and adopted in some states across the country, would distribute government-funded vouchers (typically valued between $2,500 and $7,500) to parents of school-age children, usually in a low income bracket or in troubled inner-city school districts. Parents can then use the vouchers towards the cost of tuition at private schools, including those dedicated to religious indoctrination. Neo-voucher programs essentially work in the same way as traditional school voucher programs. They are government programs providing corporate or other tax credits for donations to state authorized "scholarship organizations." These organizations provide qualifying students scholarships or vouchers to attend private schools, including those dedicated to religious indoctrination.

Superficially, school vouchers or neo-vouchers might seem a relatively benign way to increase the options poor parents have for educating their children. In fact, vouchers and neo-vouchers pose a serious threat to values that are vital to the health of American democracy. These programs subvert the constitutional principle of separation of church and state, and they threaten to undermine our system of public education.

Constitutional Issues

Proponents of vouchers and neo-vouchers are asking Americans to do something contrary to the very ideals upon which this country was founded.

Thomas Jefferson, one of the architects of religious freedom in America, said, "To compel a man to furnish contributions of money for the propagation of opinions which he disbelieves ... is sinful and tyrannical." Yet voucher programs would do just that; they would force citizens—Christians, Jews, Muslims and atheists—to have their tax dollars pay for the religious indoctrination of school children at schools with narrow parochial agendas. In many programs, 80 percent of vouchers would be used in schools whose central mission is religious training. In most such schools, religion permeates the classroom, the lunchroom, even the football practice field. Channeling public money or tax income to these institutions flies in the face of the constitutional mandate of separation of church and state.

While the U.S. Supreme Court upheld a Cleveland, Ohio school vouchers   5
program in the *Zelman v. Simmons-Harris* case, vouchers have not been given a green light by the Court beyond the narrow facts of this case. Indeed, Cleveland's voucher program was upheld in a close (5-4) ruling that required a voucher program to (among other things):

• Be a part of a much wider program of multiple educational options, such as magnet schools and after-school tutorial assistance;

• Offer parents a real choice between religious and non-religious education (perhaps even providing incentives for non-religious education); and

• Not only address private schools, but also ensure that benefits go to schools regardless of whether they are public or private, religious or not.

The constitutionality of neo-voucher programs is an open question. However, in *Arizona Christian School Tuition Organization v. Winn*, 131 S. Ct. 1436 (2011), the Court significantly limited the ability of individuals to challenge neo-vouchers programs on church-state grounds.

These decisions, however, do not disturb the bedrock constitutional idea   10
that no government program may be designed to advance religious institutions over non-religious institutions.

Finally, and of critical importance, many state constitutions provide for a higher wall of separation between church and state or other requirements pertaining to education. So voucher programs and to a lesser degree neo-voucher programs will likely have a hard time surviving litigation in state courts. For instance, in 2006 a Florida school vouchers program was struck down under a state constitutional provision concerning public education.

Vouchers and Neo-Vouchers Undermine Public Education

Implementation of voucher and neo-voucher programs sends a clear message that we are giving up on public education. Undoubtedly, vouchers or neo-vouchers may help some students. But the glory of the American system of public education is that it is for all children, regardless of their religion, their academic talents or their ability to pay a fee. This policy of inclusiveness has made public schools the backbone of American democracy.

Contrary to this policy of inclusiveness, most school voucher or neo-voucher programs allow participating private schools to discriminate in some form or another. For instance, some programs allow schools to reject applicants because of low academic achievement or discipline problems. Other programs permit participating schools to discriminate on the basis of disability, gender, religion, sexual orientation or gender identity. Furthermore, some private schools promote agendas antithetical to the American ideal.

Proponents of vouchers argue that these programs will allow poor students to attend good schools previously only available to the middle or upper classes. The facts tell a different story. A $5,000 voucher or neo-voucher supplement may make the difference for some families, giving them just enough to cover the tuition at a private school. With some private schools charging over $12,000 annual tuition, however, such families would still have to pay thousands of dollars to make up the difference between the voucher and tuition amounts. But voucher programs offer nothing of value to families who cannot come up with the rest of the money to cover tuition costs.

15   In many cases, voucher programs will offer students the choice between attending their current public school or attending a less expensive school run by the local church or other house of worship. Not all students benefit from a religious school atmosphere—even when the religion being taught is their own.

For these students, voucher or neo-voucher programs offer only one option: to remain in a public school that is likely to deteriorate even further.

As our country becomes increasingly diverse, the public school system stands out as an institution that unifies Americans. Under voucher and neo-voucher programs, our educational system and our country would become even more Balkanized than today. With the help of taxpayers' dollars, private schools would be filled with well-to-do and middle-class students and a handful of the best, most motivated students from inner cities. Meanwhile, public schools would be left with fewer dollars to teach the poorest of the poor and other students who, for one reason or another, were not able to attend or chose not to attend private schools. Such a scenario could seriously impair public education.

Finally, as an empirical matter, reports on the effectiveness of voucher programs have been mixed. Indeed, recent research reflects that "vouchers do not have a strong effect on students' academic achievement."[1]

Vouchers and Neo-Vouchers Are Not Universally Popular

When offered the opportunity to vote on voucher-like programs, the public has consistently rejected them. Since 2000, voters in three states—Michigan, California, and Utah—have rejected voucher proposals. In 1998, Colorado voters rejected a proposed constitutional amendment that would have allowed parochial schools to receive public funds through a complicated tuition tax-credit scheme. And over the last 46 years, voters have rejected vouchers and

---

[1]*Center on Education Policy, Keeping Informed about School Vouchers A Review of Major Developments and Research,* July 2011, at 3.

voucher-related proposals 22 out of 23 times. Indeed, according to a recent Gallop Poll, 65 percent of Americans oppose allowing students and parents to choose to attend a private school at public expense.[2]

Conclusion

School voucher and neo-voucher programs undermine two great American   *20*
traditions: universal public education and the separation of church and state. Instead of embracing vouchers or neo-vouchers, communities across the country should dedicate themselves to finding solutions that will be available to every American schoolchild and that take into account the important legacy of the First Amendment.

1. Suggest one or more alternative ways in which the Anti-Defamation League author might have structured the essay, keeping within the general framework of Classical organizational strategy. What may gain or lose emphasis as a result of the reordering?

2. Evaluate the author's use of facts and appeals. What additional facts and appeals, if any, might have been appropriate?

3. How convincing is the author's argument that school vouchers are constitutionally suspect?

4. How well did the author manage the data? For example, were the data clearly introduced and explained? Were there too many data or not enough to make the author's argument convincing?

---

[2]See *Highlights of the 2011 Phi Delta Kappa/Gallup Poll What Americans said about the public schools* (http://www.pdkintl.org/poll/docs/pdkpoll43_2011.pdf last visited July 16, 2012).

EXERCISE 3.3

Read "Why School Vouchers Can Help Inner-City Children," an argument by Kurt L. Schmoke, mayor of Baltimore, in support of school vouchers. Then answer the questions that follow.

Why School Vouchers Can Help Inner-City Children | The Honorable Kurt L. Schmoke

I have been a strong supporter of public education during my tenure as mayor. In 1987 I said that it was my goal as mayor to one day have Baltimore be known as

---

Source: Kurt L. Schmoke, "Why School Vouchers Can Help Inner-City Children," *Civic Bulletin* No. 20 Aug. 1999. Reprinted by permission of The Manhattan Institute.

"The City That Reads." In doing that I underscored my commitment to improving all levels of education and getting people in our city focused on lifelong learning.

The state of Baltimore's economy was one of a variety of reasons for this commitment. Thirty years before I came into office, the largest private employer in Baltimore was the Bethlehem Steel Corporation's Sparrow's Point Plant. When I entered into office, however, the largest private employer in Baltimore was the Johns Hopkins University and Medical Center.

This transition meant that though there were jobs available, they would require a level of education that was higher than that which our children's parents and grandparents had to attain. It was clear to me that a commitment to improving literacy and understanding that education is a lifelong process was vitally important to our city.

With this knowledge in mind, I worked to improve our library system and our community college. Additionally, we created a Literacy Corporation to combat illiteracy in our city. In fact, President Bush presented Baltimore with the National Literacy Award in 1992.

5   In addition to my public responsibility for the Baltimore educational system, I also have a strong private interest in our city's schools. I have two children who are graduates of city public high schools. In fact, both of my children have at some point while growing up attended both public and private schools, so I have been able to observe my own children in different educational environments.

What I've found as a result of my experiences in pursuing a better-educated Baltimore, and a better-educated family, is a major void in current school reform efforts. I believe that the issues of competition and accountability are all too often ignored in efforts to improve public education.

My years of experience in education have led me to be in favor of school choice: quite simply, I believe in giving parents more choice about where to educate their children. My support of school choice is founded in the common sense premise that no parent should be forced to send a child to a poorly performing school.

Unfortunately, however, countless parents, especially in the inner cities, are now forced to do just that. Parents in middle- and upper-class communities have long practiced school choice. They made sure that their children attended schools where they would get the best possible education. There is no reason why this option should be closed to low-income parents.

The consequences of this unfairness are not at all difficult to grasp. As one perceptive observer of urban education has written "Education used to be the poor child's ticket out of the slums. Now it's part of the system that traps people in the underclass."

10   This was part of the thinking behind what people in Baltimore call my conversion to school choice. It did not happen overnight. It evolved slowly. My belief in school choice grew out of my experiences and, yes, my *frustrations* in trying to improve Baltimore's public schools over the last twelve years.

Under my watch as mayor we have tried all sorts of programs to reform the schools. Looking back, some of these programs showed promise, and some of our schools did demonstrate that they were doing a good job of educating our children.

Our successes, however, were still the exceptions, not the norm. I feared that, unless we took drastic action, this pattern would only continue. I considered school choice to be an innovation strong enough to change the course of what was widely recognized as an ailing system.

Why school choice? Two reasons: excellence and accountability. Parents want academic *excellence* for their children. They also want to know that there is someone in their child's school who is *accountable* for achieving those high academic standards.

In most cities in this nation, however, if your child is zoned into a school that is not performing well academically, and where teachers and administrators don't see themselves as being responsible for academic performance, parents have no recourse. Parents can only send their child to that school and hope for the best.

Under a school choice plan, a parent would have options. There would _15_ be consequences for a school's poor performance. Parents could pull their children out of poorly performing schools and enroll them someplace else. If exercising this option leads to a mass exodus from certain underachieving schools, schools will learn this painful lesson: schools will either improve, or close due to declining enrollments.

Any corporation that tolerated mediocre performance among its employees, unresponsiveness to the complaints of its customers, and the promotion of a large number of failed products, would not survive in the marketplace very long. What is true of corporations should also be true of poorly performing and poorly run schools.

These are some of the ideas that I expressed when I first came out in support of school choice in a speech at Johns Hopkins University in March of 1996, not as a panacea, but as another way to improve public education. Though I thought my remarks were relatively benign, the speech sparked a great deal of controversy.

One of my own aides even joked that he wanted to see my voter registration card to see if I was still a Democrat. Well, I am still a Democrat and I have no plans to change my political affiliation. I, nonetheless, believe that the Democratic Party should reevaluate its position on school choice issues.

In actuality, choice should not be included in partisan rhetoric. School choice should be about giving our nation's children the best possible educational foundation.

The same week as my speech at Johns Hopkins, I appointed a task force to _20_ explore the idea of school choice. I asked the task force to consider the pros and cons of school choice programs in all their variations, including programs such as the system implemented in Los Angeles where parents and students have the freedom to choose any school in the public system. I also asked that they investigate private school voucher plans such as the program in Milwaukee, as well as charter and magnet schools.

The task force released a report in that year which recommended that the Baltimore school system expand magnet schools and initiate a system-wide open enrollment program as a way to provide more educational options for parents and their children.

In my view, the task force unfortunately stopped short of endorsing publicly funded vouchers as a way to achieve the goal of school choice. The group, however, did leave open the door for reconsideration of the voucher issue later on. Meanwhile, the Baltimore city public school system has now implemented a variation of the school choice idea through what is called the New Schools Initiative.

These "New Schools" are very similar to charter schools. They are publicly funded schools that are planned and operated by parents or institutions or other non-traditional sponsors.

I recently spoke at Coppin State University for commencement. Coppin State is an historically black college in Baltimore that started out as a teacher training school. Today, under one of the New School Initiatives, Coppin is managing an elementary school in its home neighborhood drawing on its teaching and research to improve that school.

25   Now, three years after that Hopkins speech, I continue to believe that choice holds the greatest hope for instilling excellence and accountability in the nation's public schools.

At that time, as a Democrat and an African-American mayor, I was considered a maverick, or worse, for expressing that idea. No longer. A groundswell of support for choice is rising all over the nation, including from some unlikely quarters. Certainly, there's no greater proof of this than the tremendous response to the Children's Scholarship Fund funded by Wal-Mart heir John Walton and financier Ted Forstmann.

Under this program, the parents of some 1.25 million low-income children across the country applied for partial scholarships to help their children attend private and parochial schools. Civil rights pioneer and former mayor of Atlanta Andrew Young wrote these words in a nationally syndicated newspaper column shortly after the results of the scholarship drive were announced: "1.25 million cries for help, voiced by poor, largely minority families, seeking something most Americans take for granted. A decent education for their children."

In that column, Young described the collective cry for help as "a moment of moral awakening" that promises to be just as pivotal in America's civil rights struggle as Rosa Park's refusal to give up her bus seat in Montgomery, Alabama more than 40 years ago.

Such moments of moral awakening, Young observed, force us to reevaluate our beliefs and finally to take action. In Baltimore, that particular scholarship program attracted twenty thousand applicants. This represents an astonishing 44 percent of city children who were eligible.

The conclusions that can be drawn from these figures are unmistakable. *30*
The *Baltimore Sun* education editor wrote, "We know now that there's a pent-
up demand for school choice in the city. And we know that poor parents do
care about the education of their children."

In fact, some low-income African-American parents in our city have shown
they care so much that they will even go so far as to look *halfway around the
world* in order to find a good school for their children. The school which I
refer to is called Baraka, which means blessings in Swahili. It's located in rural
Kenya, 10,000 miles and eight time zones from inner-city Baltimore. And it's
funded by a Baltimore-based foundation, The Abell Foundation. The Foundation recruits and selects at-risk seventh- and eighth-grade boys from the Baltimore city public schools to participate in this bold education experiment.

The kids chosen for this program are generally headed for serious trouble.
It is safe to assume that many of the boys in the Baraka program would have
ended up incarcerated, or worse, had they not been selected.

Baraka School is going to begin its fourth year of operation in the fall. With 30
graduates to date, the school is having remarkable success in boosting the academic
achievement of these at-risk youngsters and truly turning around their lives.

Because of the persistent resistance to school choice by some Maryland
politicians, however, the State Education Department has refused to fund
the Baraka School project. I do not speak of any extra funding here. I am only
talking about taking the state's cost of educating each Baraka student, which
would normally have gone to the school that they had been assigned to had
they remained in the public system, and allowing it to be used to educate the
students in this alternative environment.

The state has absolutely refused. Were it not for the support of the Founda- *35*
tion, the Baraka School, which has done such an excellent job for these young
men, would have closed.

So, despite greater acceptance of school choice it's certainly premature to
declare victory in the public opinion contest. Indeed, criticisms of school choice
are as strident as ever and I am sure you have heard the more familiar ones.

Some say that school choice, especially vouchers, will weaken public education. My response is that choice can only strengthen public education by
introducing competition and accountability into the mix. Others claim that
school choice is undemocratic. My response to them is that choice is in keeping
with the aspirations for freedom that formed the core of American democracy.
As former Delaware Governor Pete Du Pont once wrote, "It's about the liberty
to choose what's best for your children." All of us should have that choice.

Some say that school choice is elitist, or even racist. The truth is that black
low-income children are among the prime victims of the nation's failing public schools. African-American parents know this all too well. This is why they
have been so open to the idea of school choice.

A recent national poll released by the Joint Center for Political and Economic Studies found a trend toward growing support of tuition vouchers
among African-American parents.

40   Another common criticism of school choice, and especially vouchers, is that it violates the principle of separation of church and state. A properly structured voucher program is no more a violation of the principle of separation of church and state than is the GI Bill. This program allowed military veterans to use government dollars to attend any university of their choice, public or private, religious or secular.

I am convinced that with time, and through open dialogue, critics of school choice will come to see this movement for what it is: part of an emerging new civil rights battle for the millennium, the battle for education equity. We need to give poor children the same right that children from more affluent households have long enjoyed. The right to an education that will prepare them to make a meaningful contribution to society. It is that simple.

In speaking of battles, and in closing, I remind you of those few words of wisdom from Victor Hugo: "Greater than the tread of Mighty Armies, is an Idea whose Time has Come...." As we look to the future, evidence is increasingly compelling, that school choice is such an idea.

1. Compare Schmoke's method of arguing his thesis with the Anti-Defamation League's method. Is one method more effective than the other? Why or why not?

2. Critique the essay in terms of (a) the effectiveness of its introduction; (b) the strength of its evidence and appeals; (c) the strength of its refutations; and (d) its conclusion.

3. Prepare an outline of your own essay on school vouchers. What will be your thesis? What kind of evidence will you present? How will you refute challenging views?

Toulmin Argument: A Modern-Day Variation of the Classical Model

Stephen Toulmin (1922–2009), an English philosopher of science and the history of ideas, developed a system of argument that has proven useful and influential in the modern world of complex rhetorical situations where problems are not easily divided into "right" and "wrong." Toulmin's model of argument is systematic in its reasoning; at the same time, it demands that this reasoning be scrutinized for its ethical underpinnings. It is not enough to present a claim and try to "prove" it with evidence. The arguer must also examine the evidence itself to scrutinize the assumptions we make about the evidence and even to ensure that *those* assumptions are similarly scrutinized for their ethical underpinnings. Toulmin argument, then, insists that logic alone cannot resolve complex human issues. Ethics and values play as important a role in argumentation as logical reasoning.

Let's take a closer look at the elements that comprise Toulmin argument.

The Toulmin Model of Argument

The terms we encounter in the Toulmin model immediately call attention to the complexity of the social interaction required for responsible argumentation:

- An argument begins with a *claim* to be made, which must be articulated as clearly and as accurately as possible, keeping in mind that problems are often more complicated than they seem to be on the surface. The claim is the thesis or premise of your argument that you want your audience to accept.

- To accomplish this goal, you must produce compelling *data*, the grounds or evidence. It is important to keep in mind that "evidence" means different things in different disciplines. In the sciences, for example, the data probably consist of results obtained from experiments, close observations, or mathematical analyses. In other contexts, the data probably consist of rules, laws, policies, highly valued social customs, or quotations from works of literature.

- Next, you need to ask of any argument whether the data used to support the claim truly are valid and are based on a sound sense of values. In other words, you must determine one or more underlying warrants, assurances that the data are based on some sensible and ethical foundation. Anyone can

Stephen Toulmin (1922–2009) was a philosopher of science with a special interest in the role that rhetoric plays in conveying ideas about ethics and morality. His context-based theory of argument provides an influential alternative to rigid, logic-driven theories.

© Sijmen Hendricks Photography

conjure up all sorts of data and manipulate it to give the appearance of validating a claim. As Shakespeare in *The Merchant of Venice* reminds us through the mouth of the merchant Antonio, "The Devil can cite Scripture for his purpose." For example, sometimes it is not enough to cite a law; it may be necessary to decide if the law is just or unjust.

- Just as the validity of the data is reinforced and sanctioned by one or more underlying warrants, so too must the validity of the warrants be reinforced. As Stephen Toulmin himself explains in *An Introduction to Reasoning* (1979), "Warrants are not self-validating ... [and] normally draw their strength and solidity from further substantial supporting considerations" (58). These further supporting considerations Toulmin calls the *backing*. To return to the example of unjust laws, the arguer would need to ask: What *assurance* can I give that the law is unjust?

- Finally, you must be prepared to bring in one or more *qualifiers* to your claim—that is, be prepared to call attention to any exceptions to the claim under certain circumstances. Consider: "The right of free speech must be protected in all situations except when it can endanger life or safety, such as yelling 'Fire!' in a crowded theater." The qualifier—the exception to the rule—prevents the claim from losing touch with complex social situations. The ability to anticipate qualifiers to one's claim is the mark of a responsible arguer. Toulmin refers to this phase of argument as the *rebuttal*. Of course, no arguer can anticipate every possible exception, and that is why audience feedback is so important in argumentation.

The Toulmin model provides a slightly different approach to writing arguments—an alternative to the Classical model—that you can use as you consider the best approach given your audience and purpose as the writer (recall the PAWS rhetorical rhombus from Chapter 1, Figure 1.2). Let us examine each of these Toulmin model elements in more detail.

The Claim

You know this feature as the thesis, premise, or central assumption. Toulmin chooses to call it the *claim* because that term suggests a thesis or assertion that is particularly *open to challenge*. The term comes from the Latin word *clamare*, meaning "to cry out," reminding us of the spontaneity with which claims are often made and hence how easily they can reach human ears and eyes without sufficient evidence to support them. The Latin root also reminds us to pay attention to how open to public scrutiny the claim is likely to be once it is presented as a speech or as a printed document in a periodical or book, on the Internet, in a court of law, or in a college paper.

For an argument to succeed, the writer first must ensure that the claim offered is worthy of deliberation. Some claims are not arguable. For example, it would be foolish to argue seriously that, in general, red is a superior color to blue. The claim is too dependent on subjective taste to be arguable. As the Latin maxim goes, *De gustibus non est disputandum*—of taste there is no disputing. But let's say you are an interior decorator and you have studied the effects of color on mood. You might argue that particular colors work best in particular types of rooms within a house. Here the claim is based not on personal taste but on statistical fact: Researchers have shown that pale blue helps relax people; therefore, pale blue would be an appropriate color for bedroom walls.

There are two basic types of claims, objective and subjective. *Objective claims* assert that something *actually* exists and present evidence that is demonstrably factual—not only in the sense of scientifically factual but legally factual, as in the case of laws, regulations, and policies. Here are some examples of objective claims:

- Video games heighten a child's hand-eye coordination and visual perception, but they impede the development of language processing skills.
- It is a myth that science is based only on logical reasoning and that art is based only on imagination. Logical reasoning and imagination are equally important to science and to art.
- Those who wish to speak out against the U.S. Constitution have just as much constitutional right to communicate their views in public as those who support the Constitution.
- YouTube provides new artists opportunities to be seen by and signed to major recording companies.

These claims present themselves as objective truths. But they are not *self-evident* truths; they must be supported with the appropriate evidence before readers can accept them as factual. Thus, before the first claim can be accepted as factual, the arguer must show, for example, that psychologists have compared the learning behaviors of children who play video games with those children who do not and have found enough evidence to establish a causal link between video-game playing and abstract reasoning.

Before the second claim can be accepted as factual, the arguer must provide convincing examples of the way imagination works in science and the way logical reasoning works in art. For example, the arguer might refer to autobiographical statements of scientists such as Albert Einstein or mathematicians such as Jules Henri Poincaré, who at various times obtained scientific understanding through dreams or imaginary "thought experiments."

Before the third claim can be accepted as factual, the arguer must demonstrate how the Constitution, paradoxical as it may seem, actually protects the rights of those who wish to speak out against it. This proof would entail careful analysis and interpretation of selected passages from the Constitution.

Before the fourth claim can be accepted as factual, the arguer must provide examples of such artists, such as Justin Bieber, who were discovered through self-posting on YouTube. The arguer must also provide other examples and evidence that agents of major recording companies do look at YouTube videos for the express purpose of finding fresh, new talent.

Subjective claims, on the other hand, assert that something *should* exist and present evidence derived from ethical, moral, or aesthetic convictions. Someone who argues, for example, that all college students should be required to take at least one course in literature to graduate or that animals should be treated with dignity is making a subjective claim. Although each claim is based on personal values, one cannot dismiss them as a kind of anything-goes relativism. The arguer, for example, might demonstrate that the benefits derived from studying literature improve one's ability to understand human nature, a valuable asset when one interacts with people.

The Data or Grounds

The Toulmin model demands that writers take pains to ensure that the supporting evidence fully validates the claim. The word *data* suggests "hard facts"— results from experiments or statistics from surveys, as well as historical, legal, and biographical facts. For more indirect kinds of evidence, such as testimonials or interpretations, the term *grounds* is more appropriate.

Thus, we can identify five different kinds of data to authenticate a claim: (1) *legal data*, such as laws, policies, regulations, and codes; (2) *scientific data*, such as findings obtained from mathematical calculations and laboratory experiments (keep in mind that experiments such as DNA testing and ballistics analyses, used to help solve crimes, are an inherent part of legal data and are often referred to as *forensic* data); (3) *testimonial* or *experiential* data, which are based on firsthand experience, such as eyewitness testimony and oral histories as gathered by anthropologists; (4) *scholarly* or *documentary* data obtained from secondary sources published in book or electronic form; and (5) *statistical data*, which may be obtained firsthand (in which case they would be akin to but not identical to scientific data unless the statistics were derived from laboratory experiments instead of, say, opinion polls).

Like claims, data or grounds must be presented as accurately and as unambiguously as possible. Someone who argues, for example, that essay exams test student comprehension of literature better than multiple-choice exams do, and who in so arguing relies on the testimonials of students, would want to make sure that those testimonials contain clear *demonstrations* of better comprehension for students taking essay exams. Of course, the criteria for "better comprehension" would need to be clarified before they could be used as valid grounds for a claim. The criteria might include richly detailed (as opposed to generalized) recollection of the content of literary works; they might also include insightful critical assessment or comparison of the thematic material of the works (as opposed to, say, superficial explanation of its strengths and weaknesses).

The Warrant and Its Backing

A warrant is the assurance that the evidence brought in to support the claim is completely reliable and that it rests on sound principles or values. Thus, just as the data legitimate the claim, a warrant, often implicit in the argument, legitimates the data. As Stephen Toulmin writes in *The Uses of Argument*, warrants "indicate the bearing of [the] conclusion of the data already produced" (98). By "bearing," Toulmin is referring to the need for readers to recognize and accept an appropriate direction in which the argument takes shape from claim to data to warrant. Warrants remind us of the humanizing dimension of argument: An argument, no matter how "heated," must always be principled rather than stem from vague or questionable motives.

Let us see how warrants operate in a given argument. Consider an essay in which a student, Melissa, argues for the abolition of letter grades in formal education. Melissa's claim is as follows:

> Letter grades should be abolished because they result in unhealthy competition, distract students from truly learning the subject matter, and constitute an inadequate gauge of student performance.

Melissa chooses to support her claim with data that compare the performance of students in a letter-graded class with the performance of students in a Pass/ No Pass class. Melissa's warrant might go something like this: "Learning for its own sake is more satisfying to students than learning to achieve predetermined standards of proficiency." As backing for this warrant, Melissa might conclude something like the following: "The more satisfying the learning experience, the more students are likely to learn." Melissa may not need to state these sentences explicitly, but the evidence she uses to support her claim should make the warrant and backing apparent.

We might diagram the relationships among Melissa's claim, data, warrant, and backing as in Figure 3.1.

Compelling warrants are just as vital to the force of an argument as are compelling data because they reinforce the trustworthiness of the data. Unsuccessful warrants often seem disconnected from, or even contradictory to, the evidence. Consider the following claim:

> Students should not be required to attend class.

If the evidence presented is the college's pledge to inculcate self-reliance in students, then the warrant—the conviction that self-reliance is compromised when professors require students to attend class—would seem contradictory to many readers because it is often assumed that such requirements are designed to *promote* self-reliance. Similarly, backing can be faulty. For example, in an argument claiming that every sixteen-year-old who drops out of school should be denied a driver's license, a warrant might involve the conviction that there is never any legitimate justification for dropping out of school;

FIGURE 3.1

Relationships Among
the Claim, Data,
Warrant, and Backing

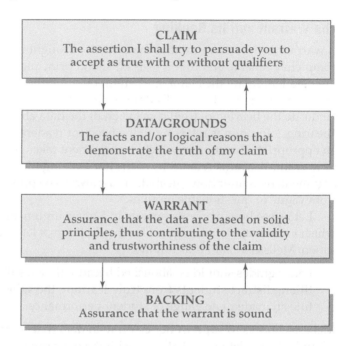

CLAIM
The assertion I shall try to persuade you to
accept as true with or without qualifiers

DATA/GROUNDS
The facts and/or logical reasons that
demonstrate the truth of my claim

WARRANT
Assurance that the data are based on solid
principles, thus contributing to the validity
and trustworthiness of the claim

BACKING
Assurance that the warrant is sound

however, it would be difficult to find backing for this warrant that would
apply in every circumstance.

There are three kinds of warrants, which roughly correspond to the three
kinds of appeals in Classical argument: logical or scientific warrants, ethical or
forensic-based warrants, and emotional or artistic-based warrants.

1. *Logical or scientific warrants.* These warrants reinforce the trustworthiness of the logical progression of scientific reasoning. If a meteorologist
   predicts a smog alert on the basis of 90-degree temperatures, little or no
   winds, and heavy traffic, her warrant would be that such a formula for
   smog predication is reliable.

2. *Ethical or forensic-based warrants.* A warrant is ethical when it relates to
   values or codes of conduct such as honor, integrity, altruism, honesty,
   and compassion. If one argues that underrepresented minorities should
   be allowed the opportunity to attend college even if their admissions
   test scores are not quite as high as those of the majority of admissions
   candidates and uses as evidence the success rate of those given such
   opportunity, the warrant is that society is ethically obligated to compensate minorities for past injustices by giving them such opportunities.
   Where affirmative action measures have become law, we could say that
   the warrant justifies enactment of that law.

3. *Emotional or artistic-based warrants.* If someone argues that profanity in films weakens instead of strengthens his enjoyment of those films and uses personal testimony as evidence, the arguer's warrant is that such negative reactions to profanity in movies is a reliable criterion for evaluating the strength or weakness of a film.

Backing may also be logical, ethical, and emotional.

When analyzing the arguments of others (and even your own arguments), keep in mind that, as stated earlier, warrants—and, consequently, backing—often remain unstated. They may be certain fundamental principles or beliefs that the writer simply assumes his or her reader shares. In fact, such principles or beliefs may well be open to challenge, thus undermining the claim of the argument. But to make such a challenge, you first have to identify the unstated warrant. In making arguments of your own, consider the possibility that a good number of your readers may not share your warrant. If that is the case, it is best to state the warrant and backing directly and perhaps even offer some defense for one or both.

The Qualifier

Claims are rarely absolute; that is, a claim may be valid in many circumstances, but not necessarily in all. If that is the case, an arguer would want to *qualify* the claim so that her readers would understand how she is limiting its range. For example, someone who claims that dress codes should be eliminated in the workplace might qualify that claim by excluding workplaces where uniforms are required for reasons of security (as is the case with police or military uniforms) or where certain articles of clothing are prohibited for reasons of personal safety (for example, someone cannot wear a necktie when operating heavy machinery). Someone writing about the negative influence of television on learning might qualify the claim by noting that watching television for the specific purpose of studying its negative effects could have a positive benefit on learning.

A radical form of qualification is known as the *rebuttal*. This is similar to refutation in Classical argument (see pages 104–105), except that in the Toulmin scheme rebuttal aims not to invalidate the claim but to show that the claim may not be valid in certain situations. Let's use the example of dress codes mentioned earlier. Instead of merely qualifying the claim that dress codes should be eliminated *except for* police uniforms, the arguer might rebut the claim entirely by agreeing that dress codes should be maintained without exception whenever there is consensus among employers and employees alike that it is necessary or desirable.

A Sample Analysis Using the Toulmin Model

Read the following argument by Virginia Woolf, noting the claim, data, warrant, and backing, as indicated by the marginal annotations.

Professions for Women | Virginia Woolf

Woolf begins by providing neces- → *sary background information for her argument*

When your secretary invited me to come here, she told me that your Society is concerned with the employment of women and she suggested that I might tell you something about my own professional experiences. It is true I am a woman; it is true I am employed; but what professional experiences have I had? It is difficult to say. My profession is literature; and in that profession there are fewer experiences for women than in any other, with the exception of the stage—fewer, I mean, that are peculiar to women. For the road was cut many years ago—by Fanny Burney, by Aphra Behn, by Harriet Martineau, by Jane Austen, by George Eliot—many famous women, and many more unknown and forgotten, have been before me, making the path smooth, and regulating my steps. Thus, when I came to write, there were very few material obstacles in my way. Writing was a reputable and harmless occupation. The family peace was not broken by the scratching of a pen. No demand was made upon the family purse. For ten and sixpence one can buy paper enough to write all the plays of Shakespeare—if one has a mind that way. Pianos and models, Paris, Vienna, and Berlin, masters and mistresses, are not needed by a writer. The cheapness of writing paper is, of course, the reason why women have succeeded as writers before they have succeeded in the other professions.

But to tell you my story—it is a simple one. You have only got to figure to yourselves a girl in a bedroom with a pen in her hand. She had only to move that pen from left to right—from ten o'clock to one. Then it occurred to her to do what is simple and cheap enough after all—to slip a few of those pages into an envelope, fix a penny stamp in the corner, and drop the envelope into the red box at the corner. It was thus that I became a journalist; and my effort was rewarded on the first day of the following month—a very glorious day it was for me—by a letter from an editor containing a cheque for one pound ten shillings and sixpence. But to show you how little I deserve to be called a professional woman, how little I know of the struggles and difficulties of such lives, I have to admit that instead of spending that sum upon bread and butter, rent, shoes and stockings, or butcher's bills, I went out and bought a cat—a beautiful cat, a Persian cat, which very soon involved me in bitter disputes with my neighbors.

What could be easier than to write articles and to buy Persian cats with the profits? But wait a moment. Articles have to be about something. Mine, I seem to remember, was about a novel by a famous man. And while I was writing this review, I discovered that if I were going to review books I should need to do battle with a certain phantom. And the phantom was a woman, and when I came to know her better I called her after the heroine of a famous poem. The Angel in the House. It was she who used to come between me and my paper when I was writing reviews. It was she who bothered me and wasted my time and so tormented me that at last I killed her. You who come of a younger and happier generation may not have heard of her—you may not know what I mean by The Angel in the House. I will describe her as shortly as I can. She was intensely sympathetic. She was immensely charming. She was utterly unselfish. She excelled in the difficult arts of family life. She sacrificed herself daily.

If there was chicken, she took the leg; if there was a draught she sat in it—in short she was so constituted that she never had a mind or a wish of her own, but preferred to sympathize always with the minds and wishes of others. Above all—I need not say it—she was pure. Her purity was supposed to be her chief beauty—her blushes, her great grace. In those days—the last of Queen Victoria—every house had its Angel. And when I came to write I encountered her with the very first words. The shadow of her wings fell on my page; I heard the rustling of her skirts in the room. Directly, that is to say, I took my pen in my hand to review that novel by a famous man, she slipped behind me and whispered: "My dear, you are a young woman. You are writing about a book that has been written by a man. Be sympathetic; be tender; flatter; deceive; use all the arts and wiles of our sex. Never let anybody guess that you have a mind of your own. Above all, be pure." And she made as if to guide my pen. I now record the one act for which I take some credit to myself, though the credit rightly belongs to some excellent ancestors of mine who left me a certain sum of money—shall we say five hundred pounds a year?—so that it was not necessary for me to depend solely on charm for my living. I turned upon her and caught her by the throat. I did my best to kill her. My excuse if I were to be had up at a court of law, would be that I acted in self-defense. Had I not killed her she would have killed me. She would have plucked the heart out of my writing. For as I found directly, as I put pen to paper, you cannot review even a novel without having a mind of your own, without expressing what you think to be the truth about human relations, morality, sex. And all these questions,

Woolf's claim emerges here through implication: Women who aspire to write must do all they can to "kill" the Angel in the House.

Woolf is more explicit about her claim here: The "Angel," if not killed, will pluck the heart out of a woman's writing.

The data (grounds) Woolf uses to support her claim: Women writers are forced to conciliate, tell lies. →

according to the Angel of the House cannot be dealt with freely and openly by women; they must charm, they must conciliate, they must—to put it bluntly—tell lies if they are to succeed. Thus, whenever I felt the shadow of her wing or the radiance of her halo upon my page, I took up the inkpot and flung it at her. She died hard. Her fictitious nature was of great assistance to her. It is far harder to kill a phantom than a reality. She was always creeping back when I thought I had dispatched her. Though I flatter myself that I killed her in the end, the struggle was severe; it took much time that had better have been spent upon learning Greek grammar; or in roaming the world in search of adventures. But it was a real experience; it was an experience that was bound to befall all women writers at that time. Killing the Angel in the House was part of the occupation of a woman writer.

Woolf's warrant, implied here, is that women writers must be free to be themselves, whatever that might be. →

But to continue my story. The Angel was dead; what then remained? You may say that what remained was a simple and common object—a young woman in a bedroom with an inkpot. In other words, now that she had rid herself of falsehood, that young woman had only to be herself. Ah, but what is "herself"? I mean, what is a woman? I assure you, I do not know. I do not believe that you know. I do not believe that anybody can know until she has expressed herself in all the arts and professions open to human skill. That indeed is one of the reasons why I have come here—out of respect for you, who are in process of showing us by your experiments what a woman is, who are in process of providing us, by your failures and successes, with that extremely important piece of information.

But to continue the story of my professional experiences. I made one pound ten and six by my first review; and I bought a Persian cat with the proceeds. Then I grew ambitious. A Persian cat is all very well, I said; but a Persian cat is not enough. I must have a motor-car. And it was thus that I became a novelist—for it is a very strange thing that people will give you a motor-car if you will tell them a story. It is a still stranger thing that there is nothing so delightful in the world as telling stories. It is far pleasanter than writing reviews of famous novels. And yet, if I am to obey your secretary and tell you my professional experiences as a novelist, I must tell you about a very strange experience that befell me as a novelist. And to understand it you must try first to imagine a novelist's state of mind. I hope I am not giving away professional secrets if I say that a novelist's chief desire is to be as unconscious as possible. He has to induce in himself a state of perpetual lethargy. He wants life to proceed with the utmost quiet and regularity. He wants to see the same faces, to read the same books, to do the same things day after day, month after month, while he is writing, so that nothing may break the illusion in which he is living—so that nothing may disturb or disquiet the mysterious nosings about, feelings round, darts, dashes, and sudden discoveries of that very shy and illusive spirit, the imagination. I suspect that this state is the same both for men and women. Be that as it may, I want you to imagine me writing a novel in a state of trance. I want you to figure to yourselves a girl sitting with a pen in her hand, which for minutes, and indeed for hours, she never dips into the ink-pot. The image that comes to my mind when I think of this girl is the image of a fisherman lying sunk in dreams on the verge of a deep lake with a rod held out over the water. She was letting her imagination sweep unchecked round every rock and cranny of the world that lies submerged in the depths of our unconscious being. Now came the experience that I believe to be far commoner with women writers than with men. The line raced through the girl's fingers. Her imagination had rushed away. It had sought the pools, the depths, the dark places where the largest fish slumber. And then there was a smash. There was an explosion. There was foam and confusion. The imagination had dashed itself against something hard. The girl was roused from her dream. She was indeed in a state of the most acute and difficult distress. To speak without figure, she had thought of something, something about the body, about the passion, which it was unfitting for her as a woman to say. Men, her reason told her, would be shocked. The consciousness of what men will say of a woman who speaks the truth about her passions had roused her from her artist's state of unconsciousness. She could write no more. The trance was over. Her imagination could work no longer. This I believe to be a very common experience with women writers—they are impeded by the extreme conventionality of the other sex. For though men sensibly allow themselves great freedom in these respects, I doubt that they realize or can control the extreme severity with which they condemn such freedom in women.

These then were two very genuine experiences of my own. These were two of the adventures of my professional life. The first—killing the Angel in the House—I think I solved. She died. But the second, telling the truth about my own experiences as a body, I do not think I solved. I doubt that any woman has solved it yet. The obstacles against her are still immensely powerful—and yet they are very difficult to define. Outwardly, what is simpler than to write books? Outwardly, what obstacles are there for a woman rather than for a man? Inwardly, I think, the case is very different; she has still many ghosts to fight, many prejudices

To provide backing to her warrant, Woolf describes her own experience as a writer to demonstrate how uncompromising one must be in communicating his or her true convictions. →

Woolf qualifies her claim by emphasizing the fact that the obstacles facing women have not yet been overcome. →

to overcome. Indeed it will be a long time still, I think, before a woman can sit down to write a book without finding a phantom to be slain, a rock to be dashed against. And if this is so in literature, the freest of all professions for women, how is it in the new professions which you are now for the first time entering?

Those are the questions that I should like, had I time, to ask you. And indeed, if I have laid stress upon these professional experiences of mine, it is because I believe that they are, though in different forms, yours also. Even when the path is nominally open—when there is nothing to prevent a woman from being a doctor, a lawyer, a civil servant—there are many phantoms and obstacles, as I believe, looming in her way. To discuss and define them is I think of great value and importance; for thus only can the labour be shared, the difficulties be solved. But besides this, it is necessary also to discuss the ends and the aims for which we are fighting, for which we are doing battle with these formidable obstacles. Those aims cannot be taken for granted; they must be perpetually questioned and examined. The whole position, as I see it—here in this hall surrounded by women practising for the first time in history I know not how many different professions—is one of extraordinary interest and importance. You have won rooms of your own in the house hitherto exclusively owned by men. You are able, though not without great labour and effort, to pay the rent. You are earning your five hundred pounds a year. But this freedom is only a beginning; the room is your own, but it is still bare. It has to be furnished; it has to be decorated; it has to be shared. How are you going to furnish it, how are you going to decorate it? With whom are you going to share it, and upon what terms? These, I think are questions of the utmost importance and interest. For the first time in history you are able to ask them; for the first time you are able to decide for yourselves what the answers should be. Willingly would I stay and discuss those questions and answers—but not tonight. My time is up; and I must cease.

EXERCISE 3.4

1. For each of the following claims, suggest at least one qualifier, two kinds of evidence, and one warrant for which you may also discover backing. Also, suggest a counterclaim with a counterdata and a counterwarrant for each.

   a. Our mayor should be removed from office because we just learned that he was once arrested for possession of marijuana.

   b. Any novel that includes the use of racial slurs should be banned from public school classrooms.

   c. Beef in restaurants should be prepared well done regardless of customer preference because of the danger of *E. coli* infection.

   d. Job seekers should use social media networking sites such as LinkedIn for the fastest and best results.

2. Work up two versions of an outline for an essay on improving conditions where you live. Use the Classical model to structure the first outline and the Toulmin model to structure the second. Which of the two outlines would you use as the basis for the paper, and why?

3. Rewrite each of the following claims by using more specific terms or references. *Example:* UFO sightings are a bunch of nonsense. *Rewrite* UFO sightings are difficult to document because trick photography is easy to accomplish.

   a. Books are an environmental problem.

   b. Cats make better pets than dogs.

   c. Students should be admitted to college on the basis of merit only.

4. Suggest one or two possible warrants for each of the following claims:

   a. All college students should be required to take at least one course in economics.

   b. Most college courses should be conducted as online courses.

   c. High school sex-education courses are inadequate.

5. Suggest at least one backing for the warrants your proposed in question 4.

EXERCISE 3.5

Read Thomas Jefferson's Declaration of Independence and identify its claim, data, warrant, and backing.

Declaration of Independence | Thomas Jefferson

When in the Course of human events, it becomes necessary for one people to dissolve the political bands which have connected them with another, and to assume among the Powers of the earth, the separate and equal station to which the Laws of Nature and of Nature's God entitle them, a decent respect to the opinions of mankind requires that they should declare the causes which impel them to the separation.—We hold these truths to be self-evident, that all men are created equal, that they are endowed by their Creator with certain unalienable Rights, that among these are Life, Liberty and the pursuit of Happiness.—That to secure these rights, Governments are instituted among Men, deriving their just powers from the consent of the governed.—That whenever any Form of Government becomes destructive of these ends, it is the Right of the People to alter or to abolish it, and to institute new Government, laying its foundation on such principles and organizing its powers in such form, as to them shall seem most likely to effect their Safety and Happiness. Prudence, indeed, will dictate that Governments long established should not be changed for light and transient causes; and accordingly all experience hath shewn, that mankind are more disposed to suffer, while evils are sufferable, than to right themselves by abolishing the forms to which they are accustomed. But when a long train of abuses and usurpations, pursuing invariably the same Object evinces a design to reduce them under absolute Despotism, it is their right, it is their duty, to throw off such Government, and to provide new Guards for their future security.—Such has been the patient sufferance of these Colonies; and such is now the necessity which constrains them to alter their former Systems of Government. The history of the present King of Great Britain is a history of repeated injuries and usurpations, all having in direct object the establishment of an absolute Tyranny over these States. To prove this, let Facts be submitted to a candid world.—He has refused his Assent to Laws, the most wholesome and necessary for the public good.—He has forbidden his Governors to pass.

Laws of immediate and pressing importance, unless suspended in their operation till his Assent should be obtained; and when so suspended, he has utterly neglected to attend to them.—He has refused to pass other Laws for the accommodation of large districts of people, unless those people would relinquish the right of Representation in the Legislature, a right inestimable to them and formidable to tyrants only.—He has called together legislative bodies at places unusual, uncomfortable, and distant from the depository of their public Records, for the sole purpose of fatiguing them into compliance with his measures.—He has dissolved Representative Houses repeatedly, for opposing with manly firmness his invasions of the rights of the people.—He has refused for a long time, after such dissolutions, to cause others to be elected; whereby the Legislative powers, incapable of Annihilation, have returned to the People at large for their exercise; the State remaining in the mean time exposed to all the dangers of invasion from without, and convulsions within.—He has endeavoured to prevent the population of these States; for that purpose obstructing the Laws of Naturalization of Foreigners; refusing to pass others to encourage their migrations hither, and raising the conditions of new Appropriations of Lands.—He has obstructed the Administration of Justice, by refusing his Assent to Laws for establishing Judiciary powers.—He has made Judges dependent on his Will alone, for the tenure of their offices, and the amount and payment of their salaries.—He has erected a multitude of New Offices, and sent hither swarms of Officers to harass our people, and eat out their substance.—He has kept among us, in times of peace, Standing Armies without the Consent of our legislatures.—He has affected to render the Military independent of and superior to the Civil power.—He has combined with others to subject us to a jurisdiction foreign to our constitution, and unacknowledged by our laws; giving his Assent to their Acts of pretended Legislation:—For quartering large bodies of armed troops among us:—For protecting them, by a mock Trial, from punishment for any Murders which they should commit on the Inhabitants of these States:—For cutting off our Trade with all parts of the world:—For imposing Taxes on us without our Consent:—For depriving us in many cases, of the benefits of Trial by Jury:—For transporting us beyond Seas to be tried for pretended offences:—For abolishing the free System of English Laws in a neighbouring Province, establishing therein an Arbitrary government, and enlarging its Boundaries so as to render it at once an example and fit instrument for introducing the same absolute rule into these Colonies:—For taking away our Charters, abolishing our most valuable Laws, and altering fundamentally the Forms of our Governments:—For suspending our own Legislatures, and declaring themselves invested with power to legislate for us in all cases whatsoever.—He has abdicated Government here, by declaring us out of his Protection and waging War against us.—He has plundered our seas, ravaged our Coasts, burnt our towns, and destroyed the Lives of our people.—He is at this time transporting large Armies of foreign Mercenaries to complete the works of death, desolation and tyranny, already begun with circumstances of Cruelty and perfidy scarcely paralleled in the most barbarous ages, and totally unworthy the Head of a civilized nation.—He has constrained our fellow Citizens taken Captive on the high Seas to bear Arms against their Country, to become the executioners of their friends and Brethren, or to fall themselves by their Hands.—He has excited domestic insurrections amongst us, and has endeavoured to bring on the inhabitants of our frontiers, the merciless Indian Savages, whose known rule of warfare, is an undistinguished destruction of all ages, sexes, and conditions. In every stage of these Oppressions We have Petitioned for Redress in the most humble terms: Our repeated Petitions have been answered only by repeated injury. A Prince, whose character is thus marked by every act which may define a Tyrant, is unfit to be the ruler of a free people. Nor have We been wanting in attentions to our British brethren. We have warned them from time to time of attempts by their legislature to extend an unwarrantable jurisdiction over us. We have reminded them of the circumstances of our emigration and settlement here. We have appealed to their native justice and magnanimity, and we have conjured them by the ties of our common kindred to disavow these usurpations, which, would inevitably interrupt our connections and correspondence. They too have been deaf to the voice of justice and of consanguinity. We must, therefore, acquiesce in the necessity, which denounces our Separation, and hold them, as we hold the rest of mankind, Enemies in War, in Peace Friends.—

We, therefore, the Representatives of the *United States of America*, in General Congress, Assembled, appealing to the Supreme Judge of the world for the rectitude of our intentions, do, in the Name, and by Authority of the good People of these Colonies, solemnly publish and declare, That these United Colonies are, and of Right ought to be *Free and Independent States;* that they are Absolved from all Allegiance to the British Crown, and that all political connection between them and the State of Great Britain, is and ought to be totally dissolved; and that as

Free and Independent States, they have full Power to levy War, conclude Peace, contract Alliances, establish Commerce, and to do all other Acts and Things which Independent States may of right do.—And for the support of this Declaration, with a firm reliance on the protection of divine Providence, we mutually pledge to each other our Lives, our Fortunes and our sacred Honor.

Reinforcing the Toulmin Model with Visuals

Visuals can reinforce a Toulmin-type argument in at least three ways: help readers visualize a claim, help readers better comprehend the data, and/or heighten awareness of the warrant. Let's consider adding illustrations to the Declaration of Independence (pages 127–130) to reinforce the warrant that the policies of the king of Great Britain against the American colonists are morally wrong. What kinds of visuals would you paste into it, and where, that would reinforce the Declaration's argument? Here are two possibilities; perhaps you can think of others:

1. To illustrate "He [the King of Great Britain] has made Judges dependent on his Will alone," create a caricature of the king's soldiers muzzling the colonial judges.

2. To illustrate the king's imposition "of taxes on us without our Consent," draw King George III as a burglar sneaking out the window of a colonist's home, a bag of money in tow.

Because the Toulmin model brings values and backing more to the forefront than does the Classical model, the kinds of visuals someone arguing in this approach might use could represent certain values with pie charts or graphs illustrating the statistics that support the claims.

EXERCISE 3.6

1. Suggest what kinds of visuals might be incorporated (and where) into Virginia Woolf's "Professions for Women," (pages 122–126).

Chapter Summary

The Classical model of argument dates back to ancient Greece and Rome, and it is still used, often adapted to incorporate modern values via the Toulmin model. Toulmin argument recognizes the logical reasoning, although necessary, is not enough to resolve the complex social issues encountered today. For that reason, it is especially suitable in courts of law and for resolving situations in which conflicting value systems are involved—situations typical of a global culture involving multiple ethnicities and religious beliefs. In effect, the Classical model (including its modern-day Toulmin variation) presents a template, a preestablished structure for framing an argument, and as such provides one pertinent model to choose from among the different ways to argue when writers address audiences that are not emotionally or intellectually vested in a particular position on the issue. The Classical model includes these elements:

- An introduction, which presents the claim to be argued and gives necessary background information
- A body of collected data or evidence and appeals, which together attempt to persuade the audience that the claim is convincing, and acknowledgment and refutation of challenging views
- A conclusion, which may summarize key points, reflect on implications and consequences, or make recommendations (if appropriate)

In addition, the content of an argument was generated by modes of thought or topics, which included definition, comparison, temporal/causal connection, circumstance, and testimony. When composing an argument using the Classical method, use the flowchart in Figure 3.2 to remind you of the key elements involved.

Argument in the ancient world was conducted mainly through oratory, the art of speechmaking. Training for a profession in which argument was part of the job included being trained in the rhetorical strategies needed for giving speeches in that profession. Hence, aspiring politicians were trained in deliberative oratory, aspiring lawyers in forensic oratory. Everyone involved in public life was probably trained in celebratory oratory, which was used for honoring individuals and events.

The Toulmin argumentation method consists of presenting a carefully articulated claim (thesis to be argued). It recognizes that a claim, whether objective (based on scientific or logical issues) or subjective (based on aesthetic, ethical, or moral issues), must be grounded by data—hard facts, statistics, experimental results, valid testimony, and/or logical analysis, depending on the nature of the claim. The claim must also be tested for possible qualifiers, exceptions to the rule; this is the rebuttal phase of an argument. Perhaps the most distinctive feature of the Toulmin method of argument is that it does not assume the data to be automatically self-justifying. Instead, the data must rest on one or more warrants, trustworthy foundations that give validity to the data. There must also be assurance—through backing—that the warrants themselves are sound.

When composing an argument using the Toulmin method, use the flowchart presented in Figure 3.1 (page 120) to remind you of the key elements involved.

FIGURE 3.2

Classical
Model
Flowchart

What *issue* am I going to investigate? [Example: The issue of visual-arts education in U.S. public schools.]

↓

What is my *claim*? [Example: Acquiring basic skills in painting, illustrating, and sculpting is as important as acquiring basic skills in math and reading.]

↓

What *grounds* (data) can I produce that would authenticate my claim? [Example: Testimonials from educational psychologists, from adults whose public-school education consisted of visual-arts training vs. adults whose education did not.]

↓

What underlying *warrant* (ethical validity) underlies my grounds? [Example: Personal testimonials are more reliable than abstract theorizing; give greater emphasis to firsthand experience.]

↓

What *backing* can I give to my warrant? [Example: Firsthand experience provides more compelling grounding because it can demonstrate better than abstract theory the impact of early learning on adult behavior.

↓

In light of challenging views, how will I need to *qualify* my claim, if at all? [Example: We should allow for individual difference in students (some are more analytically minded than others).]

↓

What *concluding reflections* can I give to my argument?

↓

Using the above information, what can I say in my opening paragraph that would best *introduce* my argument and engage my reader's attention?

Checklist

1. Does my paper include the elements of Classical argument structure in proper sequence?

2. Does my introduction clearly present my thesis and necessary background information?

3. Have I acknowledged and accurately presented challenging views? Have I refuted them thoroughly?

4. Does my conclusion summarize the key points of my argument, present insightful interpretations, or make appropriate predictions or recommendations?

5. If I have used visual aids, have I used them judiciously rather than gratuitously to reinforce my Aristotelian appeals to reason, emotion, or ethics?

6. Have I considered adapting my Classical argument approach to the Toulmin model?

Writing Projects

1. Using the Classical model of argument structure (or a Toulmin-model variation), write a three-page position paper on one of the following topics:
   a. Students should (should not) be required to take fewer core courses and allowed to take more electives.
   b. First-year composition courses should (should not) be an elective instead of a requirement.
   c. The college bookstore's buyback policy should (should not) be reformed.
   d. Publicity for extracurricular events needs to be improved.

2. Using the Classical model of argument, write an essay defending or challenging the value or usefulness of an existing law, policy, or program, such as the electoral college, the National Endowment for the Arts, the banning of prayer from public schools, or the minimum drinking age. Consider using visual aids to clarify your views or add persuasive appeal.

4 Using the Rogerian Model in Your Arguments

> The relationship which I have found helpful is characterized by ... an acceptance of [the] other person as a separate person with value in his own right, and by a deep empathic understanding which enables me to see his private world through his eyes.
>
> —Carl Rogers

In Chapter 3 we examined the art of effective argumentation as it has been practiced in Western culture since ancient times. The Classical method of argument continues to function as a versatile basis for presenting and defending a point of view, especially when the Toulmin variation, with its attention to moral and ethical complexity, is used. Toulmin-style Classical argument, one might say, is a precursor to the method of modern argument we consider in this chapter: Rogerian argument.

Carl Rogers (1902–1987) was a psychologist of the "humanist" school; he believed cooperative interpersonal relationships are key to a healthy society. As a therapist, Rogers urged self-realization and explained that to function fully as a person in society one must be open to new experiences. Rigidity of thought and defensiveness breed intolerance. The more open people are to alternative views, the likelier the possibility of cooperation—a vital asset for a world filled with cultural diversity and conflicting values. One way such openness is cultivated is through cooperative methods of communication.

The Rogerian Model of Argument

From Rogers's view, the Classical model of argument and even the more flexible Toulmin model tend to divide people into two camps: proponents and opponents, "good guys" versus "bad guys." The traditional language of argument, for example, is filled with militaristic metaphors: We *win* or *lose* arguments rather than resolve them. We *attack* someone's thesis rather than work to build consensus for resolving points of disagreement. We *marshal* evidence as if gathering troops. Even the seemingly neutral term *debate* (derived from *battre*, "to do battle") is of military origin. For Rogers, this combative approach to argument does more harm than good; it generates ill will and antagonism between discussants rather than cooperation. The Rogerian model is an option to consider when you are addressing an audience that has deep-seated opinions on the issue and may be hostile to other perspectives.

In this passage from *The Moral Landscape: How Science Can Determine Human Values*, notice how the neuroscientist and cultural critic Sam Harris strives to establish common ground between those who share his view that science, ideally, transcends gender or racial bias and those who claim that science cannot do so:

> There is no question that scientists have occasionally demonstrated sexist and racist biases. The composition of some branches of science is still disproportionately white and male (though some are now disproportionately female), and one can reasonably wonder whether bias is the cause.... One can also argue that the contributions of women and minority groups to science have occasionally been ignored or undervalued: the case of Rosalind Franklin standing in the shadows of Crick and Watson might be an example of this. But none of these facts, alone, or in combination, or however multiplied, remotely suggests that our notions of scientific objectivity are vitiated by racism or sexism.

Finding Common Ground

But, you ask, how can people cooperate or interact harmoniously if they hold diametrically opposed views about an issue? Rogers's answer is that you find a common ground and start from there. Returning to the rhetorical rhombus (see Figure 1.2), we see that Rogers emphasizes the *audience*. A paper in the Rogerian mode assumes that readers firmly hold differing views and therefore will resist hearing others' positions. Yet no matter how debatable or controversial a view is, one can locate views on the issue on which both can agree. It might take a while to find them, but they are there. Consider the controversy for and against capital punishment, for example:

- Both sides consider human life to be sacred and precious.
- Both sides feel that capital crimes must be deterred as effectively as possible.
- Both sides agree that someone convicted of a capital crime is a threat to society.
- Both sides agree that it is possible for persons to be convicted of crimes they did not commit.

Carl Rogers (1902–1987) was known for his "humanist," client-centered approach to therapy. He advocated nonthreatening methods of interpersonal communication.

The virtue of finding common ground is that one can isolate and resolve the points of opposition more effectively after identifying the points of agreement because one can reduce any hostility the audience has by demonstrating a true understanding of the audience's perspective.

It should be pointed out that finding common ground with those who disagree with you may take a good deal of preparation. A common criticism of the Rogerian method is that it is "wishy-washy"—that is, it creates the impression of making too many concessions of one's principles, of giving in, of not being assertive enough, and thereby losing respect. But this criticism is based on an inadequate understanding of those challenging views rather than on being conciliatory. Martin Luther King was intimately aware of his challengers' stances on the issues. He established common ground with them by calling their attention to matters they could not possibly disagree with, such as the biblically sanctioned importance of Christian brotherhood regardless of ethnicity. Bottom line: Do your homework! Be fully aware of the foundations of your challengers' views before invoking common ground with them.

The Rogerian model modifies the Classical model by emphasizing common ground (points of agreement) *before* calling attention to points of disagreement. The writer's goal is not to win or to prove wrong; it is to work together cooperatively to arrive at an agreed-upon truth. From its opening sentence, a Rogerian argument communicates a desire for harmonious interaction rather than combative opposition:

   I. Introduction: What is our shared problem? Let's see if we can work together to resolve it.

   II. These are the points on which we agree.

III. This is where we differ: misunderstandings, such as drawbacks or limited application to others' solutions, and the possible reasons behind these drawbacks or limitations.

IV. Possible drawbacks or limitations to the arguer's solutions, followed by greater benefits of the arguer's solutions.

V. Options for resolving our differences; or an exhortation to accept a particular option for resolving our differences together.

Considering Multiple Perspectives

Rogerian persuasion requires writers to work hard at considering multiple perspectives toward issues. You must be tolerant and respectful enough of differing viewpoints to take the time to fathom the value systems that underlie them. The first step toward achieving this goal, according to Rogers, is deceptively simple: *to listen with understanding*.

Listening with understanding is a skill that takes time to develop. You may think you are listening with understanding when you permit challengers to speak their minds, but you may only be allowing them their say rather than genuinely paying close attention to what they are telling you.

Here are some suggestions for listening with understanding, in Rogers's sense of the phrase, that also can be applied to reading with understanding:

- Be as attentive as possible. Assume that the speaker's remarks have value.

- Suspend your own judgments while listening, keeping an open mind so you do not run the risk of judging the speaker's views before you have the chance to consider them carefully.

- If anything is unclear to you or you find yourself disagreeing with anything, ask questions—but only after the person has finished speaking.

- Try to see the speaker's claims in terms of his or her warrants (underlying values or ideology on which the claims are based). One better understands and appreciates a speaker's position if one is aware of these warrants.

- Think of ways in which the speaker's point of view and your own can somehow work together, despite seeming contradictory. Even if you oppose capital punishment and the speaker supports it, both of you could approach a common ground by thinking of extreme situations on either side that would discourage an inflexible stance.

Using Rogerian argument in conversation is one thing; using it in writing is another. When writing, you do not have your audience in front of you to give you immediate feedback. Instead, you have to anticipate questions and counter-responses that challengers would have for you (in other words, automatically consider the needs of your audience). By considering the audience's needs and values and the merits of their beliefs, you will be more inclined to take a cooperative stance rather than a defensive or combative one.

In this passage from *Talking from 9 to 5: How Women's and Men's Conversational Styles Affect Who Gets Heard, Who Gets Credit, and What Gets Done at Work*, notice how psycholinguist Deborah Tannnen gathers differing views on what may legitimately constitute bias against women in the workplace:

> An academic position was advertised at a major university. Everyone was welcome to apply. But one candidate was a favorite of someone on the faculty. The faculty member saw to it that his candidate was the last one scheduled for a presentation, and he let him know when the other candidates were giving their presentations. This enabled his candidate to attend the others' presentations and gauge the reaction of his audience—what went over well, what fell flat, what concerns were reflected in the questions asked. He took this information into account in planning his own talk, and he wowed the department enough to get the job. At least one woman who had applied for the job felt that she had been locked out by an "old boy's network."... Is this illegal preferential treatment or just "mentoring" ... ? If such supporter relationships are likely to spring up between someone established in the organization and someone new to it, it is likely that the older person will be male (since he probably entered the organization when there were few or no women in it)....It is not intentional "sexism," yet it is a pattern that favors men over women—not all men, of course but it is a structure women are less likely to fit into.
>
> At the same time that we seek to understand how ways of talking can work against women, we also must bear in mind that it may be harder for women to get promoted regardless of how they speak. Marjorie and Lawrence Nadler list a number of studies that show that stereotypes work against women. They cite, for example, Lea Stewart, who found that women are often given different task assignments than men with similar positions and qualifications, and the ones they are given are not those that lead to advancement.

Arguing cooperatively also means including in your Rogerian essay specific instances in which the differing views are logically sound. That way, you show yourself to have listened well to those perspectives. This, in turn, prepares your audience for listening more carefully and sympathetically to *your* side of things. You also demonstrate your awareness of the limitations to your proposal—no position is perfect, after all—even while you show how your position works in more varied or complex or more frequent occurrences of the common problem. You and your audience both become receptive to "give and take."

Arguing from Problem to Solution

Because the hallmark of Rogerian argument is working cooperatively with those who would otherwise be characterized as "opponents," the traditional pro-versus-con combative stance, more characteristic of Classical argument, is replaced by a problem-to-solution approach. Instead of asserting, in effect, "Here's why I'm right and you're wrong," the Rogerian arguer asserts, "Let's all of us work together in an effort to reach consensus on identifying the problem, and then determining a mutually satisfactory solution."

Keep in mind that this approach will not *necessarily* vanquish opposition. The point is that the Rogerian arguer considers the issue from different perspectives, from different beliefs or value systems, without undermining his or her own moral convictions. For example, in his famous "Letter from Birmingham Jail" (see Exercise 4.2), Martin Luther King Jr., in his effort to establish common ground with his fellow clergymen, reminds them of what they presumably already are committed to: ensuring that human laws be morally consistent with God's laws to be considered just; and because laws that segregate people on the basis of race are inconsistent with God's unconditional love for humanity, they must be unjust. By means of such reasoning, King is reminding his fellow clergymen not only that they are on the same side but also that they can work together to solve the problem of racial injustice in America.

In brief, then, Rogerian problem-to-solution argument works like this:

1. The arguer first formulates the problem as a common problem and explains the problem as he or she sees it.

2. The arguer fairly considers the positions of those whose solutions differ from that of the arguer, showing how, in some instances and to certain extents, those solutions may be viable, but the arguer then modifies the solution(s) to propose the solution the arguer endorses.

3. The modified problem is then discussed in terms of a mutually satisfying solution, with points of dissent isolated and examined for their flaws in reasoning, inconsistencies, omissions, and so on.

Organizing Your Argument Using the Rogerian Model

To write an argument based on the Rogerian ideals of cooperation, find common ground with your audience regardless of their views about your claim. You need to become especially sensitive to attitudes and values other than your own. You should focus on the *issue* and the best way to resolve it, not on "winning" the argument over your "opposition."

As with the Classical and Toulmin models, begin thinking about your essay with questions about your audience, the similarities between your views and your audience's (insofar as you are aware of them), and the points at which you differ most, along with possible strategies for resolving those differences. Consider these questions:

1. Can I be objective enough to represent views and evaluate evidence fairly?

2. How much sense do the points of difference make? Do they make more sense than some of my views? If so, do I have the courage to adopt them, or at least modify them to accommodate my views?

3. Am I genuinely interested in establishing a common ground with my audience? What else can I include that could better facilitate this goal?

When constructing an outline for a Rogerian argument, think in terms of thesis, support of thesis, and concluding judgments based on that support—just as you do when using the Classical and Toulmin models. But with the Rogerian model you are more concerned with establishing common ground with readers who otherwise would reject the thesis. Here is how an argument using the Rogerian approach might take shape:

I. Introduction to the problem
   A. First scenario: A vignette that illustrates the problem
   B. Second scenario: Another vignette that illustrates the problem, but one with greater complexity that some solutions wouldn't handle well
   C. Thesis

II. Alternative views worth sharing with the target audience and why these views are worth considering

III. Points of difference, along with reflection on how to resolve them

IV. Conclusion: The implications of finding a solution in light of the evidence presented that would benefit everyone, plus discussion of the great benefits derived from the solution that all audience members would like

EXERCISE 4.1

Read the following essay in which the author uses the Rogerian method to tackle the difficult issue of sexual harassment in the early teen years. Then answer the questions that follow.

Let's Talk About Sexual Harassment in Middle School | Kimberly Shearer Palme

Like every new employee at the *Washington Post*, I was given a "Codes of Conduct" packet—the company's policies on everything from smoking to taking medical leave.[1] It was the section on sexual harassment that startled me most. Perhaps it shouldn't have.

Source: Kimberly Shearer Palmer, "Let's Talk About Sexual Harassment in Middle School," *Social Education*, May–June 2003, p. M2. © National Council for the Social Studies. Reprinted by permission.

But the prohibition against vulgar jokes and "brushing up against another's body" brought home to me the stark contrast between the informal codes of conduct my friends and I had learned to live by in middle school and what's permissible in the working world today.

The situations are very different, of course: There aren't the same sort of power relationships in school that make harassment such a complex problem in the working world. But, looking back, I'm still left wondering why so many teenagers I knew put up with unwelcome sexual behavior. And why adults consistently turned a blind eye. Twelve years ago, when I was in middle school, overt sexual advances were everyday events and usually overlooked by teachers. Boys grabbed girls' breasts in the stairwells and cafeteria as casually as they would say "hello," and our daily routines were punctuated by unwelcome slaps on the behind.

The shared sex harassment problems children in grades 8–11 have faced. →

As it turns out, my experience wasn't unusual. According to the American Association of University Women, 65 percent of girls in public school, grades eight to eleven, say they experience "touching, grabbing, and/or pinching in a sexual way."[2] My friends and I used to let boys touch, grab, and pinch us, and I don't think things have gotten all that much better. Sure, there's greater awareness: today, the districts have a sexual harassment policy that schools rely on and teachers can refer to. But the issue doesn't always reach administrators, much less the students. My recent conversations with today's teenagers suggest that it wasn't just my grade; it wasn't just my school; and it wasn't just back then. Many kids think—as my friends and I did—that the unwanted touching is just flirtation.

I have since learned to fight back when men harass me. In Paris a few years ago, when a guy grabbed my breasts, I shoved him away from me and yelled at him. After that, he left me alone. Now, when I think back to all the times in middle school when I didn't make guys leave me alone, I feel angry. So I decided to go back and find boys from my class and ask them why. I got out my old phone directory and called the same boys who would have been too cool for me to call in middle school. Most had moved, and the listed numbers were no longer valid. The ones I found shared my memories of unwanted touching in the hallways. They are, as far as I can tell, good boyfriend material. They are by all accounts sensitive and perceptive; my younger sister knows one well, and my close friend at college dated another. I found out they were just as confused as we girls were in those adolescent years.

One old classmate remembers the casual touching. "Even good guys did that," he said. "It wasn't sexual.... I don't know

what it was. I can't think it's a good thing." He also recalled walking girls to class because they felt threatened. We didn't speak in
terms of apologies, but wonderment. It seemed so very strange
that touching someone's breasts or bottom in the hallways was
considered friendly behavior. Another one of my classmates told
me that he remembered the same sorts of things. "Not until tenth
grade would guys ... realize it was not the best way to get a girl to
like you," he said. Grabbing girls was normal behavior, we both
agreed. It happened in public, in front of teachers. No one told
us it was wrong. No one even seemed worried about the possibility of lawsuits, despite the 1992 Supreme Court decision that
warned schools they could be held responsible for harassment.[3]
Maybe the teachers looked at our sometimes giggly and embarrassed
reactions and thought there wouldn't be a problem.

Basis for the
misunder- →
standings.

One male graduate told me that boys bothered girls back
then because they didn't know what else to do. "No one knows
how to act [at that age].... You're self-conscious, no one has self-
esteem." Boys, I realized, were just as insecure as I remember
feeling. We were blindly following what we assumed was routine social conduct—grabbing, pinching, being pinched. Who
knew there was another way to flirt? Boys, he told me, were just
trying to bridge the gap between girls and guys. "It wasn't meant
to hurt," he said.

Looking back now, he knows that what some boys did probably bothered some girls. But the girls didn't show it. "They probably didn't want to seem snobby or stuck up," he remembered.
As I spoke to these men, I realized how different they were from
the guy who bothered me in Paris. The rules were so blurry to
both girls and boys in middle school that neither gender really
knew when lines were crossed. For example, when my crotch was
grabbed on a school bus one afternoon, it wasn't okay with me,
but I didn't even tell my parents because at some level it seemed
so similar to what happened every day in school. I still feel mad,
but I could hardly blame my former classmates when they were
just acting out of friendship or flirtation—however misguided
that was. And the more I talked with my female friends, the
more I realized how often we gave the wrong signals. Some girls
remembered enjoying the attention, sometimes laughing along.
One recalled two boys dragging her into the boys' bathroom, as
she tried to kick her way free. But she didn't remember being
angry. "It was the only way to express ourselves," she now says.
But something else gave her further pause. She said she thought
that "teachers let it slide" like the other dumb behavior that happens among adolescents.

Fault lay with teachers who avoided dealing the problem. →

They shouldn't have. I remember only one teacher who stood in the front of her class and yelled at the boys for grabbing girls. Finally a teacher noticed, I remember thinking. Why was she the only one? And if the teacher noticed, why didn't she inform the principal, and start a school-wide discussion? My annoyance with my former classmates redirected itself as I realized that adults who could have explained and enforced the differences between right and wrong behavior—our teachers—often did not. The fact is, no one taught us the right way to act. But as Peggy Orenstein, author of *Schoolgirls: Young Women, Self-Esteem, and the Confidence Gap*, says, "It still must stop."[4] For me, it stopped as soon as I emerged from the achingly self-conscious early teenage years. Assertiveness came from the natural confidence that comes with getting rid of braces and glasses.

And yet, would early lessons have done much good? →

Shouldn't we have been helped to learn those lessons earlier? An insecure seventh-grade girl shouldn't have to deal with aggressive boys grabbing her. But I keep asking myself: What would I have wanted my parents to tell me? What could they have possibly told me? "Don't let boys touch you"? "Tell me if anyone's bothering you"? I'm sure they told me those things. I'm sure I dismissed them, way too embarrassed to talk to them about anything dealing with boy-girl relationships. How can you help a shy seventh-grade girl who doesn't even know whether to feel grateful for the attention or angry at the violation?

Admission that solutions are difficult. →

There are no easy solutions. Zero-tolerance policies make no sense, considering the level of confusion surrounding social behavior. Parents can try to teach their daughters to be tough; teachers can integrate into class discussions of what distinguishes flirtation from harassment. There's plenty of inspiration, in anything from the writings of Shakespeare to Maya Angelou, as Wellesley College sexual harassment scholar Nan Stein suggests in *Flirting or Hurting? A Teacher's Guide on Student-to-Student Sexual Harassment in Schools*.[5] And adults can talk to boys about limits.

Yet one thing remains clear. →

The fact is, my former classmates did not turn into bad men. They don't bother women at work or college. And the women I knew in school have also learned where to draw the line. But we should all have learned the rules earlier, well before it comes time to sign those company policies.

NOTES

1. This essay first appeared in the *Washington Post* on August 20, 2000. Reprinted by permission.

2. American Association of University Women, *Hostile Hallways: Bullying, Teasing, and Sexual Harassment in School* (Washington: AAUW, 2001).

3. Office of Civil Rights, "Revised Sexual Harassment Guidance" (Washington: U.S. Department of Education, 2001), http://www. ed.gov/offices//OCR/shguide/index.html.

4. Peggy Orenstein, *Schoolgirls: Young Women, Self-Esteem, and the Confidence Gap* (Landover Hills: Anchor, 1995).

5. Nan Stein, *Flirting or Hurting? A Teacher's Guide on Student-to-Student Sexual Harassment in Schools* (Washington: National Education Association, 1994).

1. What rhetorical devices—phrases, words, tone, details—suggest that Palmer is using the Rogerian method of argument?

2. What is most Rogerian about Palmer's approach to her topic? Least Rogerian?

3. Briefly, what is Palmer's position on the matter of sexual harassment in middle school?

4. Critics sometimes say that Rogerian argument is "wishy-washy." Is Palmer being wishy-washy about her middle school experiences with sexual harassment? Why or why not?

5. What, if anything, would you suggest to Palmer to strengthen her argument?

EXERCISE 4.2

In April 1963, Martin Luther King Jr. was sentenced to a week in jail because of his antisegregationalist campaign in Birmingham, Alabama. While in jail, Dr. King wrote the following letter defending his activities to eight members of the Birmingham clergy. As you read this masterpiece of persuasive writing, notice how King makes a concerted effort to seek common ground with his audience and to avoid the "good guys" versus "bad guys" combative stance. Look for specific points of emphasis and specific explanations that make his stance Rogerian. After reading, answer the questions that follow.

Letter from Birmingham Jail | Martin Luther King Jr.

APRIL 16, 1963

M y Dear Fellow Clergymen:
    While confined here in the Birmingham city jail, I came across your recent statement calling my present activities "unwise and untimely."[1] Seldom do I pause to answer criticism of my work and ideas. If I sought to answer all the criticisms that cross my desk, my secretaries would have little time for anything other than such correspondence in the course of the day, and I would have no time for constructive work. But since I feel that you are men of genuine good will and that your criticisms are sincerely set forth, I want to try to answer your statement in what I hope will be patient and reasonable terms.

I think I should indicate why I am here in Birmingham, since you have been influenced by the view which argues against "outsiders coming in." I have the honor of serving as president of the Southern Christian Leadership Conference, an organization operating in every southern state, with head-quarters in Atlanta, Georgia. We have some eighty-five affiliated organizations across the South, and one of them is the Alabama Christian Movement for Human Rights. Frequently we share staff, educational, and financial resources with our affiliates. Several months ago the affiliate here in Birmingham asked us to be on call to engage in a nonviolent direct-action program if such were deemed necessary. We readily consented, and when the hour came we lived up to our promise. So I, along with several members of my staff, am here because I was invited here. I am here because I have organizational ties here.

But more basically, I am in Birmingham because injustice is here. Just as the prophets of the eighth century B.C. left their villages and carried their "thus saith the Lord" far beyond the boundaries of their home towns, and just as the Apostle Paul left his village of Tarsus and carried the gospel of Jesus Christ to the far corners of the Greco-Roman world, so am I compelled to carry the gospel of freedom beyond my own home town. Like Paul, I must constantly respond to the Macedonian call for aid.

Moreover, I am cognizant of the interrelatedness of all communities and states. I cannot sit idly by in Atlanta and not be concerned about what happens in Birmingham. Injustice anywhere is a threat to justice everywhere. We are caught in an inescapable network of mutuality, tied in a single garment of destiny. Whatever affects one directly, affects all indirectly. Never again can we afford to live with the narrow, provincial "outside agitator" idea. Anyone who lives inside the United States can never be considered an outsider anywhere within its bounds.

5   You deplore the demonstrations taking place in Birmingham. But your statement, I am sorry to say, fails to express a similar concern for the conditions that brought about the demonstrations. I am sure that none of you would want to rest content with the superficial kind of social analysis that deals merely with effects and does not grapple with underlying causes. It is unfortunate that demonstrations are taking place in Birmingham, but it is even more unfortunate that the city's white power structure left the Negro community with no alternative.

In any nonviolent campaign there are four basic steps: collection of the facts to determine whether injustices exist; negotiation; self-purification; and direct action. We have gone through all these steps in Birmingham. There can be no gainsaying the fact that racial injustice engulfs this community. Birmingham is probably the most thoroughly segregated city in the United States. Its ugly record of brutality is widely known. Negroes have experienced grossly unjust treatment in the courts. There have been more unsolved bombings of Negro homes and churches in Birmingham than in any other city in the nation. These are the hard, brutal facts of the case. On the basis of these conditions, Negro leaders sought to negotiate with the city fathers. But the latter consistently refused to engage in good-faith negotiation.

Then, last September, came the opportunity to talk with leaders of Birmingham's economic community. In the course of the negotiations, certain promises were made by the merchants—for example, to remove the stores' humiliating racial signs. On the basis of these promises, the Reverend Fred Shuttlesworth and the leaders of the Alabama Christian Movement for Human Rights agreed to a moratorium on all demonstrations. As the weeks and months went by, we realized that we were the victims of a broken promise. A few signs, briefly removed, returned; the others remained.

As in so many past experiences, our hopes had been blasted, and the shadow of deep disappointment settled upon us. We had no alternative except to prepare for direct action, whereby we would present our very bodies as a means of laying our case before the conscience of the local and the national community. Mindful of the difficulties involved, we decided to undertake a process of self-purification. We began a series of workshops on nonviolence, and we repeatedly asked ourselves: "Are you able to accept blows without retaliating?" "Are you able to endure the ordeal of jail?" We decided to schedule our direct-action program for the Easter season, realizing that except for Christmas, this is the main shopping period of the year. Knowing that a strong economic-withdrawal program would be the byproduct of direct action, we felt that this would be the best time to bring pressure to bear on the merchants for the needed change.

Then it occurred to us that Birmingham's mayoralty election was coming up in March, and we speedily decided to postpone action until after election day. When we discovered that the Commissioner of Public Safety, Eugene "Bull" Connor, had piled up enough votes to be in the run-off, we decided again to postpone action until the day after the run-off so that the demonstrations could not be used to cloud the issues. Like many others, we waited to see Mr. Connor defeated, and to this end we endured postponement after postponement. Having aided in this community need, we felt that our direct-action program could be delayed no longer.

You may well ask: "Why direct action? Why sit-ins, marches, and so forth? Isn't negotiation a better path?" You are quite right in calling for negotiation. Indeed, this is the very purpose of direct action. Nonviolent direct action seeks to create such a crisis and foster such a tension that a community which has constantly refused to negotiate is forced to confront the issue. It seeks so to dramatize the issue that it can no longer be ignored. My citing the creation of tension as part of the work of the nonviolent-resister may sound rather shocking. But I must confess that I am not afraid of the word "tension." I have earnestly opposed violent tension, but there is a type of constructive, nonviolent tension which is necessary for growth. Just as Socrates felt that it was necessary to create a tension in the mind so that individuals could rise from the bondage of myths and half-truths to the unfettered realm of creative analysis and objective appraisal, so must we see the need for nonviolent gadflies to create the kind of tension in society that will help men rise from the dark depths of prejudice and racism to the majestic heights of understanding and brotherhood.

The purpose of our direct-action program is to create a situation so crisis-packed that it will inevitably open the door to negotiation. I therefore concur with you in your call for negotiation. Too long has our beloved Southland been bogged down in a tragic effort to live in monologue rather than dialogue.

One of the basic points in your statement is that the action that I and my associates have taken in Birmingham is untimely. Some have asked: "Why didn't you give the new city administration time to act?" The only answer that I can give to this query is that the new Birmingham administration must be prodded about as much as the outgoing one, before it will act. We are sadly mistaken if we feel that the election of Albert Boutwell as mayor will bring the millennium to Birmingham. While Mr. Boutwell is a much more gentle person than Mr. Connor, they are both segregationists, dedicated to maintenance of the status quo. I have hope that Mr. Boutwell will be reasonable enough to see the futility of massive resistance to desegregation. But he will not see this without pressure from devotees of civil rights. My friends, I must say to you that we have not made a single gain in civil rights without determined legal and nonviolent pressure. Lamentably, it is an historical fact that privileged groups seldom give up their privileges voluntarily. Individuals may see the moral light and voluntarily give up their unjust posture; but as Reinhold Niebuhr[2] has reminded us, groups tend to be more immoral than individuals.

We know through painful experience that freedom is never voluntarily given by the oppressor; it must be demanded by the oppressed. Frankly, I have yet to engage in a direct-action campaign that was "well timed" in the view of those who have not suffered unduly from the disease of segregation. For years now I have heard the word "Wait!" It rings in the ear of every Negro with piercing familiarity. This "Wait" has almost always meant "Never." We must come to see, with one of our distinguished jurists, that "justice too long delayed is justice denied."[3]

We have waited for more than 340 years for our constitutional and God-given rights. The nations of Asia and Africa are moving with jetlike speed toward gaining political independence, but we still creep at horse-and-buggy pace toward gaining a cup of coffee at a lunch counter. Perhaps it is easy for those who have never felt the stinging darts of segregation to say, "Wait." But when you have seen vicious mobs lynch your mothers and fathers at will and drown your sisters and brothers at whim; when you have seen hate-filled policemen curse, kick, and even kill your black brothers and sisters; when you see the vast majority of your twenty million Negro brothers smothering in an airtight cage of poverty in the midst of an affluent society; when you suddenly find your tongue twisted and your speech stammering as you seek to explain to your six-year-old daughter why she can't go to the public amusement park that has just been advertised on television, and see tears welling up in her eyes when she is told that Funtown is closed to colored children, and see ominous clouds of inferiority beginning to form in her little mental sky, and see her beginning to distort her personality by developing an unconscious bitterness toward white people; when you have to concoct an answer for a five-year-old son who is asking: "Daddy, why do white people treat colored people so mean?"; when you take a cross-country drive and find it necessary to sleep night after night in the uncomfortable corners of your automobile because no motel will accept you; when you are humiliated day in and day out by nagging signs reading "white" and "colored"; when your first name becomes "nigger," your middle name becomes "boy" (however old you are) and your last name becomes "John," and your wife and mother are never given the respected title "Mrs."; when you are harried by day and haunted by night by the fact that you are a Negro, living constantly at tiptoe stance, never quite knowing what to expect next, and are plagued with inner fears and outer resentments; when you are forever fighting a degenerating sense of "nobodiness"—then you will understand why we find it difficult to wait. There comes a time when the cup of endurance runs over, and men are no longer willing to be plunged into the abyss of despair. I hope, sirs, you can understand our legitimate and unavoidable impatience.

15   You express a great deal of anxiety over our willingness to break laws. This is certainly a legitimate concern. Since we so diligently urge people to obey the Supreme Court's decision of 1954 outlawing segregation in the public schools, at first glance it may seem rather paradoxical for us consciously to break laws. One may well ask: "How can you advocate breaking some laws and obeying others?" The answer lies in the fact that there are two types of laws: just and unjust. I would be the first to advocate obeying just laws. One has not only a legal but a moral responsibility to obey just laws. Conversely, one has a moral

responsibility to disobey unjust laws. I would agree with St. Augustine that "an unjust law is no law at all."

Now, what is the difference between the two? How does one determine whether a law is just or unjust? A just law is a man-made code that squares with the moral law or the law of God. An unjust law is a code that is out of harmony with the moral law. To put it in the terms of St. Thomas Aquinas: An unjust law is a human law that is not rooted in eternal law and natural law. Any law that uplifts human personality is just. Any law that degrades human personality is unjust. All segregation statutes are unjust because segregation distorts the soul and damages the personality. It gives the segregator a false sense of superiority and the segregated a false sense of inferiority. Segregation, to use the terminology of the Jewish philosopher Martin Buber, substitutes an "I-it" relationship for an "I-thou" relationship and ends up relegating persons to the status of things. Hence segregation is not only politically, economically, and sociologically unsound, it is morally wrong and sinful. Paul Tillich[4] has said that sin is separation. Is not segregation an existential expression of man's tragic separation, his awful estrangement, his terrible sinfulness? Thus it is that I can urge men to obey the 1954 decision of the Supreme Court, for it is morally right; and I can urge them to disobey segregation ordinances, for they are morally wrong.

Let us consider a more concrete example of just and unjust laws. An unjust law is a code that a numerical or power majority group compels a minority group to obey but does not make binding on itself. This is *difference* made legal. By the same token, a just law is a code that a majority compels a minority to follow and that it is willing to follow itself. This is *sameness* made legal.

Let me give another explanation. A law is unjust if it is inflicted on a minority that, as a result of being denied the right to vote, had no part in enacting or devising the law. Who can say that the legislature of Alabama which set up that state's segregation laws was democratically elected? Throughout Alabama all sorts of devious methods are used to prevent Negroes from becoming registered voters, and there are some counties in which, even though Negroes constitute a majority of the population, not a single Negro is registered. Can any law enacted under such circumstances be considered democratically structured?

Sometimes a law is just on its face and unjust in its application. For instance, I have been arrested on a charge of parading without a permit. Now, there is nothing wrong in having an ordinance which requires a permit for a parade. But such an ordinance becomes unjust when it is used to maintain segregation and to deny citizens the First Amendment privilege of peaceful assembly and protest.

I hope you are able to see the distinction I am trying to point out. In no sense do I advocate evading or defying the law, as would the rabid segregationist. That would lead to anarchy. One who breaks an unjust law must do so openly, lovingly, and with a willingness to accept the penalty. I submit that an individual who breaks a law that conscience tells him is unjust, and who

20

willingly accepts the penalty of imprisonment in order to arouse the conscience of the community over its injustice, is in reality expressing the highest respect for law.

Of course, there is nothing new about this kind of civil disobedience. It was evidenced sublimely in the refusal of Shadrach, Meshach, and Abednego to obey the laws of Nebuchadnezzar, on the ground that a higher moral law was at stake. It was practiced superbly by the early Christians, who were willing to face hungry lions and the excruciating pain of chopping blocks rather than submit to certain unjust laws of the Roman Empire. To a degree, academic freedom is a reality today because Socrates practiced civil disobedience. In our own nation, the Boston Tea Party represented a massive act of civil disobedience.

We should never forget that everything Adolf Hitler did in Germany was "legal" and everything the Hungarian freedom fighters did in Hungary was "illegal." It was "illegal" to aid and comfort a Jew in Hitler's Germany. Even so, I am sure that, had I lived in Germany at the time, I would have aided and comforted my Jewish brothers. If today I lived in a Communist country where certain principles dear to the Christian faith are suppressed, I would openly advocate disobeying that country's anti-religious laws.

I must make two honest confessions to you, my Christian and Jewish brothers. First, I must confess that over the past few years I have been gravely disappointed with the white moderate. I have almost reached the regrettable conclusion that the Negro's great stumbling block in his stride toward freedom is not the White Citizen's Counciler or the Ku Klux Klanner, but the white moderate, who is more devoted to "order" than to justice; who prefers a negative peace which is the absence of tension to a positive peace which is the presence of justice; who constantly says: "I agree with you in the goal you seek, but I cannot agree with your methods of direct action"; who paternalistically believes he can set the timetable for another man's freedom; who lives by a mythical concept of time and who constantly advises the Negro to wait for a "more convenient season." Shallow understanding from people of good will is more frustrating than absolute misunderstanding from people of ill will. Lukewarm acceptance is much more bewildering than outright rejection.

I had hoped that the white moderate would understand that law and order exist for the purpose of establishing justice and that when they fail in this purpose they become the dangerously structured dams that block the flow of social progress. I had hoped that the white moderate would understand that the present tension in the South is a necessary phase of the transition from an obnoxious negative peace, in which the Negro passively accepted his unjust plight, to a substantive and positive peace, in which all men will respect the dignity and worth of human personality. Actually, we who engage in nonviolent direct action are not the creators of tension. We merely bring to the surface the hidden tension that is already alive. We bring it out in the open, where it can be seen and dealt with. Like a boil that can never be cured so long as it is covered up but must be opened with all its ugliness to the natural medicines of air and light, injustice must be exposed, with all the tension its exposure creates, to the light of human conscience and the air of national opinion before it can be cured.

In your statement you assert that our actions, even though peaceful, must *25* be condemned because they precipitate violence. But is this a logical assertion? Isn't this like condemning a robbed man because his possession of money precipitated the evil act of robbery? Isn't this like condemning Socrates because his unswerving commitment to truth and his philosophical inquiries precipitated the act by the misguided populace in which they made him drink hemlock? Isn't this like condemning Jesus because his unique God-consciousness and never-ceasing devotion to God's will precipitated the evil act of crucifixion? We must come to see that, as the federal courts have consistently affirmed, it is wrong to urge an individual to cease his efforts to gain his basic constitutional rights because the quest may precipitate violence. Society must protect the robbed and punish the robber.

I had also hoped that the white moderate would reject the myth concerning time in relation to the struggle for freedom. I have just received a letter from a white brother in Texas. He writes: "All Christians know that the colored people will receive equal rights eventually, but it is possible that you are in too great a religious hurry. It has taken Christianity almost two thousand years to accomplish what it has. The teachings of Christ take time to come to earth." Such an attitude stems from a tragic misconception of time, from the strangely irrational notion that there is something in the very flow of time that will inevitably cure all ills. Actually, time itself is neutral; it can be used either destructively or constructively. More and more I feel that the people of ill will have used time much more effectively than have the people of good will. We will have to repent in this generation not merely for the hateful words and actions of the bad people but for the appalling silence of the good people. Human progress never rolls in on wheels of inevitability; it comes through the tireless efforts of men willing to be co-workers with God, and without this hard work, time itself becomes an ally of the forces of social stagnation. We must use time creatively, in the knowledge that the time is always ripe to do right. Now is the time to make real the promise of democracy and transform our pending national elegy into a creative psalm of brotherhood. Now is the time to lift our national policy from the quicksand of racial injustice to the solid rock of human dignity.

You speak of our activity in Birmingham as extreme. At first I was rather disappointed that fellow clergymen would see my nonviolent efforts as those of an extremist. I began thinking about the fact that I stand in the middle of two opposing forces in the Negro community. One is a force of complacency, made up in part of Negroes who, as a result of long years of oppression, are so drained of self-respect and a sense of "somebodiness" that they have adjusted to segregation; and in part of a few middle-class Negroes who, because of a degree of academic and economic security and because in some ways they profit by segregation, have become insensitive to the problems of the masses. The other force is one of bitterness and hatred, and it comes perilously close to advocating violence. It is expressed in the various black nationalist groups that are springing up across the nation, the largest and best-known being Elijah Muhammad's Muslim movement. Nourished by the Negro's frustration over the continued existence of racial discrimination, this movement is made up of people who have lost faith in America, who have absolutely repudiated Christianity, and who have concluded that the white man is an incorrigible "devil."

I have tried to stand between these two forces, saying that we need emulate neither the "do-nothingism" of the complacent nor the hatred and despair of the black nationalist. For there is the more excellent way of love and nonviolent protest. I am grateful to God that, through the influence of the Negro church, the way of nonviolence became an integral part of our struggle.

If this philosophy had not emerged, by now many streets of the South would, I am convinced, be flowing with blood. And I am further convinced that if our white brothers dismiss as "rabble-rousers" and "outside agitators" those of us who employ nonviolent direct action, and if they refuse to support our nonviolent efforts, millions of Negroes will, out of frustration and despair, seek solace and security in black-nationalist ideologies—a development that would inevitably lead to a frightening racial nightmare.

30   Oppressed people cannot remain oppressed forever. The yearning for freedom eventually manifests itself, and that is what has happened to the American Negro. Something within has reminded him of his birthright of freedom, and something without has reminded him that it can be gained. Consciously or unconsciously, he has been caught up by the *Zeitgeist*,[5] and with his black brothers of Africa and his brown and yellow brothers of Asia, South America, and the Caribbean, the United States Negro is moving with a sense of great urgency toward the promised land of racial justice. If one recognizes this vital urge that has engulfed the Negro community, one should readily understand why public demonstrations are taking place. The Negro has many pent-up resentments and latent frustrations, and he must release them. So let him march; let him make prayer pilgrimages to the city hall; let him go on freedom rides—and try to understand why he must do so. If his repressed emotions are not released in nonviolent ways, they will seek expression through violence; this is not a threat but a fact of history. So I have not said to my people: "Get rid of your discontent." Rather, I have tried to say that this normal and healthy discontent can be channeled into the creative outlet of nonviolent direct action. And now this approach is being termed extremist.

But though I was initially disappointed at being categorized as an extremist, as I continued to think about the matter I gradually gained a measure of satisfaction from the label. Was not Jesus an extremist for love: "Love your enemies, bless them that curse you, do good to them that hate you, and pray for them which despitefully use you, and persecute you." Was not Amos an extremist for justice: "Let justice roll down like waters and righteousness like an ever-flowing stream." Was not Paul an extremist for the Christian gospel:

"I bear in my body the marks of the Lord Jesus." Was not Martin Luther an extremist: "Here I stand; I cannot do otherwise, so help me God." And John Bunyan: "I will stay in jail to the end of my days before I make a butchery of my conscience." And Abraham Lincoln: "This nation cannot survive half slave and half free." And Thomas Jefferson: "We hold these truths to be self-evident, that all men are created equal...." So the question is not whether we will be extremists, but what kind of extremists we will be. Will we be extremists for hate or for love? Will we be extremists for the preservation of injustice or for the extension of justice? In that dramatic scene on Calvary's hill three men were crucified. We must never forget that all three were crucified for the same crime—the crime of extremism. Two were extremists for immorality, and thus fell below their environment. The other, Jesus Christ, was an extremist for love, truth, and goodness, and thereby rose above his environment. Perhaps the South, the nation, and the world are in dire need of creative extremists.

I had hoped that the white moderate would see this need. Perhaps I was too optimistic; perhaps I expected too much. I suppose I should have realized that few members of the oppressor race can understand the deep groans and passionate yearnings of the oppressed race, and still fewer have the vision to see that injustice must be rooted out by strong, persistent, and determined action. I am thankful, however, that some of our white brothers in the South have grasped the meaning of this social revolution and committed themselves to it. They are still all too few in quantity, but they are big in quality. Some—such as Ralph McGill, Lillian Smith, Harry Golden, James McBride Dabbs, Ann Braden, and Sarah Patton Boyle—have written about our struggle in eloquent and prophetic terms. Others have marched with us down nameless streets of the South. They have languished in filthy, roach-infested jails, suffering the abuse and brutality of policemen who view them as "dirty nigger-lovers." Unlike so many of their moderate brothers and sisters, they have recognized the urgency of the moment and sensed the need for powerful "action" antidotes to combat the disease of segregation.

Let me take note of my other major disappointment. I have been so greatly disappointed with the white church and its leadership. Of course, there are some notable exceptions. I am not unmindful of the fact that each of you has taken some significant stands on this issue. I commend you, Reverend Stallings, for your Christian stand on this past Sunday, in welcoming Negroes to your worship service on a nonsegregated basis. I commend the Catholic leaders of this state for integrating Spring Hill College several years ago.

But despite these notable exceptions, I must honestly reiterate that I have been disappointed with the church. I do not say this as one of those negative critics who can always find something wrong with the church. I say this as a minister of the gospel, who loves the church; who was nurtured in its bosom; who has been sustained by its spiritual blessings and who will remain true to it as long as the cord of life shall lengthen.

35   When I was suddenly catapulted into the leadership of the bus protest in Montgomery, Alabama, a few years ago, I felt we would be supported by the white church. I felt that the white ministers, priests, and rabbis of the South would be among our strongest allies. Instead, some have been outright opponents, refusing to understand the freedom movement and misrepresenting its leaders; all too many others have been more cautious than courageous and have remained silent behind the anesthetizing security of stained-glass windows.

In spite of my shattered dreams, I came to Birmingham with the hope that the white religious leadership of this community would see the justice of our cause and, with deep moral concern, would serve as the channel through which our just grievances could reach the power structure. I had hoped that each of you would understand. But again I have been disappointed.

I have heard numerous southern religious leaders admonish their worshipers to comply with a desegregation decision because it is the law, but I have longed to hear white ministers declare: "Follow this decree because integration is morally right and because the Negro is your brother." In the midst of blatant injustices inflicted upon the Negro, I have watched white churchmen stand on the sideline and mouth pious irrelevancies and sanctimonious trivialities. In the midst of a mighty struggle to rid our nation of racial and economic injustice, I have heard many ministers say: "Those are social issues, with which the gospel has no real concern." And I have watched many churches commit themselves to a completely otherworldly religion which makes a strange, unbiblical distinction between body and soul, between the sacred and the secular.

I have traveled the length and breadth of Alabama, Mississippi, and all the other southern states. On sweltering summer days and crisp autumn mornings I have looked at the South's beautiful churches with their lofty spires pointing heavenward. I have beheld the impressive outlines of her massive religious-education buildings. Over and over I have found myself asking: "What kind of people worship here? Who is their God? Where were their voices when the lips of Governor Barnett dripped with words of interposition and nullification? Where were they when Governor Wallace gave a clarion call for defiance and hatred? Where were their voices of support when bruised and weary Negro men and women decided to rise from the dark dungeons of complacency to the bright hills of creative protest?"

Yes, these questions are still in my mind. In deep disappointment I have wept over the laxity of the church. But be assured that my tears have been tears of love. There can be no deep disappointment where there is not deep love. Yes, I love the church. How could I do otherwise? I am in the rather unique position of being the son, the grandson, and the great-grandson of preachers. Yes, I see the church as the body of Christ. But, Oh! How we have blemished and scarred that body through social neglect and through fear of being nonconformists.

There was a time when the church was very powerful—in the time when   *40*
the early Christians rejoiced at being deemed worthy to suffer for what they
believed. In those days the church was not merely a thermometer that recorded
the ideas and principles of popular opinion; it was a thermostat that transformed the mores of society. Whenever the early Christians entered a town,
the people in power became disturbed and immediately sought to convict the
Christians for being "disturbers of the peace" and "outside agitators." But the
Christians pressed on, in the conviction that they were "a colony of heaven,"
called to obey God rather than man. Small in number, they were big in commitment. They were too God-intoxicated to be "astronomically intimidated."
By their effort and example they brought an end to such ancient evils as infan-
ticide and gladiatorial contests.

Things are different now. So often the contemporary church is a weak, inef-
fectual voice with an uncertain sound. So often it is an archdefender of the
status quo. Far from being disturbed by the presence of the church, the power
structure of the average community is consoled by the church's silent—and
often even vocal—sanction of things as they are.

But the judgment of God is upon the church as never before. If today's
church does not recapture the sacrificial spirit of the early church, it will lose
its authenticity, forfeit the loyalty of millions, and be dismissed as an irrelevant social club with no meaning for the twentieth century. Every day I meet
young people whose disappointment with the church has turned into outright
disgust.

Perhaps I have once again been too optimistic. Is organized religion too
inextricably bound to the status quo to save our nation and the world? Perhaps I must turn my faith to the inner spiritual church, the church within the
church, as the true *ekklesia* and the hope of the world. But again I am thankful to God that some noble souls from the ranks of organized religion have
broken loose from the paralyzing chains of conformity and joined us as active
partners in the struggle for freedom. They have left their secure congregations
and walked the streets of Albany, Georgia, with us. They have gone down
the highways of the South on tortuous rides for freedom. Yes, they have gone
to jail with us. Some have been dismissed from their churches, have lost the
support of their bishops and fellow ministers. But they have acted in the faith
that right defeated is stronger than evil triumphant. Their witness has been
the spiritual salt that has preserved the true meaning of the gospel in these
troubled times. They have carved a tunnel of hope through the dark mountain
of disappointment.

I hope the church as a whole will meet the challenge of this decisive hour.
But even if the church does not come to the aid of justice, I have no despair
about the future. I have no fear about the outcome of our struggle in Birmingham, even if our motives are at present misunderstood. We will reach the goal
of freedom in Birmingham and all over the nation, because the goal of America
is freedom. Abused and scorned though we may be, our destiny is tied up

with America's destiny. Before the pilgrims landed at Plymouth, we were here. Before the pen of Jefferson etched the majestic words of the Declaration of Independence across the pages of history, we were here. For more than two centuries our forebears labored in this country without wages; they made cotton king; they built the homes of their masters while suffering gross injustice and shameful humiliation—and yet out of a bottomless vitality they continued to thrive and develop. If the inexpressible cruelties of slavery could not stop us, the opposition we now face will surely fail. We will win our freedom because the sacred heritage of our nation and the eternal will of God are embodied in our echoing demands.

45   Before closing I feel impelled to mention one other point in your statement that has troubled me profoundly. You warmly commended the Birmingham police force for keeping "order" and "preventing violence." I doubt that you would have so warmly commended the police force if you had seen its dogs sinking their teeth into unarmed, nonviolent Negroes. I doubt that you would so quickly commend the policemen if you were to observe their ugly and inhumane treatment of Negroes here in the city jail; if you were to watch them push and curse old Negro women and young Negro girls; if you were to see them slap and kick old Negro men and young boys; if you were to observe them, as they did on two occasions, refuse to give us food because we wanted to sing our grace together. I cannot join you in your praise of the Birmingham police department.

It is true that the police have exercised a degree of discipline in handling the demonstrators. In this sense they have conducted themselves rather "nonviolently" in public. But for what purpose? To preserve the evil system of segregation. Over the past few years I have consistently preached that nonviolence demands that the means we use must be as pure as the ends we seek. I have tried to make clear that it is wrong to use immoral means to attain moral ends. But now I must affirm that it is just as wrong, or perhaps even more so, to use moral means to preserve immoral ends. Perhaps Mr. Connor and his policemen have been rather nonviolent in public, as was Chief Pritchett in Albany, Georgia, but they used the moral means of nonviolence to maintain the immoral end of racial injustice. As T. S. Eliot has said: "The last temptation is the greatest treason: To do the right deed for the wrong reason."

I wish you had commended the Negro sit-inners and demonstrators of Birmingham for their sublime courage, their willingness to suffer, and their amazing discipline in the midst of great provocation. One day the South will recognize its real heroes. They will be the James Merediths, with the noble sense of purpose that enables them to face jeering and hostile mobs, and with the agonizing loneliness that characterizes the life of the pioneer. They will be old, oppressed, battered Negro women, symbolized in a seventy-two-year-old woman in Montgomery, Alabama, who rose up with a sense of dignity and with her people decided not to ride segregated buses, and who responded with ungrammatical profundity to one who inquired about her weariness: "My feets is tired, but my soul is at rest." They will be the young high school and college students, the young ministers of the gospel and a host of their elders, courageously and nonviolently sitting in at lunch counters and willingly going to jail for conscience' sake. One day the South will know that when these disinherited children of God sat down at lunch counters, they were in reality standing up for what is best in the American dream and for the most sacred values in our Judeo-Christian heritage, thereby bringing our nation back to those great wells of democracy which were dug deep by the founding fathers in their formulation of the Constitution and the Declaration of Independence.

Never before have I written so long a letter. I'm afraid it is much too long to take your precious time. I can assure you that it would have been much shorter if I had been writing from a comfortable desk, but what else can one do when he is alone in a narrow jail cell, other than write long letters, think long thoughts, and pray long prayers?

If I have said anything in this letter that overstates the truth and indicates an unreasonable impatience, I beg you to forgive me. If I have said anything that understates the truth and indicates my having a patience that allows me to settle for anything less than brotherhood, I beg God to forgive me.

I hope this letter finds you strong in the faith. I also hope that circum-   *50* stances will soon make it possible for me to meet each of you, not as an integrationist or a civil-rights leader but as a fellow clergyman and a Christian brother. Let us all hope that the dark clouds of racial prejudice will soon pass away and the deep fog of misunderstanding will be lifted from our fear-drenched communities, and in some not too distant tomorrow the radiant stars of love and brotherhood will shine over our great nation with all their scintillating beauty.

—Yours for the Cause of Peace and Brotherhood,
Martin Luther King, Jr.

NOTES

1. This response to a published statement by eight fellow clergymen from Alabama (Bishop C. C. J. Carpenter, Bishop Joseph A. Durick, Rabbi Milton L. Grafman, Bishop Paul Hardin, Bishop Nolan B. Harmon, the Reverend George M. Murray, the Reverend Edward V. Ramage, and the Reverend Earl Stallings) was composed under somewhat constricting circumstances. Begun on the margins of the newspaper in which the statement appeared while I was in jail, the letter was continued on scraps of writing paper supplied by a friendly Negro trusty, and concluded on a pad my attorneys were eventually

permitted to leave me. Although the text remains in substance unaltered, I have indulged in the author's prerogative of polishing it for publication. [King's note.]

2. **Reinhold Niebuhr** Niebuhr (1892–1971) was a minister, political activist, author, and professor of applied Christianity at Union Theological Seminary. [All notes are the editors' unless otherwise specified.]

3. **justice … denied** A quotation attributed to William E. Gladstone (1809–1898), British statesman and prime minister.

4. **Paul Tillich** Tillich (1886–1965), born in Germany, taught theology at several German universities, but in 1933 he was dismissed from his post at the University of Frankfurt because of his opposition to the Nazi regime. At the invitation of Reinhold Niebuhr, he came to the United States and taught at Union Theological Seminary.

5. *Zeitgeist* German for "spirit of the age."

1. King chose to present his views in the form of a letter instead of, say, a manifesto. How might King's choice be explained from a Rogerian perspective?

2. Where do you see King making an effort to establish common ground with his audience? Explain whether you think he succeeded in doing so.

3. Do any moments in King's letter seem un-Rogerian? How so? What positive or negative effect might they have on his intended readers?

4. Does King use any of the three Aristotelian appeals of ethos, pathos, or logos described in Chapter 1? If so, which one(s)? Where do they appear? Why do you suppose King uses them?

5. Where does King most clearly reveal a special effort to reach his audience of fellow clergy?

6. Outline the key points in King's essay. Is there anything Rogerian about the way King sequences and emphasizes some of these points?

7. Should King have taken a more aggressive approach in his "Letter" (that is, used a Classical argument strategy)? Why or why not?

8. What important points regarding King's "Letter" does Matthew Neterer make in the following essay, which he wrote while a student at Ivy Tech Community College (Fort Wayne, IN)? What additional points could be made?

Matthew Neterer

English 112 - 40C Midterm exam

Professor Howard

7/9/2014

Letter from Birmingham Jail

"Letter from Birmingham Jail" is an apologia written by Martin
Luther King, Jr. in April 1963 in response to a newspaper
article published in a Birmingham newspaper about him by eight
white clergymen. The newspaper article did not specifically
mention King's name, but was directed at him and the demonstrations that he was leading in Birmingham. The article referred to
the demonstrations in Birmingham as untimely and unwise. It went
on to say that the community of Birmingham does not need help
from outsiders (referring to King who was from Atlanta, Ga). In
response to the newspaper article, King began to write an apologia to the clergymen while being housed in solitary confinement
in the Birmingham City Jail on the margins of the newspaper.
King states that he generally doesn't have time to respond to
his critics but that he feels that the clergymen are men of
genuine good will and therefore deems them worthy of a response
(184). The purpose of King's letter to the clergymen was to
respond to the claim that he was an outsider in Birmingham,
explain that he was there on behalf of those who have endured
the effects of segregation in Birmingham and to express his deep
disappointment with the southern white church leaders.

Other than the eight clergymen, King's audience consists
of the white moderate in Birmingham or as King writes "I have
almost reached the regrettable conclusion that the Negro's
greatest stumbling block is not the White Citizen's Councilor
or the Klu Klux Klanner, but the white moderate"(190). King
sees the white moderate as standing in the way of the freedom
of African-Americans in Birmingham. Despite the fact that some
of the white moderate agreed with King, they were not willing
to take action to fight segregation in Birmingham. One of the
main points of the article written by the eight white clergymen was that his demonstrations were untimely. King responded

by saying that African Americans had been waiting for over 340 years for their constitutional and God-Given rights (187).

King's essay represents a Rogerian argument because he attempts to establish common ground with the white clergymen on several different levels. The opening of the letter for example starts out with, "My Dear Fellow Clergymen." With this opening King immediately puts himself on the same level as the clergymen. In addition, King also refers to the clergymen as brothers throughout the essay. As King expresses his disappointment with the church, he first establishes the fact that he was raised as a Christian and has a deep love for the church. He states "I say this as a minister of the gospel, who loves the church; who was nurtured in its bosom; who has been sustained by it spiritual blessings and who will remain true to it as long as the cord of life shall lengthen" (194).

Several main points are emphasized in King's essay. Again, he refers to the clergymen's statement that he should have postponed the demonstrations until after the new administration was given time to get settled. King writes: "for years now I have heard the word "Wait!" It rings in the ear of every Negro with piercing familiarity" (187). Another example of how King emphasizes his feelings is contained in the longest sentence of the letter. This periodic sentence is over 300 words long and expresses some of the brutal treatment that African-Americans were experiencing in Birmingham at the time. King appeals to the audience's pathos when he describes having to tell his daughter that she can't go to the amusement park that recently opened because it is closed to black people (188).

King's support of his claims is both adequate and impressive. One claim King makes is in defense of the demonstrators who willingly broke the laws in Birmingham. King makes a claim of definition by stating that the segregation laws are unjust and therefore do not have to be followed. King claims that not only do people not have to follow unjust laws, but they have a moral responsibility to disobey unjust laws. He goes on to quote St. Thomas Aquinas: "An unjust law is a human law that is not rooted in eternal law and natural law. Any law that uplifts human personality is just" (188). King also makes several

claims of fact. In the beginning of his letter when he is
responding to why he is in Birmingham, he describes the bombings, beatings and unjust treatment in the courts that blacks
had been experiencing Birmingham.

As a minister, King uses many examples out of the Bible to
form an ethical connection to the eight white clergymen. He seems
to feel that the clergymen are good men with the best of intentions but perhaps are misguided. King quotes several religious
theologians throughout his essay such as the Apostle Paul and
Paul Tillich as a way to remind the clergymen that many of the
injustices happening in present day Birmingham were very similar
to stories in the Bible. King likely felt that the clergymen were
educated men as he was and therefore they would understand his
references to past philosophers and theologians. If King had been
addressing a non-religious or less educated audience perhaps he
would not have used as many historical references.

In conclusion, King's letter is a very moving piece of literature. Based on King's response to the clergymen, it is clear
to see he was deeply hurt and disappointed with the church
leaders and white moderate in Birmingham. King seems to feel
that his religious brothers should have been his greatest ally,
however they betrayed him and the African-American community
in Birmingham by publishing the letter in the Birmingham newspaper. King writes in the closing of his letter, "I hope that
circumstances will soon make it possible for me to meet each of
you, not as an integrationist or a civil-rights leader but a
fellow clergyman and a Christian brother (198). King's closing
seems to show his respect for the church leaders and the hope
that his letter may have opened their hearts and minds.

Reinforcing a Rogerian Argument with Visuals

Visual aids most likely to work in a Rogerian argument would illustrate cooperation and interaction among people: photographs of individuals engaged
in discussion, of planning sessions, of teamwork. An illustrated "Letter from
Birmingham Jail" (pages 184–198), for example, could include, along with
those well-known images of Martin Luther King leading a peaceful civil rights
demonstration, a photograph of citizens removing a racial discrimination sign
(for example, "Whites Only") from a restaurant window. Also, photographs of

individuals who play a role in the issue at hand would inject a human dimension to the controversy. What additional illustrations can you suggest that would capture the spirit of Dr. King's message?

Chapter Summary

A successful argument structured along Rogerian principles, like the Classical and Toulmin models, includes thorough, accurate, and relevant evidence in support of its claim; unlike these models, however, the aim of Rogerian persuasion is not to "win" the argument but to find common ground and to build consensus on an issue troubling both the writer and the audience. Instead of being considered "opponents," those with differing views are encouraged to reach cooperative dialogue to succeed; arguers need to listen with care and open-mindedness to divergent points of view. When considering taking a Rogerian approach to your argument, remember to ask yourself three questions: Can I represent challenging views and evaluate the evidence fairly and objectively? Do any of the challenging views make sense to some degree, and, if so, can I find a way to incorporate them into my own views? Am I sincere in my desire to establish common ground with those who take issue with me?

Summary and Comparison of the Classical, Toulmin, and Rogerian Models

Classical Model

- Based on philosophical ideals of sound thinking, incorporating the Aristotelian appeals of ethos (ethical principles, recognized authority, and shared values), pathos (stirring of emotions), and logos (dialectical reasoning)

- Follows a predetermined arrangement of elements: An *introduction* that states the problem and the thesis, presentation of the *evidence, refutation* of challenging views, and a *conclusion. Note that these elements do not necessarily have equal weight in the argument.*

Toulmin Model

- Based on the pragmatics of the judicial system rather than the ideals of philosophical thinking

- Approaches an argument in terms of its *claims* (which are presented more as hypotheses being open to challenge than as truths to be proven), its *data,* and its underlying *warrants,* and *backing* justifying those warrants that make the data trustworthy

- Recognizes the "real-world" complexities of an argument; gives special emphasis to refutation

Rogerian Model

- Based on humanistic values that take into account the importance of social cooperation in argument (that is, finding common ground is valued over "beating the opposition")
- Emphasizes points of agreement over points of disagreement, and treats the issue as a common problem for both the writer and the audience
- Urges arguers to cultivate multiple perspectives toward issues

When preparing an argument using the Rogerian method, consult the flowchart presented in Figure 4.1 on page 164.

Checklist

1. Do I find common ground with those whose views differ from my own?
2. Do I carefully consider the weaknesses or limitations of my point of view, as well as those of others'? Do I share these with my readers?
3. Is my tone cooperative rather than confrontational?
4. Do I encourage multiple perspectives rather than a singular one toward the issue?
5. Do I treat views with which I disagree respectfully? Do I give more emphasis to the points of agreement than to the points of disagreement?
6. Have I considered visual aids in establishing or encouraging common ground with my readers?

Writing Projects

1. Write an argumentative essay, following the Rogerian model, in which you defend or challenge one of the following issues:
   a. Books, especially textbooks, should be published online.
   b. Because the Second Amendment to the U.S. Constitution gives citizens the right to bear arms, students over the age of eighteen cannot be prohibited from bringing firearms onto campus if they feel the need for self-protection.
   c. Libraries should become media centers, using more of their budgets for electronic resources than for print resources.
   d. Tattoos demonstrate a freedom of expression and individual creativity rather than just being forms of self-scarification or emblems of endurance.

FIGURE 4.1

Rogerian Model
Flowchart

What issue am I going to investigate? [Example: The issue of visual arts education in U.S. public schools.]

What is my thesis? [Example: Acquiring basic skills in painting, illustrating, and sculpting is as important as acquiring basic skills in math and reading.]

What *common ground* exists between my views and those whose views differ from mine? [Example: We both agree that students must master those skills that will ensure success in practical "real-world" contexts; we both agree that analytical thinking and creative thinking are essential.]

What are the *challenging views* on the matter that I need to discuss? [Example: Mastery of math and reading skills must take priority over mastery of artistic skills.]

How can I most judiciously highlight the limitation of the *challenging views* and suggest a mutually agreeable way of overcoming those limitations? [Example: Giving priority to math and reading skills over artistic skills privileges analysis over creativity; yet we both agree that analysis and creativity are equally important; therefore we both agree that ways should be found to integrate math and reading skills with artistic skills in lesson plans.]

Based on shared views about my thesis, what can I add in the way of *evidence* that would be compatible with challenging views? [Example: If challengers say that math and reading skills must take priority, I can suggest that math and reading skills can be *integrated* with artistic design skills.]

What are my *concluding reflections* in light of the above?

Using the above information, what can I say in my opening paragraph that would best *introduce* my argument and engage my reader's attention?

2. Write an essay in which you use the Rogerian model to argue for one feasible way of improving living conditions with one or more roommates.

3. Write a comparative evaluation of the Classical, Toulmin, and Rogerian models of argument. Are some issues more suitable to one method than to the others? If so, what in particular would make that one method more effective?

4. Read the following essay, "Speech Codes at Private Universities," by student Kate Cooper. Then critique it in terms of her use of Rogerian persuasion.

Kate Cooper

Professor Tarnoff

English 177

11 December 2014

Speech Codes at Private Universities

Few relish the thought of someone wearing a sweatshirt that says "Fuck Women" or seeing an advertisement in a student newspaper denying the Holocaust. Such callous expressions not only offend, but also can have profound psychological effects on victims. This is especially true among disenfranchised groups. Racial discrimination, for instance, can elicit "feelings of humiliation, isolation, and self-hatred" (Delgado 137). Victims may learn to internalize degradation and doubt their self worth (Delgado 136). Hate speech silences these members by reinforcing stigmas that demean their voice (Garrett). Furthermore, a member of a disenfranchised group who experiences a verbal attack may fear that it will be followed by historical patterns of violence (Boeckmann and Turpin-Petrosino 221). These types of offensive expressions are particularly problematic on college campuses because they create a hostile environment that is distracting to student learning and counterproductive to a college's learning objective.

In an effort to minimize harassment and its damage, some call for speech codes. Speech codes are typically directed towards threats, fighting words, racial harassment, and discriminatory harassment. Punishments can range from censure to expulsion (Golding 621). Although speech codes at private universities are legitimate from a legal standpoint, their effectiveness and principles are hotly debated. Supporters of speech codes believe they help students learn that offensive expressions are not acceptable. These codes are also thought to protect students from an intimidating learning environment that interferes with a their ability to learn. Though their popularity has declined in recent years, in

2014 58 percent of the 427 schools surveyed by the Foundation for
Individual Rights in Education upheld speech codes ("Spotlight on
Speech Codes"). Proponents of these codes believe schools should
do everything in their power to cultivate a positive learning
environment, even if that means limiting free speech. Some believe
anything less is to tolerate intolerance. Supporters argue that
if universities exist to educate their students, they should not
permit this interference with their educational purpose.

Such measures are understandable—most can agree that it is
important for a university to be a place where people from all
backgrounds can learn without fear or intimidation. Moreover, proponents of either solution believe this behavior reflects problematic attitudes that we would all like to see changed. However,
private universities should opt for open discussion and education
rather than subjective speech codes that don't address underlying
beliefs, silence learning opportunities, and leave students unprepared for life in a society that upholds the freedom of speech.

Although speech codes curtail discrimination, they fail to
shed light on the attitudes that breed this behavior. A speech
code teaches students that certain expressions are unacceptable,
but it often does not explain why. Fear of punishment encourages
students to suppress prejudices where, unchallenged by discussion
or education, they are likely to persist. There is no psychological evidence that punishment causes changes in attitudes. In
fact, some evidence suggests censored speech becomes more appealing (Strossen 554). For instance, in a study at the University
of North Carolina, nearly 200 student subjects were told that
information supporting a position was being censored. Researchers
found that subjects were more interested in hearing a position
when they knew it was being censored. Furthermore, students were
more likely to agree with the censored information regardless of
their initial position (Worchel, Arnold, and Baker 227). These
results indicate that in some cases censoring speech empowers
rather than silences discriminatory expressions.

Because what's considered unacceptable speech is subjective
and has frequently been used to silence the powerless, a person
or small group of people on a college campus should not limit the

freedom of speech. For instance, a speech code at the University of Texas, Austin, defined racial harassment as "extreme or outrageous acts of communications intended to harass, intimidate, or humiliate a student or students on account of race, color or national origin and that reasonably causes them to suffer emotional stress" (qtd. in Golding 619). Such an attempt to define what should be included in a speech code reveals its inherently subjective nature. For instance, how does one define "emotional stress" and when is it "reasonably caused"? And who should be trusted to define these ambiguities? Those who make these decisions wield a large amount of power, and history shows that anti-speech laws have frequently been used to silence oppressed groups. For example, the Espionage Act was cited to justify the ten-year imprisonment of Eugene Debs for speaking at a peaceful rally for labor rights ("Freedom of Expression"). Margaret Sanger was arrested for giving a lecture that challenged the banning of birth control (Katz). In a university setting, the University of Michigan's anti-hate speech rule was frequently used by white students to charge black students with racist speech. Moreover, the only student who underwent a disciplinary hearing was black (Strossen 557). Furthermore, the necessity of speech codes to protect the individuals also seems unnecessary given that the law already protects individuals from certain forms of harmful speech, like defamatory or fighting words. It is also important to consider that what offends one student may not offend another depending on their disposition, beliefs and experiences. And in many cases it is extremely difficult to know the intention behind someone's words. In truth, "meanings change depending on the speaker, the hearer, the context, and even on who is overhearing them" (Leets and Giles qtd. in Hatfield et al. 44). It is tempting to ban speech we find offensive, but it is difficult to know where to and who should draw the line.

The appropriateness of speech codes is also questionable given that most universities value the freedom of expression and inquiry. Speech codes often contradict common university's values like the freedom to seek the truth or the freedom of expression. For instance, despite their student handbook's profession of the value of free speech, Tuft's Harassment Policy prohibits harassment and maintains its right to take disciplinary action against offenders. The definition of harassment vaguely includes verbal or written "attitudes or opinions" that create a "threat, intimidation, psychological attack, or physical assault" (Harris). When two anonymous satires of affirmative action and Islamic fundamentalism ran in a conservative student newspaper, Tufts banned anonymous pieces from the newspaper. The Committee on Student Life found these satires in violation of Tuft's harassment policy because they "psychologically intimidated" students. The committee explained that while students should "feel free" to use speech that could offend some, as a private institution Tufts had "an obligation to uphold" their "standards of behavior"(Hall 3). This contradictory language is not only confusing, but also makes the school seem more interested in protecting themselves legally by bottling up prejudices rather than airing them out with open dialogue where they can be debated and discussed to change the campus culture.

In the long run, colleges that shelter students from offensive expressions nurture unrealistic expectations for life after college in a free society. In an ideal world, no one should have to feel intimidated on the basis of his or her sexual orientation, gender, race, religious beliefs, etc. However, students who have not already been offended by some form of discrimination almost certainly will at some point in their lives. It is especially important then, for students to develop coping mechanisms for when they are intimidated or offended. Singling out a specific "zone" that limits freedom of speech may leave graduates ill prepared to respond to offensive speech that frequently occurs in a free society. While speech codes silence overt offenses, that protection dissolves as soon as students graduate and does not address a key issue: student's attitudes.

Instead, schools can encourage open discussions to dispel ignorance and address underlying assumptions. Because students come from a variety of backgrounds and because learning outside the classroom is such a key part of the college experience, a college campus is an apt setting to challenge ignorance. Despite their independence, students are still young adults who are developing their socialization and judgment skills. Offensive expressions should not be silenced but reflected on and challenged. These expressions can enhance the market place of ideas, or the free exchange of thoughts and opinions, that college campuses are valued for. When presented in "their baldest form", the weakness of these ideas can be exposed (Majeed 512). An incident can inspire a discussion around the meaning behind a word or the history of a disenfranchised group. This occurred when Sinclair Community College's Traditional Values Club invited Peter LaBarbera to speak about his belief in a LGBT community agenda. While waiting for LaBarbera to arrive, club advisers started an open discussion where, for about forty minutes, audience members were able to express their thoughts about a gay agenda. Those who found LaBarbera's position offensive articulated their views in an open dialogue among sympathizers and skeptics (Geiselman). This dialogue would not have been possible without the club's freedom to express its offensive views. Thus, college is a unique place where offenders, victims, and the campus community can bring offenses to light to expose their insensitivity. By punishing offensive behavior, speech codes give students a strong incentive to suppress their attitudes. Discussing rather than punishing offenses not only teaches students what language is unacceptable but also provides students with a greater opportunity to reconsider their underlying beliefs.

Rather than punishing offenders, a school can offer them preventive education and support offended students as they develop valuable coping mechanisms. Students should undergo some form of awareness education upon entering the university to establish a shared understanding of offensive behavior. The awareness education should teach students how to responsibly react in a situation where they may have offended others, such as issuing an apology and listening to how their actions offended someone. Instead of a speech code that prescribes a problem after the fact, this education, if done properly, can prevent offenses by combatting ignorance. A study by Hatfield et al. revealed that a Midwestern university achieved this goal when they hosted a conference about hate speech. A speaker from the Anti-Defamation League discussed the damage hate speech can have on individuals

and society. Audience members were then divided into small groups
to discuss their reactions to the speaker's ideas and reflect
on hate speech at their campus. Hatfield et al. found that students regarded hate speech as even less appropriate after the
conference and more openly expressed this new attitude. This
study illustrates how greater awareness can foster disapproval
for intolerance. Offenders could face social repercussions from
their peers who judge such offenses unfavorably. A college can
also encourage students to voluntary limit offensive expressions
with education about diversity. This could include classes that
fulfill core requirements and examine topics like the history of
racism or minority cultural and traditional practices. Finally,
the school should provide extra individual counseling to students
who may have been offended by an incident and should offer group
counseling that discuss discrimination on as well as off campus. Instead of excusing or attempting to control their student's
expressions, schools can act proactively by providing educational
resources for the student body and support for harassed students.

However, the ineffectiveness of speech codes is not an indication that verbal assaults are not as harmful as physical assaults.
Legally acceptable speech can wreak psychological damage on par
with an action's physical damage. This depends on the situation,
and in many cases this does not apply. As Chris Evans, a cyber
liberties campaign founder and lecturer explains, "there is a difference between saying you do not want blacks in the country and
trying to enforce it" (Hewett 608). Furthermore, the language of
a professor at the University of Central Florida who joked "Am I
on a killing spree or what?" after noting that his students were
"suffocating" from his difficult questions ("University of Central Florida") is not comparable to the act of a killing spree.
Yet there is a difference between hearing that type of speech and
walking into classroom in which written on the board is "A mind
is a terrible thing to waste – especially on a nigger" (Lawrence
433). This instance at the University of Michigan and others are
comparable with receiving a physical slap in the face. Unlike saying you don't want blacks in the country, such speech is both more

likely to and probably intended to prompt silence out of fear and
shock rather than a constructive discussion (Lawrence 452). Thus,
while it may not be appropriate to punish these forms of expression, it does not make them any less serious or heinous.

Punishing undesirable behavior fails to achieve the tolerance
and respect we would all like to see students develop. Furthermore, conjuring a protective bubble only strengthens a student's
unrealistic expectations about how they will be treated in a
free society. Regardless of a school's legal ability, imposing
an inherently subjective speech code to suppress student speech
is imprudent in the long term. In a country founded on the freedom of speech, private schools should allow their students to say
what they think without fear of punishment. By opting for discussion rather than punishment, schools can challenge the ignorance
from which discrimination originates.

Works Cited

Delgado, Richard. "Words that wound: A tort action for
    racial insults, epithets, and name-calling." *Harv. CR-CLL
    Rev.* 17 (1982): 135-137.

Boeckmann, Robert J., and Carolyn Turpin-Petrosino. "Under-
    standing the Harm of Hate Crime." *Journal of Social
    Issues* 58.2 (2002): 207-25. Web. 26 Oct. 2014.

"Freedom of Expression -ACLU Position Paper." *ACLU*. American
    Civil Liberties Union, 7 Jan. 1997. Web. 07 Dec. 2014.

Garrett, Deanna M. "Silenced Voices: Hate Speech Codes on
    Campus." *The University of Vermont*. The University of
    Vermont, 29 July 2002. Web. 04 Nov. 2014.

Geiselman, Kate. ""You're Leaving? Are You Effing Kidding?"
    An Anti-gay Bigot Gets Humiliated." *Salon*. Saloncom RSS,
    16 Apr. 2014. Web. 30 Oct. 2014.

Golding, Martin P. "Campus Speech Issues." The Well-Crafted
    Argument: A Guide and Reader. Ed. Fred D. White and Sim-
    one J. Billings. Boston: Wadsworth, 2014. 617-628. Print.

Hall, Sophia Gordon. "Tufts University Outcome of the Com-
    mittee on Student Life's Hearing of Complains Brought by

David Dennis and the Muslim Student Association Against *The Primary Source.*" Tufts University, 30 April 2007. Web. 7 Dec. 2014.

Harris, Samantha. "Speech Code of the Month: Tufts University -FIRE." *Foundation for Individual Rights in Education*. N.p., 2 June 2008. Web. 26 Oct. 2014.

Hatfield, Katherine L., Kellie Schafer, and Kristopher A. Stroup. "A Dialogic Approach to Combating Hate Speech on College Campuses." *Atlantic Journal of Communication* 13.1 (2005): 41–55. Web. 30 Oct. 2014.

Hewett, Caspar. "The Great Debate: Should We Censor the Internet?" The Well-Crafted Argument: A Guide and Reader. Ed. Fred D. White and Simone J. Billings. Boston: Wadsworth, 2014. 604–610. Print.

Katz, Esther. "American National Biography Online: Sanger, Margaret." *American National Biography Online*. N.p., Feb. 2000. Web. 07 Dec. 2014.

Lawrence, Charles R. "If he hollers let him go: Regulating racist speech on campus." *Duke Law Journal* (1990): 431–483. Web. 8 Dec. 2014.

Majeed, Azhar. "Defying the Constitution: The Rise, Persistence, and Prevalence of Campus Speech Codes." *Georgetown Journal of Law & Public Policy*, 7.2 (2009): 481–554. Web. 10 Dec. 2014.

"University of Central Florida: Professor Suspended for In-Class Joke." *Foundation for Individual Rights in Education*. N.p., n.d. Web. 25 Oct. 2014.

"Spotlight on Speech Codes 2014: The State of Free Speech on Our Nation's Campuses." *Issuu*. Foundation for Individual Rights in Education, n.d. Web. 20 Oct. 2014.

Strossen, Nadine. "Regulating Racist Speech on Campus: A Modest Proposal?" *Duke Law Journal* 1990.3 (1990): 484–573. *JSTOR*. Web. 3 Nov. 2014.

Worchel, Stephen, Susan Arnold, and Michael Baker. "The Effects of Censorship on Attitude Change: The Influence of Censor and Communication Characteristics." *Journal of Applied Social Psychology* 5.3 (1975): 227–239. Web. 7 Dec. 2014.

5 Reasoning: Methods and Fallacies

Come now, and let us reason together.

—Isaiah 1:18

As we have seen in the preceding chapters, argumentative writing involves the use of many skills: making rhetorical choices regarding audience, purpose, expectations, and the nature of the subject matter; outlining and drafting arguments; and deciding to use Classical, Toulmin, or Rogerian methods of argument. This chapter looks closely at another fundamental skill for writers of arguments—reasoning. By taking care to improve your ability to think critically and logically, you will be less likely to slip into errors of reasoning when supporting a claim.

Argumentative Reasoning

All arguments are imperfect to some degree. Unlike the tight logic of mathematics, in which a problem is solved methodically and objectively and is either correct or incorrect, most genuine arguments are based on complex human situations—complex because they have unpredictable or values-based elements. It is one thing to prove that force is equal to the product of mass times acceleration ($F = ma$) or that Socrates is mortal (given the fact that all humans are mortal); it is quite another matter to prove that reading to children dramatically increases their chances of college success. To argue that claim convincingly, you would first need to be aware of variables such as the availability of controlled studies on this topic, the characteristics of the students used in the studies, the types of readings the children had been exposed to, the frequency of being read to, and so on. Because of such complex variables, no argument can be 100 percent beyond dispute.

Thus, opportunities to make an argument stronger than it is always exist. Good arguers, however, strive to create not the perfect argument but the most effective one—the one that will ethically and logically persuade the readers. An argument, then, is most successful when its weaknesses are minimized as much

173

as possible. As a writer of arguments, you should familiarize yourself with the most common argumentative errors, which are known as *fallacies*. Learning to recognize fallacies does not guarantee that you will always avoid them, but it does increase the likelihood that you'll recognize them. You can use the information about fallacies to read others' arguments, resources, and your own drafts, so that your ability to recognize fallacies will eventually improve your ability to construct sound and convincing arguments.

The Nature of Fallacies

Arguers rarely use fallacies deliberately. Inadvertent lapses in judgment, fallacies usually arise from lack of experience with the subject matter, lack of familiarity with other points of view, undeveloped methods of argumentative reasoning, and hasty or insufficient revision of the argument being drafted. Let us examine each of these problems:

- **Lack of experience with the subject matter**. The more informed you are, the more material you have to defend your views. Most arguments fail to convince because they do not draw sufficiently from experience (personal experience as well as experience acquired from intensive research). You may feel passionately about the need to save the rain forests, but unless you thoroughly understand the nature of rain forests, the reasons they are so precious, and the ways in which they are so threatened, your argument will lack substance. You would have no choice but to rely on broad generalities, such as "Rain forests are filled with important species." Unless you can name and describe such species and describe their importance, readers are unlikely to be convinced that the assertion was valid.

- **Lack of familiarity with other points of view**. In addition to acquiring a knowledge base about the topic, you also need to be familiar with the range of representative views on that topic. Before you can defend your views on an issue, you need to understand challenging arguments, find reasons why those arguments are not as effective as yours, and be open to the possibility of adjusting your position if another is actually more reasonable. This may be an especially difficult hurdle because people tend to develop an emotional bond with certain views, however flawed they may be. Like heirlooms, these views may be integral to family values. Yet values change over time and circumstance; if one is to argue contemporary issues effectively, one needs to be flexible about even long-held beliefs.

- **Underdeveloped methods of argumentative reasoning**. You need to be knowledgeable about issues and familiar with the spectrum of views on those issues, and you also need to know how arguments progress logically from one point to the next. In addition to the methods of presenting an argument (the Classical, Toulmin, and Rogerian methods discussed in Chapters 3 and 4), particular *reasoning strategies* or patterns of thinking will enable you to frame an assertion logically.

- **Insufficient revision of the argument being drafted**. It is important to remember that writers must always be critical readers of their own work. This includes looking at any visual material they may have included to ensure the visuals are clear and do not contain any possible interpretations the writers had not intended.

Strategies of Reasoning

Critical thinking is actually a combination of interconnected reasoning strategies that require regular practice. The reasoning strategies most relevant to argumentative writing are as follows:

- *Deduction:* Drawing conclusions from assertions that you know to be true (insofar as you can determine); reasoning from the general to the specific
- *Induction:* Arriving at a conclusion that is based on what you judge to be sufficient (not necessarily conclusive) available evidence; reasoning from the specific to the general
- *Categorization:* Placing an idea or issue in a larger context using the strategies of definition, classification, and division
- *Analogy:* Attempting to enhance the validity of a claim by finding a similar situation in a different context
- *Authorization:* Establishing the validity of a claim by invoking authority, either in the form of personal testimonial from an expert or of preestablished policy or law
- *Plea:* Using emotionally charged expressions of feeling to aid in defending an assertion

The sections that follow look more closely at the ways in which each of these reasoning strategies operates.

Deduction

When you reason deductively, you break down an assertion into formal statements that are logically connected. A *syllogism* is one formula used in deductive reasoning, consisting of a *major premise*, a *minor premise*, and a conclusion.

Major premise:	All cats meow.
Minor premise:	Cordelia is a cat.
Conclusion:	Therefore, Cordelia meows.

As this simple example reveals, to reason deductively means to accept the major premise without question. To call the major premise into question ("Is it true that all cats meow?") is to move from deduction to induction, whereby one looks at the evidence leading up to the hypothesis to determine its truthfulness.

In commonplace arguments, an assumption often goes unstated because it is taken for granted that the audience already shares it. From the perspective of formal logic, this is considered an incomplete syllogism; but from the perspective of argumentative discourse, it is considered sufficient and is referred to as an *enthymeme*. Thus, the statement "Cordelia meows because she is a cat" is an enthymeme because the writer takes for granted that the audience accepts the unstated assumption that all cats meow.

Deductive reasoning can be especially powerful when refuting a claim. (If you need to refresh your memory about the process of refutation, review the discussion of Classical argument in Chapter 3.) For example, if a friend claims that to accept a government-run program is to reject a free-market economy, you could refute the claim by asserting that a government program and a free-market economy are not as mutually exclusive as the friend's claim implies. Such dichotomous ("either-or") thinking is a commonly occurring example of flawed deductive reasoning. By calling attention to the many-sided complexity of a problem, you raise the consciousness of your audience; you in effect *teach* your readers to recognize the gray areas that aren't as conspicuous as the black-and-white areas but that usually bring the truth much closer.

To refute a claim, you may need to do a deductive analysis of the author's reasoning strategies. Here is a five-step method for such analysis:

1. Identify contradictions.
2. Identify inconsistencies.
3. Identify omissions or oversights.
4. Reduce an unsound claim to its logical absurdity (*reductio ad absurdum*) so as to expose the flawed reasoning more conspicuously.
5. Identify oversimplifications.

Identify Contradictions   Someone asserts that making handgun sales illegal would increase crime because more guns would be obtained illegally. You could reveal a contradiction by showing (using statistics from a reputable survey) how that claim contradicts reality: that crime actually has decreased by a certain percentage in one or more places where such a law had been enacted. Similarly, if a writer asserts that playing video games excessively damages one's ability to think effectively and then proceeds to describe her own experiences with video games in an effective manner, you could point out the contradiction between the author's writing effectively and the alleged damage to her thinking skills from years of playing video games.

Identify Inconsistencies   If you claim that people should give up eating meat but then proceed to eat a bowl of chicken soup, reasoning that such a small quantity of chicken is negligible or that even vegetarians need a "meat break" now and then, you are being logically inconsistent. Or consider this somewhat more complex example: Arlene is against abortion because she equates abortion with murder. However, Arlene agrees that in cases of rape, incest, or grave danger to the mother's life, abortion is permissible. Arlene is being logically inconsistent because her exceptions seem irrelevant to her own definition of abortion as fetal murder.

Identify Omissions or Oversights   A friend advises you not to take a course from Professor Krupp because Krupp gives difficult exams, grades rigorously, and assigns a heavy reading load. At first, you think that these are pretty good reasons for not enrolling in Professor Krupp's course. But then you wonder whether any positive things about this professor might balance out the bad, so you ask: "Did you learn a lot in her course?" Your friend replies, "Oh, yes— more than in any other course I've taken." You have just identified a deliberate omission or an accidental oversight in your friend's assessment of Professor Krupp.

Reduce an Unsound Claim to Its Logical Absurdity   Someone argues against a company's policy that employees wear shirts and ties or dresses and skirts by claiming that employees can think well even when dressed casually in jeans and T-shirts. You could refute that claim by taking it to the logical extreme. Why wouldn't the first person show up in pajamas or a swimsuit for work, then? The point of the dress code is not to affect one's ability to think but to present a certain image of the company.

Identify Oversimplifications   Recall the earlier example of the friend who argues that a government-run program is never compatible with a free-market economy. This kind of dichotomous thinking oversimplifies the reality of a free-market society such as that of the United States, where government programs such as Social Security and NASA are quite compatible with a market economy. Oversimplification results from an insufficiently investigated or thought-out premise on which the argument rests.

EXERCISE 5.1

1. Examine the following four arguments and describe the method or methods of deductive reasoning that each author is using or representing.

    a. Discrimination based on beauty is rooted in the same sexist principle as discrimination against the ugly. Both rest on the power of the male gaze—the fact that men's estimation of beauty is the defining feature of the category. — Michael Kimmel

    b. If the Darwinian [evolutionary] process really took place, remains of plants and animals [that is, the fossil record] should show a gradual and continual change from one type of animal or plant into another. One of the things that worried Darwin in his day, as well as [what worries] modern evolutionists, was that the fossil record did not supply these intermediate life forms. —Donald E. Chittick

    c. Until the census is focused on individuals, not households, the situation of women and children may continue to be distorted—just as it might be if there were only one vote per household. There is such a wide range of constituencies with an interest in Census Bureau policies that journalists have coined the phrase "census politics." But social justice movements haven't yet focused on the fact that census categories also determine what is counted as work, and who is defined as a worker. —Gloria Steinem

    d. Aristotle felt that the mortal horse of Appearance which ate grass and took people places and gave birth to little horses deserved far more attention than Plato was giving it. He said that the horse is not mere Appearance. The Appearances cling to something which is independent of them and which, like Ideas, is unchanging. The "something" that Appearances cling to he named "substance." And at that moment…our modern scientific understanding of reality was born. —Robert Pirsig

2. Bring in a short article such as a newspaper editorial and discuss it in terms of its use of deductive reasoning. Point out any flaws you see in the deductive reasoning.

3. Bring in a visual, such as an editorial cartoon, and analyze what deductive conclusions it invites readers to make based on what it depicts.

Induction

You engage in inductive reasoning when you strive to make sense of things you experience. Unlike deductive reasoning, you do not begin with a premise assumed to be true and then determine a logical foundation for supporting it. Instead, you build a hypothesis out of your observations of phenomena. To return to our simple example of whether all cats meow, the inductive writer would examine the evidence—Cat A, Cat B, Cat C, and so on—until observing enough cats to warrant the conclusion, "Yes, all cats meow," or to reject it ("No, not all cats meow; Siberian tigers are cats, and they growl."), or to qualify it ("Yes, all cats meow, provided they're members of the subgenus *Felix domesticus*.").

Because in inductive reasoning the strength of the conclusion rests entirely on the sufficiency of the evidence observed, you must use an adequate number of reliable samples.

Number of Samples   How many samples must be observed before it is reasonable to make the "inductive leap"? Technically, of course, no conclusion arrived at inductively is absolutely indisputable. For that to be the case in our cat argument, for example, you would have to observe every domestic cat on earth! At some point, every inductive reasoner must say, "I have observed enough to draw a reliable conclusion." This decision can be tricky and, indeed, is a major point of disputation in science—which relies preeminently on the inductive method (better known as the *scientific method*) for testing the validity of hypotheses.

Reliability of Samples   If the purpose of your paper is to argue whether a clear correlation exists between alcohol consumption and health problems, you may decide first to conduct a campus survey to see whether health problems are more frequent among drinking students than among nondrinking ones. In addition to interviewing an adequate number of students from each group (a 20 to 25 percent response rate to your survey from the total student population would be considered substantial), you will want the sample to be reliable in other ways. For example, it should be representative of different groups within the student body. Having only women, only men, only athletes, or only Mormons included would make your sample survey on college drinking unreliable.

Strength of the Conclusion   After gathering a reasonable number of samples and determining that your samples are reliable, you must now ensure that the conclusion you reach based on your gathered evidence makes good sense. Imagine that you've been testing your suspicion that, even in the second decade of the twenty-first century, women in the professional workplace are not receiving merit-based promotions as frequently as their male counterparts. The three workplaces you have inspected have proven this to be the case. However, each workplace situation revealed a different set of variables: In workplace A, the female employee who received the very highest evaluation was promoted, but the other two female employees who also received high evaluations (but not quite as high) were not promoted. Their three male counterparts receiving correspondingly high evaluations were all promoted. In workplace B, by contrast, two female employees and two male counterparts were promoted on merit, but it turned out that the men were given 10 percent higher raises than the women. And in workplace C, one woman received a significantly greater promotion and raise based on merit, but the other three women with strong evaluations were not promoted at all. Two of their male counterparts were promoted based on mediocre evaluations and received only minimal raises. As you can see, the disparate situations in these three workplaces require the researcher to probe further into (a) specific employer criteria leading to the promotion and whether a double standard was being used; (b) differences in performance between the male and female employees that justified the disparity in promotions awarded; (c) any undisclosed evaluative criteria that may have been used in deciding against a promotion, or a raise not connected to the merit score, such as bringing a person up to parity with others who had worked at the company just as long.

EXERCISE 5.2

Describe the sequence of likely steps in inductive reasoning one might take for each of the following tasks:

1. Criteria to be used when buying a new or a used car

2. Choosing a birthday gift for a friend or parent

3. Deciding whether the prerequisites offered for a given field of study are necessary preparation for future employment in that field

4. Steps necessary in determining the chemical composition of an unknown gas

Categorization

Without systems of classification and division, we would be unable to make much sense out of reality. Perhaps the best illustration of this is the Linnaean system of taxonomy. With its binomial schema (genus name + species name, as in *Felix domesticus* or *Homo sapiens*), all life on earth has been classified. Think for a moment about how valuable such a schema is for understanding the relationship of life forms to each other.

People categorize foods into groups such as *savory* or *sweet*, or *main course* or *dessert*, to determine what they'll serve for dinner—a useful strategy for knowing what to buy for a dinner party. People break the large category of sports into basketball, baseball, and so on, and then divide those subgroups further into professional and amateur leagues. College football teams would fall into amateur leagues, which then play on their NCAA division level—IA, IAA, IIA, and so on. Imagine the injuries without such classification—an NFL football team playing a IIIA college team! Categorization in sports helps ensure a level playing field.

Categorization is just as important outside of science; for example, we can plan our day better by grouping our activities into "chores," "business transactions," "recreation," and so on. However, problems often arise. When people try to categorize human beings neatly according to ethnicity or cultural differences, the danger of stereotyping arises. Superficial differences such as skin color or manner of dress or speech are given more significance than they deserve. Racism, homophobia, and gender-based discrimination are often the ugly results. Categorizing works best when it serves as an initial gauge for differentiating A from B or A and B from C, and so forth. For example, if you were examining the study habits of college students, you might group your sample students by gender or age or major, just in case a correlation between the category selected and the kind of study habits would show up.

Another facet of categorization is definition, which is necessary for fine-tuning the distinctions between one thing and another within the same category. The very word *define* means "to determine or fix the boundaries or extent of" (*Random House Webster's College Dictionary*). Formal definitions use categorizing techniques themselves. In the definition of the word *chaplet*, for example—"a wreath or garland for the head" (*Random House Webster's College Dictionary*)—the first half of the definition ("a wreath or garland") establishes the broad category, or genus, and the second half ("for the head") pinpoints its distinguishing (specific) characteristics.

EXERCISE 5.3

1. Study the definitions of the following words in two unabridged dictionaries (for example, *The Oxford English Dictionary* and *Webster's Unabridged Dictionary*). Report the differences in the way each dictionary presents the broad category (genus) and the distinguishing (specific) characteristics:

   a. volcano

   b. emphysema

   c. magician

   d. cathedral

2. Write a brief explanation of the way knowledge is categorized in your major field of study (or in a subject you are currently studying).

Analogy

To make an analogy is to draw a correspondence between two things that are superficially different but not essentially different. Analogies are used to enhance comprehension. If you are trying to help readers understand the nature of a radio wave, for example, you might use the more familiar analogy of a water wave. A river and an artery are not superficially alike, but they behave in similar enough ways for one to say that water flows in a river the way blood flows in an artery. A more readily perceived phenomenon like a flowing river is easier to understand than the flow of blood through an artery. The author's goal is to enable ease of understanding over precision of explanation.

However, to say that people are like ants because they swarm in large numbers to sporting events is to generate a distorted (and demeaning) image of fans' behavior. Using analogy in argumentative writing is a give-and-take situation: You give your readers greater comprehension of the idea, but you take away precision. The rule of thumb, then, is to use analogies carefully.

EXERCISE 5.4

Create an analogy to help explain each of the following concepts:

1. Doppler effect
2. Cardiac function
3. Eye function
4. Heaven
5. The police brutality protests in Ferguson, Baltimore, and other American cities in 2015

Authorization

Writers sometimes need to support an assertion by including the testimony of an expert in the field in question. If you are arguing about the dangers of ultraviolet radiation and urging people to consider sunbathing a risky activity due to the alleged link between ultraviolet radiation and skin cancer, you are likely to present empirical evidence from, say, several medical studies. You could also add drama to your claim by quoting a startling statement made by a leading skin cancer expert. In such a situation, you are resorting to the ethos, or the reliable character, of the expert.

Sometimes, finding the appropriate authority to obtain testimony in support of a claim can be tricky, depending on the claim. If you wish to argue that using genetic material from human embryos is unethical, should you include testimony from geneticists or religious leaders, or other kinds of experts? It might be easy to find experts who will agree with you—but are they the right experts?

EXERCISE 5.5

Suggest appropriate credentials for one or more authority figures brought in to offer testimony for each of the following topics:

1. Depletion of South American rain forests

2. The need for greater tsunami preparedness in certain regions of the world

3. A new dieting program

4. Cultivating the habit of reading in children

5. Participation in athletic programs either undermining or enhancing academic performance. (See Cluster 2, Athletics and Academics)

Plea

Emotional response is often highly persuasive. In formal argument, therefore, you may try to persuade your audience to accept your views by way of sympathy or compassion as well as by way of logical reasoning. Thus, if your goal is fundraising for the homeless, you might tell stories about the way homeless people suffer when they have to go without eating for two or three days or shiver during cold winter nights on a park bench. If you wish to emphasize the importance of reading aloud to children, you might create a little scenario in which you dramatize the way in which listening to stories delights and heightens the intellectual curiosity of young children who are absorbed in what their parents are reading to them.

The plea strategy uses the Aristotelian appeals to emotion or to ethics. Appealing to the audience's compassion, ethical responsibility, need for security, comfort, and so on reinforces rather than counteracts the logical and analytical; for that reason, such appeals are an important rhetorical tool in the art of persuasion.

EXERCISE 5.6

Suggest possible uses of the plea strategy for each of the following topics:

1. An article on improving airport security

2. An article on preserving the individual's right to privacy

3. An article on teaching children to swim before age five

4. An article on acting to protect an endangered species, such as the blue whale

Errors in Reasoning: A Taxonomy

Now that we have examined the methods of reasoning, it is time to look closely at the pitfalls that can occur. To some degree, errors in reasoning are almost unavoidable because reasoning is a complex mental act that requires a concerted effort to perfect. Nonetheless, the more alert you become to the way in which a given line of reasoning violates a principle of logic, of ethics, or of emotional integrity, the less likely it is that your arguments will be criticized for their fallacies.

Let us begin by becoming familiar with the common fallacies; we then examine each of them in more detail and look at the ways they subtly creep into an argument. We also examine these fallacies to identify faulty logic in the sources we may consult for our topics. Seeing faulty logic in supposedly informed sources helps us to decide not to use such sources ourselves and to know what we can rebut in arguments that challenge our own.

Errors of Deduction

In this group of fallacies, the line of reasoning that stems from statements assumed to be true is flawed, or the statements themselves may be flawed. Many errors in deductive reasoning occur because the author fails to connect premises to conclusions logically. Some common types of deductive fallacies follow.

Fourth Term   Careless arguers sometimes substitute one term for another, assuming the terms mean or suggest the same things, when in fact the terms have different meanings. The way to demonstrate the illogic of such a substitution is to think about the terms in a formal syllogism (the pattern of formal deductive reasoning discussed on pages 175–178): major, minor, and middle, as follows:

	[Maj] [Maj]
Major premise:	All **dogs** are **mammals.**
	[Maj] [Maj]
Minor premise:	**Rascal** is a **dog.**
	[Maj] [Maj]
Conclusion:	Therefore, **Rascal** is a **mammal.**

In any valid syllogism, the major term is the subject that must be equated with both a generic classification (middle term) and an individual one (minor term). In the preceding example, the major term *dog* is equated with the middle term *mammal* (dog = mammal) and the minor term Rascal (dog = Rascal).

Now consider this syllogism:

All prerequisites for the major in chemistry are difficult.

Chem. 50 is highly recommended for the major in chemistry.

Therefore, Chem. 50 is difficult.

Instead of seeing the major term *prerequisites* appear in the minor premise, a substitute fourth term—*highly recommended*—appears, thus rendering the syllogism invalid (even though the conclusion may be true).

Non Sequitur   In a non sequitur ("it does not follow"), an assertion cannot be tied logically to the premise it attempts to demonstrate. Consider the premise, "Nellie is obsessed with basketball." The reason presented is "because she attends a basketball game every week." The fact that one attends a basketball game every week—or every day—does not in itself demonstrate an obsession. Nellie could be an employee at the arena, or her brother could be one of the players, or she could be a sportswriter, or she could be conducting research on the game of basketball, or she could simply love the game in a positive sense. *Obsession* implies that something in one's behavior is beyond control; if that is the case, then your statements should reflect it: "Nellie is obsessed with basketball because, despite being threatened with losing her job if she doesn't go to work rather than the basketball games, she attends them anyway."

Ad Hominem   An ad hominem ("against the individual person") is a form of non sequitur in which the arguer argues against an individual's qualifications by attacking his or her personal life or trying to create a negative link between life and work. "Sherwood would not make a good mayor because he spends too much of his free time reading murder mysteries." The reverse situation—*pro hominem*—is equally fallacious, even though it would seldom be reported: "Sherwood would make a terrific mayor because he spends a lot of his time reading the Bible."

Keep in mind that even when a public figure's personal life may seem like fair game for ad hominem attacks, such tactics would be unwarranted. For example, if a famous actor were accused of sexual misconduct, some might be tempted to argue, "We should boycott all of Rufus Lecher's films because he once was arrested for sexual harassment." Certainly, it is understandable that the public would lose respect for Lecher as a *person*, but Lecher's ability as an *actor* should not be confused with his off-screen behavior.

Denying the Antecedent/Affirming the Consequent   This fallacy occurs in hypothetical ("if–then") assertions. The first part of the assertion (the "if" clause) is called the *antecedent*; the second part (the "then" clause) is called the *consequent*. In a valid hypothetical assertion, the antecedent may be affirmed or the consequent denied—but not vice versa. Thus, in the hypothetical assertion,

If it snows today, then classes will be canceled.

the antecedent may correctly be affirmed (*It is snowing today*; therefore, classes are canceled), or the consequent correctly denied (*Classes were not canceled today;*

therefore, it must not be snowing). But asserting the opposite in each case would be fallacious, as follows:

Antecedent denied: "*It is not snowing today*; therefore, classes are not canceled." (Classes could still be canceled even if it weren't snowing—for example, teachers may have gone on strike.)

Consequent affirmed: "*Classes have been canceled today*; therefore, it is snowing." (Again, classes could have been canceled for reasons other than snowfall.)

Sometimes this fallacy is presented in a way that seems logical. Consider this example:

If more young women entering college were encouraged to study engineering, there would be more professional women engineers. According to the latest statistics, the number of female engineers today has increased over the previous year's number. One may therefore assume that more young women entering college have been encouraged to study engineering.

The consequent—that there are more professional women engineers today than there were last year—cannot logically be affirmed by the antecedent, that more young women entering college have been encouraged to study engineering. The increase could be due to other factors, such as women had been boycotting engineering firms that were disproportionately male, for example.

Errors of Induction

In this group of fallacies, the process of drawing conclusions or arriving at reliable generalizations based on observed particulars is faulty.

Unsupported Generalization   Generalizing is an important tool for critical thinkers, but a good generalization is derived from evidence. When the *evidence* is lacking, we say that the generalization is unsupported. *Evidence* in this context refers not only to statistics such as trends, tallies, or percentages but also to cases in point. For example, if you read somewhere that more physicians are being sued for malpractice in the current year than in the year preceding, you would be making an unsupported generalization if you neglected to provide statistical support for your assertion. It would also be a good idea to refer to individual cases that *demonstrated* incompetence. Why? Perhaps the increase in malpractice suits was based on other factors, such as more aggressive efforts to sue for malpractice, or perhaps the criteria defining *malpractice* had changed from one year to the next. As a critical thinker, you always need to be aware of alternative possibilities and explanations.

Another example of an unsupported generalization might be termed an assumption of hidden motive (or hidden agenda), or simply the *motive fallacy*, as the British philosopher Jamie Whyte terms it in his witty and incisive exposé of muddled thinking, *Crimes against Logic* (2004). If you're a manager and one of your employees praises you for landing an important contract, you will fall prey to the motive fallacy if you assume that the employee's motive for praise was, say, to reinforce his or her job security rather than simply wanting to praise you for your achievement. Whyte uses a courtroom example of the motive fallacy. A juror might secretly assume that a defense attorney is "motivated" to defend her client's innocence only because she is being paid to do so; but that juror obviously must consider only the evidence, not any hidden motives. "If we followed the method of the motive fallacy in civil trials," Whyte quips, "they would be rather simple. Decide against the side of the lawyer who was paid more. She has the greater corrupting motive" (12).

Hasty Generalization   A hasty generalization occurs when one leaps to a *premature conclusion*—not because the arguer provided faulty evidence or no evidence at all but because the evidence provided was insufficient to convincingly support the claim being made. Writers of argument can fall prey to hasty generalization when they do not check out enough cases before reaching their conclusion. If you claim, for example, that burglary has increased in your neighborhood and use as your only evidence the fact that two houses on your block have been burglarized, you would be guilty of a hasty generalization—*unless* you could also demonstrate that this number is greater for the same time frame of a year ago. Always make sure your evidence is thorough.

Red Herring   In British fox hunting, red herrings (very odorous) were sometimes dragged across a trail to throw the dogs off scent. This practice served as a metaphor for raising an issue that has little or nothing to do with what is being argued in order to force the argument in a new direction. For example, say that after listening to a voter's concern that the community's high school needs to receive major funds to upgrade its facilities, a candidate responds, "I understand your concern and have asked the school board to review its policies." The candidate has thrown the voter a red herring by changing the subject from inadequate facilities to the school board's educational policies.

Poisoning the Well   Like the red herring, this fallacy aims to interfere with normal argumentative progression. But whereas the red herring aims to derail an argument in progress, poisoning the well aims to corrupt the argument before it even begins—usually by passing judgment on the quality of the argument before listeners have a chance to evaluate it. If you ask your friends to listen to a debate on whether the public library should be funded for building a DVD collection but then say that one of the debaters will be presenting an argument that has already been successfully repudiated, you would be guilty of poisoning the well with your own evaluation before giving your friends the opportunity to judge for themselves.

Misreading the Evidence   One of the biggest challenges in coming up with good evidence to support a claim is interpreting it properly. Findings based on polls, for example, can qualify as valid evidence, but such findings can easily be misinterpreted. For example, if a poll reveals that the majority of people polled felt that a human mission to Mars is too expensive and should not be federally funded, you would be misreading the evidence if you interpreted that statistic as an indication that most *Americans* felt that a human mission to Mars should not be federally funded, or that most people polled felt that human exploration of space was a waste of resources, or that most people polled felt that the cost of a human expedition to Mars was much higher than the U.S. government could afford. Notice that the majority is of a subset of the population at large, so you can claim only that the majority of those polled felt a certain way.

Slighting the Opposition   It can sometimes be tempting, in an argument, to downplay points of view with which we disagree or to conveniently omit information that would make those views more persuasive and our own views less persuasive. By doing so, you commit the fallacy of slighting the opposition. Let's say you're arguing that cell phone use should not be permitted in flight, on the grounds that cell phone conversations would annoy many of the nearby passengers and that it could pose a security problem. You're aware of the counterarguments that a sizeable percentage of passengers would find cell phone conversations a more pleasant way to pass the time, would permit transacting important business, that new technology has rendered cell phone operation during flight perfectly safe, and that passengers not wanting to be seated near anyone with a cell phone would be accommodated—however, because you fear that mentioning the last counterargument would seriously undermine your own stance, you don't bother to mention it.

Post Hoc Ergo Propter Hoc   The phrase (sometimes simply *post hoc*) means "after the fact, therefore because of the fact." An effect (say, tripping and falling) is attributed to a cause (say, the sudden appearance of a black cat) only because of proximity, not because of any logical connection. The post hoc fallacy forms the basis for superstitious thinking and preempts any effort to determine a logical cause (for example, the gaping crack in the sidewalk caused the person to fall).

Begging the Question   This is an error of both deductive and inductive reasoning. As a deductive fallacy, question-begging takes the form of circular reasoning in which a conclusion is nothing more than a reworded premise, as in this example:

A required course is one that is essential for a well-rounded education.

Writing courses are essential for a well-rounded education.

Therefore, composition is a required course.

The reasoning looks sound at first glance, but nothing has been "reasoned" at all. "Required course" is just another way of saying "necessary for a well-rounded education" in the context of the above syllogism. The question that remains—that is "begged"—is "What is meant by 'necessary for a well-rounded education'"?

Question-begging can also present itself as an error in inductive reasoning. Essentially, it voices a conclusion that requires inductive testing as if the testing had already been conducted, as in the assertion, "Impractical courses like Ancient History will no longer be required for graduation." Instead of applying a test of impracticality (whatever such a test would be like) to the course in question, the speaker assumes by her phrasing that such a test would be unnecessary.

Slippery Slope   This is an example of induction run rampant. Here, a person forecasts a series of events (usually disastrous) that will befall one if the first stated step is taken. Thus, the person who asserts the following is committing a slippery slope fallacy:

> If medical researchers continue to increase human longevity, then the population will soar out of control, mass famine will occur, the global economy will collapse, and the very survival of the species will be threatened.

Factors capable of compensating for the consequences of population increase have not been considered.

Errors of Categorization

In this group of fallacies, arguers tend to see things in terms of black and white instead of color gradations, so to speak—or they confuse one group of objects or ideas with another.

False Dichotomy (Either/Or)   This error of reasoning assumes there are only two options to resolving a given situation, when in fact there may be many. Assertions such as, "If you're not part of the solution, you're part of the problem," "America: love it or leave it," or "If you love nature, then you cannot possibly support industrial development" are examples of dichotomous thinking. To address the last example mentioned, for instance, factors that complicate the industry-nature dichotomy include the fact that recycling, land reclaiming, and alternative energy use (wind, solar, geothermal, biomass) are industries.

Apples and Oranges   We often hear people comparing two things that are not comparable (because they are not part of the same category). A statement like "The physics lecture was not as good as the dinner we had at Antoine's last night" does not convey much meaning. Likewise, it is illogical to claim that Placido Domingo is a better singer than Johnny Cash, because opera and country-western are two different kinds of music, with fundamentally different criteria for excellence.

Errors of Analogy

Errors in analogies occur when the analogy distorts, misrepresents, or oversimplifies the reality.

False or Invalid Analogy   An analogy is considered false when it distorts what is essentially true about what is being analogized. If a student dislikes an instructor's strict, regimented classroom tactics and says that the classroom is like Hitler's Third Reich, the student is using a false analogy. Yes, it is true that Hitler used strict military tactics; but that fact alone cannot serve to parallel the situation in a classroom—unless the professor hired secret police agents (Gestapo), put dissenters into horrific concentration camps, and instituted mass extermination plans. Parallel activities of students and professionals often breed false analogies: "It isn't fair that I can't write on anything I want, any way I want. Nobody tells Amy Tan or Stephen King how or what to write!"

Faulty Analogy   Sometimes, the analogy we use to parallel an idea or object is something of a half-truth instead of a complete falsehood; that is, it might work in one context, but not in others. To compare human courtship rituals to those of peacocks, for example, might amusingly highlight the similarities, but the differences are too major to take the analogy seriously.

Tu Quoque   (pronounced *too qwo-kway*, Latin for "you also") You'd think that the likelihood of committing this fallacy would have vanished shortly after one's tenth birthday, but for some reason it lingers into adulthood. This is the error of analogy whereby Teddy says to Betty, "Don't you dare accuse *me* of cheating on the exam; I saw you cheating also."

Errors of Authorization

In this group of fallacies, authority figures or their testimonials are used vaguely or erroneously.

Vague Authority   In the sentence, "Science tells us that a catastrophic earthquake will strike southern California within the next ten years," we would do well to question the term *science*. (In a similar vein, recall the commercial that begins, "Four out of five doctors recommend...") We have no idea who or even what authority *science* is referring to because *science* refers to a vast body of disciplines, not any particular authority. To remove the vagueness, the author would have to say something to this effect: "Seismologists at Cal Tech [or, better yet, Dr. So-and-So, a seismologist at Cal Tech] predicts that a catastrophic earthquake will strike southern California within the next ten years."

Suspect Authority   Sometimes, it is not easy to tell whether an authority is reliable. Using the above example, if the credentials of the scientist predicting the earthquake are not disclosed—or if her field of expertise is a discipline other than seismology—we have a right to suspect her authority.

The suspect authority fallacy is encountered most frequently in advertisements and in general articles one finds on the Internet—at .com rather than .gov or .edu sites. When a film star tells us that a certain brand of shampoo gives a "deep-bodied" luster to hair, we wonder what the basis for authority possibly could be, even assuming that everyone agrees on how a "deep-bodied" luster looks.

Keep in mind, of course, that such a commercial is not an example of false advertising. The commercial never states that the film star has the proper credentials to evaluate a product's quality, only that the product is the star's personal choice. The audience is left to make any further inferences, such as, "Gosh, if Wilma Superstar uses that shampoo, then it *must* be terrific."

Errors of Pleading

These fallacies stem from erroneous or improper use of the Aristotelian appeals discussed in Chapter 1.

Appeal to Fear   Anyone who has heard commercials for security alarm systems or auto theft prevention devices is quite familiar with this appeal. The advertiser typically presents scenarios of coming home to find the place ransacked. "Better to be safe than sorry" is the common phrase brandished here. Keep in mind that this appeal becomes an error in pleading when it is excessive or when the scenarios presented are so extreme as to distort reality. If the advertiser for security alarms paints a lurid picture of you and your family being tortured or murdered by burglars, for example, such an appeal to fear likely would be excessive and thus erroneous.

There are situations in which an appeal to fear might seem justifiable. During the Ebola crisis in late 2014, for example, one country, North Korea, went so far as to prohibit all tourists from entering the country. In the United States, some politicians insisted we prohibit anyone from Liberia or Sierra Leone (where the disease had become an epidemic) from entering the country regardless of exercising medically sanctioned precautions. One could argue that this is not so much an example of the appeal to fear fallacy as it is an example of exercising excessive caution due to insufficient information.

Appeal to the Bandwagon   Appeal to the bandwagon is the fallacy behind peer pressure. "Hey, everyone else is going to the beach today; don't be a nerd and stay cooped up in the library on such a gorgeous day!" Being able to say no, to maintain your own integrity, and to do what is most responsible and best for you in the long term is hard when you are the only one following that path. If you discover that everyone has suddenly decided to take a week off from classes to attend Mardi Gras in New Orleans, the temptation is great to do likewise. It sometimes takes courage to say, "I'm going to think this out on my own and not follow the crowd."

Of course, an appeal to the bandwagon sometimes makes sense, as in the case of sound medical or health care advice: "Millions of people get their teeth cleaned regularly (because they are far less likely to suffer from gum disease if they do so), so you should get your teeth cleaned too."

Appeal to Ignorance   The basis of the appeal here is that we can decide based on what is *not* known. For example, "We have every reason to believe that Martians exist because we have no way of knowing that they *don't* exist." The problem with this kind of reasoning, of course, is that there is no way to prove or disprove the claim.

One often encounters appeals to ignorance in informal scientific speculation. Have you ever gotten into a conversation about the likelihood of intelligent life on other worlds? You might commonly hear a line of reasoning that goes something like this:

> True, we haven't the slightest blip of evidence that intelligent beings exist beyond earth; but the universe is so vast and our understanding of what the universe could contain is so meager that there must be intelligent life out there somewhere!

Although one might argue that the probability of intelligent life increases in proportion to the size of the field, that probability does not necessarily approach inevitability unless compelling evidence is uncovered (indirect evidence of intelligent habitation, such as industrial pollutants in the atmosphere of a distant planet, for example).

EXERCISE 5.7

1. What is the connection between a method of reasoning and an error in reasoning?
2. State the principal difference between inductive and deductive reasoning.
3. For each of the following passages,
   - give the method of reasoning it belongs to;
   - indicate whether it is an appropriate or erroneous use of that method; and
   - if the latter, identify the error and suggest a way to resolve it.

Note: There may be more than one error in a given passage or no errors at all.

a. Cats are just like people: They're intensely curious, and they get into trouble as a result of their curiosity.

b. The idiots who gave my car a tune-up forgot to clean the fuel injection system.

c. God is beyond logical understanding; therefore, one should never question the truth of God's existence.

d. All honors students are high achievers. José is a straight-A student. Therefore, José is a high achiever.

e. Jane: What do you think of my new boyfriend?
   Ann: I think he's a jerk.
   Jane: You just say that because you want him for yourself!

f. After interviewing a dozen students about their reading habits, I am convinced that students these days do not like to read poetry.

g. All of my friends who want to attend law school have signed up for the Advanced Argumentation course. Because you plan on going to law school, you should take this course too.

h. It's a good idea to wash fresh fruit before eating it; the last time I forgot to wash the strawberries I ate, I came down with food poisoning.

i. Music appreciation classes seem like a waste of time. I know what I like to listen to, and no music expert is going to change my mind about it.

j. Chicken is much tastier than oatmeal.

k. Libraries will soon become obsolete now that the Internet has become such a versatile research tool.

l. To answer your question about whether taxes should be raised, let me first call your attention to the fact that the unemployment rate in this state is lower than it has ever been.

m. Sound waves, just like light waves, can be low frequency or high frequency.

n. If children love to read, they will do well in school. Erika does well in school. Therefore, Erika loves to read.

o. Why should I vote? You haven't voted in years.

4. For each of the preceding passages, suggest ways in which the error, if one exists, may be corrected.

EXERCISE 5.8

Read the following commentary on the Authority Fallacy (an extension of the Suspect Authority Fallacy, discussed on page 191) by Jamie Whyte and respond to the questions that follow.

The Authority Fallacy | Jamie Whyte

"Because I say so" is something most of us were told by our parents at some time or other. Usually it was simply a threat. As an answer to "Why should I eat my peas?" for example, it is much more civilized than "Because I will beat you if you don't," and thus to be applauded. But, you may also have heard it in answer to a question about some matter of fact, such as "Why should I believe in the virgin birth?" If so, your parents erred badly, committing the Authority Fallacy.

The fallacy lies in confusing two quite different kinds of authority. There is the kind of authority our parents, football referees, and parking attendants have: the power to decide certain matters. For example, your parents have the power to decide when you will go to bed. Hence, in answer to the question "Why is 8:00 p.m. my bedtime?" the answer "Because I say so" is quite right; your parents are, quite literally, the authors of your bedtime. But it is not up to them whether or not Jesus was conceived without the help of sexual intercourse. Mary's being a virgin at the time of Jesus's birth is beyond the will of your parents, or indeed anybody else's (with the possible exception of Jesus's parents). So your father's answer "Because I say so" is quite wrong when the question is "Why should I believe in the virgin birth?" The matter exceeds the scope of his parental authority.

Yet, there is another metaphorical sense of "authority" on which the answer "Because I say so" is sometimes reasonable, even when literal authority is absent, namely, the expert kind of authority. If someone is an expert on some subject (for an authority on the topic, as it is often put) then his opinion is likely to be true—or at least more likely to be true than the opinion of a non-expert. So, appealing to the opinion of such an authority—i.e., an expert—in support of our view is perfectly OK. It is indirect evidence for your opinion.

We can't all be experts on everything. When laypeople sit around debating evolutionary biology, quantum physics, developmental economics, and the like, as the government's reckless education policies mean they increasingly do, one of the best pieces of evidence likely to be put forward is simply "Because Nobel laureate Joe Bloggs says so." And if Professor Bloggs himself is unfortunate enough to stumble into the wrong pub, then his saying "Because I say so" will do just as well, suffering only from an unpleasant air of arrogance.

The Authority Fallacy should now be clear. It occurs when the first literal type of authority, whereby someone has the power to make certain decisions, is confounded with the second metaphorical type, whereby someone is an expert and so likely to be right about some matter of fact.

Source: Jamie Whyte, "The Authority Fallacy," from *Crimes against Logic*, McGraw-Hill, 2004: 19–21. Reproduced with permission of The McGraw-Hill Companies.

Your father may decide when you will go to bed, what you will eat for dinner, and where you will go to school. But that literal authority does not make him an expert on human (or divine) reproduction. So, you would do well to demur when he tells you that you should believe in the virgin birth because he says so. It goes against everything you have learned in your school science classes and your father is a sales rep for Xerox, not a biologist or forensic archeologist. Of course, he may just be threatening you, as when you asked why you should eat your peas. But, such a threat is neither here nor there. It may motivate you to believe in the virgin birth—or to say you do*—but it provides no evidence regarding the fact of the matter. For those interested in believing the truth, the unsupported opinions of the ill-informed are of no help and are not improved upon by being offered up at gunpoint.

1. Summarize the Authority Fallacy in one or two sentences.
2. What examples of the Authority Fallacy can you recount from your own experience?
3. How would you describe Jamie Whyte's tone of voice? Serious? Satirical? Informal or colloquial? Humorous? A little of each? Does Whyte's tone enhance or interfere with your understanding of the commentary?

Chapter Summary

Argumentative writing requires careful reasoning, the ability to think critically and logically about the issues you are investigating and to recognize errors in logic. Such errors—known as *fallacies* (for example, false analogy and ad hominem)—often arise when writers are not sufficiently knowledgeable about their subject or have not thought sufficiently about possible counterarguments to their thesis. The principal strategies that constitute good reasoning in argument are deduction, induction, categorization, analogy, authorization, and plea. Deduction involves identifying contradictions, inconsistencies, omissions, and oversimplifications, as well as reducing unsound claims to their logical absurdity. Induction involves determining a sufficient quantity for the sample as well as determining the reliability of that sample. Categorization involves classifying items according to similar characteristics. Analogy is used to help readers understand a concept by comparing it to one that is simpler and more familiar. Authorization refers to the use of testimony by experts as a supplement to empirical evidence to support

---

*It is impossible to decide to believe something, even when someone menacing tells you to. You can test this for yourself. Try to believe something you now disbelieve, say, that you are heir to the throne of Croatia or that being hit by a car will not injure you. I'll bet you can't. To believe something, you normally need some reason to think it true.

claims. Plea refers to use of emotional appeals to motivate readers to take action. When learning to recognize errors in reasoning, don't worry excessively about using fallacies inadvertently; the goal is to become sufficiently familiar with them to reduce the likelihood of their occurring.

Checklist

1. Is the line of reasoning used in my argument logical and coherent?
2. Do I cover all facets of my argument?
3. Do I anticipate counterarguments?
4. Do I commit any errors in reasoning?
    a. Fallacies of deduction such as fourth term, non sequitur, and ad hominem?
    b. Fallacies of induction such as unsupported generalization, red herring, poisoning the well, and begging the question?
    c. Fallacies of categorization such as false dichotomy and mixing apples with oranges?
    d. Fallacies of analogy such as false analogy and faulty analogy?
    e. Fallacies of authorization such as vague authority and suspect authority?
    f. Fallacies of pleading such as appeal to fear, appeal to the bandwagon, and appeal to ignorance?
5. Have I used only those supporting materials that come from credible sources and that are logically sound (including any visuals that may be part of my argument)?

Writing Projects

1. Read several newspaper or magazine editorial or opinion pieces on a given topic; then, write a comparative evaluation of each piece based on the presence and frequency of deductive and inductive errors in reasoning you detect in them.
2. Write an essay on the importance of good reasoning in establishing healthy human relationships, such as romantic or business relationships, friendships, parent–sibling relationships, and so on. Focus on specific kinds of errors in reasoning that occur, using actual or representative examples.

3. Initiate an informal argument on one of the Cluster topics in Part 2 of this book with two or more of your classmates in a small group and, while you are arguing, jot down any fallacies you detect. (To be fair to your classmates, ask them to jot down any fallacies they catch *you* falling prey to.) Afterward, write up the argument, supporting the claim you feel most committed to. Do all you can to rid the argument of the detected fallacies.

6

Argument Across the Disciplines

We see–Comparatively–

—Emily Dickinson

Argument is the engine that drives intellectual inquiry in all disciplines. New discoveries or new insights resulting from original research require explanation and interpretation, and there is always more than one way to explain or interpret new information. Another researcher of equal competence can examine the same body of facts and reach very different conclusions because experts interpret findings differently. Although they describe their methodology, report their evidence, and document their sources accurately (so that other researchers may independently determine the validity of their conclusions), they may assign greater importance to some facts than to others or apply different value-based criteria to their findings.

How Argumentation Differs from Discipline to Discipline

Argumentative discourse is essential to the advancement of knowledge regardless of the field of inquiry; however, every field of inquiry has developed its own manner of argument and even its own set of criteria for what qualifies as evidence. These differences can be confusing at first to students, who soon discover that evidence in literary criticism means something quite different from evidence in physics or history or economics. By comparing the different ways in which physicists, economists, art historians, sociologists, engineers, and literary critics argue their respective ideas, you will gain a deeper understanding of how these academic disciplines operate. The aim of this chapter is to help you become familiar with these discipline-specific methods of argument and criteria for evidence.

Strategies of Argument in the Arts

A common initial reaction students may have with regard to arguing about works of art is that art is so subjective any point of view ought to be just as valid as any other.

Thus, a claim that a Jackson Pollack "splatter" canvas could just as easily have been created by a child throwing a temper tantrum with paint might be considered as legitimate as the claim that Pollack's canvases are brilliant developments in abstract expressionism. Likewise, someone might claim that a free-verse poem by, say, Ezra Pound, is utterly lacking in technique or emotional impact.

First of all, it is true that any claim is *potentially* legitimate. However, as is true of claims in any discipline, for there to be true, full argument, appropriate evidence must be brought in to support the claim. Keep in mind that evidence in the arts does not mean quite the same thing as evidence in other disciplines. Appropriate evidence in the context of the visual arts, for example, would include expert opinion by critics, historians, philosophers (aestheticians), and museum curators, all of whom ought to be specialists in the period and genre(s) in which the artist is working. For works of literature, appropriate evidence would include expert opinion by literary scholars with a specialty in Elizabethan drama, or in nineteenth-century American poetry, and so on.

Second, a work of art or literature should be placed in the context of a particular artistic or literary movement or its historical, social, and political milieu. However, such contextualizing is necessary only if the critical approach of the arguer is historical, social, or political. A work of art or literature can be the source of its own internal evidence; that is, the critic identifies and evaluates the artist's or writer's techniques, attempting to show how the aim of the work in question is successfully rendered by the effective use of those techniques.

Arguing Critically About a Painting

As anyone who has studied art history knows, the history of painting (and other arts such as theater and music) has its major movements and revolutions that often parallel history in general. When discussing a painting, for example, you generally should, regardless of the critical stance you wish to take, situate the work in its historical context and then in the context of the artistic movement in which the artist seems to be working, extending, satirizing, or otherwise rebelling against. Once this contextualizing information has been conveyed, you might then compare or contrast the painting (a) to paintings by other artists within the movement and (b) to other paintings by the same artist, perhaps to show a continuity of purpose from one work to the next. Finally, readers will want to know your own impressions of the painting, what you like or dislike about the artist's treatment of the subject, the techniques used (palette and brushwork, lighting, mood), and so on. A good critic will also call attention to other critics' assessments of the work and the reasons those assessments are faulty or limited.

Analysis of a Short Argument About a Painting

One of the most famous—and most parodied—modern American paintings is *American Gothic* (1930) by Grant Wood, an Iowa artist, influenced by Gothic and Renaissance painting, who captured rural motifs in his charming canvases.

Grant Wood, *American Gothic*
(1930)

American Gothic, 1930 (oil on board), Wood, Grant (1892-1942)/The Art Institute of Chicago, IL, USA/© DACS/The Bridgeman Art Library International

In the following commentary, note how art critic Jonathan Jones first places the painting in its historical and regional context, and then comments on the painting's ambiguous aspects.

American Gothic, Grant Wood (1930) | Jonathan Jones

Grant Wood (1892–1941) was not all he seemed. In the 1930s he became famous in the US as one of the leading figures in the Regionalist movement, an anti-modern, anti-European campaign for a purely and folklorically American art. Regionalist painters rejected the big cosmopolitan cities and depicted, in quite homely ways, rural America. This was the one American art movement that came from, and identified with, the midwestern heartland, rather than the east coast or California.

Wood hailed from and lived in small-town Iowa, and painted archaic visions of an America of little hamlets nestling in rounded hills under the beacon of a white-painted church. Yet unlike Thomas Hart Benton, the self-promoting leader of the movement, Wood was a quiet, elusive figure with a fondness for European art. In the 1920s he made four trips to Europe. His style was formed by the art he saw there, most of all northern renaissance artists such as Van Eyck, but also the 1920s German neue sachlichkeit (new objectivity) movement.

Source: The Guardian, Saturday 18 May 2002. Copyright Guardian News & Media Ltd 2011.

Wood's often dreamlike paintings recall the stories of Washington Irving, imagining a small-town world that is comforting and enclosed yet could easily be the stage for spooky nocturnal mayhem. His painting *The Midnight Ride of Paul Revere* (1931), in the Metropolitan Museum of Art, New York, despite its nationalist theme, is an eerie vision of a lonely rider hurtling through an ivory-coloured slumbering town by moonlight.

The models, dressed in clothes dating from the 1890s, are Wood's sister, Nan, and their dentist, BH McKeeby of Cedar Rapids. They pose in front of an 1880s wood-frame house—which still exists as a tourist attraction in the Iowa town of Eldon—built in the American Gothic or Carpenter's Gothic style. They are keeping us out of their world rather than showing it off. The close-packed bodies of the 19th-century farmer and his spinster daughter played by Nan and McKeeby form a wall between us and the white wooden house. The house itself is a second closing of space, its front wall impenetrably neat, with blinds pulled down over the windows. Only behind that do we glimpse the blue sky and round puffy trees of pastoral joy.

The farmer is at once genteelly studious, like a clerk, and aggressive, as if he   5
has a serious temper. He looks at us in a no-nonsense way, and that pitchfork he holds is extremely phallic and sharp: it could do you a nasty injury. Her gaze is anxiously sidelong. She might be watching some boys, wondering if they are about to steal apples, or seeing a man she had feelings for ride past with his new city wife. She wears an ornate brooch that suggests another, distant world of passion and desire, at odds with her neat white collar and tightly tied hair. Behind her ear hangs a wisp of loose, curling golden hair that suggests suppressed sensuality.

People have argued about where this painting stands on midwestern, American heartland values ever since it was first exhibited. Wood denied that it was satirical. He proclaimed his sincere belief in the values of hearth and home. And yet it is impossible to deny the strangeness of this American masterpiece, in which nothing is quite as stable as a first glance might suggest.

It is fictive in multiple ways. It is a 19th-century picture painted in the 20th century. It is an apparently naïve painting by a sophisticated artist. Even the title is ambiguous. American Gothic refers to the architecture of the house, but also unavoidably has associations with Edgar Allan Poe and big-city prejudices about in-marrying, psychopathic country folk.

The weirdest ambiguities surround the house. That pointed medieval-style window suggests to some viewers a church; indeed, were it not for the potted plants on the porch and the decorative blind, we might mistake it for a house of the Lord. But in a private house, it has other implications. Given the plain self-presentation of these people, the medieval window between their heads is incongruously flamboyant, a bit of fantasy that sits oddly with the whitewashed clapboard and the sombre dress. One feels this strange architecture might have inspired the painting—as if, seeing the house, Wood had wondered about its original inhabitants. There is something odd about that window and the concealed upstairs room behind it. Anything could go on up there.

Notice how Jones begins his critique by providing background information about Wood, and his work in relation to other regionalist painters, before presenting his own personal responses to the painting. If Jones were aiming for a scholarly audience instead of a lay audience with an interest in the arts, he probably would have compared his own reactions to the painting with those of other art critics.

EXERCISE 6.1

1. After carefully studying Grant Wood's *American Gothic*, write your own critique of the painting. What do the two figures represent to you? Why does Wood title his painting *American Gothic*? Consider as many elements of the painting as you can before working out your own response to it. What, for example, does the pitchfork represent? What do you make of the woman's expression? The man's?

2. Critique Jonathan Jones's interpretation of the painting. Which assertions do you agree with or disagree with, and why?

Arguing Critically About a Poem

People tend to react to poems with delight or confusion or both. Much modern poetry—poems written during the twentieth and twenty-first centuries—confuses general readers and creates an aversion to poetry that stays with them a long time. But modern poetry shares many characteristics with poetry from previous ages and uses poetic techniques that were developed centuries ago—techniques like irony, symbolism, figurative language, and wordplay.

Key Elements in a Critical Discussion of a Poem

As is true of writing about any work of art, it makes sense first to situate the poem in its historical and cultural context. For a critical discussion that aims solely to illuminate what the poem is "about"—its theme and the techniques the poet uses to convey the theme (what is known as formalist criticism)—historical or cultural information is usually omitted or presented as part of the introduction. For biographical, gender/feminist, or cultural critics, the larger context is the whole point. We cannot fully understand

Percy Bysshe Shelley (1792–1822)

istockphoto.com/Georgios Kollidas

a poem, these critics argue, unless we know as much as we can about the poet's life and times.

Analysis of a Short Argument About a Poem

Study the following student critique of Shelley's famous poem, "Ozymandias." First, read the poem and form your own response to it. Next, read the critique, paying attention to the way Joseph Forte structures his argument in terms of introductory remarks, presentation of thesis, defense of thesis, and conclusion. Finally, reread the critique to determine the effectiveness of Forte's argument and the ways it might be strengthened. Joseph Forte was a sophomore English minor at Santa Clara University when he wrote this essay.

Ozymandias (1818) | Percy Bysshe Shelley

I met a traveller from an antique land
Who said: Two vast and trunkless legs of stone
Stand in the desert. Near them, on the sand,
Half sunk, a shattered visage lies, whose frown
And wrinkled lip, and sneer of cold command
Tell that its sculptor well those passions read
Which yet survive, stamped on these lifeless things,
The hand that mocked them and the heart that fed.
And on the pedestal these words appear:
"My name is Ozymandias, king of kings:
Look on my works, ye Mighty, and despair!"
Nothing beside remains. Round the decay
Of that colossal wreck, boundless and bare
The lone and level sands stretch far away.

Recession-Era Reflections on Percy Shelley's *Ozymandias* | Joseph Forte

Imagine the sense of wonder that must have overcome Giovanni Belzoni, a nineteenth-century Italian explorer, when he discovered the massive statue of Ramses II (whose Greek name was "Ozymandias") dwelling inside the even larger Ramesseum temple. To Belzoni, the huge visage of Ramses must have represented the vast, age-old power and majesty of the early Egyptians. During Belzoni's life, the ancient Egyptians would have seemed mysterious and powerful indeed. In part, this was due to the European public's fad-like obsession with the Egyptians at this time

(Napoleon himself made an unsuccessful bid for the statue of Ramses). We would be naïve, though, if we did not acknowledge that the crumbling ruins of the vast empires of old still captivate us today.

British poet Percy Shelley must have been similarly captivated when he wrote *Ozymandias*. After viewing the statue at London's British Museum, Shelley and his friend Horace Smith entered into a friendly competition to see who could write the better poem about Ramses. Shelley's poem went on to achieve world renown, and for good reason. The poem's central theme of all peoples' inevitable decline has captivated generations just as the real statue of Ozymandias has. *Ozymandias's* message of human impermanence is all the more foreboding today, as America faces a century that may see its loss of international dominance. An examination of the poem's place in the Romantic movement as well as its place in Shelley's own body of work can give context that supports the poem's increasing relevance in the present.

To understand this context, we must begin with a broad understanding of what makes *Ozymandias* an essential Romantic poem. With broad strokes, we can paint Romanticism as a reaction to the norms of the Age of Enlightenment, particularly the idea that the natural world and the cosmic order could be completely explained by reason. Romanticists instead emphasized the role of intuition and emotion in experience, as well as the power of imagination. Furthermore, Romanticists found beauty and mystery in nature as well as the achievements of exotic, ancient peoples. These fundamental qualities of Romanticism can be easily observed in *Ozymandias*.

For example, the tragedy of Ozymandias' ruin showcases Romantic Poetry's strength in inspiring emotion in the reader. Shelley gives the poem an emotional core by calling attention to certain details of the desert scene. By describing Ozymandias' "frown and wrinkled lip, and sneer of cold command," he gives an inanimate object (the statue) the personal, emotional qualities of a human being. These very passions form the basis for the inscription of the statue, which is the poem's focal point. By personifying the object of ruin with the "spirit" of an ancient, mysterious despot, *Ozymandias* is able to make a powerful emotional plea in a manner very consistent with Romantic norms. The other imagery in the poem is also written to inspire great emotion. Shelley's descriptions of the desert surrounding the ruined statue are restrained in their content, yet still manage to evoke powerful feelings of wonder in the reader, perhaps because of their near-monolithic simplicity.

5   Shelley employs his mastery of diction to elicit more gut-level reactions. The traveler is from an "antique" land, not a merely "ancient" land. The sands are "lone" and level, not "desolate" and level. These word choices further pull at the reader's heartstrings, evoking the feelings of nostalgia and solitude, respectively. By imbuing every line of the poem with emotional power, Shelley enhances the personal relevance of the poem to the reader by appealing directly to his or her emotions. All this passionate use of emotion places *Ozymandias* well within the conventions of Romantic Poetry.

Yet, *Ozymandias* also delicately defies one of the Romantic Movement's ideals by implicitly disagreeing with the movement's love of nationalism. Nationalism became important to Romanticism through the movement's love for national folklore and local traditions as well as the teachings of intellectuals such as Rousseau. Eventually, Romanticism and Nationalism became intimately intertwined. For example, Delacroix's *Liberty Leading the People*, one of the most widely known Romantic paintings, explicitly supports nationalism. *Ozymandias* seems to defy this Romantic tradition. The poem's central theme of human impermanence applies to the ousting of centuries old monarchies by new national governments, but also applies to the upstarts doing the ousting.

Just as the aristocracy had grown bloated, corrupt, and unpopular, so are all forms of government subject to eventual decay and decline. The new national governments being formed on the ashes of the monarchies would, in time, be responsible for many of the injustices and cruelties the monarchies were accused of in the first place. Many of the twentieth century's acts of evil have, in fact, been the doing of democratic nations (the Holocaust, for one, was perpetrated by an elected government). Even today, wage slavery, wars of aggression, and corruption still exist. The seeds of democracy that were sewn in Shelley's time have borne fruit that is not unmarred by the wrongs of past governments. Even the loftiest ideals eventually give way to harsh realities. The nationalist movements of Shelley's time appear overconfident (even naïve) when viewed through the cynical lens of *Ozymandias*.

Ironically, *The Masque of Anarchy*, another famous work written by Shelley, appears (at first) to wholeheartedly endorse the nationalist rebellions of the time. *Masque* does not actually support nationalism, however. In fact, upon closer examination, the poem reveals itself as anti-violence and anti-rebellion. This affirms Shelley's defiance of the mainstream Romantic acceptance of nationalist revolutions.

The Masque of Anarchy (1819) | Percy Bysshe Shelley

Stand ye calm and resolute,
Like a forest close and mute,
With folded arms and looks which are
Weapons of unvanquished war.
And if then the tyrants dare,
Let them ride among you there,
Slash, and stab, and maim and hew,
What they like, that let them do.
With folded arms and steady eyes,
And little fear, and less surprise
Look upon them as they slay
Till their rage has died away

> Then they will return with shame
> To the place from which they came,
> And the blood thus shed will speak
> In hot blushes on their cheek.
> Rise like Lions after slumber
> In unvanquishable number,
> Shake your chains to earth like dew
> Which in sleep had fallen on you—
> Ye are many—they are few.

Perhaps *Masque* could be understood to support the Nationalist revolutions of Shelley's era if only history had proceeded differently. If Europe's monarchies had been toppled peacefully with a minimum of bloodshed, then *Masque*, which supports peaceful protest, would be in concord with the actions of the era's rebels. Unfortunately, history did not unfold in this fashion. For example, the French Revolution resulted in extensive death and destruction. Hugh Gough writes in his 1998 book *The Terror in the French Revolution* that up to 40,000 French citizens were executed during the reign of terror that occurred once the forces of the Revolution had seized power.

10   The cruel fact that much of the French Revolution's violence was directed at the average French citizenry surely did not escape Shelley. The systemic violence against France's own populace resembled the tyranny of the very monarchs they had overthrown. The Revolution had suffered a symbolic decline similar to Ozymandias's literal one; its original ideals of fraternity and equality had almost completely decayed. *Masque*, then, can stand beside *Ozymandias* as a critique of nationalist movements. The poem offers an alternative solution to the problems caused by Europe's monarchies. By advocating pacifism and non-violent protest, *Masque* attempts to protect would-be rebels from falling for the same traps that perverted the spirit of the French Revolution.

Examining *Ozymandias's* historical context and its relation to Shelley's other work leads us to the conclusion that even our current society, founded on principles of liberty and justice, is no more permanent than the tyranny it replaced. *Ozymandias* may seem like a rather obvious choice for an essay given our society's current trajectory: The *Wall Street Journal's* MarketWatch predicts China's GDP will overtake the USA's by the early 2020s. Now, Shelley's words seem more ominous than ever. The institutions we build for ourselves, the nations we form for protection, and the societies we create to give our lives' purpose, relate in their imperfection and impermanence. Nevertheless, this fact should not inspire feelings of hopelessness in us. On the contrary, it should inspire us to action. By realizing the limited nature of our influence, we should aim to make prudent, intelligent decisions. If we are all eventually destined to become Ozymandias, alone and forgotten, buried in the sands of time, then the least we can do is leave behind evidence of the good judgment that made us great in the first place, not the hubris that hastened our fall.

EXERCISE 6.2

1. What are the main assertions Forte makes about "Ozymandias"? How convincingly does he support these assertions? Are there any aspects of the poem that Forte overlooks? If so, what are they?

2. Write a textual explication of "Ozymandias," limiting your commentary to the text of the poem. For example, you might focus your attention on Shelley's use of symbolism and the way it helps convey the theme.

3. Compare "Ozymandias" to "The Masque of Anarchy," focusing on the similarities and differences of theme and technique used to convey the theme.

Strategies of Argument in the Natural Sciences

It is sometimes assumed that scientific discourse is purely objective, that phenomena are examined, measured, and reported without recourse to critical inquiry or debate. Although it is true that many *basics* of science can be demonstrated through indisputable experiment—like dropping two balls of unequal weight to show that all objects fall at the same rate of thirty-two feet per second or creating table salt (sodium chloride) by mixing together two poisonous substances, sodium and hydrochloric acid—more complex scientific matters such as whether salt in certain quantities can be healthful or harmful to human health are open to disputation. Indeed, scientists *welcome* disputation. In the 1996 film *Contact* (based on the novel by the late Carl Sagan), astronomer Eleanor Arroway (played by Jodie Foster) shouts to her colleagues, "Make me a liar," after detecting what she thinks is an artificial signal from interstellar space. In other words, she is asking her fellow astronomers to try to *disprove* her assumption, to think of every possible alternative explanation for the signal: a communication satellite, a secret military code, a technical glitch? Only by doing everything to disprove the assumption can one reach a reliable explanation for the phenomenon discovered.

Arguing Critically About an Issue in Space Exploration

One of the most frequent questions posed by the general public regarding space exploration is this: Why spend billions of dollars exploring other worlds, sending astronauts to the International Space Station, launching telescopes into orbit, and so on, when those funds could be used to improve the quality of life on earth? Think of what a billion dollars could do to alleviate homelessness! Think of how much food a billion dollars could purchase for starving people in Darfur. The question is entirely legitimate. Few would disagree that more could be done to combat human suffering—if not globally, at least in our own country. And yet…must one endeavor exclude another? Why can't we work harder to eliminate poverty *and* explore space? The underlying concern, of course, has to do with necessity: Why is it necessary to explore space? What benefits, if any, are derived from such an expensive and dangerous pursuit? Those are the questions that need to be carefully addressed. Although the space age is more than fifty-five years old (it officially began on October 4, 1957, when the Soviet Union launched Sputnik I, the first artificial satellite), people still tend to associate space exploration with science fiction–like fancifulness—nice for escapist entertainment but hardly relevant to solving the practical problems of the world.

A little reflection, though, will help us realize that space exploration *has* led to solving practical problems of the world. Let's start with global communications. If we had not learned to launch satellites into orbit, cellular phone and GPS technology would not exist, nor would it be possible to receive live television broadcasts from the other side of the world. A quick visit to the NASA website, www.nasa.gov, will remind us of many additional practical advances produced directly or indirectly through space exploration:

- Monitoring climate change, such as studying carbon emissions, aerosols, and other greenhouse gases; polar ice-cap shrinkage; rising sea levels
- Tracking weather systems such as hurricanes
- Changes in earth's ozone layer; amount of solar radiation reaching the surface
- Monitoring volcanoes
- Imaging natural and industrial disasters such as the oil spill in the Gulf of Mexico

Granted, you may be thinking, there are indeed some practical applications to space research, but there are also impractical ones. Some might argue that exploring space to pave the way toward colonizing the moon and Mars is an example of an impractical application. But it may be difficult to draw the line between practical and impractical. Much depends on one's values and sense of priorities. It also depends on how skillfully one can persuade others of those values and priorities.

Key Elements in a Critical Discussion of a Space Exploration Issue

As with other issues of a scientific nature, issues in space exploration will be familiar to the average reader only in the most general way. Readers may know, for example, that NASA has been developing plans for a human expedition to Mars, perhaps by 2035, but they may not be familiar with the reasons for or against such a mission—other than the most superficial pro/con reasons—for example, exploring the unknown is part of what it means to be human (pro); such an expedition would be far too expensive to fund in light of other economic needs (con). Thus, the arguer must, when dealing with a space exploration issue, provide more substantive analysis. This in turn requires not only in-depth research but also presentation of the information yielded by the research—often technical in nature—in a manner that nonspecialists can understand.

Analysis of a Short Argument on a Space Exploration Issue

Many favor robotic probes for space exploration because they are far less expensive than human explorers, and of course they do not pose a threat to human safety. But some argue that human exploration is also necessary because no robot can explore as thoroughly as a trained human scientist. Moreover, exploration is an essential human trait, a fundamental part of what it means to be human.

But how far are you willing to carry that rationale? You may agree that the human exploration of Mars, for example, would be a great adventure for humankind, and would be well worth the high cost. There are also solid pragmatic reasons for sending humans instead of robots to explore other worlds, as G. Scott Hubbard, a professor of Aeronautics and Astronautics at Stanford University and former director of NASA's Ames Research Center, argues in the following article. How compelling is Hubbard's rationale, in your opinion?

Is Space Exploration Worth the Cost? | G. Scott Hubbard

The debate about the relative merits of exploring space with humans and robots is as old as the space program itself. Werner Von Braun, a moving force behind the Apollo Program that sent humans to the moon and the architect of the mighty Saturn V rocket, believed passionately in the value of human exploration—especially when it meant beating the hated Soviet Empire. James Van Allen, discoverer of the magnetic fields that bear his name, was equally ardent and vocal about the value of robotic exploration.

There are five arguments that are advanced in any discussion about the utility of space exploration and the roles of humans and robots. Those arguments, in roughly ascending order of advocate support, are the following:

1. Space exploration will eventually allow us to establish a human civilization on another world (e.g., Mars) as a hedge against the type of catastrophe that wiped out the dinosaurs.

2. We explore space and create important new technologies to advance our economy. It is true that, for every dollar we spend on the space program,

Source: A Freakonomics Quorum (Jan. 2008). Web.

the U.S. economy receives about $8 of economic benefit. Space exploration can also serve as a stimulus for children to enter the fields of science and engineering.

3. Space exploration in an international context offers a peaceful cooperative venue that is a valuable alternative to nation state hostilities. One can look at the International Space Station and marvel that the former Soviet Union and the U.S. are now active partners. International cooperation is also a way to reduce costs.

4. National prestige requires that the U.S. continue to be a leader in space, and that includes human exploration. History tells us that great civilizations dare not abandon exploration.

5. Exploration of space will provide humanity with an answer to the most fundamental questions: Are we alone? Are there other forms of life beside those on Earth?

It is these last two arguments that are the most compelling to me. It is challenging to make the case that humans are necessary to the type of scientific exploration that may bring evidence of life on another world. There are strong arguments on both sides. Personally, I think humans will be better at unstructured environment exploration than any existing robot for a very long time.

There are those who say that exploration with humans is simply too expensive for the return we receive. However, I cannot imagine any U.S. President announcing that we are abandoning space exploration with humans and leaving it to the Chinese, Russians, Indians, Japanese or any other group. I can imagine the U.S. engaging in much more expansive international cooperation.

Humans will be exploring space. The challenge is to be sure that they accomplish meaningful exploration.

EXERCISE 6.3

1. How convincingly does Hubbard justify the high cost of space exploration? Which of his reasons are the most convincing? The least convincing?

2. Evaluate Hubbard's refutation ("There are those say that exploration with humans is simply too expensive for the return we receive...") What else might he have included in his refutation?

3. Prepare a counterargument to Hubbard's argument.

4. Suggest particular kinds of visual aids that could enhance Hubbard's article. Be prepared to explain how a particular chart, graph, diagram, or photograph would provide additional clarity or conviction to some part of the argument.

Arguing Critically About a Topic in Health/Nutrition

The most heated controversies of modern science are from biology, medicine, and health/nutrition. What are the best strategies for conquering antibiotic-resistant bacteria? Are foodstuffs like table salt, coffee, or diet soda more harmful than beneficial? What is the best strategy for tackling child obesity? Newspapers and magazines routinely report the results of new studies, but these results are often tentative or are rendered faulty or even invalid by subsequent studies. What we assume to be "the truth" in the biological sciences is usually a matter of current consensus among specialists. New findings, or new interpretations of those findings, routinely modify what is true and what is not.

Key Elements in a Critical Discussion of an Issue in Health/Nutrition

Not surprisingly, issues relating to medicine and health are of great concern to the general public. These issues concern the well-being of everyone. Thus, if you are going to write an article in this field, you must first understand your topic thoroughly enough to be able to communicate its more technical aspects in a nontechnical manner—or at least to define technical terms and concepts in a way that most readers can understand. The next order of business is to represent challenging views as fully and objectively as possible and to explain why these views or interpretations are outdated, flawed, or otherwise in error. *Caution:* Unless you have already acquired expertise in the field, you will need to rely on the findings and opinions of experts.

Analysis of a Short Argument in Health/Nutrition

Study the following article from the *U.C. Berkeley Wellness Letter* on the comparative benefits of raw versus cooked food.

The Raw vs. the Cooked | Berkeley Wellness Newsletter

The belief in the benefits of raw foods—sometimes called "living foods"—is nothing new. Sylvester Graham, for whom the cracker is named, promoted raw foods 150 years ago, just as some chefs, cookbooks, celebrities, and websites promote them today. Among other claims, raw food diets are said to eliminate headaches and allergies, improve memory and immunity, ease arthritis, and reverse diabetes. Proponents say that cooking destroys nutrients, enzymes, and the "life force" of the food itself.

Source: U.C. Berkeley Wellness Letter, April 2010.

The basics.   A raw food diet is based mostly or exclusively on uncooked and unprocessed plant foods (often organic), including fruits, vegetables, nuts, seeds, and sprouted grains. Most followers are strict vegetarians, though some eat unpasteurized dairy foods and sometimes even raw eggs, meat, and fish. Foods are prepared using blenders, processors, and dehydrators, and can be served either cold or warm, but not hot enough to cook them. Truly dedicated raw foodists shun refined sugar, vinegar, coffee, tea, soy products, most vegetable oils, dried herbs, and alcohol.

The benefits.   Raw food diets encourage people to eat lots of fresh produce and other nutritious foods that are low in saturated fat, cholesterol, and sodium, and high in fiber. Few studies have compared the health effects of a raw food diet versus other eating patterns, but vegetarians, in general, tend to have a lower risk of heart disease and are less likely to be overweight. And in a study from Roswell Park Cancer Institute in Buffalo, people who ate the most raw (as compared to cooked) cruciferous vegetables had a reduced risk of bladder cancer, possibly because the raw vegetables retain more cancer-protective isothiocyanates. Cooking, after all, does reduce some phytochemicals, including isothiocyanates, as well as many vitamins.

The drawbacks.   Some nutrients and potentially beneficial plant compounds are *less* available to the body in the raw state. Heat is needed to break down a plant's cell walls and release the compounds. Cooking a carrot releases extra beta carotene, while cooking tomatoes releases more lycopene.

5   Of more concern, some uncooked and unpasteurized foods pose a risk of food poisoning, which is especially dangerous for pregnant women, young children, the elderly, people with compromised immunity, and those with chronic medical conditions, such as liver or kidney disease. Raw sprouts, raw oysters, and raw (unpasteurized) milk products have been the cause of many outbreaks of foodborne illness in recent years. Heat kills pathogens. Depending on how strict the diet is, people on raw food diets may also need to take supplements to make up for potential shortfalls in calcium, iron, zinc, vitamin B12, and other nutrients.

What about the enzyme argument?   Raw foodists claim that the enzymes in raw foods (destroyed by cooking) aid digestion, prevent "toxicity" in the body, and have other curative effects. But these enzymes are there for the plants, not us. Moreover, they are largely inactivated by the highly acidic environment of the stomach and thus cannot aid digestion farther down in the intestines or have other benefits. And there's no evidence that the enzymes can become reactivated in the intestines, as some raw foodists say. In any case, even if some enzymes do survive, the body usually makes all the enzymes it needs to digest and absorb food. The claim by some raw foodists that our bodies have a limited lifetime supply of enzymes makes no sense, either, and is simply not true.

Cooking, the mother of inventions.   The invention of cooking was a crucial factor in the evolution of humans. Cooking, which distinguishes us from other species, makes high-protein foods softer and easier to digest, and this enabled our early ancestors to devote more energy to other activities besides hunting, gathering, and chewing raw foods all day. Besides killing bacteria and releasing healthful compounds from cell walls, cooking also allows us to more easily consume pasta, rice, wheat, corn, and potatoes.

It's true that cooking at high temperature (as in grilling meat or frying potatoes) creates potential cancer-causing substances, but most things in life carry some risk, along with benefit. If you eat a varied diet and refrain from eating a lot of charred food, this is not a problem. To retain the most nutrients, though, cook your vegetables for as short a time as possible.

A matter of balance.   Raw fruits, vegetables, nuts, and seeds are certainly good for you. But you don't need to—and should not—restrict yourself to raw foods only. There's no conclusive evidence that a pure raw food diet will prevent or cure any condition or disease. Plus, it's an extreme diet that's hard to maintain over the long run, deprives you of some of the tastiest and most nutritious foods, makes dining out difficult, and can be deficient in some nutrients.

EXERCISE 6.4

1. Critique the writer's argumentative strategy in this article, using the Rhetorical Rhombus described in Chapter 1 as a basis for your commentary. How well is the evidence for both sides of the argument presented? How convincingly are the more debatable issues (like the alleged increased cancer risk with grilled foods) resolved?

2. Discuss the level of diction used in this article. Is it too technical? Not sufficiently technical?

3. Comment on the style and formatting of the article. How helpful are the subheadings? How would you characterize the level of usage and its effectiveness?

Strategies of Argument in the Social Sciences

The social sciences, like the natural sciences, investigate phenomena as analytically and objectively as possible. Unlike the natural sciences, of course, phenomena in the social sciences (anthropology, history, international relations, law, political science, sociology) are generally too complex to reduce to axioms or laws. That's because human behavior, whether manifested individually or in groups (from families and organizations to entire cultures), is more complex. Quite commonly, the testimony of experts (cultural anthropologists, psychologists, or linguists, for example) will serve as reliable evidence to support assumptions.

Arguing Critically About an Issue in International Relations

The first challenge in writing arguments about an issue in international relations is to recognize the interdisciplinary complexity involved. Interacting with another culture—whether to establish business and trade agreements, to establish alliances or cultural exchanges, or to provide aid—requires a solid understanding of the history and customs of that culture, together with the politics and economics. The next challenge is to explore any controversies generated by the issue at hand and to decide how or whether those controversies are going to affect American interaction. If a certain country's freedom of speech is being curtailed, should we intervene? What if such intervention threatens American trade relations with the country?

Key Elements in an Argument on International Relations

A strong argument on an issue in international relations will begin by introducing the problem at hand in a larger sociopolitical context; that is, it will place the particular problem, such as the need for improved school facilities, in the context of that country's existing political and economic situation. It will look at competing scenarios, each offering different types of improvement and different timelines, and decide which scenario is the most sensible, given the degree of necessity. It might be necessary to append a breakdown of costs (for lighting fixtures, desks, blackboards, computers, textbooks, and so on).

Analysis of a Short Argument on International Relations

In the following essay, college senior Lauren Silk examines the problems underlying the failure of existing foreign aid programs to African nations and offers a possible way of making these programs more successful.

```
    Lauren Silk


             Aid to Africa: Proposed Solutions
While U.S. aid to Africa has increased by more than 60%over
the past eight years, little has been done to eradicate the
widespread poverty, disease, and famine plaguing the con-
tinent. Rather than helping to rebuild African nations, the
presence of increasing aid has slowed growth and development,
leaving over half of its population still living on under a
```

dollar a day (Moyo). While aid levels have since doubled from
$12.7 billion in 1999, African per capita incomes have yet
to budge and 400 million sub-Saharan Africans are expected to
live under the poverty line in 2015 (Smart Aid for Africa).
In 2001, roughly 46% of sub-Saharan Africans were living in
extreme poverty—a figure which has since increased to 50%
(A Dollar a Day). These statistics lead one to assume that
Africa receives very little aid—but for the past fifty years,
the U.S. has funneled over $500 billion to Africa with little
progress to show for its efforts to eradicate poverty (Lerrick). While the continent's failure to progress is partly due
to crippling debt repayments that continue to bankrupt African
governments, much more is due to mismanagement of aid by government officials. Rather than improving the quality of life
for its people, most of the aid Africa receives has gone to
supporting and sustaining corrupt governments that embezzle
state funds and exploit their people for personal gain. As
poverty continues to grow and we prepare for an even larger
and costlier aid package to Africa in an already disastrous
economic climate, policymakers must address the shortcomings
of our aid policy so that we can find a solution that will
effectively and permanently lift its people out of poverty.

As seen by our past commitments to the tune of billions of
dollars, solving Africa's problems are of great interest to the
U.S. According to the Wilson Center, six million Africans die a
year from preventable causes, 26 million are infected with HIV/
AIDS and 350 million are living on less than a dollar a day (Hamilton). While ensuring aid to Africa is largely a humanitarian
interest, it is also one of national security. Great political and
economic instability has transformed many African nations into
breeding grounds for criminal operations that threaten American
lives. Growing populations of restless and unemployed young men
with access to cheap guns has led to the growth of terrorism and
piracy. But as our deficit grows into the trillions, and the billions we have already committed have done little to help alleviate
Africa's problems, one sees the necessity of seriously reforming
our aid packages so that they effectively combat these threats and
improve economic opportunities for the African people.

As stated earlier, Africa's failure to progress is largely
due to the crippling effects that debt repayments have on their

economies. As a solution, many have called for cancelling these debts in order to provide these countries with a clean slate. While African countries won't owe anything on previous aid, they will continue to receive money in enormous amounts that they can't pay back, thus sustaining the vicious cycle of debt. If funneling billions of dollars into corrupt governments and bloated bureaucracies didn't work the first time, how can we think it will work again?

Some argue that aid has been largely ineffective in Africa because *not enough* of it has been given to adequately address their needs. Some even argue that in order to sufficiently develop these countries, current aid (already over $4 billion a year) needs to be increased by several billion dollars (Fletcher). But the current economic climate makes this request difficult to meet for both the U.S. and its allies. France, for example, has already been forced to cut aid by several billion dollars. And while countries like the UK are sustaining promised levels of aid, the decreased value in their currency makes this money worth much less than before (Kharas). According to the Brookings Institute, "the currency movement alone will wipe out $5 billion in aid in 2009" (Kharas). While a moral imperative to help these nations still exists, our ever-increasing deficit has made it so that we can't afford to increase, much less sustain, current levels.

However, some argue that it isn't our level of committed aid that's the problem, it's the fractional amount of appropriated aid that actually gets out of Washington and into Africa. Much of our committed aid has already been budgeted and accounted for, but its disbursement has been tied up in bureaucratic red tape (Kharas). In order to release this money, funds would need to be moved from "consultant contracts and slow moving projects" directly to the governments themselves (Kharas). While this would certainly speed the process of getting money out of the "bureaucratic pipeline" and into the countries themselves, history has shown that funneling free money to corrupt and bloated governments not only fuels the vicious cycle of inefficient aid but fails to guarantee that the money will even get to the populations who need it.

In light of the failure of U.S. aid to adequately assist African development, some critics have called for eliminating and replacing all aid to Africa with trade and investments (Moyo).

While trade and investments need to be ultimately part of the solution, the sudden removal of all assistance for these countries would be disastrous, and only exacerbate these countries' poverty levels. Just like the issues these countries face, the aid process is very complex and thus requires a complex solution (Joseph). No simple solution such as increasing aid or eliminating it altogether will sufficiently help solve Africa's problems. Therefore, I recommend a compromise between aid and investment. In our quest for "smarter aid," our aid must be able to balance both humanitarian needs and support the creation and flourishing of businesses and civil society (Smart Aid for Africa).

First, because much aid is embezzled by corrupt government officials and bloated bureaucracies, policymakers must commit to restoring transparency and accountability in African governments in order to facilitate movement of aid directly to the people. This effort can be done through creating incentives for African states to rebuild their governments and civil societies (Joseph). As advocated by the Millennium Challenge Corporation, these efforts require that aid be tied to the success and accountability of the government. Therefore, governments which "conduct honest elections, use available resources to improve the welfare of their people, and pursue sound economic policies" should be rewarded with greater levels of support (Smart Aid for Africa). This support should come in the form of investing in infrastructure, education and healthcare development. For low-performing states, U.S. policymakers must consult with both their governments and the international community to determine the best way to balance support between the "state and civil society" as a pre-requisite to aid (Smart Aid for Africa).

After working to build accountable and transparent African governments, the U.S. must re-structure aid to best invigorate businesses and civil society, both of which encourage healthy democracy. This can be achieved through investment in micro-loans, which would loan anywhere from about $2 to $1,500 to Africans looking to start their own businesses (Mercy Corps). An influx of microloans would fuel the African economy by invigorating the private sector and providing Africans with jobs and the opportunity to become self-sufficient. Microloans provided by American banks and businesses have already proven successful in many African countries. Not only have millions of Africans

been able to pull themselves out of poverty by their own innovation, but microloan providers see a 97% return on their investments—a much more promising statistic than that of current debt
repayments (Mercy Corps). In addition, micro-lending would help
phase out Western aid to Africa, helping it become more self-
sufficient by growing its economy from the ground up. In doing
this, we would not only succeed in our goal of reducing poverty,
but would also help Africa reach its potential and alleviate
economic pressure on the U.S. government.

In conclusion, reforming U.S. aid to Africa requires a two-
step process. First, policymakers must work to promote the same
accountability and transparency pursued in our own government in
African governments. Through providing incentives and denying aid
to those who don't meet requirements for accountability and transparency, we can ensure that money designed to help the African
people does just that. Secondly, we must invest in the African
economy. By investing in African innovation and potential, we will
help them and their countries fulfill their goal of becoming self-
sufficient. Ultimately these are the best means of achieving the
stability we have been trying to secure for the past 60 years.
By reforming African nations at the political level and investing in their people and economies, we will not only greatly reduce
impending threats to our national security, but will succeed in
our goal of restoring basic human rights to the African people.

Works Cited

"A Dollar a Day: Poverty Overview: Poverty around the
World." 2006. ThinkQuest. 28 April 2009. <http://
library.thinkquest.org/05aug/00282/over_world.htm#africa>

Fletcher, Michael. "Bush Has Quietly Tripled Aid to
Africa." *The Washington Post* 31 December 2006. 28
April 2009 < http://www.washingtonpost.com/wp-dyn/
content/article/2006/12/30/AR2006123000941.html>

Hamilton, Lee. "Helping a Troubled Continent." *Selected
Commentaries*. 5 July 2005. Woodrow Wilson International Center for Scholars. 28 April 2009 <http://www
.wilsoncenter.org/index.cfm?fuseaction=director.
thing&typeid=A687F6E6-1125-AADA-
EA0F1BD2F5FD8AEC&itemid=B0472774-1125-AADA-EABFAD9CCD-
5DBE6A>

Joseph, Richard. Interview with Jerome McDonnell. 7 April
    2009. Chicago Public Radio's Worldview. 28 April 2009.
    The Brookings Institution. <http://www.brookings.edu/
    interviews/2009/0407_africa_aid_joseph.aspx>

Kharas, Homi. "The Financial Crisis, a Development Emer-
    gency, and the Need for Aid." *The Wolfensohn Center
    for Development, The Brookings Institution.* 11 Febru-
    ary 2009. 27 April 2009. http://www.brookings.edu/opin-
    ions/2009/0211_financial_crisis_kharas.aspx

Lerrick, Adam. "Aid to Africa at Risk: Covering up Cor-
    ruption." International Economics Report. December
    2005. *Gailliot Center for Public Policy.* Carnegie Mel-
    lon University. 26 April 2009 <http://www.house.gov/
    jec/publications/109/12-09-05galliotcorruption.pdf>

"Microlending Explained." *Global Envision.* 12 May 2006.
    Mercy Corps. 28 April 2009. <http://www.globalenvision.
    org/library/4/1073/>

Moyo, Dambisa. "Why Foreign Aid is Hurting Africa." *The
    Wall Street Journal*
21 March 2009. 28 April 2009 <http://online.wsj.com/
    article/SB123758895999200083.html>

"Smart Aid for Africa." Notes from "Aid, Governance and
    Development in Africa" Conference. May 12-14 2005,
    Northwestern University. 26 April 2009. http://www.
    northwestern.edu/africanstudies/Pdfs/Smart%20Aid%20for%20
    Africa%20%20Northwestern%20conference%20statement.pdf

EXERCISE 6.5

1. How effectively does Lauren Silk introduce her thesis? If you were writing on the topic of changing the way in which the United States gives aid to Africa, how would you introduce your thesis? Explain your strategy.

2. Critique Silk's strategies of argumentation, making use of the rhetorical rhombus described in Chapter 1.

3. Compare Silk's manner of integrating her outside sources with that of the author of "The Raw vs. the Cooked" (in the *Berkeley Wellness Letter*). Suggest an underlying rationale for each method of source use.

4. Even if you agree with Silk's recommendations, suggest alternative recommendations, along with clear rationales for their implementation.

Arguing Critically About an Issue in Bioethics

As we have noted earlier, when arguing issues in one of the natural sciences such as biology, one extrapolates strictly from the phenomena themselves under scrutiny. For example, if you're investigating how a particular species of monkey evolved in a particular part of the world, you will not be arguing, say, whether evolutionary theory itself violates religious doctrines; that line of inquiry would take you out of biology and into theology. Similarly, an inquiry into the social or ethical implications of genetic engineering is not a topic in biology (although it must draw information from that scientific discipline) but rather in sociology.

Key Elements in a Discussion of an Issue in Bioethics

Any argument involving ethics necessarily involves commentary about people's values in relation to the more objective subject matter, be it law, biology, medicine, or business. A value system can be intrinsic or extrinsic, secular or religious, behavioral or pragmatic. An argument in bioethics will introduce the elements of the ethical dilemma as objectively and accurately as possible, being careful not to inject subtle biases prematurely. For example, if one wishes to argue that stem cells extracted from human embryos is a violation of human rights, one must first objectively represent the other side: that such stem cell use will possibly lead to saving lives by curing or preventing crippling genetic diseases.

Analysis of a Short Argument on an Issue in Bioethics

Study the following argument on genetic manipulation by the bioethicist Margaret McLean, PhD, director of Biotechnology and Health Care Ethics at the Markkula Center for Applied Ethics, Santa Clara University.

When What We Know Outstrips What We Can Do | Margaret R. McLean

Our genes contain information that scientists hope will help in the treatment of many diseases. Huntington's disease provides a window on the choices we face as medicine increases our ability to intervene in human genetics.

"Stop pacing, Mom. It'll be all right." Meghan and her mother, Anne, fidget nervously in the waiting area of the genetic testing center.

Source: Retrieved from: http://www.scu.edu/ethics/publications/iie/v9n2/outstrips.html

"I need to have this test, Mom," Meghan continues. "I want to know if I'm going to wind up like Uncle Harry. I want to know the chances that my children will inherit Huntington's disease." Meghan and her husband, Rick, want to start a family—a family untouched by Huntington's bizarre dances, frightening mood swings, and untimely death. "I'd rather not have children if it means sentencing them to a death like that," Meghan says.

Anne halts and faces her daughter. "I wish it wasn't this way, Meghan." Anne's family has been haunted by Huntington's since anyone can remember; those who get it always die from it. Her brother Harry was just fine until his mid- 40s—then came the depression, the twitching arms.

"I would do anything to spare you," Anne says. "But, Meghan, please   *5* understand that I don't want to be tested. 'So far, so good' is my philosophy. I'm only 42. I want to live my life and make my decisions without a Huntington's diagnosis hanging over my head."

"But Mom, you're not the one being tested; I am."

Falling into the chair next to her daughter, Anne pleads, "Don't you see? If your test is positive, it means I've got the gene, too. And I don't want to know. I have a right not to know, don't I?"

Anne and Meghan face a tentative future. Members of families with a history of Huntington's disease have long known that this neurological disorder—with its loss of motor control, personality changes, depression, dementia, and death—might eventually be their fate.

Huntington's is a genetic disease, one that can be passed down from parents to children. The gene for Huntington's is dominant, which means that a single copy of the gene from either parent triggers the disease. Children of people afflicted with Huntington's disease have a 50/50 chance of also having the disease.

Until recently, these people had no way of knowing whether they were in   *10* the unlucky 50 percent until symptoms actually appeared, usually between the ages of 30 and 50. Then, in 1993, scientists identified the gene responsible for the disorder and made possible the test Meghan wants to take.

If Meghan is tested and found to carry the gene for Huntington's disease, her mother must also have the gene. Meghan, then, will know what Anne does not want to know. What should Meghan do?

The Human Genome Project

Meghan's problem foreshadows the dilemmas many people will face as scientists learn more about genetics. In 1990, an international effort was launched to decode the language of our genes—the Human Genome Project (HGP). The United States is investing $3 billion over 15 years in this endeavor to map the complete set of genes for humans—the human genome. The project will make it easier for researchers who want to identify the genetic components both of disease and of physical and intellectual traits.

Thus far, the most obvious result of the HGP is the rapid proliferation of genetic information. As the new information pours in, the traditional questions haunt us: What should we do with this information? What does this particular genetic alteration mean personally, medically, and socially? If we can, should we intervene to correct or enhance an individual's genome? And when we cannot intervene, how do we handle diagnostic information in the absence of a cure?

Genetic screening can provide new information, not only for potential Huntington's victims but also for sufferers of the more than 4,000 other diseases of genetic origin. Additional ailments are rooted in the interaction of genes with the environment. All told, genetic disorders are the fourth leading cause of death in the United States.

15   Discovering the location of a disease-causing gene on a chromosome permits diagnosis before the onset of symptoms. It also allows testing of entire populations to identify carriers as well as those who are affected.

The long-term hope is for a precise molecular correction of the defect so that genetic disease becomes as curable as infectious disease. Such therapy might also prevent genetic pathologies from moving from one generation to the next.

The Rift Between Diagnosis and Cure

Yet despite the progress of the HGP—and, indeed, primarily because of it—disease prediction continues to outpace medicine's ability to treat or cure. The test for Huntington's disease can confirm a mutation in the Huntington's gene, but it offers no treatment for the devastating symptoms. The result is a therapeutic rift between what we know and what we can do.

Meghan and Anne fearfully straddle this crevasse, hoping against hope that it will narrow. However, it seems likely that as information flows from the HGP, this therapeutic rift will continue to enlarge for the foreseeable future. This poses profound and puzzling questions about the limits of medical knowledge and human choice.

Consider the effects of genetic information on people who, like Anne and Meghan, confront Huntington's disease. If they discover they do, in fact, have the Huntington's gene, a shadow is cast over the rest of their lives. A slight misstep becomes an omen of uncontrollable muscle movements. Feeling blue is no longer part of everyday life but a precursor of mental collapse. The person's view of life is irreversibly changed by a set of prophecies about affliction and horrifying death.

20   In *Mapping Fate*, Alice Wexler describes what it's like to live with this knowledge:

> A dancer with Huntington's disease, in her early forties, described how, long before there were any other symptoms, she began having difficulty learning dance sequences; whereas once she had no problem memorizing complicated routines, she gradually found it more and more difficult to master a series of different steps. Later on she found it increasingly difficult to organize a meal, coordinating the different dishes so that they would all come

out together. Living at risk undermines confidence, for there is no way of separating the ordinary difficulties and setbacks of life from the early symptoms of the illness. It is not like any other physical illness, where consciousness can at least continue in the knowledge that one is still oneself, despite severe pain and physical limitation. Huntington's means a loss of identity.

But long before the loss of motor control and identity, those who carry the Huntington's gene may face the loss of jobs and health coverage. Many people from families with a history of genetic disorders fear that if they are tested, the results might become public and cause employers or insurers to exclude them. Laws to prohibit such discrimination are not yet completely in place. This is the prophecy of social and medical doom that Anne is resisting.

Responsibilities to the Next Generation

But her daughter Meghan has a different set of concerns. Genetic knowledge is apt to have its greatest impact not on the lives of those who, like the stumbling dancer, are currently stricken, but on the choices to be made by those who, like Meghan, are contemplating parenthood.

If Meghan does not have the gene, then her child will not have the disease. If she does have the gene, any child she conceives has a 50 percent chance of sharing her fate.

Assuming Meghan learns that she has the Huntington's gene, what should she and her husband do? Should they take their chances with genetic roulette? Should they remain genetically childless? Should they undergo prenatal diagnosis?

Prenatal screening and diagnosis can be accomplished through methods   *25* such as amniocentesis. Sometimes genetic testing is coupled with in vitro fertilization in a technique called preimplantation genetic diagnosis (PGD). PGD is currently offered in a limited number of research facilities.

In this method, after the egg is fertilized outside the womb, the embryo is allowed to reach the eight-cell stage of development before a cell is removed. This cell is then tested for genetic components that would predispose the child to a particular disease such as Huntington's. Then, only those embryos that do not contain the disease gene are transferred to the uterus, thereby eliminating the chance of having a child with Huntington's disease.

Whatever the promise of this technique, the cost is far from trivial. It includes the fee for IVF—averaging $8,000 per cycle—plus the cost of genetic testing, which adds an estimated $2,000. Even in the rare cases when IVF expenses are paid by health insurance, the genetic component is not covered.

Costs are also likely to be high in the even more advanced procedures now being proposed. In the future, PGD might identify candidates for emerging techniques such as constructive genetic surgery and embryonic cell cloning. Constructive genetic surgery involves removing the affected gene from an embryo and replacing it with normal genetic material. But this is risky business with a failure rate of 80 percent—far too perilous to perform on a single human embryo.

Through cell cloning, however, scientists could make multiple copies of the embryo they wish to modify, increasing the genetic surgical success rate. Indeed, cellular cloning seems to hold the key to the successful genetic engineering of humans. But to what end?

30   Is Meghan's wish to prune Huntington's disease from her family tree a justified use of this future technology? Suppose parents wish to eliminate the predisposition to alcoholism. What if they want to increase a child's physical stature or intellectual acumen? Would these be reasonable requests for embryonic genetic intervention?

After all, we send our children to soccer practice and tutoring after they are born; why not give them a genetic head start? Is there an ethically relevant difference between genetic therapy and genetic enhancement?

Questions and Guidelines

Reproductive and genetic technologies are opening new medical and moral frontiers, urging us to think in new ways. As the level of medical diagnosis and treatment shifts from bodies and bones to cells and chromosomes, the level of ethical consideration must do the same.

Reaching ethical conclusions about the new genetics is challenging for two reasons: First, it is inherently difficult to understand the subtleties of genetics and the wealth of data tumbling out of the HGP. Second, it is next to impossible to foresee accurately the implications and consequences—short-term, long-term, and unintended—of intervening in the genetic "stuff of life."

The following questions may help to clarify key issues as genetic medicine comes of age:

1. What is the purpose of taking a particular genetic test? Who is affected by the results?

35   Some people undergo genetic screening simply to know their predisposition to a particular disease. Others may hope to fix that predisposition. Currently, the diagnosis of numerous genetic diseases or predispositions is possible; in most cases, however, there is no treatment or cure. Care must be taken to ensure that patients understand this rift between diagnosis and treatment and that their expectations of the testing are realistic.

Since it became possible to test for the Huntington's gene, fewer than 15 percent of those at risk have taken the test, even when it was offered free of charge. Most would rather not know. Anne, like many of us, is reluctant to find out about an inevitable future. Perhaps, out of respect for her mother's wishes, Meghan could wait to take the test, hoping that in a few more years, scientists may make progress toward a cure. Perhaps Meghan is particularly good at keeping secrets.

Traditional notions of confidentiality are profoundly challenged by medical tests that tell patients not only about themselves but also about family members. As genetic tests become readily available, respect must be given to those who, like Anne, claim a right to ignorance.

2. Who has control of genetic information?

In this era of rapid communication and data proliferation, absolute confidentiality of medical information no longer seems realistic. In a hospital, anywhere from 60 to 200 people have access to a patient's medical records. The information is also passed along to insurance carriers and health maintenance organizations. Given that complete privacy is not possible, it is important to consider who has access to genetic information and for what purpose.

People questioned about genetic testing worry that insurers will raise rates or refuse to insure them. They express concern that employers will not hire them. There is a general fear that friends and family will treat them differently or abandon them once they are "tarnished" by a deadly gene. Medicine's obligation to do no harm mandates that genetic information be used in ways that help people, not in ways that stigmatize and marginalize them.

3. What does it mean to offer genetic testing and/or therapy in the absence of universal access to health care?

This is a question of justice. What counts as a fair share of the health care pie *40* for the poor or for those without health insurance? We live in an era of limited access to childhood immunizations and routine preventive care—both of which are relatively inexpensive and medically effective. As we pour health care dollars into genetic research and treatment, we must also seek to provide basic care to those who are most vulnerable to the ravages of disease: the poor and their children.

4. On what basis should someone undertake genetic intervention such as genetic constructive surgery if and when it becomes available?

Two approaches to this question are possible. One is therapeutic; that is, such techniques should be used to correct particular diseases. The other is eugenic; that is, genetic intervention is permissible to enhance specific characteristics (e.g., intellect) or to give individuals capacities they might not otherwise have had (e.g., playing piano),

The distinction between therapy and enhancement may turn on intention. Is the purpose of the intervention to bring a person to a state of health or to go beyond health in the design of someone new or better?

With the fledgling capacity to alter the human genome comes the responsibility to think carefully about what we consider a benefit for individuals and society. Test tube racks filled with "designer genes" hold not only the promise of molecular treatments but also the age-old mischief of discrimination and exclusion. We are not yet free of the specter of forced eugenics: witness reports that up until the 1970s, an estimated 60,000 people had been sterilized in Sweden under government policies to weed out traits such as poor eyesight and "Gypsy features." What some consider desirable traits may not be a benefit in the eyes of either humanity as a whole or the affected individual.

5. For what kind of genetic future are we planning?

Genetics, by its very nature, embodies a concern for coming generations. Genetic diagnosis and intervention hold great promise. However, we need to consider carefully the power conferred on us by knowing our genetic identity and being able to alter it.

45   With great power comes greater responsibility, asking us to think carefully about the dramatic impact that genetic information and intervention might have on the future. We face not a red light but a flashing yellow as we enter the age of genetic medicine.

EXERCISE **6.6**

1. Summarize McLean's thesis in your own words. How convincingly does she support her assertions?

2. Do you agree or disagree with McLean that "we are not yet free of the specter of forced eugenics"? Why or why not?

3. Discuss whether the advantages of controlling genetic information in humans outweigh the disadvantages.

4. Comment on the way McLean has formatted her argument. In what ways does it enhance the coherence and clarity of the argument?

5. Use the preceding four prompts in this exercise to develop a Power-Point presentation, supporting or challenging McLean's thesis, for students in an introductory biology or bioethics course.

6. Compare McLean's use of evidence with that of Joseph Forte's essay on Shelley's "Ozymandias" or Lauren Silk's essay on aid to Africa. How do you account for the different approaches?

Strategies of Argument in Workplace-Related Contexts

Writing in the professional workplace is usually undertaken for strictly utilitarian reasons: to propose a new policy or project; to convey important information to colleagues or clientele, as is the case with writing a job application letter or an instruction manual; or, from the other side of the fence, writing a recommendation for hiring a particular candidate.

Arguing Critically About a Legal Issue

The law, like medicine and health, is obviously of great interest to the general public. Consider widely popular television shows like *Law and Order* and *Criminal Minds* and best-selling mystery writers like John Grisham, Scott Turow, and Michael Connelly (whose novel, *The Lincoln Lawyer*, was made into a hit motion picture). Many famous literary works are courtroom dramas, such as *Inherit the Wind*, *Twelve Angry Men*, and *To Kill a Mockingbird*, just to name a few.

Key Elements in a Critical Discussion of a Legal Issue

To risk stating the obvious, if you're going to write on a legal issue, you must thoroughly understand the law as it currently exists and then be able to translate it into nonlegalese. Arguments concerning legal issues debate not what the law is, but how the law is to be interpreted. Lawyers on either side of a case often work with the same material and facts, but they argue that readers or listeners should reach different conclusions.

What accounts for these differences? Lawyers sometimes construct theories. For example, although an act may be indisputable (a person was shot and killed), different theories may lead to different conclusions about the accountability of the one who shot the victim; the accountability may therefore be disputed.

One may cite previous acts of the defendant to show that the current act is one of many violent acts that have culminated in the utmost violent act, the taking of a life. But another may cite the actions of the deceased prior to the shooting to indicate that in this particular incident, the act of shooting a person was justified by self-defense because the deceased also had a deadly weapon and was about to use it on the defendant. Yet another might point to the upbringing and mental health of the one who shot the deceased.

Now shift that act into war: If one soldier takes the life of a soldier on the opposite side, do we use the same theories as those above to determine accountability? Is accountability even a legal issue that anyone undertakes to dispute?

In general, legal theories must be consistent with prior judgments and rulings (precedents) and should yield suitable results for future judgments and rulings. Prior cases, statutes or laws, and constitutional provisions are among the bases for legal theories, but these are not the sole bases.

Analysis of a Legal Argument

Study the following news editorial, which takes a new perspective on a long-standing legal issue: gun control.

Gun Control Debate Heats Up Again | W. E. Messamore

Today, the Assembly Public Safety Committee will take up AB 144, legislation introduced by Anthony Portantino (D-Pasadena) to ban the open carry of a handgun in the state of California. The controversial legislation has reinvigorated the decades-long debate over the effects of gun legislation on public safety.

Writing Monday at the California Progress Report, Dr. Dallas Stout, President of the California Brady Campaign to Prevent Gun Violence, argued that open carry laws actually make Californians less safe. Stout cites three anecdotes to illustrate his point: a 4-year-old boy in Maryland who shot and killed himself last month; a 2-year-old in Louisiana who used a stool to retrieve a gun in his home and shot himself in the upper right chest; and a 5-year-old from Pennsylvania who grabbed his father's firearm and shot himself in the head.

These stories are all indeed very tragic, but do little in themselves to illustrate the effectiveness of gun control laws or the danger of open carry laws. The 4-year-old who tragically killed himself in Maryland did so despite that state's stringent gun control policies. Maryland does not allow open carry without a permit, and is one of the more restrictive of the nation's relatively few "May Issue" states for carry permits. Over 30 other states are less restrictive "Shall Issue" states. As Stout also acknowledges in his article, "Authorities are trying to figure out … how the boy was able to get access to the weapon …"

Stout is also fair enough to report that the boy from Pennsylvania "climbed onto a chair near his parents' bedroom closet and grabbed his part-time police officer father's duty weapon and accidently shot himself in the head." Stricter carry laws would not have prevented this tragedy either. Anecdotes like these are subject to endless qualifications and debate, and while emotionally powerful, do not necessarily paint a statistically sound and accurate picture of how a policy actually affects the lives of the people in a given state or jurisdiction.

5   A more useful argument is Dr. Stout's assertion that a "gun is 22 times more likely to be used in a homicide, suicide or unintentional shooting than to kill in self-defense." While studies have shown that a gun owner is statistically at greater risk from his or her own weapon than they are likely to use it in self-defense, that proves only that owning a gun might make the gun owner less safe, not that more permissive gun laws make society at large less safe. In fact, the overwhelming statistical evidence to the contrary shows a powerful correlation between more permissive gun laws and lower rates of violent crime.

According to a University of Chicago interview with Dr. John Lott, economist and author of *More Guns, Less Crime*, data for all 3,054 counties in the United States during the 18 years from 1977 to 1994 demonstrate that:

> "There is a strong negative relationship between the number of law-abiding citizens with permits and the crime rate—as more people obtain permits there is a greater decline in violent crime rates. For each additional year that a concealed handgun law is in effect the murder rate declines by 3 percent, rape by 2 percent, and robberies by over 2 percent."

So while it is statistically true that owning a gun might actually make you and your household less safe, the fact that a potential criminal knows that you have the legal right to own and carry a gun makes society more safe. It doesn't take a Ph.D. economist like Lott to understand the incentives involved. A criminal has a strong disincentive to attempt a mugging in an alley when there is any reasonable chance that his victim could be carrying a gun. That's why jurisdictions with notoriously strict gun control measures paradoxically tend to suffer from the worst rates of violent crime—that is, places like Washington DC, Chicago, and even the United Kingdom.

Will gun control make California safer? That all depends on what you mean by "safe," but if we put it down to rates of violent crime, all indications from decades of data in hundreds of cities, states, and counties seem to declare a resounding "No."

EXERCISE 6.7

1. Summarize Messamore's stance on the gun control debate.

2. Compare Messamore's argumentative strategies with those of Silk and McLean. Where are they similar? Where do they differ?

3. In view of the January 2011 shootings in Tucson during which six people attending a political rally were killed by a crazed gunman, what modifications, if any, would you make to Messamore's point of view?

4. Does restricting or banning handguns violate the Second Amendment? Write a position paper supporting or defending the right to bear arms.

Arguing Critically About an Issue in Business

President Calvin Coolidge famously said that the business of America is business, but we can extend that to the entire world. Business is the engine that runs every nation on earth, from the most industrialized to the most rural.

Key Elements in a Critical Discussion of an Issue in Business

A strong business argument often relies on case studies, statistics, surveys—sources of evidence that one does not routinely find, say, in an argument on a painting or work of literature.

Whereas aesthetic bases are appropriate to arguing the value of a painting, these are not pertinent to an argument in business.

Arguments about business-related issues often present the problem at hand before they provide background information about the field and the situation leading up to the problem at hand. A time line for implementation and an analysis of costs are often included as well. Some business arguments take the form of a step-by-step guide to achieving success or (like the feature presented below) a breakdown of facts from fiction when getting started in a new business venture.

Analysis of an Argument on a Business Issue

Argumentative writing can vary in level of formality, from the scholarly to the colloquial. The following piece about running an Internet business from home is an example of the latter.

The 10 Most Popular Myths about Running a Home-Based Business Online | Elena Fawkner

Several weeks ago I finally took the plunge into the world of network marketing. I had been running an online business for almost three years by then but knew that I would have to make the leap to network marketing at some point since it was such an obvious fit with Internet marketing. And I haven't been disappointed.

One thing did surprise me though—the number of people who approached me about my network marketing business, interested in running their businesses exclusively online, but with the mistaken belief that it would be somehow easier and less expensive than establishing and running a home-based business offline.

Well, let me tell you, there's nothing easy or inexpensive about running a home-based business—online or off. The Internet is just a different way of going about it. And that's all.

Here's my top 10 myths about running an online business (and in answer to the missing Myth #11, NO, you CANNOT run a serious online business with WebTV—get a REAL computer already).

5   **MYTH #1**—It's Easy, Anyone Can Do It
  FACT—It's not easy, by any stretch of the imagination, and no, you may not
    be able to do it.
      Reality is, establishing an Internet business is a long, slow, frustrating
    process. Your first attempt at creating your own website will be an abomi-
    nation. You'll look back at it in 12 months and shudder. I know I did. You'll
    feel utterly overwhelmed by the sheer amount of information you need to
    absorb. And the fact that six different "experts" each tell you six different
    things doesn't help. (There are no "experts", by the way, just a lot of people
    with a lot of opinions. Bottom line? Do what works. For you.) The only way
    to learn is by trial and error. Some days you'll feel like you're on a roll, the

---

Source: © 2002 Elena Fawkner. A Home Based Business Online; Web.

next you'll feel like you're backsliding and FAST. No sooner do you manage a respectable ranking on Altavista, than your Yahoo listing disappears altogether, and where the hell did that number 5 listing with Google go?

After spending an ENTIRE DAY trying to work out what's going on with your search engine listings, giving up, going searching for yet another "expert" to tell you what you're doing wrong, finally realizing there is no such expert and you're going to have to learn how to do it all yourself after all (dammit to hell!) you suddenly realize that you've done absolutely nothing all day to promote your business and you still have to write the article for this week's ezine which has to go out tomorrow but you can't work your business tomorrow because you have to go work at your J.O.B......AAAARGHHHH!!!!!

Many, many people, give it up. Most, probably. It's hard work and it's frustrating. At the end of the day, most are just not prepared to do what it takes.

MYTH #2—I Can Get Wealthy Overnight   *10*
FACT—The only way to get wealthy overnight in this world is to win the Lotto. Period. It will NOT happen on the Internet. Not these days, anyway.

MYTH #3—Once I Build My Website I Can Relax And Let It Do the Work For Me
FACT—Hah. See Myth #4.

MYTH #4—Once I Build My Website The World Will Beat A Path To My Door
FACT—No. It won't.   *15*

Merely creating a website and uploading it to your host's server means that your website is available for viewing by *those who know it exists*. Only problem is, you and your web host are the only ones who know. And even your web host doesn't care (at least as long as you pay your monthly hosting fees).

You now need to submit your site to the search engines (no, they will not just find it automatically and no, your website is not just automatically added to some great universal Index once it's uploaded). Then you have to wait several weeks or months to find out whether it's been indexed. And if by some miracle it has, where and for what keywords. And then fix it. In the meantime, you have to drive traffic to your site via other means. You'll need to submit it to directories, negotiate reciprocal links with other complementary websites, start publishing a weekly ezine (electronic newsletter) and start promoting that to start developing your own opt-in list, start writing articles and submitting them wherever you can (including a link to your site in the resource box at the end is good free advertising) and, shudder, advertising. And not in the FFAs and free classifieds either. In other people's ezines. On other people's websites. In the classifieds section of newspapers (yes, the kind that leaves black stuff on your fingers when you read it). All of this costs money. Plenty of it. If you're running a network marketing business, you're also going to need to pay for leads during this period as well.

MYTH #5—I Don't Have To Spend Money To Market My Business
FACT—Yes, you do. You wouldn't expect to be able to market an offline business without financial outlay. Well, guess what? It's just the same in your online business. See Myth #4. Oh, and by the way, when you're re-reading Myth #4, keep this in mind. You haven't made a dime yet.

20   **MYTH #6**—I Can Put the Whole Thing On Autopilot And Make Money While I Sleep (Or Vacation)
FACT—True. To a point. By automating as many of your tasks as possible you necessarily free up time to do other things. You COULD use that time to sleep or vacation and you MAY make money while you're sleeping or vacationing. THIS time. But you must sow before you can reap and if you're not continually planting and growing your business, the time will come in the not too distant future when you have nothing left to harvest. You'll wake up one morning and find that, far from filling your inbox with overnight orders, your business has bitten the dust. So, instead of taking that freed up time and spending it sleeping or vacationing, spend it working your business. In other words, you'll get out of your business precisely what you put into it. Just like anything else in this world. Funny about that.

MYTH #7— I Don't Have To Deal With People, I Can Do Everything Via Email
FACT—Email is what you use to handle routine administrative issues and a tool to get prospective customers or networking partners to contact you. Once that happens, you take the relationship OFFLINE. You get on the phone and actually TALK to these people. The Internet is not an iron curtain that protects you from having to have real life conversations and relationships with people. It's just a tool that brings you together so that the real work of establishing relationships can begin. Offline.

MYTH #8—I Will Be Able to Fire My Boss And Work Where I Want, When I Want … In Six Months Or Less
25   **FACT**—Don't give up your day job just yet.

MYTH #9—When I'm Working For Myself From Home In My Online Business I Will Be Able To Spend As Much Time With My Children As I Want
FACT—When you're running a business you're running a business. It's not a pleasant little hobby that you fit in between the stuff of your REAL life. If you're not going to run your business as a business, forggeddabouddit.

MYTH #10—The Internet Is A Magic Wand
FACT—See Myths #1 through #9.

EXERCISE 6.8

1. How convincingly does Elena Fawkner distinguish between myths and facts with regard to running an online business? How adequate is the evidence that she provides?

2. How appropriate or effective is Fawker's informal diction? Identify weaknesses as well as strengths in this approach.

3. Suggest possible counterarguments to Fawkner's formulation of myths and facts about running a home-based Internet business.

4. Discuss Fawkner's argumentative strategy. For example, is her sequence of myths/facts arbitrary or purposeful? How can you tell?

5. Rework Fawkner's argument as a PowerPoint presentation. Adapt the information as you see fit—perhaps by including statistics, charts, or graphs to emphasize key points.

Arguing Critically About an Engineering Issue

Engineering students in general are surprised to discover that argumentative writing is important in this field—that engineers are responsible for procedural documents, reports, proposals, and recommendations, all of which require strategies of argumentation.

Key Features in a Critical Discussion of an Engineering Issue

The purpose of writing arguments in engineering is to convince managers or administrators to follow a particular course of action. Often a certain degree of urgency is involved. For example, following the collapse of a freeway overpass during the Loma Prieta earthquake in Northern California in 1989, civil engineers recognized the urgent need to retrofit (reinforce) existing bridges before another strong earthquake occurred. Another example involves the *Challenger* and *Columbia* space shuttle disasters of 1986 and 2003, respectively. These tragedies prompted NASA to establish special commissions to determine the exact causes of each accident and offer recommendations for redesigning the flawed systems and revamping launch protocols.

Analysis of a Short Engineering Position Paper

In his "Technical Writing for Engineers" course, Santa Clara University professor Don Riccomini assigned his students to research different reports examining the causes of the space shuttle disasters of 1986 and 2003 (students had the option of researching one or the other) and to recommend to NASA which of the reports was most accurate, reliable, and thorough. After examining the reports based on the *Challenger* disaster, Melissa Conlin, one of the students in Professor Ricomini's course, prepared the following position paper.

Date: 05/12/2010
To: Jane Doe
From: Melissa Conlin
Subject: Challenger Shuttle Disaster Recommendation

Challenger Shuttle Disaster Recommendation

Introduction Summary

You recently asked for my evaluation of three articles on the
Challenger shuttle disaster. The first was the official government commission's findings, the second the personal report of
Roger Boisjoly, and the third the personal observations of Richard Feynman. I have read these reports and in this memo I have
compared them under three main categories: author credibility,
report content, the recommendations made. Through my analysis
I have concluded that while lessons may be learned from each
report, the one by Richard Feynman encapsulates the ideas of all
three into one, easy to read paper and should be used for the
basis of future improvements.

Overview

	Author Credibility	Report Content	Recommendations Made
Rogers Commission Report	• Fourteen members of commission	• Technical problems with the design of the shuttle	• Design of some parts of the shuttle must be changed
	• Among them: Neil Armstrong, Richard Feynman and Sally K. Ride	• Analysis of the miscommunication between the managers and engineers	• Shuttle management structure should be reviewed
			• Future projects such as launch abort and escape crew

Roger Boisjoly Report	• Engineer working on improvement of O-rings at time of disaster • Argued to stop the launch of the Challenger • First-hand experience	• Ethical argument of miscommunication between engineers and managers	• Focus on establishing better communication between engineers and managers
Richard Feynman Report	• Served on Presidential Rogers Commission to investigate disaster • Nobel laureate physicist from Cal Tech	• Technical as well as ethical argument of what went wrong • Focus on technical problems as well as miscommunication	• Focus on improvements to be made in solid rockets, liquid fuel engines and avionics • Argument that disparity between management and engineer understanding must be fixed

Rogers Commission Report on the Challenger
(Official Government Report)

Author Credibility

The Commission was made up of fourteen members. Among the members were: Neil Armstrong, the first man to walk on the moon, Richard P. Feynman, winner of the 1965 Nobel Prize in Physics, Sally K. Ride, the first American woman in space, and two Air Force Generals. All of the members were important people within the United States government at the time or well known within

the scientific and space community. The authors' entire knowledge and experience combine into one long, very thorough report.

Report Content

The Rogers Commission Report is very long and extensively
detailed. In looking at the miscommunication between managers and
engineers alone there are around thirty interviews and firsthand
accounts written about and included. There are also pages upon
pages on the technical problems with the O-ring and what went
wrong in the accident. With this report there is nothing left
out, though it is informational rather than an ethical argument
of what could have been done to stop the disaster. The shuttle
design itself is examined, from the faulty Solid Rocket Motor
joint to adding a launch abort and crew escape mechanism. The
report is very formal and detailed, as the authors want nothing
to be left out in their analysis. It is much too long to be read
by the general public and would take anyone, regardless of their
interest, a long time to get through. A manager, technician, or
engineer in the specific fields discussed would find the report
very informative and useful, though they would need to search
through all the text to find the area related to their work.

Recommendations Made

The Rogers Commission Report offers very specific recommendations, added to the end of the analysis. The recommendations
revolve around the design of the shuttle as well as the structure of the management itself. The recommendations are very specific and include fixing the faulty Solid Rocket Motor joint
and seal, evaluating the Shuttle Program Management Structure,
improving communications, improving landing safety, adding a
launch abort and crew escape, and implementing maintenance safe-
guards. Even though the report itself is very long and detailed,
the recommendations presented are well thought out and there
are few enough of them that they can all be accomplished without changing too many things at once. Though with some of the
recommendations shifting towards future projects, such as launch
abort and crew escape, some of the focus could be taken off of
the problems already present within the system that need fixing. It would seem preexisting problems should be fixed before

shifting the spotlight to new areas. As the report claims, it was "An Accident Rooted in History"; old problems must be fixed before moving onto the future.

Roger Boisjoly Report

Author Credibility

Roger Boisjoly was an engineer at Morton Thiokol who was involved in an improvement effort on the O-rings used to bring a space shuttle into orbit. Before the Challenger shuttle disaster he worked vehemently to stop the launch, claiming the O-rings would not function properly in temperatures less than fifty-three degrees. His arguments were ignored, resulting in the launch of the shuttle and the eventual disaster. Boisjoly offers a reliable, first-hand account of the events leading up to the explosion and emphasizes the lack of communication between the engineers and managers in charge at the time of the disaster.

Report Content

Boisjoly's account addresses the ethical issues within the Challenger disaster, rather than focusing on the technical aspects of what went wrong. He does spend some time discussing how tests done on the O-rings indicated problems with low temperatures, but his frustration and emotion fully come out as he discusses his attempts to stop the launch of the Challenger. He mentions the lack of management support to provide resources for testing, how he and his team received no comments back on their reports against the management leading up to the disaster, and how he felt totally helpless when the decision to launch was made. His tone is conversational and there is very little technical knowledge needed to understand his report. His goal since the disaster has been to change workplace ethics and that is exactly what he focuses on here, his report making it clear that he never wants a disaster such as the Challenger to happen again through miscommunication between engineers and their managers.

Recommendations Made

Boisjoly's recommendation is ethical rather than technical. To him the lack of communication between the engineers and the managers was much more of a problem than the O-rings and technical

side of the disaster. If the communication had been better, the
problem with the O-rings could have been solved or avoided. It
doesn't matter if you have all of the evidence to support your
claims or if you know exactly how to fix a technical problem,
if you cannot communicate your knowledge to your manger nothing
will come from it. According to Boisjoly, it is the professional
responsibility, conduct and accountability that require the most
improvement. He sums up his thoughts and recommendation with his
final statement: "All of you must now evaluate your careers and
emerge with the knowledge and conviction that you have a professional and moral responsibility to yourselves and to your fellow
man to defend the truth and expose any questionable practices
that will lead to an unsafe product".

Richard Feynman Report

Author Credibility

Richard Feynman was a Nobel laureate physicist from Cal Tech who
was asked to join the Presidential Rogers Commission to investigate the Challenger disaster. Following his work for the Commission he wrote a report on his own personal observations and
interpretation of what went wrong and what current problems need
to be fixed. He does not offer a first-hand account of the events
leading up to and during the disaster, but his experiences and
interviews after provided him enough of an understanding that his
report is very reliable and contains the viewpoints of those who
were present. His technical knowledge as well as his outsider's
view of the disparity between management and engineer understanding combine to offer a very compelling argument.

Report Content

Throughout his report, Feynman switches off between an ethical
argument and a technical one. He continuously points out the disparity between management and engineers. Right from the start he
writes: "It appears that there are enormous differences of opinion as to the probability of a failure with loss of vehicle and
of human life. The estimates range from roughly 1 in 100 to 1 in
100,000. The higher figures come from the working engineers, and
the very low figures from management". As his paper continues,
he keeps pointing out the figures that the engineers have come up

with and the ones the management believes, all of them showing just as much, if not more, of a disproportion. Though along with the miscommunication he sees he also talks of the most important technical improvements that he thinks need to be put into place. He focuses on solid rockets, liquid fuel engines, and avionics. For example, in the Avionics section he points out that there have been no changes to computer hardware in fifteen years and that even after sensors have failed no changes have been made to them in eighteen months. Feynman blends both ethical and technical problems into his argument, bringing them together seamlessly in a conversational tone that can be understood by technicians and the general public alike.

Recommendations Made

Feynman recommends both technical and ethical action to improve shuttle reliability. First and foremost, managers and engineers need to be on the same page when it comes to the risks involved. Through his analysis he shows that the managers seem to have unrealistic visions of how safe the shuttles are. According to the managers, if they flew a shuttle everyday for three hundred years they would only lose one. Better communication needs to be established so that the managers know the risks as well as the engineers. Feynman also offers three main areas to be improved in the shuttle itself, giving detailed analysis of the solid rockets, liquid fuel engineers and the avionics. He feels the technology needs to be upgraded and offers specific places he could see improvement being made, such as in the fifteen-year-old computer hardware being used within the shuttles. His recommendations are specific and detailed, though he doesn't provide so many that too many things would be changed at once. His suggestions are all also already existing problems, as he focuses on fixing them before moving forward. He sums up his report with one statement, blending ethics and technology together: "For a successful technology, reality must take precedence over public relations, for nature cannot be fooled".

Conclusion

Richard Feynman's report should be read and reviewed, with his recommendations followed. Since Feynman was one of the authors of the Rogers Commission Report he addresses many of the same ideas, but in a much more condensed way. Instead of having to search through pages and pages of text, readers can read his shorter report and get an idea of what the Rogers Commission Report encapsulated. He also addresses some of the ethical issues that Boisjoly does in his report, pointing out the large discrepancies between managers' beliefs and the judgment of their engineers. Feynman's recommendations address these ethical issues as well as the technical ones that he found to be the most important from his work on the Rogers Commission Report. His recommendations also address current problems within the system, rather than shifting the focus to improvements that could potentially be made in the future. For these reasons, Richard Feynman's report should be used for the basis of future improvements.

EXERCISE 6.9

1. If you were the one evaluating the *Challenger* disaster reports, what would you do differently, or conclude differently, and why?
2. Comment on the effectiveness of the format Conlin uses in this engineering proposal, including her visual (the tabulated overview).
3. What other visual aids—charts, graphs, bulleted itemizations, photographs, drawings—might be useful in reinforcing Conlin's evaluation?
4. Compare the way Conlin organizes her argument with the way Jones organizes his argument about the Grant Wood painting.

Chapter Summary

Every discipline has its own protocols for argument because methods of research, the nature of evidence, and the manner of presenting an argument differ from one field of inquiry to another. Students writing papers on topics in the arts (for example, painting, theater, literature) need to become familiar with the different critical traditions and the changing criteria for excellence. "Evidence" in the arts often involves documents relating to the artist's or writer's life and cultural milieu, as well as to the internal evidence of the artwork or literary work itself. In the sciences and social sciences, evidence refers to demonstrable (experimentally or mathematically verifiable) results and statistics, as well as to the interpretations and recommendations of experts who base their conclusions on demonstrable results.

Checklist

1. Have I familiarized myself with the conventions of argument in the discipline I'm writing a paper in?
2. Do I understand how "evidence" is defined in a given discipline?
3. Do I understand what is appropriate and sufficient evidence in a given discipline?
4. Have I examined the ethical implications of my thesis? (See Chapter 3.)
5. Have I acknowledged challenging views, sought common ground with some of their assertions, and refuted other assertions? (See Chapters 2 and 3.)
6. Have I conducted sufficient background information to be able to argue the issue at hand?
7. Have I taken the time to explain specialized concepts in language that laypersons can understand?

Writing Projects

For Arts Majors

1. Study three paintings by the twentieth-century artist Edward Hopper and then defend or challenge the following claim: *Hopper's city scenes attempt to negate the myth of the American dream.* Hopper's paintings are accessible online. *Note:* When cutting and pasting images such as paintings from Internet sources, be sure to acknowledge the source underneath the image and on your "Works Cited" page.

2. Choose one of the following poems (accessible online) and study three critical responses to it. Write an essay in which you examine these critiques for their insightfulness and thoroughness. Call attention to aspects of the poem that were, in your opinion, misinterpreted or overlooked.

   Edgar Allan Poe, "Annabel Lee"

   Emily Dickinson, "I Heard a Fly Buzz when I Died"

   William Butler Yeats, "The Lake Isle of Innisfree"

For Science Majors

1. Study two or three explanations of a "black hole." First, in a short paper decide which explanation does the best job of conveying the concept and

why. Next, convert that short paper into a PowerPoint presentation so that you might present the argument to a high school science class.

2. Some argue that we should return to the moon because of its valuable mineral resources and/or to build colonies for future human settlement. Defend or challenge one of these proposals. A good starting source is the NASA website (www.nasa.gov).

For Social Science Majors

1. Research "social Darwinism" and then argue whether the Darwinian biological concept of "survival of the fittest" can apply to societal situations, such as warfare or workplace competition.

2. Investigate some of the challenges to *Roe v. Wade*. How valid are they, in your opinion?

For Business Majors

1. Examine the advertising strategies used to market a particular product, such as a certain make of automobile or brand of shampoo. Which advertisements (print or Internet) or television ads are most effective for the product? Least effective? What recommendations can you make to improve marketability of the product? Later, expand the project to use whatever new media are at your disposal. For example, redesign the ads with your own original photographs, videos, or drawings.

2. What criteria should be followed when preparing a resume? Obtain recommendations from your school's career counseling service as well as from two or three employment agencies. Finally, gather information from two or three employers themselves. Study the similarities and differences in the respective guidelines and make your own recommendations.

For Engineering Majors

1. Write a report on the feasibility of biofuels and biofuel systems as an automotive industry alternative for petroleum. Be sure to examine both the alleged advantages and the alleged disadvantages with equal scrutiny.

2. It has been frequently noted that a great many of America's roads are in need of repair. After surveying, say, the streets in one particular neighborhood in your community, write a proposal describing in detail the kinds of repairs needed and why the repairs are urgent. Suggestion: Use Googlemaps or a similar online resource to illustrate the urgent need for these repairs.

7 Researching Your Argument

I have always come to life after coming to books.

—Jorge Luis Borges

Much of the writing you do in college—as well as beyond—requires *research*, which refers to three interconnected activities: (1) searching for and retrieving information you need for your writing project, (2) taking notes, and (3) integrating the necessary information into your paper. These activities enable you to acquire in-depth knowledge of the subject and, in turn, to strengthen the premise of your argument.

The Nature of Research

There's no law that says research has got to be tedious. The late rhetorician Ken Macrorie (1919–2009) liked to refer to researching as "searching." It was his way of suggesting that research has an element of adventure in it: You can never fully anticipate what nuggets of information you might discover about your topic until you begin digging in the library or searching the Internet. Of course, research also has its no-nonsense aspect, that of locating the information you need to reinforce the premise of your argument. One major reason for writing an argument is to present to readers new information and insights into a topic. At the same time, however, readers need to be informed or reminded about the old information to see how the new perspective (yours) adds to the discussion of the issue and merits consideration. You therefore must learn as much as possible about your topic and know how to incorporate only the best and most relevant researched data. Sometimes students try to incorporate so much data into their papers that the papers begin to read like mere summaries of what others have written about the topic. Readers want to see your original argument *reinforced* by the findings of others.

Searching Before You Research: Taking a Mental Inventory

One of the most important steps in gathering information may seem like the least necessary: making clear to yourself how much you already know about the topic. The step is necessary because much of what you learn, if it is not used every day, ends up in the equivalent of deep storage in the brain. Some good ways for retrieving it include listing, clustering, and freewriting (predrafting strategies described in Chapter 1). These information-gathering techniques help you generate questions, ideas, and "paths" to pursue in your research.

Consider this case in point: Before Marian, a first-year composition student, sets out to research her chosen topic—possible long-term effects of secondhand cigarette smoke on children—she opens a blank document in her word-processing program and begins freewriting (rapidly recording all that she already knows or associates with the topic). Ignoring word choice, sentence correctness, or paragraph structure for the moment, Marian focuses only on content:

> My parents both smoked and I remembered coughing a lot when I was around them, and sometimes my eyes burned. I never connected my coughing and burning eyes to their smoking because I assumed that they would never do anything to undermine my health. Children can't get away from smoke. In the family, are stuck, have no choice in the matter. And then I remember that my best friend Julia's parents also smoked, even more than my parents did, and that she would cough all the time, and come down with the flu a lot. Not long afterwards (when? what year?), the Surgeon General issued a warning that ambient smoke can be just as harmful as first-hand smoke. Question: Has government done studies comparing effects on children vs. adults? I also read recently that medical researchers have established a link between secondhand smoke and chronic respiratory illnesses, such as asthma. Question: I wonder if the recent upturn in asthma rates in children relates to parents' smoking? I also know that some researchers or tobacco industry people or maybe just average smokers argue that the connection is exaggerated, people's fears get overblown—Question—how to determine how real is the danger?

Marian's freewriting inventory on secondhand smoke is not extensive, but she has written down enough for questions to start occurring to her—questions that help direct and focus the research process. Also, the freewriting gets her thinking about possible opposing views as well as helping her to establish a link between her personal experience with the topic and her more objective knowledge of it.

EXERCISE 7.1

1. Freewrite on one of the following argumentative topics:
   a. Ways to improve my local fitness center
   b. How to improve the parking situation on campus
   c. Studying to prepare for a career versus studying for the pleasure of learning
   d. News feed updates in Facebook are aids or obstacles to keep up friendships
2. Write down all that you already know about a topic you enjoy reading about; then generate a list of questions about aspects of the topic you need to know more about to increase your knowledge or expertise.

Focusing Your Research for Argumentative Essays

Once you have a sense of what you need to find out about your topic, you can guide your researching activities with sets of questions to keep your information-gathering activities in focus. Once again, recall the purpose–audience–writer–subject interconnections of the rhetorical rhombus introduced in Chapter 1 (Figure 7.1).

Generate your questions in the context of each point on the rhombus. If you are arguing against the authenticity of UFO reports, for example, you might generate sets of questions similar to those in the following four sections.

FIGURE 7.1

Rhetorical Rhombus

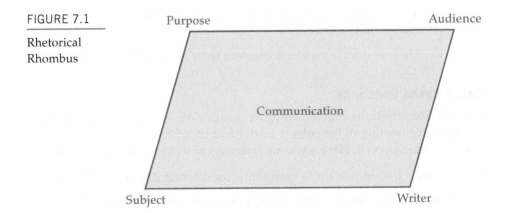

Purpose-Based Questions

Purpose-based questions are interpretive and based on values, for example:

1. What is the thesis (claim) of my essay? Is it sufficiently clear and convincing? (The next section helps you formulate a strong thesis for your papers.)
2. What values (called *warrants* in the Toulmin model) are implied by the kind of evidence I bring to the claim?
3. What larger implications are conveyed by the thesis?
4. How do I want my intended audience to think or act after reading my paper? To vote to discontinue funding of UFO research? To stop making unsubstantiated claims?

Audience-Based Questions

Audience-based questions enable you to concentrate on your readers' expectations about the subject matter, on the ways they might respond to your assertions, and on how you might counter-respond to their reactions. Here are some examples of audience-based questions:

1. Who are the readers I'd like to reach? Those who will support funding of future research on UFOs? Those who are writing the UFO reports to show them their bias?
2. What is my audience's opinion on the authenticity of UFOs? How strongly is that opinion held?
3. What kinds of sources are best suited to my audience? If uninformed, they need background information provided. If hostile, they need to be convinced that I understand their position fully and fairly.
4. What are my audience's main sources of information about UFOs? How reliable are these sources?
5. Exactly how does my audience benefit from reading this essay?

Writer-Based Questions

Writer-based questions enable you to concentrate on your existing knowledge in and understanding of the subject matter and on whether you need to gather more information on it. Here are some examples of writer-based questions:

1. Why is it so important to spend time considering this anti-UFO stance?
2. Do I actually feel strongly one way or another on this issue?
3. How much do I already know about UFO reports?

Subject-Based Questions

Subject-based questions focus on the factual content of your topic. Facts are universally verifiable; that is, they can be tested or verified by anyone. They must be distinguished from interpretations, judgments, or conclusions, which are subjective responses *derived* from your analysis of the facts. Here are some examples of subject-based questions:

1. Do existing UFO reports share common elements? Do these elements reinforce authenticity or fraud?

2. What are the *scientific* data for the claims in the most notable UFO reports? How do I know those scientific data are authentic and reliable?

3. What do I need to research to discuss or refute the claims presented by the UFO reports?

4. Do I carefully consider potential challenges to my views and the best way to interpret their validity?

You can see how the answers to questions in these four areas will affect the text, from its content to its organization to its tone.

Formulating a Strong Thesis

You already know what a thesis is: It is the main point you wish to argue, the claim you are making and are trying to persuade your audience to accept, using the strongest evidence you can find. However, you may like to gain more skill in coming up with a strong, compelling thesis for your argumentative essays. Here are three steps you can take to ensure that the thesis you come up with is a good one:

1. Write down an assertion (viewpoint, claim) on a particular topic. For example, if your topic is music censorship, you might write down, "Music censorship is wrong."

2. Ask probing questions about the clarity and specificity of your assertion, making sure that you replace vague or ambiguous language with specific, precise language. If the above statement about music censorship appeared as a thesis statement, readers would have some of the following questions:

   • What is meant by *wrong?* Unethical? Illegal? Misguided?

   • What is meant by *music?* The music itself or the lyrics to songs? If songs, then what kinds of songs? Country-western? Rap? Rock? Jazz? Rhythm and blues? Hip-hop? What about the songs do some people find objectionable? Swear words? Obscenity? Political references? Actions seemingly advocated by the lyrics?

- What is meant by *censorship?* Bleeping certain words or phrases of certain songs? Restricting sales only to those of a certain age? Banning the music altogether?

3. Turn your assertion into a well-focused, specifically worded thesis statement. For example, "Expurgating or banning rap songs because of their alleged profanity or obscenity is against the law because it violates rights guaranteed by the First Amendment."

By taking the time to examine your trial thesis statement from the point of view of its clarity and specificity, you produce effective thesis statements that in turn help you to produce more effective arguments.

EXERCISE 7.2

1. Generate three questions for each of the four elements of the rhetorical rhombus (purpose, audience, writer, subject) for an essay you have recently finished or one on which you are currently working.

2. Imagine that you are writing a paper that argues for the best ways of dealing with sexual harassment on college campuses. Generate questions in each of these categories: purpose-based, audience-based, writer-based, subject-based.

3. Revise each of the following assertions so that they can serve as strong thesis statements:

   a. Water quality needs to be improved.

   b. Males are the dominant sex because they are stronger.

   c. The university should offer more courses in ethnic studies.

Researching Using the Internet

A late-twentieth-century invention, the Internet, has evolved over the last two decades to become the most revolutionary information resource since printing was invented more than half a millennium ago. Its dramatic proliferation brings problems, however, as well as benefits. Some sources on the Net are superficial, irrelevant, or unreliable. Usually, you know right away what is junk and what isn't—but sometimes it is not so easy.

You need to acquire an eye for distinguishing between articles that are substantive and relevant and those that are not. Here are a few questions to ask about Internet articles to help you make that distinction:

1. Are the authors experts in their fields? If no biographical information about the authors is included at the site, check the library or search the web to see whether these credentials are located elsewhere.

2. Do the authors go beyond mere generalized assertions to produce useful, new knowledge about the subject? For example, if you find an article that argues either for or against the use of exit tests as a condition for high school graduation, does the author back up those assertions with actual data comparing the performance of students who have prepared for such a test with that of those who have not?

3. Do the authors provide a scholarly context for their arguments? That is, do they relate their points of view to others who have also conducted scholarly inquiry into the subject?

4. Is the subject matter treated seriously and professionally? Be wary of an amateurish tone. For example, in debates over controversial issues such as whether the state should require creationist doctrine to be given equal standing with evolutionary theory in a high school biology class, one side might easily caricature the other side as "religious fanatics" or "radical atheists." Such pigeonholing or name-calling works against the very purpose of argument, which is to examine both sides of an issue critically, carefully, and responsibly to arrive at a reasonable understanding of what really is or should be. When in doubt, weigh the tone and treatment of a questionable document with documents you know are authentic and significant.

Another criterion to consider is website domains. The .edu and .gov domains are likely to be the most reliable, although you need to be alert for the possibility that .edu articles may be the work of first-year students.

Useful Types of Internet Resources

The most useful types of information resources available on the Internet include resource guides; listservers; government information sites; encyclopedias, newspapers and magazines (many of which appear in both digital and print formats); discussion forums (sometimes referred to as bulletin boards or newsgroups), databases, and online forums.

Internet Resource Guide

A good first step for conducting Internet-based research is to consult a resource guide. The Internet Resource Guide (www.infoplease.com), for example, provides a menu of websites in the areas of Arts & Literature (such as the Library of Congress and World Wide Arts Resources); Business and Investing (such as the Better Business Bureau, the New York Stock Exchange, and the Securities and Exchange Commission); Education (such as the U.S. News Online Education Page and Family Education.com); and Entertainment (such as the All Music Guide and Entertainment Weekly Online). The U.S. government is another vast information resource; every branch of government, every government agency, has its own website. To mention just a few: the White House, the departments of Housing and Urban Development, the Central Intelligence Agency (CIA), the Environmental Protection Agency (EPA), the U.S. Commission on Civil Rights, and the: U.S. Department of Health and Human Services (HHS). These websites will, in turn, provide you with more specific links that will prove useful to you as you delve into the particulars of your research subject.

Listservers

A listserver (more commonly referred to as a *listserv*) is a discussion group subscription service in which commentary and information about a given topic are exchanged with all members of the group who are all connected by email. Listserv members often participate in ongoing conversations or debates over key issues. When a great many experts and enthusiasts from all over the world argue heatedly on a given topic, a wealth of information and viewpoints is generated. For this reason, participation in such discussion groups can be an excellent way of staying informed and developing your argumentative skills at the same time.

Newsgroups

Newsgroups (also usenets or bulletin boards) are topic-based electronic discussion groups that anyone can join. Members with an interest in, say, art history can access useful information that is arranged by subtopic and posted by other members. If you are interested in Italian Renaissance art, for example, you quite likely could find, on a homepage menu, a newsgroup devoted to that area. Many of these newsgroups archive their postings, which become valuable for research.

Newspapers, Magazines, Encyclopedias

The Internet revolution has resulted in a precipitous decline of print media, especially newspapers. However, many newspapers have adapted to the change by publishing online versions; some have even gone entirely online. Some of this material may be accessed free, but for the most part, readers must pay for subscriptions just as they would for the print versions. Keep in mind, too, that newspapers often will include more content in their online editions than in their print editions—for example, additional articles or forums for reader-response. Grammar handbooks and encyclopedias, most notably the publicly edited Wikipedia, are also published online these days.

Databases

Databases are invaluable compilations of sources in a given subject, such as a compilation of books and articles on health care, biochemistry, ancient Egyptian history, economics, or any other subject. Although many databases are accessed online, some of them, like the *Modern Language Association (MLA) International Bibliography of Language and Literature*, the *Readers Guide to Periodical Literature*, and the *Congressional Record Index* continue to be published in hard copy. See the reference librarian at your college library when uncertain about locating a particular database for your research project.

Your college library most likely subscribes to a database company that packages electronic bibliographies. The most popular is InfoTrac, which may include newspaper bibliographies (such as those for the *Wall Street Journal*, the *New York Times*, and newspapers from your local area) as well as general reference articles across the disciplines. Your librarian will be happy to inform you of the databases to which the library subscribes and may provide you with handouts describing each kind.

The catalogs of most academic and research libraries are available online. The Library of Congress's catalog is also available and contains more than twelve million items. The Library of Congress also has accessible special collections, such as the National Agricultural Library and the National Library of Medicine. Access any of the Library of Congress's catalogs at www.loc.gov.

Social Networking Sites I: Forums

A forum is an ongoing discussion group in real time. Forums exist for just about any subject matter and professional interest imaginable. Such forums can be an excellent way of finding highly knowledgeable people and learning from them, while enjoying interactive conversations with people all across the country or even the world. Be careful, however. The knowledge base of participants varies in these discussions, and some participants may purposefully or inadvertently give out misleading information. For example, the travel site TripAdvisor provides curated information about locations, such as brief travel guides, flight information, things to do, and rentals. On its site for each location is a Forum link on which any site viewer can post questions or read what other people have said about businesses and tourist destinations for a particular site, and TripAdvisor assigns some of the most frequent and reliable posters as "destination experts."

Social Networking Sites II: Blogs (Web Logs)

Blogging is a kind of opinion-oriented journalism in which you respond to issues as they're unfolding or respond to them on your own website or the websites of others and in which anyone else can do the same. Perhaps you have seen opportunities to respond to the thoughts of others when you have been reading newspaper columns or stories online. You may yourself have kept a blog as you traveled or worked to keep family and friends up to date on what you are doing.

If you consult blogs as research for any of your written arguments, however, you must read them through a critical lens. For example, "Shuggy," a forty-three-year-old educator in Glasgow, Scotland, chooses to air his opinions about politics and history, among other topics, and quite unashamedly lists as one of his interests "inflicting my insane thoughts on unsuspecting people via the blogosphere." Although Shuggy may be articulate and entertaining, no one has responded to him, and his ideas do not differ much from any layperson's.

Of course, the presence of responses alone does not guarantee accuracy of information. Although http://blog.createdebate.com encourages individuals to post issues that will engage others in conversation, one can see that not everyone posts useful statements that help to engage in formal argument. One extended blog that writers of arguments may wish to look at concerns a graphic that someone created to illustrate Paul Graham's article "How to Disagree" (http://blog. createdebate.com/2008/04/07/writing-strong-arguments).

Some blogs, though, may be quite informative. For example, one spot was created for law faculty: www.lawprofessorblogs.com. At this site, browsers can read what law professors from institutions such as Willamette have to say about environmental law. There one might see embedded photographs and links to pertinent YouTube videos, such as on the Legal Writing blog page, which has videos posted relating the history of the Legal Writing Institute. See their website, http://lawprofessors.typepad.com/legalwriting, which includes an interview with some of the pioneers in teaching legal writing.

When using information from a blog, be sure to check the source's credentials, not just to use the biographical notes for your introductory comments but also to ensure that the source is credible. Remember to credit the source on your Works Cited page.

Social Networking Sites III: Facebook, Pinterest, Twitter, LinkedIn, Instagram

According to Jonathan Zimmerman ("Hooked on Facebook," see pages 487–488), 50 to 75 percent of American teenagers have profiled themselves on one of the Internet sites dedicated to social networking, of which Facebook and YouTube are the most popular. Such sites can be useful to researchers for several reasons. For example, on Facebook one can find a site for Fulbright alumni, and its page sometimes lists what grants are available so people can tell their friends. Similar information might also be found on the official Fulbright page; however, people sometimes ask questions about fellow alumni to find contacts in another part of the world they're moving to. Sometimes people on Facebook seek to give information on a topic, such as SaxStation (www.facebook.com/saxstation), which provides a discussion area for how to improve one's ability to play the saxophone.

Another popular social networking site is Pinterest. Like Facebook, it enables online sharing; but Pinterest is better suited for bringing together things that you find on the Internet—a kind of online scrapbooking.

The rapidly growing use of smartphones for composing messages gave rise to Twitter, a social networking site that allows short (140 characters, maximum) messages that can be sent out to a wide network of followers simultaneously. Although some celebrities or friends might use Twitter just to update followers on their latest meals or parties, some professionals address serious issues in their tweets, whether current events or sharing professional accomplishments or re-tweeting others' remarks about professional issues.

For those who wish to interact in a work-related context, there is LinkedIn. If you land a job in any professional field, be it health care, investment consulting, engineering, teaching, or law, you will be able to connect with others who are engaged in similar activities. If you choose to become a member of certain groups, such as an alumni association or a special-interest forum like GrammarGirl, you and other members of the group can post links to articles in response to topics such as links to articles about gender-neutral pronouns on GrammarGirl or to articles about the evolution of creativity in universities on Higher Education Teaching and Learning.

If you follow an individual (even someone you don't know personally), then the person gives you links to what that person may be thinking about. When you log in to your LinkedIn account, the site suggests certain links based on what you may have been clicking on lately.

A relatively new, highly regarded social networking site is Instagram, where one can easily share an experience (coupled with photos and videos) with friends, family, and colleagues as it unfolds. These "to the moment" experiences can then be posted on Facebook and elsewhere.

Social Networking Sites IV: YouTube and Tumblr

According to their fact sheet, YouTube "is the world's most popular online video community, allowing millions of people to discover, watch and share originally-crafted videos" (www.youtube.com/t/about). Through YouTube, it is possible to locate videos relating to current events or hobbies and to watch scenes from a favorite television show. It is possible to insert a YouTube video into a social networking site, such as Facebook.

You may not be surprised to learn that politicians use YouTube. One politician running for office in 2010, for example, posted a video to his blog on the minimum wage, and numerous individuals posted text responses to his comments. You can find current positions on political topics such as the minimum wage not just by politicians but by sources like PBS Newsletter and university professors by putting the term in the search box of YouTube.

Those doing research on YouTube may wish to access Ted Talks <www.Ted.com>—texts of oral presentations (with accompanying videos) presented by experts on nearly two thousand topics. Here are just five examples:

- "The Career Advice You Probably Didn't Get," by Susan Golantuono, a leadership expert (September 2014)

- "How Schools Kill Creativity," by Ken Robinson, an author, educator, and creativity expert (June 2006)

- "The Workforce Crisis of 2030, and How to Start Solving It Now," by Ranier Strack, a human resources expert (October 2014)

- "Connected, but Alone?" by Sherry Turkle, a professor of social studies of science and technology at MIT (February 2012)

- "Hidden Cameras That Film Injustice in the World's Most Dangerous Places," by Oren Yakobovich, a human rights activist (October 2014)

YouTube also hosts a National Geographic channel, on which students can find topics on timely issues relating to society, archaeology, and exploration in the natural sciences.

Another popular YouTube channel is Lonely Planet, where students can learn more about cultural issues in different parts of the world. Of course, National Geographic and Lonely Planet can be accessed directly.

Tumblr is a Yahoo-owned blogging site where anyone can post music, texts, photographs, and videos on just about any topic. A good place to begin exploring the resources of this visually intensive social media site is www.tumblr .com/staffpicks with blog posts arranged in categories (Contemporary Art, Climate Change, etc.).

Students of argument may find YouTube and Tumblr useful for posting essays with visual content, or PowerPoint presentations. One student, for example, prepared a photographic essay on how habits of perception differ between males and females.

Twitter

Twitter, according to their fact sheet at http://twitter.com, "is a real-time short messaging service that works over multiple networks and devices." Once you sign up, you can send minimessages ("tweets") of no more than 140 characters (including spaces) to anyone anywhere. It is the most prevalent form of instant messaging today. People tweet from war zones to major news networks and from friend to friend anywhere in the world. Because of the brevity of these messages, tweets may help a person be aware of an issue but may not provide the sort of in-depth analysis or explanation or argument that writers will find useful to include as support of their own arguments.

Using Images in Your Web-Published Documents

Unlike an academic paper you submit as a course assignment, a document you post online is considered a publication (remember that the root meaning of "publish" is *to make public*); therefore, you must obtain permission to use an image from the copyright holder of that image. To obtain permission, contact the person or organization that produced the image (usually indicated in a source line or footnote). Describe your planned online publication in detail and include a clear reason why you are publishing it. If you receive permission, make sure that you include the sentence "Used by permission" after citing the source. Creative Commons provides visuals individuals can use with attribution, but without worry of copyright infringement. Also, if you're researching a topic using Google's search engine, click on the images button at the top of the menu that comes up; then click on the "Search Tools" button; then click on "Usage Rights" to find images that are labeled for noncommercial use. Remember that you always must provide attribution, whether the image or text in question is under copyright protection or not.

Searching on the Web

Searching for information on the web is easy—almost too easy. All you do is click on a search engine icon at your Internet service provider's homepage or enter a web address for one of the many existing search engines.

Reliable Search Engines

Some search engines are more powerful than others, however. Among the most reliable are Google, WebCrawler, Yahoo!, AltaVista, Dogpile, *Ask*, and Lycos. Here are their URL (uniform resource locator) addresses:

www.google.com

www.webcrawler.com

www.yahoo.com

www.dogpile.com

www.ask.com

www.lycos.com

http://en.wikipedia.org/wiki/Main-Page

http://scholar.google.com

www.metacrawler.com

www.hotbot.com

Every search engine is different. Some, like AltaVista and Dogpile, include brief descriptions of every site called up.

The next step is to type key words in the narrow blank rectangle provided—and here things can get a little tricky. You need to decide which three or four words come closest to the sort of information you hope to find. Use the most "official" terms you know for your subject. If you are looking for general pro–con arguments on school vouchers, for example, you might enter the key words *school, voucher,* and *programs.* If you want to find material on vouchers relating to your state, enter the name of your state in the key word field as well. If you wish to focus on specific concerns within the voucher system, you may need to enter an additional relevant key word such as *curriculum, class size,* or *teaching excellence.*

Search engines usually retrieve far more sites than you can review in a reasonable time, so you have to be selective. If you're looking for substantive, scholarly commentary, look for sites from academic institutions. (You can recognize these sites by their URL extension, *.edu.*) Or look for online magazines, or *e-zines,* as they are sometimes called.

Google has a time-saving search option, an "I'm feeling lucky" button that, when clicked on, brings up far fewer hits, but those hits are likely the most relevant to the key words you have entered.

Another problem to be aware of when searching for relevant sites is timeliness. If you require the latest information, be sure to check the dates of the sites you bring up. Some of them may be several years old.

Using Boolean Search Strategies

A Boolean search is one in which you customize your search key words using what are called *operators.* The three most common Boolean operators are

AND –

NOT –

OR –

Let's say you are searching the Expanded Academic Index (an international general database for source materials in the humanities and in social and general sciences) for articles on logging policies OR logging practices but NOT articles having to do with the history of logging. Instead of merely entering the key word *logging,* you can use the Boolean operators AND and NOT to restrict your search as follows:

```
Logging policies and practices not histories
```

Another device useful in searches is the asterisk (*), which works as a wildcard: It instructs the search engine to bring up all forms of the word attached to the word segment typed in before the asterisk. Thus, if you're looking for information about cosmology and want to bring up articles with all forms of the word *cosmology* at once instead of searching for each one separately, you would simply type in *cosm**. The search engine would then bring up database articles containing all the words bearing that segment, for example:

cosmic

cosmological

cosmologist

cosmologists

cosmology

cosmos

Of course, you would also get a lot of unwanted entries relating to words that begin with the segment *cosm* but that have nothing to do with the nature of the universe:

cosmetic

cosmetics

cosmetologist

cosmetologists

cosmetology

Useful Websites for Writers of Arguments

The list that follows gives some useful web addresses for your research. Note, however, that websites often disappear, are updated, or change their addresses. Consider using a current *Internet Yellow Pages* (available in most bookstores and libraries) to locate sources.

For Humanities Resources
   http://vos.ucsb.edu/

For Statistics from the U.S. Department of Education
   http://nces.ed.gov/pubsearch/

For Resources in Religious Studies
   www.bu.edu/sthlibrary/index.html

For Information about World History
   www.hartford-hwp.com/archives

For Health-Related Information from the Centers for Disease Control
   www.cdc.gov/

For Information about Population from the U.S. Census Bureau
   www.census.gov/

For Information about Public Policy Issues

Media Websites

www.cnn.com/	The website of the Cable News Network
www.pbs.org/	The website of the Public Broadcasting Service (educational television programming)
www.npr.org/	The website of National Public Radio
www.nytimes.com	The website of the *New York Times*
www.nytimes.com/pages/ readersopinions/index.html	This website takes you to the *New York Times* forums, where you can read numerous postings on dozens of subjects by forum members. By subscribing for free, you can post your own views and responses to the postings of others.

Finally, there are websites to help you find information on the Internet as well as to think critically about available resources:

A Tutorial for Finding Information Online
www.lib.berkeley.edu/TeachingLib/Guides/Internet/FindInfo.html
This site introduces you to the basics of web searching.

Guidelines for Evaluating Websites
www.tucolib.info/
A bibliography of online resources for evaluating websites.

EXERCISE 7.3

1. Compare the effectiveness of two different search engines, such as Yahoo!, Dogpile, or Google. Write out a description of their respective strengths and weaknesses.

2. Enter an online forum such as Salon.com on a topic that interests you and report your experience orally or in an essay. What did you learn about your topic as a result of interacting with other members of the forum?

3. Compile a list of blogs that have served as sources of information for one of your research topics. Which one of these blogs has been most useful, and why?

Researching Using Print Resources

Without doubt, the Internet is a helpful, high-speed information-accessing tool, and its resources are expanding continuously. But hard-copy resources—reference books, trade books, periodicals (specialized and nonspecialized), historical documents, maps, and newspapers—continue to be indispensable. Much if not most academic scholarship continues to be published in traditional print journals, for example. Scholars often find "hard copy" easier to consult.

Locating Articles

To locate important article sources, begin with the Expanded Academic Index in your library's electronic catalog. The listing will tell you whether your library carries the periodical containing the article. If not, you may be able to have your library obtain a fax of it for a nominal fee or obtain a book through interlibrary loan.

Other important print periodical indexes include:

Applied Sciences Index

Education Index

Environmental Index

General Science Index

Humanities Index

National Newspaper Index

Social Sciences Index

Using Additional Print Reference Works

In addition to periodical indexes, you may already be familiar with the following hard-copy reference works: encyclopedias (general and specialized), dictionaries, abstracts and digests, handbooks and sourcebooks, and atlases.

Encyclopedias   General or subject-specific encyclopedias are often a good place to begin your formal research because they offer a panoramic view of the topic with which you are working and provide references for further reading. An encyclopedia article is essentially a detailed summary of the most important facts about a topic, accompanied by a bibliography. You probably have used general encyclopedias that cover the whole spectrum of knowledge. You may not have used specialized encyclopedias, which are limited to only one subject, such as psychology or religion.

Here is just a small sampling of the kinds of encyclopedias you will find in your library's reference room:

General	Subject-Specific
Collier's Encyclopedia	*Encyclopedia of Environmental Studies*
The Columbia Encyclopedia	*Encyclopedia of Psychoactive Drugs*
Encyclopedia Britannica	*Macmillan Encyclopedia of Computers*
World Book Encyclopedia	*The Wellness Encyclopedia*

Dictionaries   A dictionary provides more than highly concise definitions and explanations; in the case of biographical dictionaries, for example, you will find profiles of notable individuals. Most dictionaries are devoted to words in general, but there are specialized dictionaries as well. Important dictionaries include:

American Biographical Dictionary

A Dictionary of Biology

McGraw-Hill Dictionary of Scientific and Technical Terms

The Merriam-Webster Book of Word Histories

New Dictionary of American Slang

The Oxford English Dictionary

Who's Who

Who's Who Among African Americans

Who's Who Among America's Teachers

Who's Who Among Asian Americans

Who's Who Among Hispanic Americans

Who's Who in American History

Abstracts and Digests   An abstract is a formal summary of a scholarly or scientific paper. Virtually all disciplines publish compilations of abstracts. Digests are summaries of less formal works such as book *reviews*. Here is a sampling of abstracts and digests:

Book Review Digest

Chemical Abstracts

Dissertation Abstracts

Ecology Abstracts

Handbooks and Sourcebooks   These types of reference books provide you with guidelines and references for particular disciplines, such as English literature, philosophy, geology, economics, mathematics, and computer science. Some handbooks and sourcebooks are:

> *A Field Guide to Rocks and Minerals* (similar field guides exist for most subjects in the general sciences)
>
> *A Handbook to Literature*
>
> *Opposing Viewpoints* (collections of pro–con position statements on a wide range of topics)

Atlases   Atlases are collections of maps (of countries, states, cities, the world) and may be historical, topographical (depicting landmasses of different elevations), or geographical (depicting regions in terms of population, natural resources, industries, and the like).

EXERCISE 7.4

1. At your library, consult *Opposing Viewpoints* (see listing under "Handbooks and Sourcebooks") and write a brief summary of each side of a particular topic that you find interesting. Decide which side is argued most convincingly and explain why.

2. Look up a single item in three different encyclopedias or dictionaries. Describe how the coverage differs from source to source.

3. Using *Book Review Digest* (see listing under "Abstracts and Digests"), locate three different reviews of a single book and write a comparative evaluation of the three reviews. Which reviewer provides the most useful information about the book's subject matter? About the author?

Gathering Information from Email, Telephone Conversations, Interviews, and Surveys

As a college student, you are part of a complex community of educators, researchers, and specialists in numerous disciplines. Name your topic, and someone on your college faculty, staff, or student body will be an expert in it. But how do you contact these individuals? Very simply: by email or telephone.

Using Email or Telephone

Obtain a campus phone directory listing faculty and staff and their respective departments or offices; there you will see each person's telephone extension number and email address, along with his or her office location. You can also check your school's website to find what specialties are listed for faculty members or to learn where the various offices and departments are on campus so that you can visit them to find out who is an expert in what. Next, email or phone that person, explain who you are and what you are researching, and ask to set up a time convenient for a telephone interview or a personal interview. If the information you require is relatively complex or the person in question is too busy to be interviewed, request an email exchange.

Conducting an Interview

An interview is a focused, carefully directed conversation on a predetermined topic, usually involving the interviewee's personal involvement in the topic being discussed. Interviews can be formal or informal, depending on the nature of the topic and the relationship between interviewer and interviewee.

Information derived from interviews is valuable for two reasons:

1. It is timely (you may be getting "cutting-edge" information before it is published).

2. It provides the opportunity for obtaining personal insights into the subject matter.

Experts can also be extremely helpful in directing you to additional sources and thinking about other aspects of the topic of which you may not be aware.

When conducting the interview, keep the following suggestions in mind:

1. Always make an appointment with the person you wish to interview and be clear about what you wish to discuss and why.

2. Prepare questions to ask during the interview, but don't use them rigidly or present them in rote fashion as in an interrogation. Rather, try to work them spontaneously into your discussion. Ask specific, well-focused questions about what you need to know.

3. It is all right to engage in "ice-breaking" small talk, but once the discussion begins try not to go off on tangents. Remember: You are there to interview the individual, not to have a casual conversation, so listen more than you talk.

4. Be alert for "spinoff" questions—unanticipated questions that occur to you in light of the way the interviewee answers a previous question. Be sure, however, that spinoff questions are relevant to the topic.

5. Avoid leading questions, whereby your manner of wording the questions reveals a bias on your part. For example, a leading question would be "Wouldn't you agree that the dangers from ozone depletion are highly exaggerated?" You want more than a *yes* or *no* response anyway.

6. Always ask for clarification of a complex idea or for definition of an unfamiliar term. Also, ask for the correct spelling of names or terms you are uncertain about.

7. If you wish to record the interview on tape, request permission to do so beforehand. But don't expect to transcribe it all. You will use the tape just to capture precise wording of an elegant or particularly apt phrase, just as when you quote a written source directly.

8. Ask the interviewee for permission to contact him or her for follow-up questions after the interview or perhaps suggest a follow-up interview.

9. Write a thank-you note to the interviewee after the interview; acknowledge that the individual is a busy person who set aside time for you. Such common courtesy is justified and appropriate. It also makes it more likely that the individual will respond if you need any follow-up help.

Conducting a Survey

To obtain information from a large number of individuals, you can conduct a survey. The first step is to prepare a questionnaire—a set of questions with room on the sheet for answers—to distribute to individuals. These questions should be carefully worded so that (1) the respondents can answer them quickly and (2) the survey will yield valid and useful information for your purposes.

The second step is to conduct the survey. This may be done via email, using a distribution list so it could be sent, for example, to the entire student body at once, or via personal distribution, where you simply question individuals directly or ask them to fill out your questionnaire while you wait. Also, it would be a good idea to check with your school's Human Subjects Board or Computer Center about any policies governing such actions.

Designing a Questionnaire

A good questionnaire is a model of relevance, clarity, and concision. Word questions carefully, making sure that binary (for example, *yes* or *no*) questions do not stem from a false dichotomy (that is, where answers other than *yes* or *no* are possible). Also, do not word questions that are leading or that conceal a bias. The following is an example of a biased question:

What percentage of old-growth forest should be logged?

_____ 10% _____ 50% _____ 75% _____ 85% _____100%

This set of options is biased because (1) there is no 0% (the opposite equivalent of 100%), and (2) there is only one option below 50% but two options above 50%.

The following is an example of a leading question:

Do you agree that the sexist practices of the labor union should be stopped?

_____ Yes _____ No _____ Not Sure

Sexist is judgmental and therefore risks leading the respondent to agree with that judgment. The question should describe actual documented actions that may or may not be judged as sexist, such as "Should the labor union continue to deny membership to women?"

It is usually a good idea to avoid questions that readers would not be sure how to answer or that would require long answers. Instead, choose questions that ask respondents to choose among the options you provide:

Which of the following long-term space exploration policies should NASA adopt? (Check all that apply.)

_____ Lunar colonization

_____ Robot probes of outer planets

_____ Human exploration of Mars

_____ Lunar-orbiting telescope

Finally, introduce your questionnaire in a brief, courteous paragraph that includes your name, the purpose of your research, and how much time you estimate it will take to answer the questions. Thank your readers in advance for their time.

Taking Effective Research Notes

The notes you take while reading outside sources for your argument-in-progress will come in handy when you decide which sources you need to integrate into the body of your paper. (See also "Incorporating Outside Sources into Your Argument" on pages 270–273.) The following suggestions will make your note taking more efficient and productive:

1. Unless you have a laptop computer to take with you into the library, or unless you work at a computer provided by your school library or public library, use index cards for taking notes (4" × 6" size is ideal): You can easily shuffle and rearrange them, as well as annotate them. Some students find that it helps to use differently colored cards for different purposes, that is, white for direct quotations, yellow for bibliography, green for the writer's own ideas. Photocopying articles and passages from books is another option, but photocopying can get expensive and

can take as much time as writing out notes. Also, photocopied pages are harder to sort through and review.

2. Write out the complete bibliographic citation for every source you use; that way, you will be able to locate the source again easily if you need to and will be able to prepare your Works Cited page more quickly. Guidelines for citing sources appear in Chapter 8, "Documenting Your Sources: MLA and APA Styles."

3. Read each source straight through to get an idea of all that it includes. Then return to the beginning and copy passages that seem most useful for your needs. Always double-check to make sure you are copying the passage accurately. If you need to omit part of a passage, indicate the omission with ellipsis dots (…). If you need to add a word or date to make a quoted passage understandable or coherent, place it in brackets:

According to the *Cedarville Gazette*, "Last year [2003], local automobile-related fatalities numbered more than 1,500."

The Role of Serendipity in Research

Writers benefit greatly from methodical research, but not all researching is methodical. Some of it results from good fortune, or a special kind of good fortune called *serendipity*.

Serendipity refers to the capacity for discovering important things in an unexpected manner or in an unexpected place. Serendipity seems most likely to occur when you are immersed in your work. Because your senses are on full alert, you pick up things you might not have otherwise noticed or make connections between two ideas that you would never have made in a less engaged state of mind.

Two students described the following serendipitous discoveries:

Student 1

> While I was working on my paper on unfair hiring practices, I happened to notice a news story on the Internet that described how frustrating it is to follow user manuals because their instructions are seldom clear enough. That made a light flash inside my head! Perhaps hiring practices are often unfair because the policies describing them are poorly written!

Student 2

> Here I was stumped about how to develop my topic on the way students can study effectively in groups. While I was eating lunch, I overheard two students discussing getting together

with their Western Civilization study group to prepare for a midterm. I introduced myself and asked them if they would tell me about how they formed their group, how beneficial they thought it was, and what sorts of pitfalls to avoid.

These examples illustrate the way in which mental alertness and engagement can help you discover new approaches to your topic in unexpected ways.

EXERCISE 7.5

1. Over the next four or five days, in addition to using methods of methodical researching, do the following:

   a. Browse for half an hour or so among the library stacks, in subject areas relevant to the topic you are working on.

   b. Listen closely for connections, however seemingly tangential, while talking with classmates or friends.

   c. Find some encyclopedia articles related to the topic you are working on and write down any ideas that might be worth incorporating into your essay.

   d. Review your lecture notes from other classes.

2. Report on any serendipitous discoveries that you were able to use for your paper. Compare your serendipity experiences with those of your classmates. If you hear of one you have not experienced, try to experience it for yourself.

Evaluating Your Sources

It is tempting to assume that just because information is published it is reliable. But that is not the case, unfortunately, so you need to ensure that the sources you incorporate into your argument are trustworthy. Evaluate every outside source you incorporate into your paper using these five criteria:

1. *Accuracy* of information presented

2. *Relevance* to your thesis

3. *Reliability* of the author and the periodical that originally published the material

4. *Clarity*

5. *Thoroughness*

The sections that follow consider each criterion in turn.

Accuracy

Factual information needs to be checked for accuracy. Data, such as population trends, the latest nutritional information about a dietary supplement, academic program policies and offerings, and so on, sometimes change so frequently that the print source at your fingertips may not be the most recent information. Carefully check dates of publication, check with the campus specialist, or search the Internet for more current information.

Relevance

Does the information you plan to use in your argument truly contribute to your thesis? If you are writing about the importance of animals in medical research but use information drawn from the use of animals in cosmetic research, there may be a problem with relevance unless you can draw a medical connection to cosmetic use (for example, certain dyes in mascara can cause an allergic reaction).

Reliability

When considering the reliability of information, think about the credentials of the author presenting it. For example, if an author is conveying information about the toxins in local ground water, that person should be a recognized authority in environmental chemistry, not just a local politician.

Clarity

Important data are sometimes presented in a way that is difficult to understand. In such cases, you may need to *paraphrase* the source material instead of quoting it directly or to quote it directly but add your own explanation afterward. Technical information, while clear to you, might be confusing to nonspecialist readers. In such cases, you may need to provide a somewhat elaborate interpretation of the data.

Thoroughness

It is important to ensure that your data are not perfunctory bits of quotations or statistics that fail to provide sufficient grounding for your claim. The more debatable your claims, the more important it is to provide sufficient data to remove any doubts from readers' minds.

Understanding and Avoiding Plagiarism

From the Latin word for "kidnapper," *plagiarism* refers to two connected acts:

1. Using someone else's work, *published* or *unpublished*, as if it were your own

2. Incorporating someone else's words or *ideas* into your own writing without explicit acknowledgment of authorship or source

You are most likely aware of the seriousness of plagiarism. Quite simply, it is a crime. People's ideas and ways of expressing them are a form of property—intellectual property—and are as worthy of protection from theft as material property. Thus, when a person plagiarizes, he or she is stealing.

Use the following guidelines to determine what kind of material should be acknowledged and what need not be:

1. Paraphrases of someone else's ideas must be acknowledged (that is, cited). Even though you are putting a passage into your own words, you are nonetheless using another's ideas. Consider this original passage and the paraphrase that follows.

   Original passage: "It is too soon to know with certainty if melting polar ice taking place right now will result in coastal flooding within the next five years" (climatologist Gail Jones).

   Plagiarized paraphrase: Will the melting polar ice currently taking place lead to coastal flooding within five years? It is too early to tell.

The author of the paraphrase gives no indication that the information conveyed was taken from the article by Gail Jones. Yes, it's possible that the author simply forgot to cite the source (sometimes referred to as *accidental plagiarism*)—but it is still full-fledged plagiarism. It is every author's responsibility to remember, and properly acknowledge, all sources. The above paraphrase must be revised accordingly. For example:

   Acceptable paraphrase: Could the melting polar ice currently taking place, climatologist Gail Jones wonders, lead to coastal flooding within five years? According to Jones, it is too early to tell.

By the way, you need also to be aware of *faulty paraphrasing*. When you recast someone else's ideas into your own words, you must be careful not to distort that original idea. Consider the following paraphrase of the Gail Jones passage:

   Faulty paraphrase: It is impossible to determine whether melting polar ice will result in coastal flooding in the near future.

This is a faulty paraphrase. Jones asserted that it was too soon to know with certainty, not that it was impossible. The paraphrase also fails to capture the fact that Jones referred to melting polar ice *that is currently taking place.*

2. Any information considered common knowledge does not require acknowledgment. Facts such as historical dates that are readily looked up in at least three different sources constitute common knowledge. The key word is *readily*. Some factual information is clearly the product of individual research and, as such, is not readily available.

3. When you need to quote verbatim (using the author's exact words), be mindful of these pointers:

a. Quote only what is necessary to convey the author's ideas. Too many or too lengthy quotations can make a paper difficult to read.

b. Do not rely on quoted material to carry your argument forward. This is a common pitfall of beginning writers. You want your paper to represent *your* way of thinking, not that of the experts you are quoting.

c. Besides quoting, *comment* on a quotation of one to two sentences or longer. Do not drop a quotation in if your reason for quoting someone else is not patently clear.

d. Use quotation marks around all material quoted verbatim. If the passage you are quoting runs more than four lines, place the passage, without quotation marks, in a separate paragraph, indented ten spaces from the main text.

EXERCISE 7.6

1. Label each of the following statements as common knowledge (not requiring acknowledgment) or not common knowledge (requiring acknowledgment):

   a. Some books should be savored slowly, others devoured ravenously.

   b. Like the 1995 flooding of the Rhine, the inundation of the upper Mississippi and Missouri Rivers in 1993 provided a dramatic and costly lesson on the effects of treating the natural flow of rivers as a pathological condition (Janet Abramovitz, *Imperiled Waters, Impoverished Future* 16).

   c. The Battle of Hastings took place in 1066 CE.

   d. Many educators these days tend to regard the Internet as a cure-all for getting students to read.

2. Choose any one of the arguments from Part 2, Reading Clusters, and evaluate in writing its evidence in terms of the five criteria: accuracy, relevance, reliability, clarity, and thoroughness.

3. Study the following passage and the paraphrases that follow. Determine which of the paraphrases (if any) are acceptable and which are unacceptable. If unacceptable, explain why (that is, faulty, plagiarized):

   The market forces of globalization are invading the Amazon, hastening the demise of the forest and thwarting its most committed stewards. In the past three decades, hundreds of people have died in land wars; countless others endure fear and uncertainty, their lives threatened by those who profit from the theft of timber and land.

   —Scott Wallace, "Last of the Amazon," *National Geographic*, Jan. 2007:43.

a. **Paraphrase A:** The forces of globalization are destroying the Amazon forests. In the past thirty years, hundreds of people have died in the land wars there; many others experience fear, their lives threatened by timber profiteers.

b. **Paraphrase B:** Worldwide market forces, notes Scott Wallace, are contributing to the rapid destruction of the Amazon forests. According to Wallace, land wars are endangering the lives of hundreds (*National Geographic* 43).

c. **Paraphrase C:** According to Scott Wallace, timber barons have all but destroyed the remaining Amazon forests and are murdering anyone who gets in their way (*National Geographic* 43).

Incorporating Outside Sources into Your Argument

The purpose of bringing outside sources into your argument is to add depth and authority to your own original insights. Make sure, then, when incorporating these sources into your paper, that you do not bury your thread of discussion, that your own voice prevails. You may be tempted to relinquish your voice to those of scholars who are recognized experts in their fields, but keep in mind that experts become so as a result of doing what you are beginning to do seriously as a writer: developing an original thesis so that other scholars will learn from you.

Notice, in the following passage, how the writer's voice becomes obscured by the voice of the authority she quotes:

> Academic integrity is taken seriously at Santa Clara University. "The University is committed to a pursuit of truth and knowledge that requires both personal honesty and intellectual integrity as fundamental to teaching, learning, scholarship, and service. Therefore, all members of the University community are expected to be honest in their academic endeavors, whether they are working independently or collaboratively, especially by distinguishing clearly between their own original work and ideas, and those of others, whether published or not" (*Undergraduate Bulletin*, 2003–05: 2). This should be a clear sign to students that academic integrity is part of the learning experience.

In that last sentence, the writer makes an important, original contribution to the conversation about academic integrity, but it is all but lost in the excessively long quotation that precedes it. It's as if the writer is saying to her audience, "Don't listen to me—I'm just a lowly student; listen to what the university administration says!" But that defeats the very reason for writing, which is to contribute new knowledge or new ways of thinking about old knowledge. Seeing her mistake, the student revised the passage as follows:

> Academic integrity at Santa Clara University is taken seriously, mainly because such integrity is part of the learning experience. That explains why the new SCU *Undergraduate Bulletin* for 2003–05 goes into elaborate detail about the issue. Administrators emphasize that the "pursuit of truth" to which the University is committed *"requires* [emphasis mine] both personal honesty and intellectual integrity" (2). In other words, you cannot truly become an educated person if you are unable or unwilling to make a clear, explicit distinction between what you know and what others know, between what you can contribute to an area of study and what others have contributed.

With this revision, the student asserts herself as a worthy contributor to the conversation on academic integrity. She has earned her stripes as an authority in her own right.

Also, all writing needs to "flow" for the points to unfold logically and smoothly for the reader. An important element in a smoothly developed argument is a clear link between each general point and the specific reference to outside sources. The writer's text should lead into the quoted material not just with a reference to who made the statement but also with the credentials of the source.

When you are incorporating others' ideas into your argument, you will want to lead into the borrowed material with signals that you are about to use a source to support your claim and that your source is a reliable one for your claim.

Finally, check to make sure that you have fully *synthesized* the material from outside sources with the new information that you have contributed. Synthesis occurs when you show that the outside (preexisting) information together with the new information that you bring to the discussion results in new understanding: $A + B = C$. Returning to our endangered Amazon forests example in Exercise 7.6, assume that the new information you want to bring into the discussion is your own sense of the global disaster that could arise if Amazon forests are depleted. That insight, combined with the factual information from Scott Wallace, might lead you to the following synthesis:

> Preserving the South American forests represent our planet's greatest hope for an environmentally sound future. If, through application of aggressive international policies, we can find a way to stop the destruction in the Amazon, we will have opened a new chapter in twenty-first-century forest stewardship that will prevent not one environmental disaster but many.

To quote or paraphrase? Generally, you should quote another's exact words when one of the following three reasons is true:

1. The precise phrasing is so elegant or apt that you wish to reproduce it intact.

2. You are going to focus on the wording itself (or some part of it).

3. You could not rephrase it without significantly changing the meaning or coming close to plagiarizing.

If none of those three reasons applies, you probably should paraphrase the source, remembering still to lead into the paraphrased material as you would a direct quotation and to provide appropriate documentation at the end of the paraphrase. Your readers should be able to tell precisely where another's ideas begin and end and where yours begin anew.

Consider the following passage:

> We may be a lot more creative than we realize. "Although we each have nearly limitless potential to live creatively, most people use only a small percentage of their creative gifts" (John Chaffee, *Critical Thinking, Thoughtful Writing*, 1st ed. 64). Therefore, we should work harder to cultivate these gifts.

Does it seem awkward or clunky to you? Can you tell what causes the awkwardness? Now read the following revision:

> We may be more creative than we realize. As John Chaffee points out in his book, *Critical Thinking, Thoughtful Writing*, "[M]ost people use only a small percentage of their creative gifts" (64). Taking the time to cultivate our creativity thus sounds like a wise investment.

This revised version makes the link between general comment and specific reference smoother and more coherent. Note that the writer trims back some of the original quotation, using only what is essential. The reader is thus able to process the information more efficiently.

Another important principle to keep in mind when you quote from outside sources is not to overquote. Use only that portion of a passage essential to making your point. Remember that you can leave out parts of a passage that seem irrelevant by using an ellipsis (…) to let readers know that words, phrases, or sentences are being omitted. Always make certain, however, that in choosing words to delete you do not distort the meaning of the original passage. In cases where you need to convey a lot of information from a source, consider combining direct quotation with paraphrase or simply rely entirely on paraphrase (making sure your paraphrase remains faithful to the essential point of the source).

EXERCISE 7.7

Examine the following passage to determine how well the writer has incorporated outside sources. Revise the passage where necessary to make it more coherent. In class, compare your revision with those of other students. You will need to consult the book being quoted to make your determination.

Libraries that receive public money should as a condition of funding be required to publish monthly lists of discards on their websites, "so that the public has some way of determining which of them are acting on behalf of their collections," recommends Nicholson Baker in his book about the way libraries have been destroying or selling off their hard-copy newspaper collections, *Double Fold: Libraries and the Assault on Paper* (New York: Random, 2001) 270. His other recommendations are that "The Library of Congress should lease or build a large building" in which to store any print materials they don't have room for; that several libraries around the country should work together to save the nation's newspapers in bound form; and that the N.E.H. should ban the current U.S. newspaper program in which newspapers are destroyed after they are microfilmed (270).

Chapter Summary

Argumentative writing often requires research, which is a dynamic, multitask process that involves searching for background information and integrating that information effectively into your paper. The research process can include many activities: searching databases to which your college library subscribes; using online search engines to search for material on the Internet; conducting surveys; interviewing specialists, such as the faculty and staff members in your university community; and using the many kinds of print sources (abstracts, atlases, bibliographies, books, government documents, indexes, and so on) available in your library. Most of your research activities should be planned and well-organized, but allow for serendipitous discovery—stumbling on unexpected sources as a result of being immersed in your planned research. By acquiring a thorough knowledge of their topics supported by careful research, writers argue their claims more authoritatively. Good research begins with taking a mental inventory and generating questions (writer-based, audience-based, subject-based, and purpose-based) about the topic that need answering. Purpose-based questions lead to formulating a strong thesis. A strong thesis, in turn, helps keep writers on track as they conduct research on the Internet, in the library, and with experts through well-prepared interviews.

Checklist

1. Do I take a thorough mental inventory of my topic?
2. Do I ask myself good purpose-, audience-, writer-, and subject-based questions about my topic?

3. Is my thesis strong and well-focused?

4. Do I analyze my Internet and print sources to make sure they meet the criteria for accuracy, relevance, reliability, clarity, and thoroughness?

5. Do I cite sources where necessary? Use proper documentation format?

6. Have I considered interviewing experts on campus or elsewhere about my topic?

7. Do I integrate researched information into my argument smoothly and clearly?

8. Do I check to ensure that I have paraphrased accurately?

9. Do I properly acknowledge the source of paraphrased as well as verbatim-quoted information?

10. Am I certain not to overlook acknowledging a source of outside information?

11. Have I considered using appropriate visual aids to strengthen my argument?

Writing Projects

1. Keep a detailed log of all your research-based activities for your upcoming writing assignment. Include idea generating, initial outlining, initial searches through various print and online reference works (list search engines used), and more methodical and focused research, interviews, and surveys. Describe your method of preparing the drafts—rough draft, first draft, and subsequent revisions.

2. Write a critical commentary on the usefulness of the Internet as a research tool. Comment on degrees of usefulness of various websites and different search engines, as well as the timeliness, reliability, and thoroughness of the information found in selected sites.

3. Write a comparative evaluation of print resources (as housed in your college library) versus Internet resources. Are both resources equally valuable? One more valuable than the other? Defend your assertions as fully as possible using specific examples.

4. Prepare a set of ten interview questions based on the topic you are currently researching or are planning to research. Next, search through your college's faculty directory or bulletin (usually available online if you do not have a print copy) to locate faculty or staff members who might serve as good interview subjects for your research.

8 | Documenting Your Sources: MLA and APA Styles

> I quote others only the better to express myself.
>
> —Montaigne

Citation of Source Material: A Rationale

You must acknowledge information and ideas taken from sources not your own (commonly referred to as *outside sources*). There are three main reasons for doing so:

1. *Original ideas are a form of property known as intellectual property.* Published material is protected from theft by copyright law. Plagiarism, which means passing off someone else's ideas or writings as your own, is, quite simply, against the law. Thus, by acknowledging your sources explicitly, you protect yourself from being accused of and prosecuted for copyright violation (see "Understanding and Avoiding Plagiarism" in Chapter 7, pages 267–269).

2. *Acknowledging your sources provides an important service to other scholars.* People who read your essays are often interested in consulting the sources you consult to obtain more detailed information.

3. *Citing your sources highlights your own original contributions to the scholarly conversation.* Think of academic or scholarly writing as advancing knowledge or heightening critical thinking about an issue. Readers will better appreciate your contributions when they are placed in the context of contributions by other scholars.

Which Documentation Style to Use?

The MLA style is commonly used to document sources in writing done within the humanities disciplines (for example, English and the foreign languages). The APA style is commonly used to document sources in writing done within the social sciences (for example, psychology and sociology). Clarify with your instructor whether you should follow the MLA style (see pages 276–296), APA style (see

275

pages 297–318), or some other system. (For example, *Chicago* style, based on *The Chicago Manual of Style*, 16th edition, is commonly used to document sources in writing done within history and sometimes other humanities disciplines.)

No one expects you to memorize all the details of any particular system of documentation, but you are expected to know how to look up and apply these details each time you write a paper that includes references to other sources. You are expected to know how to follow the instructions and examples given in documentation manuals and to make your citations complete and consistent with the recommendations of an established documentation style. Therefore, get into the habit of checking the proper format either in this chapter or in the other MLA or APA reference manuals listed in this chapter.

CAUTION: Authors of articles found online sometimes document their sources improperly. Always adhere to the standard MLA or APA formats presented in this chapter. Standard documentation formats ensure that the information and insights of other writers are clearly and accurately attributed.

A Guide to MLA Documentation Style

The following guide presents the system for documenting sources established by the Modern Language Association (MLA). For more detailed information on how to document a wide variety of both print and electronic sources with the MLA style, see *MLA Handbook for Writers of Research Papers*, 7th ed. New York: MLA, 2009; *MLA Style Manual and Guide to Scholarly Publishing*, 3rd ed. New York: MLA, 2008; and the MLA website at www.mla.org.

Remember the following about the MLA documentation system:

1. In the body of your paper, you must (a) inform readers of the last name of the author or authors for each source as you use it in your paper, and (b) give the page number where each source appears originally in a larger work. These elements of the MLA system together form what is called the *author/page in-text citation*. Note that no page numbers are needed if your source is an online one or if it is less than a page long.

2. At the end of your paper, beginning on a new numbered page, you must list in alphabetical order by authors' last names, doubled-spaced, all the sources you refer to within your paper. This list is called *Works Cited*.

Before we look at the details of how to cite various types of sources in your text and the way to list them in your Works Cited, let us look at how to present quoted material and how to paraphrase.

Presenting Quoted Material

When quoting or paraphrasing in MLA style, mention the author's surname and indicate the page number of the passage parenthetically. List the page number (or numbers) without the "p." or "pp." abbreviation. If you are citing more than one page number, indicate them in the following way: 15–16; 140–42; 201–04; 390–401.

Using Quotation Marks and Block-Style Quotation Format

Use double quotation marks around the words quoted if the passage is no more than four lines:

> According to Charles Lamb, Shakespeare's plays "are grounded deep in nature, so deep that the depth of them lies out of the reach of most of us" (7).

Lamb's name (last name first) and the title of the essay, "On the Tragedies of Shakespeare," appear in the Works Cited, along with more information about the publisher and date of the essay.

Because you are already using double quotation marks to indicate another author's work, substitute single quotation marks for any double quotations that appear in the original author's material.

> The distinguished teacher of creative writing, Brenda Ueland, insists that taking long walks is a good way to generate thoughts: "If I do not walk one day, I seem to have on the next what Van Gogh calls 'the meagerness'" (42).

The end punctuation should be placed as follows: close inner quotation, close outer quotation, insert page number of quotation in parentheses, period.

If the passage is four lines or longer, use block-style quotation. Set the passage off as a separate paragraph and indent each line ten spaces from the margin. If you are quoting two or more paragraphs in the block quotation, indent the first line of each an additional three spaces (that is, thirteen spaces from the left margin). Quotation marks are not used with block-style quotations: Consider indentation to take the place of quotation marks:

> Commenting on Shakespeare's villains, Charles Lamb notes that while we are reading any of his great criminal characters— Macbeth, Richard, even Iago—we think not so much of the crimes which they commit, as of the ambition, the aspiring spirit, the intellectual activity, which prompts them to over-leap those moral fences. (12)

The period at the end of a block quotation precedes the parenthetical information.

Quoting Verbatim

Do not change punctuation or spelling (for example, changing the British spelling of "colour" to "color"). In rare cases in which the author or printer makes a spelling or grammatical error, follow the error with the Latin word *sic* (meaning "thus") in brackets to indicate that the word appears this way in the original source. Whereas the Latin word *sic* is italicized, the brackets surrounding it are not.

Using an Ellipsis

Indicate omission of any *unnecessary* portion of the passage with an ellipsis—three dots separated from each other by a single space:

> *Original passage:* "The timing, as I mentioned earlier, had to be precise."

> *Quoted passage, using ellipsis:* "The timing...had to be precise."

Be certain that the words you omit from a passage do not alter its essential meaning.

Paraphrasing

A paraphrase is a rewording of an author's idea that presents it more concisely or clearly. By paraphrasing instead of quoting directly, you can more clearly and efficiently integrate the author's thoughts with your own. Of course, you must thoroughly understand the material you wish to paraphrase to avoid distorting it. You must also cite the author's name and a page number as if the paraphrase were a direct quotation. A paraphrase of the Charles Lamb passage quoted previously might be worded like this:

```
Lamb claims that we regard Macbeth, Richard III, and Iago
less as criminals than as high-reaching spirits marked by
great intelligence (12).
```

Make sure your readers will be able to tell which ideas are yours and which are the paraphrased ideas of another author. Do not, for example, merely list a name and page number at the end of a long paragraph. Readers will not be able to tell whether the paraphrase is the last sentence only or the entire paragraph is being paraphrased, as in the following example:

```
Revenge takes many forms. Most often it is a hot-tempered
reaction to a perceived injustice. But sometimes it is cool
and calculated, like Iago's revenge against Othello. Either
kind, though, can be thought of as a kind of wild justice
which, the more we are tempted by it, the more urgently we
must weed it out (Bacon 72).
```

The writer of the preceding passage does not make it clear whether the entire paragraph is a paraphrase of Francis Bacon's essay, just the last sentence, or even one portion of the last sentence. A simple revision clarifies the matter:

```
Revenge takes many forms. Sometimes it is cool and calculated,
like Iago's revenge against Othello. Other times it is what
Francis Bacon, Shakespeare's contemporary, once defined as
wild justice. As Bacon put it, the more we are tempted to run
to it, the more urgently we should weed it out (72).
```

Index for Citing Sources: MLA Style

Author/Page In-Text Citations

See the following pages for instruction and examples:

List of Works Cited

See the following pages for instruction and examples.

Citing Print Sources

Citing Nonprint Sources

Using Author/Page In-Text Citations

As you write the body of your paper, you will weave in references to the work of others to support or amplify the points you are making. Make sure that your readers can easily distinguish between your words and ideas and the words and ideas of others. To create this clear distinction, refer by name to whomever you are quoting or paraphrasing. You can either include the author's name in a lead-in remark:

author's full name mentioned in lead-in remark

As Eliot Asinof describes the reaction to the 1919 baseball scandal, "The American people were at first shocked, then sickened" (197).

or you can include the author's last name in parentheses with the page number after the quotation or paraphrasing:

In reacting to the 1919 baseball scandal, "[t]he American people were at first shocked, then sickened" (Asinof 197).

author's last name mentioned in parentheses no comma page number

The preferable style is to use the author's name in your lead-in.

Note the following variations on this pattern, depending on the type of source you are citing and whether you are including the author's name in a lead-in remark:

1. Author Named in Lead-in Remarks. As long as you mention the author's last name in your lead-in remarks, the only information needed in parentheses is the page number, because the full citation will appear in the Works Cited at the end of your paper.

author

According to John Jones, a colony on Mars would rapidly pay for itself (15).

page number period

author

```
In her biography of Alice James, Jean Strouse writes that the
James children "learned to see and not see, say and not say,
reveal and conceal, all at the same time" (xii).
```
quotation   page number   period

When citing a piece from an anthology or edited volume, cite the name of the author of the piece to which you are referring, not the editor or editors of the anthology.

2. Author Not Named in Lead-in Remarks.
If you do not name the author as you lead into a quotation or paraphrase, place the author's name in parentheses along with the page number of the source:

```
No one person in 1919 knew all of the factors that
contributed to the Black Sox Scandal or could tell the whole
story (Asinof 11).
```
author's last name no comma page number

3. Two or More Authors.
If you are citing a work that has two or three authors, mention all their names in your lead-in remarks or in parentheses after the reference.

```
Critical reading involves going beyond simple decoding of the
literal meanings of the written word (Cooley and Powell 3).
```
authors' last names no comma page number

If you are citing a work with four or more authors, state the first author's last name and then write "et al." (a Latin phrase meaning "and others").

4. Multiple Works by the Same Author.
If you are referring to more than one work by the same author, refer to the work's title in your lead-in remarks:

```
In Teaching a Stone to Talk, Dillard describes the drama of
the moon blocking the sun during a total eclipse by saying,
"It did not look like the moon. It was enormous and black.
...It looked like a lens cover, or the lid of a pot. It
materialized out of thin air—black, and flat, and sliding,
outlined in flame" (94).
```
page number

Alternately, you can include a short form of the title in parentheses, along with the page number.

> One observer described the mystery of the eclipse by saying, "If I had not read that it was the moon, I could have seen the sight a hundred times and never thought of the moon once" (Dillard, *Teaching* 94).
> author comma abbreviated title page number

5. Works with Anonymous or Corporate Authorship.   Cite works that name no author or editor as follows:

> According to the Consumer Protection Agency, the number of car owners who report being cheated by dishonest mechanics has dropped by 15 percent in 2000 (7).

6. Internet Sources.   For most electronic sources, it is not possible to provide a page number in the in-text citation. Instead, check to see if an author's name is given and if there are numbered paragraphs or other text divisions. If so, use these pieces of information in place of page numbers in your in-text citation:

> Some universities have been questioning their use of Aztec signs and symbols and the use of mascots like "Monty Montezuma" (Weber, par. 6).
> author comma numbered paragraph

Preparing the MLA List of Works Cited

Definition.   The list of Works Cited is an alphabetical listing of all the sources cited or paraphrased or referred to in a paper. The list of Works Cited does not include additional readings, no matter how relevant; however, your instructor may ask you to prepare a separate list of additional readings.

Purpose.   The main purpose of the list of Works Cited is to assist readers who wish to obtain more information about the topic by consulting the same sources you have. A secondary purpose is to give readers an opportunity to double-check the accuracy and appropriateness of your quotations and paraphrases. It is possible to quote someone accurately but in a way that misrepresents that author's original intentions—of course, not something you intend to do but may accidentally do.

General Procedure

1. Begin the list of Works Cited on a separate page.

2. Title the page *Works Cited* and center the heading.

3. List everything alphabetically by author's surname. List the author's surname first. If a work has more than one author, alphabetize the entry according to the surname of the author listed first. If no author is listed, enter the title alphabetically. Titles of books and pamphlets are underlined or italicized. Include the city of publication, the abbreviated name of the publisher, and the date of publication.

4. Begin each entry at the left margin. If an entry runs longer than one line, those subsequent lines are indented five spaces.

5. Do not include URLs for Internet sources. Instead, indicate "Web." Similarly, use the word "Print" for print sources.

In the following examples and in the sample student paper beginning on page 289, note the MLA style for citing various types of sources in the list of Works Cited.

Citing Print Sources

1. Single-Author Book or Pamphlet

Olsham, Matthew. *Marshlands: A Novel*. New York: Farrar, Straus & Giroux, 2014. Print.

2. Book with More than One Author

Witt, Linda, Karen M. Paget, and Glenna Matthews. *Running as a Woman: Gender and Power in American Politics*. New York: Free, 1994. Print.

When there are more than three authors, use the name of the first author and follow it with "et al."

Johnson, Eric, et al. *Smart Shopping*. Boston: Lifestyle, 1999. Print.

3. Chapter from a Book

Zelinger, Anton. "Einstein and Absolute Reality." *My Einstein: Essays by Twenty-Four of the World's Leading Thinkers on the Man, His Work, and His Legacy*. Ed. John Brockamn. New York: Pantheon Books, 2006: 121–31. Print.

4. Government Document

Author Byline Given:

> Hart, Jonathan D. *Internet Law: A Field Guide*. 6th ed. Washington: Bureau of National Affairs, 2008. Print.

No Author Byline Given:

> United States. Department of Health and Human Services. *Preventing Tobacco Use Among Youth and Young Adults: A Report of the Surgeon General*. Washington: GPO, 2012. Print.

5. Article from a Periodical

Magazine:

> Lepore, Jill. "The Last Amazon." *The New Yorker* 22 March 2014: 32–37. Print.

Academic Journal:

> Tsang, Amy. "Corporate Social Responsibility in China: A Snapshot from the Field." *Yale Journal of Sociology* 10 (Fall 2013). 56–86. Print.

Newspaper:

> Zimmer, Carl "Ocean Life Faces Mass Extinction, Borad Study Says." *New York Times* 16 Jan. 2015: A1. Print.

Letter to the Editor:

> Helms, Chris. Letter. *Boston Globe*. 6 May 2014: B22. Print.

Unsigned Editorial:

> "How Good Is the Housing News?" Editorial. *New York Times* 8 March 2012: A24. Print.

6. Book Review

Titled Review of a Work:

> Coll, Steve. "The Reporter Resists His Government." Rev. of *Pay Any Price: Greed, Power, and Endless War*, by James

Risen. *New York Review of Books*, Feb 19 2015: 16–18.
Print.

Untitled Review of a Work:

Warren, Charles. Rev. of *The Material Ghost: Films and Their
Medium*, by Gilberto Perez. *Georgia Review* 54 Spring 2000:
170–74. Print.

Citing Nonprint Sources
7. Interview

Personal Interview:

Sanders, Julia. Personal interview. 15 Oct. 2014.

Telephone Interview:

Ellis, Mark. Telephone interview. 17 Oct. 2015.

8. Correspondence

Paper Letter:

Beaumont, Clyde. Letter to the author. 10 Jan. 2013.

Email Letter:

Beaumont, Clyde. Email to the author. 10 Jan. 2013.

If a paper letter is not dated, use the date of the postmark. Email messages are
dated automatically.

9. Web Page
When your source is a web page—an electronic document from an Internet
site—include in your citation (1) the author's name; (2) the title of the document
in quotation marks; (3) information about a print version of the same document
(if any is given on the website); (4) information about the document's electronic
publication. MLA no longer recommends providing web addresses (URLs). If
an Internet source is used, indicate simply with the word "Web." The rationale
is that it is simpler to locate the article via a search engine such as Google; URLs
are cumbersome to use, and it is easy to make mistakes when entering them;
URLs will sometimes change. If you cannot locate within your electronic source
all of these four categories of information, include as much in your citation

as possible, always with the goal of allowing your reader to find your source. Finally (5), include the date on which you accessed the website because websites are frequently updated.

Document from an Internet Newspaper or Journal Site:

```
        author                 title
Stein, Charles. "After the Last Whistle: Some Workers, Towns
    Have Rebounded amid the Loss of Factory Jobs. Others
    Won't Make It."
             information about print publication    information about electronic publication
Boston Globe. Boston Globe, 23 Oct. 2003. Web. 23 Oct. 2014.
                                                      date of access
```

```
Fredman, Allen. "To the Point: The Adapted Landscape of a
    Former Baltimore Factory Stays True to Its Sudsy Past."
    Landscape Architecture. American Society of Landscape
    Architects, Nov. 2003. Web. 29 Oct. 2003.
```

Document from an Article in a Reference Database:

```
Heitz, Thomas R. "Babe Ruth." Encarta. MSN Learning and
    Research, 2003. Web. 13 Oct. 2003.
```

Article from an Online Posting:

```
Online posting. "Alient Planet 'Super-Earth' Called Best
    Candidate to Support Life." 2 Feb. 2012. Web. 3 Feb 2013.
```

Rather than citing a posting, the writer should try to locate any article cited therein at its proper web address, so readers will be able to find it. Thus, for instance, although the article "NASA Chief Predicts Scientific Tsunami" was originally discovered on the Metanews listserv, it should be cited as follows:

```
David, Leonard. Online posting. "NASA Chief Predicts
    Scientific Tsunami." SPACE.com. Space.com, 11 Oct. 2000.
    Web. 21 Oct. 2014.
```

Blog Posting:

Blog posts should be cited with access dates. Note that many blog posts are not permanent.

```
Jones, David C. "My Comments on the Republican Debates." DCJ's
    Blog. January 3, 2012. Web.
```

Article from a Magazine:

> Norton, Amy. "Video Games May Do the Aging Brain Good."
> *Psychology and Aging.* Reuters, 19 Dec. 2008. Web.
> 24 Aug. 2013.

10. Television or Radio Program

> "Senators Battle Over Judicial Nominee." Narr. Jim Lehrer.
> *Newshour.* PBS. WGBH, Boston, 23 Oct. 2003. Radio.

11. Recording

Audiocassette:

> Churchill, Winston S. *The Great Republic.* Random House
> Audiobooks, 1998. Audiocassette.

Compact Disc (CD):

> Von Bingen, Hildegard. *Canticles of Ecstasy.* Perf. Sequentia.
> Deutsche Harmonia Mundi, 1994.

Videocassette (VCR):

> *Witness.* Dir. Peter Weir. Perf. Harrison Ford and Kelly
> McGillis. Paramount, 1985. Videocassette.

MP3 Digital Files:

> Glass, Philip (composer). *Kronos Quartet Performs Philip
> Glass.* Nonesuch, 2009, MP3.

Digital Video Disc (DVD):

> *Rodgers & Hammerstein's "South Pacific" in Concert from
> Carnegie Hall.* Dir. Walter Bobbie. Perf. Reba
> McEntire, Brian Stokes Mitchell, Alec Baldwin.
> PBS, 2005. DVD.

Blu-Ray (Optical Video Disc):

> Winter, Terrence (creator) *Boardwalk Empire: The Complete
> First Season.* Episode 2. HBO, 2010. Blu-Ray.

12. Film

Boyhood. Dir: Richard Linklater. Perf: Ethan Hawke, Patricia
    Arquette. IFC Productions, 2014. Film.

13. Speech, Lecture

Chaudhuri, Haridas. "The Philosophy of History." Cultural
    Integration Fellowship, San Francisco. 7 Jan. 2007. Lecture.

14. Work of Art (Painting, Sculpture, or Photograph)

Munch, Edvard. *The Scream*. 1893. Oil, tempera, and pastel on
    cardboard. National Gallery, Oslo.

Note 1: If you are referring to a reproduction of the work in a book, cite the book instead of the location of the work, as follows:

Munch, Edvard. *The Scream*. 1893. *Edvard Munch*. Dr. Ulrich
    Bischoff. Germany: Benedikt Taschen Verlag, 1988.

Note 2: If you are citing a work of art that appears on a web page, indicate that fact with the word "Web." Including the URL of the web page is not recommended.

15. Figure (Published Chart, Graph, Table)
Note: The citation must appear directly underneath the figure (following the caption, and prefaced by the word "Source") as well as in the Works Cited page:

United Nations, World Population Prospects, the 1998 Revision.
    Population Reference Bureau.

16. Map

"Central Asia." Map. *Hammond Odyssey Atlas of the World*.
    Hammond World Atlas Corporation, 1994. 31. Print.

17. Advertisement

Cannon HD Camcorder. Advertisement. *National Geographic* Jan.
    2007: 12-13. Print.

18. Tweet or Email Message

Frost, Gary. Message to the author. September 10, 2015. Email.

Sample Student Paper: MLA Documentation Format

½⎫

Gibson 1

Daniela Gibson

Argumentation

Professor Billings

May 16, 2015

Why We Should Punish

The caning of a young American in Singapore in 1994 for minor vandalism has added new fuel to a centuries-old debate about proper forms of punishment. Logic demands, however, that prior to the decision of the proper form of punishment, we must decide on the proper aim or purpose of punishment. The views on the proper aim of punishment seem to vary widely. Writers such as Barbara Wootton and H. L. A. Hart believe that the proper aim of punishment is the rehabilitation of the criminal. Others, in contrast, argue for retribution as the proper aim of punishment. Criminal Justice professor Graeme Newman, for example, writes, "Punishment must, above all else, be painful" (40).

A third view of the proper purpose of punishment is deterrence, "removing the criminal from activity and serving as a caution to would-be-criminals" (Rottenberg 41). One recently profiled advocate of punishment as deterrence is Joe Arpaio, sheriff of Maricopa County, Arizona (Phoenix area). According to Arpaio, "Jail should be about punishment and the punishment should be so unpleasant that no one who experienced it would ever want to go through it again" (Graham 61).

The overall function of punishment is to enforce and protect the moral values of a society, a function that appears to be incompatible with the idea of retribution and only partly compatible with the ideas of deterrence and rehabilitation.

Gibson 2

Punishment linked to society's core values

The punishment and the moral values of a society
are inseparably linked by the laws of that society.
Our laws always reflect and are based on our core
values. Most societies recognize the right to life
as a core value. In the case of our American society, core values are also the ownership of property
and the freedom of speech. Consequently, America has
laws that protect private property and the freedom
of speech. Theft is against the law and so is violation of the freedom of speech. Furthermore, since
these laws are based on values, and values always
imply a right and wrong, a trespassing of these laws
must have consequences that reflect and uphold these
moral judgments. Walter Berns addresses this interdependence between morality and punishment when he
writes the following about the death penalty:

Block-style
quotation
indented ten
spaces from
margin; dou-
ble-spaced;
no quotation
marks used,
except for
those that
appear in
the original
source

> [It] serves to remind us of the majesty of the
> moral order that is embodied in our law and of
> the terrible consequences of its breach. . . . The
> criminal law must be made awful, by which I
> mean awe-inspiring, or commanding "profound
> respect or reverential fear." It must remind us
> of the moral order by which alone we can live
> as human beings. (12)

Although I do not necessarily agree with the
need for the death penalty and "reverential fear,"
Berns's observation is significant: Punishment,
indeed, must always "remind us of the moral order"
by which we live, for if the breaking of the law
would have no consequences, our moral values would
be void (85). If, for example, the violation of the
freedom of speech had no consequences, such a violation could take place again and again. But then,
it could hardly be called a value since we would
not seem to care about it and would not protect it.

Why one
scholar's
view of
punish-
ment
makes
sense

Gibson 3

Those in favor of retribution as the aim of punishment agree that a criminal act must have legal consequences for the criminal. Despite this very broad similarity between retribution and the protection of moral values, retribution appears impractical and morally wrong in the context of the American value system. Advocates of retribution often refer to Kant, who writes that the principle for legal justice is "[n]one other than the principle of equality... any undeserved evil that you inflict on someone else among the people is one that you do to yourself... Only the law of retribution can determine exactly the kind and degree of punishment" (qtd. in Berns 18). Such a view, however, is impracticable, for who would rape a rapist (and how) for retribution of the crime? In addition to these questions, it seems hardly possible that the loss of one individual can truly be retributed by the execution of the murderer.

Yet retribution is precisely the major motive behind capital punishment. The danger with this extreme form of punishment is irreversible miscarriage of justice, as when an innocent man or woman is sentenced to death (Berlow) or when racist lawyers eliminate Blacks, Hispanics, and other racial minorities as potential jurors during jury selection—which was shown to be the case with Nevada death-row inmate Thomas Nevius (Amnesty International).

But more importantly, retribution as the goal of punishment is immoral, at least in the context of our value system. Mark Costanzo, chair of the Department of Social Psychology at Claremont McKenna College, correctly identifies that

[o]ur efforts to mitigate punishments arise out of the recognition that we must not sink to the

Author presents challenging view

Reference to a source quoted by another author

Author refutes challenging view

References to Internet sources

Gibson 4

level of the criminal; raping a rapist would debase us, weaken our moral solidarity, and undermine the moral authority of the state (23).

If we punish via retribution, the danger is that we would focus too narrowly on one crime and in doing so would lose sight of the moral code that makes the crime a crime. In other words, the crime would move to the foreground and would overshadow the moral authority that it violates. For example,

if someone hits my car, I could exercise the punishment of retribution by hitting that person's car in return. However, doing so fails not only to fix my car but also to ensure me that there is a moral code and its representative law that will protect me from similar instances in the future. Hence, retribution undermines the very same moral law that punishment is supposed to uphold.

Deterrence vs. retribution as a basis for punishment

In contrast to retribution, which must be rejected as the proper aim of punishment on moral and practical grounds, deterrence appears to be partly compatible with the upholding of moral values. Ernest van den Haag, a retired professor of Jurisprudence, expresses the views of deterrence advocates when he writes that "[h]arsher penalties are more deterrent than milder ones" (114). In his explanation, he draws an analogy to everyday life situations:

All other things equal, we penalize our children, our friends, or our business partners the more harshly the more we feel we must deter them and others in the future from a wrong they have done. Social life would not be possible if we did not believe that we can attract people to actions we desire by giving them incentives, and deter them from actions we do not desire by disincentives. (115)

Gibson 5

Van den Haag's analogy works—up to a certain point. Clearly, if we care about our values, we need to protect them, and one way of doing so is to punish offenders as a means of deterrence. And in some situations, deterrence might be the only way of communicating what is right and wrong. I remember, for example, when I was three years old, I took doll clothing home from preschool. I did so because I liked to play with it more at home, and I did not understand that it was not mine. When my parents found out, they did the right thing: They told me if I ever did that again, I could no longer play with my dolls. In that situation deterrence was necessary since I was too young to understand the concept of private property and its proper relationship to right and wrong; I understood, however, that I wanted to play with my dolls and that I could no longer do so if I would take doll clothing home again.

There is a danger, however, in viewing deterrence as the only proper aim of punishment: it could disconnect what is feared from what is morally bad, what is desired from what is morally good. The *Oxford English Dictionary* defines deterrence as "deterring or preventing by fear." If I, when I was old enough to grasp the meaning of right and wrong beyond immediate desires, would have not been taught why it is wrong to take what is not mine, but instead would have been continuously motivated by fear, I could have never developed a deep respect for moral values. Rather, I would have learned to associate fear with my parents' knowledge of my "wrongdoing," but not with the wrongdoing itself. Thus, I would have most likely sought to avoid my parents'

Author addresses punishment as rehabilitation

Author qualifies her preceding claim

Gibson 6

knowledge or that of any other authority but not
to avoid the deed itself. I believe that this
example is generally applicable to deterrence
as the main purpose of punishment: Criminals
and potential criminals would be taught not that
their acts were wrong on moral grounds, but that
they should seek to avoid conflicts with authority. But such an attitude would instill in them
a distrust for the laws rather than an understanding and respect for the values that they
represent.

Another view of punishment is rehabilitation.
Rehabilitation in the sense of education seems compatible with and even part of our value system.
However, we need to ensure that rehabilitation qua
education is not conflicting with other essential
values. Costanzo points to the importance that
background and circumstances can play in a crime
(27). For example, it would seem naïve to expect
from a young man proper law-abiding behavior if
that man had suffered from "routine beatings from
an abusive father" and "grew up in a poverty-rid-
den, gang-infested neighborhood and received very
little in the way of parental guidance or supervision" (31). If that man had committed a crime,
rehabilitation that includes a positive alternative to the values or lack thereof of his childhood
upbringing seems appropriate. It might not only
protect our societal values by preventing further
criminal acts by this young man, if the rehabilitation was successful, but it would also reinforce
our values, for the effort of rehabilitation shows
that we are taking these values seriously and are
deeply caring about them.

Why rehabili-
tation cannot
be the sole
basis for
punishment

Gibson 7

Yet, as commendable as such rehabilitation efforts are, we cannot allow them to replace other important values such as responsibility and justice. By rationalizing a criminal behavior with the criminal's disadvantageous upbringing, we are in danger of denying individual responsibility, a core value of our society. Further, by granting college loans and "grants," books, "compassion and understanding," to criminals, as one former prisoner demands, we would also commit injustice (Stratton 67). For how could we explain this special treatment to all those who have abided by the law, some even despite their background, but do not enjoy grants, loans, etc.? Because these aims are potentially in conflict with each other and because our highest responsibility is to defend the values of our society, rehabilitation can be an integral part of punishment, but it should never replace punishment.

The discourse about the proper aim of punishment is indeed complex. But exactly because of this complexity, we need to approach the question of punishment step by step. It would be fatal to jump to the question of the proper forms of punishment before the question of the proper aim of punishment has been settled. It is absolutely mandatory that the question of the proper aim of punishment is addressed a priori. With respect to its answer, if the upholding of the moral values of a society is any indicator, we should dismiss retribution, and very cautiously consider deterrence and rehabilitation—but by no means should we draw any hasty conclusions.

Concluding reflections

No extra
space
between title
and first line
of text

Gibson 8

Works Cited

Amnesty International. "Serious Allegations of
Racism and Injustice in Nevada Death Penalty
Case." 6 Apr. 2001. Web. 30 Apr. 2001.

Berlow, Alan. "The Wrong Man." *Atlantic Monthly*.
Nov. 1999. Web. 6 Apr. 2001.

Berns, Walter. *For Capital Punishment*. New York:
Basic, 1991. Print.

Costanzo, Mark. *Just Revenge*. New York: St. Martin's, 1997. Print.

"Deterrence." *Oxford English Dictionary*. 2nd ed.
CD. Vers. 1.13 Oxford: Oxford UP, 1994.

Graham, Barry. "Star of Justice: On the Job with
America's Toughest Sheriff." *Harper's Magazine*
Apr. 2001: 59-68. Print.

Hart, H. L. A. *Law, Liberty, and Morality*. Stanford: Stanford UP, 1963. Print.

Newman, Graeme R. *Just and Painful: A Case for
Corporeal Punishment of Criminals*. London: Macmillan, 1983. Print.

Rottenberg, Annette T., ed. *Elements of Argument*.
6th ed. New York: Bedford, 2000. 569. Print.

Stratton, Richard. "Even Prisoners Must Hope."
Newsweek 17 Oct. 1994: 67. Print.

van den Haag, Ernest. *The Death Penalty Pro and
Con: A Debate*. New York: Plenum, 1983. Print.

Wootton, Barbara. *Crime and Penal Policy*. London:
Allen, 1978. Print.

Second
and subse-
quent lines
indented

Sources
listed in
alphabetical
order

A Guide to APA Documentation Style

The following guide presents the system for documenting sources established by the American Psychological Association (APA). For more detailed information on how to document a wide variety of sources, both print and electronic, see the *Publication Manual of the American Psychological Association*, 6th ed. (Washington, D.C.: APA, 2010) and the APA *Publication Manual* at www.apastyle.org. Remember the following about the APA documentation system:

1. In the body of your paper, you must (a) inform readers of the last name of the author or authors for each source as you use it in your paper and (b) give the year of publication. These elements of the APA system together form what is called the *author/year in-text citation.*

2. At the end of your paper, beginning on a new numbered page, you must list in alphabetical order by authors' last names, double-spaced, all the sources you refer to within your paper. This list is called *References.* Before we look at the details of how to cite the various types of sources in your text and how to list them in your References, let us look at how to present quoted material and how to paraphrase.

Presenting Quoted Material

When quoting or paraphrasing in APA style, indicate the surnames of each author, together with the year the source was published:

```
According to Freud (1900) . . .
```

At the end of the quoted or paraphrased passage, indicate the page number.

Using Quotation Marks and Block-Style Quotation Format

Use double quotation marks around the words quoted if the passage has fewer than forty words:

```
Freud (1900) notes that "in the psychic life there exist
repressed wishes" (288).
```

This passage is from *The Interpretation of Dreams,* but it is not necessary to put that information at the end of the quotation because it will appear in the References, along with other relevant publication information. Because you are already using double quotation marks to indicate another author's work, substitute single quotation marks for double quotations that appear in the original author's material:

> Henry Petroski (1992) reports that in 1900 "an American
> patent was issued to Cornelius Brosnan...for a 'paper
> clip' which has been regarded in the industry as the 'first
> successful bent wire paper clip'" (62-63).

If the passage is forty or more words long, use a block-style quotation. Set the passage off as a separate paragraph and indent each line five spaces from the margin. If you are quoting two or more paragraphs in the block quotation, indent the first line of each new paragraph an additional five spaces (that is, ten spaces from the left margin). Quotation marks are not used with block-style quotations:

> What we recollect of the dream, and what we subject to our
> methods of interpretation, is, in the first place, mutilated
> by the unfaithfulness of our memory, which seems quite
> peculiarly incapable of retaining dreams, and which may
> have omitted precisely the most significant parts of their
> content. (470)

This passage is also from *The Interpretation of Dreams.*

Quoting from Internet Sources

If the pages of document from which you are quoting are not numbered, refer parenthetically to the number of the paragraph(s) immediately after the quotation; use the abbreviation "para.":

> According to Norton (2008), adults in their 60s and 70s "who
> learn to play a strategy-heavy video game improved their
> scores on a number of tests of cognitive function" (para. 2).

For Internet documents that are paginated, indicate the page number(s) of the quoted passage, as with print documents. *Note:* The abbreviations for page(s)— p. and pp.—are no longer used.

> von Hippel, F. N. (2008, May). Rethinking nuclear fuel
> recycling. *Scientific American*, 88-93.

Quoting Verbatim

Always double-check to ensure that you have quoted the passage accurately. Do not change punctuation or spelling (for example, changing the British spelling of "colour" to "color"). In rare cases in which the author or printer makes a spelling error, follow the word with the Latin word *sic* (meaning "thus") in brackets to indicate that the word appears this way in the original source. Here's an example: "According to the *Weekly Dispatch*, 'The downtown tavern lost it's [sic] liquor license when it served beer to a minor.'"

Using an Ellipsis

Indicate omission of any *unnecessary* portion of the passage with an ellipsis—three dots separated from each other by a single space.

> **Original passage:** According to Clifford Geertz (1973), "We are, in sum, incomplete or unfinished animals who complete or finish ourselves through culture" (49).

> **Quoted passage, using ellipsis:** According to Clifford Geertz (1973), "We are...incomplete or unfinished animals who complete or finish ourselves through culture" (49).

Always check to make sure that the ellipsis does not distort the original intention of the author.

Paraphrasing

A paraphrase is a rewording of an author's idea that presents it more concisely or clearly. You must cite the author's name and the year of publication as if the paraphrase were a direct quotation. Although APA style does not require that a page number be given with a paraphrase, it suggests that you do so. A paraphrase of the Clifford Geertz passage quoted previously might be worded like this:

```
According to Geertz (1973), humans are incomplete animals who
reach completeness through culture (49).
```

Make sure your readers will be able to tell which ideas are your own and which are the paraphrased ideas of another author. Do not, for example, merely list a name and page number at the end of a long paragraph. Readers will not be able to tell whether the paraphrase is the last sentence only or the entire paragraph.

Index for Citing Sources: APA Style

Author/Date In-Text Citations

See the following pages for instructions and examples.

List of References

See the following pages for instructions and examples.

Citing Print Sources

Citing Nonprint Sources

Using Author/Date In-Text Citations

Introduce outside information smoothly and explicitly so that readers will be able to distinguish between your ideas and the outside source authors' ideas. You provide this clear distinction by referring by name to whomever you are quoting or paraphrasing, as in the following examples:

1. Author Named in Lead-in Remarks

author's full name mentioned in lead-in remark

```
According to Carolyn Heilbrun (1979), womanhood must be
reinvented (29).
```

So long as you mention the author's last name, the only other necessary information is the page number, because the full citation will appear in the References.

2. Author Not Named in Lead-in Remarks

One feminist scholar asserts that womanhood must be invented (Heilbrun, 1979, 29).

author's last name | date page number

comma

3. Two or More Authors

authors listed alphabetically separated by commas date in parens

Colombo, Cullen, and Lisle (2001) emphasize that critical thinking involves cultivating the ability to imagine and the curiosity to question one's own point of view (2).

4. Multiple Works by the Same Author

date followed by letter to indicate the different works

Jones (1998b, 130) considers colonization of space a vital step in human evolution. He even argues that our survivability as a species depends on it (1998a, 47–51).

date followed by letter to indicate the different works

The letters *a* and *b* following the date are assigned according to the alphabetized order of the publications' titles. Thus, in the list of references, Jones's 1998a publication appears alphabetically before her 1998b publication, even if the 1998b reference is cited first in the text. Works by the same author published in different years are indicated with one instance of the surname, followed by dates: (Jones, 1999, 2001). When citing two or more different authors sharing the same surname, be sure to include each author's initials: (A. Jones, 1957; C. Jones, 2001).

5. Works with Anonymous or Corporate Authorship

corporate authorship

According to the Consumer Protection Agency (2001), the number of car owners reported being cheated by dishonest mechanics dropped 15 percent in 2000 (7).

6. Internet Sources

Page from a Website:

According to the Coalition for Affordable and Reliable Energy (2001), coal fuels more than half the country's electricity.

Article from an Online Periodical:

author of online article

`Farmer` (2001) envisions a memory chip that, when implanted, will give humans the ability to process information one hundred times faster and more efficiently.

Posting from an Online Forum:

Dr. Charles Taylor (2001), a biologist, claims in an online forum that human cloning will pose no dangers to cloned persons senses of selfhood because "the mind and personality can never be cloned."

Note that you do not need to include more than the author's name and the date when citing online sources. Information such as web addresses will appear in the References.

Preparing the APA List of References

Definition.   The list of References is an alphabetical listing of all the sources cited or paraphrased or referred to in a paper. The list of References does not include additional or recommended readings, no matter how relevant; however, your instructor may ask you to prepare a separate list of supplemental readings.

Purpose.   The main purpose of the list of References is to assist readers who wish to obtain more information about the topic by consulting the same sources you have. A secondary purpose is to give readers an opportunity to double-check the accuracy and appropriateness of your quotations and paraphrases. It is possible to quote someone accurately but in a way that misrepresents that author's original intentions—of course, not something you intend to do but may accidentally do.

General Procedure

1. Begin the list of References on a separate page.

2. Title the page *References* and center the heading.

3. List everything alphabetically by author surname. List the author's surname first, followed by initials. Authors' or editors' full names are not given in APA format. If the work has more than one author, alphabetize according to the surname of the author listed first. If no author is listed, enter the title alphabetically. List the year of publication in parentheses after the authors' names. Titles of books or names of periodicals are italicized; titles of articles use neither italics nor quotation marks. Capitalize only the first word of book titles and article titles but not of

journal titles. Also, the first word after a colon, be it in the title of a book, journal, or article, should be capitalized.

4. Begin the first line of each entry flush with the left margin; turnover lines are indented five spaces.

In the following examples and in the sample student paper beginning on page 307, note the APA style for citing various types of sources in the list of References.

Citing Print Sources

1. Single-Author Book or Pamphlet

Roberts, A. (2014). *Napoleon: A life*. New York: Viking.

2. Book with More than One Author

Witt, L., Paget, K., & Matthews, G. (1994). *Running as a woman: Gender and power in American politics*. New York: Free Press.

3. Chapter from a Book

Blair, J. (1988). The Anglo-Saxon period. In K. O. Morgan (Ed.), *The Oxford history of Britain* (pp. 60–119). New York: Oxford University Press.

4. Article from a Periodical

Magazine:

Sedaris, D. (2015, January 5). Leviathon. *The New Yorker, 76*, 38–42.

Academic Journal:

Blackstock, A. (2011). Dickinson, Blake and the hymnbooks of hell. *The Emily Dickinson Journal, 20*(2), 33–56.

Newspaper:

McGreevy, P. (2015, February 15) Taxpayer activists criticize California's purchase of new cars. *Los Angeles Times*, p. A1.

Letter to the Editor:

Sharkey, J. (2014, December 28). City workers, taxpayers deserve better [Letter to editor]. *Chicago Sun-Times*, p. A15.

Unsigned Editorial:

> Flawed election in Uganda. (2001, March 16). Editorial. *The New York Times*, p. A20.

In APA format, if a journal article has more than seven authors, after the sixth author's name and initial, insert ellipses (...) to indicate additional authors, then last author's name and initial.

5. Book Review

Titled Review of Work:

> Relman, A. (2014, August 14). A challenge to American doctors [Review of the book *The American health care paradox: Why spending more is getting us less*]. *The New York Times Book Review*, p. 6.

Untitled Review of Work:

> Warren, C. (2000, Spring). [Review of the book *The material ghost: Films and their medium*]. *The Georgia Review, 54,* 170–174.

6. Government Document

Author Byline Given:

> Elkouri, F., & Asper, E. (1993). *Resolving drug issues.* Washington, DC: Bureau of National Affairs.

No Author Byline Given:

> U.S. Department of Health and Human Services. (1980, April). *Summary report of the Graduate Medical Educational National Advisory Committee.* Washington, DC: U.S. Government Printing Office.

Citing Nonprint Sources

7. Web Pages. Treat sources from the Internet just as you do print sources. Cite the author and the title of the work, publication data such as journal names and volume or issue numbers, and the publication date. In addition, however, you need to give the date the site was last updated (if different from the publication date) and the web address. The reason for the latter information is that websites sometimes disappear or the addresses change.

Periodical Article from Web Page:

> Sharlet, J. (2000, September 15). A philosopher's call
>   to end all paradigms. *The Chronicle of Higher
>   Education.* Retrieved from http://chronicle.com/
>   article/A-Philosophers-Call-to-End/34622/

Original Webpage Article:

> Williams, A. D. (1994). Jigsaw puzzles: Not just for children
>   anymore. Retrieved from www.gamesmuseum.uwaterloo.ca/
>   VirtualExhibits/puzzles/jigsaw/essay.html

Message Posted to an Electronic Mailing List or Newsgroup:

> NASA chief predicts scientific tsunami. (2000, October 20).
>   Message posted to http://metanews@meta-list.org

8. Television Program

> Turner Broadcasting. (2014, March 7). *The Situation Room with
>   Wolf Blitzer* [Television broadcast]. Atlanta: Cable News
>   Network.

9. Recording

Audiocassette:

> Churchill, W. S. (Speaker). (1998). *The great republic*
>   [Audiocassette]. New York: Random House Audiobooks.

Videocassette:

> Weir, P. (Director). (1985). *Witness* [Motion picture].
>   Los Angeles: Paramount Pictures.

Compact Disc:

> Von Bingen, H. (1994). O choruscans stellarum [Recorded by
>   Sequentia]. On *Canticles of Ecstasy* [CD]. Arles: Deutsche
>   Harmonia Mundi.

Digital Video Disc (DVD) and Blu-ray (Optical Video Disc):

> Winter, T. (creator). (2010). *Boardwalk empire: The complete
>   first season.* Episode 2. HBO. Blu-ray.

MP3 Digital Files:

> Glass, P. (composer). (2009). *Kronos quartet performs Philip Glass*. Nonesuch, MP3.

10. Film

> Nimoy, L. (Director). (1984). *Star Trek IV: The voyage home*. [Motion picture]. United States: Paramount Pictures.

11. Tweet or Email Message

> Frost, G. (2015, Feb. 10). Message to the author. [Email].

12. Do Not Include Nonprint Sources Such as Interviews or Correspondence in References.

Sample Student Paper: APA Documentation Format

1 inch
margins
left and
right

Child Molestation 1

Jarrett Green

Argumentation

Professor Billings

May 16, 2015

Running
head: short
title + page
number

Name,
course,
instructor,
date; double-
spaced

Title,
centered

Abstract

Concisely
states the
problem,
thesis, and
how the
problem can
be solved.

Child molestation has been established as a disease in both the physiological and psychological sense of the word. For this reason, prison sentences fail to cure the molester, as researchers have demonstrated. Once out of prison, molesters easily reestablish their concealed identities. Clearly, alternative measures are needed, such as forcing released molesters to publicly identify themselves as such and having the media warn the public of molesters' reestablished presence in the community.

Child Molestation 2

Quotation works as a concrete lead-in to the topic

Child Molestation: Anything but Your Typical Crime
"I've got these urges, and I can't control myself"
(Friedman, 1991, p. 2). Although these words come from
the mouth of one particular child molester, they easily
could have been uttered by thousands of others. Child
molesters come in all shapes and sizes, and live in all
types of communities—from small farming towns to large
metropolitan cities. All child molesters, however,
have one very important trait in common: They have an
intense sexual fixation with or attraction to children.
What makes this trait so dangerous is that it causes
immense damage and, at times, destruction to the lives
of countless innocent children. Child molestation,
unlike any other illegal or stigmatized act, directly
attacks our nation's youth—our nation's future. Most
states continue to simply imprison child molesters.
Some states, on the other hand, have implemented minimal publicity programs that give communities access to
information on released child molesters.

Give author's name, year, page number if author not mentioned in the sentence

The question of how to punish or deal with child
molesters is not an easy one. I, however, believe that
attaining a proper understanding of the nature of this
crime makes its solution crystal clear. Child molestation is unlike any other crime[1] for two reasons: (1)
It has been established to be a physiological and psychological disease, and (2) it requires secrecy and
identity concealment. This exceptional combination
requires that we treat molesters differently than we
treat burglars and car-jackers. More specifically, it
requires that we *publicize*[2] child molesters, not to
shame or *embarrass* them, but to *disable them*.

Explanation of unique-ness of the problem

Child molestation is anything but a typical
crime. In fact, it has been established as a physiological and psychological disease. Doctor Kieran
Sullivan, Ph.D., an Associate Professor in the Santa

Child Molestation 3

Clara University Psychology Department, explains that pedophilia (or the disorder from which child molesters suffer) "is officially recognized as a diagnostic mental disorder by the DSM IV, the psychiatrist's bible" (K. Sullivan, personal interview, March 10, 2001). More importantly, Sullivan explains that child molestation is

Block style quotations (of more than forty words) are indented five spaces from margin and double-spaced

the only crime that is actually a psychological disorder. Although we consider serial killers to be "insane," their crime is not a direct manifestation of a physiological/psychological disease. Child molesters, on the other hand, have an overwhelming inner compulsion to engage in sexual interaction with children. It is an ever-present disease that drives them and controls them. This is what makes child molesters so unique. (K. Sullivan, personal interview, April 10, 2001)

Sharon Rice is a psychiatric nurse who currently works in the Ohio Veteran's Administration Outpatient Child Clinic. She has counseled hundreds of child molesters throughout her career, both in one-on-one and group settings. Rice claims that child molesters are

Expert description of psychopathology

inflicted with a horrible disease. Nearly all of the child molesters claim that if they are released, they will be unable to not molest again. Most of them think that pedophilia should be legalized, as they believe that they are just giving children love and care. The others, though, believe their behavior is destructive and harmful toward children—and they feel incredible guilt and depression for what they have done. When asked whether or not they believe they could overcome their feelings if

Child Molestation 4

released, most believed that they could not.
They believed their yearning would eventually be
too powerful for them to control. Child molestation is really a disease that overpowers the
will of the individual. (S. Rice, telephone
interview, April 16, 2001)

Child molestation is obviously a unique crime.
The child molester suffers from a disease that
overpowers any and all restrictions (such as society's ethical standards or the molester's personal
guilt). His[3] external acts are dominated by a physiological and psychological disorder.

Explanation
of why cur-
rent strate-
gies have
failed

Because child molestation is a physiological
and psychological disease, even the harshest prison
time usually fails in deterring the molester from
recidivating. The overall rates of recidivism,
although very difficult to determine, are extremely
high. One examination, which studied 197 convicted
male child molesters, found that 42% of the men
were reconvicted within the next 31 years (Hanson,
Steffy, & Gauthier, 1993, p. 646). The study offers
the following important clarification:

Although reconviction rates were used as the
recidivism criteria in this study, it is likely
that reconviction rates underestimate the rate
of reoffending. It is widely recognized that
only a fraction of the sexual offenses against
children result in the offender being convicted.
Consequently, it is possible that all of the men
in our study could have reoffended but that only
about one half got caught. (p. 650)

Mary Sue Barone is the Assistant Prosecuting Attorney for the Criminal Division of the Wood
County District in the state of Ohio. During her
years as a prosecuting attorney she has prosecuted

Child Molestation 5

nearly every offense in the book, including numerous child molestation cases. Barone (telephone interview, April 16, 2001) claims that "recidivism rates of child molestation are consistently the highest of any crime, including drug abuse. It is a disease that plagues a child molester for his entire life." When asked whether prison is the proper solution for such a "disease," she replied, "We live in a society of politics. Families and society want to see the child molester locked up. Unfortunately, prison time doesn't seem to do much good the moment the child molester is released." I cannot stress this point enough: Child molestation is a disease—it is a sickness. Locking someone up for six to eight months is not going to suppress the disease. Even if the prison time is harsh, the child molester reenters society with a physiological and psychological urge that remains unimpeded. Thus, the prison's lesson goes in one ear, and the disease throws it out the other. Child molestation is not a typical crime.

The second reason child molestation is an atypical crime is due to the fact that it is inherently dependent on secrecy and identity concealment. Rarely are child molesters strangers who abuse random children at the playground. In nearly all cases, the child molester is the little league coach, the day-care assistant, the family friend, or the next-door neighbor. Everybody assumes that he is a harmless, good person. The child molester conceals his true self. He hides his destructive fantasies and intentions so that he can earn the trust of the child's parents. Having gained the trust of others, he commits the crime. But his crime is dependent on secrecy and concealment of his true identity.

Child Molestation 6

Our current system of throwing child molesters in prison only makes the process by which they conceal their identities easier. We catch child molesters after they have *secretly* damaged or ruined the lives of countless children. Next we *hide* them in prison cells for the length of their terms and then toss them back *without warning* into the world of children. Although mere prison time is undoubtedly a "feel-good" solution, it is really no authentic solution at all. Child molesters come out of prison and are far too easily able to reestablish their concealed identities. They once again hide their molestating selves and, once again, use this concealment to poison and destroy the lives of innocent children.

Because child molestation is a truly unique crime (since it is a *disease* that undermines prison's function as a deterrent and it is inherently dependent on identity concealment), it screams for alternative state reaction, namely, publicity. Because child molestation is a disease that plagues child molesters, we cannot release them with the expectation that they will never molest again. Consequently, we must do all that we can to decrease the ease by which the disease controls child molesters' lives and damages children's lives. Publicity is this road block. It will make it difficult for child molesters to act on hidden dangerous impulses, since others will be aware of their disease. It will prevent them from succeeding in manipulatively gaining parents' trust and children's friendships so as to satisfy their harmful desires.

Emotional appeal

If we care about the lives of our children, we must make it as difficult as possible for child molesters to satisfy their harmful impulses through identity concealment. We must prevent them from deceiving the world into trusting them. We must rob them of the tools used to molest children: secrecy and identity concealment. As I explained before, child molesters do not just molest random kids while in line for the movies. We can and must obstruct such development of loyalty and trust by *publicizing* child molesters. Each child molester, on release from prison, should be publicized by a combination of four "awareness" tactics. First, newspapers should publish the names and photographs of child molesters as they reenter society. Second, local television news programs should warn communities of the release of child molesters. News programs frequently display the names and snapshots of so-called "dangerous" citizens (such as people who are currently wanted by the police). Released child molesters are at least as dangerous and arguably more dangerous than on-the-run convicts or prison escapees (depending on the crime, of course). Third, child molesters should be forced under supervision to go door-to-door throughout their entire neighborhood (if not further) and inform people of their danger to children. Fourth, and last, child molesters should be forced to hold up signs (such as "I am a child molester and have recently been released from prison") in popular public locations (such as inside shopping malls or outside movie theatres) in their communities.

Explanation of a potential solution

   The combination of these four "awareness" tactics makes it far more difficult for the child molester reentering society simultaneously to reenter the lives of children. Because the child molester so desperately *needs* his disease covered up if he is successfully to form new relationships with children, *publicizing* his disease will make it far more difficult for him to dupe parents and children into thinking that he is harmless.

Thus, publicity does far more than shame the child molester (which it may or may not actually succeed in doing); it *disables* him by depriving him of the one tool that he needs in order to molest more children: identity concealment.

Disabling child molesters by depriving them of their necessary tool (i.e., identity concealment) is not much different than the ancient punishment of depriving pick-pocketers and thieves of their necessary tool (i.e., their fingers). Pick-pocketers and thieves obviously depended on their fingers in order to commit their crimes. Cutting off their fingers was a simple way of preventing them from repeating their crimes. Similarly, child molesters depend on the concealment of their identities in order to commit their crimes. Depriving them of their concealment via *publicity* is really the only way we can save countless children from being sexually molested. Child molestation is possibly the only crime that fully depends on (which is to say—is impossible without) the concealment of identity. For this reason, crimes such as assault and robbery (which do not depend on the secrecy and deception of identity) should not be countered by publicity. Child molestation is a unique crime. It requires a unique punishment.

Acknowledgment of challenging view

My opponents, at this time, would claim that such a punishment is unjustifiably excessive. They would argue that although publicity would disable a molester from molesting, it would also disable him from successfully seeking and holding a job. Additionally, because the child molester has already served his time, he now ought to be permitted to reestablish a normal life, which necessarily involves getting a job so that he may feed, clothe and house himself. Some, such as Judith Shepphard (1997), a journalism professor at Auburn University, argue that

Child Molestation 9

publicizing child molesters is indefensible because
it constitutes double punishment (p. 37).

I respond by arguing that we must use publicity against child molesters *in place* of full prison
terms. I am advocating a decrease in (but not elimination of) prison sentences so that publicity becomes
a normal part of "serving one's time." Thus, my opponents' argument that publicity is unfair because
child molesters have *already served* their time is
moot. The publicity with which they will be forced to
deal is not *in addition* to their time; it *is* their
time. A typical "punishment" for child molestation
should be two-pronged: It should begin with a (shortened, according to today's norms) prison sentence,
and conclude with a powerful dosage of public exposure. This public exposure is obviously not going to
help child molesters get jobs (of course, our current
system requires that molesters admit in their job
applications that they were convicted of child molestation, which doesn't help this cause much either).

Melvin Watt, the Democratic senator from North
Carolina, claims that "our Constitution says to
us that a criminal defendant is presumed innocent
until he or she is proven guilty. . . . The underlying assumption of this [argument] is that once you
have committed one crime of this kind, you are presumed guilty for the rest of your life" (Tougher
"Megan's law," 1996). Senator Watt's point demonstrates a blatant misunderstanding of the nature
of child molestation. As we established earlier in
the paper, child molestation is a physiological
and psychological disease from which child molesters suffer. It is not as if they were only *suffering* from the disease the moment they committed
the act that led to their convictions. In reality,
molesters continuously *suffer* from the disease—it

Refutation of challenging view

Child Molestation 10

When author-
ship is not
given, state
title; in this
case, no page
number is
given since
the source
is from a
website

is a mental disorder that they cannot escape. Child
molesters are not "presumed guilty" for the rest of
their lives; they are, however, presumed dangerous
for the rest of their lives. This presumption, due
to the nature of molestation, seems fair to make.

The final rebuttal that my opponents make is
that publicity violates the convicted child molester's right to privacy. Although at an initial glance
this argument appears persuasive, a proper understanding of government-enforced punishment defeats
it. If a person assaults another, he is put in
prison. Every individual in America has an inalien-
able right to liberty. We believe, however, that
an individual can sacrifice this right by behav-
ing in certain ways (such as by assaulting an innocent other). If we so easily accept that the state
can violate an individual's right to liberty, why
is it so shocking for me to suggest a punishment in
which the state violates the individual's right to
privacy? We are simply accustomed to the violation
of liberty (which, by the way, is a truly sacred
right). The fact that the right to privacy is not
regularly violated by the government (in response to
illegal behavior) does not entail that it is unjustifiable. In the case of the child molester, the
violation of this right is perfectly justifiable.

Thus, I do not support the publicity of child
molesters so that we might slowly eliminate individual rights or eventually revert back to our days
of public shaming. I support publicity because it

Restatement
of thesis and
concluding
remarks

can *disable* and *handicap* people who leave prison prepared, due to their controlling disease, to molest
more children. Although it will not put an end to
the molestation of children, it will make it far more
difficult for child molesters to reenter society and
effortlessly start up where they left off.

Footnotes

[1] If a crime exists that I am presently unaware of that satisfies each of the two stated criteria, it would also be subject to *publicity* as a "punishment."

[2] I acknowledge that this use of *publicize* is atypical; however, the need for such a use will become clear later in this paper. Also later in this paper, I will specify the exact manner in which child molesters will be publicized.

[3] Throughout this paper, I intentionally use the male pronoun in referring to child molesters since the great majority of child molesters are male.

Note use of footnotes for informational purposes

Child Molestation 12

Title is centered

References

Friedman, S. (1991). *Outpatient treatment of child molesters*. Sarasota, FL: Professional Resource Exchange.

Indent second and successive lines of each entry five spaces

Hansen, K. R., Steffy, R. A., & Gauthier, R. (1993). Long-term recidivism of child molesters. *Journal of Consulting and Clinical Psychology, 61*(4), 646–652.

Shepphard, J. (1997). Double punishment?: Megan's law on child molesters. *American Journalism Review, 19*(9), 37–41.

Tougher "Megan's law" would require notification. (1996). Retrieved from www.cgi.cnn.com/ALLPOLITICS/1996/news/9605/08/sexoffenders/index.shtml

Entries are listed in alphabetical order by author surname (or by title if no author listed)

Ampersand used before name of last author listed

First word in article title and journal title capitalized; journal title and volume number italicized

PART II

Reading Clusters

Masterpieces of Argument: What Do They Teach Us About the Art of Persuasion?

Introduction

Many of the greatest works ever written or spoken are arguments. They have appeared in all disciplines: philosophy (Plato's "Allegory of the Cave"), literature (Andrew Marvell's "To His Coy Mistress"), sociology/politics (Frederick Douglass's "I Hear the Mournful Wail of Millions," Swift's "A Modest Proposal," and Stanton's keynote address at the first Woman's Rights Convention), and photojournalism (Carter's photo of a starving Sudanese child).

What do these masterpieces of argument have in common? They all illuminate a dark corner of human or physical nature or of the relationship between the two, a corner that needs resolution. They combine clarity with subtlety, eloquence with forcefulness. As you read each of this cluster's selections, ask yourself three questions:

1. What is most effective or distinctive about the author's approach to the subject matter?

2. How has he or she combined objective factual information with subjective persuasive power?

3. Why do these arguments still make for valuable reading, even though some of them are centuries old?

What Makes a Persuasive Powerhouse?

Powerful images can have great persuasive power. During the Vietnam War, Nick Ut photoraphed terrorized Vietnamese children running from their napalmed village—an image that contributed significantly to antiwar sentiments at the time. Similarly, Kevin Carter's image of a starving child (reproduced below) has driven home the harsh reality of world hunger in ways that words alone cannot achieve. Photojournalists over the years have, intentionally or not, produced images that have influenced domestic and foreign policy.

Pulitzer Prize Photograph: Sudanese Child and Vulture | Kevin Carter

In 1993, the South African photojournalist Kevin Carter captured this unforgettable image of a starving girl in Sudan being eyed by a hungry vulture awaiting the child's death. According to Obvious magazine (http://obviousmag.org), the publisher of the photograph, the child, exhausted by hunger, was "dragging herself to a ... feeding field a kilometer away from where she was." The image captures the tragedy of famine in Africa caused by political upheaval and severe food shortages. This image earned Carter the 1994 Pulitzer Prize for Photojournalism. Three months after winning the prize, Carter, overwhelmed by the human tragedy he'd experienced in Africa, committed suicide. He was 33. The Big Bang Club was based on Carter's life.

Kevin Carter/Sygma/Corbis

Reflections and Inquiries

1. Articulate the argument(s) that Carter's photograph conveys.

2. According to *Obvious* magazine, Carter's image caused great controversy because Carter, by his own admission, did not offer assistance to the child because he was instructed not to, in light of "the possibility of disease transmission." Where do you stand on this ethical dilemma?

3. What makes this image deserving—or not—of the Pulitzer Prize?

Reading to Write

Argue whether photographs like Kevin Carter's "Sudanese Child and Vulture" serve a humanitarian purpose (for example, by shocking the public into realizing the horrors of famine in Africa) or do little more than exploit such suffering (including the suffering of the child in the photograph) for the sake of journalistic art.

Allegory of the Cave | Plato

In his masterful dialogue, The Republic, Plato (428–347 BCE) attempts to show that a rational relationship exists among the cosmos, the human soul, and the state. Qualities such as justice, good, and beautiful must coexist harmoniously in life. Politics, law, education, art, and literature are the means by which we come to perfect these qualities of the good life. In Book Seven of the dialogue, Socrates argues his case for the potential of educators to lead humanity out of the darkness of deceptions and superficial appearances into the light of higher truth. This "Allegory of the Cave," as it has come to be known, is one of the most powerful meditations on the relationship between appearance and reality and of the importance of education in society.

Socrates, Glaucon: The den, the prisoners: the light at a distance.

And now, I said, let me show in a figure how far our nature is enlightened or unenlightened:—Behold! human beings living in an underground den, which has a mouth open towards the light and reaching all along the den; here they have been from their childhood, and have their legs and necks chained so that they cannot move, and can only see before them, being prevented by the chains from turning round their heads. Above and behind them a fire is blazing at a distance, and between the fire and the prisoners there is a raised way; and you will see, if you look, a low wall built along the way, like the screen which marionette players have in front of them, over which they show the puppets.

I see.

The low wall and the moving figures of which the shadows are seen on the opposite wall of the den.

And do you see, I said, men passing along the wall carrying all sorts of vessels, and statues and figures of animals made of wood and stone and various materials, which appear over the wall? Some of them are talking, others silent.

You have shown me a strange image, and they are strange prisoners.

Like ourselves, I replied; and they see only their own shad- 5
ows, or the shadows of one another, which the fire throws on the opposite wall of the cave?

Source: Plato, "Allegory of the Cave," *The Republic*, trans. Benjamin Javett and Lewis Campbell (Oxford: Clarendon, 1894) 293–99. Book VII, 514–518.

True, he said; how could they see anything but the shadows if they were never allowed to move their heads?

And of the objects which are being carried in like manner they would only see the shadows?

Yes, he said.

The prisoners would mistake the shadows for realities.

And if they were able to converse with one another, would they not suppose that they were naming what was actually before them?

Very true.

10

And suppose further that the prison had an echo which came from the other side, would they not be sure to fancy when one of the passers-by spoke that the voice which they heard came from the passing shadow?

No question, he replied.

To them, I said, the truth would be literally nothing but the shadows of the images.

That is certain.

And when released, they would still persist in maintaining the superior truth of the shadows.

And now look again, and see what will naturally follow if 15 the prisoners are released and disabused of their error. At first, when any of them is liberated and compelled suddenly to stand up and turn his neck round and walk and look towards the light, he will suffer sharp pains; the glare will distress him, and he will be unable to see the realities of which in his former state he had seen the shadows; and then conceive some one saying to him, that what he saw before was an illusion, but that now, when he is approaching nearer to being and his eye is turned towards more real existence, he has a clearer vision—what will be his reply? And you may further imagine that his instructor is pointing to the objects as they pass and requiring him to name them,—will he not be perplexed? Will he not fancy that the shadows which he formerly saw are truer than the objects which are now shown to him?

Far truer.

And if he is compelled to look straight at the light, will he not have a pain in his eyes which will make him turn away to take refuge in the objects of vision which he can see, and which he will conceive to be in reality clearer than the things which are now being shown to him?

True, he said.

When dragged upwards, they would be dazzled by excess of light.

And suppose once more, that he is reluctantly dragged on a steep and rugged ascent, and held fast until he is forced into the presence of the sun himself, is he not likely to be pained and irritated? When he approaches the light his eyes will be dazzled, and he will not be able to see anything at all of what are now called realities.

20   Not all in a moment, he said.

He will require to grow accustomed to the sight of the upper world. And first he will see the shadows best, next the reflections of men and other objects in the water, and then the objects themselves; then he will gaze upon the light of the moon and the stars and the spangled heaven; and he will see the sky and the stars by night better than the sun or the light of the sun by day?

Certainly.

At length they will see the sun and understand his nature.

Last of all he will be able to see the sun, and not mere reflections of him in the water, but he will see him in his own proper place, and not in another; and he will contemplate him as he is.

Certainly.

25   He will then proceed to argue that this is he who gives the season and the years, and is the guardian of all that is in the visible world, and in a certain way the cause of all things which he and his fellows have been accustomed to behold?

They would then pity their old companions of the den.

Clearly, he said, he would first see the sun and then reason about him.

And when he remembered his old habitation, and the wisdom of the den and his fellow prisoners, do you not suppose that he would felicitate himself on the change, and pity them?

Certainly, he would.

And if they were in the habit of conferring honors among themselves on those who were quickest to observe the passing shadows and to remark which of them went before, and which followed after, and which were together; and who were therefore best able to draw conclusions as to the future, do you think that he would care for such honors and glories, or envy the possessors of them? Would he not say with Homer, Better to be the poor servant of a poor master and to endure anything, rather than think as they do and live after their manner?

30   Yes, he said, I think that he would rather suffer anything than entertain these false notions and live in this miserable manner.

Imagine once more, I said, such an one coming suddenly out of the sun to be replaced in his old situation; would he not be certain to have his eyes full of darkness?

To be sure, he said.

But when they returned to the den they would see much worse than those who had never left it.

And if there were a contest, and he had to compete in measuring the shadows with the prisoners who had never moved out of the den, while his sight was still weak, and before his eyes had become steady (and the time which would be needed to acquire this new habit of sight might be very considerable), would he not be ridiculous? Men would say of him that up he went and down he came without his eyes; and that it was better not even to think of ascending; and if any one tried to loose another and lead him up to the light, let them only catch the offender, and they would put him to death.

No question, he said.

The prison is the world of sight, the light of the fire is the sun.

This entire allegory, I said, you may now append, dear 35 Glaucon, to the previous argument; the prison house is the world of sight, the light of the fire is the sun, and you will not misapprehend me if you interpret the journey upwards to be the ascent of the soul into the intellectual world according to my poor belief, which, at your desire, I have expressed—whether rightly or wrongly God knows. But, whether true or false, my opinion is that in the world of knowledge the idea of good appears last of all, and is seen only with an effort; and, when seen, is also inferred to be the universal author of all things beautiful and right, parent of light and of the lord of light in this visible world, and the immediate source of reason and truth in the intellectual; and that this is the power upon which he who would act rationally either in public or private life must have his eye fixed. I agree, he said, as far as I am able to understand you. Moreover, I said, you must not wonder that those who attain to this beatific vision are unwilling to descend to human affairs; for their souls are ever hastening into the upper world where they desire to dwell; which desire of theirs is very natural, if our allegory may be trusted.

Yes, very natural.

Nothing extraordinary in the philosopher being unable to see in the dark.

And is there anything surprising in one who passes from divine contemplations to the evil state of man, misbehaving himself in a ridiculous manner; if, while his eyes are blinking and before he has become accustomed to the surrounding darkness, he is compelled to fight in courts of law, or in other places, about the images or the shadows of images of justice, and is endeavoring to meet the conceptions of those who have never yet seen absolute justice?

Anything but surprising, he replied.

Anyone who has common sense will remember that the bewilderments of the eyes are of two kinds, and arise from two causes, either from coming out of the light or from going into the light, which is true of the mind's eye, quite as much as of the bodily eye; and he who remembers this when he sees anyone whose vision is perplexed and weak, will not be too ready to laugh; he will first ask whether that soul of man has come out of the brighter life, and is unable to see because unaccustomed to the dark, or having turned from darkness to the day is dazzled by excess of light. And he will count the one happy in his condition and state of being, and he will pity the other; or, if he have a mind to laugh at the soul which comes from below into the light, there will be more reason in this than in the laugh which greets him who returns from above out of the light into the den.

40   That, he said, is a very just distinction.

But then, if I am right, certain professors of education must be wrong when they say that they can put a knowledge into the soul which was not there before, like sight into blind eyes.

The eyes may be blinded in two ways, by excess or by defect of light.   They undoubtedly say this, he replied.

Whereas, our argument shows that the power and capacity of learning exists in the soul already; and that just as the eye was unable to turn from darkness to light without the whole body, so too the instrument of knowledge can only by the movement of the whole soul be turned from the world of becoming into that of being, and learn by degrees to endure the sight of being, and of the brightest and best of being, or in other words, of the good.

Very true.

45   And must there not be some art which will effect conversion in the easiest and quickest manner; not implanting the faculty of sight, for that exists already, but has been turned in the wrong direction, and is looking away from the truth?

Yes, he said, such an art may be presumed.

The conversion of the soul is the turning round the eye from darkness to light.   And whereas the other so-called virtues of the soul seem to be akin to bodily qualities, for even when they are not originally innate they can be implanted later by habit and exercise, the virtue of wisdom more than anything else contains a divine element which always remains, and by this conversion is rendered useful and profitable; or, on the other hand, hurtful and useless. Did you never observe the narrow intelligence flashing from the keen eye of a clever rogue—how eager he is, how clearly his paltry soul sees the way to his end; he is the reverse of blind, but his keen eyesight is forced into the service of evil, and he is mischievous in proportion to his cleverness?

Very true, he said.

But what if there had been a circumcision of such natures in the days of their youth; and they had been severed from those sensual pleasures, such as eating and drinking, which, like leaden weights, were attached to them at their birth, and which drag them down and turn the vision of their souls upon the things that are below—if, I say, they had been released from these impediments and turned in the opposite direction, the very same faculty in them would have seen the truth as keenly as they see what their eyes are turned to now.

Very likely.   50

Yes, I said; and there is another thing which is likely, or rather a necessary inference from what has preceded, that neither the uneducated and uninformed of the truth, nor yet those who never make an end of their education, will be able ministers of State; not the former, because they have no single aim of duty which is the rule of all their actions, private as well as public; nor the latter, because they will not act at all except upon compulsion, fancying that they are already dwelling apart in the islands of the blessed.

Very true, he replied.

Then, I said, the business of us who are the founders of the State will be to compel the best minds to attain that knowledge which we have already shown to be the greatest of all—they must continue to ascend until they arrive at the good; but when they have ascended and seen enough we must not allow them to do as they do now.

What do you mean?

I mean that they remain in the upper world: but this must   55 not be allowed; they must be made to descend again among the prisoners in the den, and partake of their labors and honors, whether they are worth having or not.

But is not this unjust? he said; ought we to give them a worse life, when they might have a better?

You have again forgotten, my friend, I said, the intention of the legislator, who did not aim at making any one class in the State happy above the rest; the happiness was to be in the whole State, and he held the citizens together by persuasion and necessity, making them benefactors of the State, and therefore benefactors of one another; to this end he created them, not to please themselves, but to be his instruments in binding up the State.

True, he said, I had forgotten.

Observe, Glaucon, that there will be no injustice in compelling our philosophers to have a care and providence of others; we shall explain to them that in other States, men of their class are not obliged to share in the toils of politics: and this is reasonable, for they grow up at their own sweet will, and the government would rather not have them. Being self-taught, they cannot be expected to show any gratitude for a culture which they have never received. But we have brought you into the world to be rulers of the hive, kings of yourselves and of the other citizens, and have educated you far better and more perfectly than they have been educated, and you are better able to share in the double duty.

Their obligations to their country will induce them to take part in her government.

Wherefore each of you, when his turn comes, must go down to the general underground abode, and get the habit of seeing in the dark. When you have acquired the habit, you will see ten thousand times better than the inhabitants of the den, and you will know what the several images are, and what they represent, because you have seen the beautiful and just and good in their truth. And thus our State, which is also yours, will be reality, and not a dream only, and will be administered in a spirit unlike that of other States, in which men fight with one another about shadows only and are distracted in the struggle for power, which in their eyes is a great good. Whereas the truth is that the State in which the rulers are most reluctant to govern is always the best and most quietly governed, and the State in which they are most eager, the worst.

Quite true, he replied.

They will be willing but not eager to rule.

And will our pupils, when they hear this, refuse to take their turn at the toils of State, when they are allowed to spend the greater part of their time with one another in the heavenly light?

Impossible, he answered; for they are just men, and the commands which we impose upon them are just; there can be no doubt that every one of them will take office as a stern necessity, and not after the fashion of our resent rulers of State.

The statesman must be provided with a better life than that of a ruler; and then he will not covet office.

Yes, my friend, I said; and there lies the point. You must contrive for your future rulers another and a better life than that of a ruler, and then you may have a well-ordered State; for only in the State which offers this, will they rule who are truly rich, not in silver and gold, but in virtue and wisdom, which are the true blessings of life. Whereas if they go to the administration of public affairs, poor and hungering after their own private advantage, thinking that hence they are to snatch the chief good, order there can never be; for they will be fighting about office, and the civil and domestic broils which thus arise will be the ruin of the rulers themselves and of the whole State.

65   Most true, he replied.

And the only life which looks down upon the life of political ambition is that of true philosophy. Do you know of any other?

Indeed, I do not, he said.

Reflections and Inquiries

1. What is Plato's thesis in this allegory?

2. Why do you suppose Plato presents his argument as a dialogue? How does this approach contribute to the persuasive force of Plato's argument?

3. What physiological limitations of human vision does Plato use as an analogy to flawed understanding of reality? How accurate an analogy is it, in your opinion?

4. What criticism of education is Plato presenting to Glaucon?

5. How does Plato characterize the ideal legislator? How realistic a characterization is this, from your perspective?

Reading to Write

1. Reread the "Allegory of the Cave" and then present your own mini-dialogue between yourself (as a modern-day Plato) and a high school student. Topic: Why a liberal arts education is more valuable than mere training for a specific occupation.

2. Write an essay on Plato's conception of the soul, based on his discussion of it in this dialogue.

To His Coy Mistress | Andrew Marvell

Arguments can be presented poetically, as in the case of this famous late-seventeenth-century "carpe diem" poem, "To His Coy Mistress" ("mistress" meaning here "a woman of stature and authority"). Andrew Marvell (1621–1678) liked to debate difficult philosophical, political and—in the case of the following poem—moral issues poetically but without resolving them.

<table>
<tr><td></td><td>Had we but world enough, and time,</td><td></td></tr>
<tr><td></td><td>This coyness, lady, were no crime.</td><td></td></tr>
<tr><td></td><td>We would sit down, and think which way</td><td></td></tr>
<tr><td></td><td>To walk, and pass our long love's day.</td><td></td></tr>
<tr><td></td><td>Thou by the Indian Ganges' side</td><td>5</td></tr>
<tr><td></td><td>Should'st rubies find; I by the tide</td><td></td></tr>
<tr><td>*sing melancholy</td><td>Of Humber would complain.* I would</td><td></td></tr>
<tr><td>songs</td><td>Love you ten years before the Flood,</td><td></td></tr>
<tr><td></td><td>And you should, if you please, refuse</td><td></td></tr>
<tr><td></td><td>Till the conversion of the Jews.</td><td>10</td></tr>
<tr><td>*fertile, ample</td><td>My vegetable* love should grow</td><td></td></tr>
<tr><td></td><td>Vaster than empires, and more slow;</td><td></td></tr>
<tr><td></td><td>An hundred years should go to praise</td><td></td></tr>
<tr><td></td><td>Thine eyes, and on thy forehead gaze;</td><td></td></tr>
</table>

Source: Andrew Marvell, "To His Coy Mistress," *Andrew Marvell: The Complete English Poems* (New York: St. Martin's, 1974) 50–51.

15 Two hundred to adore each breast,
But thirty thousand to the rest;
An age at least to every part,
And the last age should show your heart.
For, lady, you deserve this state,
20 Nor would I love at lower rate.
But at my back I always hear
Time's winged chariot hurrying near;
And yonder all before us lie
Deserts of vast eternity.
25 Thy beauty shall no more be found,
Nor, in thy marble vault, shall sound
My echoing song, then worms shall try
That long preserved virginity:
And your quaint honor turn to dust,
30 And into ashes all my lust.
The grave's fine and private place,
But none, I think, do there embrace.
Now therefore, while the youthful hue
glow, luminescence Sits on thy skin like morning glew*
35 And while thy willing soul transpires
At every pore with instant fires,
Now let us sport us while we may,
And now, like amorous birds of prey,
Rather at once our time devour,
40 Than languish in his slow-chapped power.
Let us roll all our strength and all
Our sweetness up into one ball,
And tear our pleasures with rough strife,
Through the iron gates of life.
45 Thus, though we cannot make our sun
Stand still, yet we will make him run.

Reflections and Inquiries

1. Summarize the speaker's argument. How valid is it? How would you refute it?

2. Many consider this poem to be a satire. If so, what is it satirizing?

3. The poem uses a literary device called hyperbole (exaggeration). Where do you see examples of it? Why does the speaker use it?

4. Why does Marvell present his argument as a poem? Why not a prose manifesto instead?

5. The poem presents only one side of the argument. Why doesn't Marvell include the woman's response?

Reading to Write

1. Analyze the speaker's argument in terms of introduction, body of evidence, and conclusion.

2. Write a point-by-point counterargument (in verse or prose) from the woman's point of view.

A Modest Proposal | Jonathan Swift

Originally published as a pamphlet in 1729 with the title "A Modest Proposal for Preventing the Children of Poor People in Ireland from Being a Burden to Their Parents or Country, and for Making Them Beneficial to the Public," this bitterly satiric proposal for alleviating the famine in Ireland was sparked by Jonathan Swift's intolerance of the hypocrisy of his native Ireland that preached the joys of parenthood and the sacredness of life while at the same time permitting economic corruption and famine. Swift (1667–1745), a political journalist and the author of Gulliver's Travels (1726), was also an ordained Anglican priest in the Church of Ireland and Dean of St. Patrick's Cathedral, Dublin.

It is a melancholy object to those who walk through this great town or travel in the country, when they see the streets, the roads, and cabin doors, crowded with beggars of the female sex, followed by three, four, or six children, all in rags and importuning every passenger for an alms. These mothers, instead of being able to work for their honest livelihood, are forced to employ all their time in strolling to beg sustenance for their helpless infants, who, as they grow up, either turn thieves for want of work, or leave their dear native country to fight for the Pretender in Spain, or sell themselves to the Barbadoes.

I think it is agreed by all parties that this prodigious number of children in the arms, or on the backs, or at the heels of their mothers and frequently of their fathers, is in the present deplorable state of the kingdom a very great additional grievance; and therefore whoever could find out a fair, cheap, and easy method of making these children sound useful members of the commonwealth would deserve so well of the public as to have his statue set up for a preserver of the nation.

But my intention is very far from being confined to provide only for the children of professed beggars; it is of a much greater extent, and shall take in the whole number of infants at a certain age who are born of parents in effect as little able to support them as those who demand our charity in the streets.

Source: Jonathan Swift, "A Modest Proposal," *Gulliver's Travels and Other Writings*, ed. Lois A. Landa (Boston: Houghton, 1960) 429–36.

As to my own part, having turned my thoughts for many years upon this important subject, and maturely weighed the several schemes of other projectors, I have always found them grossly mistaken in their computation. It is true, a child just dropped from its dam may be supported by her milk for a solar year, with little other nourishment; at most not above the value of two shillings, which the mother may certainly get, or the value in scraps, by her lawful occupation of begging; and it is exactly at one year old that I propose to provide for them in such a manner as instead of being a charge upon their parents or the parish, or wanting food and raiment for the rest of their lives, they shall on the contrary contribute to the feeding, and partly to the clothing, of many thousands.

5   There is likewise another great advantage in my scheme, that it will prevent those voluntary abortions, and that horrid practice of women murdering their bastard children, alas, too frequent among us, sacrificing the poor innocent babes, I doubt, more to avoid the expense than the shame, which would move tears and pity in the most savage and inhuman breast.

The number of souls in this kingdom being usually reckoned one million and a half, of these I calculate there may be about two hundred thousand couples whose wives are breeders, from which number I subtract thirty thousand couples who are able to maintain their own children, although I apprehend there cannot be so many under the present distress of the kingdom; but this being granted, there will remain an hundred and seventy thousand breeders. I again subtract fifty thousand for those women who miscarry, or whose children die by accident or disease within the year. There only remain an hundred and twenty thousand children of poor parents actually born. The question therefore is, how this number shall be reared and provided for, which, as I have already said, under the present situation of affairs, is utterly impossible by all the methods hitherto proposed. For we can neither employ them in handicraft or agriculture; we neither build houses (I mean in the country) nor cultivate land. They can very seldom pick up a livelihood by stealing till they arrive at six years old, except where they are of towardly parts; although I confess they learn the rudiments much earlier, during which time they can however be looked upon only as probationers, as I have been informed by a principal gentleman in the country of Cavan, who protested to me that he never knew above one or two instances under the age of six, even in a part of the kingdom so renowned for the quickest proficiency in that art.

I am assured by our merchants that a boy or a girl before twelve years old is no salable commodity, and even when they come to this age they will not yield above three pounds, or three pounds and half a crown at most on the Exchange; which cannot turn to account either to the parents or the kingdom, the charge of nutriment and rags having been at least four times that value.

I shall now therefore humbly propose my own thoughts, which I hope will not be liable to the least objection.

I have been assured by a very knowing American of my acquaintance in London, that a young healthy child well nursed is at a year old a most delicious, nourishing, and wholesome food, whether stewed, roasted, baked, or boiled, and I make no doubt that it will equally serve in a fricassee or a ragout.

I do therefore humbly offer it to public consideration that of the hundred *10* and twenty thousand children, already computed, twenty thousand may be reserved for breed, whereof only one fourth part to be males, which is more than we allow to sheep, black cattle, or swine; and my reason is that these children are seldom the fruits of marriage, a circumstance not much regarded by our savages, therefore one male will be sufficient to serve four females. That the remaining hundred thousand may at a year old be offered in sale to the persons of quality and fortune through the kingdom, always advising the mother to let them suck plentifully in the last month, so as to render them plump and fat for a good table. A child will make two dishes at an entertainment for friends; and when the family dines alone, the fore or hind quarter will make a reasonable dish, and seasoned with a little pepper or salt will be very good boiled on the fourth day, especially in the winter.

I have reckoned upon a medium that a child just born will weigh twelve pounds, and in a solar year if tolerably nursed increaseth to twenty-eight pounds.

I grant this food will be somewhat dear, and therefore very proper for landlords, who, as they have already devoured most of the parents, seem to have the best title to the children.

Infant's flesh will be in season throughout the year, but more plentiful in March, and a little before and after. For we are told by a grave author, an eminent French physician, that fish being a prolific diet, there are more children born in Roman Catholic countries about nine months after Lent than at any other season, therefore, reckoning a year after Lent, the markets will be more glutted than usual, because the number of popish infants is at least three to one in this kingdom; and therefore it will have one other collateral advantage, by lessening the number of Papists among us.

I have already computed the charge of nursing a beggar's child (in which list I reckon all cottagers, laborers, and four fifths of the farmers) to be about two shillings per annum, rags included; and I believe no gentleman would repine to give ten shillings for the carcass of a good fat child, which, as I have said, will make four dishes of excellent nutritive meat, when he hath only some particular friend or his own family to dine with him. Thus the squire will learn to be a good landlord, and grow popular among the tenants; the mother will have eight shillings net profit, and be fit for work till she produces another child.

Those who are more thrifty (as I must confess the times require) may flay *15* the carcass; the skin of which artificially dressed will make admirable gloves for ladies, and summer boots for fine gentlemen.

As to our city of Dublin, shambles may be appointed for this purpose in the most convenient parts of it, and butchers we may be assured will not be wanting; although I rather recommend buying the children alive, and dressing them hot from the knife as we do roasting pigs.

A very worthy person, a true lover of his country, and whose virtues I highly esteem, was lately pleased in discoursing on this matter to offer a refinement upon my scheme. He said that many gentlemen of his kingdom, having of late destroyed their deer, he conceived that the want of venison might be well supplied by the bodies of young lads and maidens, not exceeding fourteen years of age nor under twelve, so great a number of both sexes in every county being now ready to starve for want of work and service; and these to be disposed of by their parents, if alive, or otherwise by their nearest relations. But with due deference to so excellent a friend and so deserving a patriot, I cannot be altogether in his sentiments; for as to the males, my American acquaintance assured me from frequent experience that their flesh was generally tough and lean, like that of our schoolboys, by continual exercise, and their taste disagreeable; and to fatten them would not answer the charge. Then as to the females, it would, I think with humble submission, be a loss to the public, because they soon would become breeders themselves: and besides, it is not improbable that some scrupulous people might be apt to censure such a practice (although indeed very unjustly) as a little bordering upon cruelty; which, I confess, hath always been with me the strongest objection against any project, how well so ever intended.

But in order to justify my friend, he confessed that this expedient was put into his head by the famous Psalmanazar, a native of the island Formosa, who came from thence to London about twenty years ago, and in conversation told my friend that in his country when any young person happened to be put to death, the executioner sold the carcass to persons of quality as a prime dainty; and that in his time the body of a plump girl of fifteen, who was crucified for an attempt to poison the emperor, was sold to his Imperial Majesty's prime minister of state, and other great mandarins of the court, in joints from the gibbet, at four hundred crowns. Neither indeed can I deny that if the same use were made of several plump young girls in this town, who without one single groat to their fortunes cannot stir abroad without a chair, and appear at the playhouse and assemblies in foreign fineries which they never will pay for, the kingdom would not be the worse.

Some persons of a desponding spirit are in great concern about that vast number of poor people who are aged, diseased, or maimed, and I have been desired to employ my thoughts what course may be taken to ease the nation of so grievous an encumbrance. But I am not in the least pain upon that matter, because it is very well known that they are every day dying and rotting by cold and famine, and filth and vermin, as fast as can be reasonably expected. And as to the younger laborers, they are now in almost as hopeful a condition. They cannot get work, and consequently pine away for want of nourishment

After all, I am not so violently bent upon my own opinions as to reject any offer proposed by wise men, which shall be found equally innocent, cheap, easy, and effectual. But before something of that kind shall be advanced in contradiction to my scheme, and offering a better, I desire the author or authors will be pleased maturely to consider two points. First, as things now stand, how they will be able to find food and raiment for an hundred thousand useless mouths and backs. And secondly, there being a round million of creatures in human figure throughout this kingdom, whose sole subsistence put into a common stock would leave them in debt two millions of pounds sterling, adding those who are beggars by profession to the bulk of farmers, cottagers, and laborers, with their wives and children who are beggars in effect; I desire those politicians who dislike my overture, and may perhaps be so bold to attempt an answer, that they will first ask the parents of these mortals whether they would not at this day think it a great happiness to have been sold for food at a year old in this manner I prescribe, and thereby have avoided such a perpetual scene of misfortunes as they have since gone through by the oppression of landlords, the impossibility of paying rent without money or trade, the want of common sustenance, with neither house nor clothes to cover them from the inclemencies of the weather, and the most inevitable prospect of entailing the like or greater miseries upon their breed forever.

I profess, in the sincerity of my heart, that I have not the least personal interest in endeavoring to promote this necessary work, having no other motive than the public good of my country, by advancing our trade, providing for infants, relieving the poor, and giving some pleasure to the rich. I have no children by which I can propose to get a single penny; the youngest being nine years old, and my wife past childbearing.

Reflections and Inquiries

1. Why do you suppose Swift chooses to express his views satirically? What advantage does satire have over a straightforward approach to the problem?

2. What social ills does Swift call attention to in his proposal?

3. Why does Swift refer to childbearing women as *breeders*?

4. How does Swift attempt to speak to the moral consciousness of his largely Catholic readership? What exactly is he saying to them via his proposal?

Reading to Write

Write an analysis of Swift's use of satire in this proposal. How, exactly, does it come across so powerfully?

Keynote Address at the First Woman's Rights Convention | Elizabeth Cady Stanton

Barred from a world antislavery convention in London because she was a woman, Elizabeth Cady Stanton (1815–1902), an abolitionist and cofounder (with Susan B. Anthony) of the National Woman Suffrage Association (1869), teamed up with Lucretia Coffin Mott, founder of the Female Anti-Slavery Society in Philadelphia (1833), to organize the first Women's Rights Convention (originally called the Woman's Rights Convention) in the United States in 1848. The following is an abridgment of Stanton's keynote address.

"Man cannot fulfill his destiny alone, he cannot redeem his race unaided."

We have met here today to discuss our rights and wrongs, civil and political, and not, as some have supposed, to go into the detail of social life alone. We do not propose to petition the legislature to make our husbands just, generous, and courteous, to seat every man at the head of a cradle, and to clothe every woman in male attire. None of these points, however important they may be considered by leading men, will be touched in this convention. As to their costume, the gentlemen need feel no fear of our imitating that, for we think it in violation of every principle of taste, beauty, and dignity; notwithstanding all the contempt cast upon our loose, flowing garments, we still admire the graceful folds, and consider our costume far more artistic than theirs. Many of the nobler sex seem to agree with us in this opinion, for the bishops, priests, judges, barristers, and lord mayors of the first nation on the globe, and the Pope of Rome, with his cardinals, too, all wear the loose flowing robes, thus tacitly acknowledging that the male attire is neither dignified nor imposing. No, we shall not molest you in your philosophical experiments with stocks, pants, high-heeled boots, and Russian belts. Yours be the glory to discover, by personal experience, how long the kneepan can resist the terrible strapping down which you impose, in how short time the well-developed muscles of the throat can be reduced to mere threads by the constant pressure of the stock, how high the heel of a boot must be to make a short man tall, and how tight the Russian belt may be drawn and yet have wind enough left to sustain life.

But we are assembled to protest against a form of government existing without the consent of the governed—to declare our right to be free as man is free, to be represented in the government which we are taxed to support, to have such disgraceful laws as give man the power to chastise and imprison his wife, to take the wages which she earns, the property which she inherits, and, in case of separation, the children of her love; laws which make her the mere dependent on his bounty. It is to protest against such unjust laws as these that we are assembled today, and to have them, if possible, forever erased from our statute books, deeming them

---

Source: Elizabeth Cady Stanton, "Keynote Address at the First Woman's Rights Convention, July 19, 1848," *A Treasury of the World's Greatest Speeches*, ed. Houston Peterson (New York: Simon, 1965) 389–92.

Elizabeth Cady Stanton, left (1815–1902) and Susan B. Anthony (1820–1906) were two early champions of women's rights.

Napoleon Sarony/Bettmann/Corbis

a shame and a disgrace to a Christian republic in the nineteenth century. We have met to uplift woman's fallen divinity upon an even pedestal with man's.

And, strange as it may seem to many, we now demand our right to vote according to the declaration of the government under which we live. This right no one pretends to deny. We need not prove ourselves equal to Daniel Webster to enjoy this privilege, for the ignorant Irishman in the ditch has all the civil rights he has. We need not prove our muscular power equal to this same Irishman to enjoy this privilege, for the most tiny, weak, ill-shaped stripling of twenty-one has all the civil rights of the Irishman. We have no objection to discuss the question of equality, for we feel that the weight of argument lies wholly with us, but we wish the question of equality kept distinct from the question of rights, for the proof of the one does not determine the truth of the other. All white men in this country have the same rights, however they may differ in mind, body, or estate.

The right is ours. The question now is: how shall we get possession of what rightfully belongs to us? We should not feel so sorely grieved if no man who had not attained the full stature of a Webster, Clay, Van Buren, or Gerrit Smith could claim the right of the elective franchise. But to have drunkards, idiots, horse-racing, rum-selling rowdies, ignorant foreigners, and silly boys fully recognized, while we ourselves are thrust out from all the rights that belong to citizens, it is too grossly insulting to the dignity of woman to be longer quietly submitted to. The right is ours. Have it, we must. Use it, we will. The pens, the tongues, the fortunes, the indomitable wills of many women are already pledged to secure this right. The great truth that no just government can be

formed without the consent of the governed we shall echo and re-echo in the
ears of the unjust judge, until by continual coming we shall weary him ... .

5   There seems now to be a kind of moral stagnation in our midst. Philanthropists have done their utmost to rouse the nation to a sense of its sins. War, slavery, drunkenness, licentiousness, gluttony, have been dragged naked before
the people, and all their abominations and deformities fully brought to light,
yet with idiotic laugh we hug those monsters to our breasts and rush on to
destruction. Our churches are multiplying on all sides, our missionary societies, Sunday schools, and prayer meetings and innumerable charitable and
reform organizations are all in operation, but still the tide of vice is swelling,
and threatens the destruction of everything, and the battlements of righteousness are weak against the raging elements of sin and death. Verily, the world
waits the coming of some new element, some purifying power, some spirit of
mercy and love. The voice of woman has been silenced in the state, the church,
and the home, but man cannot fulfill his destiny alone, he cannot redeem his
race unaided. There are deep and tender chords of sympathy and love in the
hearts of the downfallen and oppressed that woman can touch more skillfully
than man.

The world has never yet seen a truly great and virtuous nation, because
in the degradation of woman the very fountains of life are poisoned at their
source. It is vain to look for silver and gold from mines of copper and lead. It is
the wise mother that has the wise son. So long as your women are slaves you
may throw your colleges and churches to the winds. You can't have scholars
and saints so long as your mothers are ground to powder between the upper
and nether millstone of tyranny and lust. How seldom, now, is a father's pride
gratified, his fond hopes realized, in the budding genius of his son! The wife
is degraded, made the mere creature of caprice, and the foolish son is heavi-
ness to his heart. Truly are the sins of the fathers visited upon the children to
the third and fourth generation. God, in His wisdom, has so linked the whole
human family together that any violence done at one end of the chain is felt
throughout its length, and there, too, is the law of restoration, as in woman all
have fallen, so in her elevation shall the race be recreated.

"Voices" were the visitors and advisers of Joan of Arc. Do not "voices"
come to us daily from the haunts of poverty, sorrow, degradation, and despair,
already too long unheeded. Now is the time for the women of this country,
if they would save our free institutions, to defend the right, to buckle on the
armor that can best resist the keenest weapons of the enemy—contempt and
ridicule. The same religious enthusiasm that nerved Joan of Arc to her work
nerves us to ours. In every generation God calls some men and women for the
utterance of truth, a heroic action, and our work today is the fulfilling of what
has long since been foretold by the Prophet—Joel 2:28: "And it shall come to
pass afterward, that I will pour out my spirit upon all flesh; and your sons and
your daughters shall prophesy." We do not expect our path will be strewn with
the flowers of popular applause, but over the thorns of bigotry and prejudice

will be our way, and on our banners will beat the dark storm clouds of opposition from those who have entrenched themselves behind the stormy bulwarks of custom and authority, and who have fortified their position by every means, holy and unholy. But we will steadfastly abide the result. Unmoved we will bear it aloft. Undauntedly we will unfurl it to the gale, for we know that the storm cannot rend from it a shred, that the electric flash will but more clearly show to us the glorious words inscribed upon it, "Equality of Rights." ...

Reflections and Inquiries

1. Why does Stanton open with a reference to male and female modes of dress? What point does she make with her witty reference to the apparel of certain members of the clergy?

2. What laws does Stanton consider to be "a disgrace to a Christian republic"? Why?

3. What is the purpose of Stanton's allusion to Joan of Arc?

4. What consequences of female degradation does Stanton articulate?

Reading to Write

Examine Stanton's argument from an organizational perspective. Outline the sequence of points she makes and then suggest a rationale for this sequence in relation to her thesis. How well does her opening prepare for what follows?

I Hear the Mournful Wail of Millions | Frederick Douglass

On July 4, 1852, Frederick Douglass (1817–1895), a former slave (he escaped to New England in his twenties) and member of the Massachusetts Antislavery Society who one day would discuss slavery with President Lincoln, was invited to commemorate Independence Day in Rochester, New York, with the following speech.

Fellow citizens, pardon me, allow me to ask, why am I called upon to speak here today? What have I, or those I represent, to do with your national independence? Are the great principles of political freedom and of natural justice, embodied in that Declaration of Independence, extended to us? and am I, therefore, called upon to bring

Source: Frederick Douglass, "I Hear the Mournful Wail of Millions," *A Treasury of the World's Greatest Speeches*, ed. Houston Peterson (New York: Simon, 1965) 478–82.

our humble offering to the national altar, and to confess the benefits and express devout gratitude for the blessings resulting from your independence to us?

Would to God, both for your sakes and ours, that an affirmative answer could be truthfully returned to these questions! Then would my task be light, and my burden easy and delightful. For who is there so cold that a nation's sympathy could not warm him? Who so obdurate and dead to the claims of gratitude that would not thankfully acknowledge such priceless benefits? Who so stolid and selfish that would not give his voice to swell the hallelujahs of a nation's jubilee, when the chains of servitude had been torn from his limbs? I am not that man. In a case like that the dumb might eloquently speak and the "lame man leap as an hart."

But such is not the state of the case. I say it with a sad sense of the disparity between us. I am not included within the pale of this glorious anniversary! Your high independence only reveals the immeasurable distance between us. The blessings in which you, this day, rejoice are not enjoyed in common. The rich inheritance of justice, liberty, prosperity, and independence bequeathed by your fathers is shared by you, not by me. The sunlight that brought light and healing to you has brought stripes and death to me. This Fourth of July is yours, not mine. You may rejoice, I must mourn. To drag a man in fetters into the grand illuminated temple of liberty, and call upon him to join you in joyous anthems, were inhuman mockery and sacrilegious irony. Do you mean, citizens, to mock me by asking me to speak today? If so, there is a parallel to your conduct. And let me warn you that it is dangerous to copy the example of a nation whose crimes, towering up to heaven, were thrown down by the breath of the Almighty, burying that nation in irrevocable ruin! I can today take up the plaintive lament of a peeled and woe-smitten people!

"By the rivers of Babylon, there we sat down. Yea! we wept when we remembered Zion. We hanged our harps upon the willows in the midst thereof. For there, they that carried us away captive, required of us a song; and they who wasted us required of us mirth, saying, Sing us one of the songs of Zion. How can we sing the Lord's song in a strange land? If I forget thee, O Jerusalem, let my right hand forget her cunning. If I do not remember thee, let my tongue cleave to the roof of my mouth."

5   Fellow citizens, above your national, tumultuous joy, I hear the mournful wail of millions! whose chains, heavy and grievous yesterday, are, today, rendered more intolerable by the jubilee shouts that reach them. If I do forget, if I do not faithfully remember those bleeding children of sorrow this day, "may my right hand forget her cunning, and may my tongue cleave to the roof of my mouth"! To forget them, to pass lightly over their wrongs, and to chime in with the popular theme would be treason most scandalous and shocking, and would make me a reproach before God and the world. My subject, then, fellow citizens, is *American slavery*. I shall see this day and its popular characteristics from the slave's point of view. Standing there identified with the American bondman, making his wrongs mine. I do not hesitate to declare with all my

Frederick Douglass (1817–1895) was a self-educated former slave who discussed the evils of slavery with Abraham Lincoln and served as a U.S. minister to Haiti.

Bettmann/Corbis

soul that the character and conduct of this nation never looked blacker to me than on this Fourth of July! Whether we turn to the declarations of the past or to the professions of the present, the conduct of the nation seems equally hideous and revolting. America is false to the past, false to the present, and solemnly binds herself to be false to the future. Standing with God and the crushed and bleeding slave on this occasion, I will, in the name of humanity which is outraged, in the name of liberty which is fettered, in the name of the Constitution and the Bible which are disregarded and trampled upon, dare to call in question and to denounce, with all the emphasis I can command, everything that serves to perpetuate slavery—the great sin and shame of America! "I will not equivocate; I will not excuse;" I will use the severest language I can command; and yet not one word shall escape me that any man, whose judgment is not blinded by prejudice, or who is not at heart a slaveholder, shall not confess to be right and just.

But I fancy I hear someone of my audience say, "It is just in this circumstance that you and your brother abolitionists fail to make a favorable impression on the public mind. Would you argue more and denounce less, would you persuade more and rebuke less, your cause would be much more likely to succeed." But, I submit, where all is plain, there is nothing to be argued. What point in the antislavery creed would you have me argue? On what branch of the subject do the people of this country need light? Must I undertake to prove that the slave is a man? That point is conceded already. Nobody doubts it. The slaveholders themselves acknowledge it in the enactment of laws for their government. They acknowledge it when they punish disobedience on the part of the slave. There are seventy-two crimes in the state of Virginia which, if committed by a black man (no matter how ignorant he be), subject him to the punishment of death; while only two of the same crimes will subject a white man to the like punishment. What is this but the acknowledgment that the slave is a moral, intellectual, and responsible being? The manhood of the slave is conceded. It is admitted in the fact that Southern statute books are covered with enactments forbidding, under severe fines and penalties, the teaching of the slave to read or to write. When you can point to any such laws in reference to the beasts of the field, then I may consent to argue the manhood of the slave. When the dogs in your streets, when the fowls of the air, when the cattle on your hills, when the fish of the sea and the reptiles that crawl shall be unable to distinguish the slave from the brute, then will I argue with you that the slave is a man!

For the present, it is enough to affirm the equal manhood of the Negro race. Is it not astonishing that, while we are plowing, planting, and reaping, using all kinds of mechanical tools, erecting houses, constructing bridges, building ships, working in metals of brass, iron, copper, silver, and gold; that, while we are reading, writing, and ciphering, acting as clerks, merchants, and secretaries, having among us lawyers, doctors, ministers, poets, authors, editors, orators, and teachers; that, while we are engaged in all manner of enterprises common to other men, digging gold in California, capturing the whale in the Pacific, feeding sheep and cattle on the hillside, living, moving, acting, thinking, planning, living in families as husbands, wives, and children, and, above all, confessing and worshiping the Christian's God, and looking hopefully for life and immortality beyond the grave, we are called upon to prove that we are men!

Would you have me argue that man is entitled to liberty? that he is the rightful owner of his own body? You have already declared it. Must I argue the wrongfulness of slavery? Is that a question for republicans? Is it to be settled by the rules of logic and argumentation, as a matter beset with great difficulty, involving a doubtful application of the principle of justice, hard to be understood? How should I look today, in the presence of Americans, dividing and subdividing a discourse, to show that men have a natural right to freedom? speaking of it relatively and positively, negatively and affirmatively? To do so would be to make myself ridiculous and to offer an insult to your understanding. There is not a man beneath the canopy of heaven that does not know that slavery is wrong for him.

What, am I to argue that it is wrong to make men brutes, to rob them of their liberty, to work them without wages, to keep them ignorant of their relations to their fellow men, to beat them with sticks, to flay their flesh with the lash, to load their limbs with irons, to hunt them with dogs, to sell them at auction, to sunder their families, to knock out their teeth, to burn their flesh, to starve them into obedience and submission to their masters? Must I argue that a system thus marked with blood, and stained with pollution, is wrong? No! I will not. I have better employment for my time and strength than such arguments would imply.

What, then, remains to be argued? Is it that slavery is not divine; that God did not establish it; that our doctors of divinity are mistaken? There is blasphemy in the thought. That which is inhuman cannot be divine! Who can reason on such a proposition? They that can may; I cannot. The time for such argument is past.

At a time like this, scorching iron, not convincing argument, is needed. O! had I the ability, and could I reach the nation's ear, I would today pour out a fiery stream of biting ridicule, blasting reproach, withering sarcasm, and stern rebuke. For it is not light that is needed, but fire; it is not the gentle shower, but thunder. We need the storm, the whirlwind, and the earthquake. The feeling of the nation must be quickened; the conscience of the nation must be roused; the propriety of the nation must be startled; the hypocrisy of the nation must be exposed; and its crimes against God and man must be proclaimed and denounced.

What, to the American slave, is your Fourth of July? I answer: a day that reveals to him, more than all other days in the year, the gross injustice and cruelty to which he is the constant victim. To him, your celebration is a sham; your boasted liberty, an unholy license; your national greatness, swelling vanity; your sounds of rejoicing are empty and heartless; your denunciation of tyrants, brass-fronted impudence; your shouts of liberty and equality, hollow mockery; your prayers and hymns, your sermons and thanksgivings, with all your religious parade and solemnity, are, to Him, mere bombast, fraud, deception, impiety, and hypocrisy—a thin veil to cover up crimes which would disgrace a nation of savages. There is not a nation of savages. There is not a nation on the earth guilty of practices more shocking and bloody than are the people of the United States at this very hour.

Go where you may, search where you will, roam through all the monarchies and despotisms of the Old World, travel through South America, search out every abuse, and when you have found the last, lay your facts by the side of the everyday practices of this nation, and you will say with me that, for revolting barbarity and shameless hypocrisy, America reigns without a rival.

Reflections and Inquiries

1. How does Douglass use the special occasion of Independence Day as a foundation for his address? How effectively does it come across?

2. What is significant about the first two words of his speech from a historical/political perspective? From a rhetorical one?

3. At one point, Douglass asserts, regarding the abolition of slavery, that "there is nothing to be argued." Why does he say this?

4. How does Douglass characterize the Fourth of July from the perspective of a slave?

Reading to Write

Write a comparative analysis of Douglass's speech with Martin Luther King's "Letter from Birmingham Jail," on pages 145–157. In what ways are they similar? Different? Include a discussion of their respective rhetorical strategies.

Connections Among the Clusters

One of the most important insights gained from the study of argumentation is that any given issue is often connected to other issues. For example, injustices relating to the voting rights of minorities and women are connected to the rights of minorities and women in the workplace or in higher education. The following questions should help you to draw useful connections between the issues raised in this Cluster and those raised in subsequent Clusters.

Critical Thinking

1. If Swift's "A Modest Proposal" were made into a TV drama, it is conceivable that many would try to ban it on the basis of excessive violence. Defend or challenge this view. (See selections relating to censorship in Cluster 5.)

2. Discuss Frederick Douglass's and Elizabeth Cady Stanton's speeches in the context of multicultural learning. (See Cluster 4.)

3. How might Plato's "Allegory of the Cave" be used to resolve issues relating to multicultural learning? (See Cluster 4.)

4. Assume that a school principal refuses to allow Andrew Marvell's "To His Coy Mistress" to be taught to sixth-grade students. Defend or challenge that principal's decision. (See Cluster 5.)

Writing Projects

1. Analyze the way Plato's allegory deals with spiritual truths. How would Plato's notion of spirituality compare to that of a modern-day theologian?

2. Write an essay that satirizes a social injustice. Use Swift's "A Modest Proposal" as a possible model.

3. Write a speech that calls attention to a current injustice in civil rights. Use Douglass's or Stanton's speech as a possible model.

Suggestions for Further Reading

Speeches and Sermons

Bryan, William Jennings. "Cross of Gold" (1896). *A Treasury of the World's Great Speeches*. Ed. Houston Peterson. New York: Grolier, 1964.

Edwards, Jonathan. "Sinners in the Hands of an Angry God." From *Jonathan Edwards: Representative Selections*, ed. Clarence H. Faust and Thomas H. Johnson. New York: Hill, 1935: 155–72.

Emerson, Ralph Waldo. "Divinity School Address" (1837). *Selected Writings of Ralph Waldo Emerson*. Ed. William H. Gilman. New York: Signet, 2003.

Jesus. "The Sermon on the Mount," Matthew 5–7.

Lincoln, Abraham. "The Gettysburg Address" (1863). *A Treasury of the World's Great Speeches*. Ed. Houston Peterson. New York: Grolier, 1964.

Essays, Manifestoes, and Treatises

Arendt, Hannah. *The Origins of Totalitarianism*. New York: Harcourt, 1951; 1967.

Carson, Rachel. *Silent Spring*. New York: Houghton Mifflin, 1962.

Darwin, Charles. *On the Origin of Species* (1859). New York: Bantam, 1999.

de Beauvoir, Simone. *The Second Sex*. Trans. H. M. Parshley. New York: Knopf, 1953.

Freud, Sigmund. *Civilization and Its Discontents* (1930). Trans. James Strachey. New York: Norton, 1962.

Heilbrun, Carolyn G. "The Character of Hamlet's Mother." From *Hamlet's Mother and Other Women*. New York: Ballantine Books, 1990: 9–19.

Machiavelli, Niccolo. *The Prince* (1532). Trans. George Bull. New York: Penguin, 1961.

Mead, Margaret, and James Baldwin. *A Rap on Race*. New York: Lippincott, 1971.

Milgram, Stanley. *Obedience to Authority*. New York: HarperCollins, 1974.

Mill, John Stewart. *On Liberty* (1859). Norton Critical Edition. New York: W.W. Norton & Co., 1975.

Orwell, George. "Politics and the English Language" (1946). *Selected Essays*. New York: Penguin, 1960.

Skinner, B. F. *Beyond Freedom and Dignity*. New York: Knopf, 1971.

Thoreau, Henry David. "Civil Disobedience" (1849). *The Portable Thoreau*. Ed. Carl Bode. New York: Penguin, 1977.

Veblen, Thorstein. *The Theory of the Leisure Class* (1899). Boston: Houghton, 1973.

2 Athletics and Academics: How Do They Benefit Each Other?

Introduction

For some faculty—and students as well—"athletics" and "academics" are mutually repellant. College, they argue, should be a place for cultivating the mind, not the body. It is certainly not a place for engaging in the kinds of recruitment strategies and profiteering associated with professional sports. Athletics programs, dissenters argue, interfere with the very process of classroom education, as when student athletes skip class to participate in out-of-town competitions.

For others, however, college athletics programs are as essential to education ("education of the whole person") as any academic program; they hold that the mind–body dichotomy is a false one. If athletic programs are going to be scrapped, they argue, then why not scrap theater and dance programs as well? Moreover, athletic scholarships give many students their only opportunity to gain a foothold in academe, and successful athletic programs give many otherwise unknown institutions a chance to have a nationwide reputation. Alumni connected to the athletic programs of their alma maters are often the most generous in terms of donations to the universities—not just to the athletic programs. Top Division I academic institutions, such as Stanford, show that student athletes can excel at both. (Students from Stanford have won Olympic medals and been part of teams that have won national collegiate titles. Stanford annually supplies both Rhodes and Fulbright scholars.) In fact, some would argue that a university cannot be considered great unless it is a leader in both academics and athletics.

The issues associated with the role of sports in college are many, as the range of essays in this cluster indicates. How should we deal with the "dumb jock" stereotyping of student athletes? How do we solve the abuses in athletic programs that do indeed occur? What, exactly, should students "learn" from playing sports? How can an athletic program help the host college financially without resorting to exploitation of the athletes? What would constitute the most ethical recruitment policies?

Are Student Athletes Really Students?

A knee-jerk response to this question might be, of course they are students! But to many critics of college athletic programs, the question implies that the time and energy required for training, practice, and game participation undermine the true purpose of a college education: academics.

Game Score, Test Scores | Edward Koren

Edward Koren's cartoon depicting a scoreboard for test scores as well as for game scores whimsically calls attention to the concern of everyone—educators, parents, and sports fans, as well as the athletes themselves—that participation in sports not compromise academic achievement. Edward Koren is a prolific cartoonist, having published nearly a thousand cartoons in The New Yorker, Time, Newsweek, Sports Illustrated, and other periodicals.

Edward Koren/The New Yorker Collection/cartoonbank.com

Reflections and Inquiries

1. What serious point does Koren make with his cartoon?
2. Should GPA (as opposed to other means of determining academic excellence) be the sole criterion for determining eligibility? If so, explain. If not, what other criteria should be used?
3. What might have been Koren's rationale for depicting a basketball game (rather than, say, a football or baseball game) in his cartoon?

Reading to Write

1. Write an essay supporting or challenging the use of minimum test scores as a way of qualifying high school or college students for participation in

school-sponsored athletic events. Use the Classical, Toulmin, or Rogerian method in developing your argument.

2. Research what your school requires for its teams' minimum GPA for student athletes to play. Write an essay supporting or challenging that minimum GPA.

College Sports vs. Academics | Bryan Flynn

The debating seems interminable: Should institutions of higher learning continue to involve themselves in athletic programs that often turn out to be virtual arms races for recruiting talented players who would bring big money and prestige? Bryan Flynn covers athletic events for the Jackson (Mississippi) *Free Press.*

When people find out I'm a sports writer, they tend to ask similar questions. Most ask my opinion about this team or that player. But, every now and then, someone asks me about what I think is one of the most intriguing subjects in sports: the effect of college sports on academics and economics.

Since the early 2000s, there seems to be an "arms race" in college football to build bigger stadiums and earn more money in college athletics. But people have major concerns about the rising cost of coaches' salaries and that those salaries are rising quicker than professors' salaries. Colleges and universities want the best professors to provide quality education and research. Low pay could cause the professors to look elsewhere for employment.

Recently, Mississippi State University gave head coach Dan Mullen a significant pay raise. Mullen was making $1.5 million a year under his old contract, but after an 8-4 regular season, MSU decided their coach needed a pay increase. In a new four-year deal, Mullen will earn about $2.65 million annually.

5   Who foots that large bill?

Good question. The university will pay Mullen $250,000. Donations to the private Bulldog Foundation pay the rest of his salary.

So what does MSU pay their professors? The average salary in 2009-10 was $92,700. That would lead you to believe that Mullen makes $2.56 million more than the average professor at MSU.

But this is where it gets tricky. While professors might not make the money per year Mullen is paid, their salaries are not the grand total of their incomes. The American Association of University Professors (AAUP) does not require universities to report summer salary (summer teaching, stipends, extra load or other forms of remuneration), only contracted salary. Their contracted salaries also do not include income from research grants typically earned in the summer, or from consulting, speaking or publishing.

Source: Bryan Flynn, "College Sports vs. Academics," *Jackson Free Press*, April 16, 2011, Web.

If coaches' salaries are not a concern, people want to know how much universities spend on sports. Another tricky question.

College athletics have only two guaranteed moneymaking sports: football and men's basketball. A few exceptions exist where sports like baseball or women's basketball makes money for a school, but that's not the rule.

This generally means that football and men's basketball has to pay for all the other sports that lose money, putting more pressure to win on football and men's basketball coaches. Winning equals more booster donations, higher ticket sales (few will pay to see losing teams), higher merchandise sales and other moneymaking endeavors.

So why not get rid of all those money-losing sports? That leads us to Title IX.

Title IX is part of a federal law that provides equal opportunity in education, including in sports programs. Universities must offer equal participation in women's sports as in men's sports. For example, sports scholarships for men and women must be the same.

Not to get bogged down on specifics, but Title IX is one reason universities cannot cut money-draining athletic programs. When universities have cut athletic programs, they have usually been men's sports teams.

Universities place a bigger emphasis on football and basketball to fund their athletic programs. That leads to a bigger question: Are athletic departments funding themselves, or are they a drain on the university?

Again, this is a hard question to answer because a lot of the data are questionable at best. Most athletic departments show balancing revenues and expenditures.

Some question if athletic directors are "cooking the books" in terms of spending, says Rick Hesel, a principal of Baltimore's Art & Science Group, who helped the Knight Commission on Intercollegiate Athletics complete a study on spending on college athletics.

Studies that ask if success in athletics lead to more money for academics show mixed results. Some say sports provide no academic benefit, and others say there is a slight benefit.

Overall, though, experts admit that successful sports teams lead to increased enrollment and donations.

"Like it or not—and I generally don't—college sports is the main thing that makes alumni enthusiastic about their school," wrote publisher James Joyner on his website Outside the Beltway.

This entire subject is controversial and without easy answers.

Every time someone brings up college sports and money, I'm reminded of the movie "The Program." In one scene, James Caan's character, Coach Winter, tries to get his back-up quarterback back on the team after he's been kicked out of school.

"This is not a football vocational school. It's an institute for higher learning," the regent chairman tells him.

"Yeah, but when was the last time 80,000 people showed up to watch a kid do a damn chemistry experiment?" Caan asks.

For a 1993 film, it was ahead of its time.

Reflections and Inquiries

1. What is your reaction to the James Caan character's dichotomy between a college as a football vocational school and as an institute for higher learning? Is this a false or faulty dichotomy? Explain. You may first want to review the discussion of the either-or fallacy in Chapter 5.
2. In light of the salaries head coaches make, are college professors paid fairly or unfairly? What evidence do you use to support your claim?

Reading to Write

1. In a short essay, take a stance on the salaries of coaches versus the salaries of professors at your school.
2. Should your school increase or downsize its athletic program? Argue your premise in a four-page (1,000-word) essay.
3. How has Title IX affected your own school? Consult the resources on your campus—the Affirmative Action Office, the Compliance Officer of campus athletics—as well as the statute itself, available at www.dol.gov/oasam/regs/statutes/titleix.htm, to argue an informed piece on whether Title IX has benefited or detracted from students' opportunities for higher education.

Brawn & Brains: Student Athletes Get a Bum Rap | Dave Newhouse

Few would disagree that college should be a place where stereotyping—a major roadblock to learning—is eliminated; yet the collegiate athlete persists in being a victim of stereotyping. At the University of California, Berkeley, however, the image of the college athlete is undergoing a transformation, thanks to the efforts of Herb Simons, a professor in Cal's Graduate School of Education. He has developed a master's program called "Athletics and Academic Achievement." In the following article, Dave Newhouse, a staff writer for the San Mateo County Times *(a newspaper serving the Bay Area peninsula county just south of San Francisco), describes some of the unexpected findings of Simons's program and Cal's Athletic Study Center.*

Athletically, it goes with the turf, it's an unwritten part of every scholarship, and there's no escaping it even if you attend Cal, rated the nation's No. 1 public university.

You're a "dumb jock" regardless.

"I've done a study on this, and athletes at this university are stigmatized," said Herb Simons, a Cal professor who oversees a unique master's program that

---

Source: © Dave Newhouse, "Brawn & Brains: Student Athletes Get a Bum Rap," *Oakland Tribune* March 23, 2006. Reprinted by permission of the *Oakland Tribune.*

focuses on the academic side of student-athletes. "They're assumed to be not smart enough or interested enough."

This assumption, Simons said, is held by students and faculty.

"If you're an athlete, it's the opinion that you're not as smart as a regular   5
student," he said. "In my study, some athletes shut up in class or drop the class if the professor says something negative (about them).

"Another thing student-athletes do is try to keep their identity hidden. They don't wear their athletic clothing to class. They do not want to be known as an athlete. They try to keep it a secret."

Cal athletes qualify for NCAA tournaments and play in bowl games, but the same students who cheer them on denigrate them in the classroom.

"They hear things like, 'This test is easy. Even athletes can pass,'" Simons said. "Or, 'You're degrading my degree and my major.'"

The dumb-jock image is nothing new at Cal or at most institutions; it's a stigma that traces back to college athletics' roots in the mid-1800s. The athlete is systematically branded as lacking in intelligence.

Perhaps unfairly.   10

"Athletes are successful students," Simons emphasized. "They know how to work hard, how to deal with failure, how to manage their time. Being an athlete takes so much determination and motivation. They're interested in trying anything. They take on the task."

And, despite the negativity that student-athletes encounter from peers and professors, they're very successful in completing the task.

Derek Van Rheenen, director of Cal's Athletic Study Center, offers the following evidence: Half of Cal's 900 student-athletes have 3.0 (B) grade-point averages or higher; five of Cal's 13 men's teams and 10 of its 14 women's teams have cumulative 3.0 GPAs; of the 26 Cal football players who completed their eligibility in 2004, 22 have graduated, or 85 percent.

"Eighty-five percent is comparable to the overall graduation rate at Berkeley," Van Rheenen said. "The *Los Angeles Times* wrote last year that Cal was a model for the rest of the country in terms of the student-athlete, and if there was a Heisman Trophy for that, we would be the recipient."

The Athletic Study Center, founded in 1984, provides tutors for student-   15
athletes with the most critical academic needs. The Student Learning Center is for all Cal students. Van Rheenen reports directly to the vice provost, not the athletic department, thereby reducing pressure from coaches.

Simons, 68—a professor in the Graduate School of Education specializing in language and literacy, society and culture—has been at Cal 35 years, having chosen education over a career in optometry. He believes the general public has no concept of the rigors confronting student-athletes.

"It's the demands on the kids, which are enormous, the amount of time they have to put in," he said.

The NCAA restricts an athlete to 20 hours of participation in his or her sport weekly; however, what the NCAA dictates, it can't always see.

"There are many exceptions," Simons said of that rule. "Weight training doesn't count. Voluntary activity doesn't count; it's more like voluntary/mandatory. The more competitive the university has become playing football, the more the demands increase.

20   "It's amazing that these athletes do well academically. They get injured, they're exhausted, their sport is year-round. One athlete told me, 'You don't have to work at it all summer, but you'll be third string.'"

Non-athletes don't experience these same demands at Cal. So who's denigrating which classroom, which degree, which major? The student-athlete should serve as a beacon of education rather than as a blight.

2005 NCAA graduation chart

Beginning with the 1998–99 academic year, based on a four-year average

	All students	Student-athletes
PAC-10		
Arizona	55%	58%
Arizona State	52%	57%
Oregon	60%	64%
Oregon State	59%	57%
Cal	84%	69%
Stanford	94%	88%
USC	78%	61%
UCLA	85%	62%
Washington	71%	68%
Washington State	61%	61%
Other Bay Area Division I schools		
St. Mary's	68%	68%
Santa Clara	82%	76%
San Jose State	38%	44%
USF	66%	58%
UOP	68%	70%

	All students	Student-athletes
Various national Division I schools		
Alabama	61%	55%
Bradley	70%	77%
Connecticut	70%	62%
Duke	93%	90%
Gonzaga	77%	68%
Florida	76%	58%
Florida State	64%	62%
Georgia	71%	55%
Memphis	33%	45%
Miami Florida	67%	60%
Michigan	85%	77%
Nevada	48%	50%
Nevada-Las Vegas	38%	38%
Northwestern	92%	86%
Notre Dame	95%	90%
Ohio State	60%	62%
Oklahoma	54%	55%
Penn State	82%	80%
Tennessee	59%	55%
Texas	72%	56%
Vanderbilt	84%	77%
Virginia Tech	74%	70%
Wisconsin	76%	70%

Service academies and Ivy League schools don't offer athletic scholarships per se.
Source: NCAA

One such student-athlete was Keasara "Kiki" Williams. She started on the Cal women's basketball team, earned her master's degree in Simons' program and now is a first-year law student at Hastings in San Francisco.

"Some teachers at Cal tell students that if they can't be there for finals because of a sporting event, don't take the class," Williams said.

Despite the strict demands placed upon her athletically and academically, Williams graduated with a 3.3 GPA in sociology in four years.

25   "A lot of student-athletes are doing the same thing," she said of the four-year window. "It's a lot of time management."

Because Williams redshirted as a freshman, she began her master's work during her fifth year at Cal while completing her eligibility in basketball.

"He really cares about the athletes," she said of Simons. "He sees things we haven't thought of before, like study habits and picking whatever issue we wanted for our thesis. I did mine (in partnership) on NCAA violations and how they affect different schools and conferences differently."

Simons' master's candidates must complete 24 units in one academic year, plus write a thesis, to earn their degree from his program, called "Athletes and Academic Achievement." A minimum 3.0 GPA is required to enter any master's or doctoral program at Berkeley, but student-athletes who have entered Simons' program have a combined 3.46 GPA average.

Dumb jock, his eye.

30   "So often, student-athletes are seen as having low academics," said former Cal football player Tyler Fredrickson. "Most of the time, you hear negative things about guys barely getting into school."

In 2003, Fredrickson kicked game-winning field goals against USC and Virginia Tech in the Insight Bowl. A 3.4 GPA student in film studies, Fredrickson also produced an acclaimed documentary on that '03 Cal team for his master's thesis.

"The thing that's great about Herb is his flexibility," said Fredrickson, who recently signed with the Denver Broncos. "He wants people to pursue their academics at a higher level, and not take a ballroom dancing class like (USC quarterback) Matt Leinart.

"There's so much knowledge that a student-athlete brings to the table that the average student can't bring regarding life experience. There's so much in athletics that prepares you for a post-athletic career that you don't get from just studying in the classroom."

Simons also runs Cal's tutoring program for student-athletes. He hires graduate students as his tutors.

35   "Though the athletes we work with are the least prepared, some are very successful," he said. "There are differences in ability, never mind skills. Some are really smart kids who don't have the skills. Some are not used to writing papers. A series of drafts are surprising to them. But they should be able to get a degree if they're willing to work at it."

The NCAA's most recent graduation rates, released in 2005, cover both students and student-athletes. These graduation rates begin with the 1998–99 academic year and encompass a four-year period, although some students and student-athletes need more than four years to graduate.

The NCAA reported that 84 percent of Cal students graduated, compared with 67 percent of its student-athletes; however, athletes who transferred or left school early to pursue a professional sport or Olympic competition still counted against Cal's graduation rate, even if they graduated elsewhere. Stanford's comparable graduation rates provided by the NCAA: Students, 94 percent, student-athletes, 88 percent.

"It's no secret that Stanford has higher entrance standards for athletes than Cal," Simons said. "But private schools, traditionally, have higher graduation rates than public schools. If someone is paying $40,000 [for a child's education], they don't let them slip through the cracks."

Simons said Cal's athletic department is given exceptions by the admissions office in terms of admitting student-athletes with special needs.

"Cal can 'tag' 200 athletes it wants to get in, who vary in SAT scores," he said. "It's true everywhere that there's a certain tagging system, even in the Ivy League." Some Cal athletes are assigned one tutor; some are assigned two. These athletes meet twice weekly with a tutor, a total of three hours, and once a week with a supervisor for an hour. Plus the tutors meet with Simons weekly.

"My interest is making sure these athletes get the education they were promised when they came here," Simons said. "The (academic) turnaround can happen in a year if they're motivated."

Tutors help the athletes beyond their academic concerns. Simons discovered the athletes, mostly first-year students, will tell tutors things they don't tell anyone else. In other words, a tutorial confessional.

Simons, who has written in numerous educational journals, will retire at the end of the current academic year. He will return to Cal in the fall to work exclusively with his master's students. Van Rheenen will take over his tutoring responsibilities.

"My greatest joy has been working with the kids. I haven't met a student-athlete who was a bad kid," Simons said. "Their getting together as a group [socially], that's a different way [of fraternizing]. But every one of them has been nice and personable."

Reflections and Inquiries

1. According to Dave Newhouse, "The student athlete should serve as a beacon of education rather than as a blight." On what grounds does Newhouse rest this claim? How adequate, in your opinion, is Newhouse's evidence?
2. What function does Cal's Athletic Study Center serve? How necessary do you think this facility is?
3. What are some of the negative consequences of experiencing discrimination as a student athlete?

Reading to Write

Study the 2005 NCAA graduation chart (included with this article) in which the graduation rates of student athletes are compared to the graduation rates of all students. Compare these data to those from earlier periods (say, 1985 and 1995) as well from a more recent period (say, 2013 or 2014). What generalizations are you prepared to make about the graduation rates of student athletes in relation to types of college from which they graduate? You may need to access the websites of some of the colleges to learn more about their athletic programs. Present your conclusions in a detailed essay.

| **Academic Motivation and the Student Athlete** | Herbert D. Simons, Derek Van Rheenen, and Martin V. Covington |

In the following study, the researchers discuss their examination of 361 Division I athletes for their achievement motivation. What influence do fear of athletic failure and general commitment to athletics have on the academic motivation of these students, some of whom are revenue athletes, others nonrevenue athletes? Herbert D. Simons is an associate professor of education, Derek Van Rheenen a lecturer in education, and Martin V. Covington a professor of psychology; all teach at the University of California, Berkeley.

The researchers in this large-scale study of Division I athletes examined the achievement motivation of 361 university student athletes. The relationship of motivational orientation to academic performance and identification was investigated using a paper and pencil Likert-type scale instrument based on self-worth theory. Fear of failure and the relative commitment to athletics was found to play important roles in the academic motivation of both revenue and nonrevenue student athletes.

University student athletes present an apparent motivational contradiction. Most are highly motivated to succeed in the athletic domain, having been selected to participate in intercollegiate athletics because of their proven ability and desire to succeed. However, many of the most visible student athletes seem to lack such motivation in the classroom. Although these individuals are expected to maintain their athletic motivation at the university, they are likewise expected to demonstrate a similar motivation to succeed in the classroom. The maintenance of this academic motivation and achievement is made more difficult because of the institutional demands of their sport. Student athletes are required to devote upwards of 25 hours per week when their sport is in season, miss numerous classes for university-sanctioned athletic competitions, and deal with fatigue and injuries as a

---

Source: "Academic Motivation and the Student Athlete" by Herbert D. Simons et al. from *Journal of College Student Development* 40.2 (March–April 1999): 151–62. Reprinted by permission.

result of their athletic participation. These factors detract from the realistic like-lihood of academic success, which in turn affects their academic motivation to succeed (American Institutes for Research [AIR], 1989). Negative stereotypes about athletes' lack of academic ability only add to these motivational difficul-ties (Dundes, 1996; Edwards, 1984).

Athletic success requires an individual to work hard, be self-disciplined, exhibit perseverance and determination, be able to concentrate, stay focused, and so forth. These qualities, if transferred to the academic domain, would seem to be important for academic success. A good deal of variation was found among student athletes in their willingness and success in making this trans-fer. In general, revenue athletes (football and men's basketball) seem less will-ing to make this transfer and show an apparent lack of academic motivation (Simons, Van Rheenen, & Covington, 1997). This perceived lack of motivation is often reflected in a general disidentification with school and reduced aca-demic performance (AIR, 1989; Snyder, 1996; Snyder & Spreitzer, 1992).

On the other hand, female and nonrevenue athletes (those who played sports other than football and men's basketball) seem more willing and able than revenue athletes to make this transfer, as demonstrated by their superior academic performance. Studies have consistently shown that female student athletes are superior to male student athletes and that nonrevenue athletes are superior to revenue athletes in high school GPAs, Scholastic Aptitude Test (SAT) scores, as well as college GPAs (AIR, 1989; Purdy, Eitzen & Hufnagel, 1985; Simons, Van Rheenen, & Covington, 1997). Differences in intrinsic motivation, external rewards, and social influences favoring athletics provides some of the explanation for this seeming paradox. Adler and Adler (1991) have shown, in their longitudinal study of a Division I men's basketball team, how the pressures and rewards associated with school, sport, and peer culture lead student ath-letes to allow intercollegiate athletics to engulf their lives at the expense of their academic identification. The self-worth theory of achievement motivation (Cov-ington, 1992; Covington & Beery, 1976) provides a motivational explanation that can contribute to our understanding of this discrepancy between academic and athletic motivation. Self-worth theory builds upon the work of Atkinson (1964) and Weiner (1974). In his need achievement theory, Atkinson postulated that the motivation to achieve is a learned drive that is the result of two opposing forces: the need to approach success and the need to avoid failure. These drives are fueled by hope and pride for those who desire to approach success and shame and humiliation for those attempting to avoid failure.

Weiner reinterpreted Atkinson's theory by focusing on rational cognitive   5
thought processes rather than emotions as providing motivation for achieve-ment. He proposed attribution theory, which focuses on people's beliefs about the causes of their successes and failures. According to attribution theory, those individuals who are motivated to achieve success attribute failure to insuf-ficient effort and success to ability and effort. These attributions, which are under the individual's control, lead to greater effort following both successes

and failures. On the other hand, failure-avoiding individuals attribute failure to lack of ability and they attribute successes to luck, chance, and so forth. Because these reasons are not under their control, neither successes nor failures provide motivation to expend greater effort in attempting future tasks.

Self-worth theory further elucidates these previous conceptions of achievement motivation. According to Covington (1992), self-worth theory "assumes that the search for self-acceptance is the highest human priority, and that in schools self-acceptance comes to depend on one's ability to achieve competitively" (p. 74). Self-worth is determined by an individual's own, and others', perceptions of one's ability, perceptions that are mainly tied to successful achievement. Success indicates competence or ability and thus enhances one's self-worth. In competitive situations, where few succeed, the first priority for those who fear they may not be successful is the avoidance of failure and its implication that one lacks ability or competence. Trying hard and failing leads to the questioning of one's ability, which in turn diminishes self-worth. On the other hand, failure following a lack of effort does not reflect negatively on one's ability and self-worth as this lack of effort provides an excuse for failure that leaves the perceptions of ability and self-worth intact. This lack of effort can be disguised and rationalized by self-handicapping excuses such as procrastination, test anxiety, last-minute or inadequate study, and so forth.

On the basis of this analysis, Covington has proposed and empirically validated (Covington & Omelich, 1991) a quadripolar motivational typology based on the dual achievement dimensions postulated by Atkinson—the motivation to approach or strive for success and the motivation to avoid failure. Covington has proposed four motivational types, classified in accordance with their scores on each of these two dimensions. He has called these four motivational types: Success Oriented, Overstrivers, Failure-Avoiders and Failure-Acceptors. According to this expanded model, Overstrivers and Failure-Acceptors represent hybrid combinations of the relatively orthogonal approach and avoidance dimensions originally postulated by Atkinson. The following overview of these four types suggests that academic motivation among student athletes may be a salient factor in predicting both academic performance and identification.

Success-Oriented students score high on measures of approaching success and low on failure avoidance. These students are highly motivated to succeed without being afraid of failing. They have a strong sense of self-worth, believe they have the ability to compete academically, have good study skills, are able to accurately judge the difficulty of tasks, and therefore expect to succeed and take pride in their academic achievements. They tend to be intrinsically motivated and they work hard and efficiently to become successful students. These students have a history of strong academic performance which reinforces their feelings of self-worth and gives them confidence in their ability to succeed academically. When they do sometimes experience failure, they attribute it to factors they can control such as inadequate study. They may experience guilt because they did not put in the necessary effort. Because they are confident in their ability to succeed, the guilt arising from failure spurs them on to more effort in the future.

Failure-Avoiders score low on their motivation to approach success and high on avoiding failure. These students often have a low self-worth due to a history of academic failure. As a result, they may develop a maladjusted motivation, focusing more on the avoidance of failure than on striving for success. These students are negatively motivated by the fear of failure and the anticipation of shame in response to a failed effort. To avoid the shame and scrutiny of apparent low ability, the individual limits the effort expended. Rather than openly limiting effort, they often engage in self-handicapping behaviors such as procrastination, handing in assignments late, test anxiety, and so forth, that provide an excuse for poor performance. They rationalize that these are the factors that kept them from succeeding, rather than low ability, thus protecting an already tenuous sense of self-worth.

Overstrivers score high on both measures of approaching success and avoiding failure. Their fear of failure leads them to strive very hard to succeed, which they often do. Essentially, these students avoid failure by succeeding. They work extra hard and have good study skills. They have a higher but more fragile sense of self-worth than the Failure-Avoiders. Their success is precarious because small setbacks can have lasting effects. Because of the emotional significance of failing, they often experience test anxiety. *10*

Failure-Acceptors score low on both measures of approaching success and avoiding failure. These students are not particularly attracted to success, but neither are they concerned about failing. They have a history of failing, have a low sense of self-worth and are not very confident of their ability to succeed academically. They do not try very hard and exhibit some of the same self-handicapping behaviors and excuses as the Failure-Avoiders.

However, they are not really interested in academics and may have given up entirely on the academic enterprise. Failure-Acceptors may have at one time been Failure-Avoiders whose history of continued academic failures produced a learned helplessness (Coyne & Lazarus, 1980; Miller & Norman, 1979) that led them to give up entirely on the goal of successful academic performance. The purpose of this study was to employ self-worth theory to explore the academic motivation of student athletes. It was hypothesized that a fear of academic failure and the relative commitment to athletics was found to play important roles in the academic motivation of both revenue and nonrevenue student athletes.

Method

Participants

Participants in this study were 361 intercollegiate student athletes enrolled at the University of California at Berkeley during the 1993–1994 academic year. Participants were those student athletes who attended team meetings arranged between the authors of this study and the coaches of 22 Varsity teams. Almost two thirds of those surveyed were male (63.3%). The male student athletes participated in 11 sports, inclusive of football, basketball, baseball, track and field, cross country, soccer, swimming, water polo, tennis, gymnastics, and golf. The female student athletes (36.7%) participated in 11 sports, inclusive of basketball, softball, track and field, volleyball, cross country, soccer, swimming, tennis, crew, gymnastics and field hockey. Of the student athletes, 20.8% participated in revenue sports, whereas 79.2% participated in nonrevenue sports. All of the revenue athletes were male. Of the nonrevenue athletes, 53.5% were male. At the time of the study, 30.5% of the participants were freshmen, 26.3% sophomores, 26.4% juniors, and 16.8% were seniors. Junior college transfer students comprised 8.4% of the participants. The ethnic distribution of the participants in the survey was Caucasian (68.2%), African American (14.3%), Asian American (8.6%) , Mexican American/Latino (3.8%), Native American/Alaskan Native/Pacific Islander (3.3%), and Other (1.8%). The participants' SAT verbal scores had a mean of 489.28 with a standard deviation of 95.89. The participants' SAT math scores had a mean of 586.53 with a standard deviation of 103.15.

Measures
An instrument was constructed which consisted of 300 Likert-type scale items that measured the cognitive, noncognitive and background factors affecting the dual achievement domains of intercollegiate academics and athletics. Motivational, academic, demographic and athletic status variables were studied. Participants were asked to rate the items on a 5-point scale, from 1 (not very true of me) to 5 (very true of me).

Procedures
15   As part of a larger study (Simons et al., 1997), each team member completed a paper-and-pencil survey, which focused on academic and athletic attitudes and motivation. The surveys were completed during a scheduled team meeting. The full survey took about 40 minutes to complete.

   Background factors. Background factors included demographics and revenue/nonrevenue sport status. The demographic measures of the survey included self-reported gender, ethnicity, and social status. Ethnicity was recoded into African American and non-African American. Non-African American included Caucasian and other minorities such as Asian American, Mexican American/Latino, and so forth. Social status was measured by a scale of student's mother's educational level. Preliminary analysis showed that mother's education was a better predictor of academic performance than either father's education or participants' self-reported social status. The categories were (a) None or some high school; (b) High school diploma; (c) Some college; (d) College BA degree; or (e) Graduate degree (MBA, PhD, MD). Sport played was treated as a dichotomous variable of revenue and nonrevenue. Revenue included men's basketball and football. Nonrevenue included all other sports.

   Cognitive factors. Cognitive factors included academic performance and study. The academic data obtained from official academic records included high school GPA, SAT math and verbal scores, and cumulative university GPA.

Metacognitive study strategies are the conscious strategic deployment of cognitive resources for studying. An 11-item Likert-type scale measured several metacognitive study strategies, including comprehension monitoring, determining task difficulty, main idea comprehension, memory strategies, employing background knowledge, and self-questioning. The scale included items such as: (a) I spend more time on the difficult course material when studying for a test; (b) I study differently for different types of exams (essay, multiple choice, and so forth); (c) I make up questions to help focus my reading; (d) When I read I look for the important ideas. Cronbach's Alpha for this scale was .58.

Problems associated with reading and studying problems were measured by a 9-item Likert-type scale. The scale included the items such as (a) I often read a chapter and afterwards don't know what I have read; (b) I have trouble taking good class notes; (c) I read too slowly; Cronbach's Alpha for this scale was .61.

Motivation. Motivational factors included the Approach success-Avoid failure Achievement Questionnaire (AAAQ), Academic Self-worth, Intrinsic and Extrinsic Motivation from the Motivated Strategies for Learning Questionnaire (MSLQ), and Self-Handicapping Excuses.

The AAAQ consists of 36 Likert-type scale items that measure the two basic need achievement dimensions: the tendency to approach success and to avoid failure (Covington & Omelich, 1991). The approach scale was composed of 21 items consisting of five subscales: (a) Risk-Taking Propensity; (b) Realistic Goal Setting; (c) Intrinsic Engagement; (d) Persistence; and (e) Self-Confidence. The median score was 74. Cronbach's Alpha for this scale was .73. The avoidance scale, was composed of 13 items consisting of four subscales: (a) Unrealistic Achievement Standards; (b) Fears About Failure; (c) Doubts About One's Ability; and (d) Disposition Toward Self-Criticism as Opposed to Self-Reward. The median score was 38. Cronbach's Alpha for this scale was .77. The median split of each dimension was used to form the four motivational types. Success-Oriented individuals were above the median (74) on approach and below the median (38) on failure avoidance. Overstrivers were above the median on approach and above the median on failure avoidance. Failure-Avoiders were below the median on approach and above the median on failure avoidance whereas Failure-Acceptors were below the median in approach and failure avoidance.

Self-worth theory posits that achievement motivation is best understood in terms of attempts by individuals to maintain a positive self-image of competency, particularly when risking competitive failure. A six-item Academic Self-worth scale was composed of three items from the Rosenberg Self-Esteem measure (Rosenberg, 1965) and three items specific to academic achievement at Berkeley. The three items from the Rosenberg scale were: (a) All in all, I am inclined to feel that I am a failure in school; (b) I feel that I do not have much to be proud of as a student; and (c) On the whole I am satisfied with myself as a student. The three items developed for the current study were (d) Do you think you have the ability to succeed academically here at UC Berkeley?; (e) Compared to the average UC Berkeley student, how would you rate your overall academic ability?; and (f) Do you think you deserved to get into UC Berkeley? Cronbach's Alpha for this scale was .90.

Intrinsic motivation is defined as an individual's propensity to approach a task for its inherent challenge and interest. Four Likert-type scale items taken from the Motivated Strategies for Learning Questionnaire (MSLQ) (Pintrich,1991) were selected to measure an individual's intrinsic goal orientation in the academic domain. These four MSLQ items were: (a) The most satisfying thing in a course is trying to understand the content as thoroughly as possible; (b) I prefer course material that really challenges me so I can learn new things; (c) When I can, I choose assignments that I can learn from even if they don't guarantee a good grade; and (d) I prefer course material that arouses my curiosity, even if it is difficult to learn. Cronbach's Alpha for this scale was .60.

Extrinsic motivation is defined as an individual's propensity to approach a task to gain external rewards. Four Likert-type scale items taken from the MSLQ (Pintrich et al., 1991) were selected to measure an individual's extrinsic goal orientation in the academic achievement setting. The four MSLQ items were: (a) My main concern in my classes is getting good grades; (b) I want to get better grades in school than most other students get; (c) I want to do well in school because it is important to show my ability to others; and (d) Getting good grades is the most satisfying thing in school for me right now. Cronbach's Alpha for this scale was .64.

25   Self-handicapping excuses are maladaptive motivational responses to challenging achievement tasks that serve to protect an individual's perceived low self-worth by providing excuses for poor academic performance. A 6-item Likert-type scale measured the tendency to report excuses for lowered levels of academic effort and performance. The items were: (a) If I worked harder I would get better grades; (b) I don't have enough time to study because my sport takes up so much time; (c) I'm so disorganized that I don't get all my work done; (d) My social life interferes with my studying; (e) If my courses were more interesting, I would get better grades; and (f) I would do much better on tests if I didn't get so nervous. Cronbach's Alpha for this scale was .60

Athletic-Academic Relationship

The Athletic-Academic Relationship included the Athletic-Academic Commitment and Exploitation scales. Student athletes are expected to fill two roles, that of an athlete and a student. They vary in the degree of commitment to these roles and are often in conflict. The relative degree of commitment to athletics and academics was measured by a four-item Likert-type scale. The items included: (a) I study only hard enough to stay eligible to play my sport; (b) I care more about sports than school; (c) I put more energy into sports now because I know I've got the rest of my life to get a college degree; and (d) It is more important for me to succeed in sports than to do well in school. The higher the score on this variable, the stronger the commitment to the athletic role. Cronbach's Alpha for this scale was .79.

Student athletes are required to put a great deal of time and effort into their sport which brings prestige to the university, revenues from athletic events, and donations to the university by alumni. A 7-item Likert-type scale measured the degree to which student athletes believe they are exploited by the university for their athletic participation. The scale included items such as: (a) Sometimes I feel that I am being taken advantage of as an athlete; (b) I feel that the University cares more about me as an athlete than as a student; (c) Sometimes I feel that I am the property of the University. Cronbach's Alpha for this scale was .75.

The design of the study involved assigning the participants into the four motivational types on the basis of their scores on the AAAQ. The four types were compared in separate analyses of variance on each variable in this study. Posthoc comparisons were conducted using the Tukey test. In a second analysis, the percentage of students falling into each motivational type was compared across subgroups of participants as well as compared to the general non student athlete population.

Results

Table 1 [omitted] shows the results of the analyses of variance (ANOVAs) comparing the four motivational types on the variables in this study. All variables had significant F tests at the $p = .01$ level or below, indicating significant differences between the motivational types on these variables. Tukey posthoc tests showed a number of significant differences between pairs of motivational types.

Overall, these findings show important differences between the Success-   *30* Oriented student athletes and Overstrivers on the one hand and Failure-Avoiders and Failure-Acceptors on the other. In general, the Failure-Avoiders and Failure-Acceptors were poorer academic performers than the Success-Oriented student athletes and Overstrivers. Failure-Avoiders and Failure-Acceptors were more committed to the athletic role than the other two types and did not believe that they received enough from the university to compensate for their commitment. This may be another rationalization for their lack of academic effort. Other findings suggest that more of a commitment to athletics, less intrinsic motivation, less academic self-worth, and more self-handicapping excuses all play a role in producing lower academic performance. Academic self-worth was lower for Failure-Avoiders than Failure-Acceptors, suggesting that protection of self-worth plays a more important role for the Failure-Acceptors.

The distribution of nonathletes, athletes and subgroups of athletes in the four motivational types are shown in Table 2 [omitted]. Overall, athletes were not significantly different from nonathletes (chisquare = ns). However, females were significantly different from males: chi-square (3, N = 333) = 9.94, p = .01. Males had a larger percentage of Failure-Avoiders and a smaller percentage of Failure-Acceptors. Additionally, revenue athletes were significantly different from nonrevenue athletes: chi-square (3, N = 333) = 8.25, p = .05. Revenue athletes had a larger percentage of both Failure-Acceptors and Failure-Avoiders and a smaller percentage of Success-Oriented athletes than the nonrevenue athletes. The male nonrevenue athletes were not significantly different from the female nonrevenue athletes: chi-square (3, N = 268) = 6.86, p = .05. However, more Failure-Acceptors were found in the male group. The comparison of African American with non-African American student athletes showed that proportionately more Failure-Avoiders and fewer Success-Oriented student athletes were found in the African American group. However, the differences between the two groups were not statistically significant: chi-square (3, N = 333) = 2.81, p = .05. There were no significant differences between the four motivational types in social status, F(3, 326) = 2.45, p = .05.

Discussion

The results of the analysis of this motivational typology provides support for the validity of the self-worth model as applied to Division I student athletes. The differences between these motivational types on the cognitive and noncognitive variables are consistent with the theory's essential premise concerning approach and avoidance. Both Success-Oriented student athletes and Overstrivers, who are highly motivated to succeed academically, demonstrated higher academic performance in high school and at the university than Failure-Avoiders and Failure-Acceptors. Success-Oriented student athletes and Overstrivers also exhibited better metacognitive study strategies and were more intrinsically motivated. Success-Oriented student athletes scored the highest in academic self-worth, the lowest in self-handicapping excuses, reading and study problems. Overstrivers scored higher in their motivation to avoid failure than the Success-Oriented student athletes; they likewise reported more reading and study problems and lower academic self-worth. Failure-Avoiders are strongly motivated to avoid failure at the expense of striving for success; they exhibit the characteristics expected of this motivational type: lower academic self-worth, high self-handicapping excuses, higher reading and study problems, lower metacognitive study strategies, and less intrinsic motivation, all of which lead to lower academic performance. Failure-Acceptors are neither motivated to succeed academically nor are they trying very hard to avoid failure. As such, they are not high on failure-avoiding variables such as self-handicapping excuses, study problems, and extrinsic motivation when compared to the Failure-Avoiders.

Two noncognitive variables, athletic-academic commitment and exploitation, shed some light on the academic motivation of student athletes. Both variables were higher for Failure-Avoiders and Failure-Acceptors than Success-Oriented student athletes and Overstrivers. Failure-Avoiders and

Failure-Acceptors were more committed to the athletic role and believed they were more exploited by the university.

For all of the participants, athletic-academic commitment was negatively correlated with university GPA (r=−.50). The more commitment to the athletic role and the less to the academic role, the lower the university GPA. The nature of intercollegiate athletics, especially at Division I schools, puts pressure on student athletes to strengthen their athletic commitment at the expense of their academic commitment. This in turn lowers academic performance (Adler & Adler, 1991; Simons et al., 1997).

Many student athletes, especially revenue scholarship athletes in Division I schools, are recruited to the university mainly because of their athletic ability. This athletic ability has been developed and rewarded by parents, coaches, and peers over time, often as far back as elementary school. Thus, these student athletes come to the university with a strong athletic ability and commitment. Their academic ability and commitment may be more variable depending upon their academic ability, history of academic successes and failures, and the influences of their parents, siblings, teachers, and peers. At the university, student athletes face strong time and energy pressures from their athletic participation, as well as other less tangible factors that may put athletics in conflict with academics and enhance athletic commitment and diminish academic commitment.

Participation in intercollegiate athletics requires a substantial commitment of time and energy. While a sport is in season, student athletes generally spend between 20 and 30 hours per week, attending meetings and practices, playing games at home and on the road, and in individual weight training sessions. Depending upon the sport, and the coach's expectations or requirements, the time demands during the offseason can also be considerable.

Because athletic participation is physically strenuous, there exists the problem of fatigue that makes concentration during studying more difficult. In addition to the pain and physical discomfort that may interfere with full concentration while studying or attending class, extra time is required for the rehabilitation of both minor and major injuries.

Student athletes often decide in favor of athletics when there exist conflicts between the demands of athletics and academics (Adler and Adler, 1991; Simons et al., 1997). Missing a practice or part of a practice because of an unexpected academic commitment is generally frowned upon. Although a coach is prohibited under National Collegiate Athletic Association (NCAA) regulations from requiring a student athlete to miss an unexpected academic commitment that conflicts with practice, the coach's potential disapproval weighs heavily in the student's eyes. Because coaches possess the power to decide which athletes will play or start in the games, many student athletes believe, correctly or incorrectly, that they will be penalized by their coaches for choosing academic commitments over athletic ones. The athletes themselves are likewise reluctant to miss practice, as it may interfere with their athletic skill development, which will also place them at risk of losing a starting position. As the team often represents the central peer group for the student athlete, peer pressure to favor athletic demands over academic ones plays a strong role.

The athletic culture that student athletes inhabit informs them in subtle and not-so-subtle ways that athletics takes priority over academics. For many, staying minimally eligible to compete in their sport is the primary goal. For both Division I and II colleges and universities, athletic eligibility requires a minimum college GPA of 2.0 and completion of at least 24 semester units per academic year. The verbal shorthand for this mind-set is that "a C gets a degree," an expression vocalized by those student athletes most interested in remaining eligible and least committed to the academic role.

40   The motivation to succeed academically is further weakened by well-publicized accounts of athletes leaving school early to launch lucrative professional careers. For these few athletes, receiving a degree has been eliminated as a prerequisite for economic success and security. The fact that only a minuscule percentage of student athletes are able to enter the professional ranks appears to have little effect on dampening many student athletes' belief that they can and will become professional athletes.

Although some accommodations are made for the special demands on student athletes, such as early course enrollment, special advising and extra help in the form of tutoring and review sessions, the belief among students and faculty is that these special privileges are undeserved and that student athletes are really just athletes and are not serious students.

The belief that these individuals are being exploited by the university for their athletic ability may provide a rationalization for lower academic effort. When the combination of lower academic preparation and a greater commitment to athletics leads to poor academic performance, the student athlete may then blame the mandated athletic demands for his or her poor performance rather than his or her own lack of academic effort. Feelings of resentment emerge when student athletes believe that the university is using their athletic ability without providing the support necessary for them to become successful students. The inevitable result is poorer academic performance, as our data indicates. The fact that more Failure-Avoiders and Failure-Acceptors are found in the revenue sports suggests that these athletic pressures are more pronounced in the revenue sports. Female and nonrevenue athletes seem more able to resist the athletic pressures and put the necessary time and energy to be successful academically.

Although no differences were found between Failure-Avoiders and Failure-Acceptors in athletic-academic commitment or university GPA, there may well be two different mechanisms at work which influence their greater commitment to athletics. For Failure-Avoiders, the fear of failure is the salient motive, but Failure-Acceptors have a lack of interest in academics altogether.

45   The Failure-Acceptors are mainly interested in playing their sport, which provides a strong if not primary motivation for coming to the university. They willingly accept the athletic demands and devote most of their time

and effort to athletics. They are not especially motivated to avoid failure except as it affects their academic eligibility. Their only academic motivation is to remain minimally academically eligible to play their sport. This relative lack of motivation to achieve academically does not appear to be due to a fear of failure, for when compared to Failure-Avoiders, Failure-Acceptors are higher on academic self-worth, a variable associated with failure avoidance. They also show lower extrinsic motivation than Failure-Avoiders, suggesting that external academic motivators such as the striving for grades to demonstrate academic ability is less important for them because their interest and motivation lies elsewhere, that is sports. Self-handicapping excuses for these student athletes are employed more as an explanation for reduced academic effort than as a means of protecting self-worth. These excuses are used to conceal their lack of interest in academics, which cannot be expressed publicly. The belief that they are exploited provides an additional rationalization for lack of academic effort. The Failure-Acceptors can be said to be truly academically unmotivated. They are, however, extremely motivated in the athletic domain.

For Failure-Avoiders on the other hand, the fear of failure plays a much stronger role in leading them to put forth less academic effort and develop a greater commitment to athletics. Compared to Failure-Acceptors, they show a lower academic self-worth (lowest of all four types). The time and energy demands of athletics provide another excuse for lowered academic effort. They exhibit higher extrinsic motivation and reading and study problems than Failure-Acceptors. All these are associated with their fear of failure. They work to avoid failure by putting in less academic effort and rationalize this reduced academic effort by employing self-handicapping excuses along with the claim that they are being exploited by the university. For Failure-Avoiders, then, this need to protect their academic self-worth reinforces the commitment to athletics and diminishes their commitment to school. The Failure-Avoiders cannot be said to be unmotivated in the academic domain. Instead, they are maladaptively motivated to avoid failure rather than to achieve success. Like Failure-Avoiders, they are highly motivated in the athletic domain.

The correlational nature of the data does not allow causal inferences about the nature and development of the relationship of academic and athletic commitment for Failure-Avoiders and Failure-Acceptors. These findings do not make it clear whether the pull of athletics induces Failure-Acceptors and Failure-Avoiders to neglect academics or whether past academic failure produces more emphasis on athletics as they diminish academic effort. The relationship is likely cyclical. On the one hand, academic failure can lead to more interest and effort in athletics as the devotion of more time and energy to athletics leaves less time and interest in building academic skills. This in turn may lead to more academic failure and more devotion to athletics and so forth. Alternatively, superior athletic ability is recognized, encouraged and rewarded by adults and peers, which leads to less interest and effort in academics and the resultant academic failures.

Because sports are both intrinsically and extrinsically motivating, athletics probably provides the original impetus for both Failure-Acceptors and Failure-Avoiders to reduce academic effort. For Failure-Avoiders, academic failures play an added role. For Success-Oriented and, to a lesser extent Overstrivers, the strong pull of athletics is balanced by strong academic motivators that may come from parents, teachers, and peers, and from their early academic successes that help them develop a strong academic self-worth.

Although these results show that student athletes are distributed across motivational types in the same proportion as nonathletes, the smaller percentages of Failure-Avoiders and Failure-Acceptors for females and nonrevenue athletes supports the key role of athletic commitment. Females had higher academic commitment than the revenue males, $t(143) = -3.97$, $p = .01$, and lesser belief that they were exploited, $t(142) = -7.31$, $p = .01$. Likewise, nonrevenue athletes had a stronger academic commitment, $t(231) = 23.00$, $p = .01$, and a weaker belief that they were exploited $t(228) = 27.42$, $p = .01$.

Female athletes are less likely to come to the university primarily to play sports because of the lack of extrinsic rewards and the limited possibility of a professional athletic career. The greater emphasis that females place on academics is also shown by the higher percentage of Success-Oriented student athletes. When comparing females to revenue males, the more positive academic motivation of females is reflected in females' higher high school GPAs, $t(144) = 3.90$, $p = .01$; SAT verbal scores, $t(145) = 4.00$, $p = .01$; SAT math scores, $t(145) = 2.89$, $p = .01$; and university GPAs, $t(162) = 5.26$, $p = .01$.

50   Revenue athletes are the most highly recruited and receive more extrinsic rewards, recognition, and social support than nonrevenue athletes. For many, this can lead to more time and effort devoted to athletics and thus a stronger commitment to athletics than to academics. Revenue athletes who are Failure-Avoiders and Failure-Acceptors are the ones most likely to exhibit the discrepancy between their athletic and academic motivation. These two groups should be of most concern to educators. They are more at risk for academic failure.

To counteract these pressures, educators need to play a more prominent role in the lives of student athletes to help them see that they can succeed academically as well as athletically. In the precollege years, educators need to pay special attention to the academic needs of students who are identified as gifted athletes to balance the attention they receive for their athletic exploits. Teachers and administrators in these schools should work more closely with coaches, who play a large role in student athletes' lives, to enlist their help in emphasizing academics as well as athletics. Raising the minimum academic standards for athletic participation is one policy that provides strong extrinsic motivation to work hard academically.

At the college level, athletic administrators and coaches tend to be isolated from the intellectual life of the campus. Student athletes may also feel isolated from the other students as they spend so much time and energy participating in athletics with their athletic peers. Efforts need to be made to help student athletes see themselves as legitimate students as well as athletes.

College staff and faculty, with the cooperation of the athletic department, need to be more involved in the lives of student athletes. Faculty and academic staff need to be more involved in the athletic recruiting process so that student athletes will feel they are valued as students as well as athletes. Academic tutoring and other support services for student athletes are typically part of the athletic departments, which makes them potentially susceptible to the pressure to put athletics first. These services should be separated from the athletic department and be administratively part of academic support so that they will have some independence from the athletic department and be able to represent the academic interests of the student athlete when the inevitable conflicts arise between athletic commitments and academic ones. Early intervention for student athletes at risk of simply majoring in eligibility is also important before they decide that academics is too difficult or not important enough to pursue.

Coaches are the major adult role models for student athletes as they spend a significant amount of time with their athletes. Coaches need to see their student athletes' academic performance as part of their overall responsibility. They should be rewarded for the successful academic performance of their student athletes. Coaches also need to have more understanding of the academic demands on their athletes. They could go to some of their student athletes' classes, attend lectures, look over assignments, and so forth. More interaction with the faculty through forums, lectures, and other activities would help them to see themselves as more a part of the academic community.

As educators, we believe that academic and athletic representatives of   *55* universities must make a concerted effort to provide a more balanced picture of college life to student athletes, especially for Failure-Avoiders and Failure-Acceptors. These efforts will require the systematic involvement of faculty, academic, and athletic support staff to make clear to student athletes that they show academic, and not merely athletic, potential.

References

Adler, P A., & Adler, P. (1991). Backboards and blackboards: College athletes and role engulfment. New York: Columbia University Press.

American Institutes for Research. (1989). Summary Results from the 1987–1988 National Study of Intercollegiate Athletes. Palo Alto, CA.

Atkinson, J. W. (1964). An introduction to motivation. Princeton, NJ: Van Nostrand.

Covington, M. V. (1992). Making the grade: A self-worth perspective on motivation and school reform. New York: Cambridge.

Covington, M. V., & Beery, R. G. (1976). Self-worth and school learning. New York: Holt, Rinehart, & Winston.

Covington, M. V., & Omelich, C. L. (1991). Need achievement revisited: Verification of Atkinson's original 2 x 2 model. In C. D. Spielberger, 1. G. Sarason, Z. Kulcsar, & G. L. Van Heck (Eds.), Stress and Emotion: Anxiety, Anger, and Curiosity (Vol. 14, pp. 85–105). Washington, DC: Hemisphere.

Coyne, J. C., & Lazarus, R. S. (1980). Cognitive style, stress perception, and coping. In I. L. Kutash & L. B. Schlesinger (Eds.), Handbook on Stress and Anxiety, (144–158). San Francisco: Jossey-Bass.

Dundes, A. (1996). Two applications for admission to USC. Western Folklore, 55, ISS–163.

Edwards, H. (1984). The Black dumb jock: An American tragedy. The College Board Review, 131, 9–13.

Miller, I. W., III, & Norman, W. H. (1979). Learned helplessness in humans: A review and attribution-theory model. Psychological Bulletin, 82, 213–225.

Pintrich, P. R., Smith, D. A. F., Garcia, T., & McKeachie, W. J. (1991). A manual for the use of the motivated strategies for learning questionnaire (MSLQ). Ann Arbor, MI: The University of Michigan, National Center for Research to Improve Post Secondary Teaching and Learning.

Purdy, D. A., Eitzen, D. S., & Hufnagel, R. (1985). Are athletes also students? The educational attainment of college athletes. In D. Chu, J.O. Segrave, & B. J. Becker (Eds.), Sport and Higher Education. (pp. 221–234). Champaign, IL: Human -Kinetics Publishers.

Rosenberg, J. (1965). Society and the adolescent self image. Princeton, NJ: Princeton University Press.

Simons, H., Van Rheenen, D., & Covington, M. (1997). The dilemma of the student athlete: Balancing athletics and academics. Berkeley, CA: University of California, Education Department CA.

Snyder, E. E., & Spreitzer, E. (1992). Social psychological concomitants of adolescents' role identities as scholars and athletes: A longitudinal analysis. Youth and Society, 23, 507–522.

Snyder, P. (1996). Comparative levels of expressed academic motivation among Anglo and African American university student-athletes. Journal of Black Studies, 26, 651–667.

Weiner, B. (1974). Achievement motivation and attribution theory. Morristown, NJ: General Learning Press.

Article Credits
Herbert D. Simons is Associate Professor of Education; Derek Van Rheenen is a lecturer of Education; Martin V. Covington is Professor of Psychology, each at the University of California, Berkeley.
Correspondence concerning this article should be addressed to Herbert D. Simons, Education Department, University of California, Berkeley, CA; herbs@socrates.berkeley.edu

Reflections and Inquiries

1. Several factors generally lead student athletes to experience lower motivation for academic success than for athletic success, according to the researchers. Which of these factors seem most significant, in your opinion, and why?

2. What accounts for the differences in motivation between the success-oriented, failure-avoiding, and failure-accepting students? How might these differences best be resolved for each group?

3. To what extent is gender a factor in motivational differences among student athletes? What do you suppose contributes to these gender-based motivational differences? Apply these same questions to race/ethnicity; to socio-economic group.

4. Comment on the recommendations offered by the researchers. Are they specific enough to be useful? What more can be said about helping student athletes improve their motivation to succeed academically?

Reading to Write

Interview at least twenty student athletes, ten female and ten male, on their success (or lack thereof) in transferring their athletic-based motivation to their academic-based motivation. Use your findings to argue on behalf of your own insights into the best methods of transference.

Is Athletics Meeting Its Purpose? | John R. Gerdy

What, exactly, does a college athletic program contribute to a college education? John R. Gerdy, an education consultant based in New York City, discusses eight concerns most often raised about such programs: (1) Do they build character (and if so, what is meant by that expression)? (2) Is it true that student athletes acquire a narrower worldview while in college than that of their nonathlete fellow students? (3) Does participation in sports contribute to "good sportsmanship" in the larger sense of the term? (4) Does participation in sports interfere with the student's intellectual development? (5) What influence, if any, does an athletic program have on racial harmony? (6) Do athletic programs add to or drain the financial resources of the host college? (7) Does an athletic program add to a university's "visibility" in positive ways? Finally, (8) how valuable is the entertainment dimension of sports competitions to the host college?

There is a common belief in the value of sport, which we have chosen to view as a myth not because it is untrue, but because it is generally accepted without question. If this common understanding, this myth about sport, is valid, it ought to withstand

Source: "Is Athletics Meeting Its Purpose?" from *The Successful College Athletic Program: The New Standard* by John R. Gerdy. Oryx Press, 1997: 35–54. Copyright © 1997. Reproduced with permission of Greenwood Publishing Group, Westport, CT.

scrutiny. If it is not valid, we tax-paying citizens who make decisions about the future of our educational system need to know.... If sport does live up to the myth surrounding it, even if only in part, perhaps we should invest more heavily in sports. For example, we could make room for all students in sport, not just the athletically superior. On the other hand, what if it were demonstrated scientifically that most or all of the myths about school sport have no empirical basis, that there are no data to support them, no evidence of positive effects? As a taxpayer, parent, educator, or concerned citizen, what would your response be? What should it be?

—Andrew Miracle and C. Roger Rees

Lessons of the Locker Room

It is perhaps axiomatic that challenges to any system are scorned by those fully vested in the system. On the other hand, organizations that do not continually reevaluate their goals and their effectiveness in meeting those goals will eventually become obsolete. Critical analysis of college athletics is particularly important because a fundamental purpose of higher education is to encourage critical thinking by challenging preexisting assumptions in an effort to seek truth. Therefore, the college athletic community should not fear, resist, or ignore such scrutiny; rather, it should welcome the chance to rethink its purpose. Those who criticize college athletics should not be dismissed as simply destructive, particularly if the criticism is well formulated with suggestions for improvement.

Thus, the debate regarding whether athletics is meeting its stated purposes should not center on whether these questions should be asked, but rather on how athletics' contribution to higher education can be maximized. The credibility of any individual or organization depends upon whether the individual or organization does what it says it will. With both academe and the public questioning the role of athletics in higher education, critical debate regarding the effectiveness with which athletics accomplishes its goals should be encouraged. The following sections are intended to facilitate creative debate.

Does Athletics Build Character?

Sports is a vital character builder. It molds the youth of our country for their roles as custodians of the republic. It teaches them to be strong enough to know they are weak and brave enough to face themselves when they are afraid. It teaches them to be proud and unbending in honest defeat, but humble and gentle in victory.... It gives them a predominance of courage over timidity, of appetite for adventure over loss of ease.

—General Douglas MacArthur in Chu 1989, 65

For the past 8 years, we have been studying the effects of competition on personality. Our research began with the counseling of problem athletes, but it soon expanded to include athletes from every sport, at every level, from the high school gym to the professional arena. On the evidence gathered in this study, we can make some broad-range value judgments. We found no empirical support for the tradition that sport builds character. Indeed, there is evidence that athletic competition limits growth in

some areas. It seems that the personality of the ideal athlete is not the result of any molding process, but comes out of the ruthless selection process that occurs at all levels of sport. Athletic competition has no more beneficial effects than intense endeavor in any other field.
—Oglive and Tutko 1985, 268–269

The claim that "sports builds character" has long been a widely held assumption in the United States. This largely unquestioned belief made the sponsorship of athletic programs seem logical, not only in colleges and universities but in high schools and junior highs as well. While the lessons learned in classrooms and laboratories in English and science were important, so, it seemed, were the lessons in discipline, teamwork, and perseverance taught on the playing fields. Although thousands of former and current student-athletes will swear by the value of competitive athletics, many others look back on their intercollegiate athletic experience with bitterness and regret.

Just as I was exposed to coaches who had a tremendously positive effect on my life, I was also subject to other coaches who had no interest in my personal or academic development or in that of any of my teammates. So from my experience, while there are lessons that participation in competitive athletics teaches, there were some practices that would be hard to defend from an educational standpoint. And as the money, television exposure, and pressure to win have increased, so too have practices that would be questionable in any educational setting.

Many groups have a vested interest in promoting the principle that participation in sport is a character-building activity. To justify their place in the educational community, coaches and athletic administrators must demonstrate that sports have educational value. The widespread acceptance of the educational value of athletics secures their power and status not only in the educational community but also in the public eye.

The justification that "sports build character" serves those in the athletic establishment in another important way. An unquestioned acceptance of this ideal relieves coaches of having to be accountable for teaching in a responsible manner. A coach can justify punishing an "undisciplined" student-athlete, running a few "bad apples" off the team and out of a scholarship, or verbally abusing a student-athlete by simply stating that he or she is "teaching life lessons." Thus, teaching methods deemed unacceptable for the classroom can be justified on the playing fields in the name of "building character."

Coaches and administrators are not alone in having an interest in promoting the "sports build character" ideal. The media, bowl representatives, television executives, and others who make a living off big-time athletics all have a stake in promulgating this belief. If it were determined that participation in major college athletics had no positive educational benefits, athletics' place on the college campus would be difficult to justify. If universities no longer sponsored athletics, coaches and administrators would no longer have jobs, at least not the same jobs.

For this reason, the entire athletic community has a tremendous vested interest in promoting the "sports build character" ideal, regardless of its validity.

Not everyone has accepted without question the claim that participation in sports has significant educational benefits. Skepticism regarding the supposed benefits of athletic participation has almost been as much a part of the culture of sport as the increased heart rate and the sweat-soaked brow. In fact, the sentiment of higher education leaders that athletics was a frivolous activity prevented it from being sponsored as a university-sanctioned activity before the late nineteenth century. When it was formally incorporated into higher education, debate regarding athletics' value and place on campus intensified.

While athletics' role was debated on individual campuses for years, the issue was first raised as a national concern with the release of the Carnegie Foundation Study of American college athletics in 1929. The report addressed many concerns, including whether athletic participation had substantial educational value and whether all the attention and expense showered upon college athletic programs were justified. The report stated the following:

> To the development of the individual capacities of young men and women, their appreciation of true values, their powers of decision and choice, their sense of responsibility, and their ability to sustain it when once it comes to them—to the development of these and of all other best habits of mind and traits of character, college athletics must contribute far more than they have in the past if they are to justify the time and effort that are lavished upon them. (Savage 1929, 133–34)

Perhaps the most interesting aspect of the report was its analysis of the coach. It called into question coaches' propensity to make virtually every decision related to the game and the program themselves, leaving little opportunity for the students to develop their decision-making skills.

> The exigencies of the game forbid original thinking. Not many coaches understand what it means to let their men work out their own plays and conduct their own teams accordingly. It is a commonplace of adverse criticism of present-day coaching methods that many coaches tend to occupy too much of their men's time with fundamentals, too little with playing the game under conditions of contest. Yet, if athletics are to be "educational," the player must be taught to do his own thinking. In every branch of athletics the strategy of the game should not be beyond the capacity of the alertly-minded undergraduate. As matters now stand, no branch owes even a vestige of its strategy to the undergraduates engaged. Such matters are the affair of the coach. (Savage 1929, 176)

While the Carnegie report generated discussion, it did not result in much change. The lack of response, however, did not mean that such concerns would disappear. Since the publication of the Carnegie report, empirical data has continued to mount, indicating that the educational value of participation in intercollegiate athletics may have been greatly overemphasized. Some researchers even charge that participation in highly competitive athletics might actually hinder or arrest the development of various positive character traits.

A Narrower World View

One of the most interesting studies of the effect of athletic participation on student-athletes was conducted by sociologists Peter and Patricia Adler. The Adlers virtually became a part of a Division I basketball program for a five-year period. Their observations are outlined in their 1991 book entitled *Backboards and Blackboards: College Athletes and Role Engulfment*. Their conclusions were based upon extensive interviews and observation, and among those conclusions was the finding that after a four- or five-year intercollegiate athletic experience, student-athletes often had a much narrower "world view" than when they entered the university.

The Adlers found that upon initial enrollment, student-athletes had a   *10* broad range of interests and goals in the academic, social, and athletic areas. However, during their time on campus, they were forced to make decisions that pitted their academic and social interests against their athletic interests. Invariably, decisions were made in favor of athletic interests. For example, if a student-athlete wanted to go to a movie with a nonathlete, but the coach had planned a social event with someone who supported the athletic program, the student-athlete felt pressure to attend the team function. Or, if a coach thought a particular academic major was too demanding and would thus affect athletic performance, he would "suggest" that the student-athlete enroll in a less demanding major. Because of the intense and constant pressure to show one's "commitment to the program," student-athletes were continually forced to make decisions that would further their athletic goals, while pushing their academic and social aspirations into the background. Like the muscle that atrophies from inactivity, the result was a dwindling of student-athletes' social and academic interests in favor of athletic interests. Although certain activities, such as travel to new and exciting places, expand the student-athlete's "world view," the Adlers argued that the overall experience in some cases was actually to narrow the student-athlete's perspective.

> Despite its structural fit within the trends current in American society, the engulfment of college athletes raises questions and conflicts that cannot be easily answered. On the one hand, these young men are spending formative years sacrificing themselves to entertain and enrich others, lured by the hope of a future that is elusive at best. For other students, this kind of narrowing and intense focus may lead to a prosperous career in such fields as medicine, law, education, or business. For college athletes, however, their specialization, dedication, and abandonment of alternatives leads to their becoming finally proficient at a role that, for most, will end immediately following the conclusion of their college eligibility. For those fortunate enough to achieve a professional career, the end comes only slightly later.

It is ironic that these athletes are partly socialized to failure; although some sustained the athletic role temporarily, they were released by the system at the end of four years engulfed in a role destined to become an "ex" (Ebaugh 1988). College athletes entered the university thinking that they would expand their horizons and opportunities in a variety of ways. They ended up narrowing their selves enough that their more grandiose expectations were not met. (Adler and Adler 1991, 230)

One of the purposes of college is to broaden the scope of young people's vision and to provide youth with opportunities to make decisions for themselves and hopefully to learn from even those decisions that turned out to be mistakes. College should expand horizons and teach young people the love of learning. Is it possible that involvement in highly competitive athletics might actually do the opposite? Does participation in intercollegiate athletics actually narrow focus and self-identity of young people, and restrict decision-making opportunities?

The preliminary results of a study led by Hans Steiner, a professor of psychiatry and behavioral science at Stanford University, shed some interesting light on the issue of "focus" in athletics. The study, released in 1996, is based on a survey of more than 2,100 high school and college students. It found that high school student-athletes earned better marks on a variety of psychological tests than did their peers who were not student-athletes. But a different picture emerged of the college student-athlete. The same psychological traits that could contribute to the success of college student-athletes on the playing fields and courts also put them at increased risk of drug or alcohol abuse, or academic and personal problems. According to Steiner, student-athletes are taught to repress the notion of failure, which does not contribute to good psychological health. Steiner plans to test his conclusions further with additional student-athletes and students.

The lengths to which coaches and administrators will go to keep their student-athletes focused on their sport can at times be amusing. During my junior year at Davidson, our basketball coach took a sudden and unexpected leave of absence. We returned from our short Christmas break to find that our coach was no longer going to be with us. Worse, none of the other coaches or administrators knew where he was, or if they did, they were not telling. After practice, an administrator addressed the team as follows: "Men, your coach is gone. Don't know where he is. Thinks he's got a brain infection. Thinks he's gonna die.... But I tell ya what we're gonna do. We're gonna buy you a big 'ole [sic] steak and we're gonna go out and beat Marshall."

Our coach, for whom we all cared deeply, was missing and apparently very sick. Yet foremost on the mind of this administrator was not helping us deal with, or even understand, what had happened to him. Rather the push was to get us focused on beating Marshall. Of course, feeding us a "big 'ole [sic] steak" was supposed to help us forget that our coach was missing and to ignore the fact that no one seemed to know where he was. We lost to Marshall by 30 points.

Teaching Honesty and Sportsmanship

The promise of a fair and honest contest forms the foundation upon which   *15*
athletic competition is allegedly based. Athletic participation, it is argued,
naturally enhances a participant's moral and ethical development through the
teaching of good sportsmanship. But research supporting this assertion has, to
this point, been largely inconclusive. On the contrary, recent studies seem to
suggest that the moral and ethical reasoning skills of intercollegiate athletes
might actually be less developed than those of nonathletes.

Over the past few years, Jennifer Beller and Sharon Stoll, both of the University of Idaho's Center for Ethics, have evaluated thousands of high school
and college student-athletes and their nonathlete peers on their cognitive
moral reasoning development. Beller and Stoll have found that "revenue producing athletes, whether at NAIA, Division III, Division II or Division I are
significantly lower in moral development than their peer group, and individual and non-revenue producing athletes." Further, they found that "revenue
producing athletes are not morally, developmentally dysfunctional when they
come to athletics, rather the competitive process appears to cause a masking of
moral reasoning processes" (Stoll 1996).

The classic example of the "masking" of the moral reasoning process is
pointed out by Stephen Carter in his 1996 book *Integrity*. During a televised
football game, a player who had failed to catch a ball thrown his way hit
the ground, rolled over, and then jumped up, celebrating as if he had made
the catch. Screened from the play, the referee awarded the catch. A review
of the replay revealed that the player had dropped the ball. The broadcaster
commented, "What a heads up play!," meaning, in Carter's words, "Wow!
What a great liar this kid is. Well done!"

> By jumping up and celebrating, he was trying to convey a false impression.
> He was trying to convince the officials that he had caught the ball.... So, in
> any understanding of the word, he lied.... Now, suppose the player had
> instead gone to the referee and said, "I'm sorry sir, but I did not make that
> catch. Your call is wrong." Probably his coach and teammates and most of
> his team's fans would have been furious: he would not have been a good
> team player. The good team player lies to the referee, and does so in a man-
> ner that is at once blatant (because millions of viewers see it) and virtu-
> ally impossible for the referee to detect. Having pulled off this trickery, the
> player is congratulated: he is told that he has made a heads-up play. Thus,
> the ethic of the game turns out to be an ethic that rewards cheating. (Carter
> 1996, 5)

David L. Shields and Brenda J. Bredemeir from the University of California,
Berkeley, reviewed the body of research available regarding sport and character development in their book *Character Development and Physical Activity*. Consider the following excerpt, which calls into question the blind acceptance of
the claim that athletics builds character.

Let us state our conclusion first. The research does not support either position in the debate over sport building character. If any conclusion is justified, it is that the question that is posed is too simplistic. The term *character* is vague, even if modified with the adjective *good*. More important, sport experience is far from uniform. There is certainly nothing intrinsically character-building about batting a ball, jumping over hurdles, or rolling heavy spheres toward pins. The component physical behaviors of sport are not in themselves moral or immoral. When we talk about building character through sport, we are referring to the potential influence of the social interactions that are fostered by the sport experience. The nature of those interactions varies from sport to sport, from team to team, from one geographical region to another, from one level of competition to another, and so on.... The word *character* is often used synonymously with *personality*. Not surprisingly, then, a number of early researchers were interested in whether sport influenced the personality characteristics of participants. Most studies conducted on this question have followed one or more of three strategies (Stevenson 1975): a comparison of athletes with non-participants, a comparison of elite athletes with less-advanced sport participants or the general population, or a comparison of athletes participating in different sports. In all three cases, results are inconclusive. (Shields and Bredemeir 1995, 178)

Bredemeir and Shields went beyond assessing whether sport positively affects the "character" of participants; they reviewed the research that attempts to gauge sports participation on more narrowly defined traits such as aggression, sportsmanship, compassion, fairness, and integrity. Once again, they determined that in virtually all categories, the existing research is inconclusive.

A notable exception, however, is research indicating a negative correlation between sport involvement and delinquency; the reason for the correlation was unclear. Delinquency theory suggests that deviant behavior is learned through contact with other deviants. Thus, this correlation might be inferred by the fact that sport participation deters delinquency by encouraging less frequent, shorter, or less intense interaction with deviant others. Even this apparent positive by-product of sport participation may not result from what is being taught on the playing fields but rather from the fact that the individual simply has less contact with "bad influences." That being the case, athletic participation would be no more likely to result in preventing deviant behavior than participation in other extracurricular activities such as band, theater, or the debate club.

20   If there is one general conclusion to be made from Bredemeir and Shields' work, it is that "whatever advantages or liabilities are associated with sport involvement, they do not come from sport per se, but from the particular blend of social interactions and physical activities that comprise the totality of the sport experience" (Shields and Bredemeir 1995, 184).

Athletic Injuries to the Mind

Present-day researchers are not the only ones who have questioned the "sports build character" myth. Brutus Hamilton, track and field coach at the University of California, Berkeley, from 1933 to 1965, was one of the all-time best coaches. Hamilton was also U.S. Olympic decathlon coach in 1932 and 1936 and head U.S. track and field coach for the 1952 Olympic games in Helsinki. Hamilton, known as a coach who kept life and athletics in perspective, worried more about character development than about winning. He expressed his concern regarding sports participation and its effect on an individual's character development in a unique way at a Marin Sports Injury Conference in 1962.

Further athletic injuries to the boy's character can result in college. If he has chosen a school where sports are emphasized out of proportion to their importance he will find life easy if he performs well on the team. He will be coddled, made over, given parties by avid alumni, and even handed under-the-table payment, if not in cash then in some kind of presents. He's embarrassed at first, but soon comes to accept these things as a matter of course. The moral fiber gradually weakens and by the time his intercollegiate competition is over he is a victim of the system, a slave to gross and violent tastes, standing at the crossroads of Destiny. He was yesterday's headlines; he will be tomorrow's trivia. Now comes the harsh test as he faces the cruel pace of this competitive world in what he considers routine, humdrum chores of business. He has no headlines now; others who are younger are taking his place. Some former athletes make the adjustment rather quickly, others grope for several years and then make the adjustment, usually with the help of some good woman. Others, all too many, drift into middle age and resort to artificial stimulation to substitute for the intoxicating experiences they enjoyed in sports. Maybe sports were only partly to blame, but I believe no one would criticize a doctor who diagnosed these cases as an athletic injury to character suffered in youth....

The sad cases though are the ones which involve the eager, bright lad who goes to college on some kind of an athletic grant and is eager to become an Engineer, Lawyer, Doctor, Teacher or Architect. He becomes a victim of the intensity of the athletic training program. He misses practice to work on problem sets or to write out a book report. The coach suggests that he may be in the wrong course. Maybe he should transfer to a course which is not so demanding on his time. He certainly can't miss any more practices or his grant may be terminated. The boy has little choice, so he submits to the coach's suggestion and gives up his planned career. He may succeed gloriously in this new field but always he will wonder if he didn't make a mistake. He will always consider that he suffered an athletic injury to his mind in college whether anyone else does or not. When the training for an intercollegiate team becomes so time consuming, so intense and so exhausting that it is no longer possible for the student in the sciences or professions to participate, then something is wrong. Someone, perhaps a great many, are suffering an athletic injury to the mind. (Walton 1992, 118–20)

Los Angeles Lakers forward Elden Campbell made a related point, but much more precisely. When asked if he had earned his degree from Clemson University, he supposedly responded, "No, but they gave me one anyway."

Race and Violence

The college athletic community has also used as an educational justification the fact that a tremendous number of minority, particularly black, youngsters have benefited from the educational opportunity afforded them through athletic scholarships. Coaches often argue that athletics is the most discrimination-free enterprise in our country, insisting that the only criteria relevant in their evaluation of a student-athlete's worth is his or her performance on the field or court. The relatively large percentage of black student-athletes, particularly in the sports of football and basketball, provides some credence to the claim that athletic programs are in fact meeting this justification. According to the 1996 NCAA Division I Graduation Rate Report, 44 percent of football, 60 percent of men's basketball, and 34 percent of women's basketball student-athletes are black (National Collegiate Athletic Association 1996, 622). While these numbers are impressive, trumpeting athletics' tolerance of diversity as a significant justification for its place on campus is suspect at best, particularly given the small percentage of minorities in coaching and administrative positions, and athletics' poor record on issues relating to gender equity. . . .

Finally, there is growing concern regarding the effect of athletic participation on the participant's ability to resolve off-the-field conflicts peacefully, with particular attention being paid to violence against women. Accounts of student-athletes physically abusing women appear in our nation's newspapers far too often. One of the few studies of student-athlete violence against women was published in May 1995 in *The Journal of Sport and Social Issues*. The article reviewed 107 cases of sexual assault reported at 30 NCAA Division I institutions from 1991 to 1993. At 10 schools, male student-athletes were accused in 19 percent of the assaults, although they comprised only 3.3 percent of the male student body (Crosset, Benedict, and McDonald 1995, 126–140). Although broad conclusions should not be drawn from such limited research, the study does raise a question. Could it be that student-athletes, conditioned to resolve on-the-field conflicts with violence, have a more difficult time resolving off-the-field conflicts peacefully?

The Issue Is Environment

So what does all this mean for athletics' place within higher education? On one hand, there is the widely accepted notion that sports build character. Participation in college athletics, it is argued, teaches young people important lessons about teamwork, discipline, communication, and loyalty—all skills necessary for success beyond the playing field. For the most part, the public has bought fully into the concept. The supposed character-building benefits of sports have become a part of American folklore. From the mythical Frank Merriwell of Yale to the legendary Bud Wilkinson of Oklahoma, sports and those who play them embody the characteristics that make Americans "number one." Those who coach are sage mentors and molders of our future leaders. Those who play are inspirational heroes and role models.

On the other hand, many argue that college athletics is not about educa- 25 tion, in the sense of character development, at all; sport is about money, power, ego, and doing whatever it takes to win. As Oglive and Tutko (1985) pointed out, sport is not educational simply because it is sport. Rather it is the environment within which sports participation occurs that influences the educational, moral, and ethical development of participants. Sport that is overemphasized in relation to other fields of endeavor, particularly when it is conducted under the banner of an educational institution, is harmful. Sport kept in the proper perspective, where the process of participation (education) is not subjugated by the game's result (winning), can be extremely positive.

Along with the notion of athletics as a character builder goes the belief that coaches are effective teachers and positive educational role models. There are, however, too many examples of coaches who force their student-athletes into less demanding majors or discourage them from fully investing in their educational experience. These coaches are more interested in winning next week's game than preparing their student-athletes for life after athletics. Far too many student-athletes discontinue their participation in college athletics after becoming disillusioned with "the system." These dropouts are dismissed as "not having what it takes to be a winner." The successes are a product of the system; the failures are the result of the individual's shortcomings. Coaches refuse to admit the fact that often the individual succeeds despite the system or that it can be the system, rather than the individual, that fails. Therefore, along with questioning sports as inherently character building, we must also accept the fact that a whistle around the neck does not serve to qualify a coach as an educator.

For close to 100 years, we have claimed that big-time athletics is linked to the educational mission of the university, that participation is educational for the student-athlete, and that coaches and athletic administrators are educators. That assumption, however, can no longer be accepted without question. The purpose in highlighting the rather inconclusive research regarding sports participation's effect upon personality development is, once again, not to attack athletics or to minimize its potential to influence young people positively, but rather to caution the athletic community regarding its cavalier use of the "sports build character" justification. If education is a primary justification for athletics being on the college campus, then the question we must concern ourselves with is whether the environment in our programs is conducive to the positive educational and personal development of the student-athlete. It is time for the college athletic community to seriously rethink how this component of its mission is approached and realized.

Does Athletics Make Money?

Concern regarding making ends meet financially has been as much a part of the history of American higher education as the classroom lecture. As noted earlier, the never-ending search for new revenue streams was the driving force behind athletics' acceptance into the higher education community.

> With the introduction of athletics to the already economically hard-pressed colleges and universities of late 19th and 20th century America, the doctrine of good works [that revenues generated by intercollegiate athletics are so much greater than the cost of the sport that the entire college benefits financially] offered some hope of relief from further financial hardships. Along with claims concerning the educational value of athletics—that sport participation builds character and that it helps student grades—the financial rationale for sport programs eased the entry onto campus of athleticism, a program previously foreign to the cognitively oriented college and university of the era. (Chu, Segrave, and Becker 1985, 289)

A widely held belief is that major college athletic programs generate a huge surplus of revenue for universities through gate receipts, television revenue, and alumni contributions. Even at universities where programs operate at a deficit, the exposure generated through television and the media is thought to increase the institution's stature and generate public interest in the university. Such visibility, it is said, results in increased applications and curries favor with legislators and the surrounding community. The facts, however, paint a different picture.

When institutional support (salaries, cash, tuition waivers, etc.) is not included on the revenue side of the financial ledger, most Division I college athletic programs lose money. According to an NCAA-sponsored report, only 28 percent of Division I programs generate more revenues than they expend. Further, only 46 percent of the 89 Division I-A schools reporting generated a profit. (The total number of Division I-A programs, those with "big-time" football, is 108; Division I-AA has 119 members and I-AAA has 78.) Without general institutional support, barely more than one in four Division I athletic programs would be solvent. A more detailed accounting of the financial statistics from this report follows (Fulks 1995, 19, 33, and 47):

	Profit	Deficit	Even
Division I-A (n=89)	46%	52%	2%
Division I-AA (n=72)	13%	85%	2%
Division I-AAA (n=45)	18%	82%	0%

And, as institutions begin to appropriate the long-overdue resources neces- 30
sary to meet the demands of Title IX and gender equity, future financial figures
may become more sobering.

There is more to the issue of athletics as a sound institutional business investment. The National Association of College and University Business Officers (NACUBO) conducted an analysis of college athletics' finances
in its 1993 report entitled *The Financial Management of Intercollegiate Athletics
Programs*. The analysis brought to light additional concerns regarding university accounting procedures as they apply to athletic operations. The report concluded that current costs, as high as they are, may not yet be telling the entire
financial story. Specifically, the report questioned the practice of institutions
paying many indirect or overhead costs generated by the athletic department.

The report identified six data elements that represent indirect expenditures.

- Amortization of facilities (if owned by the university)

- Student support services (academic and financial assistance) provided by
  the institution

- Student health services provided by the institution

- Athletic staff salaries and benefits for staff employed in other departments

- Proportion of buildings and grounds maintenance

- Proportion of capital equipment used

The report went on to state that

> Interviews with personnel in 18 institutions across all athletics divisions
> showed that only one of these data elements, amortization of facilities, could
> be calculated with any degree of accuracy, and even then this could be done
> only by the four Division I-A institutions in the study. Given this difficulty, it
> seems likely that many indirect or "overhead" expenses attributable to ath-
> letics activities are borne by the university as a whole. In institutions that
> require other programs or divisions to bear their share of indirect costs,
> allowing athletics to escape this burden creates a basic inequity. (National
> Association of College and University Business Officers 1993, 20)

We can easily conclude that were athletics' accounting held to a common business standard where all direct and indirect expenses are charged against revenues, significantly fewer than the 28 percent of all Division I institutions would
report an athletic department profit.

Inasmuch as athletics was formally and primarily incorporated into higher
education for financial and business reasons, it is ironic that more often than
not this "business proposition" is a bad one. A successful business generates
more money than it expends. After looking at the numbers, the argument can
be made that except for the elite programs, athletics actually drains financial
resources from the university.

A review of the reports published over the past decade indicates that, as a whole, American intercollegiate athletics programs are unable to support themselves and that most programs run a deficit. This finding is not surprising in colleges that designate varsity sports as part of the educational budget and make no claim to seek massive crowds. It does warrant concern, however, when one looks at institutions that have established varsity football and/or basketball as major, self-supporting activities intended to produce revenues, with large arenas and stadia and with television audiences. (Thelin and Wiseman 1989, 15)

Due largely to reports of huge television deals and corporate sponsorship agreements, it is easy to assume that major college athletic programs are rolling in money. But based upon actual figures, the claim that athletic programs make money for the university is largely untrue. Yes, athletic programs generate revenue. And yes, occasionally we read about an athletic department writing a check to the university's library or general scholarship fund. But what is not as readily reported is that major college athletic programs also spend a tremendous amount of money, particularly in the sports of football and basketball.

Further, no conclusive evidence exists to prove that a successful athletic program results in increased alumni giving or applications. Yet, the athletic community continues to use the claim as a primary justification for its own existence. While a successful athletic program can be a factor in alumni giving and student applications, it is unlikely that it is as much of a factor as claimed by those in the athletic community. While an institution may experience an immediate, short-term jump in applications or financial support (more than likely earmarked specifically for the athletic program) after a particularly successful football or basketball season, the fact remains that most institutions will continue to attract quality students who, when they graduate, will donate money to their alma maters, with little regard to the quality or even existence of a big-time athletic program.

Does Athletics Generate Positive Visibility?

35   Despite the probability that collegiate athletics does not generate monies for the university in general, athletic programs do provide significant regional and national visibility and exposure for the university. Games are broadcast on radio and television to a national audience, and newspaper coverage is often extensive. "By 1900, the relationship between football and public relations had been firmly established and almost everywhere acknowledged as one of sport's major justifications" (Rudolph 1990, 385). Clearly, athletic programs generate significant public exposure for universities. What is not so clear, however, is whether that exposure contributes positively to public relations.

The truth has been well documented: all exposure generated through major college athletic is not positive. A striking example of this dichotomy occurred at Florida State University. In winning a national football championship by defeating the University of Nebraska in the 1994 Orange Bowl, FSU garnered a tremendous amount of positive publicity. A national championship in football was evidence of the university's commitment to excellence. FSU was the best in the nation. There was no reason to expect other programs offered by the university were of lesser quality.

But how quickly things can change. Shortly after the Orange Bowl victory, allegations that student-athletes were provided clothes and cash by agents while coaches "looked the other way" quickly changed the type of exposure the football program was generating. If winning a national football championship meant that Florida State University was a winner, what did allegations that the football program won the national championship while breaking NCAA rules mean?

Questions regarding the supposed positive effect of athletic department visibility on the university go beyond the bad publicity associated with a scandal.... [T]he argument can be made that the exposure generated through athletics has little to do with advancing positive educational or institutional messages, but that instead such visibility is used simply to promote the specific goals of the athletic department.

Again, the purpose here is not to criticize unduly or to dismiss the positive impact an athletic program can have on a university, financially or otherwise. A well-run program can contribute to the mission of a university in ways that might not show up in the institutional balance sheet. Visibility and stature within the state legislature may in many cases have a positive impact on institutional efforts to attract state funding. And despite inconclusive evidence, a successful athletic team and the visibility it brings has the potential to attract students to campus on an occasional basis. In fact, ... such contributions must be given greater consideration when evaluating an institution's return on investment in athletics.

Given the financial statements and the inconclusive research regarding *40* alumni giving and applications, however, coaches and athletic administrators can no longer assert without question that athletics is a positive financial proposition for the institution. That being the case, they must be prepared to address this financial reality as they are challenged to justify athletics' place on campus. Like golfing partners who, when playing for money, make each other putt those short distances that are "gimmes" when playing for fun, college athletics no longer has the benefit of the "financial gimme."

Now That's Entertainment

For millions of people, intercollegiate athletic contests provide enjoyable, exciting entertainment. Whether attending a women's tennis match or watching the Final Four on television, the pageantry and spectacle of college athletics offers an exciting reprieve from the ordinary. If there is one thing about college athletics that almost everyone—critics and proponents, fans and faculty—can agree upon, it is that college sports is good entertainment.

College sports is also Big Entertainment. Simply consider the NCAA's current seven-year, $1.7 billion contract with CBS for the television rights to the NCAA Division I Basketball Tournament as proof that college sports is an entertainment Goliath. If that is not proof enough, stand outside any Southeastern Conference or Big Ten football stadium on a Saturday afternoon in the fall and feel the excitement of 80,000 fans preparing for a big game. Concession stands, T-shirt sales, program sales, tailgating, and ticket scalpers—all turning a buck on college athletics. Merchandising, television ratings, corporate sponsors, shoe contracts, media coverage, crowds cheering ... now that's entertainment!

Entertaining students, alumni, and the surrounding community is indeed a valuable service that higher education provides the public; it should not be trivialized. Higher education's purpose is to serve the needs of society, and athletics' unqualified success in providing this service should be celebrated.

As university enrollments have increased and diversified, athletic teams have promoted institutional unity and "the old college spirit." The entire university family, from faculty, students, and local fans, to alumni living in faraway places, can usually rally around "Ole State" U's football team. And while the firing of a controversial coach or an NCAA investigation can splinter a campus, athletics usually serves a unifying function for the university community. At what other function does so much of the university community gather to rally around the institution? As Paul "Bear" Bryant, the legendary University of Alabama football coach, allegedly said, "Fifty thousand people don't come to watch English class."

> At games, students and other members of the community come together for a common purpose. They are united, at least for the duration of the contest. Personal differences, politics, even business matters may be put aside. Those gathered view themselves as the community, united against another community. Everyone pulls together, and in so doing, the community generates uncommon energy and commitment. With community members acting in unison with the force of passion, for the very dignity of the community is at stake, the whole is more than the sum of its parts. (Miracle and Rees 1994, 160)

There are, however, risks in relying on athletic teams to unify the campus community. Institutions that use athletics to solve the problems of a fragmented community run the risk of making athletics, and not academic excellence, the primary purpose of the institution. Although a football or basketball program can unite a university community in a way that an English department cannot, the primary purpose of the institution remains educational. In short, a winning football team does not make a quality educational institution.

45   Further, placing such a heavy emphasis on the unifying function of sports promotes a community mind-set that college athletics is more about the fans and campus community than it is about the participation of student-athletes. A successful team in terms of a won-loss record, although pleasing to fans,

alumni, and the media, may cover up fundamental problems within an athletic program, such as low graduation rates, illegal activities, or abusive coaches. While a few wins may unite the campus community in the short term, it may result in long-term disintegration of community trust if the athletic department is not meeting its fundamental educational responsibilities to its student-athletes or if it contradicts broader institutional goals.

Thus, the question remains: Are the entertainment and unifying functions of athletics enough to justify athletics' prominence in the university educational system?

What Does All This Mean?

So where does this analysis of principles, missions, and justifications leave us? After having reviewed athletics' three primary justifications for being a part of the higher education community, the answer is still mixed. Whether athletic departments are meeting their fundamental educational and personal-development responsibilities to student-athletes is questionable. Certainly, many coaches and athletic administrators are committed and effective teachers as well as positive educational role models. And thousands of student-athletes earn a quality, well-balanced academic and athletic experience. But unfortunately, as a result of the "win-at-all-cost" mentality that drives the athletic culture, some lessons learned through athletic participation are not positive. Thus, the assertion that participation in college athletics is a positive educational experience can no longer be accepted without question.

Regarding the claim that athletics generates money and visibility for the university, the data are again mixed. While athletic programs generate revenue, most do not generate more than they expend. And finally, not all the visibility that an athletic program brings to the university is positive. Just ask any president of a school that has been placed on NCAA probation.

Thus, only one of the justifications for athletics being a part of higher education is being fully met—the justification of providing entertainment. And ironically, even when using the current standard of measuring the success of an athletic program—championships won—the vast majority of universities fail miserably. The very nature of sport dictates that for every winner there is a loser. Only one team in every league hangs up the championship banner at season's end.

If our athletic programs are not successful in meeting their primary reasons *50* for existence within higher education, we must reconsider how they can justify their existence. Moreover, because so few of our athletic programs achieve success as it is currently defined, we should reconsider whether the current standards of success—championship banners won and revenue generated—are reasonable and relevant. In short, we must go back to the drawing board and consider in fundamental terms just what our athletic programs should be about, what the people associated with these programs should represent, where these programs fit overall within higher education, and, most important, how their success should be measured.

References

Adler, Patricia A., and Peter Adler. *Backboards and Blackboards: College Athletes and Role Engulfment.* New York: Columbia University Press, 1991. Print.

Carter, Stephen L. *Integrity.* New York: Basic Books, 1996. Print.

Chu, Donald. *The Character of American Higher Education and Intercollegiate Sport.* Albany, NY: State University of New York Press, 1989. Print.

Chu, Donald, Jeffrey Segrave, and Beverly Becker. *Sport and Higher Education.* Champaign, IL: Human Kinetics Publishers, 1985. Print.

Crosset, Todd W., Jeffrey R. Benedict, and Mark A. McDonald. "Male —Student Athletes Reported for Sexual Assault: A Survey of Campus Police Departments and Judicial Affairs." *Journal of Sport and Social Issues* 19.2 (1995). Print.

Ebaugh, Helen R. *Becoming an Ex.* Chicago: University of Chicago Press, 1988. Print.

Fulks, Daniel L. *Revenues and Expenses of Intercollegiate Athletic Programs: Financial Trends and Relationships.* Overland Park, KS: NCAA, 1995. Print.

Miracle, Andrew, and C. Roger Rees. *Lessons of the Locker Room: The Myth of School Sports.* Amherst, NY: Prometheus Books, 1994. Print.

National Association of College and University Business Officers. *The Financial Management of Intercollegiate Athletics Program.* Washington, D.C.: NACUBO, 1993. Print.

National Collegiate Athletic Association. *1996 NCAA Division I Graduation-Rates Report.* Overland Park, KS: NCAA, 1996. Print.

Oglive, Bruce, and Thomas Tutko. "Sport: If You Want to Build Character, Try Something Else." *Sport and Higher Education.* Eds. Donald Chu, Jeffrey Segrave, and Beverly Becker. Champaign, IL: Human Kinetics Publishers, 1985. Print.

Rudolph, Frederick. *The American College and University: A History.* Athens, GA: University of Georgia Press, 1990. Print.

Savage, Howard J., et al. *American College Athletics.* New York: Carnegie Foundation, 1929. Print.

Shields, David L., and Brenda J. Bredemeir. *Character Development and Physical Activity.* Champaign, IL: Human Kinetics Publishers, 1995. Print.

Steiner, Hans. Research results reported in *Stanford Daily.* 7 May 1996. Print.

Stevenson, C.L. "Socialization Effects of Participation in Sports; A Critical Review of the Research." *Research Quarterly* 46 (1975): 287–301. Print.

Stoll, Sharon. *Letter to John Gerdy.* 19 July 1996.

Thelin, John R., and Lawrence L. Wiseman. "The Old College Try: Balancing Athletics and Academics in Higher Education." *Report No. 4.* Washington, D.C.: The George Washington University, 1989. Print.

Walton, Gary M. *Beyond Winning: The Timeless Wisdom of Great Philosopher Coaches.* Champaign, IL: Leisure Press, 1992. Print.

Reflections and Inquiries

1. Do you agree or disagree with Douglas MacArthur's description of sports as a character builder, quoted on page 374? Explain.
2. What contributes to the skepticism that usually greets the formulaic assertion that sports builds character?

3. What did the findings of Jennifer Beller and Sharon Stoll, of the University of Idaho's Center for Ethics, reveal about the influence of sports on the moral development of students?
4. Weigh the validity of the Adlers' findings, described on pages 377–378.

Reading to Write
After researching possible ways in which participating in sports can build character, write an essay in which you discuss the character-building potential of college athletics (or one of the other seven questions Gerdy addresses). Does your data confirm or disprove Gerdy's assertions?

Issues for Further Research: The Intrinsic Value of College Athletics

Student Essay

Paradox of Payment | Bryan Crook

A biology major at Santa Clara University, Bryan Crook was a first-year student when he wrote this essay. As a multitalented student athlete, Bryan not only maintained a nearly perfect GPA in his first year of studies but also ran on the Division I cross-country and track teams for the university. Bryan interacted both with student-athletes and with fellow members of the University Honors Program, so he brings a broad perspective to the debate over whether student-athletes should be paid for playing their sports for their universities.

Public service announcement: College Sports are a BIG deal. Scratch that, they are a huge deal. Colossal might be the most indicative adjective for the presence of college sports in our daily lives. No matter, anyone who has ever hovered over one of the seemingly endless variations of ESPN on television has seen coverage of Nick Saban's all-star recruiting class or projections for whether Andrew Luck's pro-day will help or hurt his status as the likely number one draft pick. Heck, anyone who doesn't live under a rock has heard of how Joe Paterno was willing to sacrifice his morals and the safety of children to save the face of his football program at Penn State. Collegiate athletics aren't just a big deal; they are just as big of a business. As the business of college sports grows, many coaches, players, and journalists are becoming increasingly vocal in asserting that full-ride scholarships aren't just compensation for the money these athletes make for their schools. Some have even gone so far as to call athletes exploited and draw parallels to slavery. As this topic gains attention, the question needs to be answered: should college athletes be paid to play or do critics underestimate the true value of an education?

Back before the intense commercialization of collegiate athletics, nobody called for student-athletes to be paid. This question has only arisen in the past 30 or so years as the amount of money being raked in by top programs has grown dramatically with the help of increased attention made possible by media outlets like ESPN and conference networks. The situation of student-athletes reached a spearhead recently with an article written by Taylor Branch in *The Atlantic* and a week-long special on ESPN. The numbers don't lie. College sports, more specifically the "revenue sports" which consist of men's football and basketball (unless you attend Connecticut or Tennessee, where the women's teams turn a profit as well) are at a level of unprecedented financial success. According to Seth Davis in an article for *Sports Illustrated* titled "Should College Athletes Be Paid? Why, They Already Are," the "SEC recently surpassed the $1 billion mark for football receipts" and "the football programs at Texas, Florida, Georgia, Michigan and Penn State earn between $40 million and $80 million each year in profits." Additionally, the NCAA recently signed a contract with CBS and Turner to televise March Madness worth $10.8 billion through 2024. These numbers are staggering, and they don't even include the financial excesses of the BCS system which is under federal investigation for possible anti-trust violations.

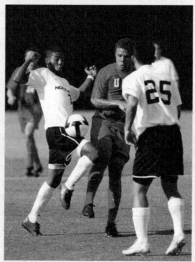

Prakash Singh/AFP/Getty Images

John J. Klaiber Jr/Shutterstock.com

Considering the huge sums of money involved, both sides of this debate should be heard out. Proponents of paying players have taken a few angles in attempt to sway the NCAA. One of their main arguments is that student athletes would be better defined as employees of their university. The expectations and requirements of a collegiate athlete are certainly similar to those of an employee. Athletes are expected to dedicate a considerable amount of their time and effort to their sport, and some athletes can spend in the ballpark of 40 hours per week on training and competing during the height of their seasons, numbers that can compare with many full-time jobs. Colleges make money from this time and effort, so in the most basic logic collegiate athletes may be loosely considered employees. If they qualify as employees, then the argument predictably follows that they must be compensated for their work.

Similarly, proponents argue that athletes are taken advantage of when these programs make money from the sale of memorabilia. Every university in the country has at least one store that sells sportswear and other items supporting its teams, and if one of those items has a specific player's name or number on it, then there is something to be said for giving them a cut of the profit. Selling anything they get from the school (clothing, gear, etc.) is strictly prohibited, and scandals involving athletes selling or trading personal memorabilia have racked the NCAA recently, capturing stars like Terrelle Pryor and A.J. Green in a net of sanctions. The argument heard from players regarding these sales is that since their hard work makes their jersey popular, they should get a cut of the profits the school is making off of them. Likewise, proponents are in an uproar regarding the use of athletes' likenesses to sell their university and their athletic events. This is a form of endorsement that they get no compensation for, yet the school still benefits. Even if

athletes can't get compensated for advertising their own university, those who support paying athletes argue that they should be allowed to pursue endorsement deals outside of their school.

5   No matter which of the above strategies people use to argue for the payment of college athletes, almost all arguments claim the same thing: full scholarships don't legitimately cover the actual "cost of attendance." The "cost of attendance" argument includes costs like entertainment, food, and clothing as expenditures that student athletes shouldn't have to pay for. Those who argue the necessity of helping students pay such expenditures claim that athletes need these funds to keep from going into debt. They are especially in danger of debt since they have less time to pursue jobs to earn spending money with the time-consuming combination of their studies and workouts, along with mandatory summer practices that interfere with their ability to hold a job over the summer.

Proponents of paying athletes for their services do not all agree on how exactly they want to do this. Proposed methods of payment include giving athletes a stipend or allowance, paying them at market value, giving "full-cost" scholarships, or allowing them to pursue endorsement deals. Most suggestions for a stipend range from around $2,000 to $5,000 per season to allay the "cost of attendance." Allowances offered would likely be a few hundred dollars per week, and Steve Spurrier, a coach at South Carolina, has gotten support from many coaches in the SEC for his proposal to pay such allowances out of their own salaries (which generally are in the ballpark of $2–$6 million) according to Mark Schlabach of ESPN. Schlabach also notes, however, that "the NCAA would never go for Spurrier's plan" and SEC commissioner Mike Slive said that this proposal is "something that obviously can't be done" (Schlabach). The Universities could still provide an allowance to players if the NCAA allowed them to do so. "Full-cost" scholarships would likely have an extra $2,000 to $5,000 built in for living expenses according to Big Ten commissioner Jim Delany (Schlabach), and are endorsed by the commissioners of the Pac 12 and Big 12 as well.

Perhaps the most drastic proposal for how to compensate athletes for their efforts is to pay them market value salaries. The argument here is that most professional sports pay their athletes in the form of a salary and since college sports make just as much money as professional ones, college athletes deserve compensation determined in a similar manner. This would land collegiate athletes more money than any of the other proposals. Seth Davis mentioned an NCPA (National College Players Association) study in his article which "found that, at the highest end, the fair market value for a football player at the University of Texas is $513,922" (Davis). Allowing players to be paid free-market salaries would mean open season for recruiting and would result in top high school talents essentially being auctioned off. This change would also increase the financial risk to athletic departments because this money would be lost if a player gets hurt or doesn't play up to the level expected of him or her. Finally, critics call for athletes to be allowed to pursue any endorsement deal that they can get, citing it as their right to lend their likeness for advertising purposes. Although most athletes would not benefit if allowed to pursue endorsement deals, the few stars who would could foreseeably earn six- or seven-figure amounts or more annually from local sports stores, car dealerships, and even top clothing companies like Nike, Adidas, or Under Armour.

These proposals further vary based on their inclusiveness as to who should be paid and who is out of luck in college athletic departments. Some call for only the athletes who are making their schools money to be paid, and there is some sense to that argument since a rower has nothing to do with the football team selling out their stadium. Others are more inclusive and insist that all athletes should be paid regardless of whether they are in a revenue sport or not. To return to an earlier argument, if athletes are considered employees, then all athletes must be paid since they all put in the time and effort that is required for their sport. Additional complications to these proposals are that there are many schools and conferences in the NCAA that cannot afford to shell out the money required to pay their athletes. Frank Deford insists that this shouldn't be an issue, and proposes that schools that can't afford to pay their athletes should cut their athletic programs entirely. He defends his position by claiming "either make the economic model work fairly, or get out of the business" (Deford). In this model of college athletics Deford imagines, athletic departments would consist of men's football and basketball teams, along with just enough women's teams to make the programs meet Title IX regulations.

While these proposals are very optimistic in the logistics of their implementation, there are many factors that complicate the prospect of paying college athletes. The first of these roadblocks is Title IX, a federal law aimed at promoting equal opportunity between genders in collegiate athletics. Many of these payment plans completely ignore the issue that whatever payment is allotted to men has to be given equally to women in each athletic department. Some writers confront Title IX with the attitude that it should be scrapped and vehemently argue that women shouldn't be paid since they don't generate revenue for the school. The problem here is that paying athletes would simply become an avenue to circumvent equality among genders and divert money to men's sports. Eventually, this would spell the end for women's sports as athletic departments would become increasingly bold in paying their male, revenue-producing athletes. This end is similar to the side effect of the proposals like Deford's that have athletic departments cutting all sports that can't turn a profit.

10   These proposals and calls to cut sports completely miss the point of college athletics and the community that a full athletic program fosters. On the NCAA's website, under "core values," the NCAA and its member institutions pledge a commitment to "[the] supporting role that intercollegiate athletics plays in the higher education mission and in enhancing the sense of community and strengthening the identity of member institutions." This vow can be broken into two key values, complete education and community. The athletes themselves are not the only ones who share this sense of community; those who support them and follow their progress compose a crucial part of the larger community. Most students who have attended a school basketball game have also probably gone to a volleyball or baseball game as well, and the bonds between students at one are no stronger or weaker than between those at another. By professionalizing college sports and emphasizing business over participation, athletic departments would be destroying the communities that they play a large role in forming.

Besides the obstacle imposed by Title IX or the prospect of hurting the college community, there are serious logistical limitations to the proposed plans for paying athletes. The biggest of these is the apparently ignored statistic provided by the NCAA that contends only 12 athletic programs in the nation actually turn a profit. Armed with this piece of information the question becomes where the money for paying college athletes should come from. Since most schools help fund their athletic departments, they are the next logical source to turn to for the money to pay athletes. Private Universities could technically choose to do so if the NCAA changes its bylaws, but public Universities can't justify diverting taxpayer dollars to make sure Vince Young was paid handsomely for his National Championship winning effort during the 2005 season. The answer to this predicament provided by many people is to cut nonrevenue sports, specifically men's teams, to stay within the boundaries of Title IX, and give the money that used to be diverted to them to those who play revenue sports. As previously discussed, that is a bad idea because it disturbs the college community. Additionally, collegiate athletics are the primary training ground for our Olympic hopefuls aged 18–22. Many of these nonrevenue sports do not have very competitive professional leagues, so cutting college programs would make America less competitive at the international level and would force promising young athletes aged 18–22 to make the choice between an education and an attempt to make the Olympics. Taking away Michael Phelps's 15-gold-medal contribution to the American haul over the last two Olympics is a consequence supporters of Deford's view of college sports should consider before axing collegiate swim programs.

Although the various proposals for paying athletes seem enticing and the sheer majority of media members in support of pay-for-play can fatigue readers into agreement, I find the severe undervaluation of the student-athlete experience shocking and offensive as a student-athlete myself. For starters, anyone who claims that student athletes get nothing for their time completely overlooks the significance of full-ride scholarships, which can value over $200,000 over four years. Athletes on full scholarship benefit from a free education: one that many would not have had access to if it weren't for collegiate athletics. Additionally, for all of the talk about "fair wages" and the "cost of attendance," very few people ever talk about the "benefit of attendance." As I mentioned earlier when talking about the core values of the NCAA, the NCAA is interested in promoting the complete education of its athletes, not assuming a role as a minor league supplier to professional leagues.

When I refer to complete education, I am talking about experiential learning that is such a crucial part of the college experience along with the traditional sense of academic success. As far as traditional academics are concerned, college athletes benefit from much more than just the dollar amount of a scholarship. Along with any services available to regular students, athletes at virtually any Division I school have additional academic advisors that monitor their progress and help them transition to college and manage their time. If an athlete is struggling in any class, the athletic department will arrange for them to meet with a tutor at their convenience. As an athlete myself, I have benefitted from the help of my academic advisor in choosing classes and have enjoyed priority registration for classes, giving me the advantage of choice between professors and class times. There is also an academic support center in the Leavey Center which serves as a study room that I can go to if the library is full or I need a quiet place to work. This center pales in comparison to similar centers at big sports schools like the University of Oregon. Oregon has a 40,000-square-foot, state-of-the-art facility called the John Jaqua Center that is almost exclusively dedicated to athletes. There are many areas and even floors of this building (which is similar in size to the Santa Clara [University] library) that are off limits to anyone except athletes. Services and facilities like this are funded with a portion of the money made by athletic departments, so nobody can argue that athletes aren't seeing the benefit of their on-field success.

Besides tangible benefits like advising, priority, and study rooms, athletes also benefit from the collegiate athlete experience in ways that are impossible to quantify. College is an ideal venue for learning the complexities of a particular sport. In his essay "The Dark Night of the Soul," Richard Miller outlines the importance of such experiential learning in our world. In Miller's concluding paragraph, he imagines a world where "the first year writing course become(s) a place where we engage productively with the dark realities of our time: violence, suicide, war, and terrorism, as well as fraudulence, complicity, and trauma?" Between injury, team tragedy, and eating disorders, a sports team is the perfect place to be exposed to certain lessons instead of a classroom. As a freshman, I can already rattle off a list of life lessons I've learned and the ways I've matured as a result of my experiences as a Division I cross-country runner. These include such things as dealing with disappointment and adversity when you have invested so much into a venture, being flexible when things don't go according to plan, and learning to help a teammate through tragedy. My sports experience has taught me more about accountability for my own actions and responsibility to others than any class ever could.

15   Albeit slightly abstract, the experience of being a collegiate athlete also compares nicely to Miller's analysis of Chris McCandless' adventure into the Alaskan wild. Miller claims, "McCandless was killed off by a reading practice that placed too much faith in books, a practice that forgets that the world in all its infinite complexity and particularity will always exceed the explanatory grasp of any single text and, indeed, of all texts taken in their totality" (Miller, 431). Classrooms cannot teach students everything, and athletes are given plenty of all-expenses-paid learning experiences. Going to out-of-town competitions is one such example, where athletes are put up by their schools and learn how to adapt and become comfortable in unfamiliar situations. The experience of traveling to an unknown city and staying in a hotel the night before a big race helps prepare young athletes for doing the same thing before giving a presentation to potential investors later on in their lives. These learning experiences are guided by coaches, who are paid quite a bit to be life mentors to their athletes just as much as they are to be teachers of their sport. Coaches serve as role models and parental figures to their players more so than professors do because of their mutual investment in the same goal and the sheer time they spend with their athletes. I attribute a significant part of my growth as a person over the past six months to lessons and examples my coaches Felipe and Chantelle have set, and I consider them equal parts coach, parent, and guidance counselor.

Considering all of the benefits college athletes get from playing sports in college, proponents of pay-for-play certainly can't argue that they get nothing for their work. Besides, going to college and playing sports is a choice, and contrary to popular belief among sportswriters, the primary purpose of university attendance is education. If an athlete is capable of playing professionally and wants to be paid, they have a choice of doing so instead of going to college. In fact, the reason athletes choose not to play for pay in Europe or go to the minors in preparation for the big leagues is the college experience. In their own cost-benefit analysis, the college experience is more valuable than the money they would earn playing professionally. This does not mean that they don't see any of the money made from their efforts.

Recently, the issue of paying collegiate athletes has been one of the most heated and polarized controversies in American sports. Many proponents of paying collegiate athletes cite capitalism and fairness as reasons for compensation and draw parallels between players and unpaid laborers. The problem with their arguments, however, is that they fail to consider the ramifications of the changes they propose or the true state of the student-athlete. People can argue all they want about whether or not collegiate athletes deserve to be paid, but they can't deny the numerous benefits playing collegiate sports gives them and they certainly can't assume that any change would be good change. College athletics as they are now promote community and help dedicated student-athletes get the most out of a multifaceted education, and the privilege of playing a sport at the collegiate level is one that collegiate athletes should be grateful for.

Works Cited

Cooper, Kenneth J. "Should College Athletes Be Paid To Play?" *Diverse Issues In Higher Education* 28.10 (2011): 12–13. *OmniFile Full Text Mega (H.W. Wilson)*. Web. 5 Mar. 2012.

Davis, Seth. "Should College Athletes Be Paid? Why They Already Are." *Rebutting Taylor Branch Belief in Paying Student-athletes*. Web. 10 Mar. 2012. <http://sportsillustrated.cnn.com/2011/writers/seth_davis/09/21/Branch.rebuttal/1.html>.

Deford, Frank. "Bust The Amateur Myth." *Chronicle Of Higher Education* 58.17 (2011): A8. *OmniFile Full Text Mega (H.W. Wilson)*. Web. 5 Mar. 2012.

Miller, Richard. "The Dark Night of the Soul." In *Ways of Reading: An Anthology for Writers*, 9th edition, ed. David Bartholomae and Anthony Petrosky. Boston: Bedford/St. Martins, 2011.

"National Collegiate Athletic Association." *NCAA Public Home Page*. Web. 7 Mar. 2012. <http://www.ncaa.org>.

Schlabach, Mark. "Examining Pay-for-play proposals." *ESPN*. ESPN Internet Ventures. Web. 10 Mar. 2012. <http://espn.go.com/college-sports/story/_/id/6768411/pay-play-proposals-ncaa-student-athletes>.

Voepel, Mechelle. "Title IX a Pay-for-play roadblock." *ESPN*. ESPN Internet Ventures. Web. 10 Mar. 2012. <http://espn.go.com/college-sports/story/_/id/6769337/title-ix-seen-substantial-roadblock-pay-play-college-athletics>.

Wilbon, Michael. "College Athletes Deserve to Be Paid." *ESPN*. ESPN Internet Ventures. Web. 10 Mar. 2012. <http://espn.go.com/college-sports/story/_/id/6778847/college-athletes-deserve-paid>.

Wolff, Alexander. "An Honest Wage." *Sports Illustrated* 80.(1994): 98. *OmniFile Full Text Mega (H.W. Wilson)*. Web. 5 Mar. 2012.

Reflections and Inquiries

1. According to Crook, Title IX's guarantee of gender equality would spell the end for women's sports if a pay-for-play policy were implemented. Evaluate Crook's reasons for this assertion.
2. How accurately does Crook represent each of the play-for-pay proposals?
3. Which method of argument—Classical, Toulmin, or Rogerian (discussed in Chapters 3 and 4)—best characterizes Crook's essay? How can you tell?
4. Defend or refute Crook's claim that a college education is not complete unless it includes experiential learning.

Reading to Write

1. In a six- to eight-page essay, defend or challenge Crook's assertion that "by professionalizing college sports and emphasizing business over participation, athletic departments would be destroying the communities they play a large role in forming."
2. Crook finds offensive "the severe underevaluation of the student-athlete experience." Drawing from your own experience with college athletics, argue why you share Crook's sentiment or not.

Connections Among the Clusters

The issues relating to the athletics vs. academics controversy overlap with other issues such as the representation of minorities and women in sports, or the role of athletics in multicultural education, or the impact of media on college athletic programs.

Critical Thinking

1. What influence can college athletic programs have on student diversity and multicultural learning? (See Cluster 4.)
2. What kinds of media regulation or censorship might arise in the context of broadcasting or writing about college sports? How might they be prevented? (See Cluster 5.)
3. Suggest possible connections between college athletics and media coverage of college athletic programs. (See Cluster 5.)

Writing Projects

1. Review your college athletic program's policy on academic standards. What modifications or additions to the existing policy do you recommend, and why? Write an essay in which you identify problems and make specific recommendations.

2. Write an essay on the position that participation in a college athletic program benefits or hinders academic performance. You may want to obtain testimonies from several students, as well as from coaches and professors, to support your assertions.

Suggestions for Further Reading

Ashley, Bob. "Can Athletics, Academics at Duke Coexist?" *Herald-Sun* 16 June 2006. Print.

Benedict, Jeff, and Armen Keteyian. *The System: The Glory and Scandal of Big-Time College Football*. New York: Anchor, 2014.

Branch, Taylor. "The Shame of College Sports." *The Atlantic*, October 2011: 81–110. Print.

Cotton, H. F., *A + A = F: Academics Plus Athletics Equals Failure*. Bloomington, IN: XLibris Corp., 2009.

Funk, Gary D. *Major Violation: The Unbalanced Priorities in Athletics and Academics*. Champaign, IL: Leisure Press, 1991. Print.

Gerdy, John R. *Sports in School: The Future of an Institution*. New York: Teachers College, 2000. Print.

Nixon II, Howard L. *The Athletic Trap: How College Sports Corrupted the Academy*. Baltimore: Johns Hopkins Univ. Press, 2014.

Sack, Allen L. *Counterfeit Amateurs: An Athlete's Journey through the Sixties to the Age of Academic Capitalism*. University Park: Penn State UP, 2008. Print.

Schulman, James L., and William G. Bowen. *The Game of Life: College Sports and Educational Values*. Princeton: Princeton UP, 2001. Print.

Smith, Jay M., and Mary Willingham. *Cheated: The UNC Scandal, the Education of Athletes, and the Future of Big-Time College Sports*. Lincoln: Potomac Books / Univ. of Nebraska Press, 2015.

Snyder, H., and E. Spreitzer, "Social Psychological Concomitants of Adolescents' Role Identities as Scholars and Athletes: A Longitudinal Analysis." *Youth and Society* 23 (1992): 507–522. Print.

Yost, Mark. *Varsity Green: A Behind the Scenes Look at Culture and Corruption in College Athletics*. Stanford: Stanford UP, 2010.

Zimbalist, Andrew. "A Conversation with Andrew Zimbalist." *U.S. Society and Values*. Dec. 2003. Print.

Zimbalist, Andrew, and Bob Costas. *May the Best Team Win: Baseball Economics and Public Policy*. Washington, D.C.: Brookings Institution, 2004. Print.

International Relations, Immigration Reform, and the Global Economy: What Are the Key Issues?

Introduction

Kipling's Victorian-era jingle, "East is East and West is West and never the twain shall meet," implying that ethnic and cultural differences will always keep people separate even if they come together (as they did during the era of British imperialism), has long since proven to be a falsehood. The United States is often portrayed as a land of different cultures that not only interact harmoniously but enrich and influence one another, sometimes to the point of "flattening" the world, Thomas Friedman's metaphor for the globalized world that is becoming technologically and industrially homogenized. Along with globalization, however, comes increased concern over national security, especially border security and immigration control. Nothing is more precious to America than its freedom (national as well as individual), and strong security measures protect that freedom. However, too much emphasis on security can have the opposite effect, undermining freedom and America's moral integrity.

What Happens to National Boundaries and Cultures Once Globalization Begins?

The word "globalization" implies a movement toward international cooperation at least in terms of trade and cultural exchanges, but economic disparities and different social customs can prove to be obstacles that must be overcome. What factors might lead to better cooperation among nations?

"We've Lost Control of Our Borders" | Mike Luckovich

One important benefit of globalism is abandoning a provincial perspective regarding human communities with a global or intercultural perspective. It used to be assumed, for example, that "Western culture" and "culture" were synonymous. Today, we call that view "Eurocentric." Perhaps the most blatant expression of Eurocentrism was the notion that Columbus had "discovered" America, as if the entire Western hemisphere had been some uninhabited, isolated place before 1492. Today, we know that the Americas had been home to hundreds of nations of indigenous peoples for centuries before the present nations of Europe even existed. In the following editorial cartoon, Mike Luckovich reminds us of the importance of nurturing a global perspective on contemporary issues like immigration. Luckovich, a graduate of the University of Washington, is an editorial cartoonist for the Atlanta Journal Constitution; he won the Pulitzer Prize in 1995.

Mike Luckovich/The Cartoonist Group

Reflections and Inquiries

1. What underlying point is Luckovich making by the way the individual in the first panel specifically phrases his assertion about "losing control of our borders"?

2. Why is the speaker's appearance obscured in the first panel?

3. How does this cartoon affect the traditional notion of "borders"?

Reading to Write

Discuss the validity of the analogy, suggested by Luckovich's cartoon, between Native Americans/whites and Mexican immigrants/American citizens.

Issues for Further Research:
Privacy vs. National Security

One of the most heated debates in the post-9/11 era is where to draw the line between national security and the individual's right to privacy. Too much emphasis on the former could lead to a police state; too much emphasis on the latter could lead to anarchy.

Candorville | Darrin Bell

*What price are we willing to pay for security? To what extent are we willing to sac-
rifice privacy for protection? Is the government going too far when it monitors the
way American citizens use the Internet or the public library? If we agree that this
kind of snooping into our private business is going too far and violating our First
Amendment rights, what is to prevent domestic terrorists from using the Internet
to make bombs or to interact with terrorist cells around the world? In this Candorville strip, Darrin Bell takes a humorous approach to the way such snooping
might get out of hand. Darrin Bell is the cocreator of the comic strip Rudy Park,
syndicated to eighty newspapers and websites. A graduate in political science from
the University of California, Berkeley, Darrin Bell has been a staff cartoonist for
the Daily Californian and a regular contributor to the Los Angeles Times, San
Francisco Chronicle, and Oakland Tribune.*

Reflections and Inquiries

1. What would you say is the central argument of Bell's *Candorville* strip?
   Where does it come through most clearly?

2. All political cartoons and comic strips exaggerate or satirize to convey their
   premises humorously as well as emphatically. The possibilities for unjustifiable
   exaggeration exist, of course. Does Bell exaggerate unjustifiably or not? Explain.

3. Reflect on the way in which Bell depicts his characters. What correlation, if any, do you detect between their physical appearance and their roles?

Reading to Write

Examine Darrin Bell's other work by accessing his portfolio at www.bellcartoons.com or www.candorville.com. Then write an essay explaining Bell's social or political views on one specific topic and argue for the effectiveness (or lack of effectiveness) of the use of visual argument to convey that particular viewpoint.

Big Brother Is Listening | James Bamford

The NSA has the ability to eavesdrop on your communications—landlines, cell phones, emails, BlackBerry messages, Internet searches, and more—with ease. What happens when the technology of espionage outstrips the law's ability to protect ordinary citizens from it?

The conflict between protecting the security of the United States and protecting the privacy rights of U.S. citizens is ongoing. Many agree that in our post-9/11 era, heightened security measures are needed, but how much is too much? James Bamford, who has joined the American Civil Liberties Union in its lawsuit asking the courts to end the National Security Agency's spying without warrants, has published two books on the NSA and another on intelligence agencies generally: The Puzzle Palace: A Report on NSA, America's Most Secret Agency (Random House, 1982); Body of Secrets: Anatomy of the Ultra-Secret National Security Agency (Random House, 2001); and A Pretext for War: 9/11, Iraq and the Abuse of American Intelligence Agencies (Random House, 2005). The following essay was first published in 2006.

On the first Saturday in April of 2002, the temperature in Washington, D.C., had taken a dive. Tourists were bundled up against the cold, and the cherry trees along the Tidal Basin were fast losing their blossoms to the biting winds. But a few miles to the south, in the Dowden Terrace neighborhood of Alexandria, Virginia, the chilly weather was not deterring Royce C. Lamberth, a bald and burly Texan, from mowing his lawn. He stopped only when four cars filled with FBI agents suddenly pulled up in front of his house. The agents were there not to arrest him but to request an emergency court hearing to obtain seven top-secret warrants to eavesdrop on Americans.

As the presiding justice of the Foreign Intelligence Surveillance Court, known as the FISA court, Lamberth had become accustomed to holding the secret hearings

---

Source: James Bamford, "Big Brother Is Listening," from *The Atlantic Monthly*, April 2006. Reprinted by permission of International Creative Management, Inc. © 2006 by James Bamford.

in his living room. "My wife, Janis ... has to go upstairs because she doesn't have a top-secret clearance," he noted in a speech to a group of Texas lawyers. "My beloved cocker spaniel, Taffy, however, remains at my side on the assumption that the surveillance targets cannot make her talk. The FBI knows Taffy well. They frequently play with her while I read some of those voluminous tomes at home." FBI agents will even knock on the judge's door in the middle of the night. "On the night of the bombings of the U.S. embassies in Africa, I started the first emergency hearings in my living room at 3:00 a.m.," recalled Lamberth. "From the outset, the FBI suspected bin Laden, and the surveillances I approved that night and in the ensuing days and weeks all ended up being critical evidence at the trial in New York.

"The FISA court is probably the least-known court in Washington," added Lamberth, who stepped down from it in 2002, at the end of his seven-year term, "but it has become one of the most important." Conceived in the aftermath of Watergate, the FISA court traces its origins to the mid-1970s, when the Senate's Church Committee investigated the intelligence community and the Nixon White House. The panel, chaired by Idaho Democrat Frank Church, exposed a long pattern of abuse, and its work led to bipartisan legislation aimed at preventing a president from unilaterally directing the National Security Agency or the FBI to spy on American citizens. This legislation, the 1978 Foreign Intelligence Surveillance Act, established the FISA court—made up of eleven judges handpicked by the chief justice of the United States—as a secret part of the federal judiciary. The court's job is to decide whether to grant warrants requested by the NSA or the FBI to monitor communications of American citizens and legal residents. The law allows the government up to three days after it starts eavesdropping to ask for a warrant; every violation of FISA carries a penalty of up to five years in prison. Between May 18, 1979, when the court opened for business, until the end of 2004, it granted 18,742 NSA and FBI applications; it turned down only four outright.

Such facts worry Jonathan Turley, a George Washington University law professor who worked for the NSA as an intern while in law school in the 1980s. The FISA "courtroom," hidden away on the top floor of the Justice Department building (because even its location is supposed to be secret), is actually a heavily protected, windowless, bug-proof installation known as a Sensitive Compartmented Information Facility, or SCIF. "When I first went into the FISA court as a lowly intern at the NSA, frankly, it started a lifetime of opposition for me to that court," Turley recently told a group of House Democrats looking into the NSA's domestic spying. "I was shocked with what I saw. I was convinced that the judge in that SCIF would have signed anything that we put in front of him. And I wasn't entirely sure that he had actually *read* what we put in front of him. But I remember going back to my supervisor at NSA and saying, 'That place scares the daylights out of me.'"

5   Lamberth bristles at any suggestion that his court routinely did the administration's bidding. "Those who know me know the chief justice did not put me on this court because I would be a rubber stamp for whatever the executive

branch was wanting to do," he said in his speech. "I ask questions. I get into the nitty-gritty. I know exactly what is going to be done and why. And my questions are answered, in every case, before I approve an application."

It is true that the court has been getting tougher. From 1979 through 2000, it modified only two out of 13,087 warrant requests. But from the start of the Bush administration, in 2001, the number of modifications increased to 179 out of 5,645 requests. Most of those—173—involved what the court terms "substantive modifications."

This friction—and especially the requirement that the government show "probable cause" that the American whose communications they are seeking to target is connected in some way to a terrorist group—induced the administration to begin circumventing the court. Concerned about preventing future 9/11-style attacks, President Bush secretly decided in the fall of 2001 that the NSA would no longer be bound by FISA. Although Judge Lamberth was informed of the president's decision, he was ordered to tell no one about it—not even his clerks or his fellow FISA-court judges.

Why the NSA Might Be Listening to *You*

Contrary to popular perception, the NSA does not engage in "wiretapping"; it collects signals intelligence, or "sigint." In contrast to the image we have from movies and television of an FBI agent placing a listening device on a target's phone line, the NSA intercepts entire streams of electronic communications containing millions of telephone calls and e-mails. It runs the intercepts through very powerful computers that screen them for particular names, telephone numbers, Internet addresses, and trigger words or phrases. Any communications containing flagged information are forwarded by the computer for further analysis.

The NSA's task is to listen in on the world outside American shores. During the Cold War, the principal targets were the communications lines used by the Soviet government and military—navy captains calling their ports, fighter pilots getting landing instructions, army commanders out on maneuvers, and diplomats relaying messages to the Kremlin. But now the enemy is one that communicates very little and, when it does, uses the same telecommunications network as everyone else: a complex system of wires, radio signals, and light pulses encircling and crisscrossing the globe like yarn. Picking up just the right thread, and tracing it through the maze of strands, is difficult. Sometimes a thread leads back inside the United States. An internal agency report predicted a few years ago that the NSA's worldwide sigint operation would demand a "powerful and permanent presence" on the global telecommunications networks that carry "protected American communications." The prediction has come true, and the NSA now monitors not only purely "foreign" communications but also "international" ones, where one end of the conversation might be in the United States. As a result, the issue at hand since the revelation last December of the NSA's warrantless spying on American citizens is not the agency's access to the country's communications network—it already has access—but whether the NSA must take legal steps in preparing to target the communications of an American citizen.

10   It used to be that before the NSA could place the name of an American on its watch list, it had to go before a FISA-court judge and show that it had probable cause—that the facts and circumstances were such that a prudent person would think the individual was somehow connected to terrorism—in order to get a warrant. But under the new procedures put into effect by Bush's 2001 order, warrants do not always have to be obtained, and the critical decision about whether to put an American on a watch list is left to the vague and subjective "reasonable belief" of an NSA shift supervisor. In charge of hundreds of people, the supervisor manages a wide range of sigint specialists, including signals-conversion analysts separating HBO television programs from cell-phone calls, traffic analysts sifting through massive telephone data streams looking for suspicious patterns, cryptanalysts attempting to read e-mail obscured by complex encryption algorithms, voice-language analysts translating the gist of a phone call from Dari into English, and cryptolinguists trying to unscramble a call on a secure telephone. Bypassing the FISA court has meant that the number of Americans targeted by the NSA has increased since 2001 from perhaps a dozen per year to as many as 5,000 over the last four years, knowledgeable sources told *The Washington Post* in February. If telephone records indicate that one of the NSA's targets regularly dials a given telephone number, that number and any names associated with it are added to the watch lists and the communications on that line are screened by computer. Names and information on the watch lists are shared with the FBI, the CIA, the Department of Homeland Security, and foreign intelligence services. Once a person's name is in the files, even if nothing incriminating ever turns up, it will likely remain there forever. There is no way to request removal, because there is no way to confirm that a name is on the list.

In December of 1997, in a small factory outside the southern French city of Toulouse, a salesman got caught in the NSA's electronic web. Agents working for the NSA's British partner, the Government Communications Headquarters, learned of a letter of credit, valued at more than $1.1 million, issued by Iran's defense ministry to the French company Microturbo. According to NSA documents, both the NSA and the GCHQ concluded that Iran was attempting to secretly buy from Microturbo an engine for the embargoed C-802 anti-ship missile. Faxes zapping back and forth between Toulouse and Tehran were intercepted by the GCHQ, which sent them on not just to the NSA but also to the Canadian and Australian sigint agencies, as well as to Britain's MI6. The NSA then sent the reports on the salesman making the Iranian deal to a number of CIA stations around the world, including those in Paris and Bonn, and to the U.S. Commerce Department and the Customs Service. Probably several hundred people in at least four countries were reading the company's communications. The question, however, remained: Was Microturbo shipping a missile engine to Iran? In the end, at the insistence of the U.S. government, the

French conducted a surprise inspection just before the ship carrying the mysterious crate was set to sail for Iran. Inside were legal generators, not illegal missile engines.

Such events are central to the current debate involving the potential harm caused by the NSA's warrantless domestic eavesdropping operation. Even though the salesman did nothing wrong, his name made its way into the computers and onto the watch lists of intelligence, customs, and other secret and law-enforcement organizations around the world. Maybe nothing will come of it. Maybe the next time he tries to enter the United States or Britain he will be denied, without explanation. Maybe he will be arrested. As the domestic eavesdropping program continues to grow, such uncertainties may plague innocent Americans whose names are being run through the supercomputers even though the NSA has not met the established legal standard for a search warrant. It is only when such citizens are turned down while applying for a job with the federal government—or refused when seeking a Small Business Administration loan, or turned back by British customs agents when flying to London on vacation, or even placed on a "no-fly" list—that they will realize that something is very wrong. But they will never learn why.

More than seventy-five years ago, Supreme Court Justice Louis Brandeis envisioned a day when technology would overtake the law. He wrote:

> Subtler and more far-reaching means of invading privacy have become available to the government.... The progress of science in furnishing the government with means of espionage is not likely to stop with wiretapping. Ways may some day be developed by which the Government, without removing papers from secret drawers, can reproduce them in court, and by which it will be enabled to expose to a jury the most intimate occurrences of the home.... Can it be that the Constitution affords no protection against such invasions of individual security?

Brandeis went on to answer his own question, quoting from an earlier Supreme Court decision, *Boyd v. U.S.* (1886): "It is not the breaking of his doors, and the rummaging of his drawers that constitutes the essence of the offence; but it is the invasion of his indefeasible right of personal security, personal liberty, and private property."

Eavesdropping in the Digital Age

Today, the NSA's capability to eavesdrop is far beyond anything ever dreamed of by Justice Brandeis. With the digital revolution came an explosion in eavesdropping technology; the NSA today has the ability to scan tens of millions of electronic communications—e-mails, faxes, instant messages, Web searches, and phone calls—every hour. General Michael Hayden, director of the NSA from 1999 to 2005 and now principal deputy director of national intelligence, noted in 2002 that during the 1990s, e-communications "surpassed traditional communications. That is the same decade when mobile cell phones increased

15

from 16 million to 741 million—an increase of nearly 50 times. That is the same decade when Internet users went from about 4 million to 361 million—an increase of over 90 times. Half as many land lines were laid in the last six years of the 1990s as in the whole previous history of the world. In that same decade of the 1990s, international telephone traffic went from 38 billion minutes to over 100 billion. This year, the world's population will spend over 180 billion minutes on the phone in international calls alone."

Intercepting communications carried by satellite is fairly simple for the NSA. The key conduits are the thirty Intelsat satellites that ring the Earth, 22,300 miles above the equator. Many communications from Europe, Africa, and the Middle East to the eastern half of the United States, for example, are first uplinked to an Intelsat satellite and then downlinked to AT&T's ground station in Etam, West Virginia. From there, phone calls, e-mails, and other communications travel on to various parts of the country. To listen in on that rich stream of information, the NSA built a listening post fifty miles away, near Sugar Grove, West Virginia. Consisting of a group of very large parabolic dishes, hidden in a heavily forested valley and surrounded by tall hills, the post can easily intercept the millions of calls and messages flowing every hour into the Etam station. On the West Coast, high on the edge of a bluff overlooking the Okanogan River, near Brewster, Washington, is the major commercial downlink for communications to and from Asia and the Pacific. Consisting of forty parabolic dishes, it is reportedly the largest satellite antenna farm in the Western Hemisphere. A hundred miles to the south, collecting every whisper, is the NSA's western listening post, hidden away on a 324,000-acre Army base in Yakima, Washington. The NSA posts collect the international traffic beamed down from the Intelsat satellites over the Atlantic and Pacific. But each also has a number of dishes that appear to be directed at domestic telecommunications satellites.

Until recently, most international telecommunications flowing into and out of the United States traveled by satellite. But faster, more reliable undersea fiber-optic cables have taken the lead, and the NSA has adapted. The agency taps into the cables that don't reach our shores by using specially designed submarines, such as the USS *Jimmy Carter*, to attach a complex "bug" to the cable itself. This is difficult, however, and undersea taps are short-lived because the batteries last only a limited time. The fiber-optic transmission cables that enter the United States from Europe and Asia can be tapped more easily at the landing stations where they come ashore. With the acquiescence of the telecommunications companies, it is possible for the NSA to attach monitoring equipment inside the landing station and then run a buried encrypted fiber-optic "backhaul" line to NSA headquarters at Fort Meade, Maryland, where the river of data can be analyzed by supercomputers in near real time.

Tapping into the fiber-optic network that carries the nation's Internet communications is even easier, as much of the information transits through just a few "switches" (similar to the satellite downlinks). Among the busiest are MAE

East (Metropolitan Area Ethernet), in Vienna, Virginia, and MAE West, in San Jose, California, both owned by Verizon. By accessing the switch, the NSA can see who's e-mailing with whom over the Internet cables and can copy entire messages. Last September, the Federal Communications Commission further opened the door for the agency. The 1994 Communications Assistance for Law Enforcement Act required telephone companies to rewire their networks to provide the government with secret access. The FCC has now extended the act to cover "any type of broadband Internet access service" and the new Internet phone services—and ordered company officials never to discuss any aspect of the program.

The NSA won't divulge how many people it employs, but it is likely that more than 38,000 worldwide now work for the agency. Most of them are at Fort Meade. Nicknamed Crypto City, hidden from public view, and located halfway between Washington and Baltimore, the NSA's own company town comprises more than fifty buildings—offices, warehouses, factories, laboratories, and a few barracks. Tens of thousands of people work there in absolute secrecy, and most never tell their spouses exactly what they do. Crypto City also houses the nation's largest collection of powerful computers, advanced mathematicians, and skilled language experts.

The NSA maintains a very close and very confidential relationship with   *20* key executives in the telecommunications industry through their membership on the NSA's advisory board. Created shortly after the agency's formation, the board was intended to pull together a panel of science wizards from universities, corporate research labs, and think tanks to advise the agency. They keep the agency abreast of the industry's plans and give NSA engineers a critical head start in finding ways to penetrate technologies still in the development phase.

One of the NSA's strategies is to hire people away from the companies that make the critical components for telecommunications systems. Although it's sometimes difficult for the agency to keep up with the tech sector's pay scale, for many people the chance to deal with the ultimate in cutting-edge technology and aid national security makes working for the NSA irresistible. With the help of such workers, the agency reverse-engineers communication system components. For example, among the most crucial pieces of the Internet infrastructure are routers made by Cisco. "Virtually all Internet traffic," says one of the company's television ads, "travels across the systems of one company: Cisco Systems." For the NSA, this is an opportunity. In 1999, Terry Thompson, then the NSA deputy director for services, said, "[Y]ou can see down the road two or three or five years and say, 'Well, I only need this person to do reverse-engineering on Cisco routers (that's a good example) for about three or five years, because I see Cisco going away as a key manufacturer for routers and so I don't need that expertise. But I really need somebody today and for the next couple of years who knows Cisco routers inside and out and can help me understand how they're being used in target networks.'"

The Temptations of Secrecy

The National Security Agency was born in absolute secrecy. Unlike the CIA, which was created publicly by a congressional act, the NSA was brought to life by a top-secret memorandum signed by President Truman in 1952, consolidating the country's various military sigint operations into a single agency. Even its name was secret, and only a few members of Congress were informed of its existence—and they received no information about some of its most important activities. Such secrecy has lent itself to abuse.

During the Vietnam War, for instance, the agency was heavily involved in spying on the domestic opposition to the government. Many of the Americans on the watch lists of that era were there solely for having protested against the war. Among the names in the NSA's supercomputers were those of the folk singer Joan Baez, the pediatrician Benjamin Spock, the actress Jane Fonda, the civil-rights leader Martin Luther King Jr., and the newspaper editor David Kahn, whose standard history of cryptology, *The Codebreakers*, contained information the NSA viewed as classified. Even so much as writing about the NSA could land a person a place on a watch list. The NSA, on behalf of the FBI, was also targeting religious groups. "When J. Edgar Hoover gives you a requirement for complete surveillance of all Quakers in the United States," recalled Frank Raven, a former senior NSA official, "and when Richard M. Nixon is a Quaker and he's the president of the United States, it gets pretty funny."

Of course, such abuses are hardly the exclusive province of the NSA; history has repeatedly shown that simply having the ability to eavesdrop brings with it the temptation to use that ability—whatever the legal barriers against that use may be. For instance, during World War I, the government read and censored thousands of telegrams—the e-mail of the day—sent hourly by telegraph companies. Though the end of the war brought with it a reversion to the Radio Act of 1912, which guaranteed the secrecy of communications, the State and War Departments nevertheless joined together in May of 1919 to create America's first civilian eaves-dropping and code-breaking agency, nicknamed the Black Chamber. By arrangement, messengers visited the telegraph companies each morning and took bundles of hard-copy telegrams to the agency's offices across town. These copies were returned before the close of business that day.

25   A similar tale followed the end of World War II. In August of 1945, President Truman ordered an end to censorship. That left the Signal Security Agency (the military successor to the Black Chamber, which was shut down in 1929) without its raw intelligence—the telegrams provided by the telegraph companies. The director of the SSA sought access to cable traffic through a secret arrangement with the heads of the three major telegraph companies. The companies agreed to turn all telegrams over to the SSA, under a plan code-named Operation Shamrock. It ran until the government's domestic spying programs were publicly revealed, in the mid-1970s.

The discovery of such abuses in the wake of the Watergate scandal led Congress to create select committees to conduct extensive investigations into the government's domestic spying programs: their origin, extent, and effect on the public. The shocking findings turned up by the Church Committee finally led to the formation of permanent Senate and House intelligence committees, whose primary responsibility was to protect the public from future privacy abuses. They were to be the FISA court's partner in providing checks and balances to the ever-expanding U.S. intelligence agencies. But it remains very much an open question whether these checks are up to the task at hand.

Who Watches the Watchmen?

Today, the NSA has access to more information than ever before. People express their most intimate thoughts in e-mails, send their tax returns over the Internet, satisfy their curiosity and desires with Google searches, let their hair down in chat rooms, discuss every event over cell phones, make appointments with their BlackBerrys, and do business by computer in WiFi hot spots.

NSA personnel, the customs inspectors of the information superhighway, have the ultimate goal of intercepting and reviewing every syllable and murmur zapping into, out of, or through the United States. They are close to achieving it. More than a dozen years ago, an NSA director gave an indication of the agency's capability. "Just one intelligence-collection system," said Admiral William O. Studeman, referring to a listening post such as Sugar Grove, "can generate a million inputs per half hour." Today, with the secret cooperation of much of the telecommunications industry, massive dishes vacuuming the airwaves, and electronic "packet sniffers," software that monitors network traffic, diverting e-mail and other data from fiber-optic cables, the NSA's hourly take is in the tens of millions of communications. One transatlantic fiber-optic cable alone has the capacity to handle close to 10 million simultaneous calls. While most communications flow through the NSA's electronic net unheard and unread, those messages associated with persons on the agency's watch lists—whether guilty or innocent—get kicked out for review.

As history has shown, the availability of such vast amounts of information is a temptation for an intelligence agency. The criteria for compiling watch lists and collecting information may be very strict at the beginning of such a program, but the reality—in a sort of bureaucratic law of expansion—is that it will draw in more and more people whose only offense was knowing the wrong person or protesting the wrong war.

Moreover, as Internet and wireless communications have grown exponen-   30
tially, users have seen a corresponding decrease in the protections provided by the two institutions set up to shield the public from eavesdroppers. The first, the FISA court, has simply been shunted aside by the executive branch. The second, the congressional intelligence committees, have quite surprisingly abdicated any role. Created to be the watchdogs over the intelligence community, the committees have instead become its most enthusiastic cheerleaders. Rather than fighting for the public's privacy rights, they are constantly battling for more money and more freedom for the spy agencies.

Last November, just a month before *The New York Times* broke the story of the NSA's domestic spying, the American Bar Association publicly expressed concern over Congress's oversight of FISA searches. "The ABA is concerned that there is inadequate congressional oversight of government investigations undertaken pursuant to the Foreign Intelligence Surveillance Act," the group stated, "to assure that such investigations do not violate the First, Fourth, and Fifth Amendments to the Constitution." And while the administration did brief members of Congress on the decision to bypass FISA, the briefings were limited to a "Gang of Eight"—the majority and minority leaders of the House and Senate and the chairmen and ranking members of the two intelligence committees. None of the lawmakers insisted that the decision be debated by the joint committees, even though such hearings are closed.

Frank Church, the Idaho Democrat who led the first probe into the National Security Agency, warned in 1975 that the agency's capabilities

> could be turned around on the American people, and no American would have any privacy left, such [is] the capability to monitor everything: telephone conversations, telegrams, it doesn't matter. There would be no place to hide. If this government ever became a tyranny, if a dictator ever took charge in this country, the technological capacity that the intelligence community has given the government could enable it to impose total tyranny, and there would be no way to fight back, because the most careful effort to combine together in resistance to the government, no matter how privately it is done, is within the reach of the government to know. Such is the capacity of this technology.

It was those fears that caused Congress to enact the Foreign Intelligence Surveillance Act three years later. "I don't want to see this country ever go across the bridge," Senator Church said. "I know the capacity that is there to make tyranny total in America, and we must see to it that [the National Security Agency] and all agencies that possess this technology operate within the law and under proper supervision, so that we never cross over that abyss. That is the abyss from which there is no return."

Reflections and Inquiries

1. How does the NSA gather surveillance information? What, if anything, concerns you about this method?

2. Explain the literary reference in Bamford's title. How accurate a reference is it?

3. What did law professor Jonathan Turley find so frightening about the FISA court? Do you share Turley's apprehension? Explain.

4. The NSA often obtains documents without a warrant. Do you agree or disagree that this is a necessary procedure? Support your view as fully as you can, keeping aware of counterarguments.

Reading to Write

Go to the NSA's website, www.nsa.gov, to learn more about the organization. For example, you can learn about the history of signals intelligence (SIGINT). Next, compare the way the NSA represents itself to the way James Bamford represents it in at least one of his books, mentioned above. Finally, using Academic Search Elite or your library's electronic catalog, locate a third perspective on the NSA, ideally one that has been published within the last five years and that differs from Bamford's perspective. Then write an essay in which you assess the ethical foundations of the NSA's surveillance practices.

Issues for Further Research: Immigration Reform

America is a nation of immigrants—this we know; but the debate over immigration reform focuses mainly on the influx of immigrants from our neighbors to the south, especially from Mexico and Central America. This calls into question whether current immigration policies discriminate unfairly against immigrants from these countries by claiming, say, that they threaten the jobs of native workers, or that they make contribute to higher crime rates.

America is a nation of immigrants—this we know—but the debate over immigration reform focuses mainly on the influx of immigrants from our neighbors to the south, especially from Mexico and Central America. This calls into question whether current immigration policies discriminate unfairly against immigrants from these countries by claiming, say, that they threaten the jobs of native workers, or that they may contribute to higher crime rates.

Does Immigration Harm Working Americans? | David Frum

The answer that some economists give to David Frum's question is "no"—but other economists worry that the problem is much too complex to answer without careful qualification. David Frum is a senior editor of The Atlantic, *where this article first appeared. In 2001–2002, he served as a speech writer for President George W. Bush.*

The job news is increasingly good: 321,000 jobs created in November. Yet the national economic mood remains grimly bleak.

Many Americans feel a sharp distinction between what's said about "the" economy and what they experience in "their" economy. At the top of the income distribution, wages are rising. In the middle and bottom, wages stagnate. Jobs are created, yes—but native-born Americans are not hired for them.

Last month, the Center for Immigration Studies released its latest jobs study. CIS, a research organization that tends to favor tight immigration policies, found that even now, almost seven years after the collapse of Lehman Brothers, 1.5 million fewer native-born Americans are working than in November 2007, the peak of the prior economic cycle. Balancing the 1.5 million fewer native-born Americans at work, there are 2 million more immigrants—legal and illegal—working in the United States today than in November 2007. *All the net new jobs created since November 2007 have gone to immigrants.* Meanwhile, millions of native-born Americans, especially men, have abandoned the job market altogether. The percentage of men aged 25 to 54 who are working or looking for work has dropped to the lowest point in recorded history.

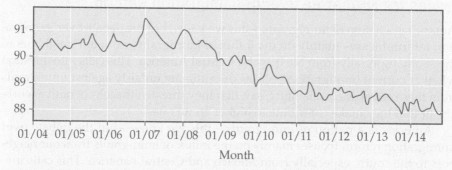

Month

Labor Force Participation Rate Among Men Aged 25 to 54, 2004–2014.
Source: Bureau of Labor Statistics.

It's said again and again that immigrants do not take jobs from natives. Here's *National Journal*, reporting just last year, under the headline "Left and Right Agree: Immigrants Don't Take American Jobs":

5   That immigrants take the jobs of American-born citizens is "something that virtually no learned person believes in," Alex Nowrasteh, an immigration expert at the libertarian Cato Institute, said at a Thursday panel. "It's sort of a silly thing."

Most economists don't find immigrants driving down wages or jobs, the Brookings Institution's Michael Greenstone and Adam Looney wrote in May. In fact, "on average, immigrant workers increase the opportunities and incomes of Americans," they write. Foreign-born workers don't affect the employment rate positively or negatively, according to a 2011 analysis from the conservative American Enterprise Institute. And a study released Wednesday by the liberal Center for American Progress suggests that granting legal status to undocumented workers might even create jobs.

So there you have it. Experts say it's impossible. Can't be happening. And if actual observed data from the real economy seem to suggest that the impossible *is* happening—well, Albert Einstein himself answered that one. If the material universe doesn't support the theory: "Then I'd feel sorry for the good Lord. The theory is correct."

Before deciding whom to trust on this issue, the economists or your lying eyes, it helps to understand how the economists reached their conclusion.

Since the time of Adam Smith, economists have agreed that the secret of economic growth is specialization. Rather than everyone baking his or her own bread and sewing his or her own clothes, everyone chooses one occupation and then trades for the products others make. The more individuals specialize, the more productive everyone becomes. The more people trade, the more widely the benefits of productivity are shared.

Immigration economists apply this insight to the domestic labor market. One of the most eminent specialists in the field of immigration economics, Giovanni Peri of the University of California at Davis, offers this homely analogy: *10*

> An extreme example of this would be if you have an engineer and you add a construction worker. With the engineer by himself you're not going to do much. But with an engineer plus a construction worker, you can build a building. Therefore, the productivity of the engineer goes up a lot. And the wages for both workers increase.

The technical term for the situation Peri is describing is "complementarity." The labor of the engineer and the labor of the construction worker each complement the other. Immigration economists argue that immigrant labor likewise complements native-born labor. As Peri assured readers in a 2010 paper for the San Francisco Federal Reserve, "Immigrants expand the U.S. economy's productive capacity, stimulate investment, and promote specialization that in the long run boosts productivity. Consistent with previous research, there is no evidence that these effects take place at the expense of jobs for workers born in the United States."

So long as everyone imagines that low-wage immigrant workers are paired off with high-wage natives, such assurances seem credible. The foreign-born nanny enables her college-educated employer to return to the workforce earlier, raising wages for both nanny and employer. The foreign-born gardener mows the lawn, freeing his accountant employer to spend Saturday morning billing clients.

Even as the encounter between low-paid immigrants and highly paid natives becomes more distant and abstract, the complementary relationship of their labor seems to hold. Immigrant labor enables middle-class Americans to buy a roasted chicken and pre-washed salad at the supermarket or to check a box and have their holiday presents arrive at their door already gift-wrapped. Upper-income Americans live easier and more efficient lives thanks to millions of low-paid immigrant workers they never see and whose names they never know.

But what about everybody else? The promise of the immigration economists is not that *some* Americans, the already successful, would be enriched even further. The promise is that *all* Americans would be made better off, even if they don't employ nannies, even if they mow their own lawns, even if they can't afford the rotisserie chicken, even if they shop at the thrift store rather than Amazon. How can that be possibly be true? *15*

The answer embedded in the economic models is that immigration prods even less affluent natives to shift away from immigrant-dominated economic niches and find new work that pays better. The immigrant groundskeeper can't speak English very well, so the lawn service hires a bilingual Mexican-American to supervise him. The rising numbers of immigrant nannies call forth specialized payroll firms that hire native-born workers to process checks and pay taxes. More supermarkets operating more chicken rotisseries causes local governments to hire more health officers to confirm the chicken meets sanitary standards. More immigrants wrapping presents in L.L. Bean's warehouses mean more native-born UPS drivers delivering presents.

Everybody wins!

Yet three things have to be said about the above story.

First: The story about immigration benefiting all (or almost all) native workers could be true. But that doesn't mean it *is* true. Economists prove their claims about immigrant law by drawing regression curves that compare ratios between data sets based upon the number and the pay of immigrant and native workers. Have they drawn their data sets correctly? Did they choose the correct basis for comparison?

20   These technical decisions at the beginning of the calculation have huge impacts on the final conclusion at the end. Between 1990 and 2006, the wages of non-college-educated Americans declined. The less education the worker had, the steeper the decline. How much was immigration responsible? The data the economist chooses to look at will determine the answer.

Let's go to the fine print, relying on a critique of Giovanni Peri's work by George Borjas, of Harvard's Kennedy School. Aggregate high-school dropout and high-school graduates together, and immigrant labor accounted for 13.2 percent of the increase in hours worked between 1990 and the onset of the Great Recession: big, but not cataclysmic. But if you take more care to compare like with like, you begin to see huge supply shocks. Among high-school dropouts only, immigrants accounted for 23 percent of the increase in hours worked between 1990 and 2006. Among high school dropouts in their 30s and 40s, immigrants accounted for over one-third of the increase in hours worked.

Here's what that means for economic modeling. If you assume that all low-education workers are potential substitutes for each other—the 23-year-old recent arrival from Guatemala with the 53-year-old who proceeded from high school to the Army—then your model will show a less dramatic effect of immigration on wages. If, however, you assume that the 23-year-old Guatemalan is competing with 20- and 30-something native-born workers who lack diplomas, then your model will show a very big effect.

A model based on unrealistic assumptions can still achieve perfect internal consistency. It just won't describe the real world very accurately. Which seems to be precisely what is happening with immigration economics.

Second: If the economists are right about the complementarity of immigrant and native labor, it's important to understand how and why. Back in the 20th century, there were presumably many accountants who would have preferred to spend Saturday mornings finishing their work rather than mowing the lawn. There were many new mothers who would have returned to work if nanny services had been more widely available. What changed between, say, 1970 and 2005? The short answer is that the cost of employing people in these immigrant-dominated niches plummeted, in real terms. Because the cost plummeted, more hiring occurred in those niches, enabling the mothers to return to work, the accountants to spend Saturday mornings at the office.

Economic popularizers passionately deny that immigration causes wage declines and job displacement. From the point of view of several actual economists, however, these reassurances are so much uninformed propaganda. As the technical economists understand, wage cuts and job displacement are the exact and only ways that immigration confers any benefits on native workers at all. It is wage decline and job displacement that drives natives to shift to higher-paid sectors. No wage cuts, no job displacement. No jobs displaced, no benefit to natives. Here's Peri saying just that: "Large inflows of less educated immigrants may reduce wages paid to comparably-educated, native-born workers. However, if less educated foreign- and native-born workers specialize in different production tasks, because of different abilities, immigration will cause natives to reallocate their task supply, thereby reducing downward wage pressure."

When economists minimize the impact of immigration on wages, they aren't denying that immigration pushes wages down in the jobs that immigrants take. They concede that immigration does do that. They celebrate that immigration does that. Instead, they join their celebration of immigration's wage-cutting effects with a prediction about the way that the natives will respond.

But what if the prediction is wrong? What if natives respond to immigrant competition by shifting out of the labor market entirely, by qualifying for disability pensions? The proportion of the population receiving disability pensions doubled between 1985 and 2005 and jumped by another 20 percent during the Great Recession. 14 million Americans now receive disability pensions. The evidence is compelling that disability applications rise when the job market weakens.

Why? Economists talk too blithely about natives shifting to more skilled and remunerative work. Up-skilling costs time, effort, and money. It can oblige a worker to move away from family and friends. It forces older workers to begin again at a time in their lives when they felt settled, to risk failure at a time in life when risk is not appreciated. It's not highly surprising that many displaced workers would opt to give up on work altogether instead.

The exit of native-born men from the workforce—at least arguably because of immigration—has the curious side effect of tilting the immigration models in a pro-immigration direction. Remember, the models are based on ratios of hours worked and wages paid. If a native-born janitor earning $18 an hour is displaced by an immigrant and then shifts to a $12 an hour retail job, the models capture that change as a harm to native-born workers. But if the displaced native-born janitor exits the labor force, he disappears from the model altogether, and with him, the evidence of the harm. It may seem crazy, but it's the way the model is built.

25

30   Third: Economists habitually regard the free movement of investment, goods, and people as the natural order of things. They don't feel much need to explain such movements, any more than lawyers ask why people violate contracts or doctors ask why people fall off ladders.

Yet immigration is inescapably a political act. Nations can regulate immigration, can make choices about which immigrants they allow and how many, about how strictly labor laws will be policed and what will be done with lawbreakers.

Theoretically, a nation could determine that high-skill labor is complementary to low-skilled labor and make decisions such as the following:

"If we admit a lot of foreign-born surgeons, we could hugely drive down the cost of major medical operations. American-born doctors would shift their labor to fields where their language facility gave them a competitive advantage: away from surgery to general practice. This policy would hugely enhance the relative purchasing power of plumbers and mechanics, enabling them to eat out more often and buy more American-made entertainment, increasing GDP and creating jobs."

Or: "The ratio of CEO pay to other workers has skyrocketed. Obviously we are suffering from a glut of workers and massive CEO scarcity. We should issue work permits automatically to any executive with a job offer that pays more than $500,000 a year. Americans with organizational skills will be pressed to shift to the public sector, improving the quality and lowering the cost to taxpayers of government services."

35   But that's not how things are done. In the United States, the hypothesis of native-immigrant complementarity is deployed to justify policies that intensify competition for the lower and middle echelons of the society, rarely near the top. Perhaps it doesn't have to be that way, yet somehow it always is.

Reflections and Inquiries

1. Frum calls attention to what he sees is a disparity between what is reported and what is actually experienced in the job market—more specifically, that instead of stimulating job growth as reported, the influx of immigrants undermines it. How convincingly does Frum support his premise, in your opinion?

2. Discuss Frum's assertion that some economists use immigrant-native complementarity "to justify policies that intensify competition for the lower and middle echelons of society." What other methods can be used to describe the impact of immigrants on the U.S. job market?

3. For Frum, the hypothesis that greater immigrant employment leads to greater native specialization is flawed. How well does Frum make his case?

Reading to Write

Write an essay in which you weigh the potential benefits versus the potential liabilities of immigrant hiring for the American job market.

Point Counterpoint: Scholarly Debate on the Use of Rhetoric in Establishing Immigration Reform Policy

Rhetoric, as is apparent throughout this textbook, is relevant to any area of inquiry; that's because language is the requisite transmitter of information, and language is governed by rhetoric. The two pairs of scholars in their respective articles that follow explicitly invoke the way in which argumentative rhetorical strategies—specifically those developed by Aristotle (see Chapter 3, Using the Classical Model in Your Arguments) are exploited by political leaders like Governor Jan Brewer of Arizona in determining immigration policy for her state. The focus of the debate lies in the manner and degree to which those rhetorical strategies are used.

Economic Globalization and the "Given Situation" Jan Brewer's Use of SB 1070 as an Effective Rhetorical Response to the Politics of Immigration

Kevin A. Johnson and Jennifer J. Asenas*

Immigration, legal or illegal, is a staple issue in American politics. Since at least the 1830s, many Americans began expressing a "growing concern" about "the increasing volume of immigration in both absolute terms and relative to the US population and the facts that more of the arrivals were Catholic and unskilled" (Cohn).[1] These concerns resulted in the passage of the Chinese Exclusion Act in 1882 followed by other laws in the 20th century;[2] however, those efforts pale in comparison to the fury of anti-immigration legislation post-9/11, especially at the state level.[3] According to the "Immigrant Policy Project" report, 2010 was a record year for state laws concerning immigration: "Forty-six state legislatures and the District of Columbia enacted 208 laws and adopted 138 resolutions for a total of 346." Perhaps the most (in)famous of those laws was Arizona's SB 1070 (the Support Our Law Enforcement and Safe Neighborhoods Act), which became a focal point for advocates seeking a more aggressive approach to deterring illegal immigration.

On April 23, 2010, Arizona Governor Jan Brewer signed SB 1070 into law. The intent of the law was to reduce Arizona's illegal immigrant population by allowing state and local law enforcement agencies to determine the legal status of an alien if they had "reasonable suspicion" that the individual was in the country illegally and to impose penalties on those "hir[ing], ... transporting, moving, concealing, harboring, or shielding ... unlawful aliens" (SB 1070 1, 5). Supporters of the law claimed it was necessary to safeguard citizens from the criminal conduct of

*Kevin A. Johnson, Center for First Amendment Studies, California State University, Long Beach. Jennifer J. Asenas, Dept. of English, California State University, Long Beach.

illegal aliens and from the drain on public resources their presence posed (Brewer, "Statement"; Pearce). Critics of the law claimed that it would legalize racial profiling (Woods qtd. in Schwartz and Archibold; Obama qtd. in Hough).

There are numerous ways to analyze the importance and impact of SB 1070, but the purpose of this article is to assess how Governor Brewer used SB 1070 as a rhetorical response to generate and maintain political support from her constituents, state industries, and wealthy contributors who might have conflicting social and economic interests. Working from Aristotle's definition of rhetoric as "the faculty of observing in any given situation the available means of persuasion," we believe that Governor Brewer's given situation should not be limited to Arizona's political situation (Bizzell and Herzberg 151). To understand how bills like SB 1070 function as rhetorical responses for politician-rhetors requires an assessment of the "given situation" that includes the realities of economic globalization.

Economic globalization is a term that "describes a set of processes whereby production and consumption activities shift from the local or national scale to the global scale" (O'Brien and Leichenko 225). This "intensification and stretching of economic interrelations across the globe" creates "new linkages among national economies" ("Globalization"). Rising levels of international trade, foreign direct investment, and multinational production processes integrate even local economies in important ways. For example, a multinational hotel chain might host a meeting for a group of US and non-US investors strategizing the expansion of their business in Arizona whose rooms are cleaned by and meals prepared and served by undocumented immigrants. While the meeting would bring business to Arizona, not all of the money spent would benefit or employ the citizens of that state.[4] The previous scenario is not hard to imagine and demonstrates how economic globalization produces some of the conflicting interests that influence economic decisions elected officials must make. From this vantage point, our argument is that whether by design or accident, SB 1070 was both a fitting response and tremendous rhetorical resource for Governor Brewer, who needed to increase her political popularity. We begin by briefly describing the importance of emphasizing the "given situation" segment of Aristotle's definition of rhetoric and then outline the impact globalization has on the political process in the United States. We then turn to Governor Brewer's specific political situation and how she used SB 1070 as an effective way to balance the interests of her constituents and corporations within the context of economic globalization to gain political popularity.

The "Given Situation" of Economic Globalization, Illegal Immigration, and the Political Process

Translations of Aristotle's definition of rhetoric differ slightly. For example, rather than the "given situation," George A. Kennedy's translation refers to "any given case": "the faculty of observing in any given case the available means of persuasion" (7). What remains consistent is that rhetorical resources arise from specific contexts. For, as Thomas Farrell noted, "unless we believe that means of persuasion are fixed and that cases are eternally recurring, what the rhetorician 'sees' must vary with the times" (324). Given this focus, the "given situation" is not simply a catalog of preexisting persuasive resources but instead a context that makes certain rhetorical strategies (un)available. The given situation of state and national politicians is one in which the influence of economic globalization on campaigning, political popularity, and economic policy is pervasive.

Economic globalization creates a complicated situation that politicians must negotiate while trying to obtain or maintain political popularity. As multinational corporations have acquired increasing global power, international corporate interests have played an active role in domestic policy agendas, a situation exacerbated by the Citizens United decision that prohibits the government from restricting independent political expenditures by corporations and unions.[5] Most politicians rely on financial backing from wealthy contributors who have accumulated their wealth through investment in markets that maximize profits, in part, by minimizing labor costs.[6] Once (re)elected, politicians must maintain the political support of their constituencies whose interests and/or agendas might run counter to those of their wealthy contributors. We suggest that illegal immigration is an issue in which politician-rhetors are pressured to accommodate the conflicting interests that are exacerbated by economic globalization.

Balancing Perception and Profits: Creating Synergistic Immigration Laws

Effectively balancing the desires of constituents and the economic impact of restricting illegal immigrant labor is difficult. Illegal immigration is difficult for governments to control, in part, because it pits governments against market forces (Naim). In states in which opposition to undocumented immigrants is strong, elected officials must respond to the concerns of some of their constituents. Strict immigration laws might be ideologically pleasing to some members of the population, but they might also have negative consequences for the economy. Such was the case with HB 87, Georgia's immigration enforcement law, which created labor shortages in 2011. These shortages "triggered an estimated $140 million in agricultural losses" and "affected the hotel and restaurant industries" (Powell).

Unlike HB 87, SB 1070 might have created a symbiotic relationship between industries that would detain undocumented immigrants through greater enforcement and those reliant on exploitable labor pools. Prison corporations, including Corrections Corporation of America (CCA), have had a hand in drafting the legislation and have contributed millions of dollars to the bill's sponsors (Hoy; Roth). Perhaps in anticipation of increased arrests and detainment of undocumented immigrants, Governor Brewer allocated $98 million to private prison corporations (Hoy; Roth). Tanya Roth reported the following: "According to the *Arizona Daily Star*, the [CCA] runs six private prisons in the state. If more illegal immigrants are detained as a result of the law, [then] the corporation stands to make more money." In an investigative report for National Public Radio, Laura Sullivan reported that "hundreds of pages of campaign finance reports, lobbying documents and corporate records" revealed that the CCA expects "to bring in 'a significant portion of [its] revenues' from Immigration and Customs Enforcement, the agency that detains illegal immigrants."

Other industries that might use illegal immigrant labor in Arizona are either unaffected or might benefit from SB 1070. Perhaps the biggest indicator that SB 1070 would not significantly impact these industries is that few, if any, used their resources to contest the bill. SB 1070 was written in a way that would appear to be "tough on illegal immigration" while creating a synergistic relationship between multiple industries. These features of SB 1070 enabled Governor Brewer to use it as an available means of persuasion to her given situation to increase her political popularity.

SB 1070 and Governor Brewer's Available Means

Governor Brewer's interest in illegal immigration is relatively recent. Prior to her 2010 campaign, she had never made immigration an issue of any significance in her 25 years of public service (Archibold); however, analysis of Jan Brewer's reelection situation reveals how championing an illegal immigration bill was an effective response to her waning political appeal. SB 1070 was in the interest of some of her campaign donors, it was ideologically pleasing to many of her constituents, and it created future opportunities in which she could fund-raise and address a national audience.

Like most politicians, Governor Brewer had to fund-raise for her reelection campaign. Some of her donors were board members and employees of the Corrections Corporation of America (CCA), the country's largest for-profit prison company, which operates six prisons in Arizona—three of which list US Immigration and Customs Enforcement as a client (Lemons). The CCA's political action committee also contributed to Proposition 100 (Loew), which was "considered by many to be the linchpin for a Brewer victory in November" (Lemons). Governor Brewer's spokesman, Paul Senseman, and her campaign manager, Chuck Coughlin, also had ties to CCA (Loew; Sullivan). Regardless of the influence her advisers might or might not have had on Governor Brewer, increasing the numbers of detained undocumented immigrants is big business, and the CCA stood to benefit from SB 1070.

Signing SB 1070 also benefitted Governor Brewer's political popularity. In his blog for the *Phoenix New Times,* James King wrote that most political pundits "would have laughed in your face" if you had asked them if they had "anticipated attending Brewer's second inauguration.... Then SB 1070 happened, and Brewer's signature ... made her the Conservative darling behind which Arizona's predominantly Republican electorate could rally." Indeed, many Arizonans have favored tough illegal immigration policies. In 2010, a poll by Arizona State University's Morrison Institute for Public Policy found that "81 percent of [Arizona] registered voters approved of requiring people to produce documents that show they are in the country legally" ("More than 80%"). SB 1070 gave Governor Brewer opportunities to speak, and a controversial topic to speak about, with little risk of failure in the two most important areas of her campaign: political support and economic/financial interests.

The national attention SB 1070 received also created opportunities to increase Governor Brewer's popularity and fundraising opportunities. After signing the bill, she gained private audience with President Obama in June of 2010. Although Governor Brewer initially called the meeting "very, very cordial" (qtd. in Feldmann), in her book *Scorpions for Breakfast*, she claimed that President Obama was condescending toward her. The supposed tension between the two was photographed in January of 2012 when Governor Brewer (in)famously wagged her finger at President Obama on the Phoenix-Mesa Gateway Airport tarmac.[7] The next day, Governor Brewer appeared on the Fox News show *Hannity* and received praise from interviewer Monica Crowley. The image was also featured as a backdrop at Republican fundraising events at which Governor Brewer was the keynote speaker. And, not surprisingly, sales of her book skyrocketed after the incident (Rough).

The inevitable Supreme Court decision on SB 1070 also afforded Governor Brewer with opportunities to generate popularity. Ultimately, the Court's decision handed Governor Brewer the best possible outcome—a highly moderate policy necessary to sustain the synergistic cycle of economic interests, political support, and an unfinished cause to champion. If we could retroactively posit the possibility that Governor Brewer knew the Supreme Court would overrule most, if not all, of SB 1070, then we might conclude that Governor Brewer is a political genius; however, the more modest claim is that the situation given to Governor Brewer by the Court's decision provided the best rhetorical possibilities to advance her political interests. SB 1070, it seems, is a rhetorical gift that keeps on giving.

Economic Globalization and the Health of Democracy

Through our analysis of the politics surrounding SB 1070, we have argued that the realities of economic globalization are an essential feature of the political given situation on issues of immigration. In the past, immigration to the United States might also have been about the global labor market, but the current context of economic globalization presents politician-rhetors with a qualitatively different situation that might pit the needs and desires of their constituents against the economic will of the industries in their state, nation, and the international marketplace.

Our analysis of SB 1070 leads to troubling questions about the role of economic globalization and the accountability of elected officials. Voters might keep politicians accountable if they can "discern whether [elected officials] are acting in their interest and sanction them appropriately" (Manin, Przeworski, and Stokes 40). When elected officials' given situations require them to "enter into a web of symbiotic relationships with powerful special interests," democracy suffers (Canova 59). As a Senate staffer in the 1980s, Timothy Canova "saw firsthand how important it was for incumbent members of Congress to court powerful financial contributors and then to curry favor with their lobbyists" (59). To court the favor of industry and their constituents, politicians exploit ideological differences that exacerbate an already divisive political climate. In this way, economic globalization erodes voters' abilities to discern whether elected officials are acting in their interests both actually and perceptually, further reducing government accountability to the electorate (Hellwig and Samuels 297). SB 1070 confronts all Americans with the status of democracy in the context of economic globalization. If we are to respond effectively to this crisis of democracy, then we must consider the extent to which a globalized economy influences our political system. This consideration is a first step toward finding the available means of persuasion to counter the consequences of SB 1070 and exploitable pools of labor.

Endnotes

1. Cohn, Raymond. "Immigration to the United States." *EH.net*. Economic History Association, Web. 2 Aug. 2012. <http://eh.net/encyclopedia/article/cohn. immigration.us>. Prior to 1830, anti-immigrant sentiments were more broadly conceived. Notably, the first use of "illegal alien" in a legal sense did not occur until the early 1900s. See Mae M. Ngai, *Impossible Subjects: Illegal Aliens and the Making of Modern America* (Princeton, NJ: Princeton UP, 2004).

2. Other attempts to restrict immigration in the 20th century include the following: the adoption of a literacy test in 1917, the Quota Act of 1921, The National Origins Act of 1924, and the Immigration and Nationality Act of 1965.

3. According to the Immigrant Policy Project report generated by the National Conference of State Legislatures, 2011 found a dramatic increase in state laws: see <http://www.ncsl.org/issues-research/immig/2010-immigration-related-laws-and-resolutions-in-t.aspx>.

4. For articles that analyze the impact of spending at locally owned versus national or multinational corporations, see <http://www.ilsr.org/key-studies-walmart-and-bigbox-retail/>.

5. For example, this tension existed for the 2012 Obama campaign in which Obama supported, but did not solicit for, the Priorities USA super-PAC. George Zornick. "Obama Unleashes His Super-PAC." *The Nation*. 7 Feb. 2012. Web. 6 July 2012. <http://www.thenation.com/blog/166109/obama-unleashes-his-super-pac>.

6. See Robert Reich's analysis in "Employment Will Come Back in America; It's Just Pay that Won't." *Business Insider*. Web. 2 June 2014. <http://www.businessinsider.com/robert-reich-the-future-of-american-jobs-2010-4#ixzz33VWFOa4W><http://www.businessinsider.com/robert-reich-the-future-of-american-jobs-2010-4>.

7. Image link, as follows: <http://guerillawomentn.blogspot.com/2012/01/angry-gov-jan-brewer-wags-her-finger-in.html>.

Works Cited

Arizona v. United States, 567 U.S. (2012). Web. 2 Aug. 2012.

Brewer, Janice. "Brewer: Supreme Court's Arizona Decision a 'Victory for the Rule of Law.'" *FOXNews.com*. 25 June 2012. Web. 19 July 2012.

—. "Inaugural Address." Phoenix, AZ. 3 Jan. 2011. Web. 1 Aug. 2012.

—. *Scorpions for Breakfast: My Fight Against Special Interests, Liberal Media, and Cynical Politicos to Secure America's Borders.* New York: Broadside, 2011. Print.

—. "Statement by Governor Jan Brewer." 23 Apr. 2010. Web 1 Aug. 2012.

Calmes, Jackie. "In Border City Talk, Obama Urges G.O.P. to Help Overhaul Immigration Law." *New York Times.* Web. 10 May 2011.

Canova, Timothy A. "Campaign Finance, Iron Triangles and the Decline of American Political Discourse." *Nexus, A Journal of Opinion: Chapman's Journal of Law and Policy* 12 (2007): 57–83. Web. *LexisNexis* 2 Aug. 2012.

Citizens United v. Federal Election Commission, 558 U.S. 50 (2010).

Cohn, Raymond L. "Immigration to the United States," *EH.net.* Operated by the Economic History Association, Web. 29 July 2012.

Farrell, Thomas B. "Rhetoric in History as Theory and Praxis: A Blast from the Past." *Philosophy & Rhetoric* 41.4 (2008): 323–36. Web. 29 July 2012.

Feldmann, Linda. "Obama-Brewer Summit on Illegal Immigration Eases Tensions; Though They Continue to Differ on Illegal Immigration Issues, Including Comprehensive Reform and Border Security, Arizona Gov. Jan Brewer and the White House Described the Meeting as Cordial." *Christian Science Monitor* 3 June 2010. Web. *LexisNexis* 3 Aug. 2012.

"Globalization." *The Encyclopedia of Political Science.* Ed. George Thomas Kurian. Washington, DC: CQ, 2011. 677–81. *SAGE knowledge.* Web. 28 May 2014.

Hellwig, Timothy, and David Samuels. "The Electoral Consequences of Globalization." *Comparative Political Studies* 40 (2007): 283–306.

Hough, Mary. "President Obama on The Supreme Court's Ruling on Arizona's Immigration Law." 25 June 2012. Web. 2 Aug. 2012.

Hoy, Seth. "Prisonomics 101: How the Prison Industry Got Arizona's SB10780 onto Gov. Jan Brewer's Desk." *LA Progressive.* Web. 30 Oct. 2010.

Immigrant Policy Project: 2010 Immigration-Related Laws and Resolutions in the States (January 1–December 31, 2010). *National Conference of State Legislatures.* 5 Jan. 2011.

King, James. "Jan Brewer Sworn In as Arizona's 22nd Governor—Compliments of SB 1070." *Phoenix New Times.* Web. 3 Jan. 2011.

Lemons, Stephen. "Jan Brewer's CCA Money and Her Possible Conflict of Interest Over SB 1070." *Phoenix New Times.* Web 15 Sept. 2014.

Loew, Morgan. "Brewer Linked To Private Prisons Housing Illegal Immigrants 9-01-2010." CBS5AZ.Com. Web. 15 Sept. 2014.

Manin, Bernard, Adam Przeworski, and Susan C. Stokes. "Elections and Representation." In *Democracy, Accountability, and Representation.* Ed. Adam Przeworski, Susan C. Stokes, and Bernard Manin. NY: Cambridge UP, 1999. Print. 29–54.

"More Than 80% Back Tougher Immigration Law in Arizona," *The Nation.* (4 Sept. 2010). Web. *LexisNexis* 2 Aug. 2012.

Naim, Moises. "The Five Wars of Globalization." *Foreign Policy.* 134 (2003): 28–36. Web. 4 June 2014.

Ngai, Mae M. *Impossible Subjects: Illegal Aliens and the Making of Modern America.* Princeton, NJ: Princeton UP, 2004. Print.

O'Brien, Karen L., and Robin M. Leichenko. "Double Exposure: Assessing the Impacts of Climate Change within the Context of Economic Globalization." *Global Environmental Change* 10 (2000): 221–32. Web. 30 May 2014.

Pearce, Russel. "Enough Is Enough: What Does It Take. (Also Below A Short List Of Deaths, Maimings, Crime, And Some Of The Cost)." Email Message to John Huppenthal. 30 June 2009. Web. 1 Aug. 2012.

Powell, Benjamin. "The Law of Unintended Consequences." Editorial. *Forbes* 17 May 2012. Web. 1 Aug. 2012.

Roth, Tanya. "Private Prisons Helped Draft Arizona's SB 1070." *LawInfo.com*. Web. 29 Oct. 2010.

Rough, Ginger. "Gov. Jan Brewer's Most Memorable Moments in Office." AZCentral. Web. 15 Sept. 2014.

Schwartz, John, and Randal C. Archibold. "A Law Facing a Tough Road Through the Courts." *The New York Times* 27 Apr. 2010. Web. 2 Aug. 2012.

Sullivan, Laura. "Prison Economics Help Drive Ariz. Immigration Law." National Public Radio. 28 Oct. 2012. Web. 31 July 2012.

Support Our Law Enforcement and Safe Neighborhoods Act. S.B. 1070. 49th Legislature. Second Regular Session. (2010).

Zornick, George. "Obama Unleashes His Super-PAC." *The Nation*. 7 Feb. 2012. Web. 6 July 2012.

Contexts of Lived Realities in SB 1070 Arizona: A Response to Asenas and Johnson's "Economic Globalization and the 'Given Situation'"

Cruz Medina and Aja Y. Martinez

Arizona matters to us. Arizona is what Jacqueline Jones Royster would call our "home place."[1] We studied together at the University of Arizona during the passing of SB 1070, which legalized racially profiling Latin@s "reasonably suspected" of being undocumented, and HB 2281, which outlawed Mexican American Studies in Tucson Unified School District. Because of our research and Arizona ties, we are responding to the recent *Present Tense* article, "Economic Globalization and the 'Given Situation': Jan Brewer's Use of SB 1070 as an Effective Rhetorical Response to the Politics of Immigration" by Jennifer J. Asenas and Kevin A. Johnson. Our purpose is to problematize, complicate, and personalize the discussion presented by Asenas and Johnson. We feel that the article would have benefitted significantly from critical inquiry that engaged with the situation on the human level as well as taking into consideration the history of Arizona as the "given situation." As a demonstration of a methodology based on lived experiences, we also provide a counternarrative to further emphasize ethical considerations that were overlooked by Asenas and Johnson's use of logocentric strategies to discuss the dehumanizing policy of SB 1070.

Although Asenas and Johnson's argument engages policy that connects the macro-context of global economics, we believe a more biting critique of SB 1070 is required due to the micro-context of the lived experiences of the people framed by this ultraconservative rhetoric reified into law. Asenas and Johnson explain that "the purpose of this article is to assess how Governor Brewer used SB 1070 as a rhetorical response to generate and maintain political support for her constituents, state industries, and wealthy contributors." On its surface, the application of Aristotle's definition of rhetoric to the contemporary controversy surrounding SB 1070 only seems to rearticulate without complicating or extending Karl Marx's arguments about the relationship between the political superstructure and the economic base to reproduce the conditions for production. By focusing specifically on rhetorical strategies for fluctuating poles or ego-driven concerns of "political popularity," the authors miss an important opportunity to consider the human experience and civic action that makes democracy possible.

Asenas and Johnson focus on Brewer's popularity resulting from rhetorically pandering to businesses that include "state industries"; however, we argue that the efficacy of Brewer's decision was as short-lived as it was inhumane and shortsighted. Reporting on the backlash to SB 1070, the *New York Times'* Marc Lacey noted, "musicians canceled Arizona concerts, tourists canceled Arizona vacations and convention organizers bypassed Arizona in favor of less politically toxic states." The success of the Arizona boycott affected hotel and convention business, resulting in Arizona business leaders urging state lawmakers to back off future immigration legislation (Lacey). Although Asenas and Johnson pinpoint their argument on transnational businesses, we would also point out the hotel and music industries identified in the *Times* article are neither uniquely local to Arizona, nor exclusive to U.S. ownership.

While the purpose of Asenas and Johnson's article is to evaluate a piece of legislation as a response in a "given situation" to global economics, there is much more to this context than Governor Brewer's political popularity. Asenas and Johnson acknowledge the crucial importance of context, yet the discussion moves quickly from the local to the abstract. We, however, advocate for a needed awareness and focus on the criminalizing of brown and black bodies within the borderlands.[2] Asenas and Johnson explain that the "given situation [context] of state and national politicians is one in which the influence of economic globalizations on campaigning, political popularity, and economic policy is pervasive." Context as central to a political situation is briefly addressed within the Aristotelian definition of rhetoric: "Working from Aristotle's definition of rhetoric ... we believe that Governor Brewer's given situation should not be limited to Arizona's political situation." Although the purpose of "Economic Globalization and the 'Given Situation'" is to analyze the rhetorical efficacy of a senate bill vis-à-vis global economics, we argue that more attention needs to be paid to the "given situation" of Arizona's history and culture.

In *Present Tense*'s second issue, Victor Villanueva[3] makes a point about the interplay between politics and economics *and* attends to Arizona and its tradition of scapegoating people of color. Villanueva draws attention to the racial component of Arizona's political history: "Arizona's bid for statehood at the turn of nineteenth to the twentieth century had been denied several times on the basis of its Mexican population." Additionally, Villanueva addresses the more contemporary failure of Arizona to acknowledge Dr. Martin Luther King Jr. Day with the Super Bowl pulling out of Arizona as a result, as well as the state passing an English-only law in 1995. Asenas and Johnson's focus on the logic of Brewer's decision-making during the passage of SB 1070 fails to account for the ethics related to a historical trajectory of racial discrimination, in which this particular situation is merely a moment.

We appreciate that Asenas and Johnson explain the connection between Corrections Corporation of America (CCA) and Jan Brewer's campaign. This connection possesses the potential for problematizing the prison industrial complex and militarizing police enforcement, yet their argument instead focuses on the logic of appealing for donations from CCA: "increasing the number of detained undocumented immigrants is big business, and the CCA stood to benefit from SB 1070." We are concerned that there is no critique—or acknowledgement—of the dehumanizing assumption that economic interests justify instituting what amounts to Jim Crow style laws that institutionalize second-class citizenship for non-whites.[4] This is especially important because of the dehumanizing reality that Arizona's policy undergirds. Arizona's ultra-conservative political culture is one that authorizes abuses of power such as the over-enforcement of undocumented people by the re-elected Maricopa County (Phoenix area) Sheriff Joe "America's Toughest Cop" Arpaio.[5]

Returning to Royster's criticism that the experiences of friends have been carelessly mishandled,[6] we draw attention to our colleague Dr. Ersula Ore, Assistant Professor of Rhetoric and Composition at Arizona State University, who was stopped and forcibly arrested by ASU Police Officer Stewart Ferrin. On a street with construction on one end and no cross-traffic, Dr. Ore was singled out by Officer Ferrin in the middle of the street at night among the semi-regular foot traffic. When Dr. Ore asked why she was being stopped and did not produce identification when Officer Ferrin ignored her initial inquiry, he violently threw her across the hood of his patrol car and pinned her down with her skirt forced up, exposed to on-lookers. It is heartbreaking that a white police officer would feel justified in escalating a jaywalking stop to a physical violation of an African American professor, but the history and culture of white supremacy that dominate the mythos of the Southwest[7] reveal this as a reality to people of color through lived experience. We understand it can be difficult to write rhetorical scholarship about a policy that affects the material lives of many, so we suggest scholarship from the emerging body of knowledge on post-SB 1070 Arizona. For example, Cruz's recent book[8] engages both SB 1070 and House Bill 2281 through the analytical lens of pop culture, which in itself could seem to diminish the severity of these issues. However, Cruz and others devoting scholarly attention to these policies address the *human level* through autobiographical connections, ethnography, observation, or interaction with the people affected by these policies (Acosta 2014; Ribero 2013; Serna 2013a, 2013b; Villanueva 2011). When Asenas and Johnson mention the nameless, faceless examples of hotel workers and food preparers targeted by SB 1070 they confuse cliché for experience:

> For example, a multinational hotel chain might host a meeting for a group of US and non-US investors strategizing the expansion of their business in Arizona whose rooms are cleaned by and meals prepared and served by undocumented immigrants. While the meeting would bring business to Arizona, not all of the money spent would benefit or employ the citizens of that state. (2)

This hypothetical example of undocumented hotel workers only serves to mimic—even if unconsciously—the tired rhetoric of "they're stealing our jobs," rather than critically evaluating it and its material effects. Our concern is that audiences who read these hypothetical examples uncritically may follow the logic without recognizing the embedded assumptions in the stereotypical representation.

Beyond the hypothetical, and as an illustration of policy-driven actions and lived realities of people of color in Arizona, we advocate for employing a narrative methodology that can counter dominant methods that dismiss or decenter racism and the lives affected daily by it.[9] As Aja has argued in previous scholarship,[10] counterstory functions as a method for marginalized people to intervene in research methods that would form master narratives based on ignorance and on assumptions about minoritized peoples like Chican@s. As an example of research that draws from personal experience, we offer Aja's humanizing counternarrative for consideration:

> It's 6:30AM, still dark outside, with a winter chill in the desert air. As I turn the ignition switch to my dad's sleek Mercedes E class, I increase the heat to a cozy 76, and my dad, in the passenger seat teases, "What you're cold? I thought those upstate New York winters made you tough. A badass." I laugh and rub my eyes, sleepy. It's the holidays and I'm in Arizona, my borderlands home of 30 years. Working as an assistant professor, I now live in the northeast and I've missed my southwest home. I've romanticized it, written about it, and taught about its incendiary policies on immigration and ethnic studies to my mostly horrified and unknowing New York City and Long Island students. From that safe distance I've critiqued the seemingly endless affronts by the Arizona legislature toward its populace and I've grown more sensitive to, yet less experienced, in the everyday effects of living in this space.

> As I round the curved roads near the San Xavier Mission, my dad says, "Rides real smooth, huh?" He's referring to his new Mercedes, a car he worked hard his whole life to buy, a car he is proud of and that he wants me to drive so I can share in his accomplishment. My dad was born in Nogales, Arizona and grew up in a south-side Tucson barrio, one of ten siblings. His mother was born in the cotton fields of Buckeye, Arizona to a family of migrant farm workers; his father was Mexican from Sonora but became a US citizen in the 1990s. After serving in the US Marine Corps during Vietnam, my father earned two associates degrees in digital electronics and business management and went directly to work as an electronic technician for a local defense contractor. He has spent more than thirty years working alongside and *training* recent graduates with

10

BAs in engineering to do a job he knows by experience and heart, but can't officially perform due to his lack of a four-year degree. For more than thirty years, my dad has supported my academic pursuits—acutely aware of the second-class citizenship his community college degrees have afforded him. He has steadily worked to provide his family with a comfortable life and opportunities. So, on this winter morning, with his daughter the PhD and professor, driving him to work in a car he's worked a lifetime to afford, he's proud.

As I make the left-hand turn onto the company facility site, I fumble with my wallet and New York driver's license. From years of dropping off my dad, I know that ID is required for entry. I am prepared for the usual exchange with the guard:

Guard: Where you headed?
Me: Building 501.
Guard: You know the way?
Me: Yes, thank you.
Guard: Have a nice day.

15 However, this guard, a young rosy-cheeked white male, mid-to-late 20s, wearing a guard's coat and skull cap against the chilly morning air, says instead: "Are you two US citizens?"

At first my dad and I laugh, both out of surprise, and I think because we really did believe the guard was telling a joke. But the guard does not laugh. He does not crack a smile. "Oh God, he's serious," I realize. As my stomach drops, I look to my dad in the passenger seat and his face is confused and defiant. Like I had my New York ID extended toward the guard, my dad has his company badge held out in plain sight. You see, because this company is a national defense contractor, you must be a citizen to be hired. You must be a citizen to hold a badge.

Embarrassed and flustered, I answer, "Yes, we're citizens." The guard looks at my dad, who says in an annoyed tone, "Yes, I'm a citizen." The guard holds our gazes for a few moments more and I hold my breath. He finally says, "Okay, have a nice day." He waves us through and I exhale.

"What an asshole," my dad mutters.

As I drove back toward my parents' home, I wracked my brain for answers to this experience. Being that it was so early in the morning, I noted that I was still in my pajamas, with my hair, a frizzy tangled mess, tied into a quick ponytail. Was that why? I thought about my dad's Mercedes, my NY ID, my dad's badge, and his dismissive "asshole" response about the guard. *When and how did this security gate become a border checkpoint? What was it about me that prompted this question? Why do I feel so ashamed? Why was my dad so numb?*

20 From this experience I've come to terms with a few things:

1. The lived experience of people of color in the borderlands of Arizona is *always* subject to scrutiny regarding their legality in the land. So much so, that people like my Mexican American father become numb and desensitized to the continual assaults on their humanity under this legislation.

2. Because I have moved away to a space where my legal status is not constantly surveilled and of reasonable suspicion, I am privileged. Being questioned is not my everyday lived reality as it is for my family, friends, and countless other people of color in AZ.

3. In a state like Arizona, my titles, degrees or even the car I drive do not matter when my brown skin is of enough reasonable suspicion to the law.

4. Because I teach about, critique, and engage in conversations about Arizona legislation such as SB1070 and HB2281, I must remember, even if this is through painful and humiliating personal assaults, that I have a responsibility to always consider and include the discussion of human life affected under this jurisdiction.

Although we both write from outside Arizona and its systemic inequality, we write out of love for our family and friends who feel the daily reverberations of political theater and quarterly earnings reports that support the rejection of culture, history, knowledge, and decades of work loyalty. We aim to create a dialogue about our work and the responsibility that we believe rhetorical teacher-scholars must insert as ethical considerations into public discourse that concerns economic policies diminishing the value of human life. Our goal is not to lay claim to, or knowledge of (nor to seek an apology for) Asenas and Johnson's *intent* in their essay's analysis. We seek only to raise the awareness of the realities facing our "home place" of Arizona, so that both authors and the audience of their article will further consider the complex dimensions of personal experience, race, and colonialism endemic to this given situation. Beyond politics and economics, and above all, human lives matter to our work.

Endnotes

1. In "When the First Voice You Hear Is Not Your Own," Royster explains her disbelief at the level of disrespect that has happened in research about people of color: "when you visit other people's 'home places,' especially when you have not been invited, you simply cannot go tramping around the house like you own the place, no matter how smart you are, or how much imagination you can muster, or how much authority and entitlement outside the home you may be privileged to hold" (32).

2. See Samuel Huntington's fear-based essay concerning his perceived risks to national identity due to our increasing Latin@ population: "The Hispanic Challenge" http://foreignpolicy.com/2009/10/28/the-hispanic-challenge/.

3. "Of Ideologies, Economies, and Cultures: Three Meditations on the Arizona Border."

4. Laws such as SB 1070 provide a highly subjective "probable cause" for an already over-militarized law enforcement, as we have seen in Maricopa County's Sheriff Joe Arpaio's racial profiling and over-enforcement outside of his jurisdiction of suspected undocumented persons (Hesson).

5. Sheriff Arpaio is known for his immigration raids and tent city prison that has received Human Rights criticism and federal crackdowns on his racial-profiling (Hesson).

6. With regard to how news organizations have covered Dr. Ore's case, we find Royster's assertion fitting: "I have found it extremely difficult to allow the voices and experiences of people that I care about deeply to be taken and handled so carelessly and without accountability by strangers" (31). The representations of Dr. Ore in media reports following her arrest repeatedly use the photo from her mug-shot, as opposed to the more flattering images of the police officer. The message communicated by her arrest photo support the dominant narrative perpetuated about Dr. Ore, portraying her as the one at fault. As with all messages, the narrative of Arizona media is shaped by the expectations of its ultraconservative Arizona audience.

7. Though outsiders may argue that Officer Ferrin's termination did not come as a result or prove his racially motivated abuse of Dr. Ore, our relationship with Dr. Ore and our experiences in Arizona teach us otherwise.

8. *Reclaiming Poch@ Pop: Examining the Rhetoric of Cultural Deficiency.*

9. Counterstory as a research method comes out of Critical Race Theory. Scholars such as Derrick Bell examined the intersections of law, race, and power with knowledge derived from lived experience as a guiding principle.

10. See Martinez's "A Plea for Critical Race Theory Counterstory: Stock Story versus Counterstory Dialogues Concerning Alejandra's 'Fit' in the Academy."

Works Cited

Acosta, Curtis. "Huitzilopochtli: The Will and Resiliency of Tucson Youth to Keep Mexican American Studies Alive." *Multicultural Perspectives* 16.1 (2014): 3–7. Print.

Asenas, Jennifer J. and Johnson, Kevin A. "Economic Globalization and the "Given Situation": Jan Brewer's Use of SB 1070 as an Effective Rhetorical Response to the Politics of Immigration." *Present Tense* 4.1 (2014): n. pag. Web. 5 Nov 2014.

Hesson, Ted. "Judge Says Sheriff Joe Arpaio Racially Profiled Latinos." *ABC News Internet Ventures.* 24 May 2013. Web. 1 Dec. 2014.

Lacey, Marc. "Immigration Advocates Split Over Arizona Boycott." *New York Times.* 14 Sept. 2011. Web. 13 Jan. 2015.

Levine, Sam. "Rand Paul Thinks Taxes Are Partly to Blame for Eric Garner's Death." *Huff Post: Politics.* Huffington Post, 3 Dec. 2014. Web. 10 Dec. 2014.

Lorde, Audre. "The Master's Tools Will Not Dismantle the Master's House." *Sister Outsider* 110 (1984): 81–102. Print.

Martinez, Aja Y. "A Plea for Critical Race Theory Counterstory: Stock Story versus Counterstory Dialogues Concerning Alejandra's 'Fit' in the Academy." *Composition Studies* 42.2 (2014): 33–55. Print.

—. "Critical Race Theory Counterstory as Allegory: A Rhetorical Trope to Raise Awareness About Arizona's Ban on Ethnic Studies." *Across the Disciplines.* Fall (2013). 26pp. 12 Dec 2014.

Marx, Karl. *A Contribution to the Critique of Political Economy*. No. 1. International Library Publishing Company; London, Kegan Paul, Trench Trubner, Limited, 1904. Print.

Medina, Cruz. "Nuestros Refranes: Culturally Relevant Writing in Tucson High Schools." *Reflections: A Journal of Public Rhetoric, Civic Writing, and Service Learning* 12.3 (2013): 52–79. Print.

—. *Reclaiming Poch@ Pop: Examining the Rhetoric of Cultural Deficiency* (Latino Pop Culture Series). New York: Palgrave Macmillan, 2015. Print.

Neel, Jasper P. *Aristotle's Voice: Rhetoric, Theory, and Writing in America*. SIU Press, 1994. Print.

Ribero, Ana Milena. "'In Lak'Ech (You Are My Other Me):' Mestizaje as a Rhetorical Tool that Achieves Identification and Consubstantiality." *Arizona Journal of Interdisciplinary Studies* 2 (2013): 22–41. Print.

Royster, Jacqueline Jones. "When the First Voice You Hear Is Not Your Own." *College Composition and Communication* (1996): 29–40. Print.

Serna, Elias. "The Eagle Meets the Seagull: The Critical, Kairotic and Public Rhetoric of Raza Studies Now in Los Angeles." *Reflections: A Journal of Public Rhetoric, Civic Writing, and Service Learning* 12.3 (2013a): 80–93. Print.

—. "Tempest, Arizona: Criminal Epistemologies and the Rhetorical Possibilities of Raza Studies." *The Urban Review* 45.1 (2013b): 41–57.

Van Dijk, Teun. *Elite Discourse and Racism*. Newbury Park: Sage P, 1993. Print.

Villanueva, Victor. "Of Ideologies, Economies, and Cultures: Three Meditations on the Arizona Border." *Present Tense* 1.2 (2011): n. pag. Web. 2 Dec 2014.

Reflections and Inquiries

1. Defend or challenge Medina and Martinez's assertion that Asenas and Johnson should have given more attention to the human context of the immigration issue—specifically "the criminalizing of brown and black bodies within the borderlands."

2. What insights into the immigration reform issue are gained by examining it from a rhetorical perspective?

3. Medina and Martinez introduce personal experience into their critical response. How successful is this approach, in your opinion?

4. After reading both articles, what is your own reaction to Governor Jan Brewer's immigration bill?

Reading to Write

1. Write an essay addressing the claim that current immigration policy along the U.S.-Mexican border violates human rights.

2. Conduct your own critical examination of SB 1070 to determine whether or not it is a "dehumanizing" policy. Be sure you make clear your definition of "dehumanizing."

Student Essay

NSA's Global Leviathan | Joseph Cotter

First-year computer science major Joseph Cotter investigated NSAs activities in 2015, nine years after Bamford's essay on the NSA was published (see pages 405–414). Cotter found that the agency had not reduced but increased its surveillance thanks to developing technology, and he claims that the NSA has in fact gone global in its interests.

Joseph Cotter
Professor Billings
ENGL 2H
3/13/15

NSA's Global Leviathan

As it stands, the NSA's global surveillance network, if unchecked, has the capability to decompose the United States (if not the world) into totalitarian dystopia. We are surely close to this irrevocable milestone; the NSA, with little or no regard for the legality of its actions, already has the ability to intercept, analyze, and document nearly every iota of electronic information being passed into, out of, or through the United States. The issue has gone beyond Locke's social contract (that the people must cede rights to their government in return for safety)—the documents leaked by Edward Snowden make it certain that the National Security Agency uses its Orwellian capabilities for a hell of a lot more than matters of national security. Human beings, flawed, cannot be trusted with powers of omnipotence. If we are to retain any sort of digital privacy in the future, the NSA must be made a heavily supervised, legal, and more transparent agency.

Bryan Bedder/Getty Images

The public would likely know nothing about the NSA's practices if not for one man—Edward Snowden. A former NSA employee, Snowden began courageously leaking top secret NSA documents to the public in 2013. His actions have split public opinion, with some considering him a heroic   Edward Snowden whistleblower and others a traitor to his country. Regardless, his dissidence has sparked a debate in the United States and elsewhere regarding mass surveillance and the balance of national security and individual privacy. He is currently receiving asylum in Moscow; if he returns to the United States he faces up to 30 years in prison. Nearly all of the information in this essay comes from documents leaked by Snowden, and I hope that by substantiating the NSA's wrongdoing I will also vindicate his innocence and patriotism.

According to documents released by Snowden, as much as 90% of those under NSA surveillance are ordinary Americans, not legally targeted foreign threats (Gellman). Yet, on August 6, 2013, President Obama appeared on national television assuring the public that "We [the United States] don't have a domestic spying program" and "There is no spying on Americans." With these things in mind, let us now delve into the disarray that is the NSA's global surveillance network.

So, the NSA is supposed to apply for a warrant from this thing called the FISA court anytime they wish to conduct surveillance on someone currently within U.S. borders. The court was established to protect Americans; the only problem is, of the 33,949 warrant requests submitted since the court was established in 1979, a total of 12 have been rejected (Federation of American Scientists). This is frightening for a couple of reasons. First, it is obvious that the FISA court is little more than a rubber stamp; second, the fact that warrants are only needed to surveil people in the United States means that the NSA can spy on foreign targets in any way it pleases with absolutely no oversight.

Even when the NSA wants to conduct espionage on people in the United States, however, it often completely disregards the FISA court. And they always gets away with it. Why is this possible, you ask? It breaks down like this: following the terrorist attacks of September 11th, 2001, everyone was scared shitless. Including the government of the United States. So, they did what any reasonable government would do: they poured billions of dollars into their national security program and told it to do what it needed to in order to keep the United States safe. And the NSA *has* kept the United States safe. Which is why so many people do not support Edward Snowden's actions; they believe that by leaking our country's espionage secrets he has inadvertently given malicious parties our playbook, thus endangering the lives of countless Americans. However, there is no publicly revealed evidence that the NSA has prevented much of anything, let alone a terror plot on the scale of 9/11. Of the 227 people convicted of acts of terrorism/conspiracy to commit acts of terrorism against the United States since 2001, only 17 were caught by NSA surveillance (Neal). Of these 17, only one man was convicted by evidence obtained from the NSA's domestic espionage program. He was charged with sending money to a terrorist organization in Somalia. There was never any threat of physical attack. The other 210 people convicted of terrorism were caught by traditional investigative means, such as informants, tips, or good ol' fashioned law enforcement (Neal).

These statistics suggest that, at the very least, the NSA's sweeping dragnet of internal data collection is of little use. In fact, President Obama's advisory panel determined that the NSA's domestic digital espionage is "not essential to preventing attacks" (Serwer). And yet, the National Security Agency continues to spy on American citizens in a number of alarming ways. The NSA pays private tech companies (such as Skype, Microsoft, Google, Yahoo, Apple, and YouTube to name a few) hundreds of millions of dollars for "clandestine access" to their communications networks (Timberg). The NSA then uses this backdoor access to harvest millions of email and instant messaging contact lists (many belonging to innocent Americans), as well as to sift through the actual email content of United States citizens.

Tomorrow's United States could very well be the dystopia envisioned in George Orwell's 1984.

The NSA doesn't pay for access if it can avoid it, though; they simply have the FISA court draw up a warrant demanding that companies like Verizon turn over their user's phone records on a daily basis (Greenwald).

The NSA also engages in more bizarre forms of espionage against United States Citizens, such as creating fake *Second Life* and *World of Warcraft* accounts to spy on users by hiding in plain sight (Elliott). The NSA also monitors the online sexual activity of those they affectionately term "radicalizers" in hopes to discredit them (Gallagher). These people are generally targeted for attempting to forward incendiary opinions on a public platform. Thus far, each of these so-called radicalizers has been Muslim.

Perhaps the most shocking espionage against United States citizens comes from NSA employees operating independently from the agency itself. These employees use the powers they are endowed with to monitor the online activity of their friends, family, or love interests (Gorman). Though this practice is formally condemned by the NSA, it still occurs, and often goes undetected. These employees can uncover their acquaintances' most highly personal information with the ease of a few clicks—power cannot be so consolidated. The chance for abuse is simply too great. Something must change.

Perhaps even more unsettling than the NSA's domestic practices are its practices abroad. Documents leaked by Snowden suggest that the NSA engages in outright economic espionage. Said documents detail the NSA's heavy surveillance of Brazil's top oil company, *Petrobras*, as well as charities such as *Unicef* and *Medecins du Mond* (Watts). It seems the National Security Agency believes it should have its hand in matters far beyond that of national security; there is no excuse for such blatant disregard of behavioral axioms.

Another revelation of the Snowden documents is that the NSA spies on some of the U.S.'s closest allies, including France, Britain, China, Mexico, Spain, and Germany (Baker). In addition to this, the NSA monitors the internet and phone activity of "high profile individuals from the world of business and politics," including at least 35 world leaders. Among them is German Chancellor Angela Merkel, who remarked that "spying among friends is not at all acceptable" and compared the NSA to the secret Stasi police force of East Germany, where she grew up (Baker). Here lies likely the greatest damage done by Snowden: not in giving the terrorists an advantage, but in justly alienating the allies of the United States.

We treat our allies poorly enough, but they are subjected to relatively little infringement of rights when compared to our enemies. The NSA uses GPS tracking software to pinpoint enemy cell phones and then calls in drone strikes on these locations (Gander). This is a remarkably callous tactic; the NSA waits for the phone of a suspected terrorist to make a call, and then, without certainty of the users identity, calls in the strike. Not only could the call possibly have been made by an innocent third party, but other, unintended targets may very well be in the caller's vicinity. Regardless of the caller's potential status as a threat to the United States, this method of remote extermination should be abolished due to the innocent lives it surely takes.

National Reconaissance Office; US Government

The actual logo of a government surveillance project. Literally a giant octopus sucking on the face of the North American continent. Not doing much for the NSA's image.

Said a former drone operator, the NSA's drone strikes have "absolutely" killed innocent people (Gander). All without a warrant.

Snowden's leaks also revealed what is perhaps the NSA's most outrageous plan to date: to infect millions of computers with "implants" that would allow NSA agents to remotely access the computer's webcam and microphone capabilities (Gallagher). Though not directed at American citizens, this plan, if implemented, would give the NSA direct access to the information on the implanted computer rather than the secondary access afforded to them by their method of intercepting and sifting through massive amounts of data. The operation has already been effected on a small scale, with implants in a few hundred to a few thousand individually targeted computers. But the new plan, codenamed "Turbine" would systematically infect whole populations in an automated process that implants large groups of computers at once.

It is difficult to conceive of a greater breach of digital privacy than Turbine. Supporters of this and other NSA espionage operations ("many" of which have yet to be disclosed, according to Snowden) argue that if you have nothing to hide, you have nothing to fear. However, there are a few glaring problems with this oft-recycled argument. To begin with, everyone has something to conceal. Those who do not admit so are lying, and in actuality are probably worse than those who acknowledge the skeletons in their closets. Privacy expert David Flaherty argues, "There is no sentient human being in the Western world who has little or no regard for his or her personal privacy; those who would attempt such claims cannot withstand even a few minutes' questioning about intimate aspects of their lives without capitulating to the intrusiveness of certain subject matters" (Solove).

The nothing-to-hide argument also fails to address one sizeable effect of mass surveillance: it leads to a government with greater social control over its citizens. Surveillance of the magnitude the NSA engages in changes not only the power dynamic between people and their governmental institutions, but also the very nature of interpersonal relationships. Mass surveillance serves to frustrate the individual by manifesting a sense of powerlessness.

It is for this reason that our privacy must somehow be preserved. The NSA is seeking absolute power; their mission statement, found in a document leaked by Snowden, sounds like something straight out of 1984: "To dramatically increase mastery of the global network" and "acquire the capabilities to gather intelligence on anyone, anytime, anywhere." To "Collect it all, Process it all, Exploit it all, Know it all" (Cole). If the NSA achieves these goals, the United States will fall into a chasm from which there is no escape. And the American people have very little say in the matter; the power to change the NSA rests solely in the hands of policy makers in Washington. One would think that the abuses which the NSA has been found guilty of would move our government to tighten its grip on the rogue agency, but precious little has changed since Snowden began leaking documents in 2013. And much of the public has simply swept the NSA and its distasteful practices under the rug since that time. Others, however, still actively protest and petition our government to provide the NSA with strict supervision and semi-transparency. However, as time slips into the future and still nothing changes, citizens of America and the world have begun to take matters into their own hands. These people hope that by using advanced encrypting methods on their personal information they can evade the NSA or at the very least make it financially inviable for the agency to accrue information in the manner it has been. As Snowden himself put it, encryption is "the defense against the dark arts for the digital realm"

(Meyer). Sadly, for every brilliant mind working to outsmart the NSA, there is an even more brilliant mind already working for it. And even if the encryption methods do work, the majority of Americans would have to use them for any change to occur. So, at the moment, the best way to safeguard our future is to spread information about the NSA's practices. If enough people demand change, our government may listen. And if it doesn't, perhaps new encryption methods will save us from dystopia. Somehow, the NSA must be turned away from its tyrannical course and reminded of what it means to be human.

Works Cited

Baker, Luke and Rinke, Andreas. "Merkel Frosty on the U.S. Over 'unacceptable' Spying Allegations." *Reuters.com*. 24 Oct. 2013. Web. 9 Mar. 2015.

Cole, David. "'No Place to Hide' by Glenn Greenwald on the NSA's Sweeping Efforts to 'Know it All.'" *washingtonpost.com*. The Washington Post, 12 May 2014. Web. 9 Mar. 2015.

Elliott, Justin. "World of Spycraft: NSA and CIA Spied in Online Games." *propublica.org*. 9 Dec. 2013. Web. 9 Mar. 2015.

Federation of American Scientists. "Foreign Intelligence Surveillance Act Court Orders 1979-2014." *epic.org*. 1 May 2014. Web. 9 Mar. 2015.

Gallagher, Ryan and Greenwald, Glenn. "How the NSA Plans to Infect Millions of Computers with Malware." *firstlook.org*. 12 Mar. 2014. Web. 9 Mar. 2015.

Gallagher, Ryan, Greenwald, Glenn, and Grim, Ryan. "Top-Secret Document Reveals NSA Spied On Porn Habits As Part Of Plan To Discredit 'Radicalizers'". *huffingtonpost.com*. 26 Nov. 2013. Web. 9 Mar. 2015.

Gander, Kashmira. "NSA Drone Strikes Based on Mobile Phone Data." *theindependent.co.uk*. The Independent, 10 Feb. 2014. Web. 9 Mar. 2015.

Gellman, Barton. "In NSA-intercepted Data, Those Not Targeted Far Outnumber the Foreigners Who Are." *washingtonpost.com*. The Washington Post, 5 Jul. 2014. Web. 9 Mar. 2015.

Gorman, Siobhan. "NSA Officers Spy on Love Interests." *wsj.com*. The Wall Street Journal, 23 Aug. 2013. Web. 9 Mar. 2015.

Greenwald, Glenn. "NSA Collecting Phone Records of Millions of Verizon Customers Daily." *theguardian.com*. The Guardian, 6 Jun 2013. Web. 9 Mar. 2015.

Meyer, David. "A Year into the Snowden Leaks, Here's Something Useful We Can All Do." *gigaom.com*. 5 Jun. 2014. Web. 9 Mar. 2015.

Neal, Meghan. "You'll Never Guess How Many Terrorist Plots the NSA's Domestic Spy Program Has Foiled." *vice.com*. 13 Jan. 2014. Web. 9 Mar. 2015.

Serwer, Adam. "NSA's Metadata Program 'not essential' to Thwarting Attacks." *msnbc.com*. 18 Dec. 2013. Web. 9 Mar. 2015.

Solove, Daniel. "Why Privacy Matters Even if You Have 'Nothing to Hide.'" *thechronicle.com*. The Chronicle of Higher Education, 15 May 2011. Web. 9 Mar. 2015.

Watts, Jonathan. "NSA Accused of Spying on Brazilian Oil Company Petrobras." *theguardian.com*. The Guardian, 9 Sep. 2013. Web. 9 Mar. 2015.

Timberg, Craig. "NSA Paying U.S. Companies for Access to Communications Net works." *washingtonpost.com*. The Washington Post, 19 Aug. 2013. Web. 9 Mar. 2015.

Reflections and Inquiries

1. What are Cotter's principal concerns about NSAs surveillance tactics?

2. Based on what you learn from your own research about Edward Snowden, argue whether or not Cotter's characterization of Snowden's whistleblowing actions are warranted.

3. How would you characterize Cotter's argumentative strategies— Aristotelian? Rogerian? Could he have been more persuasive in his premise? If so, how?

4. How convincing is Cotter's refutation of the "nothing to hide" rationale for increased surveillance?

5. Do you agree with Cotter that NSA tactics are Big-Brother-like, and that America could become the kind of dystopia Orwell depicts in his novel *Nineteen Eighty-Four*?

Reading to Write

How should America draw the line between surveillance for security and surveillance that jeopardizes an individual's (or a group's) right to privacy? Write a position paper in which you give equal attention to both the security and the privacy sides of the issue.

Connections Among the Clusters

Issues of globalization inevitably give rise to other issues that affect society such as educational reform, access to health care, and media access.

Critical Thinking

1. To what extent do issues of globalization or immigration affect issues relating to multicultural learning? (See Cluster 4.)

2. Can we draw the line between necessary and unwarranted kinds of speech censorship (see Cluster 5) for purposes of international cooperation? Explain.

3. Consider the influence of globalization on scientific research generally, or biomedical research specifically. (Review the material in Cluster 6.)

4. How might media regulation, especially regulation of the Internet, be enhanced or restricted as a result of globalization? (See Cluster 5.)

Writing Projects

1. Write an essay in which you explore the role ethics should (or should not) play in developing an effective national security policy.

2. What kinds of international trade would be most affected (for better or worse, in your opinion) by changes in U.S. immigration policy? Be sure to weigh the strengths and shortcomings of challenging views in developing your paper.

3. Using Classical/Aristotelian, Toulmin, or Rogerian methods of argument, propose—and establish a rationale for—a national security policy for a nation known to possess (or suspected of possessing) nuclear materials (for example, North Korea, Iran, or Pakistan).

4. Propose changes to your college's core curriculum in light of issues raised by globalization. For example, what kinds of language, ethnic studies, or ethics courses ought to be required of all undergraduates, and why?

5. Take a stance on how individual privacy should best be protected, if at all, in the context of contemporary methods of information flow and online social networking via such sites as Facebook and LinkedIn. Note that that their privacy settings can be modified by users but that the privacy policies for such sites occasionally change, as users know.

Suggestions for Further Reading

Calomiris, Charles W., and Stephen H. Haber. *Fragile by Design: The Political Origins of Banking Crises and Scarce Credit.* Princeton: Princeton University Press, 2014.

Catan, Thomas. "Myth and Reality about the Euro Crisis." *Wall Street Journal,* Dec. 9, 2011. Web.

Cole, David, et al. *Terrorism and the Constitution: Sacrificing Civil Liberties in the Name of National Security.* New York: New Press, 2002. Print.

Diffie, Whitfield, and Susan Landau, *Privacy on the Line: The Politics of Wiretapping.* Cambridge: MIT Press, 1998. Print.

Friedman, Thomas L. *The Lexus and the Olive Tree: Understanding Globalization.* New York: Farrar, Straus and Giroux, 1999. Print.

Friedman, Thomas L. *The World Is Flat 3.0: A Brief History of the Twenty-First Century.* New York: Picador, 2007.

Gonzales, Alberto R., and David N. Strange. *A Conservative and Compassionate Approach to Immigration Reform: Perspectives from a Former U.S. Attorney General.* Lubbock: Texas Tech University Press, 2014.

Gray, Colin S., *National Security Dilemmas: Challenges and Opportunities.* Herndon, VA: Potomac Books, 2009.

Grewal, David Singh. *Network Power: The Social Dynamics of Globalization.* New Haven: Yale University Press, 2009. Print.

Kulish, Nicholas, "Central Bank becomes an Unlikely Hero in Euro Crisis." *New York Times*, Jan. 20, 2012. Web.

Mayer, Jane. *The Dark Side: The Inside Story of How the War on Terror Turned into a War on American Ideals*. New York: Anchor Books, 2008. Print.

Pisari-Ferry, Jean. *The Euro Crisis and Its Aftermath*. Oxford: Oxford University Press, 2014.

Rothkopf, David J. *Running the World: The Inside Story of the National Security Council and the Architects of American Power*. New York: Public Affairs, 2005. Print.

Schwab, William A., and G. David Gearhart. *The Right to DREAM: Immigration Reform and America's Future*. Fayetteville: University of Arkansas Press, 2013.

4

Multicultural Learning: What Are the Priorities?

Introduction

Ideas about education, like ideas about religion and politics, tend to be categorized as "conservative" or "liberal." Thus stereotyped, they tend to become oversimplified as well. While it is true that to be conservative generally means to find value in traditional practices and that to be liberal generally means to be willing to change existing practices in light of changing values and circumstances, it does not necessarily follow that one view must exclude the other.

Multiculturalism—the study of the way different cultures and groups interact in a particular context (educational, economic, political)—has shed important light on the possibilities of human progress and cooperation. In education, it has called attention to possible correlations among cultural heritage, sexual orientation, socioeconomic background, and learning; between proficiency in a primary or secondary language and learning; between culturally bound teaching methods and learning.

The following selections address some of the key issues regarding multicultural education: Who, if anyone, benefits from instruction that incorporates multicultural perspectives on language, literature, social studies, and history? What obstacles do minority students continue to face in U.S. schools? What is the relationship between multiculturalism and globalization? What can be done to engage students who have been disenfranchised as a result of cultural, linguistic, or ethnic barriers? Can standardized testing be improved to better meet the needs of minority students?

Bilingual Education

To some, the reasoning is simple: the United States was founded by English speakers; hence, English should be the official national language. To others, however, today the United States reflects and promotes cultural diversity, which includes language diversity. And so the debate continues.

English: The National Language | John Darkow

Many people think English is the official language of the United States, but the United States does not have an official language—nor should it, some will argue, because it is a nation of immigrants, a pluralist society in which many languages are spoken, as John Darkow's cartoon makes dramatically clear. John Darkow is an editorial cartoonist for the Columbia (MO) Daily Tribune.

Reflections and Inquiries

1. What is ironic about Darkow's cartoon?

2. How might the cartoon be altered to reflect support of the English-as-a-national-language movement?

3. Compare Darkow's approach to the issue to Monte Wolverton's in the cartoon on the next page. What aspects of the issue does Wolverton's cartoon allude to that Darkow's does not, and vice versa?

Linguistic Police | Monte Wolverton

Reading to Write

What are the advantages and the disadvantages to making English the official language of the United States? Before arguing your premise, research both sides of the debate.

Bilingual or Immersion? | Kendra Hamilton

To some educators, the question posed by the title of this article is the wrong question to ask about teaching English to nonnative speakers. The real concern is the quality of instruction. Kendra Hamilton, a poet, journalist, and regular contributor to Diverse: Issues in Higher Education, *discusses the efficacy of this point of view in the following article.*

Source: Kendra Hamilton, "Bilingual or Immersion?" *Diverse: Issues in Higher Education* 23.5, April 20, 2006: 23–26, including sidebar, "Six Myths About Bilingual Education." Reprinted with permission from *Diverse: Issues In Higher Education*, www.DiverseEducation.com.

A new group of studies is providing fresh evidence that it's not the language of instruction that counts, but the quality of education.

Eight years ago, Proposition 227 virtually eliminated bilingual education in California's K–12 schools. Since then, the English-only approach has made inroads in states like Arizona and Massachusetts, where ballot initiatives have created even more restrictive "English immersion" programs than California's. In Colorado, backers of a failed ballot initiative are trying again, this time with a campaign for a constitutional amendment.

But a group of new studies is providing fresh evidence of what many researchers have been saying all along: English immersion has more political appeal than educational merit.

"We're saying it's not possible given the data available to definitively answer the question 'which is better—bilingual or immersion?'" says Dr. Amy Merickel, co-author of "Effects of the Implementation of Proposition 227 on the Education of English Learners K–12." The five-year, $2.5 million study was conducted for the state of California by the American Institutes for Research and WestEd.

"We don't see conclusive evidence that bilingual education is superior to English immersion, and we don't see conclusive evidence for the reverse," Merickel says. "We think it's the wrong question. It's not the model of instruction that matters—it's the quality."

5   Dr. Tim Shanahan, professor of curriculum and instruction at the University of Illinois–Chicago and director of its Center for Literacy, agrees. Shanahan and a team of more than a dozen researchers from institutions across the nation recently completed a synthesis of all the available research on literacy, including second language literacy for the U.S. Department of Education.

"When we looked at all the past attempts to get at this issue and analyzed their data, essentially what we concluded was that, in fact, kids did somewhat better if they received some amount of instruction in their home language," Shanahan says. "How much? It was not clear from the available data. What should it look like? That wasn't entirely clear either. But across the board, the impact of some instruction in home language seemed to be beneficial."

"But one of the things that surprised me and that stood out for me was the sheer volume of the research that was not devoted to these issues," he adds. "If you look at the data, most of the research is on [which] language of instruction [is better]. That issue has so sucked up all the oxygen that all those other issues of quality clearly are being neglected."

Such conclusions run sharply counter to the assertions of many defenders of English immersion. In 1997, millionaire Ron Unz began a campaign against bilingual education, forming an advocacy organization with a simple name and message—English for the Children. That organization helped push Proposition 227 to a landslide victory in California, claiming 61 percent of the vote.

Two years later, citing dramatic gains on test scores for immigrant children, the English for the Children movement moved to Arizona, where Proposition 203 notched 63 percent of the vote. In 2002, Massachusetts followed suit with Question 2, which was passed with 70 percent support. But in Colorado, voters rejected the English-immersion philosophy, turning it down 55 percent to 44 percent at the polls.

But the movement began to fizzle after 2002. The offices of English for the Children have closed, and studies have consistently been punching holes in core tenets of the English-only argument.

First to fall were the "dramatic gains" in test scores. Proponents of English-immersion stated emphatically that test scores for immigrant students had shot up 40 percent between 1998 and 2000. But research teams from Stanford University, Arizona State University and others pointed out that scores had risen for all students during that period. They also noted that the rising test scores were due to the fact that California had introduced a new achievement test and not to the effects of Prop 227. *10*

More damning was the failure of Prop 227 to hold up its central promise. English for the Children had repeatedly claimed that results could be achieved with only a one-year transition period for English learners.

"The one-year limit is a fantasy," says Dr. Stephen Krashen, professor emeritus at the University of Southern California's Rossier School of Education. "In California and Arizona, English learners are currently gaining less than one level per year out of five, where level five means 'ready for the mainstream.'"

"That means that a child starting with no English will take at least five years before 'transitioning.' In Massachusetts, after three years of study, only half of the English learners are eligible to be considered for regular instruction," he says.

Merickel's AIR/WestEd research team noted several exemplary programs during the course of their study. Some of the programs were bilingual, others were English immersion and some were "dual immersion"—providing instruction in both Spanish and English.

Prop 227 has actually been a useful tool, she says, for forcing the state to focus much-needed attention on the non-English speaking population. Some former foes of the proposition, she says, "have come to see it as a positive thing." *15*

But Shelly Spiegel-Coleman, president of Californians Together, an advocacy coalition formed in 1998, isn't willing to go so far.

"The truth is Prop 227 was a horrible blow for us, but if that was all that happened to us since 1998, we could have galvanized attention, made our points" and worked to ease the law's most restrictive elements, she says.

But Prop 227 was the first of a wave of reform movements, each more restrictive than its predecessor. First came a flurry of one-size-fits-all, skill-based reading programs, crafted to meet the curricular needs specified in Prop. 227.

"They allow no accommodation for non-native speakers, and they're sweeping the country," Spiegel-Coleman says.

20   And then there are the harsh accountability systems mandated by No Child Left Behind.

"There are these people who have so much invested in these English-only reading programs and accountability systems who do not want to admit that what they're doing is wrong for kids," Spiegel-Coleman says.

Indeed, the stakes in these political battles over education could not be higher. According to U.S. Census figures, the number of children living in homes where English is not the primary language more than doubled from 1979 to 1999, from 6 million to 14 million. California was home to more than 1.4 million English learners—or nearly 40 percent of all such public school students in the nation (excluding Puerto Rico).

These "language minority" students face formidable obstacles in school, according to the National Center for Education Statistics. The dropout rate is 31 percent for language minority children who speak English, compared with 51 percent for language minority kids who do not and only 10 percent for the general population.

"At some point," says Shanahan, "we better get serious about immigration, about integrating immigrants as productive, tax-paying and social security-supporting parts of our work force. To do these things, they have to be able to do the work that we do in the United States—that means we have to be making quality choices to provide them with a quality education."

25   But the discussion about quality has only begun, says Shanahan, noting that his review found only 17 studies concerned with educational quality, compared with more than 450 studies examining types of reading programs.

Meanwhile the discussion about the language of instruction—a discussion Shanahan says is deeply political—seems never-ending.

Six Myths About Bilingual Education

Myth 1: Bilingual programs are mostly concerned with maintaining the ethnic culture of the family.

Response: While some bilingual programs encourage development of a student's native language after English has been mastered, the major goal of bilingual education is the rapid acquisition of English and mastery of academic subjects.

Myth 2: Bilingual education doesn't work; it prevents children from acquiring English.

Response: Scientific studies consistently show that children in bilingual programs typically score higher on tests of English than do children in all-English immersion programs. In fact, three major reviews coming to this conclusion were published last year in professional, scientific journals.

Myth 3: Children languish in bilingual programs for many years, never learning enough English to study in mainstream classes.

Response: According to a recent report from New York City for children entering school at kindergarten and grade 1, only 14 percent were still in bilingual education after six years. From data provided by the state of Texas, I have estimated that for those who started at kindergarten, only 7 percent were still in bilingual education after grade 5.

Most students in bilingual programs in upper grades are those who came to the United States at an older age. These late-comers face a daunting task: Many come with inadequate preparation in their country of origin, and need to acquire English as well as assimilate years of subject matter knowledge.

Myth 4: Bilingual programs teach only in the native language.

Response: Some critics have claimed that bilingual education requires that children spend five to seven years mastering their native language before they can learn English. This is not correct. In properly organized bilingual programs, English is introduced immediately. ESL [English as a Second Language instruction] begins from the first day, and subjects are taught in English as soon as they can be made comprehensible. Research confirms that English is not delayed by bilingual education. According to one study of bilingual programs, by the time children are in third grade, 75 percent of their subject matter is in English, and it is 90 percent by grade 5.

Myth 5: Immigrants, especially Spanish-speakers, are refusing to learn English.

Response: They aren't refusing to learn English. According to the most recent census, only 7 percent of those who said another language was spoken at home cannot speak English. These figures include newcomers. Census data also tells us that Spanish speakers are acquiring English at the same rate as other groups.

Spanish speakers born in the United States report that they speak, read, and write English better than they do Spanish by the time they finish high school. One does, of course, occasionally run into immigrants who don't speak English. These are usually new arrivals, or those who have not been able to find the time or opportunity to acquire English.

Myth 6: Bilingual education is not done in other countries, only in the United States.

Response: Bilingual education is not the most widely used approach for children acquiring a second language, but it is widespread. Most European countries provide bilingual education for immigrant children, and studies done by European scholars show that children in these programs acquire the second language of the country as well as and usually better than those in "immersion" programs. There are also numerous programs for the languages spoken by indigenous minority communities. No member of the European Economic Community has passed the equivalent of California's Proposition 227.

Source: Dr. Stephen Krashen, Professor Emeritus, Rossier School of Education, University of Southern California.

Reflections and Inquiries

1. What was faulty about the "dramatic gains in test scores" initially reported by the English for the Children group (immersion advocates)?

2. What caused the failure of California's Prop 227?

3. Despite the fact that researchers are uncertain about the superiority of one mode of English instruction over another, the "Six Myths About Bilingual Education" Hamilton appended to her essay reveals her stance on the matter. How convincingly do her responses to the "myths" support the idea that bilingual education is the best approach?

Reading to Write

After reviewing current research in scholarly education journals such as the *International Journal of Bilingual Education and Bilingualism*, and perhaps interviewing students who have taken bilingual or immersion classes, write an essay discussing what would constitute "quality" in teaching English to nonnative speakers.

Two Languages Are Better Than One	Wayne P. Thomas and Virginia P. Collier

Some educators argue that bilingual education fails because teachers cannot properly teach students to be experts in the language of instruction while simultaneously learning the subject of instruction. But Wayne P. Thomas and Virginia P. Collier set out to prove that thesis wrong. According to these educators, students serve as peer tutors for each other and are able to stimulate natural language acquisition because they keep the level of interaction intellectually stimulating. Thomas is professor of research and evaluation methods at George Mason University. Collier is professor of bilingual, multicultural, and ESL education at George Mason University. Both authors are researchers with the U.S. Department of Education's Center for Research on Education, Diversity, and Excellence.

Among the underachieving youth in U.S. schools, students with no proficiency in English must overcome enormous equity gaps, school achievement tests in English show. Over the past three decades, schools have developed a wide range of programs to serve these English learners. After much experimentation, U.S. schools now have

Source: "Two Languages Are Better Than One," by Wayne P. Thomas & Virginia P. Collier (1997/1998), *Educational Leadership* 55(4), pp. 23–26. ©1997 by ASCD. Reprinted with permission. Learn more about ASCD at www.ascd.org.

clear achievement data that point to the most powerful models of effective schooling for English learners. What is astounding is that these same programs are also dynamic models for school reform for all students.

Imagine how the 21st century will look. Our world will surely be in constant change, for we are facing this pattern now. The predictions of the near future also depict an interconnected world, with global travel and instant international communications. Right now, many U.S. businesses seek employees proficient in both English and another language. Students who graduate with monocultural perspectives will not be prepared to contribute to their societies, for cross-cultural contact is at an all-time high in human history as population mobility continues throughout the world (Cummins in Ovando and Collier 1998). Thus, majority and minority language students together must prepare for a constantly changing world.

Tapping the Power of Linguistic Diversity

For more than three decades, as we have struggled to develop effective models for schooling English learners, we have mostly considered the choices available to us from a deficit perspective. That is, we have often viewed English learners as a "problem" for our schools (oh, no—they don't know English), and so we "remediate" by sending them to a specialist to be "fixed." In the remedial program, English learners receive less access to the standard grade-level curriculum. The achievement and equity gap increases as native English speakers forge ahead while English learners make less progress. Thus, underachieving groups continue to underachieve in the next generation.

Unfortunately, the two most common types of U.S. school services provided for English learners—English as a Second Language (ESL) pullout and transitional bilingual education—are remedial in nature. Participating students and teachers suffer often from the social consequences of this perception. But when the focus of any special school program is on academic enrichment for all students, the school community perceives that program positively, and students become academically successful and deeply engaged in the learning process. Thus, enrichment programs for English learners are extremely effective when they are intellectually challenging and use students' linguistic and cultural experiences as a resource for interdisciplinary, discovery learning (Chiang 1994, Ovando and Collier 1998, Thomas and Collier 1997). Further, educators who use the enrichment models that were initially developed for English learners are beginning to see the power of these models for *all* students.

A History of Bilingual Enrichment

These innovative enrichment models are called by varying names—*dual language, bilingual immersion, two-way bilingual,* and *developmental bilingual education.* We recommend these models as forms of mainstream education through two languages that will benefit all students. Let's examine the history of their development and some basic characteristics of these models.

Initially, the first two 20th-century experiments with bilingual education in the United States and Canada in the early 1960s came about as a result of parental pressure. Both of these experiments were enrichment models. In Canada, English-speaking parents who wanted their children to develop in both French and English initiated what became known as immersion education. Immersion is a commitment to bilingual schooling throughout grades K–12 in which students are instructed 90 percent of the school day during kindergarten and grade 1 in the *minority* language chosen for the program, and 10 percent of the day in the majority language (English). The hands-on nature of academic work in the early grades is a natural vehicle for proficiency development of the minority language.

Immersion programs emphasize the less dominant language more than English in the first years, because the minority language is less supported by the broader society, and academic uses of the language are less easily acquired outside school. Gradually, with each subsequent grade, the program provides more instruction in the majority language until children learn the curriculum equally through both languages by grade 4 or 5. By grade 6, students have generally developed deep academic proficiency in both languages, and they can work on math, science, social studies, and language arts at or above grade level in *either* language. From the 1960s to the 1990s, immersion bilingual schooling has grown immensely popular in Canada and has achieved high rates of success with majority and minority students, students of middle- and low-income families, as well as students with learning disabilities (Cummins and Swain 1986, Genesee 1987).

About the same time that the first immersion program started in Canada, Cubans arriving in Miami, Florida, initiated the first U.S. experiment with two-way bilingual education in 1963. The term *two-way* refers to two language groups acquiring the curriculum through each other's languages; *one-way* bilingual education refers to one language group receiving schooling through two languages (Stern 1963). Intent on overthrowing Fidel Castro and returning to their country, the Cuban arrivals established private bilingual schools to develop their children's English and maintain their Spanish. The public schools, losing significant enrollment, chose to develop bilingual classes to attract students back. As English-speaking parents enrolled their children in the classes, two-way, integrated bilingual schooling emerged as a new program model in the United States. These classes provided a half day of the grade-level curriculum in Spanish and a half day in English, now known as the 50–50 model of two-way.

Over time, these two experiments have expanded to many states in the United States as school communities recognize the benefits for all students. The immersion model, originally developed in Canada for majority language speakers, has become known as the *90–10* two-way model in the United States because during the first two years both language groups receive 90 percent of the instruction through the *minority* language.

Students as Peer Language Models

Key to the success of all two-way programs is the fact that both language groups   10
stay together throughout the school day, serving as peer tutors for each other.
Peer models stimulate natural language acquisition for both groups because
they keep the level of interaction cognitively complex (Panfil 1995). Research has
consistently demonstrated that academic achievement is very high for all groups
of participants compared to control groups who receive schooling only through
English. This holds true for students of low socioeconomic status, as well as
African-American students and language-minority students, with those in the
90–10 model achieving even higher than those in the 50–50 model (Lindholm
1990, Lindholm and Aclan 1991, Thomas and Collier 1997).

The Role of Careful Planning

What are other essential characteristics of this school reform? An important
principle is clear curricular separation of the two languages of instruction. To
maintain a continuous cognitive challenge, teachers do not repeat or translate
lessons in the second language, but reinforce concepts taught in one language
across the two languages in a spiraling curriculum. Teachers alternate the language of instruction by theme or subject area, by time of day, by day of the
week, or by the week. If two teachers are teaming, each teacher represents one
language. When two teachers share and exchange two classes, this is a cost-
effective, mainstream model that adds no additional teachers to a school system's budget. In contrast, ESL pullout is the most costly of all program models
for English learners because extra ESL resource teachers must be added to the
mainstream staff (Crawford 1997).

Successful two-way bilingual education includes

- a minimum of six years of bilingual instruction;
- focus on the core academic curriculum rather than on a watered-down version;
- quality language arts instruction in both languages;
- separation of the two languages for instruction;
- use of the non-English language for at least 50 percent of the instructional time and as much as 90 percent in the early grades;
- an additive bilingual environment that has full support of school administrators;
- a balanced ratio of students who speak each language (for example, 50–50 or 60–40, preferably not to go below 70–30);
- promotion of positive interdependence among peers and between teachers and students;
- high-quality instructional personnel; and
- active parent-school partnerships (Lindholm 1990).

Demographics influence the feasibility of two-way programs, because the students in each language group serve as peer teachers for each other. A natural choice for many U.S. schools is a Spanish-English two-way program, because Spanish speakers are most often the largest language group. In the 204 two-way bilingual schools identified in the United States in a 1997 survey, other languages of instruction in addition to Spanish include, in order of frequency, Korean, French, Cantonese, Navajo, Japanese, Arabic, Portuguese, Russian, and Mandarin Chinese (Montone et al. 1997).

Closing the Equity Gap Through Bilingual Enrichment

What makes these programs work? To answer this question, let's look at the students who are initially the lowest achievers on tests in English. Most school policymakers commonly assume that students need only a couple of years to learn a second language. But while these students make dramatic progress in English development in the first two years, English language learners are competing with a moving target, the native English speaker, when tested in English.

15   The average native English speaker typically gains 10 months of academic growth in one 10-month school year in English development because first language acquisition is a natural work in progress throughout the school years, not completed until young adulthood. Although some score higher and some lower, on average they also make a year's progress in a year's time in mathematics, science, and social studies. Thus students not yet proficient in English initially score three or more years below grade level on the tests in English because they cannot yet demonstrate in their second language all that they actually know. These students must outgain the native speaker by making one and one-half years progress on the academic tests in their second language for each of six successive school years (a total of nine years progress in six years) to reach the typical performance level of the constantly advancing native English speaker.

When students do academic work in their primary language for more than two to three years (the typical support time in a transitional bilingual program), they are able to demonstrate with each succeeding year that they are making more gains than the native English speaker—and closing the gap in achievement as measured by tests in English across the curriculum. After five to six years of enrichment bilingual schooling, former English learners (now proficient in English) are able to demonstrate their deep knowledge on the academic tests in English across the curriculum, as well as in their native language, achieving on or above grade level (Thomas and Collier 1997).

Bridging the Gap to a Better Tomorrow

Why is such progress for English learners important for our schools? Language-minority students are predicted to account for about 40 percent of the school-age population by the 2030s (Berliner and Biddle 1995). It is in our pragmatic self-interest to ensure their success as young adults, for they will be key to a robust economy to pay retirement and medical benefits for today's working adults. We must close the equity gap by providing enrichment schooling for all. For native English speakers as well as language-minority students, the enrichment bilingual classes appear to provide a constant stimulus and intellectual challenge similar to that of a gifted and talented class. The research evidence is overwhelmingly clear that *proficient* bilinguals outperform monolinguals on school tests (Collier 1995). Crossing cultural, social class, and language boundaries, students in a bilingual class develop multiple ways of solving human problems and approach ecological and social science issues from a cross-national perspective. These learners acquire deep academic proficiency in two languages, which becomes a valuable resource in adult professional life. And they learn to value each other's knowledge and life experiences—leading to meaningful respect and collaboration that lasts a lifetime.

References

Berliner, D. C., and B. J. Biddle. (1995). *The Manufactured Crisis: Myths, Fraud, and the Attack on America's Public Schools.* Reading, Mass.: Addison Wesley.

Chiang, R. A. (1994). "Recognizing Strengths and Needs of All Bilingual Learners: A Bilingual/Multicultural Perspective." *NABE News* 17 4: 11, 22–23.

Collier, V. P. (1995). *Promoting Academic Success for ESL Students: Understanding Second Language Acquisition for School.* Elizabeth: New Jersey Teachers of English to Speakers of Other Languages-Bilingual Educators.

Crawford, J. (1997). *Best Evidence: Research Foundations of the Bilingual Education Act.* Washington, D.C.: National Clearinghouse for Bilingual Education.

Cummins, J., and M. Swain. (1986). *Bilingualism in Education.* New York: Longman.

Genesee, F. (1987). *Learning Through Two Languages: Studies of Immersion and Bilingual Education.* Cambridge, Mass: Newbury House.

Lindholm, K. J. (1990). "Bilingual Immersion Education: Criteria for Program Development." In *Bilingual Education: Issues and Strategies,* edited by A. M. Padilla, H. H. Fairchild, and C. M. Valadez. Newbury Park, Calif.: Sage.

Lindholm, K. J., and Z. Aclan. (1991). "Bilingual Proficiency as a Bridge to Academic Achievement: Results from Bilingual/Immersion Programs." *Journal of Education* 173: 99–113.

Montrone, C., D. Christian, and A. Whitcher. (1997). *Directory of Two-Way Bilingual Programs in the United States.* Rev. ed. Washington, D.C.: Center for Applied Linguistics.

Ovando, C. J., and V. P. Collier. (1998). *Bilingual and ESL Classrooms: Teaching in Multicultural Contexts.* 2nd ed. New York: McGraw-Hill.

Panfil, K. (1995). "Learning from One Another: A Collaborative Study of a Two-Way Bilingual Program by Insiders with Multiple Perspectives." *Dissertation Abstracts International* 56-10A. 3859 (University Microfilms No. AA196-06004).

Stern, H. H., ed. (1963). *Foreign Languages in Primary Education: The Teaching of Foreign or Second Languages to Younger Children.* Hamburg, Germany: International Studies in Education, UNESCO Institute for Education.

Thomas, W. P., and V. P. Collier. (1997). *School Effectiveness for Language Minority Students.* Washington, D.C.: National Clearinghouse for Bilingual Education.

Reflections and Inquiries

1. What "enormous equity gaps" must students with no English proficiency overcome? What would be the best way to overcome such equity gaps, according to Thomas and Collier?

2. The authors assert that program enrichment rather than the students' learning problems should be the focus of a bilingual education classroom. What is the point of changing emphasis in this manner? How valid is such a change in emphasis, in your opinion?

3. Why do the authors advocate peer-teacher models? How do they work best?

4. What does it mean when the level of peer–student interaction is kept "cognitively complex"? Why is this important?

Reading to Write

Review Thomas and Collier's criteria for "quality instruction" in a successful bilingual education program. Then discuss in a short essay which two or three of these criteria are most important and why.

Point/Counterpoint: Two Student Essays About English as the National Language

Many educators agree that bilingualism is an admirable goal. But the controversy centers on the classroom: should English be the sole language of instruction ("immersion" approach), or should English and Spanish (or another foreign language) be equally used ("bilingual" approach)?

Although both Regina Patzelt, a Santa Clara University junior, and Yung Le, a recent graduate, received bilingual education instruction, their views about the effectiveness of this mode of learning English differ dramatically. Patzelt in "Education in English: The Proven Benefits of a Bilingual Academic Program" argues for bilingual education; Le in "English First" [see following essay] supports an emphasis on English. What conclusions, if any, can you draw about the intrinsic effectiveness of bilingual instruction based on the experiences of these students, both of whom have clearly developed an admirable degree of proficiency in English?

Student Essay

Education in English: The Proven Benefits of a Bilingual Academic Program | Regina Patzelt

[M]ajority and minority language students together must prepare for a constantly changing world.
—Wayne Thomas and Virginia Collier (443)

With the great influx of minorities in the American population in the past fifty years, education for these students as well as majority students has become the foremost concern for upcoming generations. Obviously, the children need to be taught English if they are to achieve any sort of success in this country; however, therein lies the problem of how best to teach English to these nonnative speakers while simultaneously including their cultural heritage in the education of all the students. Although a few methods do this, it has become apparent that bilingual education is the method that is most beneficial not only to the ESL students but to the English-speaking students as well, for the process inherently allows for mastery of language on both sides. In order to teach children English while maintaining their personal culture, schools need to use a program of bilingual education for this is the most successful way to teach English while also achieving an incorporation of minority students' cultures.

Bilingual education is a program that requires various aspects in order for it to be successful. There are two main types of educational programs: 90–10, in which 90 percent of the school day is taught in the minority language and 10 percent in the majority language, usually English, and the 50–50 model wherein the school day is split equally between the two languages. Both programs require certain basic characteristics to work in the academic setting. One of the main ideas is keeping the English and non-English speaking students together in all the classes so they "serve as peer tutors for each other" (Thomas and Collier 445). This way, the students hear the more formal language of the teachers coupled with the informal language of the native speakers, which promotes a greater understanding and learning of the language. Another important part to the program is the planning of where and when to use the languages so that they complement each other and provide "a continuous cognitive challenge" (445) so that they don't repeat lessons and classes in the opposite language but switch between the languages depending on theme and subject matter as well as day to day or week to week (445). Finally, the program only works if implemented early and continued for 6 or more years. The earlier the students start, the easier it is for them to learn a second language, as proven by psychological research. Learning a language before the age of 12 ensures much more efficient learning and better comprehension due to the fact that even one's first language is not fully mastered until the age of 12. Adding another language earlier serves to promote quicker and fuller fluency. The aforementioned aspects constitute the only basic necessities for making two-way educational programs work, for there are also several minor necessary parts. These include such things as support of administration and parents, an almost equal ratio of students who speak the two languages, quality instruction, etc. (446). In general, all these aspects must be combined to create an efficient and successful program.

The other, formerly popular, type of ESL educational program, remedial education, does not work nearly as well as bilingual education and consequently has become much less common. Remedial education is inherently flawed in many ways, beginning with the central premise that it is built on. In this program, children who do not speak English as their first language are seen as "problems" that need to be "remedied," which automatically categorizes these students as inferior. This results in their being seen as negative "issues" that need to be dealt with, when in reality they are just children who happen to be disadvantaged by not knowing the language of the majority. Then, these "problems" are segregated by being placed into separate, special classes where they are supposed to be taught English. However, often there are many problems with their curriculum, as Mike Rose points out in his essay *The Politics of Remediation*. Two minor problems with the curriculum he mentions are a lack of continuity with the lessons he taught and a self-enclosed curriculum that automatically excludes the use of the children's own culture in the exercises such as storytelling. But, as Rose points out, the main problem with the program is that there is no space in the program "to explore the real stuff of literacy" (Rose 673). Because there is so much focus on the very precise, dry, categorical parts of grammar, Rose says that there is a lack of emotion, so the children lose the chance to explore fully the language. Thomas and Collier agree with Rose on this point, saying, "In the remedial program, English learners receive less access to the standard grade-level curriculum" (Thomas and Collier 443–448). All of these problems combined result in an ineffective program and a poor choice for teaching English to students. Additionally, remedial education ignores the diverse cultures of the students, preventing them from making connections between the new ideas and themes in English and their own background.

The strictly "white" approach to teaching English in remedial education programs leads to the ignoring of the cultural heritage of the students. Because of the parameters the program places on the subjects covered, students cannot incorporate familiar aspects of their private life into their learning, an inability that limits their ability to comprehend the subject matter. So the students are forced to forget both their first language as well as most of their cultural familiarities. Yet, the incorporation of their cultural knowledge can supplement the learning of the students and improve their ability to grasp the new concepts. In Leslie Marmon Silko's essay *Language and Literature from a Pueblo Indian Perspective*, she explains the difference between the linear, flat, logical style of English writing and the web-like, interconnected style of Pueblo writing. This difference makes it challenging for Pueblo students to learn English because it is so opposite to the language and writing they are used to. However, she points out how incorporating aspects of Pueblo language in English would benefit the language. It would also probably make it easier for Pueblo students to learn English because they could use their cultural knowledge during the challenging process of learning a new language. This idea that the use of one's own culture in the learning of a new language creates greater and quicker comprehension can extend to students of all cultural backgrounds.

5   Not only are there are numerous benefits to a bilingual educational program, it also solves the problems found in remedial educational programs. First, it addresses the segregation issues associated with remedial education as it places both ESL and non-ESL students in the same classrooms. This placement also solves the problem of excluding other cultures because they are inherently involved in the bilingual curriculum. In this program the students teach each other about both their language and their culture in a two-way

exchange. A second benefit to two-way education is that it solves the predicament of the "moving target" (447), where by the ESL student must compete with the ever-advancing native English speaker who starts out ahead and widens the gap with each passing year. This program starts the students out on equal footing as native speakers from both languages continually mentor each other. This prevents anyone from advancing too quickly as they rely on each other throughout the learning experience. The third advantage to this type of program is that it can be used both ways: English speakers can learn a second language through their ESL peers as the ESL students learn English and teach their language. It ends up being a mutually beneficial situation; the parties involved gain knowledge of another language and culture. Testing statistics have proven the effectiveness of this approach, showing "proficient bilinguals outperform monolinguals on school tests" (Thomas and Collier 447). Overall, research has shown time and again that having fluency in two languages promotes higher achievement in all areas of life, especially academically and occupationally. Truly, bilingual education has shown to have numerous benefits and essentially no disadvantages.

There seems to be only one major disadvantage that opponents bring up, that the program can contribute to the loss of cultural heritage, for the students may forget their past if they are not reminded of it. Rodriguez addresses this point when he laments that he "would have been happier about my public success had I not sometimes recalled what it had been like earlier, when my family had conveyed its intimacy through a set of conveniently private sounds [Spanish]" (Rodriguez 453). Yet he goes on to explain that "loss implies gain" (454) and that by learning English he could "seek the rights and opportunities" (454) that are present in America. So even though he lost some of his culture, he gained a sense of individuality and competency in America. Silko also speaks of this issue and what happens with Native Americans attending English schools by offering a powerful anecdote. In the story, she goes into an English class of Laguna and Acoma Pueblos and asks the students if they know of a particular Pueblo story because storytelling is so fundamental to their culture. She is shocked and pleasantly surprised to discover that most of the students knew of the story, proving "that storytelling continues on" (Silko 416) and displaying that despite their English education the students still were well aware of their heritage. These two authors who have had experience with the bilingual education program show that culture loss is not a great issue with the program.

Overall, it has been proven that bilingual education is one of the most effective ways to teach English to ESL students and to introduce and promote fluency in a second language for native English speakers. Through the various essays, an abundance of evidence and examples proves the success of bilingual education. The world is changing and by the 2030s 40 percent of the school-age population will be language minority students (Thomas and Collier 447); it would be foolish now not to implement more bilingual educational programs. Ignoring the facts and the inevitable increase of minorities in America will only harm the country in the end. It is often said the future lies in the school, and if this is true, we should really try to offer only the best education available to all students. It will benefit the entire American population and prove even more clearly that two-way education is a most effective academic program.

Works Cited

Rodriguez, Richard. "Speaking a Public Language." *The Well-Crafted Argument*. 3rd ed. Ed. Fred D. White and Simone J. Billings. Boston: Houghton Mifflin, 2008. Print.

Rose, Mike. "The Politics of Remediation." *The Well-Crafted Argument*. 2nd ed. Ed. Fred D. White and Simone J. Billings. Boston: Houghton Mifflin, 2005. Print.

Silko, Leslie Marmon. "Language and Literature from a Pueblo Indian Perspective." *The Well-Crafted Argument*. 3rd ed. Ed. Fred D. White and Simone J. Billings. Boston: Houghton Mifflin, 2008. Print.

Thomas, Wayne P., and Virginia Collier, "Two Languages Are Better Than One." *The Well-Crafted Argument*. 3rd ed. Ed. Fred D. White and Simone J. Billings. Boston: Houghton Mifflin, 2008. Print.

Student Essay

English First | Yung Le

Bilingual education prevents one from learning English. English is arguably the hardest language to learn; even native English speakers struggle with it. Like all languages, English involves continually learning new vocabularies and usage: each new subject is a discovery of the English language. The U.S. public school system, especially on the elementary level, should not stunt the development of a student's English by teaching a bilingual curriculum. Students and their respective families who wish to foster their native language should do so outside of the education system or as an elective.

By no means am I implying that all languages besides English are inferior or that I do not see value in learning a native language or any other languages for that matter. I myself am bilingual without the bilingual education. I do not credit elementary bilingual education for learning another language; I credit my family, outside classes, and foreign language classes throughout high school and college. However, I do credit my English-only education system for learning English, for being able to communicate in all its entailments, and for developing and honing my English throughout my education. My English skills would have never been acquired had I been allowed to use my native language as a handicap in learning and communicating in English at the same level as a native English speaker.

English-only instruction stresses the importance of English skills in a society that is predominately English speaking. The school system, at least at the elementary level, should not compromise developing English skills by teaching curriculum in another language. If another language is taught, a student will not develop either of the languages fully. For instance, if social studies is taught in Spanish instead of English, students will not learn new ideas and words associated with that subject in English—missing pertinent English language development. In essence, a bilingual education system consisting of 50 percent English and 50 percent Spanish (for example) will only be teaching its students 50 percent of the content and ideas in English. Rather than being adept in one language, students are inept in two.

In elementary school we learn to be adept in English so we can develop our public persona and communicate effectively in society. This development happens regardless of the subjects taught: math, science, or history. Students just entering school have yet to develop their rudimentary English skills, or even their native language. It is unfair to compromise the learning of English—one of the purposes of going to school—to try to accomplish another goal that can be done outside or as an elective. Why should the school system attempt to develop multiple personas when it has a hard time developing one effective persona?

In his autobiography, *Hunger of Memory*, Richard Rodriguez, the son of a   5
Mexican immigrant worker, supports English-only instruction in American schools. He asserts that English-only instruction allowed the development of his public identity: "how long could I have afforded to delay [speaking English]?—learning the great lesson of school, that I had a public identity" (449). Sure, teaching in the student's native language would've made the transition easier, but it would've slowed down the English learning process. As Rodriguez says, "it would have pleased me to hear my teacher address me in Spanish.... I would have felt much less afraid.... But I would have delayed—for how long postponed?—having to learn the language of public society" (449). From English-only instruction Rodriguez understood the importance of learning English, as all elementary students in the United States need to understand and learn. It is not the school system's concern to worry about a private persona, or any other persona, when one persona is yet to be fully developed. The underdevelopment of English is demonstrated by low English literacy in the United States.

Statistics show that students do not understand English at their level. "A stunning 40 percent of America's 4th graders continue to read below the basic level on national reading assessments" (http://www.edu-cyberpg.com). Why is the school system going to confuse students further by mixing in another language? The literacy rate in the United States is astoundingly low: according to the Children's Literacy Foundation, "one in five American children grows up functionally illiterate" and "three out of four American school children do not have the knowledge or skills needed to write stories and reports proficiently" (http://www.clifonline.org). Shouldn't we focus on trying to teach successfully English to our kids before we insist that they learn another language? In the United States high school students are now required to pass an exit exam—consisting of reading and writing—in order to graduate. How is learning a foreign language in conjunction with English a foundation to passing the exit exam?

The elementary foundation is shaken up further as bilingual education confuses not only the students but also the school system. How is the school system supposed to decide on what language to teach in addition to English? Majority vote? The second most popular language based on demographics? What will happen if the population is split between Spanish and Chinese speakers? The United States is a melting pot of different cultures and ethnicity; in one school district we can find a whole array of languages: who's going to decide which language is more important? If a school decides that Spanish will be the second language, is a Chinese native speaker supposed to learn Spanish, English, and the native language that he or she speaks at home? In essence, the student will be immersed in three different languages—none of which the student knows fluently. Now that's confusing. Imagine the difficulties in crossing over pronunciations, sound, and tone. Even I have to remind myself to make the "th" sound in "the" instead of "duh," and I had an English-only elementary education.

In addition, there are so many opportunities to learn another language at any age or level of learning. Implementing a mandatory bilingual education in elementary schools is counterproductive and unnecessary. Students who wish to master language other than English can take extra classes, such as Saturday school (which I did) or as a school elective. Sure, the students may not develop the other language to the same level as English; but can you really develop another language at the same level as English, when we live in an English-speaking society? For those who want to immerse themselves into a foreign language, there are many opportunities. Students can travel in the summer, take required foreign language classes in high school and college, study abroad, or even go on field trips to areas such as Chinatown or Little Italy. There is no reason to sacrifice pivotal English learning, regardless of subject, when students are able to pursue a foreign language on their own time.

So please, if you're thinking of voting for bilingual education in elementary schools, don't. If you're thinking you're doing bilingual students like me a favor, you're not. If you're worried that not learning another language will give your children less of a competitive edge, don't. There are so many opportunities to learn a foreign language outside an English-only curriculum. Statistics show that our future generations aren't learning English proficiently. We don't need to add another language. We need more qualified teachers and English assistance so students can fully learn the language of English and can effectively communicate their beliefs.

Works Cited

Ellis, Karen. "Educational CyberPlayGround." *Edu-cyberg.com*. 1996. Web. 8 June 2006.
Rodriguez, Richard. "Speaking a Public Language." *The Well-Crafted Argument*. 3rd ed. Ed. Fred D. White and Simone J. Billings. Boston: Houghton Mifflin, 2008. 449–454. Print.
"Statistics on Children's Literacy." *Clifonline.org*. Web. 8 June 2006.

Reflections and Inquiries

1. Summarize Patzelt's and Le's respective viewpoints regarding bilingual education. Is one student's evidence supporting her view more convincing than the other's? Explain.

2. How useful is the information Le provides about her family background?

3. Comment on each student's use of outside sources in supporting their views.

Reading to Write

Contact several students who have studied English as a second language and see if you can determine the extent to which non-classroom language experiences have contributed to their mastery of English. Use your findings in an essay to support your views on the influence of non-classroom language experience on developing English proficiency.

Issues for Further Research: Who, If Anyone, Benefits from Multicultural Education?

How exactly is ethnic diversity beneficial to education? The following selections address that issue.

Family Tree | Signe Wilkinson

Study-abroad programs are a splendid enhancement to any undergraduate education, a way of immersing students in a new culture and often in a new language in the process of being mastered. Of course, there is always the temptation of forgetting about the "studies" aspect of the learning experience abroad—or even before going abroad, as Signe Wilkinson humorously reminds us in the following comic strip.

Reflections and Inquiries

1. Comment on the irony underlying Ingrid's plan to aim for a *lower* grade in Spanish as a means of persuading her parents to finance her studies abroad. Is Wilkinson indirectly commenting on parental resistance to finance such a project for their son or daughter? What might be their underlying reasons for such resistance?

2. Compare Ingrid's attitude with that of most students in study-abroad programs, including your own. What really motivates most students to participate in such programs? What about you?

Reading to Write

1. Conduct a survey of student performance in study-abroad programs, before and after. How do such programs contribute to gaining insight into a different culture? To enhancing one's classroom performance?

2. What is the true purpose behind study-abroad programs? Argue your premise in a four- to five-page analysis.

17 Scary Stats on Minority Education in America | Online Colleges

Over the past twenty years, online education has become an important alternative for students as well as workplace professionals. Onlinecolleges.net is an information resource designed to help learners make informed decisions about choosing colleges where online courses are offered. Current staff writers include professional educator Jill Rooney, PhD, and Anna Schumann, a cum laude graduate from Texas Tech University. In the following piece, Rooney and Schumann have gathered together persistent problems that minority students face in high schools and colleges around the country, problems that could help them decide whether online education might serve them better.

Although the past century witnessed swelling educational opportunities for America's minority students, a history of unjust marginalization means serious work still needs doing. Even today. While many issues associated with minority schooling enjoy steady improvements deserving accolades, that doesn't lessen the imperative to constantly strive towards equality anyway. The following statistics, by no means comprehensive, illustrate some areas where the education system needs to

Source: Online Colleges, "17 Scary Stats on Minority Education in America." Sept. 19, 2011. Web.

pay serious attention. Administrators, teachers, policymakers, parents and students must all do their part to ensure every American child and teen receives the viable education to which he and/or she is fully entitled.

1. Stereotyping impairs performance

A startling Ohio State University study exploring the effects of racial stereotyping uncovered some very unfortunate truths. Nearly 160 African-American students were asked to write an essay about an average college student, either named "Tyrone" or "Erik," with the implication being that the former is black and the latter white. Those assigned Tyrone scored an average of 4.5 on a standardized test, while Team Erik ended up with 6.2. Although possessing equal academic aptitude, researchers believe prevailing stereotypes negatively impact performance—thus creating an unjust cycle reinforced by students and teachers alike.

2. Hispanic high school students had the highest dropout rate in 2009

The National Center for Educational Statistics shows that 17.6% of Hispanic high school students drop out before completing their diplomas or GEDs. Reasons vary from kid to kid, of course, and do not necessarily denote poor grades or discipline. On a positive note, however, Hispanic dropout rates decline steadily every year, with 2008 seeing 18.3% of the high school population leaving before graduating.

3. Minorities comprise 32% of undergraduate enrollees

Undergraduate enrollment has actually increased among all racial and ethnic demographics, although minorities remain heavily underrepresented on American college campuses. Only 32% of postsecondary students are minorities as of 2004 statistics, but their numbers increase yearly—certainly a positive trend. Between 1976 and 2004, Asians and Pacific Islanders experienced the highest rate of increase, boasting a whopping 461%. So while the number still seems low these days, minorities are definitely catching up on campus and enjoy more opportunities to have their voices heard and heeded.

4. Minorities comprise 25% of graduate enrollees

With increased minority undergraduate enrollment came more representation in graduate programs, though at a slower pace. 2004 statistics showed that 25% of master's and doctoral students were minorities, up from 11% in 1976. The most rampant increase occurred among Hispanics, at 377%. Once again, there's absolutely nothing "scary" about more opportunities and representation in higher education. But the numbers could definitely be higher, especially since more enrollees means more imperative to address diverse needs.

5. Black, non-Hispanic, or Latino students are the most bullied middle and high-school students

Just over 29% of Caucasian students between the ages of 12 and 18 say they've been bullied, with black, non-Hispanic or Latino almost tying them at 29.1%—a negligible difference, really. During the 2008-2009 school year, 45.1% of instances took place "in a hallway or stairwell," followed by 38.4% "in a classroom." Across all demographics, more bullying takes place in 6th grade (39.4%) and are lobbed at students from low-income households (32.3% at the $7,500 to $14,999 level).

6. Nearly 80% of Hispanic 4th graders qualify for free or reduced-price lunch

The statistics—77% only cover public schools, however. And that 77%? That represents the total. A staggering 84% of Hispanic 4th graders in town areas come from homes qualifying them for free or reduced-price lunches, compared to 82% of urban, 70% suburban and 72% rural.

7. Minorities comprise 10.2% of private school principals

In total, of course, as statistics vary rapidly depending on what—if any—denomination owns and operates the schools in question. Seventh-Day Adventist institutions lead the way, with 26.4% minority principals. Administrators of black, non-Hispanic or Latino descent are most prevalent, particularly in Seventh-Day Adventist (17.7%) and Pentecostal (14.7%) schools. They also make up 5.2% of total minority principals. When it comes to private education, more needs doing to ensure minority students and staff alike see their requests properly met.

8. The majority of black and Hispanic students attend high-poverty schools

Statistics from 2005 school year revealed that black and Hispanic students populate high-poverty schools more than any other minority. The National Center for Education Statistics considers "high-poverty schools," which are those with 75% or more attendees receiving free or reduced-price lunches. Forty-eight percent of black and 49% of Hispanic 4th graders hail from such desperately wanting institutions, while Asians and Pacific Islanders are more evenly distributed across economic demographics.

9. Hispanic and black students are less likely to have internet access at home

Because of this, they adapt to classroom technology at a slower pace than their white, Asian and Native American peers. Twenty-six percent of Hispanic and 27% of black students use the internet at home, compared to 58% of Asian and 47% of Native American kids, resulting in a very unfortunate achievement gap. Numbers are improving, of course, but there's still a ways to go before the gulf starts shrinking.

10. Asian and Hispanic students struggle most with speaking English

No matter the grade level, English proves most challenging for Asian and Hispanic students who speak another language at home. The most vulnerable, at 18.8%, are Hispanics in kindergarten through 8th grade, followed by 16.9% of Asians in the same age range. Once the former hits high school, the percentage drops to 14.5%, while the latter only improves its English language skills by .3%. With so many students admitting they grapple with speaking something unfamiliar, schools must find more ways to reach out and help them catch up in a way that doesn't impede their other lessons.

11. Schools with black or Hispanic majorities are more likely to hire underqualified or novice teachers

In fact, 25% of math educators at schools with 50% or more black students do not hold a degree or any other qualifications in the subjects they teach—probably the most egregious example. And once said teachers rack up the experience, they usually flee to more affluent (and white) areas. Such an unfortunate and enduring phenomenon plays a major role in perpetuating, if not outright widening, the achievement gap. Without knowledgeable, experienced and engaged teachers, students in affected schools typically lag behind and never receive the academic opportunities that should be afforded all youngsters.

12. Native American students significantly lag behind on taking AP exams

Although every demographic—including whites—sees more and more students participating in AP exams yearly, those of Native American descent are far less likely to go for it. In 2008, only 7,750 across the States sat down for the intensive tests. Hispanic students boasted the higher turnout, with a turnout of 209,721, and their black peers enjoyed the highest increase over the past decade. The year 1999 saw 31,023 black students show up for AP exams, compared with 108,545 in 2008, meaning their participation improved by 249.9%.

13. More black students repeat grades than any other racial or ethnic demographic

Both genders, too. In 2007, 25.6% of black males and 15.3% of black females between kindergarten and 12th grade had repeated at least one grade. These numbers, though, only reflect the issue as it relates to public school students.

14. More black students receive suspensions and expulsions than any other racial or ethnic demographic

Between 6th and 12th grades, the 2007 school year saw 49.5% of black males and 34.7% of black females reporting that they had received at least one suspension in their academic careers. When it comes to expulsions, 16.6% of males and 8.2% of females said they had been dismissed from school at least once.

15. Hispanic teenagers have the highest pregnancy rate

In 2007, 81.7 out of every 1,000 Hispanic teenage girls gave birth—more than any other race or ethnicity. Across all demographics, however, the numbers are steadily decreasing. This probably has something to do with improved sex education and easier access to necessary birth control devices, though the problem still requires considerable intervention. Especially since popping out babies as a high schooler is all trendy these days.

16. Mixed-race students who never completed high school experience the highest unemployment rate

And the most vulnerable demographic consistently remains those between the ages of 16 and 24. In 2008, a shocking unemployment rate settled at 33.8% of mixed-race individuals within the temporal and educational criteria. Amongst all races, the unemployment rate shrinks in correlation with the level of schooling completed.

17. Native Hawai'ian and Pacific Islander students are more likely to bring a weapon to school

Typically, students of all races' motivations lay far more with self-defense than causing any real trouble. By the 2007 school year, 9.5% of Native Hawai'ian and Pacific Islander high school students admitted to carrying a weapon on campus. Considering 38.5% of them—the highest percentage amongst all racial and ethnic demographics—know drugs are available practically in their classrooms, such measures make perfect sense.

Reflections and Inquiries

1. Which of the seventeen problems seem to you to be most in need of resolving, and why?

2. Try to identify the causes underlying each of these seventeen problems. Which causes are easiest to identify? Which are most difficult?

Reading to Write

Select one of the seventeen problems identified by onlinecolleges.net. Conduct an in-depth inquiry into the origins of the problem, how the problem has been handled by educators (if at all), and what should be the best course of action toward resolving the problem.

Perspectives: Improving Race Relations One Journalism Class at a Time

Breea C. Willingham

Eliminating racial discrimination often seems like an overwhelming challenge, even after more than half a century of civil rights reforms. But according to Breea C. Willingham, a former newspaper reporter and now a journalism professor at St. Bonaventure University in Allegany, New York, one must not overlook the small steps. One of the most important of these small steps is simply to talk about race—but, as Willingham explains in the following article, that is not as simple as it sounds.

I was standing in line in the Dollar Tree store recently when a blonde-haired little girl who looked to be about 5 years old flashed a toothless smile at me. "Hello," she said. "You have a black face. How did you get that black face?"

I'm usually quick with a comeback, but the girl caught me off guard. After pausing for a few minutes I simply replied, "I was born with it just like you were born with your white face."

"Oh," the little girl said, and went about her business.

Imagine that little girl in my classroom 13 years from now. I recognize that little girl in a few of my students. I'm an African-American faculty member on a predominantly White campus in a town where less than 5 percent of the population is minority.

Many of my students are from White suburban communities or small towns, where diversity is not an issue because there is none. For many of them, their first experiences with minorities and discussions about race happen in my classroom. 5

Getting my students to talk about race is challenging, at best, on most days.

And on the days when my students write papers where they call Black people "coloreds" or say the majority of crimes in the United States are committed by Black men, that goal seems more frustrating than attainable.

The biggest challenge for me is figuring out how to use those frustrations as learning tools and examples of precisely why diversity is needed across the curriculum. Just as newsrooms across the nation celebrate Time Out for Diversity and Accuracy once a year, journalism educators need to be reminded why they have to bring these issues to the classroom.

I've always been passionate about issues dealing with race, ethnicity and diversity, and how they relate to the media. I covered these matters as a reporter for the *Times Union* in Albany, and I work hard to incorporate them into my courses.

Source: Breea C. Willingham, "Perspectives: Improving Race Relations One Journalism Class at a Time," *Diverse Online*, September 28, 2006. Reprinted with permission from *Diverse: Issues in Higher Education*, www.DiverseEducation.com.

10   For instance, during an exercise in my "Women, Minorities and the Media" class I drew four columns on the blackboard and labeled each one African-American, Asian American, American Indian or Hispanic. I then asked the students to call out stereotypes for each group.

The students had no problem calling out stereotypes such as "lazy," "like to eat fried chicken" and "can't speak English well." But when I drew a fifth column for White people and asked for the stereotypes, the students were hard pressed to find any. I repeated the exercise asking for positive attributes for each group; the lists for the minorities were considerably shorter.

At the end I asked my students why it was so easy for them to point out the negatives and not the positives. They all blamed the media for portraying negative images of minorities.

I try to teach my students that before they can even begin to report on and write about race-related issues, they have to be willing to talk about them first and confront their prejudices.

Teaching that lesson isn't always easy, and I even became discouraged when I read course evaluations from last fall semester where some students criticized me for talking about diversity too much in class.

15   But then I read one student's paper in the spring semester. "Because of this class I feel better prepared to deal with many social issues and situations, especially race, on a day-to-day basis," the student wrote. I felt an overwhelming sense of satisfaction knowing I at least reached one.

My efforts so far have taught me that adding diversity to the curriculum is more than just adding a new course to the roster, and simply having a "Women, Minorities and the Media" course is not enough.

I'm learning it's more about changing the way students think about and look at diversity issues, and challenging their biases. Professors also need to learn before they can deal with these issues as an educator; they need to acknowledge and challenge their own biases.

Although I have my moments when I feel like I want to give up trying to teach diversity to the next generation of journalists, my passion for the issue won't let me.

And on the days when I feel my efforts are in vain, I remember the advice a colleague recently gave me: "You're the only education some of these students will ever get on race issues. I don't know if that's more frustrating than consoling, but I see it as a legitimate chance for you to make a difference in some of their lives and in the world around you. Yeah, it seems small-scale, but if the world's gonna change, it's going to be one person at a time. At least you're doing some good things to try to initiate that change. Keep at it." And so I do.

Reflections and Inquiries

1. What point does Willingham attempt to convey with her opening anecdote, and how effectively does she convey it? If you had encountered a young child who asked the same question about your skin color, how would you have responded, and why?

2. Reflect on the role that language plays in race relations.

3. What do you suppose contributes to so much misinformation about race?

4. Comment on the teaching methods Willingham uses in her classes. What other methods can you think of that might also work to raise student consciousness about race relations?

5. Discuss this article from the standpoint of the three Aristotelian appeals of ethos, pathos, and logos. You might want to review "Using Appeals in Argument" in Chapter 1.

Reading to Write

After obtaining testimonials from teachers on how they help their students acquire understanding and appreciation of racial diversity, write an essay on what you consider to be the most effective teaching methods, and why. Consider consulting your campus study-abroad office and multicultural center or equivalent to ask whether they have any opinions on this matter.

Student Essay

The Importance of Multicultural Education in Global Society | Chris Garber

In a multicultural society, educators have come to realize, one's social identity cannot be ignored. One's race, cultural heritage, gender, and socioeconomic milieu are fundamental ingredients in acquiring a sense of self. Without finding ways of connecting this sense of self to what one is being taught in the classroom, learning may be impeded. In the following essay, Chris Garber, a first-year business major at Santa Clara University, critiques the arguments against multicultural education and calls attention to its benefits.

People speak as if race is something blacks have, sexual orientation is something gays and lesbians have, gender is something women have, ethnicity is something so called "ethnics" have.... Thus, if persons do not fit "neatly" into the aforementioned categories, they are not acknowledged as sharing group membership in any particular group. Moreover, if they do not openly identify with the above categories, people assume that they do not have any worries about the various identities.
—Henry Louis Gates (Ferguson and Howard-Hamilton 284)

By 2030, educators estimate language-minority students will make up 40 percent of children in school (Thomas and Collier 26). This statistic represents not only the increasing diversity of the population in the United States, but also a pressing need within the educational community to reevaluate its focus. Currently, an entire portion of the school age population does not benefit from the system of education in our country. Since this group grows larger every year, curriculum needs to be adapted to meet the needs of a more diverse group of students.

Although a concrete, universal definition remains elusive, most educators understand that multicultural education is a method of teaching that exposes students to a wide variety of cultures, traditions, and social groups in an attempt to help them better understand how they fit into society. This also includes bilingual education, which seeks to increase students' proficiency in English while at the same time maintaining their connection with their first language. Multicultural education has grown in popularity throughout the past 15 years as student populations have grown increasingly diverse. The need stems from the fact that "traditional student affairs and psychological research historically has excluded or minimized the importance of the individual's social identities (i.e., ethnicity, gender, sexual orientation) and their relationship within individuals' psychological, interpersonal, leadership, and social development" (Ferguson and Howard-Hamilton 293). It is detrimental to assume that a child who does not know English would benefit from the same type of education as a student who has been speaking English his or her entire life. Multicultural education seeks to allow all students to benefit equally from education.

The debate on this issue remains complex, and as a result it is easier to avoid rather than discuss or address. Activists bring up the fearful image of the "melting pot" in argument against multicultural education. In this social model, programs use education to mold the various cultures of America into one homogeneous group deemed socially acceptable by dominant society. This results in the loss of the history and traditions of the many ethnic groups who inhabit our nation. Supporters believe in order to "make it" in society, minority students are forced to abandon their heritage, thus giving up their personal and cultural identities (Nieto 10). They fear that multicultural education will serve only to destroy the cultural differences making each of us unique. Another accusation against multicultural education is it completely undermines the integrity of the history of Western thought and achievement. Critics shrug off multiculturalism as an identity crisis of the minority population which threatens to destroy Western culture (Giroux 505).

In his book, *The Disuniting of America*, Arthur M. Schlessinger states a contrasting argument as he explores the effects of multiculturalization on society. He comes to the conclusion that while cultural diversity promotes human interaction, the overemphasis of these differences leads to conflict. First, it creates a group Schlessinger refers to as the "militants of ethnicity"—people caught up in upholding cultural differences who become alienated from society and instill social unrest. Second, cultural separation results in "balkanization": a disuniting of society that eventually leads to social breakdown on the premise that no one will be able to relate to any cultural group but their own. Schlessinger argues that the only way to achieve social diversity without the fragmentation of society is to create an education system that lifts up cultural differences and teaches tolerance and understanding. Only through a system of multicultural education can people gain the cross-cultural experience necessary to interact in today's international world.

Multicultural education benefits and improves our society. In "Two   5
Languages Are Better than One," Wayne P. Thomas and Virginia P. Collier argue for multicultural education because, "in the remedial program, English learners receive less access to the standard grade-level curriculum. The achievement and equity gap increases as native English speakers forge ahead while English learners make less progress" (23). The current system of education proves culturally inadequate since it widens the gap in student achievement rather than closes it. Our current programs for bilingual education involve either separating English learners from the school population or minimizing their exposure to core material. Both options alienate them from their peers and deny them the education they need and deserve.

In his book *Hunger of Memory*, Richard Rodriguez writes about the changes in his life as a result of bilingual education. He explains that the biggest barrier in the English learner's quest for acceptance in society remains the sense of separation between his or her culture and the American life he or she is pursuing. Rodriguez insists, "full individuality is achieved, paradoxically, by those who are able to consider themselves members of the crowd. Thus it happened for me: Only when I was able to think of myself as an American, no longer an alien in *gringo* society, could I seek the rights and opportunities necessary for full public individuality" (27). An educational program making all members feel like they belong builds a stronger and less fragmented community. Once a sense of public identity is achieved, the individual understands his or her societal role and can better interact with other people. In this way, education represents the pathway to becoming a member of society.

The argument against multicultural education has taken a number of different forms. Henry A. Giroux's essay, "Democracy and the Discourse of Cultural Difference: Towards a Politics of Border Pedagogy," emphasizes one of the more powerful movements by conservative intellectuals who claim multiculturalism works against the entire institution of Western thought. They argue multicultural proponents hold distorted attitudes that emphasize bigotry and prejudice in Western culture rather than its great achievements. Furthermore, they label multiculturalism as a crisis within the value system of American culture that destroys the "common culture" that has resulted from hundreds of years of shared international discovery. Giroux quotes Roger Kimball, who states:

> Implicit in the politicizing mandate of multiculturalism is an attack on the idea of common culture, the idea that, despite our many differences, we hold in common an intellectual, artistic, and moral legacy, descending largely from the Greeks and the Bible, supplemented and modified over centuries by innumerable contributions from diverse lands and peoples. It is this legacy that has given us our science, our political institutions, and the monuments

of artistic and cultural achievement that define us as a civilization. Indeed, it is this legacy, insofar as we live up to it, that preserves us from chaos and barbarism. And it is precisely this legacy that the multiculturalist wishes to dispense with. (519)

Kimball points out that discoveries of people from all nations founded the modern world. Thus, he explains, modern civilization is by definition diverse and emphasizing these differences is unnecessary. Kimball sees multiculturalism replacing the shared identity developed through humankind's achievements. Furthermore, he concludes, the emphasis of cultural differences does not provide common ground, and therefore it dismantles the foundation of modern civilization.

Gloria Anzaldúa, in her book *Borderlands/La Frontera: The New Mestiza*, argues a different point with ramifications similar to Kimball's. She explains that American education forces other cultures to give up their identities for the sake of fitting into popular society. While her ideas place importance on customs and heritage, she does not support multicultural education. She sees it as a method of assimilation diluting the full importance of cultural independence. She explains, "Chicanos and other people of color suffer economically for not acculturating. This voluntary (yet forced) alienation makes for psychological conflict, a kind of dual identity—we don't identify with the Anglo-American cultural values and we don't totally identify with the Mexican cultural values" (43). Anzaldúa claims that forcing outside rules on minority cultures does not draw them in as expected, but rather pushes them away through the destruction of their social identity. As a result, they cannot relate to other social groups and move to the fringes of society. In addition, by losing their cultural identity, they have difficulty if they want to go back to their original beliefs.

10   Both Anzaldúa's and Kimball's ideas assume multicultural education cannot provide the benefits found in either the institution of Western thought or the cultural history of minority populations. Kimball's statement ignores the argument that accepted Western thought ignores the ideas of minorities while claiming to represent the entire population. The argument is not what would happen if multicultural education is widely implemented, but rather what will happen if it is not. Giroux states, "what is at stake is not the defense or repudiation of a common culture, but the creation of a democratic society in which differences are affirmed and interrogated rather than dismissed as essentialist or disruptive" (509). Without a broader education base, our society will not gain the cultural acceptance necessary for the coming age of diversity, and Schlessinger's fear of "balkanization" could become a reality.

Anzaldúa's pessimistic view of multicultural education can be counterargued by Rodriguez, who wrote, "Those middle-class ethnics who scorn assimilation seem to me filled with decadent self-pity, obsessed by the burden of public life. Dangerously, they romanticize public separateness and they trivialize the dilemma of the socially disadvantaged" (27). He explains separatists have become convinced that minorities cannot emerge as members of mainstream society. By citing personal examples, his story argues that one gains personal identity through cultural acceptance and understanding. Further, he states while his family life at home changed as a result of his learning English, "there are two ways a person is individualized" (26). While an individual's private sense and his or her dependence on cultural heritage diminishes with multicultural education, this loss makes the gain of a greater understanding of the self in relation to the rest of the world possible. In the end, the gain results in the forming of a public identity—a sense of belonging within mass society, which Rodriguez claims is essential to being an active member of a community.

For students in the multicultural age of America, English cannot be a second language. It needs to be a tool that, when combined with a student's first language, not only makes the student a part of American society but allows him or her to achieve at a higher level than possible without it. In light of this, there are a number of ways multicultural education could be implemented to best improve each student's experience.

For example, in "Strength Through Cultural Diversity," multicultural expert Ronald Takaki proposes that courses encouraging diversity should be offered at universities to fulfill social science or humanities requirements as core classes. In this way, students would receive diversity education without having to take extra classes or commit more time to study (Heuberger, Gerber, and Anderson 109). Angela D. Ferguson and Mary F. Howard-Hamilton call for a similar solution in their discussion of college diversity but assert that faculty need to reaffirm their commitment to supporting a diverse student population. They also seek the implementation of courses and programs that not only support diversity but also "emphasize the idea of diversity as including multiple identities [and] sensitize students to becoming aware that people do not exist under one identity" (291). This argument seeks not only a broader curriculum base but also seeks programs supporting ethnic students as well as those of different sexual orientations. It reminds us that a classroom experience can cover only so much information and that the variables included in a person's identity are infinite, necessitating personalized support and interaction. Furthermore, Leslie Marmon Silko writes from a Pueblo Indian perspective, a culture based in storytelling. She states, "if you begin to look at the core of the importance of the language and how it fits in with the culture, it is the *story* and the feeling of the story which matters more than what language it's told in" (58). Multicultural education should not emphasize the evident differences in language and customs but rather accentuate the common themes that can be better explored by bringing in diverse works. Commenting on a broad scale, Thomas and Collier see that bilingual education would be beneficial to the entire school age population, not just communities including English learners. "The research evidence is overwhelmingly clear that *proficient* bilinguals outperform monolinguals on school tests" (26). With this in mind, multicultural education represents an improvement on the modern education system not only for minority students but for all. A wide-scale implementation of multicultural and bilingual programs can serve only to enhance the experience of English-speaking students while at the same time rectifying the crime being committed by a system serving only the majority.

It is essential that the American education system keep up with the changing needs of our students. As globalization spreads throughout the modern world, contact and interaction with other cultures will become part of daily life. Students need to be given the tools to allow intercultural relations to take place. This can be accomplished by changing curriculum and implementing programs that broaden the scope of topics covered, as well as enacting bilingual programs to make education more effective for the entire school age population. The result is a student who is not only better educated but ready to critically assess, with an open mind and an open heart, situations involving people from all walks of life.

Works Cited

Anzaldúa, Gloria. "How to Tame a Wild Tongue." *Ways of Reading: An Anthology for Writers.* Ed. David Bartholomae and Anthony Petrosky. 5th ed. Boston: Bedford, 1999. 36–45. Print.

Ferguson, Angela D., and Mary F. Howard-Hamilton. "Addressing Issues of Multiple Identities for Women of Color on College Campuses." *Toward Acceptance: Sexual Orientation Issues on Campus.* Ed. Vernon A. Wall and Nancy J. Evans. Lanham: UP of America, 2000. 283–97. Print.

Giroux, Henry A. "Democracy and the Discourse of Cultural Difference: Towards a Politics of Border Pedagogy." *British Journal of Sociology of Education* 12 (1991): 501–20. Print.

Heuberger, Barbara, Diane Gerber, and Reed Anderson. "Strength Through Cultural Diversity." *College Teaching* 47 (1999): 107–14. Print.

Nieto, Sonia. "Affirming Diversity." *National Education Association Today* 18 (2000): 10. Print.

Rodriguez, Richard. *Hunger of Memory.* Boston: Godine, 1982. Print.

Schlesinger, Arthur M. *The Disuniting of America: Reflection on a Multicultural Society.* New York: Norton, 1991. Print.

Silko, Leslie Marmon. "Language and Literature from a Pueblo Indian Perspective." *English Literature: Opening Up the Canon.* Ed. Leslie A. Fiedler and Houston A. Baker. Baltimore: Johns Hopkins UP, 1981. 52–58. Print.

Thomas, Wayne P., and Virginia P. Collier. "Two Languages Are Better than One." *Educational Leadership* 55 (Dec. 1997–Jan. 1998): 23–26. Print.

Reflections and Inquiries

1. What are Garber's principal arguments against multicultural education? How convincingly does he refute them?

2. Garber argues that English cannot be a second language for students in the United States. Why not? Do you agree or disagree?

3. According to Garber, "A wide-scale implementation of multicultural and bilingual programs can serve only to enhance the experience of English-speaking students." Defend or challenge this assertion.

Reading to Write

After reading about multicultural education programs, curricular and extracurricular, investigate your school's programs. Examine any brochures and catalogs associated with these programs. What do you see as their strengths and shortcomings? Write an essay evaluating one or more of these programs, suggesting improvements if you feel they are warranted.

Connections Among the Clusters

Many connections can be made between the issues related to multicultural learning and those related to, say, globalization, right to privacy, athletics, or health and medicine.

Critical Thinking

1. What connections can you make between issues in international relations (see Cluster 3) and multicultural learning?
2. What issues in media regulation (see Cluster 5) emerge when we consider bilingual education methods?
3. How important are the traditional values of a culture in the context of a formal education today? (See Cluster 3.)

Writing Projects

1. Visit your campus's multicultural center or a minority-student organization and obtain information about its most pressing problems. Then write an essay in which you examine these problems, their effect on student learning and student life, the efforts to solve the problems, and the work that remains to be done.
2. Examine the course offerings in your major from the perspective of multicultural learning. Write an essay in which you propose changes, such as adding new courses that focus on minorities and their works or revising existing courses so they embrace multicultural matters.

Suggestions for Further Reading

Banks, James A., and Cherry Banks. *Multicultural Education: Issues and Perspectives*. New York: John Wiley, 2004. Print.

Bloom, Allan David. *The Closing of the American Mind: How Higher Education Has Failed Democracy and Impoverished the Souls of Today's Students*. New York: Simon, 1987. Print.

Gandara, Patricia. *The Latino Education Crisis: The Consequences of Failed Social Policies*. Cambridge: Harvard University Press, 2009.

Darling-Hammond, Linda. *The Flat World and Education: How America's Commitment to Equity Will Determine Our Future* [Multicultural Education Series]. New York: Teacher's College Press, 2010.

Gorski, Paul C., and Seema G. Pothini. *Case Studies on Diversity and Social Justice Education*. New York: Routledge, 2013.

Harper's Symposium. "Who Needs the Great Works?" *Harper's* Sept. 1989: 43–52. Print.

Hays, Pamela A., PhD, *Addressing Cultural Complexities in Practice: Assessment, Diagnosis, and Therapy*, 2nd Edition. Washington, DC: American Psychological Association, 2007. Print.

Moya, Paula. *Learning from Experience: Minority Identities, Multicultural Struggle*. Berkeley: U of California P, 2002. Print.

Nieto, Sonia. *Light in Their Eyes: Creating Multicultural Learning Communities*. New York: Teachers College P, 1999. Print.

Potowski, Kim. "Situational Context of Education: A Window into the World of Bilingual Learners." *International Journal of Bilingual Education and Bilingualism* 9.2 (2006): 281–83. Print.

Spring, Joel. *Deculturalization and the Struggle for Equality: A Brief History of the Education of Dominated Cultures in the United States*. New York: McGraw-Hill, 2009. Print.

Suarez-Orozoco, Carolo, et al. *Learning a New Land: Immigrant Students in American Society*. Cambridge: Harvard University Press, 2008.

Tatum, Beverly Daniel. *Why Are All the Black Kids Sitting Together in the Cafeteria?: A Psychologist Explains the Development of Racial Identity*, Revised Edition. New York: Basic Books, 2003. Print.

Vavrus, Michael. *Diversity and Education: A Critical Multicultural Approach*. New York: Teachers College Press, 2014.

Walqui, Aida. "Scaffolding Instruction for English Language Learners: A Conceptual Framework." *International Journal of Bilingual Education and Bilingualism* 9.2 (2006): 159–80. Print.

Media Matters: What Are the Key Issues?

Introduction

The influence of the Internet on society has been nothing short of profound. The distinction between public and private identity has blurred as a result of the extraordinary influence of social networking sites. Thanks to smartphones, we can rapidly access information anywhere at any time. But this amazing digital technology comes with a price: we are more vulnerable to invasion of privacy, to being bullied, to identity theft, and to becoming addicted to social media and 'Net surfing—concerns that the following selections address.

Is Speed and Convenience Trumping Thoroughness in Communication?

Today's digital tools have revolutionized the way we communicate—but are we losing the willingness (if not the ability) to develop our thoughts as thoroughly as we should?

The I.M.s of Romeo and Juliet | Roz Chast

Humorists often generate laughs through the use of anachronisms. In Mark Twain's comic satire, A Connecticut Yankee in King Arthur's Court, *for example, Hank Morgan, who winds up in the Middle Ages after getting bopped on the head, bedazzles and educates (with ironic consequences) superstitious medieval folk with his knowledge of late-nineteenth-century science and technology. Roz Chast, one of the most prolific and admired of contemporary New Yorker cartoonists and the winner of the 2015 National Book Critics Circle Award in Autobiography for her graphic memoir* Can't We Talk about Something More Pleasant? *suggests what might happen to Shakespeare's famous young lovers if they had had access to a certain staple of twenty-first-century technology.*

© Roz Chast/Cartoonbank.com

Reflections and Inquiries

1. Aside from generating laughs, what serious point is Chast making by placing Romeo and Juliet in a twenty-first-century milieu with access to computers and instant-messaging technology?

2. What do the content and format of Romeo and Juliet's messages suggest about the ways in which technology can influence communication, even intimate communication?

3. Compare Romeo and Juliet's conversations in Shakespeare's play with their conversation in the cartoon. What "statement" do you suppose Chast is making (if any) about the language or communication skills of today's youth?

Reading to Write

In an essay, reflect on the influence of text messaging on language use. Identify what you consider to be positive as well as negative aspects of this kind of communication. Draw from personal experience as well as from the experiences of fellow students.

Literacy Learning in the 21st Century [NCTE Policy Brief] | National Council of Teachers of English

Although English teachers, especially high school English teachers, are the target audience for the following position statement on what twenty-first-century literacy learning should involve, it is important for students to be part of the conversation. Students, after all, know a thing or two about the role technology plays in communication. As you read this official policy statement, prepared by the largest organization for teachers of English in the United States, consider whether all aspects of the topic have been properly or sufficiently addressed, if included at all.

To be successful in the 21st century requires skills that an earlier generation never imagined. Fundamental changes in the economy, jobs, and businesses have reshaped industry and the nature of work. Today, employees engage with a technology-driven, diverse, and quickly changing global economy that requires new and different skills. Literacy demands have changed along with these changes in society and technology.

Technology has increased the intensity and complexity of literate environments, and the 21st century demands that a literate person possess a wide range of abilities and competencies. Twenty-first century readers and writers need to be able to:

- Develop proficiency with the tools of technology;

- Build relationships with others to pose and solve problems collaboratively and cross-culturally;

- Design and share information for global communities to meet a variety of purposes;

- Manage, analyze, and synthesize multiple streams of simultaneous information;

- Create, critique, analyze, and evaluate multi-media texts; and

- Attend to the ethical responsibilities required by these complex environments.

Because students build 21st century literacies essential for their future through access to technology and to instruction and practice in these literacies, the National Council of Teachers of English supports efforts by Congress to increase the federal investment in programs that address 21st century literacy teachers and learners. As Congress reauthorizes the Elementary and Secondary Education Act (NCLB) and considers a comprehensive literary policy and other legislation affecting our nation's schools, attention needs to be paid to research on 21st century literacies. This document describes important research-based approaches and recommendations for policymakers in order to prepare students to become informed citizens, prepared workers, and life-long learners in the 21st century.

Research-based Practices

Aligning literacy efforts in preschool and early grades with middle and high school assures a continuum of instruction and learning.

Interventions with low-income preschoolers offer the highest potential returns in terms of later school success because achievement gaps between low-income and more affluent children begin well before kindergarten and increase with each school year.[1] With appropriate instruction, including new technologies, children three to five years of age can develop understandings about the appearance of print, the connection between marks and language, the ways different kinds of writing shape the form and meaning of texts, and the ways readers and writers see and understand one another.[2]

5   Once students enter middle and high school they must develop the ability to read and comprehend complex texts and multimedia texts, to write to diverse audiences in varied ways, and to use a variety of media forms to make meaning. Just when students need support to reach these higher literacy levels, most schools stop providing literacy instruction. Accordingly, secondary teachers need to explicitly address the specific and specialized literacy demands of each discipline. Creating a comprehensive literacy program across academic levels and providing professional development across content areas would support continuity and high-quality literacy instruction in all content areas.

Twenty-first century students need to gather information from multiple sources, evaluate their reliability, and apply their findings effectively.

Most students like to use the Web, but often lack skills necessary to find information or to use that information effectively. Teachers need to provide explicit instruction on strategies such as formulating a research question, evaluating information, evaluating the search process, and assimilating information.[3] Therefore, professional development about information literacy is crucial.

Twenty-first century technologies can engage students in learning.

Research shows that computer technology and other multichannel digital technologies can reduce the isolation of school work from real-world contexts.[4] Students' natural interest in the use of various media outside of school can be tapped to engage them in reading and writing in school. Accordingly, professional development is needed in order to effectively incorporate technologies in pedagogy and curriculum.

Twenty-first century assessment will be different because of technology.
Research shows that newer forms of assessments, such as portfolio and performance-based assessment, can motivate student learning.[5] Portfolio-based assessment fosters reflection which, in turn, enhances student awareness of and engagement in learning.[6] Performance-based assessment reveals how students can apply their knowledge in real world settings.

Recommendations for Policymakers

Teachers need both intellectual and material support for effective 21st century literacy instruction. Accordingly, federal and state legislators need to support schools in providing continuing opportunities for professional development as well as up-to-date technologies for use in literacy classrooms.

- Create and fund a comprehensive early childhood through grade 12 literacy program.

- Provide funding for professional development to help teachers learn ways to support student progress in the full range of 21st-century literacies, and provide assistance to schools for professional development to help teachers incorporate literacy learning in all content areas.

- Make performance-based assessments of 21st-century literacies a priority. Teachers should contribute to the choice of appropriate assessments and have access to assessment data in a timely fashion so they can use it to shape instruction.

- Ensure that schools are equipped with a 21st-century technology infrastructure and 21st century technology tools.[7]

For more than ninety-five years, the National Council of Teachers of English has been devoted to improving the teaching and learning of English and the language arts at all levels of education. We value your efforts to enact policies that support this goal. If you have questions or need further assistance, please contact Stacey Novelli, NCTE Legislative Associate, at snovelli@ncte.org.

Notes

1. Perez-Johnson, I. & Maynard, I. (2007). The case for early, targeted interventions to prevent academic failure. *Peabody Journal of Education 82(4)*, 587–616.

2. Rowe, D.W. (2008). Social contracts for writing: Negotiating shared understandings about text in the preschool years. *Reading Research Quarterly 43(1)*, 66–95; Harste, J., Woodward, V., & Burke, C. (1984). *Language stories and literacy lessons*. Portsmouth, NH: Heinemann.

3. Kulper, E., Colman, M., & Terwel, J. (2005). The web as an information resource in K–12 education: Strategies for supporting students in searching and processing information. *Review of Educational Research 75(3)*, 283–328.

4. Moje, E.B., Ovrby, M., Tysvaer, N. & Morris, K. (2008). The complex world of adolescent literacy: Myths, motivations, and mysteries. *Harvard Educational Review 78(1)*, 107–158; Yi, Y. (2008). Relay writing in adolescent online community: Relay writing can serve as a new and valuable window into online literacy as well as adolescent literacy practices outside of school. *Journal of Adolescent & Adult Literacy 51(8)*, 670–681.

5. Hargreaves, A., Earl, L., & Schmidt, M.(2002). Perspectives on alternative assessment reform. *American Educational Research Journal 39(1)*, 69–95.

6. Scott, T. (2005). Creating the subject of portfolios: Reflective writing and the conveyance of institutional prerogatives. *Written Communication 22(1)*, 3–35.

7. The Partnership for 21st Century Learning Skills. Retrieved on December 8, 2008, from http://www.21stcenturyskills.org.

Reflections and Inquiries

1. Which of the six abilities and competencies identified by NCTE as essential for a literate person to possess do you consider most important, and why? What, if anything, would you add to the list? What would you exclude?

2. What do you consider to be "appropriate instruction" in new technologies for students in elementary grades? In middle school? In high school?

3. The policy brief claims that most students "lack skills necessary to find information or to use that information effectively." From your perspective as college students, how accurate is that claim? What information-gathering or information-using skills do you feel most students lack by the time they graduate from high school?

4. Evaluate the policy statement's four recommendations for teachers. Which do you consider to be most important, and why?

Reading to Write

Look back on the writing instruction you received in high school. Write an essay on what you consider to be the crucial skills that contributed to the development of your writing ability. Possible skills might include preparing a portfolio, computer-based research and document-design skills, and locating and using material from online and database resources. In preparing your essay, make use of some of the sources listed in the policy statement's endnotes.

Hooked on Facebook | Jonathan Zimmerman

Drug addiction analogies crop up frequently in commentary relating to online social networking—or for that matter, in commentary relating to any kind of computer-based activity. In the following op-ed piece, Jonathan Zimmerman, who teaches history and education at New York University, explains why he thinks parents should be worried about their teenagers' addiction to online social networking sites like Facebook—and it has little to do with predators.

Imagine a drug that made American teenagers think and talk more about the timeless concerns of adolescence: Who's cool, who's cute, and who's going out with whom. Then imagine that millions of teens were taking this drug, every day. Actually, you don't have to. The drug already exists, and it's called "MySpace." There's a competitor drug, too, known as "Facebook."

Between one-half and three-quarters of American teens already have a profile on an Internet social networking site, where they spend hours per week—nobody really knows how many—sharing pictures, gossip and jokes. And we should all be worried about that, although not for the reasons that you might suspect.

That's because the newspapers keep reminding us about "online predators" and other malfeasance on the Net, which makes us miss the digital forest for the trees. In this medium, the real danger doesn't come from depraved adults. It's much subtler than that, and it comes from teenagers themselves—specifically, from their insatiable desire to hang out with each other. And the key word here is "insatiable."

After all, teens have *always* wanted to hang out with each other. But the Internet lets them do it 24/7, transforming the social world of adolescence into an omnipresence. Consider last year's report by the MacArthur Foundation on "digital youth," which confirmed that most teens communicate online with kids they already know—and they're doing it more than ever. "Young people use new media to build friendships and romantic relationships as well as to hang out with each other as much and as often as possible," the report found.

As the teenagers would say, duh! Then they would ask, what's the problem with that?

Nothing, really, except for what it replaces: solitude.

Once you're "always on," as the kids describe it, you're never alone. That means you're less likely to read a book for pleasure, to draw a picture, or simply to stare out the window and imagine worlds other than your own. And as any parent with a teenager could testify, you're also less likely to communicate with the real people in your immediate surroundings. Who wants to talk to family members, when your friends are just a click away?

5

Source: "Hooked on Facebook," by Jonathan Zimmerman from *San Francisco Chronicle,* March 30, 2009, p. A19. Reprinted by permission.

True, many teens do communicate with strangers on the Net. But adolescents are also very adept at sniffing out "creepy" adults, whose threats have been vastly overblown by media reports. Consider all the ink spilled over Lori Drew, the Missouri woman who used a phony MySpace account to trick a teenager into believing that Drew was a male suitor. When the fake suitor dumped the teen and she committed suicide, you would have thought every kid in America was somehow in danger. They're not, at least not from strangers.

Although 32 percent of American teens say they have been contacted on the Net by someone they don't know, according to the Pew Research Center, just 7 percent report feeling "scared or uncomfortable" as a result.

10   And when teens do feel hurt by something on the Internet, it usually comes from—surprise!—other adolescents at their schools. About one-third of teenagers say they have been the target of "online bullying," such as threatening messages or embarrassing pictures. But two-thirds of teens say bullying is more likely to happen offline than online. The Internet just makes it easier to do—and harder to escape.

If social networking sites had existed when I was a kid, I would have used them every bit as much as my teenage daughter does. With my own Facebook or MySpace page, I would have focused even more upon all of the natural worries that permeated my adolescence: Am I cool? Am I cute? Will my peers like me? And it would have taken me a lot longer to become an adult.

So what should today's adults do, in the face of this new challenge? We can try to limit our teenagers' computer time, of course, but that's probably a lost cause by now. The better solution, as always, comes from the kids themselves. Teens around the country have started a small online movement against social networking sites, trying to make them seem *un*-cool. My best friend's daughter just took down her Facebook page, for example, insisting that the site was "for losers."

So pass the word, to every teen you know: social networking is for losers. Just don't tell them I said so.

Reflections and Inquiries

1. Explain why you agree or disagree with Zimmerman that online social networking acts like a literal drug on teenagers.

2. Zimmerman worries that online social networking interferes too much with solitude. Do you agree or disagree with the value he places on solitude? Why?

3. Comment on Zimmerman's concluding reflections.

4. Do you detect any logical fallacies in Zimmerman's argument? What are they?

Reading to Write

Conduct a survey of your fellow students' involvement with online social net-working and compare your findings with those of other researchers. You may want to review the guidelines for preparing a questionnaire and conducting a survey in Chapter 5. Also, use an online search engine and your library's online catalog to locate books and articles about Facebook, Skype, Google+ hangouts, Google chat functions, and other online social networking sites.

How Should the First Amendment's Freedom of Speech Guarantee Be Applied?

Issues of censorship are interwoven with issues of individual freedom, as well as of freedom of speech and the press, which are protected by the First Amendment to the Constitution. But is there ever such a thing as too much free speech?

Speech Overview | Rodney Smolla

Whenever free speech seems threatened, people quickly invoke the First Amendment, which guarantees that no law shall infringe on each citizen's right to free speech. In the following article, Rodney Smolla, dean of the University of Richmond's School of Law, provides a detailed explanation of the implications of the First Amendment and of why it protects speech (including images) considered to be hateful, anti-American, or even criminal.

The First Amendment to the Constitution of the United States declares that "Congress shall make no law … abridging the freedom of speech." What does and should this mean? Justice Oliver Wendell Holmes, in his famous *Abrams v. United States* (1919) dissenting opinion, began what may be the single most poetic paragraph ever written by a Supreme Court justice on the meaning of freedom of speech. Here is that improbable opening line: "Persecution for the expression of opinions seems to me perfectly logical." What could Holmes have been thinking?

Perhaps Holmes was expressing the view that all of us, individually and col-lectively, have within us a kind of censorship-impulse. Governments are espe-cially prone to censor. As Holmes went on to put it: "If you have no doubt of your premises or your power and want a certain result with all your heart you naturally express your wishes in law and sweep away all opposition." Censorship is thus a kind of social instinct. As caring and responsible citizens of society, *especially* good and decent citizens of a good and decent society, we are likely to want *many* results with all our hearts. We want security, we want freedom from fear, we want order,

---

Source: "Speech Overview," by Rodney Smolla, Dean, University of Richmond School of Law, August 2003. Reprinted by permission of the author.

civility, racial and religious tolerance, we want the well-being of our children. We want these things with all our hearts, and when others express opinions that seem to threaten these aspirations, who can blame us for being tempted to express our wishes in law and sweep away the opposition? It is perfectly logical. And that is what, at bottom, freedom of speech is all about.

Over the course of roughly the last 50 years the U.S. Supreme Court has set our nation on a remarkable experiment, often construing the First Amendment in a manner that strenuously defies the natural and logical impulse to censor. In scores of decisions, the Supreme Court has interpreted the First Amendment in a manner that to most of the world seems positively radical. Those decisions are numerous and cover a vast and various terrain, but consider some highlights. Americans have the right to:

- Desecrate the national flag as a symbol of protest.

- Burn the cross as an expression of racial bigotry and hatred.

- Espouse the violent overthrow of the government as long as it is mere abstract advocacy and not an immediate incitement to violence.

- Traffic in sexually explicit erotica as long as it does not meet a rigorous definition of "hard core" obscenity.

- Defame public officials and public figures with falsehoods provided they are not published with knowledge of their falsity or reckless disregard for the truth.

- Disseminate information invading personal privacy if the revelation is deemed "newsworthy."

- Engage in countless other forms of expression that would be outlawed in many nations but are regarded as constitutionally protected here.

Such First Amendment decisions reject the impulse to censor; they are therefore striking as legal doctrines. Perhaps more striking, however, is that these decisions have gained widespread currency within American culture as a whole. The Supreme Court is not alone in its commitment to the free-speech project. While undoubtedly any one decision will often be controversial with the public, which may be deeply divided on topics such as flag-burning or sex on the Internet, on balance what is extraordinary about the evolution of freedom of speech in America over the last 50 years is that it has taken such a strong hold on the American consciousness, a hold that seems to cut across party labels such as "Democrat" or "Republican" or ideological labels such as "liberal" or "conservative." On the Supreme Court itself, for example, justices with hardy conservative credentials such as Antonin Scalia or Clarence Thomas have often been as committed to expansive protection for freedom of speech as justices famous for their liberal views, such as William Brennan or Thurgood Marshall. Appointees of Republican presidents, such as Anthony Kennedy or David Souter, have been as stalwart as appointees of Democratic presidents, such as

Stephen Breyer or Ruth Bader Ginsburg, in their articulation of strong free-speech doctrines. So too, in the political arena, views on free-speech issues often do not track along traditional party lines or classic ideological divisions.

This is not to say that in some simplistic sense everybody in America   5
believes in freedom of speech, and certainly it is not to say that everybody in America believes that freedom of speech means the same thing. But it is to say that in a sense both deep and wide, "freedom of speech" is a value that has become powerfully internalized by the American polity. Freedom of speech is a core American belief, almost a kind of secular religious tenet, an article of constitutional faith.

How do we account for the modern American reverence for freedom of speech? Why is this value so solidly entrenched in our constitutional law, and why is it so widely embraced by the general public? Over the years many philosophers, historians, legal scholars and judges have offered theoretical justifications for strong protection of freedom of speech, and in these justifications we may also find explanatory clues.

An obvious starting point is the direct link between freedom of speech and vibrant democracy. Free speech is an indispensable tool of self-governance in a democratic society. Concurring in *Whitney v. California* (1927), Justice Louis Brandeis wrote that "freedom to think as you will and to speak as you think are means indispensable to the discovery and spread of political truth."

On a communal level, free speech facilitates majority rule. It is through talking that we encourage consensus, that we form a collective will. Whether the answers we reach are wise or foolish, free speech helps us ensure that the answers usually conform to what most people think. Americans who are optimists (and optimism is a quintessentially American characteristic) additionally believe that, over the long run, free speech actually *improves* our political decision-making. Just as Americans generally believe in free markets in economic matters, they generally believe in free markets when it comes to ideas, and this includes politics. In the long run the best test of intelligent political policy is its power to gain acceptance at the ballot box.

On an individual level, speech is a means of participation, the vehicle through which individuals debate the issues of the day, cast their votes, and actively join in the process of decision-making that shape the polity. Free speech serves the individual's right to join the political fray, to stand up and be counted, to be an active player in the democracy, not a passive spectator.

Freedom of speech is also an essential contributor to the American belief   10
in government confined by a system of checks and balances, operating as a restraint on tyranny, corruption and ineptitude. For much of the world's history, governments, following the impulse described by Justice Holmes, have presumed to play the role of benevolent but firm censor, on the theory that the wise governance of men proceeds from the wise governance of their opinions. But the United States was founded on the more cantankerous revolutionary principles of John Locke, who taught that under the social compact sovereignty always rests with the people, who never surrender their natural right to

protest, or even revolt, when the state exceeds the limits of legitimate authority. Speech is thus a means of "people-power," through which the people may
ferret out corruption and discourage tyrannical excesses.

Counter-intuitively, influential American voices have also often argued
that robust protection of freedom of speech, *including speech advocating crime
and revolution*, actually works to make the country more stable, increasing
rather than decreasing our ability to maintain law and order. Again the words
of Justice Brandeis in *Whitney v. California* are especially resonant, with his
admonition that the framers of the Constitution "knew that order cannot be
secured merely through fear of punishment for its infraction; that it is hazardous to discourage thought, hope and imagination; that fear breeds repression;
that repression breeds hate; that hate menaces stable government; that the path
of safety lies in the opportunity to discuss freely supposed grievances and proposed remedies; and that the fitting remedy for evil counsels is good ones."
If a society as wide-open and pluralistic as America is not to explode from
festering tensions and conflicts, there must be valves through which citizens
with discontent may blow off steam. In America, we have come to accept the
wisdom that openness fosters resiliency, that peaceful protest displaces more
violence than it triggers, and that free debate dissipates more hate than it stirs.

The link between speech and democracy certainly provides some explanation for the American veneration of free speech, but not an entirely satisfying
or complete one. For there are many flourishing democracies in the world, but
few of them have adopted either the constitutional law or the cultural traditions that support free speech as expansively as America does. Moreover,
much of the vast protection we provide to expression in America seems to bear
no obvious connection to politics or the democratic process at all. Additional
explanation is required.

Probably the most celebrated attempt at explanation is the "marketplace
of ideas" metaphor, a notion that is most famously associated with Holmes'
great dissent in *Abrams*, in which he argued that "the best test of truth is the
power of the thought to get itself accepted in the competition of the market."
The marketplace of ideas metaphor does not posit that truth *will* emerge from
the free trade in ideas, at least not instantly. That would be asking too much. It
merely posits that free trade in ideas is the best *test* of truth, in much the same
way that those who believe in laissez-faire economic theory argue that over
the long haul free economic markets are superior to command-and-control
economies. The American love of the marketplace of ideas metaphor stems in
no small part from our irrepressible national optimism, the American "constitutional faith" that, given long enough, good will conquer evil. As long as
this optimism is not blind naiveté, but is rather a motive force that encourages us to keep the faith in the long view of history, it can be a self-fulfilling
prophecy. Just as we often have nothing to fear but fear, hope is often our best
hope. Humanity may be fallible, and truth illusive, but the hope of humanity
lies in its faith in progress. The marketplace metaphor reminds us to take the
long view. Americans like to believe, and largely *do* believe, that truth has a

stubborn and incorrigible persistence. Cut down again and again, truth will still not be extinguished. Truth will out, it will be rediscovered and rejuvenated. It will prevail.

The connection of freedom of speech to self-governance and the appeal of the marketplace of ideas metaphor still, however, do not tell it all. Freedom of speech is linked not merely to such grandiose ends as the service of the democracy or the search for truth. Freedom of speech has value on a more personal and individual level. Freedom of speech is part of the human personality itself, a value intimately intertwined with human autonomy and dignity. In the words of Justice Thurgood Marshall in the 1974 case *Procunier v. Martinez*, "The First Amendment serves not only the needs of the polity but also those of the human spirit—a spirit that demands self-expression."

Many Americans embrace freedom of speech for the same reasons they   15
embrace other aspects of individualism. Freedom of speech is the right to defiantly, robustly and irreverently speak one's mind just because it is one's mind. Freedom of speech is thus bonded in special and unique ways to the human capacity to think, imagine and create. Conscience and consciousness are the sacred precincts of mind and soul. Freedom of speech is intimately linked to freedom of thought, to that central capacity to reason and wonder, hope and believe, that largely defines our humanity.

If these various elements of our culture do in combination provide some insight into why freedom of speech exerts such a dominating presence on the American legal and cultural landscape, they do not by any means come close to explaining the intense and seemingly never-ending legal and cultural debates over the *limits* on freedom of speech.

There *are* limits. The major labor of modern First Amendment law is to articulate the points at which those limits are reached. This ongoing process is often contentious and difficult, and no one simple legal formula or philosophical principle has yet been discovered that is up to the trick of making the job easy. Americans thus continue to debate in political forums and litigate in legal forums such issues as the power of society to censor offensive speech to protect children, the power to arrest speakers spreading violent or hateful propaganda for fear that it will foment crime or terrorism, the permissibility of banning speech that defeats protection of intellectual property, the propriety of curbing speech to shelter personal reputation and privacy, the right to restrict political contributions and expenditures to reduce the influence of money on the political process, and countless other free-speech conflicts.

Yet while the country continues to struggle mightily to define the limits and continues to debate vigorously the details, there is surprisingly little struggle and debate over the core of the faith. Americans truly *do* embrace the central belief that freedom of thought, conscience and expression are numinous values, linked to our defining characteristics as human beings. While limits must exist, American culture and law approach such limits with abiding caution and skepticism, embracing freedom of speech as a value of transcendent constitutional importance.

Reflections and Inquiries

1. How does Smolla, by way of Oliver Wendell Holmes, explain the impulse to censor?

2. Smolla calls attention to First Amendment Supreme Court decisions within the last fifty years that "strenuously def[y]" the natural impulse to censor. By what line of reasoning have such activities as hate speech, dissemination of information invading personal privacy, or flag burning become worthy of First Amendment protection? Do you challenge any of these rulings, and if so, why?

3. Explain the rationale behind the analogies Smolla makes between freedom of speech and democracy and between freedom of speech and a market economy.

4. The framers of the Constitution, Justice Brandeis wrote in *Whitney v. California*, understood "that it is hazardous to discourage thought." Explain.

Reading to Write

Should there be constraints of some kind on the exercise of free speech? In other words, is there a legitimate basis for censoring certain kinds of speech in special cases? Why or why not? Present your argument in an essay, making sure that you illustrate with cases in point and that you fairly represent and challenge dissenting views.

Issues for Further Research: Book Banning

Even among those who defend First Amendment rights, book banning is sometimes urged when it is assumed that certain books offend particular religious, moral, or political views. Are such calls for book censorship ever justified?

A Letter to the Chairman of the Drake School Board | Kurt Vonnegut Jr.

One of America's best-loved novelists, Kurt Vonnegut (1922–2007), is famous for novels that satirize the human condition from unusual perspectives. His most famous novel, Slaughterhouse-Five, *which focuses on the brutality of World War II, has been banned from numerous schools and libraries primarily because of its use of offensive language. In 1973, after the school board in Drake, North Dakota, literally burned the book, Vonnegut wrote the following letter to the chairman of the Drake school board.*

My novel *Slaughterhouse-Five* was actually burned in a furnace by a school janitor in Drake, North Dakota, on instructions from the school committee there, and the school board made public statements about the unwholesomeness of the book. Even by the standards of Queen Victoria, the only offensive line in the entire novel is this: "Get out of the road, you dumb motherfucker." This is spoken by an American antitank gunner to an unarmed American chaplain's assistant during the Battle of the Bulge in Europe in December 1944, the largest single defeat of American arms (the Confederacy excluded) in history. The chaplain's assistant had attracted enemy fire.

So on November 16, 1973, I wrote as follows to Charles McCarthy of Drake, North Dakota:

Dear Mr. McCarthy:

I am writing to you in your capacity as chairman of the Drake School Board. I am among those American writers whose books have been destroyed in the now famous furnace of your school.

Certain members of your community have suggested that my work is evil. This is extraordinarily insulting to me. The news from Drake indicates to me that books and writers are very unreal to you people. I am writing this letter to let you know how real I am.

I want you to know, too, that my publisher and I have done absolutely nothing to exploit the disgusting news from Drake. We are not clapping each other on the back, crowing about all the books we will sell because of the news. We have declined to go on television, have written no fiery letters to editorial pages, have granted no lengthy interviews. We are angered and sickened and saddened. And no copies of this letter have been sent to anybody else. You now hold the only copy in your hands. It is a strictly private letter from me to the people of Drake, who have done so much to damage my reputation in the eyes of their children and then in the eyes of the world. Do you have the courage and ordinary decency to show this letter to the people, or will it, too, be consigned to the fires of your furnace?

5

AP Images

Kurt Vonnegut

I gather from what I read in the papers and hear on television that you imagine me, and some other writers, too, as being sort of ratlike people who enjoy making money from poisoning the minds of young people. I am in fact a large, strong person, fifty-one years old, who did a lot of farm work as a boy, who is good with tools. I have raised six children, three my own and three adopted. They have all turned out well. Two of them are farmers. I am a combat infantry veteran from World War II, and hold a Purple Heart. I have earned whatever I own by hard work. I have never been arrested or sued for anything. I am so much trusted with young people and by young people that I have served on the faculties of the University of Iowa, Harvard, and the City College of New York. Every year I receive at least a dozen invitations to be commencement speaker at colleges and high schools. My books are probably more widely used in schools than those of any other living American fiction writer.

If you were to bother to read my books, to behave as educated persons would, you would learn that they are not sexy, and do not argue in favor of wildness of any kind. They beg that people be kinder and more responsible than they often are. It is true that some of the characters speak coarsely. That is because people speak coarsely in real life. Especially soldiers and hard-working men speak coarsely, and even our most sheltered children know that. And we all know, too, that those words really don't damage children much. They didn't damage us when we were young. It was evil deeds and lying that hurt us.

After I have said all this, I am sure you are still ready to respond, in effect, "Yes, yes—but it still remains our right and our responsibility to decide what books our children are going to be made to read in our community." This is surely so. But it is also true that if you exercise that right and fulfill that responsibility in an ignorant, harsh, un-American manner, then people are entitled to call you bad citizens and fools. Even your own children are entitled to call you that.

I read in the newspaper that your community is mystified by the outcry from all over the country about what you have done. Well, you have discovered that Drake is a part of American civilization, and your fellow Americans can't stand it that you have behaved in such an uncivilized way. Perhaps you will learn from this that books are sacred to free men for very good reasons, and that wars have been fought against nations which hate books and burn them. If you are an American, you must allow all ideas to circulate freely in your community, not merely your own.

10   If you and your board are now determined to show that you in fact have wisdom and maturity when you exercise your powers over the education of your young, then you should acknowledge that it was a rotten lesson you taught young people in a free society when you denounced and then burned

books—books you hadn't even read. You should also resolve to expose your children to all sorts of opinions and information, in order that they will be better equipped to make decisions and to survive. Again: you have insulted me, and I am a good citizen, and I am very real.

Reflections and Inquiries

1. How would you describe the tone of Vonnegut's letter to Charles McCarthy? Is it angry? Upset? Respectable? Sarcastic? A little of each? Something else? What is noteworthy about the tone of the letter?

2. What do you consider to be the most important point that Vonnegut makes in his letter? How convincingly does it come across?

3. Imagine that you are a member of a junior high school's book-selection committee. Would you vote to ban Vonnegut's book on the basis of the sentence that he quotes from it? Why or why not?

4. To what extent does Vonnegut consider the views of the Drake school board? Should he have been more sympathetic to them? Explain. You may wish to review Rogerian argumentative strategies in Chapter 4.

5. What seem to be the major factors underlying a public school board's decision to ban books? Which of these factors, if any, seem valid to you?

Reading to Write

Write a letter to Vonnegut in which you support or take issue with his response to the Drake school board.

Point/Counterpoint: Two Student Essays on Book Censorship

Is book censorship bad or good? Bad in some cases but good in others? What criteria should be used in judging one way or another? The matter is complicated by the fact that there are many motives for censorship and many situations in which it isn't even clear whether works have been censored or not. In the case of the traditional Western canon, is the relative absence of works by women or persons of color the result of censorship? What about censoring certain kinds of books for children of a certain age? The very term "censorship" becomes problematic. In their respective essays, Santa Clara University seniors Kiley Strong and Gaby Caceres take very different views on censorship in schools: Strong on the myth of book censorship and Caceres on when censorship is and is not necessary.

Student Essay

The Myth of Book Censoring Within the American Education System | Kiley Strong

The traditional literary canon has come under fire in recent years for the exclusion of works by females and cultures outside the western hemisphere. However, some school boards in the United States have aimed the ammunition at some of the literature's content rather than the homogony of the works' authors. For example, students in Savannah, Georgia, in 1999 had to obtain a signed permission slip from parents to read *Hamlet*, *Macbeth*, or *King Lear*. Since when does Shakespeare meet the qualifications of literature which needs to be censored from students? Conservative parents, teachers, and educators should be aware that carrying censorship too far will only result in cheating students of a well-rounded education. The banning of books should not be permitted in the secondary level of public education because the lack of specific criteria makes the process too subjective and limits the ideologies and opinions to which students are exposed.

What exactly does book banning consist of? The Modern Library Association cites two statuses books can be in, based on complaints and recommendations of readers. The first is books which are challenged by educators for their content and are considered books which should be taken off of reading lists in schools and out of public libraries. While these books supposedly contain questionable material, they still remain readily available to the public. If a book is successfully challenged, it becomes a "banned" book, meaning it is removed from public libraries and is not allowed to be sold in bookstores due to its content. The history of book censorship in the United States is interesting and provides a foundation for the arguments against censorship at secondary level in schools. Books have been banned from the public sphere since before the United States existed for reasons ranging from obscenity to racism to curse words to antidemocratic sentiments. Some past banned books include *Hamlet*, *The Communist Manifesto*, *Lady Chatterley's Lover*, and *Moll Flanders*. To a contemporary, this censorship of classic literature is laughable.

Many Americans willingly accept freedom of speech and recognize the option they have to view the book or not to view it, much like pornography. However, the issue gains heat when considering how students of varying perspectives, backgrounds, and maturity levels will react to literature that contains mature content. In modern American society the media expose children to sex, cursing, violence, and a wide range of political ideologies on a daily basis. Educators and parents naively believe that students' first exposure to this content is through reading books which contain this material. Conservative parent and educator groups who insist on sheltering important ideas and viewpoints from a generation which has already long been exposed to the "real world"—some probably even by watching *The Real World*.

Book censorship remains a mysterious process which does not have any real criteria and remains a local rather than a national level issue. These two facts detract from the credibility of such decisions. Who decides which books should be banned? Mostly it is parents and school board members who are outraged that teachers try to introduce such topics in a classroom setting. School boards then vote to remove books from the libraries only for the reason that parents or faculty believe they are too obscene, too racy, too racist, or too anti-America for children to handle. And if books are to be banned, why is this only done at a local level? If a book is considered inappropriate for 16-year-olds in one county, why not for 16-year-olds across the board? The answer to this question is obviously that there are regional differences in beliefs. But really whose beliefs are these? They are mostly the beliefs of the parents and educators, not the students. Given the chance, most students would rather read a controversial book than, say, *Moby Dick*. If definitive criteria existed by which a book could be judged, then I think the process would seem fairer to everyone and more practical. But how can a book be judged inappropriate in one place, and taught in another?

While the lack of criteria makes banning wrong on a logical level, the real   5
issue at hand is that students could possibly miss out on important and eye-opening experiences. When a teacher chooses a book to teach in an English class, it is usually because the book is an example of fine literature and style and also contains universal themes. Reading provides students with the opportunity to understand other people's perspectives and walk in another person's shoes. For example, *Black Boy* by Richard Wright, a book banned a few decades ago, gives students a chance to experience what it is like to grow up in the South as a black man. By banning this book from schools, it cheated students of the chance for an eye-opening reality check of what life in the South was actu-

ally like. And even if the reality presented is harsh, its [*sic*] better for students as American citizens to be aware of the reality, as opposed to having an idyllic view of Southern society in the past. Another reason books that discuss sex, racism, and other hot topics should be taught to students is that the classroom provides a much better setting

Richard Wright

to learn about and discuss these topics than anywhere else. Within a structured classroom environment students can hear honest viewpoints provided by teachers and classmates and partake in discussions about what they are reading. This option is preferable to students just hearing about sex and racism from their peers or the media, which most likely would provide exaggerated, untrue, or stereotyped information.

So before teachers and parents start urging the removal of books from school libraries and classrooms, they should take a second look at what ideologies they are exactly removing. By preventing the free consumption of ideas, parents and educators are acting in the same manner as the Chinese government. According to a recent issue of *Time* magazine, when Tiananmen Square is Googled in China, the only images which pop up are tourist photos or one of a congressman posing in the square. This kind of censorship is outrageous to Americans and parents should not think that solely exposing children to ideas and hot issues through literature is going to incite children to act in a certain manner or develop certain ideas; rather books give students ideas to think and mull over in their own heads and form their own ideas and not eat the ideals parents forcefeed them.

Student Essay

Censorship of Books for Public High Schools: When Necessary, When Not | Gaby Caceres

It's not just the books under fire now that worry me. It is the books that will never be written. The books that will never be read. And all due to the fear of censorship. As always, young readers will be the real losers.
—Judy Blume

Censorship is a heated issue affecting all aspects of speech and media. Particularly among school boards, censorship is a longstanding debate with no easy or obvious resolution that will please all board members, teachers, students, parents, and anyone else with connections to these schools. School boards must make many decisions about what is allowed to be taught in classrooms and what is not allowed in the curriculum. Especially among public high school textbooks, censoring of books is a topic of extensive discussion and argument. Obviously not all works are appropriate *required* reading for public high school students—for example, pornographic literature or books advocating devil worship. But because the censorship of schoolbooks has become so prevalent, removing the censorship of schoolbooks in public high schools could not only lead to a broader knowledge for these teenagers but also help these young adults feel more accepted within their family and society.

Many feel that censorship is a thing of the past, but a close look into the complexities and controversies that arise from censorship or attempted censorship reveal that it is a longstanding problem still present in many high school systems, leading to problems for not only high school students but also for their families and teachers. Prominent publishers of public high school textbooks such as Scott, Foresman; McGraw-Hill; and many others delete or reword material that certain groups or authors would most certainly object to. The censorship of high school written material has even developed such strict guidelines and regulations that in some states rejection or significant changes have been made in one-half to two-thirds of the material proposed for use. Publishers use censorship as a way to protect themselves and the readers of their books from reading material that others could claim to be damaging to the readers: reference to possible negative exposure of material that shows sex and drug use; literature showing children challenging parents and authorities; discussion of evolution and/or creationism; racist and/or sexist views. But these issues are not the only reason for censorship. Right-wing conservatives also pressure publishers, as do left-wing liberals, each supporting their views of what should and should not be included in schoolbooks. These influences are supposed to help young adolescents become well educated, but what is really happening is the development of problems that will negatively affect high school students.

One of the main reasons the removal or censoring of school books published for public high schools is seen as necessary is that such books run the risk of misleading and of misrepresenting material. Many publishing companies are scared of the negative publicity from lawsuits that arise from publishing sensitive or offensive material. Publishers are responding to this fear by eliminating or changing large amounts of written material submitted for use in their textbooks. Although publishers must protect themselves from lawsuits, they are now deleting or rewording so much written material that it is jeopardizing the textual integrity of their schoolbooks. For example, one publisher of a high school anthology deleted over three hundred lines of Shakespeare's *Romeo and Juliet*. This is a large quantity of material to eliminate from a play consisting of less than three thousand lines, and it is hard to believe that the substance and meanings behind the play are fully preserved under these conditions. Many critics agree that changing such a large part of this play leads to the corruption and distortion of a famous literary classic. Anne Ravitch, author of *The Language Police*, states "The history texts are reluctant to criticize any dictator unless they are long dead. And even then, there are exceptions like Mao who is praised in one text for modernizing China but his totalitarian rule is not mentioned." Ravitch has also shown her disproval of certain textbooks which display photos of Saudi women working as doctors and nurses, because of the implication that they have gender equality, which everyone knows is not the case.

The publishers' problem is not only the fact that they alter the information published in their textbooks but also that they usually do not note these changes, or simply mention them on the bottom of the acknowledgements page. Many times, even acknowledged alteration of written material is not specific on what or where the changes are.

5   Another reason to prohibit censorship of school books is that the reading material that publishers consider to be unfit for a public high school curriculum could actually help students better understand themselves, their families, and their societies. Censorship is such a highly subjective issue that publishers are afraid to publish anything. If one group advocates a certain issue in a text, another group denounces that issue and demands its removal, forcing publishers to "dumb down" the books they distribute to avoid any conflict.

Some of the many topics that are constantly challenged and removed from schoolbooks are the ones that deal with issues relevant to today's teenagers and young adults. Any references to sex, drugs, alcohol, violence, or children challenging their parents almost never make their way into literature provided for public high school students. In this day and age, adolescents are going through many changes and are beginning to experience many pressures and desires that will help form their characters in the years to come. Thus, high school students could definitely gain from exposure to some literature discussing these controversial issues. All teenagers question themselves and their place in society; at some point all teenagers wonder whether or not they are normal or whether or not they are living a normal lifestyle. Reading literature that deals with these issues could certainly help young adults relate to issues that are so pertinent to their age group. Adolescents could use this exposure to not only help themselves feel that they are acceptable within their families and society, but also to educate themselves about the dangers and consequences of sex, drugs, alcohol, and violence. Also, this kind of literature can help reduce tensions felt by so many teenagers and can reassure them that it is normal to feel certain pressures and desires at their age. With opportunities to realize that they are normal, to have books to turn to, and to help them relate to certain issues, students can relieve themselves of their anxieties and focus more attention on academics.

The censorship of schoolbooks also has a negative impact on the preparation of future college students and current high school teachers. Since censorship does not substantially affect the textbooks or literary works taught at college level, many high school students, teachers, and college faculty are faced with problems over the preparation of prospective college students. Joan DelFattore, professor of English Education at the University of Delaware, understands the negative effects of censorship and says, "When twelfth-grade textbooks present the following year's college freshman with versions of *The Right Stuff* without expletives, Chaucer without bawdiness, *Hamlet* without overt sexual relations between Gertrude and Claudius, and 'The Train from Rhodesia' without 'piccanins,' these textbooks are giving the students neither an accurate factual background in literature nor adequate preparation to discuss the complexities and controversial elements of the unadulterated literature taught in college."

High school students should be fully prepared for their future schooling at the university level, and the censorship of high school texts unquestionably deters students from achieving that necessary level of preparation. Of course, not all high school graduates attend college, but even when a student will not continue his or her schooling at a higher level, censorship can still leave a negative influence. A student that is taught misrepresented or misleading information will never know that what he or she learned in high school was not accurate information.

Since oftentimes acknowledgements of censored material are not mentioned in high school books or are inconspicuously printed, teachers are left uninformed on the subjects to be taught. Thus, they can not [sic] adequately teach their students, much less properly plan their discussions.

Many argue that censorship of material for high school students is absolutely   *10* necessary to have a diverse multicultural education and to avoid the corruption of teenagers. A closer look at these arguments reveals that these claims are false. Liberals argue that censorship is the only way minority authors have the chance to place their works in high school texts; however, since right wing conservatives more commonly lead the pressures that influence publishers, works that represent women and minority writers such as Frederick Douglass and Harriet Beecher Stowe are often replaced by more traditional ones like those written by dead white European males such as Nathaniel Hawthorne and Henry David Thoreau to please the greater pressures of the conservatives. School boards and publishers also challenge or ban books proposed for distribution for a high school curriculum for fear that certain material corrupts teenagers. Even books such as J. K. Rowling's Harry Potter series have been challenged and banned from some school districts because of the claim that they promote witchcraft and deal with dark subjects such as death and evil too often.

Although censorship is a good way to protect students from offensive material, the censorship of one book leads to the censorship of another and another, creating a slippery slope in which students become deprived of the privilege to read books that ultimately encourage the use of their imagination and critical thinking skills. Often schools and publishers also bring too much negative publicity to challenged books, resulting in a motivating factor for students to seek out these books and read them, not the result the censors intended.

Perhaps developing a compromise between those who are against censorship and those who deem it necessary will resolve the longstanding problems that are affecting students across the nation. First and foremost, publishers must be more specific as to what contents they have altered or deleted. Acknowledgements of these alterations should be explicit on each literary work affected so students and teachers can be aware of these changes. Also, allowing students to read certain material that has been considered objectionable should be allowed as long as teachers and parents abide by strict guidelines that might help their students. Teachers and parents should be able to carefully examine the material they propose for students to read and help the students to distinguish between literal and literary ideas. Teachers should also allow themselves to be open to discussion about the uncensored material so that students can discuss their readings and feelings on the taboo issues that affect teenagers each day. If teachers and parents can openly discuss the material that their students read at school, censorship of high school texts would not be such a controversial issue because schools would not have as much to fear for their students.

As a controversy, censorship will not be resolved anytime in the near future. It will, in fact, be a more frequent issue every day. It has a profound impact on students across the United States. Over time, censorship has not only become a personal issue but has led to federal disputes. Authors around the world are deterred from writing about certain things for fear of the detrimental effects others may claim are being imposed on students and the possible lawsuits that could arise against them. If publishers would stop worrying about making the greatest possible profit, high school texts might be more sensitive in teaching tolerance, honor, and courage, all necessary for shaping the future leaders of our nation. High schools need to realize the negative affects [*sic*] of distributing censored material and need to act in order to help high school students learn to their full potential.

Reflections and Inquiries

1. How convincingly does Kiley Strong support her claim that banning books from secondary public schools should not be permitted?

2. What problem does Strong see in the differing regional criteria used to determine whether a book should be banned?

3. According to Caceres, when can censorship of certain books in public high schools be beneficial? When can it be a problem?

4. Caceres states that a "compromise" between those who advocate censorship and those who are against it could "resolve the longstanding problems that are affecting students across the nation." What kind of compromise? What longstanding problems does Caceres have in mind?

5. Do you find one essay easier to read than the other? Are the ideas in one essay clearer than those in the other? What contributes to these differences?

Reading to Write

Examine the arguments both for and against the censoring of *one* particular book in public high schools, and take a stance on the issue—either for censorship of the work or against it.

Issues for Further Research: Plagiarism

Issues of plagiarism can be confusing at times. It is important that such issues be made clear.

The Rules of Attribution | Deborah R. Gerhardt

Ignorance of the law—including intellectual property law—is no excuse, as the cliché goes. For anyone who takes pen to paper (or fingers to keyboard)—students and professional authors alike—it pays to learn about the way intellectual property is protected. Using the case of Harvard undergraduate Kaavya Viswanathan, whose novel How Opal Mehta Got Kissed, Got Wild, and Got a Life *(published by Little, Brown in 2006) was shown to contain unattributed passages from two novels by Megan McCafferty, Deborah R. Gerhardt argues that existing copyright laws are counterintuitive and that teachers need to do more to clarify these laws if they want to prevent plagiarism. Part of the problem, it seems—and this is one of the points Gerhardt raises—has to do with the complexity of copyright law. Deborah Gerhardt is the director of copyright and scholarly communications at the University of North Carolina, Chapel Hill.*

Why do smart students commit plagiarism? Why would a top high-school writer—so accomplished that she would eventually attend Harvard—commit professional suicide by publishing text copied from another author's popular novel? In reading the gotcha press coverage on Kaavya Viswanathan's novel *How Opal Mehta Got Kissed, Got Wild, and Got a Life,* I can't help wondering how much Ms. Viswanathan knew about copyright infringement and plagiarism while she was writing. We don't send our high-school basketball stars onto the court without teaching them the rules of the game, but I fear that too often we send our high-school writing stars to college and graduate school without teaching them the academic and legal rules that govern their creative work.

Ms. Viswanathan's book was inspired by two novels that resonated with her own experience: Megan McCafferty's *Sloppy Firsts* and *Second Helpings.* She readily admits to having read the novels three or four times. Many passages are so similar that last month the young novelist was accused of plagiarism and copyright infringement, and her public comments about those charges reflect genuine contrition and confusion. She told *The New York Times:* "All I really want to do is apologize to Ms. McCafferty. I don't want her to think I intended to cause her distress, because I admire her so much." This month she was accused of using content from another author's work as well.

In college basketball, the rules are not taught once during a brief orientation and then forgotten. They are repeatedly discussed as the season progresses. As we push young writers into the creative arena, the rules of the writing game should get the same attention. Plagiarism rules are not there just to deter literary thieves. They are codes of honor designed to nurture academic integrity by teaching students to honor the voices of others on the way to finding their own.

Copyright law cannot be understood without thoughtful reflection, because it contains many contradictions. Copyright protection is not supposed to extend to

---

Source: Deborah R. Gerhardt, "The Rules of Attribution," *Chronicle of Higher Education* 52, May 26, 2006. Reprinted by permission of Deborah R. Gerhardt.

facts, ideas, or general plot lines, yet the copyright laws tell us that the right to create derivative works—for example, a movie from a novel—belongs exclusively to the author. Copyright laws provide broad protection for authors and publishers by assuring that their work will not be copied without compensation, yet they still permit fair use, such as copying excerpts for criticism, comment, or parody. Trying to define the scope of fair use can be a maddening endeavor, but we would serve our students well by at least alerting them to the known ends of the spectrum, to give them some compass to guide them in determining when and how they may use another's content.

5   We should not expect our students to absorb these complex rules on their own. If we stop to look at our cultural environment through the eyes of Ms. Viswanathan and her peers, we will see that the concepts of plagiarism and copyright are counterintuitive. Copying is essential to learning. When a toddler repeats a word, it is great cause for celebration. That same child will learn to write by copying letters seen in print. In high school and college, students memorize their lecture notes and redeliver this content back to professors on exams, often without the expectation of attribution. The ability to repeat back what they learned (generally without attribution) is richly rewarded.

We encourage our students to recycle objects and ideas they get from others. Discarding paper and plastic in appropriate receptacles has become a routine responsibility in our schools. Students create collages and sculptures from discarded items such as milk jugs and magazines. We assign them to groups to share ideas. We teach them that great writers recycled ideas they found in other great works. A high-school student will learn that Shakespeare brilliantly recast the plot of Tristan and Isolde to create Romeo and Juliet. She may also learn that Thomas Jefferson could not have drafted the Declaration of Independence without recasting the thoughts of other great philosophers such as John Locke. We would serve our students better if we enriched these lessons with discussions about plagiarism and copyright laws so our students would understand the principles that govern their work in different contexts. They need to learn that they can still work within those principles to create new works inspired by their creative heroes.

When the school day ends, students are inundated with an infinite quantity of recycled content in popular culture. They listen to music that uses famous riffs from other songs. They read books that are turned into movies, and then the characters from those movies appear on an endless array of products, such as breakfast cereals, clothing, toys, and video games. Most students do not know that it takes hours of negotiation and boxes of trademark and copyright licenses to make all this borrowing appear so seamless. The recording industry's lawsuits against students who pirate digital music may have taught our students that copying an entire work can get them in trouble. We must alert our students to the reality that sometimes copyright laws also prohibit copying smaller portions of a work.

It is quite possible—and I believe likely—that Ms. Viswanathan's editors and advisers pushed her to write and publish without first taking the time to explain to her the basic principles of plagiarism and copyright. Much of the alleged copying in her work is not verbatim lifting but the creative recycling of ideas. The rules of what can be borrowed and when attribution must be given are complex and require vigilant attention. She confessed to *The New York Times*: "I feel as confused as anyone about it, because it happened so many times." It is so unfortunate to see a promising young writer taken out of the game because she did not understand the rules. My hope is that this incident will motivate parents and educators to remember that creative work has its rules, and if they want to stay in the game, our students should know them.

Reflections and Inquiries

1. According to Gerhardt, what can teachers learn from basketball coaches in teaching students about plagiarism?

2. What makes copyright law so difficult to understand? What strategy might teachers use to get around this problem?

3. If "copying is essential to learning," as Gerhardt points out, why do you suppose plagiarism is such a serious offense?

Reading to Write

Locate three or four additional articles on plagiarism; then write an essay in which you distinguish between fair use of existing ideas (for example, taking a well-known plot such as that of *The Wizard of Oz*, either in L. Frank Baum's 1900 book or the 1925 or 1939 Hollywood film adaptations) and using them as the basis for an "original" work, such as Gregory Maguire's novel, *Wicked: The Life and Times of the Wicked Witch of the West* (HarperCollins, 1995).

Plagiarism Lines Blur for Students in Digital Age | Trip Gabriel

In the eyes of many students these days, material from the Internet, often published without bylines (such as Wikipedia entries) falls outside the domain of "intellectual property" protected by copyright and therefore freely available for cutting and pasting into one's own work without attribution.

But this is a misconception. The rules for citing print sources also apply to Internet sources.

However, as Trip Gabriel makes clear in the following article, confusion over what is considered to be intellectual property, whether protected by copyright or in the public domain, is not the most serious problem. Instead, it is the passing off of someone else's original thoughts and words as one's own—hardly a learning experience.

Trip Gabriel (also known as Bertram Gabriel III), who holds a degree in philosophy from Middlebury College, has written for Rolling Stone, Outside, *and* GQ *magazines before becoming a reporter for* The New York Times. *A developer and fashion editor of that newspaper's Style section, Gabriel currently reports on education-related issues.*

At Rhode Island College, a freshman copied and pasted from a Web site's frequently asked questions page about homelessness—and did not think he needed to credit a source in his assignment because the page did not include author information.

At DePaul University, the tip-off to one student's copying was the purple shade of several paragraphs he had lifted from the Web; when confronted by a writing tutor his professor had sent him to, he was not defensive—he just wanted to know how to change purple text to black.

And at the University of Maryland, a student reprimanded for copying from Wikipedia in a paper on the Great Depression said he thought its entries—unsigned and collectively written—did not need to be credited since they counted, essentially, as common knowledge.

Professors used to deal with plagiarism by admonishing students to give credit to others and to follow the style guide for citations, and pretty much left it at that.

5 　 But these cases—typical ones, according to writing tutors and officials responsible for discipline at the three schools who described the plagiarism—suggest that many students simply do not grasp that using words they did not write is a serious misdeed.

It is a disconnect that is growing in the Internet age as concepts of intellectual property, copyright, and originality are under assault in the unbridled exchange of online information, say educators who study plagiarism.

Digital technology makes copying and pasting easy, of course. But that is the least of it. The Internet may also be redefining how students—who came of age with music file-sharing, Wikipedia and Web-linking—understand the concept of authorship and the singularity of any text or image.

"Now we have a whole generation of students who've grown up with information that just seems to be hanging out there in cyberspace and doesn't seem to have an author," said Teresa Fishman, director of the Center for Academic Integrity at Clemson University. "It's possible to believe this information is just out there for anyone to take."

Professors who have studied plagiarism do not try to excuse it—many are champions of academic honesty on their campuses—but rather try to understand why it is so widespread.

In surveys from 2006 to 2010 by Donald L. McCabe, a cofounder of the   *10* Center for Academic Integrity and a business professor at Rutgers University, about 40 percent of 14,000 undergraduates admitted to copying a few sentences in written assignments.

Perhaps more significant, the number who believed that copying from the Web constitutes "serious cheating" is declining—to 29 percent on average in recent surveys from 34 percent earlier in the decade.

Sarah Brookover, a senior at the Rutgers campus in Camden, New Jersey, said many of her classmates blithely cut and paste without attribution.

"This generation has always existed in a world where media and intellectual property don't have the same gravity," said Ms. Brookover, who at 31 is older than most undergraduates. "When you're sitting at your computer, it's the same machine you've downloaded music with, possibly illegally, the same machine you streamed videos for free that showed on HBO last night."

Ms. Brookover, who works at the campus library, has pondered the differences between researching in the stacks and online. "Because you're not walking into a library, you're not physically holding the article, which takes you closer to 'this doesn't belong to me,'" she said. Online, "everything can belong to you really easily."

A University of Notre Dame anthropologist, Susan D. Blum, disturbed   *15* by the high rates of reported plagiarism, set out to understand how students view authorship and the written word, or "texts" in Ms. Blum's academic language.

She conducted her ethnographic research among 234 Notre Dame undergraduates. "Today's students stand at the crossroads of a new way of conceiving texts and the people who create them and who quote them," she wrote last year in the book "My Word!: Plagiarism and College Culture," published by Cornell University Press.

Ms. Blum argued that student writing exhibits some of the same qualities of pastiche that drive other creative endeavors today—TV shows that constantly reference other shows or rap music that samples from earlier songs.

In an interview, she said the idea of an author whose singular effort creates an original work is rooted in Enlightenment ideas of the individual. It is buttressed by the Western concept of intellectual property rights as secured by copyright law. But both traditions are being challenged.

"Our notion of authorship and originality was born, it flourished, and it may be waning," Ms. Blum said.

She contends that undergraduates are less interested in cultivating a unique   *20* and authentic identity—as their 1960s counterparts were—than in trying on many different personas, which the Web enables with social networking.

"If you are not so worried about presenting yourself as absolutely unique, then it's O.K. if you say other people's words, it's O.K. if you say things you don't believe, it's O.K. if you write papers you couldn't care less about because they accomplish the task, which is turning something in and getting a grade," Ms. Blum said, voicing student attitudes. "And it's O.K. if you put words out there without getting any credit."

The notion that there might be a new model young person, who freely borrows from the vortex of information to mash up a new creative work, fueled a brief brouhaha earlier this year with Helene Hegemann, a German teenager whose best-selling novel about Berlin club life turned out to include passages lifted from others.

Instead of offering an abject apology, Ms. Hegemann insisted, "There's no such thing as originality anyway, just authenticity." A few critics rose to her defense, and the book remained a finalist for a fiction prize (but did not win).

That theory does not wash with Sarah Wilensky, a senior at Indiana University, who said that relaxing plagiarism standards "does not foster creativity, it fosters laziness."

25   "You're not coming up with new ideas if you're grabbing and mixing and matching," said Ms. Wilensky, who took aim at Ms. Hegemann in a column in her student newspaper headlined "Generation Plagiarism."

"It may be increasingly accepted, but there are still plenty of creative people—authors and artists and scholars—who are doing original work," Ms. Wilensky said in an interview. "It's kind of an insult that that ideal is gone, and now we're left only to make collages of the work of previous generations."

In the view of Ms. Wilensky, whose writing skills earned her the role of informal editor of other students' papers in her freshman dorm, plagiarism has nothing to do with trendy academic theories.

The main reason it occurs, she said, is because students leave high school unprepared for the intellectual rigors of college writing.

"If you're taught how to closely read sources and synthesize them into your own original argument in middle and high school, you're not going to be tempted to plagiarize in college, and you certainly won't do so unknowingly," she said.

30   At the University of California, Davis, of the 196 plagiarism cases referred to the disciplinary office last year, a majority did not involve students ignorant of the need to credit the writing of others.

Many times, said Donald J. Dudley, who oversees the discipline office on the campus of 32,000, it was students who intentionally copied—knowing it was wrong—who were "unwilling to engage the writing process."

"Writing is difficult, and doing it well takes time and practice," he said.

And then there was a case that had nothing to do with a younger generation's evolving view of authorship. A student accused of plagiarism came to Mr. Dudley's office with her parents, and the father admitted that he was the one responsible for the plagiarism. The wife assured Mr. Dudley that it would not happen again.

Reflections and Inquiries

1. According to educators who study plagiarism, "concepts of intellectual property, copyright, and originality are under assault." Under assault in what way? What are the factors, in your opinion, that contribute to some students' rejection of, or difficulty in understanding the nature of, intellectual property or the need for its protection?

2. Gabriel reports that the number of undergraduates who believe that plagiarism from the Internet constitutes serious cheating has declined from 34 percent earlier in this decade to 29 percent more recently. What do you suppose has contributed to this decline?

3. How serious a problem is Internet plagiarism (in relation to print plagiarism), in your opinion? What, if anything, should teachers do to prevent it?

Reading to Write

Conduct a survey on your campus to determine students' attitudes toward Internet plagiarism—whether they consider it ethical or unethical, legal or illegal—and their reasons behind those attitudes. Based on your survey, what conclusions are you willing to draw regarding the seriousness of Internet plagiarism on your campus? What, if anything, should be done to prevent Internet plagiarism, and why?

Connections Among the Clusters

Media issues call attention to issues in education and national security. The common denominator, of course, is language, the basic tool for transmitting information.

Critical Thinking

1. What potential national security issues, if any, might arise if certain kinds of information, such as information about explosives, were freely available on the Web? What measures should or should not be taken in light of this potential security problem? (See Cluster 3.)

2. How might online social networking serve multicultural learning objectives? Consult the readings in Cluster 4. Consider the different groups one can join in Facebook and LinkedIn.

3. Discuss the limitations of Internet-based learning in the context of multicultural education. (see Cluster 4). One limitation may be the lack of firsthand experience of, say, a city or a work of art. See the full-color American Airlines ad, "You Just Can't Download This" in Chapter 1 on page 32.

Writing Projects

1. Write an essay on the role, if any, that ethics should play in determining intellectual property policy.
2. Are U.S. copyright laws fair or unfair? Write an essay in which you take a stance but in which you also give careful consideration to views that challenge your own. Look up the precise copyright laws you wish to discuss.
3. Take a stance on Internet music downloading in light of your views regarding intellectual property. That is, to what degree should recording artists and composers retain copyright protection for their creative works in light of the claim that the public has a right to free access to music?

Suggestions for Further Reading

Abagnale, Frank W. *Stealing Your Life: The Ultimate Identity Theft Prevention Plan.* New York: Broadway Books, 2007. Print.

Andrews, Lori. *I Know Who You Are and I Saw What You Did: Social Networks and the Death of Privacy.* New York: The Free Press, 2012.

Angwin, Julia. *Dragnet Nation: A Quest for Privacy, Security, and Freedom in a World of Relentless Surveillance.* New York: Times Books, 2014.

Arvidsson, Adam. *Brands: Meaning and Value in Media Culture.* London: Routledge, 2006. Print.

Burgess, Jean, et al., *YouTube: Online Video and Participatory Culture.* Cambridge, UK: Polity, 2009. Print.

Holtzman, Linda, and Leon Sharpe. *Media Messages: What Film, Television, and Popular Music Teach Us about Race, Gender, and Sexual Orientation,* 2nd Edition. New York: Routledge, 2014.

Kirkpatrick, David. *The Facebook Effect: The Inside Story of the Company That Is Connecting the World.* New York: Simon & Schuster, 2011. Print.

Parmelee, John H., and Shannon L. Richard. *Politics and the Twitter Revolution: How Tweets Influence the Relationship between Political Leaders and the Public.* Lanham, MD: Lexington Books, 2013.

Russell, Matthew A. *Mining the Social Web: Analyzing Data from Facebook, Twitter, Linkedin, and Other Social Media Sites.* Sebastopol, CA: O'Reilly Media, 2011. Print.

Solve, Daniel J. *Nothing to Hide: The False Tradeoff between Privacy and Security.* New Haven: Yale University Press, 2013.

Stickley, Jim. *The Truth about Identity Theft.* Upper Saddle River, NJ: FT Press, 2009. Print.

Whitlock, Warren, *Twitter Revolution.* Las Vegas, NV: Xeno Press, 2008. Print.

6 | Biomedical Research: What Role Should Ethics Play?

Introduction

The human genome has been mapped. A mother can test her unborn child for genetic defects. Implantation of embryonic stem cells (and perhaps other types of stem cells) may someday reverse the effects of paralysis, Alzheimer's, and neuromuscular diseases. Consciousness has now become a subject of scientific scrutiny. "Questions once confined to theological speculations and late-night dorm-room bull sessions," writes Harvard psychologist Steven Pinker in his article "The Mystery of Consciousness" (part of *Time*'s January 29, 2007, special issue on the human brain), "are now at the forefront of cognitive neuroscience" (60). Exciting? Frightening? Yes to both, many would agree.

Others would insist that we are going too far: Certain aspects of our being—like our cellular beginnings or the domain of the soul (where consciousness is traditionally located)—should not be anatomized by the icy rationality of science. To delve into what many consider to be the sacred mysteries of life is to risk dehumanization through eugenics, mind control, and transforming human beings (or their organs) into marketable commodities. Many insist, to put it more bluntly, that such research is flat-out immoral (for example, because it puts people in the role of tampering with what should occur naturally in humans and animals), despite the arguments that such research is profoundly moral because it can alleviate suffering and help us to better know ourselves.

As the following cluster of articles suggests, the debate is far from resolved. As with any controversy, it is important to examine all points of view with care, understanding, and objectivity, no matter how tempting it is to dismiss those views with which we disagree. When it comes to issues of a scientific nature, there's an additional challenge: lack of familiarity with the scientific topic in question. This does not mean that one has to be a biochemist or neurologist to be able to pass judgment on the ethics of stem cell or brain research. But it does mean that before agreeing or disagreeing, say, that destroying embryonic stem cells is tantamount to destroying living human beings, one needs to have at least a grounding in prenatal biology as well as a grounding in bioethics. Pursuing one without the other is to risk flawed, biased judgment.

Can Biomedical Issues Be Separated from Politics?

Because so much of biomedical research raises ethical issues, political intervention becomes unavoidable—which may be a good thing. Congressional leaders, for example, feel it is their duty to alert the public on, say, advances in genetic modification of meats and vegetables.

Political Science/Politicized Science | Dave Coverly

A good editorial cartoon can, through exaggeration and wordplay, bring out aspects of a controversy that would otherwise be difficult to articulate. In the case of Dave Coverly's cartoon, reproduced here, the cause in question is the blurring of the distinctions between politics and science that commonly occur in the popular media. Dave Coverly is the creator of the successful syndicated cartoon series Speed Bump, *which appears in more than 200 periodicals. He has twice received a Reuben Award (in 1995 and 2003) for the best newspaper panel by the National Cartoonists Society. Coverly's website is www .speedbump.com.*

Reflections and Inquiries
1. What is the basis of the humor in this cartoon?

2. How would you distinguish between "political science" and "politicized science"? Why do you suppose political science is so named, instead of, say, "political studies"? How does the idea of science change from political science to the so-called hard sciences, such as chemistry or physics?

3. Comment on the "books" on the rack. In what ways have stem cell research, contraception, global warming, and air pollution been politicized?

4. What other "books" of politicized science would you be willing to place on the rack?

Reading to Write
Write an essay on whether you believe a particular science should be "politicized." If so, what kinds of legislation would you consider appropriate for the scientific research, and why? If not, what would be your reasons for keeping the science insulated from governmental control?

Inside the Meat Lab
A handful of scientists aim to satisfy the world's growing appetite for steak without wrecking the planet. The first step: grab a petri dish. | Jeffrey Bartholet

How willing are you to sit down to a steak dinner or hamburger that was created in a laboratory? Despite the stated advantages—avoiding the slaughter of livestock, diminishing environmental degradation caused by raising cattle, pigs, chickens, and the like—many people would hesitate to consume lab-produced food. Perhaps this Scientific American *article by Jeffrey Bartholet, a former Newsweek bureau chief, will help you change your mind.*

In Brief
Meat grown in a laboratory could provide high-protein food sources free of the environmental and ethical concerns that accompany large-scale livestock operations. **Yet progress** has been slow, in no small part due to the difficulty scientists

have securing funding for their research. **One promising strategy** involves growing embryonic stem cells from livestock in a culture, then coaxing them to transform into muscle cells. **Even if research is successful,** some people question whether the public would ever develop a taste for meat engineered in the lab.

It is not unusual for visionaries to be impassioned, if not fanatical, and Willem van Eelen is no exception. At 87, van Eelen can look back on an extraordinary life. He was born in Indonesia when it was under Dutch control, the son of a doctor who ran a leper colony. As a teenager, he fought the Japanese in World War II and spent several years in prisoner-of-war camps. The Japanese guards used prisoners as slave labor and starved them. "If one of the stray dogs was stupid enough to go over the wire, the prisoners would jump on it, tear it apart and eat it raw," van Eelen recalls. "If you looked at my stomach then, you saw my spine. I was already dead." The experience triggered a lifelong obsession with food, nutrition and the science of survival.

One obsession led to another. After the Allies liberated Indonesia, van Eelen studied medicine at the University of Amsterdam. A professor showed the students how he had been able to get a piece of muscle tissue to grow in the laboratory. This demonstration inspired van Eelen to consider the possibility of growing edible meat without having to raise or slaughter animals. Imagine, he thought, protein-rich food that could be grown like crops, no matter what the climate or other environmental conditions, without killing any living creatures.

Under normal conditions, 10 cells could grow into 50,000 metric tons of meat in just two months. One such cell line would be sufficient to feed the world.

If anything, the idea is more potent now. The world population was just more than two billion in 1940, and global warming was not a concern. Today the planet is home to three times as many people. According to a 2006 report by the Food and Agriculture Organization, the livestock business accounts for about 18 percent of all anthropogenic greenhouse gas emissions—an even larger contribution than the global transportation sector. The organization expects worldwide meat consumption to nearly double between 2002 and 2050.

Meat grown in bioreactors—instead of raised on farms—could help alleviate planetary stress. Hanna Tuomisto, a Ph.D. candidate at the University of Oxford, co-authored a study last year on the potential environmental impacts of cultured meat. The study found that such production, if scientists grew the muscle cells in a culture of cyanobacteria hydrolysate (a bacterium cultivated in ponds), would involve "approximately 35 to 60 percent lower energy use, 80 to 95 percent lower greenhouse

gas emissions and 98 percent lower land use compared to conventionally produced meat products in Europe."

As it is, 30 percent of the earth's icefree land is used for grazing livestock and
growing animal feed. If cultured meat were to become viable and widely con-
sumed, much of that land could be used for other purposes, including new forests
that would pull carbon out of the air. Meat would no longer have to be shipped
around the globe, because production sites could be located close to consumers.
Some proponents imagine small urban meat labs selling their products at street
markets that cater to locavores.

The Only Choice Left

Even winston churchill thought in vitro meat was a good idea. "Fifty years hence,
we shall escape the absurdity of growing a whole chicken in order to eat the breast
or wing by growing these parts separately under suitable medium," he predicted
in a 1932 book, *Thoughts and Adventures*. For most of the 20th century, however,
few took the idea seriously. Van Eelen did not let it go. He worked all kinds of
jobs—selling newspapers, driving a taxi, making dollhouscs. He established an
organization to help underprivileged kids and owned art galleries and cafes. He
wrote proposals for in vitro meat production and eventually plowed much of his
earnings into applying for patents. Together with two partners, he won a Dutch
patent in 1999, then other European patents and, eventually, two U.S. patents. In
2005 he and others finally convinced the Dutch Ministry of Economic Affairs to
pledge €2 million to support in vitro meat research in the Netherlands—the largest
government grant for such research to date.

By that time, an American scientist had already succeeded in growing a piece
of fish filet in a lab. Using a small grant from NASA, which was interested in
developing food sources for deepspace voyages, Morris Benjaminson removed
skeletal muscle from a common goldfish and grew it outside the fish's body. Then
an associate briefly marinated the explants in olive oil, chopped garlic, lemon and
pepper, covered them in bread crumbs and deep-fried them. "A panel of female
colleagues gave it a visual and sniff test," says Benjaminson, now an emeritus professor at Touro College in Bay Shore, N.Y. "It looked and smelled pretty much the
same as any fish you could buy at the supermarket." But NASA, apparently convinced there were easier ways to provide protein to astronauts on long deep-space
voyages, declined to further fund Benjaminson's research.

The Dutch money was used by van Eelen and H. P. Haagsman, a scientist at
Utrecht University, to fund a consortium that would aim to show that stem cells
could be taken from farm animals, cultured and induced to become skeletal muscle
cells. The team included a representative from meat company Meester Stegeman
BV, then part of Sara Lee Corporation in Europe, and top scientists at three Dutch
universities. Each university studied different aspects of in vitro meat production.
Scientists at the University of Amsterdam focused on producing efficient growth
media; a group at Utrecht worked on isolating stem cells, making them proliferate
and coaxing them into muscle cells; and those at Eindhoven University of Technology attempted to "train" the muscle cells to grow larger.

The scientists made some progress. They were able to grow small, thin strips of muscle tissue in the lab—stuff that looked like bits of scallop and had the chewy texture of calamari—but several obstacles remained to commercial-scale production. "We gained knowledge; we knew a lot more, but we still didn't have [something that tasted like] a T-bone steak that came from a petri dish," says Peter Verstrate, who represented Meester Stegeman in the consortium and now works as a consultant. In time, the Dutch money ran out.

Van Eelen now fumes that one scientist involved was "stupid" and others just milked him and the Dutch government for money. "I don't know what they did in four years-talking, talking, talking—every year taking more of the money," he says. For their part, the scientists say that van Eelen never understood the scale of the challenge. "He had a naive idea that you could put muscle cells in a petri dish and they would just grow, and if you put money into a project, you'd have meat in a couple of years," says Bernard Roelen, a cell biologist who worked on the project at Utrecht.

Van Eelen was not the only one who imagined a revolution. In 2005 an article in the *New York Times* concluded that "in a few years' time there may be a lab-grown meat ready to market as sausages or patties." A couple of months before the story appeared, researchers had published the first peer-reviewed article on cultured meat in the journal *Tissue Engineering*. The authors included Jason G. Matheny, co-founder of the lab-produced meat advocacy group New Harvest. He understands the challenges better than most. "Tissue engineering is really hard and extremely expensive right now," he says. "To enjoy market adoption, we mainly need to solve the technical problems that increase the cost of engineered meat." That will take money, he notes, and few governments or organizations have been willing to commit necessary funding.

To the scientists involved, that failure seems shortsighted. "I think [in vitro meat] will be the only choice left," says Mark J. Post, head of the physiology department at Maastricht University. "I'm very bold about this. I don't see any way you could still rely on old-fashioned livestock in the coming decades."

Assembly Required

In theory, an in vitro meat factory would work something like this: First, technicians would isolate embryonic or adult stem cells from a pig, cow, chicken or other animal. Then they would grow those cells in bioreactors, using a culture derived from plants. The stem cells would divide and redivide for months on end. Technicians would next instruct the cells to differentiate into muscle (rather than, say, bone or brain cells). Finally, the muscle cells would need to be "bulked up" in a fashion similar to the way in which animals build their strength by exercising.

For now there are challenges at every stage of this process. One difficulty is developing stem cell lines that can proliferate for long periods without suddenly deciding they want to differentiate on their own. Another challenge is to be sure that when stem cells are prompted to differentiate, the overwhelming majority of them turn into muscle as instructed. "If 10 cells differentiate, you want at least

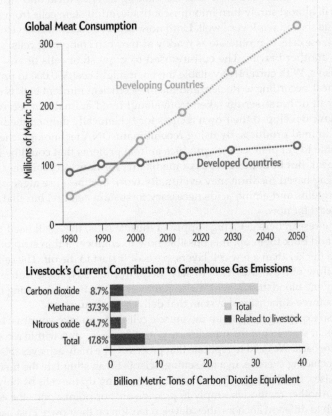

Meaty Problems

The rich world already eats a lot of meat; the developing world is catching up. One reason is that as more people move to cities, improved infrastructure means that meat can be kept cold throughout its journey from the slaughterhouse to the kitchen. Yet as demand for meat increases, so will the environmental consequences. Livestock farming already accounts for 17.8 percent of all anthropogenic greenhouse gas emissions.

Global Meat Consumption

Developing Countries

Developed Countries

Millions of Metric Tons

300

200

100

0

1980 1990 2000 2010 2020 2030 2040 2050

Livestock's Current Contribution to Greenhouse Gas Emissions

Carbon dioxide	8.7%
Methane	37.3%
Nitrous oxide	64.7%
Total	17.8%

Total

Related to livestock

0 10 20 30 40

Billion Metric Tons of Carbon Dioxide Equivalent

seven or eight to turn into muscle cells, not three or four," Roelen says. "We can achieve 50 percent now."

The Utrecht scientists tried to extract and develop embryonic stem cell lines from pigs. Such cells would, in normal conditions, be able to duplicate every day for long periods, meaning 10 cells could grow into a staggering amount of potential meat in just two months—more than 50,000 metric tons. "Culturing embryonic stem cells would be ideal for this purpose since these cells have an (almost) infinite self-renewal capacity," according to a 2009 report by the Utrecht team. "In theory, one such cell line would be sufficient to literally feed the world."

Until now, however, such cell lines have been developed only from mice, rats, rhesus monkeys and humans. Embryonic cells from farm animals have had a tendency to differentiate quickly—and of their own accord—into specialized cells. In the report, Utrecht team's porcine cells often veered toward "a neural lineage"—brains, not bacon.

The Utrecht group also worked with adult stem cells, which have the advantage of being largely preprogrammed. These cells exist within skeletal muscle (as well as other parts of the body) with a specific mission: to do repair work when tissue is injured or dies off. So if you are making in vitro meat and want stem cells that will almost surely turn into muscle tissue, adult stem cells from skeletal muscle tissue should work very well. Until now, however, scientists have not been able to get these cells to proliferate as readily as they can embryonic cells.

Cost is another barrier. The culture used to grow stem cells of any kind is very expensive. With currently available media, it might cost $50,000 to produce a pound of meat, according to Roelen, and the most efficient nutrient bath is derived from fetal calf or horse serum taken from slaughtered animals. In recent years scientists have developed their own recipes for "chemically defined media" that include no animal products. By using recombinant-DNA technology, they have also been able to get plant cells to produce animal proteins that could be used to grow the meat. But both these types of media are, for now, prohibitively expensive. An algae-based medium may eventually work best because algae can produce the proteins and amino acids necessary to sustain cell life, but that, too, is costly—at least for now.

Once the researchers get a big supply of muscle cells, they will need to keep them alive and bulk them up. It is possible now to engineer a thin strip of tissue, but if it gets thicker than a few cell layers, parts of it start to die off. The cells need a constant flow of fresh nutrients to stay alive. In the body, these nutrients are delivered by the bloodstream, which also removes waste. Post is working on how to develop a three-dimensional system that delivers such nutrients.

He is also exploring bulking up the muscle cells. "If you take your cast off after a bone break, it scares you: the muscles are gone," he says. "But within a couple of weeks they're back. We need to replicate that process." The body achieves this in several ways, including exercise. In a lab setting, scientists can stimulate the tissue with electrical pulses. But that is costly and inefficient, bulking up the cells by only about 10 percent. Another method is simply to provide anchor points: once the cells are able to attach to different anchors, they develop tension on their own. Post has made anchors available by providing a scaffold of sugar polymers, which degrades over time. But at this stage, he says, "We're not looking at Schwarzenegger muscle cells."

He has one more method in mind, one he thinks might work best. But it is also more complex. The body naturally stimulates muscle growth with tiny micropulses of chemicals such as acetylcholine. These chemicals are cheap, which is part of what makes this approach appealing. "The trick is to do it in very, very short pulses," Post says. The hurdles to that arc technological, not scientific.

Breakthroughs in all these areas will take money, of course. In 2008 People for the Ethical Treatment of Animals (PETA) offered $1 million to the first person or persons who could grow commercially viable chicken in a lab by 2012. But that was mainly a publicity stunt and no help to scientists who need money to get research done now. More seriously, the Dutch government recently pledged roughly €800,000 toward a new four-year project that would continue the stem cell research at Utrecht—and also initiate a study on the social and moral questions related to in vitro meat.

The Ick Factor

Some see social acceptance as the biggest barrier of all to producing in vitro meat on a commercial scale. "I've mentioned cultured meat to scientists, and they all think, 'great idea;" says Oxford's Tuomisto. "When I talk to nonscientists, they are more afraid of it. It sounds scary. Yet it's basically the same stuff: muscle cells. It's just produced differently."

Cor van der Weele of Wageningen University is heading up the philosophical aspects of the new Dutch study (for example, is cultured meat a moral imperative or morally repugnant, or some combination of the two?). She has been intrigued by the emotional reactions that some people have toward the idea. "We call it the 'yuck response;" she says. "People initially think that it might be something contaminated or disgusting."

But that perception can change quickly, van der Weele observes. She notes that people often associate cultured meat with two other ideas: genetically modified foods—which are often seen, particularly in Europe, as a dangerous corporate scheme to dominate or control the food supply—and negative perceptions of the meat industry in general, with its factory farms, disease and mistreatment of animals. Once people realize that cultured meat is not genetically modified and could be a clean, animal- friendly alternative to factory farms, she says, "the scared, very negative response is often very fleeting."

Such observations are only anecdotal, of course. The study will assess popular responses to in vitro meat in detail—comparing reactions across different regions and cultures—and will determine ways to frame the issue that might enhance consumer interest. Proponents imagine a day when governments will levy special environmental taxes on meat produced from livestock or when consumers will be able to opt for in vitro meat that is labeled "cruelty-free."

"I don't think you want to know about the hygienic conditions in the majority of slaughterhouses in the U.S. or the efficiency of euthanasia," says Post, who spent six years at Harvard University and Dartmouth College before returning home to the Netherlands in 2002. Another outbreak of disease—like mad cow or bird flu—could make cultured meat seem all the more appetizing. "We are far from what we eat," Roelen says. "When we're eating a hamburger, we don't think, 'I'm eating a dead cow.' And when people are already so far from what they eat, it's not too hard to see them accepting cultured meat."

Post has a bold scheme to attract new funding: he aims to create an in vitro sausage just to demonstrate that it is possible. He estimates that it will cost

€300,000 and take six months of work by two doctoral students using three incubators. "We'll take two or three biopsies of a pig—say, 10,000 stem cells," Post says. "After 20 population doublings, we'll have 10 billion cells." The students will use 3,000 petri dishes to produce many tiny bits of porcine muscle tissue, which then will be packed into a casing with some spices and other nonmeat ingredients to give it taste and texture. In the end, scientists will be able to display the sausage next to the living pig from which it was grown.

"It's basically a stunt to generate more funds," Post says. "We're trying to prove to the world we can make a product out of this." But will it taste like a sausage? "I think so," Roelen says. "Most of the taste in a chicken nugget or a sausage is artificially made. Salt and all kinds of other things are added to give it taste."

Van Eelen, who regards himself as "the godfather of in vitro meat," is not a fan of the sausage proposal. He is a diehard idealist and thinks it is important to launch the in vitro revolution with meat that looks, smells and tastes just like anything you would buy off the farm. Van Eelen probably also realizes that time is running out to realize a dream that he has pursued nearly his entire life. "Every time you talk to him, he's speaking about someone else he's found who will be the top scientist who will solve his problems," Roelen says. "I can understand his point of view. But I can't change the laws of the universe."

More To Explore

Production of Animal Proteins by Cell Systems. H. P. Haagsman, K. J. Hellingwerf and B.AJ. Roelen. University of Utrecht, October 2009.

Livestock Production: Recent Trends, Future Prospects. Philip K. Thornton in *Philosophical Transactions of the Royal Society B*, Vol. 365, No.1554, pages 2853-2867; September 27,2010. Food: A Taste of Things to Come? Nicola Jones in Nature, Vol. 468, pages 752-753; 2010. Animal-Free Meat Biofabrication. B. F. Bhat and Z. Bhat in *American Journal of Food Technology*, Vol. 6, No.6, pages 441-459; 2011. New Harvest: www.new-harvest.org

Scientific American Online

Listen to an interview about the future of cultured meat at ScientiflcAmerican.com/jun2011/meat

Reflections and Inquiries

1. How convincingly does Bartholet make the case for laboratory-produced meat? What obstacles to this technology can you think of? How might livestock farmers respond to this technology?

2. Would the reduction in greenhouse gas emissions resulting from lab-grown meat be worth the change? Why or why not?

3. How effective are Bartholet's references to Willem van Eelen, Winston Churchill, and PETA in making the case for in-vitro meat?

Reading to Write

Make the case for or against replacing (completely or partially) traditional livestock farming with lab-produced meat. Be sure to consider the advantages and disadvantages.

Bioengineering and Self-Improvement | Arthur Caplan

Many people feel uncomfortable using modern-day technology for self-improvement, especially when such improvement involves enhancing one's physical appearance. In the following essay, Arthur Caplan, professor of bioethics at the University of Pennsylvania and director of the university's Center for Bioethics, identifies the reasons behind people's associating self-improvement with unethical behavior and explains why using biotechnology to enhance one's physical well-being is not unethical.

I walked by a laser-eye-surgery clinic in a shopping mall recently. There was a sign high up over the door. I could not read it, so I put on my glasses. The sign said, "Our latest techniques are safe, easy, painless and quick—you may see better than 20/20." Which got me to thinking—is there anything wrong with using medicine and biological engineering to modify our brains and bodies to improve or enhance them?

Very few people have 20/20 vision. Being able to see well is crucial to success in some sports. Those who have extraordinary vision, better than 20/20, turn out to be especially good at hitting a baseball or catching a lacrosse ball. On the whole, few of us see 20/20, and almost none of us sees better than that. The clinic was claiming that, in only a few hours in the mall, they could make those with lousy vision see as well as or better than most of humanity ever has! Is there anything immoral about doing that? Surprisingly, a lot of people think the answer to that question is yes.

There has been a lot of interest on the part of President George W. Bush's Council on Bioethics in the subject of human improvement. They have spent a considerable amount of time in recent years pondering the question of whether it is right to improve or enhance ourselves using new biological knowledge.

Just over a year and a half ago, the council issued a report titled *Beyond Therapy* that wrestles with the question of what we are going to do with the explosion of knowledge about the brain—some biochemical (e.g., drugs that affect the brain), some technological (implants that might go into the brain), and some related to scanning and diagnostics (ways to see the brain and make forecasts about propensities or abilities). What should we do in the face of this new area of knowledge?

5   The Council isn't alone in having worries about the wisdom of whether it is right to use bioengineering to try to improve ourselves. Writers such as Carl Elliott, Michael Sandel, Bill McKibben, and Francis Fukuyama are made quite nervous by the prospect of people choosing bioengineering to enlarge their breasts, smooth out their wrinkles, mellow out their moods, and pep up their memories. We might dub these people "anti-meliorists" and their doubts "anti-meliorism."

What the anti-meliorists argue is that, if we don't put a stop to things like laser surgery and liposuction, who knows where it will all end? Our children, or their children, will all have been slugging down chemical concoctions of who knows what in the incessant pursuit of perfection, concoctions fobbed off on them by a greedy pharmaceutical industry. Worse still, the chase for betterment is vain (as in narcissistic), unfair, and doomed to fail.

One aspect of improvement that seems to really gall anti-meliorists is their conviction that trying to improve yourself is vain. Accept yourself as you are, rather than letting Madison Avenue, Joan Rivers, *Town and Country*, or *Vogue* tell you how you ought to be. But it doesn't just have to be a matter of vanity. If it's really all vain, then why don't we just take off our clothes, throw away the makeup, get rid of the fashion industry, and reconcile ourselves to grubbing around in grass skirts? We know that, to some extent, part of what gives us pleasure is trying to control our appearance, to control how others see us. But it may be something in which we can overindulge. I would grant that the person who undergoes her or his twentieth cosmetic-surgery procedure (I have a certain aging pop singer in mind here) may be abusing the idea of improvement. But that doesn't show that it is vain if you want to remove a port-wine-stain blemish from your face, to see better through laser surgery, to wear contacts rather than glasses, or even to remove your wrinkles.

I'm not arguing that it's right for fourteen-year-olds to get breast augmentation surgery. I think you should learn to decide whether you like your body or not, and you're not ready at that age to make such a decision. But, it is not self-evident that all pursuit of beauty or looks or appearance is vain in and of itself. And certainly, vanity has nothing to do with interest in trying to think faster or have more memory, or in the decision about whether one wants to be stronger or to be able to increase aptitudes and capabilities. That's not vanity; that's self-regard.

It is true that we in the developed world could find ourselves having access to biological engineering that poor people in poor nations do not. It's also true that we in rich countries could find ourselves with a lot of people unable to buy or purchase many of these things that might lead to improvement or enhancement.

I'm not in favor of inequity. But, if I said, "We're going to guarantee to   *10*
anyone who wants it access to a chip that can be put into somebody's head
and improve his memory"—if, in other words, equity is taken off the table—
then worries about equity evaporate. Inequity is bad. But it's not bad because
it might be connected to biological engineering. Inequity is immoral because it
is unfair.

Well, the anti-meliorists fret, can you really be happy through biological
tinkering? If we wind up using biological knowledge to engineer ourselves
so that we can think more quickly in solving a problem, have more memory,
figure out problems better than we could before, because we've taken a drug,
in what sense have we earned or do we merit these improvements?

If we swallow a cup of coffee or tea every morning as a stimulant, should
those who do so all feel morally bad for a while? Cheap thrills may be cheap,
but they can still be thrilling. Some people do think that the only way to get to
the top of the mountain is to hike or bike up there. I don't have a problem with
that. If they like doing that, that's fine. Me, I like a helicopter. View's the same.
I don't care. I get to the top.

Not all forms of pleasure have to be earned to be pleasurable. There are
plenty of things that you and I are all happy about that we have nothing to
do with the creation or attainment of, that we don't struggle, practice, earn,
fight for, or do anything to attain. They just happen, and we say, "Well, that's
good fortune." It is only a bizarre form of puritanical, capitalistic hedonism,
which seems to have infected the anti-meliorists, that supports the view that
only earned happiness is authentic happiness.

The drive to improve ourselves using bioengineering is not immoral in
principle. So, why shouldn't we try to improve ourselves both biologically and
socially? I find no convincing arguments why, in principle, we shouldn't try to
improve ourselves at all. I don't find it persuasive that to say you want to be
stronger, faster, or smarter makes you vain, unfair, or doomed to be dissatis-
fied. I have yet to meet anyone who has had laser surgery with good results
who says he or she feels unsatisfied because a laser did the work.

If we limit ourselves in the way that many anti-meliorists are suggesting
that we do now, then we will rob ourselves and our descendants of some of the
most exciting opportunities that the biological revolution presents.

Reflections and Inquiries

1. How does Caplan refute the position of the anti-meliorists that enhancing
   ourselves through laser surgery, liposuction, and the like is vain and futile?
   How convincingly does he refute them?

2. Caplan admits that controlling our appearance "may be something in which
   we can overindulge." What do you suppose he means by "overindulge" in
   the context of his defense of self-improvement?

3. Do you agree or disagree with the anti-meliorists that only earned happiness is authentic happiness?

4. If you had an opportunity to enhance your memory through biotechnology, would you take advantage of it? Would your response be different if the enhancement were aimed at improving some aspect of your physical appearance? Explain.

5. What is Caplan's aim in his opening and concluding paragraphs? How well does the opening paragraph set the stage for what follows? How, specifically, does the concluding paragraph serve to achieve closure?

Reading to Write

1. Use "Suggestions for Further Readings" at the end of this cluster to gain a wider understanding of the ethical issues involved in biotechnological applications for self-improvement; also conduct a survey to determine student attitudes toward the use of biotechnology for intellectual enhancement and for physical enhancement. Use your findings from both sources of data to argue your stance on biotechnological applications for self-improvement.

2. Write an essay about self-improvement (through surgery or drugs) from a religious perspective. After obtaining theological or scriptural reasons either for or against it, argue for or against these reasons.

The Stem Cell Debate | John W. Donohue, S.J.

One of the most divisive issues of the twenty-first century is whether embryonic stem cells should be cultivated and used for medical research and, potentially, for curing devastating diseases like Alzheimer's, neuromuscular disorders, and Down syndrome—and possibly even for spinal cord regeneration that would restore movement to paralyzed people. The problem, of course, is that embryos are considered by some to be human, every bit as sacred as postembryonic human life. Who has the authority to say that this is, or is not, the case?

In the following article, John W. Donohue, S.J., a priest and the associate editor of America magazine, gives a succinct overview of the controversy, revealing his own position in the process.

Source: John W. Donohue, "The Stem Cell Debate," reprinted from *America*, Nov. 13, 2006 with permission of America Press Inc. © 2006. All rights reserved. For subscription information, visit http://www.americamagazine.org.

Why is there an irreconcilable division between two groups of thoughtful and sympathetic people?

Orrin Hatch, Utah's Republican senior senator, is a firm opponent of abortion. He is also a firm supporter of research on embryonic stem cells, even though this involves destruction of the embryos. The senator's reasons for this latter position are mainly two. He believes, as he has said, that life starts in the womb, "not in a petri dish," and he believes this research on embryos has promise of developing regenerative therapies for such devastating afflictions as Alzheimer's and Parkinson's diseases and for the injuries that produce paraplegics. On July 18, Mr. Hatch was one of the 63 senators who voted for substantial increases in federal funding for embryonic stem cell research.

On the other hand, President George W. Bush and the 37 senators who voted against that bill, along with the members of the U.S. Conference of Catholic Bishops and millions of other citizens, are opposed to enlarging federal grants for research on embryonic stem cells. They are just as compassionate as Senator Hatch and just as hopeful that scientific inquiries will find cures for crippling sicknesses. All the same, they oppose research even on 5- or 6-day-old embryos, because it regularly destroys human life in its earliest stages. On this account, President Bush on July 19 vetoed that bill, which would have removed the restrictions he imposed in 2001 when he limited embryonic stem cell research to the 22 authorized stem cell colonies already in existence.

How does it happen that on this issue there is an irreconcilable division between two groups of thoughtful and sympathetic people? No doubt the answer is complex, but it includes the difference between those whose thinking is dominated by the imagination and those who think more abstractly. Publicists for embryonic stem cell research often point out that the embryos used for this research are no larger than the dot at the end of this sentence. Not only do they not

Stem cells for treating cancer in microtubes.

look like a fetus; they cannot be imagined as looking like anything at all and cannot be fancied as human.

On the other hand, opponents of stem cell research can detach themselves from fancy. They know, as a wise scientist once said, that if 100 first-rate biologists were gathered together, they would all agree that even an eight-cell embryo is living. They might not agree on the definition of life, but they would agree that if this embryo were to nest in a womb, it would normally grow into a baby ready for birth. Those who view the question from this perspective have formed an intellectual judgment that science itself has established. They also argue that research on embryonic stem cells should not be federally funded because it offends the consciences of many Americans.

5   President Bush made the right decision when he vetoed the stem cell bill. Nevertheless, as Representative Mike Pence, Republican of Indiana, remarked at the signing of the veto, he and other opponents of embryonic stem cell research are losing the argument with the American people. Where does that argument stand today? At this point in history, a few conclusions are reasonably certain.

By now, the question of funds for embryonic stem cell research is practically moot. This research is already amply supported by such private sources as university institutes and biotechnology companies, along with monies from some states. It is worth noting, however, that so far none of this research has produced those miraculous therapies that have been predicted. Speaking of these promises, the best that Douglas A. Melton, director of the Harvard Stem Cell Institute could say not long ago was, "We haven't learned anything that makes us think this won't work."

It is known, however, that research on adult stem cells has produced some therapeutic experiments that do work. For instance, the Sept. 21 issue of the *New England Journal of Medicine* reported a study that found that adult stem cells from patients' own bone marrow had improved those patients' cardiac function after a heart attack. Research on these adult stem cells is morally unobjectionable, because they are derived without harm to the donor. The National Institutes of Health currently supports this adult stem cell research and take the position that government funding for it should be substantially increased.

The success of work with adult stem cells will not, however, satisfy those who think no boundaries should be imposed on scientists and their research. This was pointed out by Robert George, a professor of jurisprudence at Princeton University, who is also a member of the President's Council on Bioethics. On the July 17 broadcast of the "NewsHour with Jim Lehrer," Mr. George called the Senate debate about stem cells a sideshow. The real debate now, he said, is about the next step in embryonic stem cell research—a debate about the creation of cloned human embryos that are a match for a particular patient and will be destroyed once their stem cells have been harvested for regenerative medicine. A law that banned federal funding for this "fetal farming" would clearly represent a choice of life over death.

Reflections and Inquiries

1. What is Donohue's thesis? How does he convey it?

2. Why do you suppose Donohue begins his article with Utah Senator Orrin Hatch's supportive stance on stem cell research?

3. What are Donohue's reasons for supporting President Bush's veto of the bill that would have supported stem cell research? Explain why you agree or disagree with the veto.

Reading to Write

Donohue alludes to the possibility of using adult stem cells instead of embryonic stem cells. How promising are adult stem cells according to the latest research? In an essay, argue whether adult stem cells or embryonic stem cells seem most promising for future research.

Issues for Further Research: Genetic Engineering

"Genetic engineering" carries many negative connotations: creating monstrosities, dangerous tinkering with food, and so on. How warranted are such fears? Do the authors of the following selections dispel or reinforce them?

The Need to Regulate "Designer Babies" | Editors of *Scientific American*

Most people are uncomfortable with the word designer being applied to human beings, particularly to babies. The word connotes artificiality, mechanization—the stuff of science fiction scenarios, not to mention Nazi-style eugenics programs. As the editors of Scientific American imply in the editorial that follows, these scenarios may be exaggerated, but in light of the growing demand for parental control over their children's genetic destiny, there ought to be in place a set of guidelines to regulate such procedures.

More oversight is needed to prevent misuse of new reproductive technologies

On March 3 the cover story of the *New York Daily News* trumpeted a simple imperative to "Design Your Baby." The screaming headline related to a service that would try to allow parents to choose their baby's hair, eye and skin color. A day later the Fertility Institutes reconsidered. The organization made an "internal, self regulatory decision" to scrap the project because of "public perception" and the "apparent negative societal impacts involved," it noted in a statement.

The change of heart will do nothing to stymie the dawning era of what the article called "Build-A-Bear" babies. The use (and abuse) of advanced fertility technology that evokes fears of Gattaca, Brave New World and, of course, the Nazis' quest for a blonde, blue-eyed race of Aryans apace. A recent survey found that about 10 percent of a group who went for genetic counseling in New York City expressed interest in screening for tall stature and that some 13 percent said they would be willing to test for superior intelligence. The Fertility Institutes is still building the foundation for a nascent dial-a-trait catalogue: it routinely accepts clients who wish to select the sex of their child.

The decision to scrap the designer baby service came just a few weeks after Nadya Suleman, a single, unemployed California mother living on food stamps, gained notoriety after giving birth to octuplets through in vitro fertilization. The Suleman brouhaha showed that even routine uses of reproductive technologies can be fraught with issues that bear on ethics and patient safety.

The preimplantation genetic diagnosis (PGD) technique used by the Fertility Institutes to test embryos before implantation in the womb has enabled thousands of parents to avoid passing on serious genetic diseases to their offspring. Yet fertility specialists are doing more than tiptoeing into a new era in which medical necessity is not the only impetus for seeking help. In the U.S., no binding rules deter a private clinic from offering a menu of traits or from implanting a woman with a collection of embryos. Physicians who may receive more than $10,000 for a procedure serve as the sole arbiters of a series of thorny ethical, safety and social welfare questions. The 33-year-old Suleman already had six children, and her physician implanted her with six embryos, two of which split into twins. American Society for Reproductive Medicine (ASRM) voluntary guidelines suggest that, under normal circumstances, no more than two embryos be transferred to a woman younger than 35 because of the risk of complications.

5   Of course, any office consultation with a fertility doctor will likely neglect the nuances of more encompassing ethical dilemmas. Should parents be allowed to pick embryos for specific tissue types so that their new baby can serve as a donor for an ailing sibling? For that matter, should a deaf parent who embraces his or her condition be permitted to select an embryo apt to produce a child unable to hear? Finally, will selection of traits perceived to be desirable end up diminishing variability within the gene pool, the raw material of natural selection?

In the wake of the octuplets' birth, some legislators made hasty bids to enact regulation at the state level—and one bill was drafted with the help of antiabortion advocates. The intricacies of regulating fertility technology requires more careful consideration that can only come with a measure of federal guidance. As part of the push toward health care reform, the Obama administration should carefully inspect the British model.

Since 1991 the U.K.'s Human Fertilization and Embryology Authority (HFEA) has made rules for in vitro fertilization and any type of embryo manipulation. The HFEA licenses clinics and regulates research: it limits the number of embryos implanted and prohibits sex selection for nonmedical reasons, but it is not always overly restrictive. It did not object to using PGD to pick an embryo that led to the birth of a girl in January who lacked the genes that would have predisposed her to breast cancer later in life.

HFEA may not serve as a precise template for a U.S. regulatory body. But a close look at nearly two decades of licensing a set of reproductive technologies by the country that brought us the first test-tube baby may build a better framework than reliance on the good faith of physicians who confront an inherent conflict of interest.

This story was originally published with the title "Designing Rules for Designer Babies."

Reflections and Inquiries

1. Do you agree that a genetic regulating body like the U.K's Human Fertilization and Embryology Authority can effectively monitor proper use of embryonic manipulation? Why or why not?

2. Where would you draw the line, if at all, between what would be permitted or not permitted with regard to embryonic manipulation? How would you justify your limitations, if any?

3. From the perspective of natural evolutionary progression, what concerns are raised by our ability to control the genetic destiny of our children? In other words, if natural selection can be preempted by human intervention, is that a good thing or a bad thing, and why?

Reading to Write

Write an essay weighing the advantages against the disadvantages of embryonic manipulation. What are your conclusions and recommendations with regard to the continuation of this biotechnology?

Patenting Life | Michael Crichton

Patenting genetically altered animals for laboratory research may seem like a good idea from an intellectual property point of view. After all, if a scientist creates a microorganism capable of, let us say, absorbing pesticide traces that have been absorbed into harvested crops or traces of mercury that have been absorbed by fish, shouldn't that scientist's right of ownership (and the remuneration resulting

---

from it) be protected? No, insists Michael Crichton (1942–2008), for the reasons he explained in the following op-ed piece. Crichton, the creator of the television series ER and famous for his blockbuster science fiction novels The Andromeda Strain, Jurassic Park, and Next, was a graduate of Harvard Medical School and served as a postdoctoral fellow at the Salk Institute.

You, or someone you love, may die because of a gene patent that should never have been granted in the first place. Sound far-fetched? Unfortunately, it's only too real.

Gene patents are now used to halt research, prevent medical testing and keep vital information from you and your doctor. Gene patents slow the pace of medical advance on deadly diseases. And they raise costs exorbitantly: a test for breast cancer that could be done for $1,000 now costs $3,000.

Why? Because the holder of the gene patent can charge whatever he wants, and does. Couldn't somebody make a cheaper test? Sure, but the patent holder blocks any competitor's test. He owns the gene. Nobody else can test for it. In fact, you can't even donate your own breast cancer gene to another scientist without permission. The gene may exist in your body, but it's now private property.

This bizarre situation has come to pass because of a mistake by an underfinanced and understaffed government agency. The United States Patent Office misinterpreted previous Supreme Court rulings and some years ago began—to the surprise of everyone, including scientists decoding the genome—to issue patents on genes.

5   Humans share mostly the same genes. The same genes are found in other animals as well. Our genetic makeup represents the common heritage of all life on earth. You can't patent snow, eagles or gravity, and you shouldn't be able to patent genes, either. Yet by now one-fifth of the genes in your body are privately owned.

The results have been disastrous. Ordinarily, we imagine patents promote innovation, but that's because most patents are granted for human inventions. Genes aren't human inventions, they are features of the natural world. As a result these patents can be used to block innovation, and hurt patient care.

For example, Canavan disease is an inherited disorder that affects children starting at 3 months; they cannot crawl or walk, they suffer seizures and eventually become paralyzed and die by adolescence. Formerly there was no test to tell parents if they were at risk. Families enduring the heartbreak of caring for these children engaged a researcher to identify the gene and produce a test. Canavan families around the world donated tissue and money to help this cause.

When the gene was identified in 1993, the families got the commitment of a New York hospital to offer a free test to anyone who wanted it. But the researcher's employer, Miami Children's Hospital Research Institute, patented the gene and refused to allow any health care provider to offer the test without paying a royalty. The parents did not believe genes should be patented and so did not put their names on the patent. Consequently, they had no control over the outcome.

In addition, a gene's owner can in some instances also own the mutations of that gene, and these mutations can be markers for disease. Countries that don't have gene patents actually offer better gene testing than we do, because when multiple labs are allowed to do testing, more mutations are discovered, leading to higher-quality tests.

Apologists for gene patents argue that the issue is a tempest in a teapot,   *10* that patent licenses are readily available at minimal cost. That's simply untrue. The owner of the genome for Hepatitis C is paid millions by researchers to study this disease. Not surprisingly, many other researchers choose to study something less expensive.

But forget the costs: why should people or companies own a disease in the first place? They didn't invent it. Yet today, more than 20 human pathogens are privately owned, including haemophilus influenza and Hepatitis C. And we've already mentioned that tests for the BRCA genes for breast cancer cost $3,000. Oh, one more thing: if you undergo the test, the company that owns the patent on the gene can keep your tissue and do research on it without asking your permission. Don't like it? Too bad.

The plain truth is that gene patents aren't benign and never will be. When SARS was spreading across the globe, medical researchers hesitated to study it—because of patent concerns. There is no clearer indication that gene patents block innovation, inhibit research and put us all at risk.

Even your doctor can't get relevant information. An asthma medication only works in certain patients. Yet its manufacturer has squelched efforts by others to develop genetic tests that would determine on whom it will and will not work. Such commercial considerations interfere with a great dream. For years we've been promised the coming era of personalized medicine— medicine suited to our particular body makeup. Gene patents destroy that dream. Fortunately, two congressmen want to make the full benefit of the decoded genome available to us all. Last Friday, Xavier Becerra, a Democrat of California, and Dave Weldon, a Republican of Florida, sponsored the Genomic Research and Accessibility Act, to ban the practice of patenting genes found in nature. Mr. Becerra has been careful to say the bill does not hamper invention, but rather promotes it. He's right. This bill will fuel innovation, and return our common genetic heritage to us. It deserves our support.

Reflections and Inquires

1. According to Crichton, just as we "can't patent snow, eagles or gravity," we "shouldn't be able to patent genes, either." Comment on the soundness of this analogy.

2. Crichton argues that gene patenting could be used to block innovation and hurt patient care. What evidence does Crichton present to support his claim, and how convincing is it, in your opinion?

3. What is the current status of the Genomic Research and Accessibility Act? Explain why you would support or challenge this congressional effort to make the benefits of the decoded genome accessible.

Reading to Write

1. In Crichton's view, the counterargument that patents are readily available at minimal cost is "simply untrue." After learning more about current costs involved in using patented organisms in biomedical research, write a position paper supporting or defending the practice of gene patenting.

2. Write an essay in which you consider the ethical implications of patenting genetically altered organisms.

The Debate over Genetically Modified Foods | Kerryn Sakko

Kerryn Sakko, currently a senior systems engineer at Sage Automation in Melbourne, was an undergraduate at the University of Adelaide (South Australia) majoring in chemical engineering and mathematics/computer science when she published the following article weighing the benefits against the risks of genetically modifying crops.

Food can be engineered to prevent disease

Before their release, genetically modified (GM) foods require more encompassing tests to assess their effect on human health, their impact on the environment, and their overall benefits or risks to society. The following benefits may be derived from genetic modification:

- Rice with built-in Vitamin A that can help prevent blindness in 100 million children suffering from Vitamin A deficiency;

- A tomato that softens more slowly, allowing it to develop longer on the vine and keep longer on the shelf;

- Potatoes that absorb less fat when fried, changing the ever-popular french fries from junk food into a more nutritional food;

Conventional breeding is a slow, unpredictable process

- Strawberry crops that can survive frost;

- An apple with a vaccine against a virus that causes childhood pneumonia.

Source: Kerryn Sakko, "The Debate over Genetically Modified Foods," May 2002.

These are some of the benefits promised by biotechnology. The debate over its benefits and safety, however, continues. Do we really need to fear mutant weeds, killer tomatoes, and giant corn and will the benefits be delivered?

Conventional Breeding Versus Genetically Modified (GM) Crops

For thousands of years farmers have used a process of selection and cross breeding to continually improve the quality of crops. Even in nature, plants and animals selectively breed, thus ensuring the optimum gene pool for future generations. Traditional breeding methods are slow, requiring intensive labor: while trying to get a desirable trait in a bred species, undesirable traits will appear and breeders must continue the process over and over again until all the undesirables are bred out.

In contrast, organisms acquire one specific gene or a few genes together through genetic modification, without other traits included and within a single generation. However, this technology too is inherently unpredictable and some scientists believe it can produce potentially dangerous results unless better testing methods are developed.

The fallacy of equating gene-splicing with traditional breeding

Traditional breeding is based on sexual reproduction between like organisms. The transferred genes are similar to genes in the cell they join. They are conveyed in complete groups and in a fixed sequence that harmonizes with the sequence of genes in the partner cell. In contrast, bioengineers isolate a gene from one type of organism and splice it haphazardly into the DNA of a dissimilar species, disrupting its natural sequence. Further, because the transplanted gene is foreign to its new surroundings, it cannot adequately function without a big artificial boost.

Biotechnicians achieve this unnatural boosting by taking the section of DNA that promotes gene expression in a pathogenic virus and fusing it to the gene prior to insertion. The viral booster (called a "promoter") radically alters the behavior of the transplanted gene and causes it to function in important respects like an invading virus—deeply different from the way it behaves within its native organism and from the way the engineered organism's own genes behave.... Consequently, not only does the foreign gene produce a substance that has never been in that species, it produces it in an essentially unregulated manner that is uncoordinated with the needs and natural functions of the organism."[11]

60% of U.S. grocery food contains GM ingredients

One of the main differences between conventional and genetically modified crops is that the former involves crosses either within species or between very closely related species. GM crops can have genes either from closely related species or from distant species, even bacteria and viruses. A typical example of a GM crop in the market in Australia is cotton known as Ingard.[6] This cotton has a gene from a naturally occurring soil bacterium known as *Bacillus thuringiensis* (Bt). The Bt gene renders the cotton resistant to the heliothis caterpillar, a major threat to the cotton industry. In this example, an appropriate and selected gene (in a construct containing a promoter, transcription terminator, selection marker, etc. genes) was inserted into the cotton, unlike in conventional breeding where not only the appropriate gene was inherited in breeding but other genes as well.[10]

When combining two crops using standard agricultural techniques, genes are allowed to mix at random. A typical example is Triticale, a synthetic hybrid between wheat and rye grown in Europe, which is the result of combining 50,000 largely untested genes, 25,000 from each species.[10] GM crops, in contrast, have specific genes inserted to produce the same desired effect.

Biotech plants are now grown on about 130 million acres in 13 countries, including Argentina, Canada, and Germany. In 2001, 3.6 million acres were used for GM crops in the U.S. More than 60% of all processed foods in the U.S. contain ingredients from GM soybeans, corn, or canola.[1]

Benefits: One Side of the Debate

Economical

Growing GM crops is initially costly but cheaper in the long run

GM supporters tell farmers that they stand to reap enormous profits from growing GM crops. Initially, the cost is expensive but money is saved on pesticides. To produce the GM crops, modern biotechnology is used which requires highly skilled people and sophisticated and expensive equipment.[7] Large companies need considerable investments in laboratories, equipment and human resources, hence the reason why GM crops are more expensive for farmers than traditional crops. GM crops, farmers are told, are a far better option. It takes a shorter time to produce the desired product, it is precise and there are no unwanted genes.

Herbicide-resistant crops

Farmers need less herbicides in GM fields

So what other advantages do GM crops hold for farmers? GM crops can be produced to be herbicide resistant. This means that farmers could spray these crops with herbicide and kill the weeds, without affecting the crop. In effect, the amount of herbicide used in one season would be reduced, with a subsequent reduction in costs for farmers and consumers. For Ingard cotton, pest resistance was built into the cotton, hence reducing and even removing the use of pesticides, which are not only expensive but, more importantly, harmful to the environment.

Biotechnology companies are even experimenting with crops that can be genetically modified to be drought and salt-tolerant, or less reliant on fertilizer, opening up new areas to be farmed and leading to increased productivity. However, the claims of less herbicide usage with GM crops have till now not been independently supported by facts.

Better quality foods

No safety studies have been done on GM salmon

Even animals can be genetically modified to be leaner, grow faster, and need less food. They could be modified to have special characteristics, such as greater milk production in cows. These modifications again lead to improved productivity for farmers and ultimately lower costs for the consumer. Modified crops could perhaps prevent outbreaks such as foot and mouth disease, which has devastated many farmers and local economies.

No such products have been released to date; however, some are under consideration for release. For example, GM salmon, capable of growing almost 30 times faster than natural salmon, may soon be approved by the FDA (Food and Drug Administration) in the U.S. for release into open waters without a single study on the impact on human health or the environment.[5]

The following are some examples of food plants that are undergoing field trials:[10]

- apples that resist insect attack

- bananas free of viruses and worm parasites

- coffee with a lower caffeine content

- cabbage that resists caterpillar attacks

- melons that have a longer shelf life

- sunflowers that produce oil with lower saturated fat

Risks: The Other Side of the Debate

The major concerns of those who oppose GM foods center on the:

- potential danger to the environment

- possible health risks to humans

Environmental damage

Will herbicide resistance pass on to weeds?

The problem with GM crops is that there is little known about what effect they will have in, say, 20 years time. The genetic structure of any living organism is complex and GM crop tests focus on short-term effects. Not all the effects of introducing a foreign gene into the intricate genetic structure of an organism are tested. Will the pests that a crop was created to resist eventually become resistant to this crop?

Then there is always the possibility that we may not be able to destroy GM crops once they spread into the environment. In Europe, for example, a strain of sugar beet that was genetically modified to be resistant to a particular herbicide has inadvertently acquired the genes to resist another.[7] This was discovered when farmers attempted to destroy the crop in Britain, France and the Netherlands, where it was being tested, and 0.5% of the crop survived.[7] More noxious herbicides had to be used to remove the remainder of the plantation. What if this herbicide resistance passed on to weeds?

Risk to food web

The Skylark and the Monarch butterflies were affected by GM crops

A further complication is that the pesticide produced in the crop may unintentionally harm creatures. In Britain, a native farm bird, the Skylark, was indirectly affected by the introduction of GM sugar beets designed to resist herbicides. In planting this crop, the weeds were reduced substantially. However, since the birds rely on the seeds of this weed in autumn and winter, researchers expect that up to 80% of the Skylark population would have to find other means of finding food.[4]

GM crops may also pose a health risk to native animals that eat them. The animals may be poisoned by the built-in pesticides. Tests in the U.S. showed that 44% of caterpillars of the monarch butterfly died when fed large amounts of pollen from GM corn.[8]

Cross-pollination

Will genes from GM plants transfer to other organisms?

Cross-pollination is a concern for both GM crops and conventional breeding, especially with the more serious weeds that are closely related to the crops. With careful management this may be avoided. For example, there is a type of maize that will not breed with other strains and scientists are hoping that it could help to prevent cross-pollination.[3] Genetic modification to herbicide resistant crops could insert the gene that prevents the problem. The number of herbicide-tolerant weeds has increased over the years from a single report in 1978 to the 188 herbicide-tolerant weed types in 42 countries reported in 1997.[6] They are an ever-increasing problem and genetic engineering promises to stop it. But will genes from GM plants spread to other plants, creating superweeds and superbugs we won't be able to control?

GM mix-ups

The taco scandal in the U.S. heightened awareness of GM risks

Humans can inadvertently eat foods that contain GM products meant as animal feed, i.e., crops modified for increased productivity in animals. This happened in the U.S., where traces of a StarLink GM crop, restricted for use only in feed, were found in taco shells.[2] Apparently no one became ill but other such occurrences may lead to health problems.

Allergies and toxins

Very little scientific information exists about the risk of GM food on human health. One major report by Dr. Arpad Pusztai, published on this web site, explains how GM foods could trigger new allergies and contain toxins that may be harmful.[9]

Disease

Will GM products increase the problems with resistance to antibiotics?

Another concern is disease. Since some crops are modified using the DNA from viruses and bacteria, will we see new diseases emerge? What about the GM crops that have antibiotic-resistant marker genes? Marker genes are used by scientists to determine whether their genetic modification of a plant was successful. Will these antibiotic-resistant genes be transferred to microorganisms that cause disease? We already have a problem with ineffective antibiotics. How can we develop new drugs to fight these new bugs?

Conclusion

Proponents of GM crops claim that advantages may be many, such as:

- improved storage and nutritional quality
- pest and disease resistance
- selective herbicide tolerance
- tolerance of water, temperature and saline extremes
- improved animal welfare
- higher yields and quality

However, until further studies can show that GM foods and crops do not pose serious threats to human health or the world's ecosystems, the debate over their release will continue. Living organisms are complex and tampering with their genes may have unintended effects. It is in our common interest to support concerned scientists and organizations, such as Friends of the Earth who demand "mandatory labeling of these food products, independent testing for safety and environmental impacts, and liability for harm to be assumed by biotech companies."[5]

References

1. Ackerman, Jennifer. 2002. "Food: How Safe? How Altered?" *National Geographic*, May issue.

2. Boyce, Nell. 2000. "Taco Trouble." *New Scientist*: Vol. 169, No. 2259, 7 October.

3. Boyce, Nell. 2000. "A Breed Apart." *New Scientist*: Vol. 168, No. 2261, 21 October.

4. Firbank, Les E. and Frank Forcella. 2000. "Genetically Modified Crops and Farmland Biodiversity. *Science*: Vol. 289, No. 5484, 1 Sept.

5. Friends of the Earth. 2002. "Petition to President Bush: Don't Turn Your Back!"

6. Gene Technology Information Service provided by Biotechnology Australia in partnership with the University of Melbourne.

7. Gene Technology in Australia website. http://genetech.csiro.au/. Accessed 6/02.

8. Biotechnology Australia website. http://www.biotechnology.gov.au. Accessed 6/02.

9. Pusztai, Arpad. June 2001. "GM foods: Are they a risk to animal/human health?" http://www.actionbioscience.org/biotech/pusztai.html. Accessed 6/02.

10. National Centre for Biotechnology Education website. http://www.ncbe.reading.ac.uk/. Accessed 6/02.

11. Druker, Steven M., Exec. Dir. of Alliance for Bio-Integrity. "Why concerns about health risks of genetically modified food are scientifically justified." http://www.biointegrity.org/health-risks/health-risks-ge-foods.htm. Accessed 6/02.

Reflections and Inquiries

1. Which of the benefits of genetically modified food, as Sakko presents them, seem to you most important? Which of the risks seem the most serious?

2. Evaluate Sakko's conclusion in light of your own assessment of the benefits and risks of genetically modified food.

Reading to Write

1. One of the risks of genetically modifying crops is harm to the environment. After researching the latest information available on this risk, argue in a

four- to five-page paper whether there may or may not be effective ways to ensure against such environmental harm.

2. Conduct a critical evaluation of the benefits versus the risks of genetic modification of crops and decide whether benefits outweigh risks or vice versa. Start with Sakko's lists of benefits and risks but check to see if there are other benefits and risks that have been identified by scientists since 2002, when Sakko published her essay. Consider interviewing faculty members in the biology, environmental studies, and agribusiness departments, or in programs at your school.

William Paton
Dr. Simone Billings
English 2H
March 12, 2015

Student Essay

The Role of Genetically Modified Organisms in a Shrinking World | William Paton

Genetic modification of crops is nothing new. As William Paton, an undergraduate at Santa Clara University majoring in Bioengineering, points out, humans have been modifying crops for three thousand years. Yet modern-day genetic manipulation gives us pause. Are the reasons for hesitation justified?

When the first *Homo sapiens* walked on Earth, nature was forever changed. With our ability to become the ultimate predator in any environment, we quickly rose to the top of the food chain, altering countless ecosystems. We have built dams and canals to divert major rivers. Our urban areas have displaced innumerable populations of wild animals. Our hunting practices have caused many animal species to go extinct. Humans have scarred the face of the earth with mining and quarrying, and depleted the nutrients from millions of acres of soil through farming. With the exponential increase in the global human population during the last 500,000 years, the effects on the Earth have become more and more significant. Now we are faced with overpopulation, and we are pushing the limits of naturally-occurring resources. In order to sustain this growing population, we have been forced to search for novel strategies to make these resources renewable and plentiful; many of which have destroyed natural environments. One of the most important resources that a significant proportion of the world's individuals lacks is food. According to Hans Rosling, we must double our food production by 2030 to adequately feed the entire global population.

This Assyrian relief carving from around 870 BCE shows artificial pollination of date palm plants.

Background

The Importance of Agriculture. At the end of the last ice age, humans profoundly altered the course of Earth's history: about 10,000 years ago various populations began to domesticate different crops. Consequently, humans began to provide food for themselves with agriculture, rather than through hunting and gathering. Agriculture was born in Sumer, located between the Tigris and Euphrates rivers in what is now Iraq, home to the earliest known civilization ("Sumer"). Cultivating fields caused humans to become civilized by differentiating roles in society, rather than individually foraging for food. Job specialization created time for more complex modes of thinking such as philosophy, mathematics, engineering, politics, ethics and history, to name a few ("origins of agriculture"). Ultimately, the advent of agriculture has been the one of the most significant catalysts for human development thus far.

The History of Genetic Modification. Fast-forward to Assyria about 3,000 years ago: farmers were manually pollinating date palm plants in order to cross-breed them with the cream of the crop ("origins of agriculture"). This was the first case of genetic modification of plants: selective breeding to produce a superior crop. However, it was not until Gregor Mendel's 1865 paper *Experiments on Plant Hybrids* that humans understood the science behind selective breeding. After extensive experimentation on peas, Mendel was able to explain how specific phenotypes could be produced by dominant and recessive alleles ("Gregor Mendel"). A century later, James Watson and Francis Crick determined the molecular structure of DNA, allowing humans to better understand how to manipulate DNA molecules ("genetic engineering"). Then, in 1986, the first genetically modified tobacco plant was created by inserting an herbicide-resistant gene from a bacterium into a tobacco plant (James and Krattiger). In 1995 genetically modified foods were approved for human consumption by the FDA, and by the end of 2010 almost one-tenth of the world's farmland was covered by GM crops ("genetically modified organism (GMO)").

Types of GMO Crops

Insect-Resistant Crops. When Rachel Carson wrote her groundbreaking book *Silent Spring* in 1962, she predicted that many pests would evolve to become resistant to

DDT and other toxic chemicals used by farmers. In the 1940s, agricultural workers in the United States and elsewhere had limited access to pesticides, losing about seven percent of their crops as a result. However, despite the increased use of pesticides, approximately fifteen percent of US crops have been lost since the 1980s, validating Carson's prediction (WGBH Educational Foundation). In order to combat this growing issue, scientists have inserted genes from certain bacteria in order to kill pests without the need for toxic chemicals. Since the mid-1990s, potatoes, corn and cotton have been modified with *Bacillus thuringiensis* (*Bt*) in order to protect them from caterpillars, corn borers, budworms and potato beetles. In 1999, 29 million acres of *Bt* corn, potatoes and cotton were grown across the world; the use of *Bt* cotton that year was estimated to save the United States approximately $92 million. In addition to their insect resistance, *Bt* crops protect farm workers and non-target organisms from exposure to harmful pesticides. *Bt* does not kill insects such as flies, bees, allowing them to pollinate these crops without being harmed, as can be the case when crops are sprayed with synthetic insecticides (Chien and Aroian).

However, similar to Carson's prediction, harmful insects may become resistant to *Bt*, so farmers must take many steps towards preventing this potential catastrophe. One such method is planting "refuge acreage," which involves planting a portion of the fields with wild-type plants that are meant to be eaten by pests. Another difficult issue some farmers have encountered when planting *Bt* crops is that of "secondary pests," which can gradually erode their benefits. This issue is especially prevalent in agricultural communities that are not familiar with secondary pest problems. Researchers from the American Agricultural Economics Association illustrated that many Chinese cotton farmers who adopted the use of *Bt* seeds did not anticipate secondary pests; in fact, the potential benefits of using these seeds were completely eroded by the presence of secondary pests (Just, Wang, and Pinstrup-Andersen). Because *Bt* crops pose threats to farmers and the agricultural industry, laws requiring farmer education programs should be instituted to prevent insect resistance and secondary pest issues. These laws will improve the safety and efficacy of *Bt* crops throughout the world.

Herbicide-Tolerant Crops. The most common GMO crops have been engineered to tolerate the harsh effects of herbicides, particularly glyphosate. In the 1980s, agricultural scientists attempted to conventionally breed herbicide-tolerant (HT) crops, but failed. This came as no surprise; only a handful of grasses and a single broadleaf plant species had developed a natural resistance to herbicides in the field. In 1996, Monsanto—a multinational agricultural and biotech corporation—introduced genetically modified soybeans that were resistant to Roundup, an herbicide used in both commercial farms and residential lawns. Now, Roundup can be used in fields where these seeds are planted in order to eliminate unwanted foliage without harming crops. This is a more cost-effective form of weed control than previous techniques because farmers only have to use one product to kill all weeds, without worrying about killing their own crops. It has resulted in an increase in soybean yield by 30% in Romania, and an increase in corn in Argentina and the Philippines by 9% and 15%, respectively (Brookes and Barfoot). The use of HT crops has also been important in maintaining the integrity of topsoil: farmers no longer have to over-till their fields to remove weeds, which can expose them to wind and water erosion. In the United States, approximately 86 percent of HT soybean acres utilize conservation tillage techniques, compared to a mere 36 percent of non-HT soybean acres. This is important because conservation tillage has been shown to reduce soil degradation and water and chemical runoff while increasing water retention: this decreases the amount of work that farmers must put in at the beginning of each growing season, as well as reducing their carbon footprint. Thus, the advent of herbicide-tolerant crops has helped to reduce the risk of another period like the Dust Bowl of the 1930s, where a drought exacerbated the negative effects of farming without using conservation tillage techniques. The no-tillage cycle also shortens the production cycle of many crops; farmers in South America can now plant a crop of soybeans immediately after a wheat crop in the same growing season. This second crop increased the soybean production in Argentina and Paraguay by 67.5 million tons from 1996 to 2007 (Brookes and Barfoot).

Some argue that the introduction of herbicide-tolerant (HT) crops has caused an unhealthy increase in the use of herbicides across the globe. While it is true that the amount of glyphosate has doubled in use from 90 million pounds in 2001 to 180 million pounds in 2007 (Brookes and Barfoot), other herbicides have been used significantly less, resulting in a modest increase in herbicide use. While increased herbicide use is not ideal, using glyphosate instead of other herbicides is. It is

During the Dust Bowl, also known as the "Dirty Thirties," farmers did not use dryland farming techniques to prevent wind erosion.

significantly less persistent and less toxic than traditional herbicides; thus, the adoption of HT crops has lead to an overall positive impact on the environment, including a reduction in health risks to farm workers. Another point that many anti-GMO bring up about Roundup Ready and other HT seeds is that Monsanto and other biotech companies prohibit replanting in order to maintain annual revenue. However, according to Kent Bradford, a plant scientist at the University of California Davis, large-scale commercial growers do not typically save seeds: "The quality deteriorates—they get weeds and so on—and it's not a profitable practice" (Borel). Therefore the main concerns regarding herbicide-tolerant crops are the increased and sometimes excessive use of toxic herbicides (however harmless), as well as the eroding benefits of HT crops. Ultimately, this issue can be mitigated by imposing calculated restrictions on amount of tolerated herbicide use per acre of farmed land, as well as further development of HT crops. The future is bright in this regard: approximately 800 new GMO crops have been tested in the US each year since 2002 (Fernandez-Cornejo, Wechsler, and Livingston).

Improved Nutritional Content. While citizens of wealthy countries such as the United States rely on a variety of foods to obtain their nutrition, many populations can only afford to eat a limited diet of certain staple foods. In Southeast Asia and Africa, dependence on rice as a primary food source is common among the poor. Rice and other carbohydrate-rich foods are generally lacking in micronutrients. An especially significant drawback of rice is that it does not contain any beta-carotene, a pigment that is converted by the human body into Vitamin A. Consequently, Vitamin A Deficiency (VAD) is a major issue among those who consume it as a primary food source. According to the World Health Organization, approximately 250 million preschool children were affected by VAD in 2012 (World Health Organization). Providing those children with vitamin A could prevent a third of deaths of children under the age of five, amounting to 2.7 million children. Young children are especially susceptible to micronutrient deficiencies, and VAD can lead to blindness and eventual immune system impairment, resulting in death. In 2002, "Golden Rice" was developed by Syngenta, a Swiss biotechnology company. They found a way to insert the vitamin A-producing gene from carrots into rice, resulting in a food that could potentially save millions of people in the developing world from blindness or death (Paine et al.). The company even handed over the intellectual property rights to the nonprofit organization The Golden Rice Project: Syngenta didn't want groups who oppose GMO foods because biotech companies profit from them to resist this lifesaving technology. In 2009, Golden Rice was successfully tested on humans in the United States, and in 2013 Pope Francis gave his personal blessing to Golden Rice (Ropeik). However, environmental organization Greenpeace has been leading a campaign to block the use of Golden Rice, calling it a "fake remedy for Vitamin A Deficiency" (Cotter with Greenpeace). According to a study by two agricultural economists from the Technical University of Munich and the University of California, Berkeley, "the delayed application of Golden Rice in India alone has cost 1,424,000 life years since 2002" (Ropeik). Even Dr. Patrick Moore, who was a co-founder of Greenpeace, is campaigning for the production

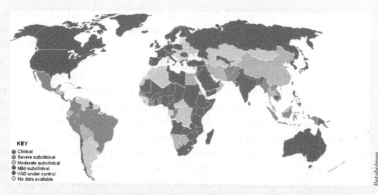

This map shows global prevalence of Vitamin A Deficiency. VAD is most severe in Africa and Southeast Asia where the diets of about 400 million poor people consist primarily of rice.

of Golden Rice. David Ropeik summarized the issue well: "When advocates get so passionate in the fight for their values that they potentially impose harm on others, it puts us all at risk, and we have the right to call attention to those potential harms and hold those advocates accountable. And this is much broader than just GMOs" (Ropeik).

The Future of GMOs

It is undoubtedly true that GMOs lie in our future; 93 percent of soy cultivated in the US is GM, as is 90 percent of corn and cotton produced here (GMO Compass). Passing legislation to phase out the use [of] these crops would be incredibly difficult, especially because of their demonstrated economic benefits for farmers. Genetically modified crops are a polarizing issue; agronomists tout the proven as well as the potential benefits of GM crops, while ecologists argue the present and future risks of their use. One thing is clear: the future of GMOs is uncertain.

Possible Dangers to Human Health. There is no doubt that there are numerous potential benefits in the future for GM foods. According to Dr. Dean DellaPenna from Michigan State University, the ideal future of agriculture includes:

> ... tomatoes and broccoli bursting with cancer-fighting chemicals ... wheat, soy, and peanuts free of allergens; bananas that deliver vaccines; and vegetable oils so loaded with therapeutic ingredients that doctors "prescribe" them for patients at risk for cancer and heart disease. (Ackerman)

On the other hand, humans have not been consuming GMO foods long enough to observe any long-term health issues associated with them. However, many people fear that GMO foods already pose a threat to human health. When Star-Link, a genetically modified variety of corn approved only for livestock, had an allergy scare in 2000, many scientists and consumer groups became worried about more allergy-related issues in the future. While there is a legitimate possibility that some unknown allergenic protein may present itself as the result of genetic modification of a crop, there is also the possibility that such a protein could turn up in conventionally bred foods and go undetected. According to Steve L. Taylor of the University of Nebraska, there are currently no cases of GM crops being linked to allergic reactions or any other health issues in humans (Ackerman).

Necessity for Future Food Security. Hans Rosling has been called a "data visionary." As a global health expert with the access to and ability to interpret massive amounts of data, he has significant insight into the future of global population growth. He describes the growth of the world population in terms of the poorest section of the population, which has a very low rate of child survival. This problem causes parents to have many children in order to rear some who survive. He argues that "only child survival will stop population growth," and that population growth can stop at 9 billion with higher rates of child survival. This is an interesting point in the context of the GMO debate: of the 10.9 million children under the age of five that die in these developing countries every year, over 6.5 million perish from malnutrition and hunger (United Nations Children's Fund). Therefore, improved food production seems to be the best option for improving child survival and ultimately keeping the global population in check.

However, Earth does not have enough resources for humans to simply increase the acreage of farmland. Humans use 50 percent of Earth's freshwater, 70 percent of which is used for agriculture, and agriculture already covers 40 percent of earth's land surface. There is no room for us to expand into the remaining lands, sensitive ecosystems that would be destroyed by the introduction of agriculture. According to Jonathan Foley of the Institute on the Environment at the University of Minnesota, we need to farm the lands we have better, especially in Africa, Latin America, and Eastern Europe (Foley). While GMOs may not be the silver bullet that scientists hope they are, different types of GMOs can be used alongside targeted public health initiatives like "silver buckshot" as a multi-faceted approach to solving the food and environmental security needs of the future. Using GMOs, humans can produce better yields with reduced use of toxic pesticides, while growing more nutritious crops that may contain a host of health benefits in the future. Posing no overwhelming concerns to human nor environmental health, GMO foods should be supported in comprehensive, integrated governmental food policies that aim to eradicate global hunger [and] promote the economic, social, and intellectual development of emerging [countries] while combating overpopulation.

Works Cited

A Black Blizzard over Prowers CO. 1937. Western History Collection, University of Oklahoma. *The Dust Bowl.* Web. 09 Mar. 2015.

Ackerman, Jennifer. 'Food: How Altered?'. *National Geographic* May 2002. Web. 2 Mar. 2015. <http://environment.nationalgeographic.com/environment/global-warming/food-how-altered/>.

Borel, Brooke. 'http://www.popsci.com/article/science/core-Truths-10-Common-Gmo-Claims-Debunked'. *Popular Science* 11 July 2014: n. pag. Print.

Brookes, Graham, and Peter Barfoot. 'Global Impact of Biotech Crops: Socio-Economic & Environmental Effects 1996–2007'. *The Journal of Agrobiotechnology Management and Economics* 12.2 (2009): 184–208. Web.

Chien, Karen, and Raffi Aroian. 'Bacillus Thuringiensis'. *University of California San Diego*. N.p., n.d. Web. 8 Mar. 2015. <http://www.bt.ucsd.edu/index.html>.

Cotter, Janet with Greenpeace. *Golden Illusion: The Broken Promises Behind 'Golden' Rice*. Ed. Steve Erwood. Amsterdam: Greenpeace International, 2013. Print.

Date Palm Pollination in Assyria. Digital image. *The Fruits of Caravaggio*. Purdue University, n.d. Web. 09 Mar. 2015.

Fernandez-Cornejo, Jorge, Seth James Wechsler, and Michael Livingston. 'Adoption of Genetically Engineered Crops by U.S. Farmers Has Increased Steadily for Over 15 Years'. *United States Department of Agriculture Economic Research Service*. N.p., 4 Mar. 2014. Web. 9 Mar. 2015. <http://www.ers.usda.gov/amber-waves/2014-march/ adoption-of-genetically-engineered-crops-by-us-farmers-has-increased-steadily-for-over-15-years.aspx#.VQIXyUIwyZN>.

Foley, Jonathan. 'The Other Inconvenient Truth'. *TED*. N.p., Oct. 2010. Web. 8 Mar. 2015. <http://www.ted.com/talks/jonathan_foley_the_other_ inconvenient_truth?language=en>.

'Frequently Asked Questions on Genetically Modified Foods'. *World Health Organization*. N.p., 9 Dec.2014. Web. 5 Mar. 2015. <http://www.who.int/foodsafety/ areas_work/food-technology/faq-genetically-modified-food/en/>.

"genetic engineering." *Encyclopaedia Britannica. Encyclopaedia Britannica Online Academic Edition*. Encyclopædia Britannica Inc., 2015. Web. 12 Mar. 2015. <http:// academic.eb.com/EBchecked/topic/228897/genetic-engineering>."genetically modified organism (GMO)." *Encyclopaedia Britannica. Encyclopaedia Britannica Online Academic Edition*. Encyclopædia Britannica Inc., 2015. Web. 12 Mar. 2015. <http:// academic.eb.com/EBchecked/topic/897705/genetically-modified-organism>

GMO Compass. 'USA: Cultivation of GM Plants, 2013'. *gmo-compass.org*. N.p., 21 May 2014. Web. 9 Mar. 2015. <http://www.gmo-compass.org/eng/agri_biotechnology/ gmo_planting/506.usa_cultivation_gm_plants_2013.html>.

"Gregor Mendel." *Encyclopaedia Britannica. Encyclopaedia Britannica Online Academic Edition*. Encyclopædia Britannica Inc., 2015. Web. 12 Mar. 2015. <http://academic. eb.com/EBchecked/topic/374739/Gregor-Mendel>.

James, Clive, and Anatole Krattiger. *Global Review of the Field Testing and Commercialization of Transgenic Plants: 1986 to 1995*. N.p., 1996. Print.

Just, David, Shenghui Wang, and Per Pinstrup-Andersen. 'Tarnishing Silver Bullets: Bt Technology Adoption, Bounded Rationality and the Outbreak of Secondary Pest Infestations in China'. *American Agricultural Economics Association Annual Meeting*. N.p., 2006. Print.

"origins of agriculture." *Encyclopaedia Britannica. Encyclopaedia Britannica Online Academic Edition*. Encyclopædia Britannica Inc., 2015. Web. 8 Mar. 2015. <http://academic.eb.com/EBchecked/topic/9647/agriculture>.

Paine, Jacqueline A. et al. 'Improving the Nutritional Value of Golden Rice through Increased pro-Vitamin A Content'. *Nature Biotechnology* 23.4 (2005): 482–487. Web.

Prevalence of Vitamin A Deficiency. Digital image. *Wikipedia.org*. N.p., 5 Nov. 2008. Web. 10 Mar. 2015.

Ropeik, David. 'Golden Rice Opponents Should Be Held Accountable for Health Problems Linked to Vitamin A Deficiency'. *Scientific American*. N.p., 5 Mar. 2014. Web. 10 Mar. 2015. <http://blogs.scientificamerican.com/guest-blog/2014/03/15/golden-rice-opponents-should-be-held-accountable-for-health-problems-linked-to-vitamain-a-deficiency/>.

Rosling, Hans. 'Global Population Growth, Box by Box'. *TED*. N.p., June 2010. Web. 8 Mar. 2015. <https://www.ted.com/talks/hans_rosling_on_global_population_growth>."Sumer." *Encyclopaedia Britannica. Encyclopaedia Britannica Online Academic Edition*. Encyclopædia Britannica Inc., 2015. Web. 13 Mar. 2015. <http://academic.eb.com/EBchecked/topic/573176/Sumer>.

United Nations Children's Fund. *State of the World's Children 2007*. N.p., 2006. Print.

WGBH Educational Foundation. 'Evolution: Library: Pesticide Resistance'. *pbs.org*. N.p., 2001. Web. 9 Mar. 2015. <http://www.pbs.org/wgbh/evolution/library/10/1/l_101_02.html>.

World Health Organization. 'Micronutrient Deficiencies'. *who.int*. N.p., 9 Dec. 2013. Web. 10 Mar. 2015. <http://www.who.int/nutrition/topics/vad/en/>.

Reflections and Inquiries

1. After reading the advantages and disadvantages of creating and consuming herbicide-tolerant crops, how should genetically modified crops be regulated, if at all?

2. What do you consider to be the principal risks involved in consuming GM crops?

3. How effectively did Paton structure his argument? For example, what is the purpose, if any, of the introduction to the history of agriculture? Is it covered in the right amount, too much detail, or too little detail? You may find yourself discussing purpose in your response.

Reading to Write

After researching the latest information on genetically modified crops, write an essay defending or challenging the necessity to manipulate the herbicide resistance or nutritional value of various foods.

Connections Among the Clusters

Issues in biomedicine and bioethics inevitably touch upon other issues, such as national security, education, and individual privacy.

Critical Thinking

1. How do issues in bioethics relate to issues in multicultural learning? (See Cluster 4.)

2. Suggest ways in which genetic engineering or stem cell research could become an issue of national security. (See Cluster 3.)

3. How might issues in biotechnology relate to issues in athletics? (See Cluster 2.)

Writing Projects

1. Write an essay in which you weigh the potential benefits and potential liabilities of gene therapy, genetic engineering, animal patenting, or stem cell research; then present your own position on the issue in light of your examination of both sides.

2. How do the essays in this cluster affect your views of biomedical research? Should such research be restricted? If so, how, and by whom?

Suggestions for Further Reading

http://www.geneticsandsociety.org/index.php

Anthes, Emily. "Don't Be Afraid of Genetic Modification." *The New York Times*, March 10, 2013: SR 4.

Blair, Robert, and Joe M. Regenstein. *Genetic Modification and Food Quality: A Down to Earth Analysis*. Hoboken, NJ: Wiley, 2015.

DeGrazia, David, Thomas Mappes, Jeffrey Ballard. *Biomedical Ethics*, 7th Ed. New York: McGraw-Hill, 2010. Print.

Fountain, Henry. "Building a $325,000 Burger." *The New York Times*, May 14, 2013: D1.

Harris, John. *Enhancing Evolution: The Ethical Case for Making Better People*. Princeton: Princeton University Press, 2007.

Holland, Suzanne, Karen Lebacqz, and Laurie Zoloth, eds. *The Human Embryonic Stem Cell Debate*. Cambridge: MIT Press, 2001. Print.

Kalb, Claudia. "Ethics, Eggs and Embryos." *Newsweek* 145, June 20, 2005: 52–53. Print.

Khademhosseini, Ali, Joseph P. Vacanti, and Robert Langer. "Progress in Tissue Engineering." *Scientific American*, May 2009: 64–71. Print.

Lauritzen, P., ed. *Cloning and the Future of Human Embryo Research*. New York: Oxford UP, 2001. Print.

Levine, Carol, ed. *Taking Sides: Clashing Views on Biomedical Ethics*, 4th Ed. New York: McGraw-Hill/Dushkin, 2011. Print.

O'Brien, Robyn, with Rachel Kranz. *The Unhealthy Truth: One Mother's Shocking Investigation into the Dangers of America's Food Supply—and What Every Family Can Do to Protect Itself.* New York: Three Rivers Press, 2010. Print.

Park, Alice. "Stem Cells: The Quest Resumes." *Time* 9 Feb 2009: 36–43. Print.

Rosen, Jeffrey, "The Brain on the Stand: How Neuroscience Is Transforming the Legal System." *New York Times Magazine,* March 11, 2007: 49–53, 70, 77–82, 84. Print.

Ruse, Michael, and Christopher A. Pynes, eds. *The Stem Cell Controversy: Debating the Issues.* Amherst, NY: Prometheus, 2003. Print.

Sandel, Michael J. *The Case against Perfection: Ethics in the Age of Genetic Engineering.* Cambridge: Belknap Press of Harvard University Press, 2007.

Wolfson, Elissa. "Animal Patenting." *E Magazine: The Environmental Magazine* 5.2; March/April 1994: 25–26. Print.

GLOSSARY OF RHETORICAL TERMS

Active reading. A form of critical reading, conducted in groups, for the purpose of determining the rhetorical techniques, strengths, and weaknesses of a given selection. Active reading can also refer to the reading one does on one's own, by questioning and commenting on the rhetorical elements of a selection.

Ad hominem fallacy. Literally, argument directed against the person. An error of reasoning in which the arguer attacks an individual's character or person as a way of attacking his or her ideas or performance, as in "Adam Stone does not deserve an Oscar for Best Film Editing; he has been diagnosed as psychotic."

Affirming the consequent fallacy. For the outcome of a hypothetical statement ("If x, then y") to be valid, the antecedent (the "if" clause) must be affirmed or the consequent (the "then" clause) denied. It is a fallacy, however, to say that if the consequent is affirmed, then the antecedent must be denied. Consider this hypothetical statement: "If taxes are raised, the economy will prosper." To affirm the consequent—that is, to say "the economy is indeed prospering; therefore, taxes were raised"—is a fallacy (the economy, given the framework of the statement, could have prospered for other reasons). One can only deny the consequent: "The economy did not prosper; therefore, taxes were not raised."

Analogy. Comparison made, for purpose of clarification, between two ideas sharing similar characteristics.

Analysis. Breakdown of an idea into its constituent elements to facilitate comprehension.

Appeals. The three means of persuasion described by Aristotle: *ethos* (referring to persuasion through character, ethics, values); *pathos* (referring to persuasion through emotions, feelings); and *logos* (referring to persuasion through logical reasoning). The three appeals often overlap in an argument.

Apples and oranges. An error of reasoning in which a comparison is made between two things that are not comparable (because they are not part of the same category).

Argument. A discussion in which a claim is challenged or supported with evidence in an effort to get at the truth of the matter insofar as it is currently perceived. *See also* Persuasion.

Backing. In Toulmin argument, support for the *warrant*, which is not, in itself, self-validating. The more substantial the backing, the more compelling the warrant.

Bandwagon fallacy. The assumption that if an opinion is shared by a majority, the opinion must be correct. Example: "So many people are buying hybrid cars, therefore hybrid cars must be superior."

552

Begging the question fallacy.   (1) An error of reasoning in which the "evidence" used to support a claim is merely a rephrasing of the problem, as in, "Imprisonment does not deter crime because it does nothing to discourage criminal activity"; (2) presenting a disputable claim in a manner that suggests it is beyond dispute, as in, "Her whimsical ideas should not be taken seriously."

Brainstorming.   A form of prewriting in which one spontaneously records or utters ideas for a topic.

Categorization.   Arrangement or classification according to shared similarities.

Claim.   The idea or thesis that forms the basis of an argument.

Classical (or Aristotelian) argument.   A model of argument that follows a pre-established structure consisting of an introduction to the problem, a statement of the thesis or claim, a discussion of the evidence in support of the thesis, a refutation of opposing views, and a conclusion.

Clustering.   A form of prewriting in which one spontaneously writes down similar ideas and examples in circled groupings or clusters to generate content for an essay.

Common ground.   In Rogerian argument, determining which points or values writer and audience agree on despite the larger difference of opinion. *See also* Redundancy.

Composing process.   A reference to the multiple (but not necessarily sequential or otherwise orderly) activities of a writer in the act of completing a writing task. These activities typically involve such prewriting activities as brainstorming, freewriting, listing, and clustering; drafting activities such as preparing a first draft, revising, rerevising, and copyediting; and proofreading.

Concision.   Using as few words as possible without losing clarity or readability. In fact, concision improves clarity and readability. Example: "The article titled 'On Improving Memory,' which was written by Sam Smith, was published in today's *Oakville Gazette*," can be made more concise as follows: "Sam Smith's article, 'On Improving Memory,' appears in today's *Oakville Gazette*"—11 words instead of 18.

Data.   Another word for *evidence*. It can also refer to statistical evidence as opposed to testimonial, mathematical, or observational evidence.

Database.   An electronic list of references grouped by subject matter.

Deduction.   A mode of reasoning that begins with what is known to be true and seeks to determine the elements or premises that demonstrate the validity of that truth. *See also* Induction.

Definition.   In argumentative writing, definitions of technical terms are often necessary when the claim involves a specialized topic in law, the sciences, technology, business, or industry. A definition often includes reference to a word or expression's origin (etymology) and usage history, as well as a standard lexical meaning.

Denying the antecedent fallacy.   *See* Affirming the consequent fallacy.

Development.   Examining an idea in depth, using illustrations, cases in point, analysis, statistics, and other means of supporting assertions.

Discourse.   Sustained communication through oral or written language. There are three modes of discourse: (1) expository (or referential), which refers to explanation and analysis; (2) expressive, which refers to descriptive and dramatic writing; and (3) persuasive, which refers to the use of the Aristotelian appeals, Toulmin warrants, or Rogerian strategies for finding common ground to change readers' minds about something. *See also* Appeals.

Either-or fallacy.   An error of reasoning in which a many-sided argument is presented as having only two sides. Also known as the *false dichotomy*. Example: "Either you're for us or you're against us."

Enthymeme.   In deductive reasoning, a syllogism in which one of the premises goes unstated because it is assumed to be understood. In the enthymeme, "Socrates is mortal because he is a human being," the omitted—because understood—premise is "All human beings are mortal." *See also* Syllogism.

Ethos.   *See* Appeals.

Evidence.   Support for a claim. Evidence may be direct (data from surveys, experiments, research studies, and so on) or indirect (mathematical or logical reasoning). *See also* Prove.

Fallacy.   An error or flaw in logical reasoning.

False analogy or faulty analogy.   An error of reasoning that assumes the accuracy of an inaccurate (false) or inappropriate (faulty) comparison.

False dichotomy.   *See* Either-or fallacy.

Fourth-term fallacy.   An error of reasoning in which one term is carelessly or deceptively substituted for another to force the assumption that both terms mean the same thing (thereby adding a "fourth term" to a syllogism, which can contain only three terms in their respective premises: major, middle, and minor). *See also* Syllogism.

Freewriting.   A form of prewriting in which one writes spontaneously and swiftly without regard to organization, development, usage, or mechanics.

Generalization.   A nonspecific, summative statement about an idea or situation. If a generalization does not account for some situations, it is said to be *hasty* or *premature*. If a generalization is not accompanied by particular examples, it is said to be *unsupported*.

Glosses.   Notes, such as comments or cross-references, in the margins of texts that enhance understanding as well as help to develop a critical stance on the ideas presented.

Hasty generalization.   *See* Generalization.

In-depth reading. In critical reading, the stage of reading involving close attention to complexities of the topic, to subtle meanings and inferences; follows previewing. *See also* Previewing.

Induction. Form of reasoning whereby one attempts a generalization or hypothesis after considering particular cases or samples, not before. *See also* Deduction.

Linking. In critical reading, the connecting of one part of a sentence with another to determine meaning and continuity of idea.

Listserv. An online discussion group, acquired through subscription.

Mediation. A form of argument that attempts to fairly present an objective discussion of opposing views before helping others to reach a conclusion.

Misreading the evidence fallacy. Accidental or deliberate misinterpretation or misrepresentation of data as part of an effort to discredit a challenging view.

Newsgroup. An electronic bulletin board or forum. Also known as *usenet*.

Non sequitur fallacy. Error in reasoning in which an assertion cannot logically be tied to the premise it attempts to demonstrate. Example: "I lost my keys because you made me so angry."

Paraphrase. *See* Quotation.

Peer critiquing. A draft workshopping activity whereby the participating writers share similar backgrounds; for example, they are all first-year college students.

Persuasion. A form of argument that relies on using emotional, rational, or ethical appeals more than logical analysis to get readers or listeners to change their minds about something.

Plagiarism. The use of others' ideas as if they were one's own. Plagiarism is a violation of international copyright law and therefore illegal. Also, it is possible to plagiarize from yourself if you present material as original and new that you included in another assignment.

Poisoning the well fallacy. Attempting to corrupt an argument before the argument begins.

Post hoc fallacy. Shortened form of *post hoc ergo propter hoc* ("after the fact, therefore because of the fact"). An error of reasoning in which one attaches a causal relationship to a sequential one. Example: "Because I spilled salt, I had a long string of bad luck."

Premature conclusion. *See* Generalization.

Previewing. The initial stage of critical reading consisting of prereading, skim-reading, and postreading. *See also* In-depth reading.

Proofreading. Reading semifinal draft copy for errors in grammar, spelling, punctuation, capitalization, and the like.

Prove.   To provide evidence involving mathematical deduction or the presentation of indisputable facts.

Qualifier.   In Toulmin argument, a limitation imposed on a claim that makes it valid only under some or most circumstances, but not all. *See also* Toulmin argument.

Quotation.   The words of an authority used in argumentative writing to reinforce one's own views on a given topic. Direct quotation refers to verbatim citation of the author's words, which are placed in quotation marks. Indirect quotation or paraphrase refers to the author's idea without quoting verbatim. Both forms of quotation must be properly documented.

Red herring fallacy.   An error of reasoning in which one introduces an unrelated but similar-seeming bit of information to throw one off the track of the issue being argued. Example: "Do I think global warming is a hoax? It seems that we need better weather forecasting."

Redundancy.   Words that unnecessarily repeat a thought already conveyed by other words in the passage. Examples: "She spoke in a soft whisper" instead of "She whispered"; "The tiles were gray in color and had rectangular shapes" instead of "The tiles were gray and rectangular."

Refutation.   The technique of representing fairly and then demonstrating the shortcomings of assertions that challenge your own.

Research.   The process of searching, retrieving, and integrating information from outside sources to authenticate or reinforce one's argument.

Review.   A critical evaluation of an artistic work, a new product, or a restaurant.

Revising.   Substantive development or restructuring of a draft. *See also* Proofreading.

Rhetoric.   The art of or the techniques used in writing or speaking effectively. Aristotle defined rhetoric as the art of finding the best available means of persuasion in a given case.

Rhetorical rhombus.   A schematic for showing the elements involved in written or oral communication: Purpose, Audience, Writer, Subject.

Rogerian argument.   A mode of argument established by Carl Rogers in which arguers are urged to cooperate, to seek a common ground on which to negotiate their differences.

Serendipity.   In research, a fortunate coming together of ideas through unexpected discovery.

Slighting the opposition fallacy.   An unfair downplaying of a challenger's claim, despite its potential validity.

Slippery slope fallacy.   An error of reasoning in which one alludes to a sequence of highly unlikely consequences resulting from an observed or proposed situation. Example: "If physicists continue to search for exotic subatomic particles, they will unleash unknown forces of nature which in turn could destroy the earth."

Summary.   A highly condensed version of a work using or paraphrasing only the work's key points.

Suspect authority.   An error of authorization in which an authority's credentials do not prove his or her expertise on the topic.

Syllogism.   A form of logical argument consisting of a major premise ("All stars are suns"), a minor premise ("Sirius is a star"), and a conclusion ("Therefore, Sirius is a sun").

Thesis.   The claim or main idea or premise of an argument.

Topic.   The specific subject of a paper.

Toulmin argument.   A strategy of argument developed by philosopher Stephen A. Toulmin, in which it is understood that any claim is arguable because it is based on personal ethical values or warrants as well as on outside evidence or data.

Tracking.   In critical reading, shifting the perspective of meaning from sentence to word or from sentence to paragraph or from paragraph to whole essay.

***Tu quoque* fallacy.**   Literally, "you too." An error of reasoning whereby one asserts that an action (or refusal to take action) is validated by the fact that the other person acted or refused to act. "Why should I obey the rules when you're always breaking them?"

Tweet.   A post on Twitter (a service for microblogs limited to 140 characters) that enables users to send or read updates on news or personal information. Tweets may be sent from mobile phones, computers, or tablets.

Unsupported generalization.   *See* Generalization.

Vague authority.   An error of authorization in which an ambiguous entity, such as a concept or discipline, is cited as a figure of authority.

Visual aids.   Images such as charts, diagrams, or photographs used for illustrating and reinforcing a claim. Can also refer to presentation formats such as PowerPoint or Prezi.

Warrant.   *See* Toulmin argument.

INDEX OF AUTHORS AND TITLES

INDEX OF TERMS